Junípero Serra

BEFORE GOLD
California under Spain and Mexico
VOLUME 3

ROSE MARIE BEEBE & ROBERT M. SENKEWICZ
Series Editors

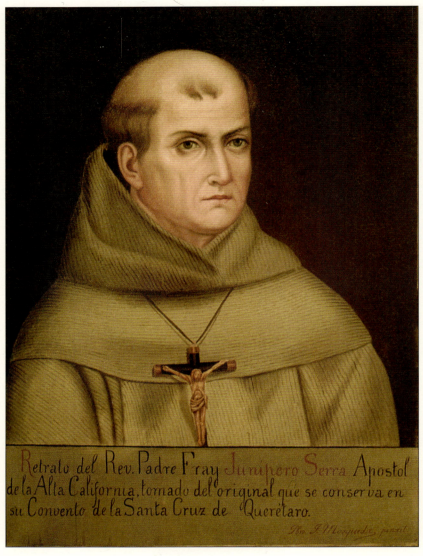

FRONTISPIECE. Portrait of Rev. Padre Fray Junípero Serra. This portrait has come to be one of the standard representations. It was done in the early twentieth century by a Mexican priest, Fr. José Mosqueda, who said that he copied it from a work that had hung in the Colegio de la Santa Cruz in Querétaro. If the painting to which Mosqueda referred was genuine and originally done in Querétaro, it may have dated from the 1750s, when Serra served as president of the missions in the Sierra Gorda, near Querétaro; or from 1767, when Serra stopped at the Colegio de la Santa Cruz on his way to Baja California; or from 1774, when Serra stopped there again on his return from Mexico City to Alta California. *Courtesy of the Santa Bárbara Mission Archive-Library.*

Junípero Serra

California, Indians, and the Transformation of a Missionary

Rose Marie Beebe & Robert M. Senkewicz

University of Oklahoma Press ❋ Norman

Published in cooperation with
the Academy of American Franciscan History
Mission San Luis Rey, Oceanside, California

Library of Congress Cataloging-in-Publication Data
Beebe, Rose Marie.
　Junípero Serra : California, Indians, and the transformation of a missionary / Rose Marie Beebe & Robert M. Senkewicz.
　　pages cm. — (Before gold : California under Spain and Mexico ; v. 3)
　　Includes bibliographical references and index.
　　ISBN 978-0-8061-4868-7 (hardcover : alk. paper)
　1. Serra, Junípero, 1713–1784. 2. Missionaries—California—Biography. 3. Franciscans—California—Biography. 4. Missions, Spanish—California—History. 5. California—History—To 1846. [1. Indians of North America—Missions—California.]
I. Senkewicz, Robert M., 1947– II. Title.
　　F864.S44B44 2015
　　979.4′01092—dc23
　　[B]
2014029599

Junípero Serra: California, Indians, and the Transformation of a Missionary is Volume 3 in the series Before Gold: California under Spain and Mexico.

The paper in this book meets the guidelines for permanence and durability of the Committee on Production Guidelines for Book Longevity of the Council on Library Resources, Inc. ∞

Copyright © 2015 by the University of Oklahoma Press, Norman, Publishing Division of the University. Manufactured in the U.S.A.

All rights reserved. No part of this publication may be reproduced, stored in a retrieval system, or transmitted, in any form or by any means, electronic, mechanical, photocopying, recording, or otherwise—except as permitted under Section 107 or 108 of the United States Copyright Act—without the prior written permission of the University of Oklahoma Press. To request permission to reproduce selections from this book, write to Permissions, University of Oklahoma Press, 2800 Venture Drive, Norman, OK 73069, or email rights.oupress@ou.edu.

3 4 5 6 7 8 9 10

for
W. Michael Mathes

Contents

List of Illustrations 9
List of Color Plates 13
Acknowledgments 15

Introduction 17
  1. Mallorca 39
  2. New Spain 67
  3. Baja California 133
  4. San Diego and Monterey 205
  5. Journey to Mexico City 227
  6. Return to Carmel 245
  7. Serra-Rivera Correspondence 275
  8. San Diego 323
  9. A Series of Setbacks 343
  10. Mission among the Chumash 379
  11. Final Years 391
Conclusion 423

Appendix: Four Sermons 427
Glossary 459
Bibliography 467
Index 493

Illustrations

Rev. Padre Fray Junípero Serra, by Fr. José Mosqueda . . . *frontispiece*

FIGURES
1. María del Buen Año baptismal record, 1782 38
2. Village of Petra, Mallorca 43
3. Patio of the Convento de San Francisco, Palma, Mallorca, 1860, by Charles Clifford 50
4. Colegio de la Santa Cruz de Querétaro, by Robert Michels and Stephanie Daffer 75
5. Colegio de San Fernando, Mexico City, by Fr. Maynard Geiger, OFM. 76
6. Frontispiece of *La mística ciudad de Dios*, by an anonymous artist . 82
7. *Funeral Portrait of Don José de Escandón, Conde de Sierra Gorda*, by Andrés de Islas 97
8. *Procession of Monks and Flagellants*, by Giambattista Tiepolo. . . 104
9. Inquisitorial interrogation scene, by Constantino Escalante . . . 118
10. Church of Santo Domingo, Mexico City, by Fr. Maynard Geiger, OFM 131
11. Miguel Venegas's map of Baja California, 1757 134
12. Gaspar de Portolá, by an anonymous artist 139
13. José de Gálvez, ca. 1787 145
14. Autographs from the Portolá expedition 146
15. Ship *San Carlos*, by Raymond Aker 151
16. Mission San Francisco Javier de Viggé-Biaundó, by Harry W. Crosby 154
17. Mission Nuestra Señora de Loreto Conchó, 1750 155
18. Mission San José de Comondú, by Harry W. Crosby . . . 158
19. *Mules and Indian Boy*, by Louis Choris 163
20. El Camino Real midway between San Ignacio and Santa Gertrudis, by Harry W. Crosby 164

21. Mission Santa Gertrudis de Cadacamán, by
    Fr. Maynard Geiger, OFM 167
22. El Cajón, by Harry W. Crosby 168
23. Mission San Fernando Rey de España de Velicatá, by G. W. Hendry 171
24. Cattle in the *tinaja* at Rancho del Zorrillo, by Harry W. Crosby . . 174
25. María de Jesús de Ágreda woodcut, by an anonymous artist . . . 177
26. "Women and Men of California," from Miguel Venegas, *Noticia de la California* 190
27. "The Manner and Caring for the Sick in California" and "Sorcerers of California," from Miguel Venegas, *Noticia de la California* . . . 190
28. Page of Serra's Baja California diary 203
29. Bernardino de Jesús baptismal entry, 1770 223
30. *Reception of La Pérouse at the Mission of Carmel in Monterey*, by José Cardero 224
31. Pedro Fages 231
32. *Mission San Luis Obispo*, by Edward Vischer 234
33. *Antonio María de Bucareli y Ursúa*, by an anonymous artist . . . 239
34. *View of the Convent, Church, and Rancherías of the Mission of Carmel*, 1791 (view 1), by José Cardero 256
35. *Mission of Carmel at Monterey*, 1791 (view 2), by José Cardero . . 256
36. *Church, Mission, and Ruins of Mission San Antonio de Padua*, by Edward Vischer 259
37. *Indian Woman from Monterey*, 1791, by José Cardero 270
38. *Indian Man from Monterey*, 1791, by José Cardero 280
39. *View of Monterey Presidio*, 1791, by José Cardero 287
40. *Indians Dancing at Mission San José*, 1806, by Georg Heinrich von Langsdorff 292
41. *Mission San Luis Rey*, 1827, by Auguste Duhaut-Cilly . . . 293
42. *How California Indians Fight*, 1791, by Tomás de Suría . . . 331
43. Drawing of the Presidio of San Diego, by Mariano Guadalupe Vallejo 336
44. Map of the Pueblo de San José, 1781, by Joseph Moraga . . . 347
45. Plan of the Royal Presidio of San Carlos of Monterey, by Miguel Costansó 350
46. *Plaza of the Presidio of Monterey*, 1791, by José Cardero . . . 351
47. Confirmation Register at Mission Santa Clara 373
48. Chumash artifacts 382–83
49. *Mission San Buenaventura*, 1856, by Henry Ford Miller . . . 386
50. *Mission Santa Clara*, 1842, by Gustavus M. Waseurtz af Sandels . . 407
51. *Mission San Francisco de Asís*, by Henry Chapman Ford . . . 408

52. Painting of Serra seated on the *equipal*, by Fr. Andrés Caymari . . 415
53. Fr. Serra's silk burial stole 419
54. Fr. Serra's cross, the "Cruz de Caravaca" 419
55. Ceremonial opening of Fr. Serra's tomb, 1882, by Charles Pierce . . 420
56. Mission San Carlos Borromeo, 1949, by Manuel Mallafré Sunyer . 425

Maps

1. Serra's Mediterranean travels, 1749 62
2. The Iberian peninsula 79
3. The Sierra Gorda region 90
4. Serra's domestic missions between 1758 and 1768 103
5. The Huasteca region 111
6. Baja California missions 136
7. Indigenous linguistic groups in Baja California 142
8. Rumsen village locations, Monterey Bay region 220
9. Portolá expedition 228
10. The ten missions in Las Californias 322
11. Chumash settlements along the central Alta California coast . . 380
12. Spanish and indigenous communities of the Santa Bárbara region . 389

Color Plates

following page 226

A. Allegory of the Llullian doctrine
B. *Brother Junípero and the Beggar*, ca. 1646, by Bartolomé Esteban Murillo
C. *Fray Juan Duns Escoto*, by an anonymous artist
D. *María de Jesús de Ágreda*, by an anonymous artist
E & F. *Rendition of a Chichimeco* and *Rendition of a Chichimeca*, 1711, by Manuel Arellano
G. Illumination from the eighteenth-century work *Crónica de la Provincia de los Santos Apóstoles S. Pedro y S. Pablo de Michoacán*, by Fray Pablo de Beaumont
H & I. Missions Santa María del Agua de Landa and San Miguel Concá, by Robert Michels and Stephanie Daffer
J. Mission Santiago de Jalpan, by Robert Michels and Stephanie Daffer
K. Mission Nuestra Señora de la Luz de Tancoyol, by Robert Michels and Stephanie Daffer

following page 274

L. Escudo or shield of the Mexican Inquisition
M. Agnus Dei (Lamb of God) medallion
N. *Rendition of a Mulata*, 1711, by Manuel Arellano
O. *De chino cambujo e india, loba*, 1763, by Miguel Cabrera
P. Jaguar warrior, photograph by Robert H. Jackson
Q. Mission Santiago, by Fr. Ignacio Tirsch, SJ
R. Farm at Mission Santiago, by Fr. Ignacio Tirsch, SJ
S. Killing a deer, by Fr. Ignacio Tirsch, SJ
T. California Indian woman, by Fr. Ignacio Tirsch, SJ
U. *Indians of California*, 1769, by Alexandre-Jean Noël
V & W. Plants of Baja California, by Fr. Ignacio Tirsch, SJ
X. Heathens coming out of the wilderness, by Fr. Ignacio Tirsch, SJ
Y. *Soldado de cuera*, by Raymundo Murillo

Color Plates

following page 378

Z. *How Missionaries Cross Rivers*, by Fr. Florián Paucke, SJ
AA. Lord's Prayer in hieroglyphics
BB. *Mission San Gabriel in 1832*, by Ferdinand Deppe
CC. *La Dolorosa (Our Lady of Sorrows)*, by an anonymous artist
DD. *Mission San Carlos Borromeo del Río Carmelo*, ca. 1899, by Edwin Deakin
EE. *The Flagellation of Hernán Cortés by Franciscan Friars*, by an anonymous artist
FF. Pictograph from Burro Flats
GG. Pleito Creek: Chumash painted shelter facing east and Chumash painted shelter detail, photographs by Rick Bury
HH. *Santa Bárbara Presidio Chapel, 1855*, by James Madison Alden
II. *Junípero Serra Receives the Viaticum, 1785*, by Mariano Guerrero

Acknowledgments

During the years that we have been researching the life, words, and worlds of Junípero Serra, we have been assisted by many people and organizations. Our greatest debt is to the Academy of American Franciscan History, especially its director, Dr. Jeffrey Burns. Jeffrey and the board of directors of the Academy awarded us several grants, which enabled us to lighten our teaching responsibilities during a few academic quarters. We were also able to present some of our developing ideas at conferences and symposia organized or supported by the Academy, especially the conference "From La Florida to La California: The Genesis and Realization of Franciscan Evangelization in the Spanish Borderlands," held at Flagler College in March 2011. We were also assisted by a generous grant from the Program for Cultural Cooperation between Spain's Ministry of Culture and United States Universities.

The overwhelming number of documents that we consulted are housed at the Santa Bárbara Mission Archive-Library. Two successive directors, Lynn Bremer and Dr. Mónica Orozco, provided us with a series of documents and other resources from that indispensable repository. They were generous and unstinting in their support of this project. Lynn and Mónica both worked alone, without any paid staff. They were assisted by a series of wonderful volunteers, notably Brian Burd and Gary Matz. In the midst of innumerable details that constantly pressed them from all sides, Lynn and Mónica always made time for our seemingly interminable requests for a copy of "just one more document." We are deeply grateful to both of them.

At Santa Clara University, the Office Manager of the History Department, Judy Gillette, generously managed many of the logistics of this project, such as travel, copying, and supplies. Her support and efficiency contributed greatly to this project's completion.

As she has done for us in the past, Susan Snyder, Head of Public Services at The Bancroft Library, was enormously helpful and supportive, especially in gathering graphics from that institution's vast repository and making them available to us.

At the University of Oklahoma Press, Robert Clark was instrumental in developing the series in which this book is appearing. Bob's extensive background in publishing materials about the American West proved to be a tremendous gift to us, especially as we were conceptualizing this project in its initial stages. After Bob left Norman, Oklahoma, and returned to the Pacific Northwest, we were fortunate to be able to work with Charles Rankin, Associate Director/Editor-in-Chief of the University of Oklahoma Press, who helped us enormously as we shepherded this project to completion. We would also like to acknowledge the great assistance given to us by Bethany Mowry (Press Editorial Assistant), Stephanie Attia (Senior Manuscript Editor), Christi Stanforth (freelance copyeditor), and Francine Cronshaw (freelance indexer) as we moved into the production phase.

We have benefited from the insights of other scholars who read or listened to us present earlier versions of some of the material that appears in this volume. We would like to thank Steven Hackel, whose invitation for us to participate in two conferences at The Huntington Library, "Alta California: Peoples in Motion, Identities in Formation" in September 2006 and "Junípero Serra: Context and Representation, 1713–2013" in September 2013, allowed us to present some of this material and receive helpful and constructive critiques from the wide variety of scholars in attendance. We also thank Dr. Jeffrey Burns and Fr. Francisco Morales, OFM, for inviting us to participate in a conference on the history of the Franciscans in Colonial New Spain that was held in Cholula, Mexico, in 2007.

In addition, a series of scholars and friends have reacted to different versions of this material in manuscript form over the past few years. We are especially grateful for the insights offered by Dr. William Taylor, Dr. James A. Sandos, and Dr. Carol Higham at a crucial point in the development of this project.

We received generous and indispensable assistance in locating and receiving permission for using the graphics in this volume from Eder Arreola, Dr. Clara Bargellini, Carmen Boone Canovas, Harry W. Crosby, Dr. Cristina Cruz González, Dr. Iris Engstrand, Fr. Carl Faria, Marilyn Fedewa, Gail Sheridan, and Edward Vernon. We are grateful to Fr. Joseph Chinicci, OFM, for his support of this project over the years. And to the one who was with this project from its inception, Conde Duque de Olivares, better known to us and his friends as Ollie, "canine supervisor par excellence," we hope that you will enjoy the fruits of your boundless patience from your Heavenly perch.

We are dedicating this volume to the memory of a dear friend and mentor, W. Michael Mathes. Mike was one of the people who introduced us to Colonial New Spain and the "Borderlands" more than two decades ago, and his consistent support, suggestions, and enthusiasm kept us going at a number of difficult junctures. Indeed, one of the last conversations we had with him, just a few weeks before his passing, enabled us to understand some of the more obscure terms Serra was using when he was talking about cattle at the missions. You truly were ¡excelente!

Introduction

In a drenching downpour in December 1776, a group of Chumash people, one of California's most numerous and intimidating native coastal groups, suddenly confronted a small Spanish party in the foothills along the Santa Bárbara Channel. The Chumash controlled a vast expanse between San Gabriel and San Luis Obispo. Indeed, their territory represented the largest area south of Monterey in Alta California still untouched by a Spanish colonial establishment. No mission or presidio had yet been established there, and hostilities between the Chumash and Spanish colonizers had been widespread. The group of Spaniards slogging ponderously through the mud that day had little doubt they had just walked into a well-designed ambush.

Among the group were two Spanish priests: Junípero Serra and Fermín Francisco de Lasuén. Accompanying them was a small number of mestizo soldiers. Serra in particular had reason to be concerned. As the head of the seven small, roughly constructed missions now established in Alta California between San Diego and San Francisco, he knew California as well as anyone. He realized he was in one of the most densely populated native regions of California, but he had only been through this area twice before, and on both those occasions he had had the benefit of a significantly larger military presence. In 1772, he had accompanied the military commander Pedro Fages and a large group of soldiers through the region on a journey that resulted in the founding of Mission San Luis Obispo. In 1774, on his way back to Monterey from the south, he and Juan Bautista de Anza, who led a well-equipped military party, were in the area at the same time.

Serra came to California to work among the native peoples, and in December 1776 these people were very much on his mind. He was returning from San Diego, where he had supervised the beginning of the reconstruction of the mission there after its destruction and the killing of one of its priests by a large band of Kumeyaay people. He had long been eager to attempt to evangelize the Chumash, but recent signs had not been promising. His companion, Lasuén, had been on a similar journey in the region a year and a half before, and his traveling party was attacked after an encounter between the soldiers and the Indians. Lasuén's experience was a vivid example of how volatile the relations between the native peoples and their colonial occupiers could be. He reported that one moment he was dismounted and distributing glass beads to some Chumash children, whose mothers had brought them to see the Spaniards pass through, and the next moment he was being attacked by a large group of Indians who were shooting arrows at the party. "I tried to mount my mule," he recounted, "but found I could not do so, for the animal had become very restive because of the vociferous yelling." He said, "It was only because three soldiers rushed to my rescue [that] I was able to make my escape on foot, and although it was difficult because of my weight, with God's help I found myself very shortly beyond the range of their shafts." The arrival of additional soldiers turned the tide: some of them were slightly ahead of the party attending to the pack train, and others were escorting additional horses in the rear. The soldiers opened fire, and at the end of the fight, six Indians lay dead. Lasuén was shaken by the incident and came away believing, "These Channel Indians know that they are strong and they act on the principle that whoever harms them will have to pay a price."[1]

In light of all of these concerns, any journey through Chumash territory was not to be taken lightly. December was the rainy season and a severe storm made matters worse. Furious winds and high waves made traveling along the coastal beaches impossible. As Serra recounted, "Strong winds, heavy rains, much mud, and rough, high seas did not allow us to set foot on the beach, which would have made for a shorter and easier walk." So the party was forced to seek higher ground and travel along the foothills farther from the beach. But the swollen streams and creeks they encountered made the journey even more perilous, and the mud created by the storm made it difficult for the horses and mules to proceed. The soldiers and missionaries were well aware that this was the perfect occasion for an ambush. Sure enough, the Chumash soon appeared. Serra did not record his or his companions' immediate reaction to their presence, but what happened next confounded his expectations and made a lasting impression on him.

Instead of attacking, the Indians began to assist the beleaguered Spanish group. Serra was the oldest member of the party, and his Franciscan garb gave him a distinctive appearance. So he found himself the special object of native attention as they did everything they could to help him out. "Since I could not travel on foot or on horseback," he wrote a few months later, "with one person on each side, they took hold of my arms and carried me over the muddy hills. I was not able

---

1. Guest, *Fermín Francisco de Lasuén*, 62; Lasuén, *Writings*, 1:46–47.

to repay them for their efforts and their act of compassion, nor do I think I will ever be able to repay them as I would hope to do." A year later the memory of the episode was still strong, and he elaborated on it in another letter: "One time, when the ground was so muddy (because shortly before it had rained heavily), since I could not travel on foot or on horseback, with one person on each side, they took hold of my arms and carried me a great distance until they could set me down on firmer ground." Groups of native people remained with the traveling party for the next few days, and Serra did everything he could to try to interact with them. He remembered, "When I was able to sing, a large number of them would happily join in and accompany me. When we stopped, I blessed those who had helped me and then a second group came over and asked me to bless them as well. A number of them accompanied us for many days." Serra concluded his account by recording the intense feeling he had for these people: "And for me, this served to deepen the compassion I have felt for them for quite some time."[2]

For Junípero Serra, this encounter on a stormy winter day symbolized what he hoped to achieve in California. The natural human bond between Chumash and Spanish, with one group seeing another in need and spontaneously offering to come to its aid, was the foundation for the kind of evangelization he hoped to carry out along the Pacific slope. Serra hoped this human bond would allow contact and dialogue and that California's native peoples would gradually come to understand and accept the truth of Christianity. As the founder of his religious order, Francis of Assisi, had respectfully preached to Sultan Melek el-Kamel in Egypt in the thirteenth century, so Serra believed he could respectfully and successfully spread the Christian Gospel among the indigenous peoples with whom he had freely chosen to spend the rest of his life. That belief had led him to America a quarter century earlier, and it continued to animate everything he did.

Unlike Francis, however, Serra did not travel alone. He was embedded in an elaborate, complicated, and often violent colonial project that stretched back almost three hundred years. This project had created the first global empire emanating from Europe. But it had also resulted in the deaths of millions of the original inhabitants of the Americas. Junípero Serra spent the final half of his life, from the moment he arrived in Mexico City on January 1, 1750, until his death at Carmel on August 28, 1784, struggling to live out his own beliefs in the midst of that complex and bloody colonial reality. The manner in which he did so was controversial in his own day and remains no less controversial today.

---

2. These letters of Serra are quoted more fully in chapter 10.

Junípero Serra is the most widely known figure who lived in pre–U.S. California. Schools, streets, freeways, even a mountain bear his name. A life-sized statue of him greets visitors at some of California's most visited tourist attractions, the Spanish era missions whose establishments he initiated. More words have been written about him than about anyone else who lived in pre–gold rush California. Indeed, the same is probably true about most people who lived in California after it was acquired by the United States. Serra, along with Ronald Reagan, represents California in the National Statuary Collection in the United States Capitol in Washington, D.C.

Like all historical figures, Serra has been remembered in a variety of ways. He has been celebrated and condemned. Various interpreters have found him inspiring, repulsive, or puzzling. He elicits such a range of reactions because so many of the facts of his life are known. Indeed, Serra has been fortunate in his biographers. His closest friend published a laudatory biography of him a mere three years after his death. The book was published in Mexico City, the largest city in the Americas and the cultural capital of New Spain. In its pages an idealized Serra continued to live on for decades and centuries. In more modern times, the Franciscan order freed one of its greatest historians from all other responsibilities for years at a time so that he could scour three continents for documents on Serra. Father Maynard Geiger's two-volume biography, published in 1959, reconstructed the particulars of Serra's life in the greatest detail. On those terms, it will probably never be surpassed.

The sheer volume of information we possess about Junípero Serra has made it much easier for subsequent generations to interpret him through their own experiences and cultural presuppositions. Those interpretations have at times been grounded in evidence, both creative and imaginative. But all too often they have had the inadvertent effect of flattening him, of making him two-dimensional, almost a cardboard figure. This is deeply unfortunate, for the flattening of Serra has had the effect of flattening our understanding of an important aspect of the colonial history of the American Southwest. Junípero Serra helped direct the beginning of the final expansion of the Spanish frontier. He contained in himself many of the ideas and practices that had animated almost three centuries of the Spanish presence in the Americas. Examining his life and trying to ascertain what made him do what he did can offer us a unique picture of the complex development of California and the American Southwest.

History is never written in a vacuum, and the history devoted to such a widely studied individual as Junípero Serra proves that point dramatically. The contemporary figure of Serra the man is surrounded by more than two centuries of contradictory interpretations. We must begin our study of this man by entering the interpretive mist that has come to surround him.

Junípero Serra was the subject of the first published book written in Alta California. In September 1784, a week or so after he had celebrated Serra's funeral Mass, Francisco Palóu, Serra's former student and closest friend, returned to his post at Mission San Francisco de Asís. He spent the next months writing Serra's biography, which he titled *Historical Account of the Life and Apostolic Labors of the Venerable Father Fray Junípero Serra*. Palóu took this manuscript with him when he returned to Mexico City in the summer of 1785. He circulated it among a number of his companions at the Colegio de San Fernando. At their suggestion he added a final chapter that dealt with Serra's virtues. The completed book was published by the Mexico City publishing house of Don Felipe de Zúñiga y Ontiveros in 1787.[3]

Palóu had multiple purposes in writing this biography. A chief one was personal. Junípero Serra had been his teacher, mentor, and friend. Palóu's preservation of Serra's memory was an act of personal homage, what the ancient Romans might have called *pietas*. The relationship between Palóu and Serra had been extremely close. At the beginning of the final chapter Palóu spoke of "the intimate friendship and love I owed him" from the time they first met in Mallorca almost half a century before. Palóu was the first person to whom Serra had confided his desire to go to America as a missionary. They worked together in the Sierra Gorda for eight years. They were slated to go to Texas together, but the destruction of Mission San Sabá in 1758 by a Wichita, Comanche, and Caddo force thwarted that assignment. They both worked out of the Colegio de San Fernando for the next eight years, and then they spent a year close to each other in Baja California before Serra left for Alta California in 1769. When the Franciscans transferred the Baja California missions to the Dominicans in 1773, Serra begged Palóu, then in Baja California, not to go back to Mexico City. He hoped that Palóu would go to Alta California so that "we should live and die there together." They spent considerable time together at Mission San Carlos before Palóu founded Mission San Francisco in 1776. And Palóu was the person who entered Serra's room at Mission San Carlos in 1784 and discovered his lifeless body. For Palóu, writing Serra's biography was an act of devotion to his closest companion. He presented Serra as a dedicated and selfless priest, impelled only by love for all of God's children to spread the message of salvation and civilization to the farthest corners of the globe.[4]

Palóu also had a wider purpose in writing Serra's biography. Serra had spent a good part of the last seven years of his life struggling against Governor Felipe

---

3. Palóu, *Relación histórica*.
4. Palóu, *Palóu's Life of Fray Junípero Serra*, 259, 135, 241. On Palóu's work, see also Beebe and Senkewicz, "Constructing California."

de Neve, a colonial official who shared a growing view among many officials in New Spain that missions were anachronistic institutions that retarded the civic development of the Spanish empire by inhibiting the assimilation of the native peoples. Neve tried to reduce the influence of the missions in California, to restrict the number of missionaries, and to limit their power over the Indians.[5]

Palóu attempted to create a master narrative to contest these official policies. His biography made Junípero Serra the central character in the establishment of the Spanish empire in the far northwestern frontier. Toward the end of his book he anointed Serra the true founding father of Alta California: "In this northern and new California, previously inhabited only by gentiles, he left fifteen settlements, six inhabited by Spaniards or *gente de razón*, and nine by full-blooded native neophytes baptized by His Reverence and his missionary companions." The "nine" settlements were the missions and Serra was indeed their founder. But the rest of Palóu's sentence was a dramatic overstatement. For the "six" settlements "inhabited by Spaniards or gente de razón" were four presidios and two pueblos. In fact, Serra had endured a frosty relationship with the presidios and had opposed founding the pueblos. In Palóu's formulation, however, Serra became the prime mover behind all the Spanish institutions in the province.[6]

Palóu's biography succeeded in both respects. The picture he painted of his friend, of a loving and fervent missionary, persisted. By the early twentieth century writers were building on Palóu's notion that Serra was the major figure of the era. Over time Serra became progressively identified with the place and became a virtual symbol for everything that occurred in Spanish California.

This process began even before the acquisition of California by the United States. For instance, the first English book written about California was published in 1839 by Alexander Forbes, a British merchant who resided in Tepic, Mexico. Forbes's treatment of the founding of Alta California relied heavily on Palóu and concluded with a direct quote from the biography that praised Serra's "glorious actions." Similarly, an 1846 volume, *Life in California*, by Alfred Robinson, who spent fifteen years in Mexican Alta California, described early California as exhibiting "the success and triumph of the Cross." Robinson spoke of the mission system in very positive terms: "The neophyte was protected, conquests increased, and the abundance of the warehouses and granaries continued to be distributed with . . . liberality."[7]

The first generation of American historians of California, writing in the latter decades of the nineteenth century, also accepted Palóu's personal portrait of

---

5. Beilharz, *Felipe de Neve*; Taylor, *Magistrates of the Sacred*, 83–86; Weber, *Bárbaros*, 107–109; Osante, *Testimonio acerca de la causa formada en la colonia del Nuevo Santander*, x, xxix; Osante, *Orígenes del Nuevo Santander*, 147, 234; Osante and Alcaraz Cienfuegos, *Nuevo Santander*, 82.
6. Palóu, *Palóu's Life of Fray Junípero Serra*, 257.
7. Forbes, *California*, 79–130; Robinson, *Life in California*, 18. See also Osio, *The History of Alta California*, 3.

Serra. Yankee Protestants did not regard Catholic Alta California as a particularly attractive place, however, and consequently they did not identify Serra with California as thoroughly as Palóu did.

In 1878 John S. Hittell published *A History of the City of San Francisco*. In this work he introduced a number of themes that would come to characterize a considerable amount of nineteenth-century American historical writing on Serra and the missions. While he regarded Serra as personally honorable, he thought that both he and California had been significantly inhibited by Catholicism. He wrote: "Junípero Serra was a typical Franciscan, a man to whom his religion was everything. . . . Art or poetry never served to sharpen his wits, lighten his spirits, or solace his weary moments. . . . He knew nothing of the science and philosophy which threw all enlightened nations into fermentation a hundred years ago." A man with such views was basically incapable of establishing a system that would benefit anyone, especially California's native peoples. Hittell wrote, "The Indians of California did not thrive anywhere under the care of the Friars." He continued, "It is a mistake to suppose that the Missions were prosperous institutions until their secularization. They were not even self-supporting. They were for a long time a burden on the government." Hittell believed in enlightenment and progress, and he did not see how a man with Serra's closed and retrogressive views could have made much of a contribution to California.[8]

The next significant work of California history to appear was Hubert Howe Bancroft's monumental seven-volume *History of California*. The volumes were written by multiple authors, which perhaps accounts for the somewhat variant assessments of Serra that appear in their pages. Serra appears most completely in the first volume, which tended to replicate John Hittell's judgments: Serra was a good man in the service of a flawed system. Bancroft wrote that Serra was "a great and remarkable man. Few who came to California during the missionary regime were his equal in devotion to and success in his work." He continued, "His faults were those of his cloth." Bancroft's view of the mission system was at times contradictory. At one point he argued that "down to 1800 and considerably later the natives were as a rule most kindly treated." But he also criticized the amount of coercion that existed within the missions, and he faulted Serra for never doubting "his absolute right to flog his neophytes for any slight negligence in matters of the faith."[9]

In *California Pastoral*, which was published after the early volumes of the *History of California* had been completed, Bancroft tended to soften his personal critiques of Serra while at the same time sharpening his critiques of the mission

---

8. Hittell, *A History of the City of San Francisco*, 35, 50, 58–59.
9. Bancroft, *History of California*, 1:415–16, 437, 596.

system. "Father Junípero, blessed and just!" he exclaimed in the overwrought prose that consistently marred this volume. "Serra was," Bancroft summarized, "a good and great man." But he also judged that the effects of the mission system were disastrous: "Those first pure priests who came hither, devoted ministers of the living God, who really desired the welfare of the aboriginals, desired them to live and not die; these with their comforts and their kindness killed as surely as did Cortés and Pizarro with their gunpowder, steel, and piety."[10]

Thus toward the end of the nineteenth century a clear historiographical consensus about Junípero Serra had emerged in American California. But that consensus was soon challenged. The challenge did not come from within the historical profession; rather it came from a cultural movement now known as the Spanish Revival. The writings associated with this movement retained the positive Hittell-Bancroft judgment about Serra's personal character. In addition, these authors applauded mission-era California and aggressively identified Serra with what it regarded as the blessings of the mission system. They also extended Palóu's judgment about Serra's influence over the entire sweep of California history during the Spanish and Mexican eras.

The groundwork for this movement was laid in the 1880s by Helen Hunt Jackson. In 1883 she published an essay entitled "Father Junípero and His Work" for the *Century Magazine*.

Her condemnation of the American betrayal of the Indians, which she had chronicled in her 1881 work *Century of Dishonor*, led her to project the California missions as an idealized alternative. Serra benefited from that projection. In the essay, she described his fifteen years in Alta California as "a history of struggle, hardship, and heroic achievement. The indefatigable Serra was the main spring and support of it all. There seemed no limit to his endurance, no bound to his desires; nothing daunted his courage or chilled his faith." He was, in short, "the foremost, grandest figure in the mission's history. If his successors in their administration had been equal to him in spirituality, enthusiasm, and intellect, the mission establishments would never have been so utterly overthrown and ruined."[11]

Jackson moved from this effusive praise of Serra to an almost iconic portrayal of life at the missions as it was understood during the Spanish Revival: "The picture of life in one of these missions during their period of prosperity is unique and attractive. The whole place was a hive of industry: trade plying indoors and outdoors; tillers, herders, vintagers by hundreds, going to and fro; children in schools; women spinning; bands of young men practicing on musical instruments; music, the scores of which, in many instances, they had themselves written out;

---

10. Bancroft, *California Pastoral*, 168, 174.
11. H.H. [Helen Hunt Jackson], "Father Junípero and His Work," 11, 18.

at evening, all sorts of games of running, leaping, dancing, and all throwing, and the picturesque ceremonies of the religion which has always been wise in availing itself of beautiful agencies in color, form, and harmony."[12]

Jackson's writings sparked an outpouring of celebration of Serra and the mission system in popular culture. Mrs. Jane Stanford, who had contributed money for the restoration of Mission San Carlos in Carmel in the 1880s, commissioned a statue of Serra, which was dedicated in Monterey in 1891. Jackson's essay was republished in 1902 and included a series of drawings by Henry Sandham. That same year Charles Fletcher Lummis published a translation of Serra's diary from Baja California to San Diego in *Out West*. In his introduction to the translation, Lummis wrote: "It is full, not only of the humility and faith and quenchless courage of the greatest missionary who ever trod the soil of the United States, it is also vital with his quiet humor." Former San Francisco mayor James Phelan spearheaded an effort to have a statue of Serra placed in San Francisco's Golden Gate Park, and the heroic representation of the missionary was dedicated in 1907. That same year, Frank Miller, owner of the Glenwood Mission Inn in Riverside, erected a "Serra Cross" at the summit of Mount Rubidoux outside of Riverside. In 1913, to celebrate the two hundredth anniversary of Serra's birth, both Phelan and Miller helped George Wharton James fund and publish the first complete English translation of Palóu's biography, which was done by C. Scott Williams.[13]

A plethora of laudatory popular biographies of Serra soon appeared. Racine McRoskey's 1914 volume *The Missions of California*, in which Serra was described as "the greatest and most wonderful disciple of Saint Francis," was heavily dependent on Helen Hunt Jackson's 1883 essay. Some of these biographies were influenced by contemporary American politics. After the Spanish-American War, some Americans had ironically and probably unknowingly adopted the rationale of the Spanish empire to justify annexation of the Philippines. A remark attributed to President McKinley by one of his supporters in 1903 may not actually have been spoken by the president, but it did express widespread public sentiment. The president is said to have told a group of ministers that it was America's task to "civilize and Christianize" the Filipinos, who were "our fellow men for whom Christ also died."[14]

In this context Serra was Americanized as the person who first did in California what the United States was said to be doing in the Philippines. As a 1914 work by A. H. Fitch, *Junípero Serra: The Man and His Work*, stated, "Whatever was done to further the cause of civilization in California was done by him." While

---

12. H.H. [Helen Hunt Jackson], "Father Junípero and His Work," 200.
13. Jackson, *Father Junípero and the Mission Indians of California*; Lummis, "Diary of Junípero Serra," 293; Palóu, *Francisco Palóu's Life and Apostolic Labors of the Venerable Father Junípero Serra*.
14. McRoskey, *The Missions of California*, 11; Gould, *The Spanish-American War*, 109.

some historians, such as James M. Guinn, struggled to keep alive the complex version of Serra that had become prevalent in nineteenth-century California histories, the popular picture of Serra and the missions became even more heroic and one-dimensional. As the Franciscan historian Francis Guest later quipped, in Spanish Revival writings "the missionaries were portrayed as a kind of collective Santa Claus, as it were, distributing among the California Indians the blessings of western culture and civilization."[15]

The great Franciscan historian Zephyrin Engelhardt provided an impressive scholarly foundation for some of these popular perceptions. His master work, the four-volume *Missions and Missionaries of California*, was published between 1908 and 1915. He followed that with a series of local studies, and he was able to complete sixteen volumes in this series before his death in 1934.[16]

Engelhardt used the documents that had come to Mission Santa Bárbara as the backbone for his many studies. Herbert Eugene Bolton shared with him many documents that Bolton collected on research trips to Mexico. Engelhardt also researched in the Archive of California, which was in San Francisco and from which the Bancroft staff made a series of abstracts that filled sixty-three handwritten volumes in the 1870s. Engelhardt may have been one of the last scholars to use that original collection before it was destroyed in the fire following the San Francisco earthquake of 1906.

Engelhardt was upset at what he took to be the anti-Catholic bias in the writings of the California historians of the later nineteenth century. As we have seen, many of those historians were critical of the mission system, and Engelhardt wrote passionately in response.[17]

Serra was not an actor in those sections of his volumes where Engelhardt wrote most intensely. These sections involved the secularization of the missions in the 1830s, which Engelhardt interpreted through the prism of the anticlericalism of the Mexican Revolution of the 1910s. He regarded secularization primarily as an attack on the Catholic Church and secondarily as a betrayal of the Indians. But Serra was the dominant figure in Engelhardt's treatment of the first fifteen years of the Alta California missions. Engelhardt's Serra was the selfless and dedicated hero depicted by the Spanish Revival authors. He termed Serra "guileless." His devotion to the missions and to the Indians was boundless. At one point, describing life at Mission San Carlos, Engelhardt said that Serra was "thoroughly at home in philosophy and theology, and turn[ed] to something altogether outside

---

15. Fitch, *Junípero Serra*, 356; Sandos, "Junípero Serra, Canonization, and the California Indian Controversy," 319; Guest, "The Cause of Junípero Serra," 14.
16. Pilarcik, "Out of the Ruins," 35–40, 50–70.
17. Bancroft, *History of California*, 1:418–20; Engelhardt, *Missions and Missionaries*, 2:69, 404.

of his sphere as a priest, but under the circumstances of more urgent importance—to cereals, vegetables, and livestock. How he must have loathed it; yet for the sake of his beloved Indians, he devoted himself to that department of Indian missionary existence as though he loved that too." He also remarked that Serra's "forbearance of Neve's impertinence bordered on the heroic."[18]

The other side of the coin of Engelhardt's glorification of the missionaries was his denigration of the culture of the California Indians. Most nineteenth-century American writers regarded the native Californians as uncivilized and brutish, and Engelhardt cited such opinions about the Indians offered by Franklin Tuthill, Bancroft, and Theodore Hittell. But Engelhardt also had his own purpose in emphasizing what he took to be the lack of genuine culture among California's native peoples. The lower the Indians were on the scale of human development, the more heroic the missionaries could become in his pages, as he described their leaving their homelands and giving up everything as they embraced their ministry to such people, who were widely regarded, he said, "as among the most stupid, brutish, filthy, lazy and improvident of the aborigines of America." The only exception Engelhardt allowed were the Chumash along the Santa Bárbara Channel, who "seem to have been somewhat brighter and more industrious." In such a desolate landscape, the missionaries were indeed heroic. Their aim was "none other than the conversion of the savages to Christianity," and "they have given up relatives, friends, property, prospects, and mother country for the sake of attracting souls to Christ," a task that was, in Engelhardt's view, "superhuman."[19]

One result of Engelhardt's prodigious research in primary sources was to provide additional documentation on the missions that could be used to assist in enhancing Serra's burgeoning reputation. In 1927 Willa Cather worked into her novel *Death Comes for the Archbishop* Palóu's story about Serra's encounter with a hospitable family that he took to be an apparition of Joseph, Mary, and Jesus. In the same year, in a move that epitomized the degree to which Serra had become formally identified with California, the California legislature established a commission to select who should represent California in Statuary Hall. Serra was chosen, along with Unitarian minister Thomas Starr King. The statues were unveiled in 1931. The main speaker for Serra was prominent Los Angeles Catholic layman and lawyer Isidore Dockweiler. While acknowledging that "Serra represented a theory of colonial government, which is obsolete today," Dockweiler eulogized Serra as "our country's first civilizer of our western coasts."[20]

---

18. Engelhardt, *Missions and Missionaries*, 2:145, 315; 3:341–42; Engelhardt, *Mission San Carlos Borromeo*, 87.
19. Engelhardt, *Missions and Missionaries*, 2:224, 234, 242, 245.
20. Cather, *Death Comes for the Archbishop*, 292–96; *Acceptance and Unveiling of the Statues of Junípero Serra and Thomas Starr King*, 37, 40, 43. California decided to replace the King statue with one of Ronald Reagan after the former president's death in 2004.

The Serra Cause, the effort to advance him on the road to formal canonization as a saint by the Catholic Church, began in 1934. It was a direct outgrowth of Serra's growing prominence in popular culture. The cause owed a great deal to romantic writers like Helen Hunt Jackson, Spanish Revivalists like Lummis, and influential and wealthy Catholic laymen like Dockweiler. It also sparked a tremendous outpouring of scholarly activity, notably in the person of the modern founder of Serra studies, Father Maynard Geiger, OFM. As Engelhardt's successor at Santa Bárbara, Geiger undertook a Herculean series of journeys seeking Serra documentation on three continents. These journeys were supported by wealthy Catholic laypeople and foundations. The hundreds of documents that he collected and copied form the core of the invaluable Junípero Serra Collection at the Santa Bárbara Mission Archive-Library. Geiger published a series of articles in the late 1940s in *The Americas*, the journal of the Academy of American Franciscan History. He published a new translation of *Palóu's Life of Junípero Serra* in 1955, and his monumental two-volume biography of Serra appeared in 1959. As an example of how close the identification between Serra and California had become, Geiger titled his chapter on Serra's 1769–70 sojourn in San Diego "Here California Began." Geiger broke little conceptual new ground on Serra, for his volumes followed the broad outlines of Palóu's account. But he created a picture of Serra and his times that was broader, deeper, and much more nuanced than anything that had come before.[21]

It is perhaps appropriate that Geiger's magisterial biography was published in 1959, for the decade that began the following year witnessed a seismic shift in many aspects of the writing of history in the United States. As the title of one anthology from the late 1960s said, Americans were beginning to construct a "new past." Groups who had hitherto been acknowledged only on the margins of historiography began to claim much more central spaces. Native Americans were one such group, and early California history was dramatically altered by their being restored to the foreground. As native Californian historians, anthropologists, and others influenced by this change in perspective began to produce scholarly works, much of the conventional history of the California missions was called into question. Since Junípero Serra had become the preeminent emblem of the mission era, the reevaluation of the missions resulted in a reevaluation of him.[22]

In California this development had been anticipated in the writings of Sherburne F. Cook. Research that he conducted early in his career on diseases suffered by native peoples of Baja California led him to a wider investigation of population trends among California Indians. Cook published the results of

---

21. Geiger, *Life and Times of Fray Junípero Serra*, 1:228–38.
22. Bernstein, *Towards a New Past*.

this research in a series of seminal articles in the early 1940s. Cook documented the rapid and consistent population decline experienced by the native peoples of California during the mission era and the ways in which that decline was especially pronounced among Indians who were part of the mission system. He was critical of what he argued were systematic forced conversions of Indians by the missionaries and by the use of excessive corporal punishment within the missions. In 1946 Carey McWilliams seized on Cook's research and compared the missions to "concentration camps." The California Indian occupation of Alcatraz from 1969 to 1971 brought the California Indians' loss of their lands into greater public consciousness and spurred even more California historians to take a fresh look at this issue.[23]

Native American historian Jack D. Forbes was already a pioneer in this endeavor. A series of articles about native peoples in Sonora and the American Southwest in the late 1950s served as a background for an important essay he published in *The Americas* in 1963, which was titled "The Historian and the Indian: Racial Bias in American History." This was followed by a series of seminal books and articles on California and Southwest Indians over the next two decades. One of the earliest scholar-activists, Forbes was a leader in the development of Native American Studies programs. He also wrote fiction and poetry.[24]

A number of scholars who followed Forbes focused their attention on the relationship between the missions and the native peoples. Notable among them were Florence Shipek and Robert H. Jackson. Starting with her 1977 dissertation at the University of Hawaii on the Luiseño people, Shipek devoted her entire career to the experiences of the native peoples of Southern California. She focused her work on the Kumeyaay. Jackson began his publishing career with studies of what the mission registers in northern Mexico and Baja California revealed about the Indian presence in those regions. He centered his research on the incidence of disease and the death rates of the native peoples and he published a series of important studies on the catastrophic decline of the Indian population in California and elsewhere. Since much of the evidence for significant population decline was taken from mission registers recorded decades after Serra's death, Serra himself did not figure directly in much of this research. But by that time he was tightly identified with everything that happened in California before the American conquest. Furthermore, as a result of the Serra Cause, the writings of Geiger, and the work of the Academy of American Franciscan History, there was more information available on Serra than on any other California missionary.

---

23. Cook, "Population Trends"; Cook, "The Conflict between the California Indian and White Civilization," i–iv.
24. Forbes, "Historical Survey of the Indians of Sonora"; Forbes, "Unknown Athapaskans"; Forbes, "The Historian and the Indian."

This solidified his popular status as a symbol of everything that had happened during the entire mission era. Serra's centrality was reinforced when, as the two hundredth anniversary of his death approached in 1984, a number of California Catholics organized the Serra Bicentennial Commission and sought, among other things, to move the Serra Cause forward.[25]

The mid-1980s was a period of great contention as this new scholarship and a renewed emphasis on Serra's beatification and canonization coincided with international planning for the Columbus quincentenary in 1992. Native peoples and others throughout the Americas were determined to ensure that this anniversary be commemorated not as a celebration of European expansion (as the 1892 anniversary had been), but as a stark remembrance of the catastrophic (some preferred the term "genocidal") population decline and extreme cultural dislocation that many Native American groups experienced after 1492. In California, Carey McWilliams's "concentration camp" analogy was widely employed, and Serra was sometimes portrayed as the grisly architect of a death-dealing system. One professor in the California State University system was quoted as saying that Serra was a "sadist" and a "fanatic." A native Californian who taught at a community college near Santa Cruz stated, "The missionaries were sent here by the Spanish monarchy along with the military to work hand-in-hand to colonize this so-called virgin territory. And to bring the Indian people through the baptismal into slavery." Another opponent stated, "To make a man a saint after he helped in the genocide of Native Americans in this part of the country is a contradiction of the words the religion preaches."[26]

As this controversy began to intensify, the Academy of American Franciscan History decided to commemorate the two hundredth anniversary of Serra's death with a conference at the American Historical Association meeting in Chicago in December 1984. The American Catholic Historical Association and the Conference of Latin American Historians cosponsored the gathering. The Academy decided to try to break the tight link between Serra and California. As Antonine Tibesar, OFM, stated, the focus was "on the frontier of Northwestern New Spain during Serra's time, 1750–1825, as well as on his work in Upper California." The conference proceedings were published in *The Americas* the next year and also as a separate volume by the Academy. The controversy was certainly present in the proceedings, especially in the sharply opposing essays by Florence C. Shipek and

---

25. Shipek, "A Strategy for Change"; Shipek, "A Native American Adaptation to Drought"; Shipek, "Kumeyaay Socio-political Structure"; Jackson, "Epidemic Disease and Population Decline"; Jackson, "The Last Jesuit Censuses of the Pimería Alta Missions"; Jackson, "Demographic Patterns in the Missions of Northern Baja California"; Jackson and Castillo, *Indians, Franciscans, and Spanish Colonization*; Castillo, "The Assassination of Padre Andrés Quintana"; Castillo, "An Indian Account of the Decline and Collapse of Mexico's Hegemony."
26. See, for instance, "Activist Threatens to Resist Canonization; To Many Indians, Serra Was No Saint," *Los Angeles Times*, March 26, 1986; Associated Press, "Report Responds to Serra Critics," *Modesto Bee*, November 27, 1986.

Harry Kelsey, but the conference as a whole adopted a much broader framework. The keynote address, by Mexican historian Miguel León-Portilla, focused on the interrelationship between Serra and Spanish official José de Gálvez, while other contributions focused on events in Spain and over the entire reach of northwestern and northern New Spain. A final essay by Louis J. Luzbetak, SVD, focused on the manner in which aims and methods of Catholic missionary activity had dramatically changed since the eighteenth century.[27]

This broader approach was the hallmark of the third great Franciscan archivist-historian, Father Francis Guest. The first of this group to receive historical training in a secular university, he earned a doctorate from the University of Southern California. Significantly, his dissertation was not on one of the missions or one of the friars. Rather, in "Municipal Institutions in Spanish California, 1769–1821," he chose to focus on the entity in Alta California that most displeased Serra: the *pueblo*. Guest's masterwork was his authoritative biography of the often underappreciated Fermín Francisco de Lasuén, Serra's successor as president of the missions.

However, as the beatification process moved forward, this broader approach was overshadowed for a time by a tighter focus on Serra and California. In 1986 Monterey bishop Thaddeus Shubsda arranged for the publication of "The Serra Report," whose core was interviews of eight leading historians and anthropologists. They all attempted to place Serra in a wide context, but the thrust of the interview questions generally tended to direct the discussion back to Serra's personal behavior as a missionary in California and his personal relationship to the Indians. The interviewers insisted, correctly, that there was little evidence that Serra himself personally abused the Indians with whom he directly dealt and that there was also little evidence of widespread forced conversions during the time he was missionary president. Those interviewed tried to keep a distance from the controversy. One said, "I don't know whether Serra's a saint or not. That's not my business to judge." But the controversy, and the link between Serra and the entire experience of pre-American California which animated it, was never far from the surface. One participant echoed Palóu's assertions about Serra as the founder of and emblem for all of Alta California. He praised Serra's ability to "coordinate the settlements of a whole new frontier. . . . We have somebody here who took a whole brand-new frontier, did not know anything about it, and in four years had taken it and converted it into a functioning organized frontier." But since the aim of the report was to clear the ground for Serra's eventual beatification, the parts of the report that most focused on Serra himself earned the most widespread public attention.[28]

---

27. Tibesar, "Editor's Note," *The Americas* 41.4 (1985): 426.
28. The report may be found at The Bancroft Library, BANC MSS 87/208c. Large sections also appear in Costo and Costo, *The Missions of California*, 222.

The report was answered the very next year with the publication of a provocatively titled work, *The Missions of California: A Legacy of Genocide*. This volume vigorously argued that Spanish colonialism had an extremely negative effect on California's indigenous communities, which were numerous and thriving before the arrival of the Europeans. As enthusiastic agents of Spanish colonialism, and as the founders and directors of the twenty-one places along the California coast in which the Indian death rates dramatically and routinely exceeded birth rates, Serra, along with the missionaries, bore primary responsibility for this demographic catastrophe. The volume was a mix of scholarly articles and powerful personal testimonies by a number of native Californians, including one who was a Catholic priest.

After Pope John Paul II beatified Serra in Rome in 1988, the controversy continued to rage for a few years. But then more scholars began to look at Serra from the wider perspective that the Academy of American Franciscan History had urged in the mid-1980s. A 1992 volume by Bartoméu Font Obrador and Norman Neuerburg, *Fr. Junípero Serra: Mallorca, México, Sierra Gorda, Californias*, was in this vein. This trilingual work (English, Spanish, and Catalán) delved even more deeply into Serra's Mallorcan roots. Obrador and Neuerburg placed Serra's youth in the context of popular devotion on that island.[29]

Two recent Franciscan historians, Lino Gómez Canedo and José Luis Soto Pérez, have made important contributions to the study of Serra and his work by emphasizing the non-California aspects of his life and efforts. Other historians have related Serra to larger trends. For instance, Steven W. Hackel's *Children of Coyote, Missionaries of St. Francis* focused on the Monterey Bay region during the Spanish and Mexican periods. Serra appeared often, especially toward the beginning of the volume, and his writings and actions were taken as emblematic of the larger Franciscan approach to the native peoples. But Hackel's main concern was what he called the "dual revolutions"—demographic and ecological—that dramatically transformed the experiences of the native peoples of California. Craig Russell devoted a chapter to Serra in *From Serra to Sancho: Music and Pageantry in the California Missions*. Russell demonstrated how music was central to the rituals and conventions associated with the founding of the missions. He analyzed the religious background and evangelical meaning of the hymns that Serra indicated were sung on those occasions. James Sandos's pioneering study *Converting California* was in the same vein. Sandos sharply distinguished between baptism and conversion and sensitively examined the different fashions in which the missionaries and native peoples understood what was happening when native people became members of various mission communities. Steven Hackel's 2013 biography of Serra joined much of this recent research with Hackel's own extensive

---

29. Font Obrador and Neuerburg, *Fr. Junípero Serra*.

archival investigations to present the first scholarly account of Serra's entire life since Geiger's effort sixty years previously. In 2014 Gregory Orfalea offered a generally sympathetic portrayal of Serra from a literary and speculative perspective.[30]

Junípero Serra's life and career have thus generated an immense and rich body of interpretive writings. Indeed, in the two centuries since his death, writers have enlisted Junípero Serra's participation in a series of controversies—about the Bourbon reforms in Colonial New Spain, the significance of the American conquest of Mexican California, the Spanish revival movement, and the social and cultural conflicts of the 1960s and after. On the one hand, this is not surprising. History is always a dialogue between past and present, and historical figures of the past are inevitably and properly interpreted through the prism of the present. But present and past must be held in balance. In the case of Serra, the present has often overwhelmed the past, and the actual lived experience of Junípero Serra has at times been obscured by the interpretive controversies that have surrounded him. In this volume, we attempt to redress that balance.

We focus on Serra the man and on two aspects of his life and work that have not been brought together systematically in the voluminous historiography his career has spawned. Those are (1) his sense of self-identity, that of an eighteenth-century Roman Catholic missionary priest, and (2) his relationships with the native peoples he encountered in the Americas. We believe that these two aspects of Serra's life and work, more than any others, defined him and provided him with a meaning and purpose for virtually everything he did after he left his homeland in 1749. While various authors have made important contributions by examining one or other of these aspects, we believe that the core of Junípero Serra can be discovered only when these two aspects are thoroughly analyzed and placed side by side. This was how he defined himself.

In this work we seek to present Junípero Serra as he was. We attempt to relate him to the people and the social and cultural realities of his age. At the same time, however, because the writing of history inevitably looks to both past and present, we attempt to access his significance within the framework of today's interpretive trends relating to the ethnohistory of northern New Spain.

For the past two decades, we have been involved in recovering and translating the writings of men and women who lived in California before the gold rush.

---

30. Gómez Canedo, *Sierra Gorda*; Gómez Canedo, *Evangelización, cultura y promoción social*; Gómez Canedo, *Evangelización y conquista*; Palóu, *Cartas desde la península de California*; Palóu, *Recopilación de noticias*; Hackel, *Children of Coyote*; Russell, *From Serra to Sancho*; Sandos, *Converting California*; Hackel, *Junípero Serra*; Orfalea, *Journey to the Sun*.

That experience has led us to believe that people's language is one of the best windows into their psyches, beliefs, and values. So, in our attempts to present Serra as he was, we turn to what he wrote. And he was a voluminous writer. That predilection stemmed partly from the fact that he was an academic before he became a missionary, so writing came somewhat easily to him. It also grew out of the fact that, as president of the Alta California missions, he had to write what seemed to him to be an interminable series of reports. Finally, for Serra, writing was at times a way of thinking. For all of these reasons, he has left us a rich body of writings from his own hands.

The present volume is built around the words of Junípero Serra. However, those words have survived in an intermittent way, thus they cannot be uniformly placed throughout our volume. Serra spent the first half of his life in Mallorca, and he probably did not write very many letters during those thirty-five years. Mallorca itself was a relatively small island, and Serra traveled widely throughout it. He was able to maintain contact with family and friends on a more personal, face-to-face basis. What writing he did was generally academic, consisting of the notes he took as a student and the lecture notes he composed as a faculty member. Only fragments of these actual writings have survived. The other type of writing Serra did while he was in Mallorca was religious. He preached widely in Palma and in many villages throughout the island. Three of his sermons, along with part of a fourth, have survived. Of these writings from the first half of his life, we present in an appendix the four sermons that have survived.

Serra wrote much after he arrived in America, but those writings have survived in the same intermittent fashion. For the eight years he spent in the Sierra Gorda, only one substantial letter has been found. A few letters survive from the time he returned from the Sierra Gorda in 1758 to the time he arrived in Baja California in 1768. Records of an interrogation of two women he conducted for the Inquisition in 1766 are also extant.

Serra's writings exist in the most systematic fashion from the period after he arrived in Baja California, and the overwhelming majority of his extant correspondence and writings dates from the time he was president of the missions in Alta California. For the time Serra was stationed in Alta California, his own voice is more consistently present in the documentary record, and we try to present his experiences in his own words.

This pattern of the survival of Serra's correspondence means that a volume like the present one, built around his words, has to diverge from the traditional way in which documentary history is presented. For almost three-quarters of his life, we have only a few documents from his own hand. Because Serra's actions in Alta California from 1769 onward seem to have been fundamentally shaped by the values and standards he acquired before he arrived there, we use our own words to try to reconstruct his pre-California experiences. Since this part of Serra's life is less well-known, we have supplemented our text describing these years with a large number of illustrations, to help the reader gain a visual sense of what Serra's worlds were like.

Serra's writings touch on a number of topics. In fact, very few of his letters from California are about only one thing, a consequence of the manner in which he composed them. He generally wrote letters when it was possible to send them. So when a boat arrived or he was told that a military courier was heading south, he would compose a series of long letters to Mexico City or to other missions, in which he would try to cover everything that had happened since he composed his last letters. Because he was never sure that these previous letters had reached their destinations by the time he was composing the new ones, he would often repeat some information he had put in previous letters, just to be sure. His letters, therefore, tended to be filled with repetitive information on a myriad of topics, ranging from liturgical happenings to the health of the mules at the mission, from questions about rations for the servants to the number of sacraments administered. While our focus in this volume is on religious identity and indigenous people, we have included parts of some letters that dealt with these other topics. We believe the reader should have a sense of the day-to-day activities that took up so much of Serra's time. Also, the existence of the diary of military commander Fernando de Rivera y Moncada allows us to reconstruct some of the correspondence between him and Serra in the mid-1770s. As a result the reader can get a "slice of life" sense of the matters that engaged Serra from day to day.

For many years the writings of Junípero Serra were accessible only in their original Spanish form. But thanks to the painstaking work of mid-twentieth-century scholars, these documents were transcribed and translated and thus became accessible to a wider audience. As approaches to scholarship on Serra have changed in the intervening half century, so has the way we translate original documents. Living languages are constantly evolving. Translation is an art, not a science. Translations that were appropriate in the 1950s may not be as fitting for the twenty-first century. Indeed, the word-for-word method of translation that was used by some scholars in the past had its downside. In their quest to preserve the "flavor" of the original document, the end product was sometimes stilted, hard to understand, and misleading. In some instances the living language of the original documents was obscured or lost. That being said, experienced translators know that there is no such thing as a perfect translation. We, as researchers, value the outstanding contributions of these scholars and strive to build on their efforts to gain a deeper understanding of Junípero Serra.

For the present volume, we offer new translations of Serra's Spanish writings. We have used both originals and various copies of Serra's documents at the Santa Bárbara Mission Archive-Library, as well as the transcriptions in the authoritative four-volume bilingual set of Serra's writings published by the Academy of American Franciscan History between 1955 and 1966. We have attempted to render the living language of the eighteenth century—Serra's living language—into the language we speak today.[31]

Through his writings, Serra displayed a wide range of human emotions. For example, before setting sail from Cádiz to cross the Atlantic, Serra wrote a letter to a priest in Mallorca in which he expressed how he felt as he was faced with the probability of never seeing his aging parents again. His language conveyed a poignant mix of joy and sadness, anticipation and regret, enthusiasm and melancholy:

> My beloved friend, I am at a loss for words, yet overwhelmed by emotion as I depart. I beg you once again to comfort my parents. I know they will be greatly affected by my leaving. I wish I could instill in them the great joy that I am experiencing because I believe they would urge me to go forth and never turn back.

Junípero Serra had a complex sense of humor. He could be witty, dry, or sarcastic, even at times childlike. In the following example taken from Serra's Baja California diary, he describes what happened to a burro and plays on the word "homicide":

> June 19. . . . On today's journey, one of the Señor Gobernador's servants, a Genoese cook, showed the strength of his sword by thrusting it through the hindquarters of a she-ass because the animal had the audacity to cut in front of the cook when he was riding, thus slowing him down. The she-ass died at the cook's feet. The Señor Gobernador was convinced a crime had been committed based on the statements of eyewitnesses and the confession of the man who committed the "burricide."

Serra also experienced anger, but he made every effort to keep that anger within the boundaries of diplomacy and tact. When he felt that he was being unjustly attacked or criticized, he would respond in a forceful but contained manner. For example, Governor Felipe de Neve once remarked to Serra that he believed the priests were more concerned about themselves than about the welfare of the Indians. Serra minced no words in his response to Neve. He was polite, but his anger was not far from the surface:

---

31. Serra, *Writings*.

If our request for the advancement of the missions and for the equitable payment of what is due them appears to be excessive, one must keep in mind that this was achieved through the toil of many poor and wretched Indians. And if advocating effectively on their behalf has the appearance of greed, many saints who have come before us and who have surpassed us, will not be free from that accusation. If the clothing and provisions requested are to stave off hunger and cover the Indians' nudity, doing so should appear as an act of charity. And that being so, it should not be harshly criticized as being excessive, since the charity of God Himself is praised as such. We work for the good of these poor people, without harming others and without duplicity, of which, it seems, some have accused us.

In our quest to present a multidimensional picture of Junípero Serra—a complex individual living in a complex era—we found ourselves mediating between two cultures, our own and that of the eighteenth-century Spanish empire. Also, since any type of translation compels the translator to be both active (constantly making the interpretive, contextual, and linguistic judgments on which the translation depends) and passive (ensuring that the author's voice is primary), our interdisciplinary study of Junípero Serra takes place at the intersection of history, culture, and linguistics. Through this study and these new translations we have tried to preserve and convey the power and nuances of Serra's voice and, ultimately, the impact of the man through his writings.

As with any translation project, some words and phrases do not have a precise English equivalent, such as words that name positions in an official bureaucracy, food, measurements, or items of clothing. We have left these words untranslated and have provided a glossary for them. In the case of Serra's writings, we have done the same thing for the semi-official titles and adjectives he uses when he refers to particular people, such as the viceroy, the governor, or the military commander. We believe that translating these titles would bestow on Serra's letters an inaccurate tone and flavor. To fill a translation of one of his letters with phrases like "The Most Illustrious Gentleman" or "The Most Excellent Lord" or "Your Grace" would give that translation a tone of obsequiousness that the original Spanish did not have. When Serra used these phrases, he was not groveling or affecting a false sense of humility. These phrases were simply the normal polite phrases of the day, for which we really do not have an equivalent meaning in American English of the twenty-first century. So we have left them untranslated and placed them in the glossary as well.

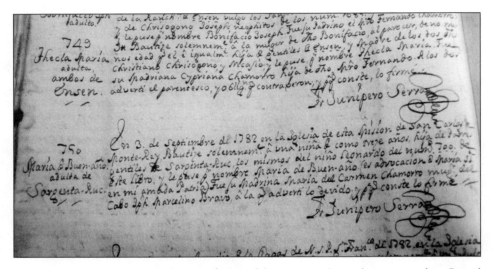

FIGURE 1. Serra's record of the baptism of María del Buen Año, September 3, 1782, when Carmel was experiencing the prospect of a poor harvest. *Courtesy of Rev. Carl Faria, Diocese of Monterey, in California Archives.*

CHAPTER 1

Mallorca

Junípero Serra's life began and ended at the edge of empire. He was born on the fringes of Spain and died on the fringes of the Spanish empire. Except for an eight-year period during which he was headquartered just outside of Mexico City, the capital of the viceroyalty of New Spain, he spent his entire life as a man of the periphery.

Serra spent the first half of his life on the island of Mallorca, the largest of the Balearic Islands. Serra's life was influenced by the island's culture—a culture that was dynamic and outward looking. The island's location on a number of Mediterranean trade routes made it a center of cartography during the Middle Ages. In addition, the largely Jewish members of what came to be called the "Mallorcan school" produced some stunning masterpieces, such as the 1375 Catalán Atlas. Even though the island was small by conventional measures, with slightly over 100,000 inhabitants at the beginning of the eighteenth century, it always prized its connections to the larger world. Junípero Serra's life on Mallorca consisted of a series of moves into larger theaters. He started in a small agricultural town, then moved to the capital. He entered the Franciscan order and quickly ascended through its ranks to become one of the leading professors and preachers among Mallorcan Franciscans. But he found that he was not satisfied and, like many of his countrymen before him, was driven to leave his island home for what he hoped would be broader horizons.[1]

BEGINNINGS

Serra was born on November 24, 1713, in the rural village of Petra, on the western side of Mallorca. His parents, Antoní Serra and Margarita Ferrer, christened him Miquel Josep. He was the third child born to the couple, who had been

---

1. Vicedo, *La casa solariega de la familia Serra*, 245; Santamaría Arández, "Mallorca en el siglo 14," 273–75; Xamena Fiol, "El siglo 16," 281.

married six years earlier. The first two children, a boy and a girl, both died in infancy. Petra was a small agricultural village of approximately two thousand people, and its roots may have stretched back to Roman times. Serra was proud of its history. Shortly before he left for the Americas, he boasted that it was one of the four oldest *villas* on the island.[2]

Serra's father owned and tended six small parcels of land scattered around the outskirts of Petra, and young Miquel worked the land with him. He thus grew up close to the land in a region where the forces of nature determined much about the quality of life. Cycles of drought had long been a fact of life on Mallorca. During the Middle Ages, Mallorca won the right to alleviate famines by trading for food among the Muslims of southern Spain and northern Africa. Engaging in such commerce made the island a center for trade and cartography. This form of commerce became one of the traditional privileges (*fueros*) of the island. The residents of Petra were no strangers to drought. One of the major religious devotions in the village involved the veneration of the Virgin Mary under the title of Our Lady of Bonany, which was Catalán for *buen año*, or "good year." The devotion dated from 1609, a year of bountiful harvests after a number of years of drought. The "good year" was attributed to the villagers' prayers to Mary. A chapel to Mary was built outside Petra to commemorate the happy result. Serra always cherished this devotion, and he always remained, at least in part, a resident of Petra. For instance, in 1782, when Serra was sixty-eight years old, the harvest at Mission San Carlos was projected to be a poor one. On September 3 of that year, Serra baptized a child at Mission San Carlos in Carmel. He recorded it in the baptismal register as follows:

> On September 3, 1782, in the church of this mission, San Carlos de Monterrey, I solemnly baptized a girl, about thirteen years old, the daughter of gentile parents from Sargenta-Ruc, the same parents of the boy Leonardo, number 300 in this book. I gave her the name María de Buen-año, (in honor of Most Holy Mary of my beloved homeland). Her godmother was María del Carmen Chamorro, wife of Corporal José Marcelino Bravo. I advised her of her responsibilities. And in order for it to be on record, I signed it.
>
> Fr. Junípero Serra

This baptismal record suggests that Serra hoped the Virgin would act in Monterey Bay as he believed she had acted in Petra.[3]

---

2. Geiger, *Life and Times of Fray Junípero Serra*, 1:3–8; Serra, *Writings*, 4:298–99.
3. This record is baptism SC [San Carlos] 00750 in the Early California Population Project database, http://www.huntington.org/Information/ECPPmain.htm. The sacramental register in which the full record is contained is located in the Archives of the Diocese of Monterey, in Monterey, California. We thank Br. Lawrence Scrivani, SM, for locating this record for us when he served as archivist; Lladó Ferragut, "El siglo 17 en Mallorca," 209–17.

Drought likely featured among Serra's last memories of Mallorca. In 1747, two years before he left for the Americas, the harvests began to fail. By the end of the 1740s, the island's farmers were bringing in only one-sixth of the amount of wheat they had harvested just a few years earlier. A number of the wealthier Mallorcan families left for the mainland, and their absence appears to have contributed to a significant decline in the local economy. By January 1749 special prayers for rain were ordered to be said in all of the churches of the island. The skies did not open until the second week of May. By then, Serra was in Cádiz on the Spanish mainland, where he was awaiting passage for America.[4]

These Mallorcan agricultural catastrophes left a permanent mark on Serra. His correspondence from California repeatedly demonstrated his insatiable desire to leave no detail of the agricultural and economic development of the missions unattended. Large sections of his famous 1773 *representación* to the viceroy, which is mostly remembered for Serra's successful appeal to get Pedro Fages replaced as military commander of Alta California, were devoted to the issues of maintaining and supplying the struggling missions. Serra's remarks covered a range of topics, such as the necessity of immediately readying a new frigate, the best way for invoices to be drawn up, and the reasons the missions needed another forge and a blacksmith. Drought had taught Serra that agricultural enterprises could be very fragile.[5]

There was another aspect of life in Petra that continued to influence Serra. After around 1720, it appears that the production of textiles increased notably in the rural areas of the island. In Mallorca, as elsewhere in Europe, most of this work was done by women. Figures are hard to come by, but it appears that between 1720 and 1755, when Serra was growing up in Petra, studying and teaching in Palma, and traveling widely throughout the Mallorcan countryside as a preacher, textile exports from the island almost tripled. Women therefore played an especially important economic role in the communities in which Serra lived and worked during this period. For Serra and the Mallorcans who accompanied him to the New World, the well-ordered rural community included women who were engaged in weaving and other forms of domestic production. In his laudatory biography of Serra, his fellow Franciscan Francisco Palóu described his and Serra's missionary activities in the Sierra Gorda from 1750 to 1758 in terms that harked back to their experiences in the Balearic Islands. Under Serra's leadership, he said, "the harvests increased and became so abundant that some was left over," and the native women were employed "in tasks befitting their sex, such as spinning, weaving, making stockings, knitting, sewing, and so forth."

---

4. Piña Homs, "Del decreto de Nueva Planta a las Cortes de Cádiz," 321; Alomar Esteve, *Ensayos sobre historia de las Islas Baleares*, 365–66; Campaner y Fuertes, *Cronicon Mayoricense*, 538.
5. Bancroft, *History of California*, 1:416; Serra, *Writings*, 1:294–329.

In some ways, Serra's journey to the New World represented a continuity of his traditions in Petra.[6]

Franciscan Student

Serra attended a primary school in Petra that was run by the Franciscans. He left his home village when he was fifteen years old and spent a year studying with one of the canons of the cathedral in Palma. He was most likely encouraged to do so by the Franciscans in Petra, who were always on the lookout for bright young boys who might join the order. Indeed, between 1607 and 1835 a total of seventy-nine boys from the town became Franciscans. Serra did not disappoint them. He applied for admission to the Franciscans soon after he celebrated his sixteenth birthday, but his petition was denied. The reason may have been that people named "Serra" had been identified and punished by the Mallorcan Inquisition from the end of the fifteenth century until at least the beginning of the seventeenth century. Serra's paternal grandmother was named Juana Avram [Abraham] Salom, and this perhaps increased suspicions about the possibility of Jewish roots somewhere in the family history. An ecclesiastical investigation into his background may have ensued. However, Serra was able to reapply about six months later and was accepted. He spent a year as a novice; during this period he lived in a Franciscan community and studied Franciscan spirituality. In September 1731, he formally became a Franciscan by taking solemn vows of poverty, chastity, and obedience. On this occasion, he changed his given name to Junípero.[7]

It was not unusual for young religious to take the name of a favorite saint or a holy person when they took their vows. In this way they were expressing their devotion to a significant figure in their religious development. The young religious might add that name to their given name, as a type of middle name. However, it was unusual for them to use that new name in place of their given name. Of all the Mallorcan Franciscans who came to the New World, Serra seems to have been the only one to have done that.

What was the significance of this choice? Brother Junípero was one of the companions of Francis of Assisi, the founder of the Franciscan order. The stories about Brother Junípero in the Franciscan tradition Serra imbibed as a novice also emphasized the brother's simplicity. This trait could easily come across to various audiences, even to his fellow religious, as foolishness. In one story Junípero

---

6. Manera, "Manufactura téxtil y comercio en Mallorca, 1700–1830"; Manera, "Mercado, producción agrícola y cambio económico en Mallorca durante el siglo 18"; Jover Avellà and Manera Erbina, "Producción y productividad agrícolas en la Isla de Mallorca, 1590–1860"; Palóu, *Palóu's Life of Fray Junípero Serra*, 32–33.
7. Vicedo, *La casa solariega de la familia Serra*, 249; Geiger, *Life and Times of Fray Junípero Serra*, 1:10, 18–22; Sandos, *Converting California*, 33; Braunstein, *The Chuetas of Majorca*, 139–81.

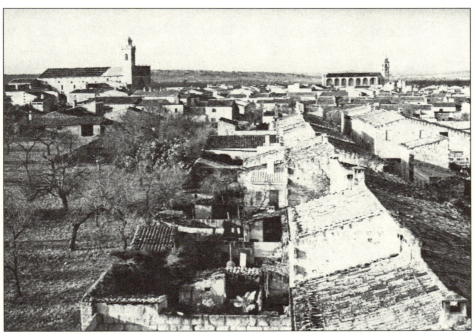

FIGURE 2. Serra was baptized in the church on the right, San Pedro, in the village of Petra, Mallorca. He attended grammar school at the church on the left, San Bernardino. *Courtesy of the Santa Bárbara Mission Archive-Library.*

gave away half his cloak to a beggar and was then viewed with "contempt and indignity" by a group of young men. On another occasion, he so rejoiced to suffer for the love of God that he refused to defend himself when he was unjustly accused of being a low criminal. Brother Junípero was saved only when recognized at the last minute by another friar as a companion of Francis. Another story recounted how he was so embarrassed by people's devotion to him as a saintly man that he began to play seesaw with some children and continued to do so until all his admirers left in confusion. Other Franciscan sources emphasized Brother Junípero's patience and humility. One thirteenth-century Franciscan author said of him, "Brother Junípero shone with such a gift of patience that no one ever saw him disturbed even when he was experiencing many difficulties." Another early Franciscan author said that Junípero "achieved the perfect state of patience because he always kept in mind the perfect truth of his low state and the ardent desire to imitate Christ through the way of the cross." In the early

Franciscan tradition, Brother Junípero was, in short, a man of patience, humility, and simplicity. None of these are qualities that one spontaneously associates with Junípero Serra. Perhaps Serra knew himself well enough to realize that these were qualities that he would always have to struggle to attain. If so, then his choice of name suggests that he anticipated that life as a member of a religious order would be a challenging struggle to reach a series of ideals.[8]

Brother Junípero also appeared in the second part of a fourteenth-century devotional work, *The Little Flowers of St. Francis*. This volume was one of the most widely read books about St. Francis, and Serra undoubtedly read it. The account of the life of Brother Junípero in this volume stretched over fourteen chapters, each of which recounted an episode from his life. The first story contained most of the themes that animated the rest. The story recounted that Brother Junípero was ministering to a sick brother, who asked Junípero if he could find a pig's foot for him to eat. Brother Junípero went out and saw a herd of swine, caught one, cut off one of its feet, and ran off with it. When he got back home, he cooked it and gave it to the sick brother.

The owner of the swine had seen what had occurred and came to the friars' residence denouncing Brother Junípero as a hypocrite and a thief. Saint Francis and the other friars came together and made excuses for Brother Junípero, who they already knew was possessed of "indiscreet zeal," but they failed to assuage the owner of the swine. Francis then confronted Junípero, who freely admitted what he had done and said he had done so out of charity for the sick brother. Junípero volunteered that God would certainly be pleased by his action. Francis told Junípero to go find the man, apologize, and offer to make amends. Brother Junípero, even though he thought temporal things such as the swine possessed no value in and of themselves, agreed to do so. He found the man, but failed to move him. He told his story over and over again and finally flung himself on the man, who then came to understand that Junípero had done what he had done because of charity and love. At this point the man's heart changed; he agreed with Brother Junípero, went and killed the swine, cut it up, and brought it to the friars. This moved Francis, noting Junípero's simplicity and patience under such great adversity, to say, "Would to God, my brothers, that I had a forest of such junipers!"[9]

The qualities exhibited by Junípero in the story—a single-mindedness to do what the protagonist regarded as good, a conviction that social rules were of less importance than religious motivation, the belief that good intentions will eventually triumph over the stubbornness and short-sightedness that is rooted

---

8. Geiger, *Life and Times of Fray Junípero Serra*, 1:20–21; Geiger, "The Mallorcan Contribution to Franciscan California"; Armstrong, Hellmann, and Short, *Francis of Assisi*, 3:36, 125, 333.
9. Brown, *The Little Flowers of St. Francis*, 219–22.

in social conventions—would come to characterize the actions of Junípero Serra in Alta California.

Serra may very well have also been attracted by the general connotation of strength in Francis's statement about the forest of junipers. Perhaps this aspiration was also personal, for Serra himself was small and slight and always seemed to be pushing himself to compensate for a lack of physical prowess. As a novice, he was embarrassed that he was too short to reach a lectern to perform a regular duty of the novices—turning the pages of the book for the friar who was leading the chant. Finally, a local variety of the juniper plant, *ginebró*, flourished in the Mallorcan countryside. The choice of the name thus may also be another reference to his childhood and his place of birth—Serra's way of saying that his new identity as a Franciscan would incorporate his older one as a resident of rural Mallorca.[10]

For centuries Spaniards and other Europeans had been changing indigenous names of people and places in the Americas to European names as an expression of the new colonial relationship. As we have already seen, Serra did the same thing in California in connection with the sacrament of baptism, but he first did this to himself. Serra was a man for whom adopting a new name to express a new identity and a new relationship was a normal part of life.

After Serra finished his novitiate on the outskirts of Palma, he moved into the city. He spent the next eighteen years studying and teaching at the university named for one of the most famous Mallorcans, Ramón Llull. Theologian, philosopher, mystic, poet, scholar, and the author of over one hundred works, Llull was born in Mallorca in 1232 and died in 1315. He was a member of the third order of Saint Francis, a group designed for those who wished to cultivate Franciscan spirituality in their lives without becoming priests, brothers, or sisters. Llull's tomb was in the great Franciscan Church of San Francisco in Palma, in whose residence Serra lived for almost twenty years.[11]

Llull was very interested in missionary work to the Muslims of North Africa. He traveled there a number of times to engage Muslim scholars and leaders in conversation and to preach there. In 1276, Llull even started a school on Mallorca to train missionaries in Arabic.[12] Llull's reputation in official church circles waxed and waned over the centuries after his death, but in Mallorca he was always regarded very favorably. The university in Palma, founded in 1483, was named the Estudio General Lulliano. Even after its name was officially changed in 1526 to the Imperial and Royal University, it continued to be called the "Lullian

---

10. Palóu, *Palóu's Life of Fray Junípero Serra*, 5, 321; Alomar Esteve, *Ensayos sobre historia de las Islas Baleares*, 393.
11. Peers, *Ramón Lull*; Bonner, *Doctor Illuminatus*.
12. Escandell Bonet, *Baleares y América*, 292–93; McCarty, "Before They Crossed the Great River"; Bonner, *Doctor Illuminatus*, 13.

University." In 1721 a definitive edition of Llull's works was completed in Germany, and this gave rise to what one Llull scholar has termed a "flurry" of publications in Mallorca. Between 1720 and 1750, at least forty-three editions of various Llull works were published on the island.[13]

This growing interest in Llull was part of a larger cultural development in Mallorca in the first decades of the eighteenth century. Since being conquered by King Jaime I of Aragón in 1229, Mallorca's primary association with the Spanish mainland had been with that northeastern region of the Iberian Peninsula. Like most Aragón-related jurisdictions, in the succession controversy at the beginning of the eighteenth century, Mallorca favored the claim of the Hapsburg Archduke Charles to the Spanish throne over that of Philip, the Bourbon Duke of Anjou. Mallorca felt that the Hapsburgs would be more likely than the Bourbons to retain the traditional local fueros that the island had enjoyed. When the War of Spanish Succession (1701–13) ended with Philip on the throne, the victorious monarch was quick to extend his control over Mallorca. In 1714 the royal fleet appeared off Palma and an army landed on the eastern coast. In 1715 the army entered Felanitx, about ten miles south of Petra. The conquest was achieved in short order, and the traditional fueros were superseded by a decree known as the Nueva Planta, issued in 1715. This was one of a series of edicts propagated in a number of localities by which the Bourbons imposed their central authority. The Mallorcan version of the Nueva Planta reduced local power, including the power of the Church.[14]

The new authorities took additional steps to exert control over the island. In 1721 the commander general ordered his troops to fan out through the countryside to put down remnants of local resistance. In the countryside, people often took refuge in churches, but the Bourbon troops disregarded the right of sanctuary and routinely entered churches to make arrests. And in 1747, two years before Serra left for the New World, the army swept through Palma and forcibly conscripted a large number of young men who were sent to join the royal forces in the siege of Naples.[15]

In the context of these events the revival of interest in Llull can be seen as part of the reassertion of what one historian has termed an "insular nationalism" in the face of Bourbon initiatives. In another cultural assault, the Bourbon centralizers and the early patrons of the Spanish Enlightenment who were associated with them tended to disparage local cults and heroes, such as Ramón Llull. Benito

---

13. Palóu, *Palóu's Life of Fray Junípero Serra*, 309; Bonner, *Doctor Illuminatus*, 59, 69–70. The number forty-three was derived from the online card catalogue of the Biblioteca Nacional de España, at http://catalogo.bne.es/.
14. Piña Homs, "Del decreto de Nueva Planta a las Cortes de Cádiz," 292–308.
15. Piña Homs, "Del decreto de Nueva Planta a las Cortes de Cádiz," 263–64, 319–21; Alomar Esteve, *Ensayos sobre historia de las Islas Baleares*, 364.

Jerónimo Feijóo, one of the leading exponents of this trend, ridiculed Llull's most significant work, the *Ars Magna*, scornfully noting that in Mallorca, Llull was venerated as a saint and his words were regarded as "the trumpet of the Holy Spirit." Antoní Ramón Pascual, a colleague of Serra's at the Lullian University, published a two-volume response to Feijóo and defense of Llull in 1749–50.[16]

As a result of the association of Llull with Mallorcan pride, one of the major annual events in Mallorca became the sermon preached on Llull's feast day, January 25, in the Church of San Francisco. On January 25, 1749, that sermon was preached by none other than Junípero Serra. A copy of it has not survived, but Palóu tells us that a retired faculty member said the sermon should be "printed in letters of gold." The sermon connects Serra very closely with the local tradition of Mallorca and suggests that he was among those who opposed the Bourbon centralization and the military efforts that were used to enforce it.[17]

By the time Serra arrived in New Spain, the tensions between missionaries and soldiers had a long history. Indeed, events in New Spain are sufficient to explain the quarrels between Serra and a series of military officers in Alta California. Serra's antipathy to the military, however, was particularly intense compared with that of other missionaries. It figured in a number of conflicts, but perhaps most forcefully in the disputes he had with the military commanders he dealt with in central New Spain in the 1750s and in Alta California after 1769. As a Mallorcan, Serra came to the New World with a preexisting antipathy toward the Bourbon military, and part of the ferocity with which he quarreled with military leaders in the New World stemmed from that.

As in many places in Spain, Mallorca's own identity was closely associated with struggles against the "other," notably Jews and Moors. The Inquisition had been set up on the island at the same time that it was established in the rest of the Iberian Peninsula in the fifteenth and sixteenth centuries. But at least in its formal activities, the Inquisition was less active after about the middle of the sixteenth century. The next hundred years were a time of economic troubles for both Spain and Mallorca. This period climaxed around 1650, when a plague ravaged the island, killing as much as 20 percent of the population. Prosperity began to return to Spain in the second half of the seventeenth century. The coastal areas were the first to experience this, and Mallorca participated in it. However, the gradual rise in prosperity appears to have increased tensions on the island, sparking some resentment against the *converso* (baptized Catholics of Jewish descent) families who were members of Palma's commercial class. These people found themselves targeted with accusations, common to the Spanish Inquisition,

---

16. Peers, *Ramón Lull*, 391; Bonner, *Doctor Illuminatus*, 70–71.
17. Palóu, *Palóu's Life of Fray Junípero Serra*, 6.

that their conversions to Christianity were fraudulent and that they continued their Jewish practices in secret.[18]

In 1675 the Inquisition condemned a Jewish man fleeing from North Africa to be burned alive in Palma. In 1679 it conducted mass arrests and trials, and in a 1691 auto-da-fé it executed three conversos by burning them. The Inquisition also seized large amounts of property as part of this persecution. According to one leading scholar these confiscations were the largest in all three centuries of the Spanish Inquisition. The moves against the conversos, who were called *chuetas*, a derogatory term probably derived from the diminutive of an old Mallorcan word for "Jew," basically involved the seizure and redistribution of much of the commercial wealth of Palma.[19]

During the entire eighteenth century, conversos could live only in a specific part of the city. Autos-da-fé were held in Palma in 1722 and 1724, although no one was executed in connection with them. However, open hostility to the conversos continued throughout the eighteenth century. For example, in 1755 the Inquisition in Mallorca published a list of all the people on the island whom it had punished since 1645. Also in 1755, a 1691 book by the Jesuit Francisco Garau, describing in gruesome detail the executions at the end of the seventeenth century, was republished in Palma. In 1772 the chuetas of Mallorca addressed a formal petition and protest to King Carlos III, who issued three decrees in the 1780s forbidding various forms of discrimination against them.[20]

During the 1740s Serra was a *comisario* (investigator) of the Inquisition. Within two years of arriving in the New World he requested and received a similar appointment in the Mexican Inquisition. His clear desire to participate in this body was perhaps related to the questions about his possible Jewish heritage and his judgment that being an active member of the Inquisition would put these questions to rest. His formal participation in the Mallorcan Inquisition mainly involved examining works for their orthodoxy to determine whether they should be published—a task not explicitly related to the treatment of conversos.[21]

However, living in a city with a large and identifiable converso population affected how Serra and Spaniards with similar experiences looked on conversion,

---

18. Kamen, "Vicissitudes of a World Power," 166; Phillips, "Economy and Society in the Iberian Atlantic," 23–24; Alomar Esteve, *Ensayos sobre historia de las Islas Baleares*, 359; Lynch, *Bourbon Spain, 1700–1808*, 8; Lea, *A History of the Inquisition of Spain*, 1:335, 3:306.
19. Kamen, *Inquisition and Society*, 232; Kamen, *The Spanish Inquisition*, 150; Braunstein, *The Chuetas of Majorca*, 69–70; on the term *chueta*, see Moore, *Those of the Street*, 22. Families of those who were persecuted by the Inquisition in Mallorca suffered discrimination up to the twentieth century. See Moore, *Those of the Street*, 159–204.
20. Selke, *The Conversos of Majorca*, 3–5; Kamen, *Inquisition and Society*, 234; Lea, *A History of the Inquisition of Spain*, 2:213, 3:307; Braunstein, *The Chuetas of Majorca*, 122, 125.
21. On aspects of the Inquisition in Spain, see Nalle, "Inquisitors, Priests, and the People during the Catholic Reformation in Spain."

which was the fundamental task of a missionary. To put it simply, association with the Inquisition and residence in a city known for its anti-converso actions inculcated in Serra and those like him a sensibility of suspicion about conversions to Christianity. The more the Inquisition took action against so-called *judaizantes*, the more it raised doubts about the sincerity of the "conversion" of the conversos. In California, Serra would have the same doubts about the authenticity of some Indian conversions.

Teacher

Serra spent most of his time in Palma in the academic world. After he took his vows, he moved to the Convento de San Francisco in the heart of the city, which was to be his home for the next eighteen years. There he began a formal course of studies in philosophy (1731–34) and theology (1734–37). He was ordained a priest at the end of 1737, then began advanced studies in theology and also taught a three-year philosophy course during 1740–43. As he was teaching that course, he finished his theology studies and received a doctorate. From 1744 to 1749, he held the Chair of Scotistic Theology at the Llullian University.[22]

The chair was named for the thirteenth-century Franciscan theologian John Duns Scotus. In the broad sweep of medieval theology and philosophy, Scotus was not typical. Indeed, he was rather eccentric, which was why the sarcastic name given to the followers of Duns Scotus has survived in the word "dunce." For instance, he rejected the widely held synthesis of one of the most influential Christian medieval theologians, Anselm of Canterbury, about the doctrine of the redemption wrought through Christ, since he thought it placed insufficient emphasis on the boundless love of God for humanity. In his theology, Scotus, in common with many Franciscans, emphasized the will over the intellect. His philosophy and theology also tended to emphasize the qualities of relationships and aesthetics over the more static Scholastic categories of substance and judgment. For Scotus, goodness and beauty were almost co-extensive with each other and with being itself. He explicitly understood moral goodness in terms of musical harmony and used the image of chords on a harp to underscore his insistence that morality involves, above all, a proper relationship among human actions. In another passage he spoke of the morally good act as a work of art, in which proportion and balance combine to produce something that is aesthetically pleasing. He spoke of God as a type of divine artist.[23]

---

22. Geiger, *Life and Times of Fray Junípero Serra*, 1:30–36; Geiger, "The Scholastic Career and Preaching Apostolate of Fray Junípero Serra."
23. Ingham, *The Harmony of Goodness*, 55–72; Ingham, *Scotus for Dunces*, 83. Kovach, "Scholastic Challenges," 97, 103, 108.

FIGURE 3. The patio of the Convento de San Francisco in Palma, Mallorca, in 1860. Serra spent almost twenty years in residence at this convent. Photograph by Charles Clifford, 1819–63. *Courtesy of the Biblioteca Nacional de España.*

Serra's insistence on the catechetical benefits of art and music and his almost obsessive concern with obtaining good works of art from Mexico for the California missions stemmed in part from his absorption with Scotus. In addition, Scotus's emphasis on relationships and his insistence on the Trinity as the model of relationships gave Serra's experience of growing up in the stable agricultural community of Petra a philosophical and theological grounding. Well-ordered communities did no less than reflect the very nature of God.[24]

Serra was an active academic. Besides teaching, he heard over one hundred oral exams in theology, both at the baccalaureate and doctoral levels. During the course of one such examination, he even became involved in a dispute with another professor over which of them outranked the other. Like many other European Franciscan academics of the time, when school was not in session Serra

---

24. See, for instance, Serra, *Writings*, 1:187, 221, 225; 2:311, 431; 3:55, 91.

would often travel to parishes and other churches to preach and hear confessions. He also preached on various occasions in the city of Palma itself.²⁵

We have a general idea about how Serra taught and preached during these years. One of his students kept extensive notes from the philosophy course, so we have an idea of what and how he taught. In addition, four Lenten homilies that he preached at a convent of Poor Clares in Palma in 1744 have survived. Also extant is an approbation of a 1749 funeral sermon composed by Serra and another faculty member.²⁶

Considered as a whole, this academic and theological body of writings and notes is markedly different from the more administrative writings Serra produced when he was president of the Alta California missions. Serra's Mallorca writings help us fill out the picture of the man and offer examples of the intellectual and religious currents that helped to shape his missionary strategy.

The works that Serra penned on his home island reveal that he was a widely read individual. For instance, the funeral sermon he was assessing in the 1749 essay was about the death of an eminent Mallorcan Franciscan, Antonio Perelló, a native of Petra who served three terms as provincial (chief Franciscan) of the island. The sermon rested on the classical myth of the Phoenix, and Serra and his coauthor used that myth to praise Perelló, who had attained many high honors within the Franciscan order, for not being seduced by those honors and remaining true to his humble roots. The essay in which he evaluated the sermon was replete with classical allusions. Serra and his coauthor quoted from Virgil, Seneca, Plutarch, and Quintillian. Serra apparently liked Virgil, whose emphasis in the *Aeneid* on *pietas* and duty made him one of the medieval Church's most favored classical authors. Serra ended his philosophy course in 1743 with a quotation from that epic poem.²⁷

The course Serra was assigned to teach was a standard survey course of Scholastic philosophy. This course was built on the thought of the classical Greek and Roman thinkers, especially Aristotle, whom the medieval Scholastics termed simply "the philosopher," and on some early Christian thinkers, especially Augustine. In the Middle Ages this large body of thought was approached somewhat differently by the Dominicans, who followed the Aristotelian synthesis

---

25. Geiger, *Life and Times of Fray Junípero Serra*, 1:32, 33–35; Font Obrador and Neuerburg, *Fr. Junípero Serra*, 67–68.
26. The Santa Bárbara Mission Archive-Library contains a typescript of a student's notes from the first year ("Logic") and part of the second year ("Physics") of the philosophy course. See Junípero Serra, "Compendium Scoticum" (Palma de Mallorca, 1743), Junípero Serra Collection, no. 34, Santa Bárbara Mission Archive-Library. The original is in Mallorca. In the eighteenth century, most Franciscan philosophers and theologians had developed an eclectic rather than a rigidly Scotistic approach. The title "Compendium Scoticum" was probably not an original part of the student's notes and was added later: Fernández-Largo, "Junípero Serra, escotista inédito," 540–41; Serra, *Writings*, 4:292–301; Serra, "Four Sermons" (Palma de Mallorca, 1744), Junípero Serra Collection, no. 15, Santa Bárbara Mission Archive-Library.
27. Geiger, *Life and Times of Fray Junípero Serra*, 1:28.

of Thomas Aquinas in emphasizing the philosophical analysis of the intellect, and the Franciscans, who tended to follow the Augustinian path of Bonaventure and Scotus in focusing on an analysis of the heart and will.[28]

On the first day of class, as a good teacher, Serra shared something about himself as a means of establishing a rapport with his students. He told them that he was a student of John Duns Scotus. Indeed, most eighteenth-century Spanish Franciscan theologians were followers of Scotus, whose complexity of analysis had earned him the title of the "Subtle Doctor." Serra informed his students that he was very pleased that the influence of Scotus's ideas appeared to be increasing within the Church. One of those ideas was a notion championed by Scotus that Mary, the mother of Jesus, was conceived without original sin. Serra was able to tell his students that even though the idea of the Immaculate Conception had not yet been officially adopted as a formal doctrine by the Church, it was gaining greater acceptance and steadily advancing toward official recognition. Mallorcan Franciscans were especially devoted to this concept. Indeed, part of the vow formula Serra recited as a young Franciscan in 1731 contained an oath to defend the concept of the Immaculate Conception.[29]

This idea was controversial during the Middle Ages. A good number of Catholic theologians argued that if Mary had never been stained by original sin, then she logically would not have needed to be saved by Christ's redemptive suffering. But, these theologians continued, that would contradict the Christian doctrine that Christ was the universal savior of all mankind. Scotus attempted to answer this objection by arguing that Mary was immaculately conceived only by virtue of Christ's redemptive sacrifice. This view gradually gained favor, especially in Spain. By the seventeenth century, the Hapsburg monarchy adopted this view and used devotion to the doctrine as a way of fostering greater religious unity in the country.[30]

After sharing this personal introduction with his students, Serra turned to the business at hand—the traditional course he had been assigned to teach. He immediately plunged into the first topic of his logic presentation, "De operationis intellectus," a consideration of the way in which the intellect works. Serra developed the course around the dialectical style that would have been familiar to any student in a Franciscan Scholastic philosophy course in Europe. The

---

28. Fernández-Largo, "Junípero Serra, escotista inédito"; Copleston, *Medieval Philosophy*, 112; Cirino and Raischl, *A Pilgrimage through the Franciscan Intellectual Tradition*, 53–68.
29. Geiger, *Life and Times of Fray Junípero Serra*, 1:22; Sánchez Gil, "Teología y teólogos franciscanos españoles," 715, 731.
30. Martínez, "The Banner of the Spanish Monarchy." We thank Margo Gutiérrez, Librarian for U.S. Latina/o Studies, Benson Latin American Collection, University of Texas Libraries, for finding a copy of this article for us.

content was also quite traditional in that the authorities he most often cited were Aristotle, Scotus, and Aquinas. When we remember that Serra was working on his advanced theology studies at the same time he was teaching this course, the standard nature of the course content should come as no surprise. Serra was directing his intellectual energies elsewhere during these three years, and we do not glean that much in terms of his own thoughts from these class notes.

Three years later he ended the course in a similarly personal fashion. The students were all much younger than he was, so he told them that at some point in their lives they would probably hear the news that he had died. He said, "I desire nothing more from you than this, that when news of my death shall have reached your ears I ask that you say for the benefit of my soul 'May he rest in peace,' and I shall not fail to do the same for you so that all of us will attain that goal for which we have been created. Amen and farewell.... I am no longer your professor but rather your most humble servant, Fray Junípero Serra of the Order of Friars Minor."[31]

Preacher

Whereas Serra was somewhat constrained in his philosophy classroom by the relatively conventional nature of the material he was assigned to teach, we can get a better sense of the religious views that he would take to America from the four surviving sermons he preached in Mallorca in 1744. Serra was an active preacher on his native island for much of the time that he was a teacher at the university, preaching both in the capital and in at least thirteen villages. Some of his preaching tended to be dramatic and extravagant. As we have seen, he was embarrassed by his small stature. During his novitiate, Serra often suffered from poor health and was weak, which bothered him because he frequently had to be excused from the house chores that were routinely assigned to the novices. Perhaps as a way of compensating for these conditions, he developed a boisterous and theatrical pulpit persona. Palóu reported in his biography that during a sermon in Mexico City in the 1760s Serra took out a chain and began to flog himself with it.[32]

Palóu admitted that Serra's sermons could be very long, which could be a "source of annoyance" for his listeners. In addition, he said that during Serra could get "carried away" as he delivered his sermons. Both the length and the emotion of his preaching style were evident in Mallorca. For instance, a sermon in the village of Selva in 1747 created a scene. Palóu reported that Serra told him a woman stood up during "the most fervent part of one of his sermons" and shouted at him, "Keep on yelling! Keep on yelling! But you will not finish this Lent." Serra told Palóu

---

31. Geiger, *Life and Times of Fray Junípero Serra*, 1:28.
32. Palóu, *Palóu's Life of Fray Junípero Serra*, 5, 41–42.

that the woman, possessed by the devil, was telling him he would die before the end of the forty days of Lent. More plausibly in a stage whisper designed to be heard by the preacher, the woman was sarcastically wondering if Serra was going to finish his seemingly interminable sermon before the end of Lent.[33]

In 1744 Serra was invited to preach a series of sermons during Lent at the Convent of Santa Clara in Palma. Lent was a forty-day season of prayer and repentance preceding the celebration of the feast of Christ's resurrection on Easter Sunday. The scripture passages read during the various liturgies of the season offered preachers a wide variety of ways in which they could reflect on the central meanings of the Christian faith. The Convent of Santa Clara was founded in the thirteenth century. When Serra preached at the convent, there were sixty-one cloistered nuns in residence. These nuns were the primary audience for his sermons. However, the sermons were most likely heard as well by persons in attendance in the more public areas of the church. Serra preached five sermons at the convent. The first three seem to have survived more or less in their entirety. A large part of the fourth sermon appears to have survived as well. The fifth sermon is lost. In these sermons Serra developed his own spiritual views at some length, and they offer important indications of the religious views that animated his missionary activities in the Americas.[34]

In a few places the sermons were rhetorically boisterous. For instance, Serra began the third sermon by exclaiming, "A full and vibrant trumpet call ought to resound in this church today before I begin my sermon, for I am going to issue a public call and publish a royal decree. Congratulate yourselves a thousand times over, you happy vassals!" But the overall style of the sermons was quite academic. Serra was always ready to quote various authorities to bolster whatever point he was making. As might be expected, he quoted liberally from the Jewish and Christian scriptures. A number of the Church Fathers, including Saints Augustine, Jerome, John Chrysostom, and Gregory the Great, made their way into the sermons. In addition, Saint Francis, Saint Bonaventure, the seventeenth-century Conceptionist nun Sor María de Jesús de Ágreda, and others from the Franciscan tradition were quoted. But Serra did not ignore the secular world: the very first person quoted in the first sermon was the well-known former king of Aragón, Alfonso el Sabio. Aristotle, with whom Serra was very familiar from his philosophy studies, was also cited. Toward the end of the fourth sermon, Serra extensively paraphrased a section of the Old Digest from the legal code of Justinian.

---

33. Palóu, *Palóu's Life of Fray Junípero Serra*, 6–7, 282.
34. Serra, "Four Sermons" (Palma de Mallorca, 1744), Junípero Serra Collection, no. 15, Santa Bárbara Mission Archive-Library. These Catalán sermons were translated into Spanish in Font Obrador, *El apóstol de California, sus albores*. In our translations of the sermons into English, we used the texts in both languages.

Serra was a university professor, and these sermons were quite academic in another sense. At times he spoke as if he were in a classroom. All of the sermons required his listeners to compare and contrast a number of concepts. In the first sermon he asked the nuns and the other listeners to ponder that the human person consists of two parts: "an inferior or sentient part, which he shares with irrational creatures," and "a superior or rational part, which he shares with the angels." In the second sermon he declared that "the yoke of the divine law" was very soft and gentle in two complementary respects: "first, in its intrinsic nature and, second, because of various extrinsic circumstances," such as the nature of God, the example of Christ, the presence of divine grace, and the hope of heavenly glory. In the third sermon, he stated that the trials and tribulations people suffer in this life are actually quite gentle in two senses: a priori, because "sufferings come from the paternal and infinite love that the Lord has for us," and a posteriori, "because of the eternal and heavenly prize they allow us to reach." And in the fourth sermon, Serra argued that God's mercy was boundless both intensively and extensively. "In terms of its intention," he stated, it was boundless "because of the intense and intrinsic affection with which he [God] pardons us." On the other hand, the divine mercy was extensive "because of the great multitude of sins which God's mercy reaches." In the same sermon, Serra quoted Saint Anthony of Padua to the effect that God's mercy is his greatest virtue, since it is infinite. But Serra wondered aloud: How can the saint say that? Are not all of God's virtues infinite by definition? To explain this seeming contradiction, Serra put on his best academic hat. He told his listeners that here we must "make a distinction." One wonders if his listeners were taking notes through all of this! But Serra was trying to use these academic conventions to make the point that his God was accessible and loving, not remote and harsh.

As he had done in his philosophy class, Serra began the sermons by attempting to establish a rapport with his congregation by asking them to reflect on their own experiences. He encouraged them to think about the different types of people they had met and to imagine people in their own lives whose temperaments were both harsh and gentle. Then he established a bond with his audience by citing Alfonso, a beloved king of Aragón, the area of the Iberian Peninsula with which the island of Mallorca had the most intricate history.

The first sermon established a general tone of tempered moderation that characterized all four of the sermons that have survived. The overarching theme was taken from a verse from Psalm 34: "Taste and see that the Lord is good." When he spoke, Serra quoted the verse from the Latin Vulgate: "Gustate, et videte quoniam suavis est Dominus." Then he played with the Latin word that is usually translated into English as "good"—*suavis*. He announced that his theme was going to be God's *suavidat*—a Catalán word that means "softness" or "mildness" and connotes "gentleness" or "sweetness." Then, picking up on the beginning of the verse ("taste"), Serra introduced the word *dulzura* (sweetness) as a virtual synonym for suavidat.

At the beginning of this first sermon Serra outlined for his audience the themes of the five sermons. Each would be devoted to a different way in which this suavidat of God is manifest: in the words with which he calls people, in his law that he orders them to observe, in the sufferings he sends them, in the mercy with which he pardons them, and in the glory with which he will reward them. He called these five aspects "the five rungs of the ladder of divine gentleness." Serra said that in the course of his sermons "I will name the ladder, rung by rung."

The first sermon concerned the words of God. Serra stated that he would elaborate on "the gentleness of the divine voice by which the Lord calls us to his love." He stated that God spoke to people with two types of voices: "interior voices in our hearts" and "exterior voices to our ears, through his ministers." Serra insisted that God could be directly experienced by human beings and that this experience was like coming across a type of hitherto-unknown culinary delicacy: "Those who do not know anything about this sweetness and do not taste it do not have any appetite for it. But someone who has tried it just once finds that he has an increasing appetite for it and finds it very soothing." This notion that the encounter with God would awaken in people aspects of themselves that they had not realized before would inform Serra's missionary strategy in the New World.

Serra also insisted that the exterior voices of God's ministers deserve the same attention and had the same urgency as the interior voices of the divinity itself: "Whoever the minister who speaks the word of God might be, to scorn the minister is to scorn God Himself." In the New World, he never doubted that this dictum applied to the words of himself and his fellow missionaries.

In his second sermon Serra argued vigorously that the law of God was not harsh and vindictive but easy and gentle. He began the homily by saying that too many people believed the "common error" that keeping God's commandments is "difficult." His main text came from Matthew 11, where Jesus said, "My yoke is easy and my burden is light." Serra insisted that this verse contained the essence of God's law. But as he said in the first sermon, this truth can only be discovered by experience. Where he had previously argued that God's sweetness could only be discovered through actually tasting it, here he argued that the gentleness of God's law can only be discovered through actually observing its decrees. The farther away one is from God's law, the more difficult and demanding it seems. But the more one follows it, the easier it becomes. "The path of the holy and divine law," he stated, "should not be called narrow, because it is not. It only seems that way when you look at it from a distance and have not actually undertaken it." He continued, "That path seems difficult to you because you do not have the kind of love you ought to have for the Lord and for divine matters."

Serra marshaled a wealth of quotations from a number of Christian authors to support his position, since this view of God's law was not original with him. However, it would play an important role in his life as a missionary, for this interpretation of divine law was one of the theological bases for the missionary policy of reduction, that is, forcing native peoples to live together under what the missionaries benignly termed the "sound of the bell." If people were compelled at the beginning of their Christian experience to live by God's laws, they would gradually come to see that these laws were actually sweet and gentle. The coercion and violence that was an integral part of the missionization process stemmed from that perspective.

In the light of this coercion and violence, the theme of Serra's third sermon was especially relevant. The third sermon concerned "the pains and labors which the Lord sends us in this life," and the "punishments" he sometimes metes out. In part of the sermon Serra was at pains to insist that it was not always legitimate to regard people's suffering as simply a punishment that God was visiting on those who deserve it. This surely resonated with his listeners on an island where extreme drought and devastating plagues were a normal part of existence.[35]

The overall thrust of the sermon was Serra's insistence that what people often regard as punishment might better be regarded as a gift from God. The reason was that if God punished people, the intent of this punishment was to make them better and bring them closer to their eternal salvation. In this sense God was very much like a responsible parent in whom "love and strictness are in harmony." When this analogy was transported to the Americas, it had the inevitable effect of infantilizing the native peoples.

Serra also used other analogies to drive home the same point. He asked his listeners if they would want a doctor who told them everything was fine, or a doctor who occasionally had to hurt them to cure them of their infirmities. The answer to this rhetorical question was obvious. He also compared punishments to what happened when a glassblower did his craft. There was fire and destruction, but the final result was a thing of beauty: "The glass maker takes a flint, places it in the fire, keeps it up in open air until it is melted and purified and becomes very fine glass. That is what the Lord does with you, because He loves you and desires your salvation."

---

35. One book has argued that Palma was afflicted by a plague at the very time Serra was preaching these sermons. See Font Obrador and Neuerburg, *Fr. Junípero Serra*, 68–70. That appears to be inaccurate, for, although the city was hit by plague in 1744, it did not break out until the fall, well after the season of Lent had concluded. See Font Obrador, *El apóstol de California*, 31, 142–43.

Even though he probably did not realize it at the time, Serra's use of the parent-child analogy fit very well into the developing conceptions of the relationship between colonizers and the native inhabitants of the Americas. The earliest Spanish academics tended to base their ideas about the native peoples in America on the thought of Aristotle. That thinker interpreted the conventional Greek distinction between themselves and others (often termed "barbarians" or *barbaroi*, since their languages sounded to Hellene ears as an unintelligible series of "bar," "bar" sounds) as a distinction between those who were fully human and those who were not. In Aristotle's famous phrase, fully human beings were "political"—that is, they lived in a *polis*, a city, a civic and structured human community. Those who did not live in this fashion were not fully human or rational and were thus destined by nature for slavery. So philosophical discussions about the Native Americans in the early sixteenth century revolved around the question of whether the native peoples were rational beings or natural slaves. This was the precise point argued in the famous 1550–51 Valladolid debates between Bartolomé de las Casas and Juan Ginés de Sepúlveda.[36]

However, in the practical realm, Spanish activities after the mid-sixteenth century tended to be based on a negative view of the Indians. The natural slavery argument was buttressed by the view that non-Christian natives were under the dominion of the devil. This view legitimized the "wars of fire and blood" waged by the conquistadors against the peoples on the frontiers of New Spain and Peru during the latter part of the sixteenth century.[37]

By the eighteenth century the situation was changing. Thinkers in Spain and the New World gradually became more influenced by the relativistic anthropology expounded by writers such as the Spanish Jesuit Juan de Acosta. Clerical writing in New Spain in the eighteenth century, for instance, tended to reflect Acosta's argument that non-Christian Indians were in a state of natural infancy rather than natural slavery. This state held out the promise of their eventual growth and development in a way in which the state of natural slavery denied.[38] Serra's use of the parent-child analogy in his third sermon fit neatly into this developing conception of the nature of Indians in America. When Serra landed in New Spain in 1749, he entered a world of Spanish discourse that had both somewhat humanized and somewhat infantilized the Indians he would be encountering.

The incomplete fourth sermon presented Serra with a bit of a dilemma. The three previous sermons analyzed matters that were normally regarded by believers

---

36. Pagden, *The Fall of Natural Man*, 41–50; the Valladolid debates are analyzed in Hanke, *All Mankind Is One*.
37. Cervantes, *The Devil in the New World*, 8; Keen, *The Aztec Image in Western Thought*, 173.
38. Pagden, *The Fall of Natural Man*, 146–197; Taylor, "'. . . de corazón pequeño y ánimo apocado,'" 8–11, 33; Taylor, Introduction, 18; Katzew, "'That This Should Be Published,'" 75.

as strict and harsh: commandments, laws, and sufferings. But this sermon was going to analyze something normally thought to be sweet and gentle, namely God's mercy. So it was difficult for him to create the dialectical tension that had animated his three previous efforts. Serra solved this by arguing at the outset that the reception of God's mercy depended on the attitude of the human sinner. One who sinned repeatedly and calculated that a merciful God would send forgiveness would find that God is not gentle but harsh. "The divine mercy should not be extolled to the extent that some do, those who use it as an excuse to commit more sins," he warned. "These people are completely unworthy of God's mercy and they ought to fear for their salvation." There was always a potential tension between God's gentle mercy and any sinner's hard and calculating attitude. Serra argued that God's mercy was not free but, rather, had to be earned through genuine contrition and repentance. But in the Americas, Serra encountered people for whom this type of contrition and repentance were alien concepts.

Departure

Serra spent over eighteen years in academic life in Palma as a student and a teacher. He did extremely well in that career, yet at some point in the 1740s, when he was entering his mid-thirties, he seems to have begun to become disenchanted with academics. The academic life was not measuring up to his expectations, and he felt that his own spiritual life was becoming stale. As a Mallorcan Franciscan who walked by the tomb of the missionary Ramón Llull almost every day, for Serra the path to rekindling his religious zeal lay across the sea. We only have Palóu's account of Serra's interior struggle, but it was obviously based on intimate conversations between the two men. According to Palóu, Serra "rekindled in his heart those desires which had stirred him as a novice, but which had been deadened because of his preoccupation with study." In other words, for Serra the attraction of missionary life was that it offered a path to personal and spiritual renewal.[39]

In this crisis Serra chose as his model the recently canonized seventeenth-century Franciscan missionary Francisco Solano. Like Serra, Solano was an accomplished and well-known priest in the region of Spain where he lived before he decided to volunteer for the missions. A preacher and confessor, Solano had a reputation as a wonder worker and healer in Andalucía. According to a biography of Solano with which Serra was probably very familiar, Solano's desire to go to the missions was partly due to his success in his own career. Solano felt that his spiritual well-being was endangered by so many people calling him a saint, since

---

39. Palóu, *Palóu's Life of Fray Junípero Serra*, 8.

it made him vulnerable to the sin of pride. Thus moving to the remote missions of Peru would be a way of renewing his own religious zeal. This line of reasoning may well have resonated with Serra, who was quite successful in his own career. Also, the fact that Solano became a missionary at the then advanced age of forty was probably a further motivation for Serra, who, at age thirty-five, was very likely near the midpoint of his own life. Finally, Solano was spurred to go to the missions when King Felipe II issued a recruiting call for more Franciscans to go to South America. At the end of the 1740s, two Franciscan recruiting expeditions from missionary colleges in Mexico City and Querétaro were making their way through the Iberian Peninsula. Neither expedition visited Mallorca, but word of their activities had reached the island. So, in many ways, Serra found in Solano a model that was possible for him to emulate.[40]

While Serra's decision to go to the Americas was rooted in his personal experience, it was also part of a much larger phenomenon. During the entire Spanish colonial period (1493–1822), over fifteen thousand priests and members of religious orders left Spain to work in the New World. The overwhelming majority of these men did so because they felt called on some level to respond to the summons of Christ in the Gospel according to Matthew, "Go and make disciples of all nations, baptizing them, and . . . teaching them to observe all I have commanded you." For most Spaniards, whose emerging national identity was tied up with the Reconquista, there was little meaningful difference between responding to this biblical summons to make indigenous people Christian and making those same people Hispanic.[41]

This intertwining of two areas that the modern Western world generally regards as distinct ("church" and "state") was heightened by the Patronato Real, the system through which the Spanish monarchy controlled ecclesiastical finances and personnel. This system was initiated even before the discovery of the Americas. At first it applied to the newly conquered Canary Islands and Granada. It was extended to the Caribbean in 1508 and continued throughout the Spanish empire in America for the next three centuries. Thus, in the practical order, all Spanish missionaries were colonial officials, which on occasion put some missionaries, including Serra, in difficult situations, because they sometimes felt they were being asked to serve two masters who did not always issue compatible commands.

The decision to become a missionary also implied a willingness to be killed by those one was attempting to convert. For centuries it was almost an article of Christian faith that the spread of Christianity in the Roman Empire had been possible

---

40. Córdoba y Salinas, *Vida, virtudes, y milagros*, 25–26.
41. Borges Morán, *El envío de misioneros a América*, 478–535; Matthew 28:19–20.

because of people's willingness to sacrifice their lives for the faith. This view was encapsulated in the saying of Tertullian, a second-century Christian apologist, that "the blood of martyrs is the seed of the Church." In the thirteenth and fourteenth centuries, the missionary activity of the Franciscans in Africa and Asia resulted in a number of their members being killed, and this strengthened in the minds of many Franciscans the notion of a close link between the concepts of mission and martyrdom. At times the very desire for martyrdom could be presented as a good reason for a person's desire to become a missionary. Such a motive, for instance, was attributed to Francisco Solano by his biographer. While Serra's writings do not indicate that he personally wished for this kind of death, his reactions to the killing of missionaries in Texas in 1768 and San Diego in 1775, which we shall encounter later in this volume, demonstrated that he shared this general view.[42]

After some correspondence between Palma and Madrid it was determined that Serra and another faculty member, Rafael Verger, and two of their former students, Francisco Palóu and Juan Crespí, would be assigned to the expedition from the Colegio de San Fernando in Mexico City, which was led by veteran missionary Pérez de Mezquía. Serra and Palóu left Palma before the other two. They traveled on an English vessel that took them as far as Málaga. From there they took a Spanish vessel to Cádiz. There they met Pedro Pérez de Mezquía, a missionary who had worked in both Texas and the Sierra Gorda. Serra was described in an official document as "35-years old, of medium height, swarthy, dark eyes and hair, slight beard."[43]

Before his vessel set sail for the trip across the Atlantic, Serra wrote a letter to the Franciscan parish priest at Petra. Serra had actually been engaged in preaching in his home town of Petra when he received word that his application to become a missionary in America had been accepted. But he left Petra without informing his parents that he was departing from the island. Less than a week after leaving the village, he was on a vessel bound for Spain. Serra most likely felt that his parents would not accept his decision and that they would beg him not to leave them. But he knew that he could never be dissuaded, and he wanted to spare all three of them the pain of such a disagreeable departure. However, he could only imagine the sense of betrayal his parents felt when they learned that he had gone and that they would most likely never see their eldest child again. So he asked the priest to console his parents by reading them his letter. His parents were advanced in years (his father was seventy-three and his

---

42. Johnson, "Franciscan Passions," 485–94; Córdoba y Salinas, *Vida, virtudes, y milagros*, 23; For similar views of Jesuits about martyrdom, see Clossey, *Salvation and Globalization*, 125.
43. Geiger, *Life and Times of Fray Junípero Serra*, 1:58.

MAP 1. Serra's Mediterranean travels from 1749. *Map by Tom Jonas.*

mother was seventy-two), and Serra probably felt that they would not support his decision to leave them. But, he wrote, if they realized "the great joy that I am experiencing," then "they would urge me to go forth and never turn back." In words that recall his sermons from 1744, he said of his parents, "They should not attribute their sadness to anyone except our Lord God, and they will see how gentle His yoke can be. And what they now may be experiencing as great sorrow will be turned into grand consolation for them." He asked his cousin to tell his parents that he was leaving for the missions "to become a good religious," which he believed was his parents' deepest desire for him. This letter, one of only four in all of Serra's extant correspondence that were addressed to people on Mallorca, offers a glimpse into the mix of emotions—enthusiasm, anticipation, regret, and loss—that Serra carried to the New World.[44]

---

44. Serra's father, Antonio Nadal Serra Avram, was born on December 25, 1675, and his mother, Margarita Ferrer Fornés, was born on March 5, 1677. See Vicedo, *La casa solariega de la familia Serra*, 250–51; Palóu, *Palóu's Life of Fray Junípero Serra*, 275.

※ *Letter to Padre Francesch Serra, August 20, 1749*

Jesús, Mary, Joseph

Dearest friend in Jesus Christ, Padre Francesch Serra:

This is a letter of farewell, since we are about to leave this city of Cádiz and sail to Mexico. I do not know the exact day but the trunks with our belongings are locked. They say that within two, or at the most three or four days, the *Villasota*, the ship on which we will be traveling, will set sail. We thought it would have been sooner and that is why I wrote that we would leave close to the feast day of San Buenaventura, but the trip has been delayed until now.

My beloved friend, I am at a loss for words, yet overwhelmed by emotion as I depart. I beg you once again to comfort my parents. I know they will be greatly affected by my leaving. I wish I could instill in them the great joy that I am experiencing because I believe they would urge me to go forth and never turn back.

They should realize that the role of apostolic preacher is so much more when it is put into practice. This is the most they could hope for, that is, to see me fulfill my responsibilities well.

Because they are so old, their life is now very fragile and most likely they will not live much longer. If they are able to compare what life they have left with eternity, they will clearly see that it is but an instant. And that being so, it is most appropriate and very much in accordance with the holy will of God that they notice only slightly that I will be of little help to them in terms of the benefits of this earthly life, so that if we do not see one another again in this life, our Lord God will deem us worthy of being together forever in eternal glory.

Tell them I still feel badly that I am not able to stay in close proximity with them as I was before, in order to console them. But I am also thinking "first things first." Above all else, our first obligation is to do the will of God and fulfill it. I have left them because of the love of God, and with His grace I have the resolve to leave them. The case may be that they too, because of the love of God, will be happy without my being there to keep them company.

Help them understand what the confessor tells them about this and they will see that God has now truly entered their home. With holy patience and resignation to the divine will, they will take charge of their souls and will attain eternal life.

They should not attribute their sadness to anyone except Our Lord God and they will see how gentle His yoke can be. And what they now may be experiencing as great sorrow will be turned into a grand consolation for them.

It is no longer the time to get upset or lament anything of this earthly life but rather submit completely to the will of God, as we try to prepare ourselves to die well, which is the only thing that matters in terms of all the things that exist in this life. If one dies well, it is of little importance if all else is lost. And if one does not attain this, all the rest is of no use.

May it please them to have a priest for a son, even though he is bad and a sinner, who prays for them with his entire being each day in the Holy Sacrifice of the Mass. Many a day he offers Mass only for them so that the Lord will help them and they will not lack what they need to survive; that God grant them patience to endure their hardships; that they resign themselves to His holy will; that they be at peace and live in harmony with everyone; that they have the courage to resist the temptations of the devil; and finally, when the time is right, that they experience death clearly and in His holy grace.

If I, with the help of God's grace, manage to become a good religious, my prayers would be more effective and my parents would benefit greatly. The same applies to my dear sister in Christ, Juana, and my brother-in-law Miguel. The only way they should think of me now is in terms of commending me to God so that I can become a good priest and a good minister of God.

This is what most concerns all of us and this is what is important. I remember when my father had that very serious illness and they gave him the last rites. At that time I was already a religious and was attending to him, thinking that he was dying. When he and I were alone he told me, "My son, what I want from you is for you to be a good religious of the Padre San Francisco." Well, father, know that those words are never far from my thoughts, as if I had heard you utter them at this very instant. And also know that I have undertaken this path to try to become a good religious.

Do not feel sad, for I am doing as you wish, which is also the will of God. I also know that my mother has never failed to commend me to God with the same affection so that I might become a good religious. Well, dear mother, if by chance God has put me on this path because of your prayers, be happy with what God has put into motion. And whenever you experience hardships, always say, "Blessed be God and may His holy will be done."

My sister Juana already knows it was not long ago that she found herself at death's door. And through the goodness and intercession of Most Holy Mary, the Lord restored her to perfect health. If she had died, she would not be upset now as to whether I am in Mallorca or not. She should give thanks to the Lord and respect what He provides since what He provides is what is appropriate. And it is quite conceivable that the Lord restored her health so she would be able to comfort the old folks, since I would be leaving.

Let us bless God for God loves us and He cares for all of us. Brother-in-law Miguel and sister Juana: I beg you in earnest to do what I previously asked, that is, continue to live together with great peace and tranquility. Try to respect, bear with patience, and console the old folks. And take the utmost care to raise your children well. And I ask you all to be mindful about going to church to confess and take communion frequently, pray the Stations of the Cross, and try as hard as you can to be good Christians.

I trust that as you have done until now, you will continue to commend me to God from here on out. As we pray to the Lord, I for them and they for me, may the Lord Himself help all of us and bestow His holy grace upon us in this life and glory when this life is over.

Goodbye, dear father! Goodbye, dear mother! Goodbye, Juana, my sister! Goodbye, Miguel, my brother-in-law! Make sure that Miguelito becomes a good Christian and a good student, and that the two girls become good Christians. Trust in God that your uncle might be of some worth. Goodbye, goodbye!

Dearest brother Padre Serra, goodbye. My letters from here on out will be, as I have said, less frequent. With respect to consoling my parents, sister, and brother-in-law, look after them with great affection as I have said to you. To you, first and foremost, and then to the Padre Vicario, the Padre Guardián, and Padre Mestre, I ask of you and trust that *epistola mea comnes vos estis*.[45] Padre Vicario and Padre Mestre, if possible, please be present when this letter is read. This would be of great comfort to them. And do not allow others to join in. It should only be you and the four of them: father, mother, sister, and brother-in-law.

And if anybody else might want to hear the letter, let it be cousin Juana, our neighbor. Please give my warmest greetings to her, cousin Roig, her husband, Aunt Apolonia Boronada Xurxa, and the other relatives.

My greetings to each member of the community of Petra, without forgetting a single one, especially Fray Antonio Vives.

My greetings to Dr. Fiol, his brother; to Señor Antonio, his father, and the rest of the family.

---

45. "You are all my letter," a paraphrase of 2 Corinthians 3:2. "Vicario" and "Guardián" were titles of Franciscan officials in Petra. Padre Mestre was either Pera Mestre or Juan Bautista Mestre, both Mallorcan Franciscans. Serra, *Writings*, 1:409 (note 4).

Very special greetings to Amón Rafael Moragues Costa and his wife; to Dr. Moragues, his brother, and his wife, and the same to Dr. Serralta; to the Señor Vicario Perelló; Señor Alzamora, Señor Juan Nicoláu and his brother, regidor Bartolomé, and the rest of the family. In short, greetings to all my friends.

Tell Padre Vicario that I trust that the book about the black saint will arrive.[46] If it has not arrived from Madrid by the time I leave, I have left instructions here to have the Fornaris take it to him when they go to Mallorca. And try to persuade him to promote devotion to my patron San Francisco Solano.

The enclosed letter is for Medo Maxica, a neighbor of the convent. It is from her son Sebastián who has arrived from the Indies. He seems to be a nice fellow.

Finally, may the Lord bring us together in glory and until then, keep Vuestra Reverencia many years. That is my prayer.

From this house of the holy mission in the city of Cádiz, August 20, 1749.

Lector Palóu sends Vuestra Reverencia many greetings. Please extend these greetings on our behalf to Señor Guillermo Roca and his family.

Your dear friend in Christ,
Fray Junípero Serra, most unworthy priest
Reverendo Padre Fray Francisco Serra, Religious Minor

---

46. The "black saint" was San Benito de Palermo (known in English as Benedict the Moor). He was a Sicilian Franciscan whose parents were African slaves. The volume to which Serra was referring was most likely *Sombra ilustrada con la razón, demonstración, y verdad, admirable vida, virtudes, y milagros de el Beato Benito de San Fradello, conocido por el Sto. Negro de Palermo* by Diego Alvarez, OFM (Alcalá, 1747). Mallorcan Franciscan interest in San Benito may have been because he was a Mediterranean Franciscan who had been beatified only a few years earlier, in 1743. Also, the penitential garb worn by those punished by the Inquisition was called a *sanbenito*, although the name derives from the sixth-century Italian founder of the Benedictines.

CHAPTER 2

New Spain

Serra and Palóu left Cádiz at the end of August aboard the vessel *Villasota*. They were part of a group of twenty Franciscans and seven Dominicans heading for the Americas. The ship arrived at San Juan, Puerto Rico, on October 18. The San Juan that greeted Serra and Palóu was a frontier port. Located at the eastern extremity of the greater Antilles and the northern extremity of the lesser Antilles, Puerto Rico was in the midst of trade routes traveled by ships from a number of European countries, including England, France, and Holland, in addition to Spain. Smuggling and contraband trade were a normal part of the island's life. Indeed, Alejandro O'Reilly reported in 1765 that what prosperity existed on the island was due largely to these extralegal activities. San Juan itself contained slightly over four thousand people, of whom roughly 20 percent were African slaves.[1]

Serra described the journey and his stay in Puerto Rico in a letter to Father Francesch Serra that he composed when he finally reached Veracruz on the Mexican mainland in December. He did not have much to say about the journey except to confess that he had not borne all its difficulties with patience. His struggle to attain that virtue, which had most likely led him to choose the name Junípero in 1731, would last the rest of his life.

Serra stated that the would-be missionaries on board, after having been cooped up for six weeks on the longest sea voyage most of them had ever undertaken, were anxious to engage in evangelical activity. So they decided to organize a domestic mission, along the lines of the popular preaching exercises that were so prevalent in Spain during the eighteenth century. These exercises were often elaborate pageants, with street corner exhortations, religious processions, emotional preaching, and long lines in front of the confessionals dominating the public life of a city for the space of a few days.

The formal preaching usually fell into two categories. Someone would be designated to preach an emotional call to repentance, which was intended to stimulate

---

1. Morales Carrión, *Puerto Rico*, 45–47; Jiménez de Wagenheim, *Puerto Rico*, 78–81, 89.

feelings of guilt, anxiety, and contrition among the listeners as they contemplated the gravity of their sins. Someone would also be designated to preach a doctrinal sermon, which was intended to refresh the congregation about some of the more basic points of Christian belief and behavior to which the sinners affected by the first sermon were attempting to recommit themselves. Serra, who had developed a theatrical pulpit persona during his preaching journeys throughout the island of Mallorca, was one of those chosen to preach the emotional call to repentance. As Serra freely acknowledged in the following letter, his preaching experience did not go well. Indeed, it was significant that Serra was willing to share what he regarded as a personal failure with his friend on Mallorca. He did not begin his time in the New World with an unbridled success. He realized that he had been unable to engage in effective evangelization in San Juan. The style that had served him so well in the rural areas of Mallorca did not seem to work in the more freewheeling setting of San Juan.

Serra characteristically attributed the lack of his preaching prowess to personal failings, his lack of "interior fervor" that would have truly spoken to his congregations. In the ascetic tradition that animated Serra, a lack of such "interior" fervor was often due to one's paying too much attention to the "exterior," that is, to one's physical senses and physical comfort. Serra's decision, when he landed in Veracruz on December 6, to walk from Veracruz to Mexico City—a decision that had serious long-term physical consequences for him—was an attempt to recover his interior fervor by disciplining and punishing his body. Puerto Rico had taught him that the New World was going to present him with a series of very steep challenges, and he wanted to be as ready as he could be.

When the friars drew lots to decide which saints to pray to during a storm on the way from Puerto Rico to Veracruz, Serra's choice of Francisco Solano indicates that this saint, whose life had provided a model for him during his own spiritual crisis during his last years on Mallorca, continued to be at the forefront of his consciousness.

❋ *Letter to Padre Francesch Serra, December 14, 1749*

Dearest friend in Jesus Christ, Padre Fray Francisco Serra, Master and Señor,

Thanks be to God, after a very lengthy voyage I finally find myself at the desired port in this city of Veracruz, on the eve of our departure for Mexico [City] which is eighty leagues away by land. I think our departure will be tomorrow or the day after.

The story of this voyage is much too long to recount, but in a few words I can say that for us, it was pleasant, albeit long. We only experienced a few difficulties, and for me the worst of them all was my not being able to handle them with patience.

We boarded ship on August 29 at night and set sail on Saturday, the 30th. On September 8, the feast of María Santísima,[2] we found ourselves opposite the Canary Islands. We continued sailing without any crosswinds and there were a few periods of dead calm. The only time the sea was quite rough was on the eve of the feast of San Miguel,[3] which worried the pilots somewhat. But it passed before becoming a storm of any note.

On the feast of Nuestra Señora del Rosario,[4] fearing that there would not be enough water, we were all given rationed amounts. The rationing was so strict that it amounted to a glass the size of those in the dining room at Petra. We were given water at each of the two daily meals. And the glasses were never filled to the top. They were always about a fingerbreadth short of the top. We could not drink chocolate even though we had some with us because they did not give us water to prepare it. This enforced rationing lasted for fifteen days until we landed in the city of Puerto Rico, which is 1,200 leagues from Cádiz.

This tribulation with the water was the worst of it. There were moments when I would have drunk from the filthiest puddle in the street. I would have drunk anything at all. But on occasions a Mallorcan sailor would come to our aid. Sometimes he would obtain an extra ration for me and Palóu, either by sheer cleverness or because he gave us his own ration.

With this difficulty, which if we had approached it with patience could have given us much joy, we arrived and disembarked in the city of Puerto Rico on Saturday, October 18, the feast of San Lucas. There our lodging was at the hermitage of La Purísima Concepción de María, which is in the center of the city. That night we recited the Rosary in the church with a large crowd of people.

The following night I recited the mysteries and added a short sermon about the preaching of missions in the days to come, as the Padre Presidente had ordered me to do. The next day we left to preach throughout the city and its plazas, which produced tremendous excitement. Since the church of the hermitage was more or less the same size as that of the Convento de Jesús in Palma, it would not be able to hold one-third of those gathered, so the Señor Vicario General[5] begged us to hold the mission at the cathedral. And that is what happened. The cathedral was filling up with people and they did not

---

2. September 8 is the feast of the birth of the Virgin Mary.
3. September 29 is the feast of Saint Michael the Archangel.
4. October 7 is the feast of Our Lady of the Rosary.
5. The Vicario General was the senior church official in San Juan.

even fit there. The series of sermons were distributed as follows: a missionary from Sahagún would preach the doctrines, and the Padre Presidente (who is another missionary from Sant Espíritu) and I would preach the mission.[6]

And that was how it was done. I preached the first sermon in the cathedral, and then the Padre Presidente and I would take turns. There is no doubt that it was merely an honor that the Padres wanted to bestow on me, but I was confused by this because my way of preaching was so different than that of those Padres, like the difference between straw and gold, fire and ice, and day and night. The night the Padre Presidente was preaching there was such a commotion—tears, sighs, breast beating, and more; so much so, that for a long time after he had descended from the pulpit, you still could not hear anything in the church because of the wailing and crying of those who were heading back to their homes.

And the same thing happened with some sermons the missionary Padre gave at the hermitage, days after we had finished preaching the mission, for our departure was delayed and we ended up staying longer than intended. However, when I would preach, whether it be on horrific subjects or shouting myself hoarse, you could not even hear a sigh. It was made public that I was the only one who did not possess that interior fervor that is so necessary to instill words with passion to stir the hearts of those who are listening. This was a blow to my pride.

I hope that Vuestra Reverencia will take pity on me and commend me to God so that I can learn how to love Him with my entire being and in this way the Lord can prepare me for such an important ministry.

Whether it was the preaching of such laborers as the reverend missionary Padres or the zeal demonstrated by the others in the confessional, which was an example for all of us, the mission produced such fruit that we heard confessions morning and night. We would sit down in the confessional at three or four o'clock in the morning and hear confessions until midnight.

The people were very enthusiastic and sent so many gifts of food and beverages that there was not enough room in the house for everything. I will tell you, in short, that we had arranged with the ship captain that he would provide us with everything we needed during our stay, but he reneged on the agreement. So twenty religious and three servants went ashore without a maravedí[7] for food. We spent eighteen days eating better than we would have

---

6. In preaching missions like this to those who were already baptized, there were often two types of discourse: the elaboration of various theological and religious points (the doctrines) and the verbal summons, often delivered in an emotional sermon, to integrate these points into one's life and conduct (the mission).
7. A copper coin of small value.

in any convent. Everyone drank chocolate. There was tobacco for smoking as well as snuff; as much lemonade as you wanted in the afternoon as a refreshment. The brother who came with us still has forty pesos left. And with regard to spices, we loaded on board as much as we thought we would want for the rest of the voyage. We did all this while continuously saying we did not want any gifts.

As soon as we arrived, two or three men, who appeared to us to be important gentlemen, asked if there was a Mallorcan Padre at the mission. And seeing that there were two of us, they immediately began to offer us all kinds of things, but seeing that we would not accept anything, they gave the community an overly abundant amount of fruit, preserves, money to buy meat, tallow candles for light since oil is not used here for that purpose, and other things. They honored us greatly. In addition to these two men who distinguished themselves so much that the entire mission sang the praises of the Mallorcans, another fellow, named Don Juan Ferrer, also came and presented us with gifts. He is the nephew of Padre Definidor Botellas and manages the royal warehouses.[8]

We finally boarded ship on the 31st. The ship struggled to get out of the port and could not do it. The ship was close to crashing against the rocks in two fathoms of water, more or less. We signaled for help by firing a cannon. Those who were in the city thought we had already perished. There was so much wailing and crying on behalf of the religious that the governor immediately ordered all available boats to head out toward the ship. Before doing anything else they were to rescue the religious and take them to shore.

Most of us went ashore. The people realized we would not have food or a place to sleep that night, so when we arrived at the small plaza of the hermitage we found the people already there. Some brought food, others chocolate, and others brought beds. That night we had leftovers of everything, chocolate for the morning, and there was even enough left to take on board.

That night we preached and heard confessions after reciting the rosary. And in the morning, All Saint's Day, we sang a Mass of thanksgiving to honor María Santísima. We boarded ship that day, which was Saturday, and safely left the port. We continued our voyage toward the city of Veracruz. At the end of this second voyage, which was as exceedingly long as the first one due to the weight of our ship, we experienced a number of hardships. On December 2, when we saw that we were getting closer to Veracruz, we thought that if we did not enter the port that afternoon, we would surely

---

8. Antonio Botellas was a Mallorcan Franciscan. The title "Definidor" indicated that he was a member of the advisory council to the Provincial of the Mallorca.

enter early the following day, at first light. However, we were caught by a north wind, which is very dangerous along this coast, and we got turned around and ended up sailing away from the shore where we wanted to be. For days we sailed farther and farther away and the terrible storm caused the ship to take on a lot of water. It was a miracle that the main mast withstood all of this.

Our twenty religious and the seven Dominican Padres who were headed for Guadalajara met. We discussed *quid resolvendum*[9] whether we should make some sort of promise so that the Lord would take pity on us. It was agreed that each person would write down on a slip of paper the name of his favorite saint, without telling anybody. We would put the papers in a jar, and after invoking the Holy Spirit and reciting the prayer of Todos los Santos,[10] we would draw lots, hoping to be lucky enough to draw our own patron saint and protector. If that happened, as we landed we would celebrate in community a solemn Mass and sermon. I wrote down San Francisco Solano and Lector Palóu chose San Miguel, but neither one was drawn. Santa Bárbara was the winner. Padre Ferrer, from Valencia, had written her name. As soon as that slip of paper was drawn we all exclaimed ¡Viva Santa Bárbara! Her feast day was that very day, December 4. That night the ship turned to return to port and we were all happy yet confused. In fact, the crosswind had ceased and a favorable one was blowing, which allowed us to sail toward the port. We dropped anchor on Saturday, the 6th. We piously believed that we had been saved through the intercession of María Santísima on whose feast days we have always experienced solace. Santa Bárbara also interceded for us. For after we landed we noticed gaping holes in the ship and the main mast was gone, a condition that would render a ship incapable of sailing for even a day without very serious risks.

On the 10th we celebrated the feast of our seraphic father San Francisco at this convent.[11] The Padre Prior of the Dominicans officiated. Members from each of the communities assisted and I was entrusted with the sermon, for which I felt inadequate.

Everyone, help me thank God for so many benefices and commend me to Him so that I will know how to be grateful to Him.

---

9. "What must be resolved." A standard phrase that appeared in many moral theology handbooks of the day.
10. The prayer of the liturgy of All Saints' Day, November 1, the day on which the voyage had begun.
11. In the book of Isaiah, seraphs were angelic beings who attended the throne of God. One of them purified the prophet by placing a burning coal on his lips (Isaiah 6:1–7). In the Franciscan tradition, after Francis received the stigmata (the wounds of Christ in his own body), he was attended by a seraph. Hence he was often called "Our Seraphic Father" in the Franciscan tradition. See Armstrong, Hellmann, and Short, *Francis of Assisi*, 3:727.

I send my father, mother, sister, brother-in-law, etc. many greetings. Tell them to be happy in Christ for I never forget to pray for them every day at Mass. I find myself in good health and nothing new has happened to me, except for the fact that I was the only religious from our order and the Dominican order, as well as the servants, who did not get seasick. When the rest were almost dead, I could not even tell that we were at sea. And that is the truth.

Greetings to the Padre Guardián and to dear Padre Vicario, to all of the Padres. I send Vuestra Reverencia 1,000 embraces, trusting that you will commend us all to God, as I implore you to do, so that we will meet again in Heaven, if not on this earth. Amen.

Veracruz, December 14, 1749
Your servant and friend in Christ,
Fray Junípero Serra, your most unworthy priest

Colegios Apostólicos

When Serra arrived in Veracruz, most of the friars whose destination was Mexico City availed themselves of the horses that were provided to them by the government for the journey to Mexico City. However, Serra and one other friar elected to make the journey on foot. During this walk he developed an infection in his leg that bothered him periodically for the rest of his life. He generally refused medical treatment for the infection and quoted in defense of this refusal remarks attributed to a third-century martyr, Saint Agatha, "I have never used carnal medicine for my body."[12]

In his biography of Serra, published thirty-seven years later, Palóu cast the story of this journey on foot as a lesson in God's providence. On a number of occasions, the two friars were hungry and without resources, yet they were always helped at the last minute by an unexpected stranger who appeared seemingly out of nowhere. On one occasion Serra and his companion even gave the meager food they had to a poor man they met. But at the end of the day, a man on horseback appeared and gave them some bread. Some of these stories were quite similar to stories about Saint Francis that appeared in Bonaventure's *The Life of Saint Francis*. For instance, one night Francis and his companions were hungry and without food when a man appeared out of nowhere and gave them bread. Potential Franciscan missionaries, who were one of the intended audiences for Palóu's biography, would have instantly recognized the similarity. Serra

---
12. Palóu, *Palóu's Life of Fray Junípero Serra*, 274.

suspected or perhaps hoped that one of these unexpected benefactors who gave them a pomegranate was actually San José appearing to them.[13]

By December 31 Serra and his companion were at Guadalupe, a shrine commemorating what many believed was an appearance in 1531 of the Virgin to an Indian named Juan Diego. Guadalupe was one of the most sacred spots in Catholic Mexico. At nine o'clock in the morning the following day, they reached the Colegio Apostólico de San Fernando on the outskirts of Mexico City.

These colegios were a comparatively recent development among the Franciscans in New Spain. They were an attempt to help the order recover for itself the intensity and perceived successes of the sixteenth-century golden age of missionary activity after what was regarded as a stagnant time in the seventeenth century. These schools were modeled on colegios founded on the Iberian Peninsula starting in 1680. The Iberian missionary colegios were created to train and support the increasing number of men then engaged in itinerant ministry within Spain itself, preaching in the countryside to renew religion among the faithful.[14]

The colegios were brought to the New World by a Mallorcan, Antonio Llinás. Like Serra, Llinás was something of a dissatisfied academic. He was twice turned down for positions at the university in Palma and went to New Spain to accept a lectureship there. After teaching at Franciscan schools in Querétaro, Celaya, and Valladolid, Llinás experienced a religious transformation in 1675. He related that he had a vision in which God had shown him "the manifest deceptions of this miserable world." So he went to Spain and consulted with the minister general of the order. Llinás convinced him and other Franciscan authorities that the opening of colegios apostólicos in the Americas could be an important way of renewing the Franciscan missionary enterprise there. Among Llinás's first recruits for this new enterprise were twelve Mallorcan Franciscans who enlisted in the cause in 1682. In the eighteenth century Llinás continued to be well known among Franciscans in Mallorca, and he served, along with Llull, as a model for Serra. For instance, while Serra was at Cádiz awaiting transport to America in 1749, he spent some time reviewing a manuscript he had brought with him on his trip. The manuscript was prepared by a Mallorcan notary and dealt with some miracles attributed to Llinás.[15]

---

13. Palóu, *Palóu's Life of Fray Junípero Serra*, 17–20. Armstrong, Hellmann, and Short, *Francis of Assisi*, 2:550; Fogelquist, "The Discourse of Saints' Lives," 236. More than half a century later Alexander von Humboldt called the road from Veracruz to Mexico City "the most difficult perhaps in all America." Archer, *The Army in Bourbon Mexico*, 39.
14. McCloskey, *The Formative Years of the Missionary College of Santa Cruz*; Sáiz Díez, *Los colegios de Propaganda Fide*; Mujal, "Out of the Apocalypse to Alta California," 155–69.
15. McCloskey, *The Formative Years of the Missionary College of Santa Cruz*, 16; Escandell Bonet, *Baleares y América*, 241–43; Castro, "Texto autógrafo latino."

FIGURE 4. Interior of the Colegio de la Santa Cruz de Querétaro. Founded in 1683 by Mallorcan Antonio Llinás, this was the first *colegio apostólico* in the New World. *Photograph by and courtesy of Robert Michels and Stephanie Daffer.*

The first colegio was founded in Querétaro. Llinás had developed an interest in organizing missionary activity in the highlands of the Sierra Gorda, and Querétaro was the gateway to that region. The colegio was named Santa Cruz, after a local devotion to a miraculous stone cross that was associated with the conquest and Christianization of the region in the sixteenth century. Thus the founders of the first colegios consciously harked back to an earlier period of missionary activity. Friars from Santa Cruz eventually founded two other colegios apostólicos in Mexico: Nuestra Señora de Guadalupe in Zacatecas in 1707 and San Fernando in Mexico City in 1733. When Serra arrived at San Fernando he found his perfect match—a man seeking personal renewal found an institution, the colegio apostólico, dedicated to institutional renewal.[16]

16. Espinosa, *Crónica de los colegios de propaganda fide de la Nueva España*, 103–39; Gunnarsdóttir, *Mexican Karismata*, 98; Taylor, "Placing the Cross in Colonial Mexico," 167–71.

Figure 5. Colegio de San Fernando, Mexico City. It was founded in 1733, and Serra arrived there on January 1, 1750. He remained affiliated with it for the rest of his life. Photograph by Fr. Maynard Geiger, OFM. *Courtesy of the Santa Bárbara Mission Archive-Library.*

When Llinás returned to the New World, he brought more than the authorization to begin colegios apostólicos. He also brought a devotion to Sor María de Jesús de Ágreda, a well-known Franciscan sister who died in 1665. At the time, Sor María was best known for a biography she had written about the Virgin Mary, *La mística ciudad de Dios*. But Llinás also brought documents that indicated that Sor María and some Franciscans had said that she had bilocated in Spain and New Mexico in the 1620s and early 1630s and had preached the Gospel to various groups of native peoples there.

The story began in 1629 when a supply expedition from Mexico City reached Santa Fe. The expedition contained twenty-nine friars who had recently arrived from Spain and were to be stationed in the missions of New Mexico. One of the friars brought with him a contemporary painting of Sor Luisa de la Ascensión, a well-known Franciscan nun who resided at the convent of Santa Clara in the town of Carrión de los Condes. Sor Luisa had a widespread reputation as a mystic and healer in northern Spain, and she had been credited with a number of bilocations in Spain, generally in connection with her miraculous healing powers. There was an upsurge in such reports of mystical journeys to distant places, especially journeys undertaken by women religious in Spain, in the first few decades of the seventeenth century. Between 1614 and 1629 Sor Luisa herself was popularly credited with at least thirty healing miracles. The arrival of the picture of Sor Luisa caused a sensation among the missionaries in New Mexico, and they soon reported that a group of native people from the Jumano group was saying to them that they themselves had been visited by a woman who looked like the figure in the newly arrived picture, except that she was a much younger person.[17]

The chief of the newly arrived missionaries was Father Estevan de Perea. He had served a previous term as head missionary in New Mexico, and like many other New Mexico Franciscan authorities during this period, he had vigorously quarreled with the governor. Perea's aims had been thwarted by instructions from the viceroy in 1621, but he continued to press his case in ecclesiastical circles. He prevailed upon the Inquisition to appoint a special officer for New Mexico as a way of increasing the Church's authority there. That friar, Alonso de Benavides, also served for a time as the chief Franciscan official in New Mexico, and this made him a very important figure in the area. So Perea's return to New Mexico in 1629 was a triumphant homecoming of sorts for him. He and Benavides apparently decided that this was a good time to try to press their advantage. Benavides was dispatched back to Spain with the goal of convincing the civil and

---

17. Benavides, *Benavides' Memorial of 1630*, 58; Tar, "Flying through the Empire," 280–83; Egido, "Religiosidad popular y taumaturgia," 18–19. For a study of the actual missionary approach to the Jumanos in the 1620s, see Hickerson, *Jumanos*, 86–102.

ecclesiastical authorities to make the New Mexico missionary region a diocese unto itself. At some point Benavides seems to have decided that he would make an excellent first bishop for this diocese.[18]

Benavides arrived in Spain in 1630 and presented a report to Bernardino de Sena, the minister general of the Franciscans, who was residing in Madrid. The report was filled with accounts of miraculous events that accompanied the Franciscan evangelization effort in New Mexico, including the story of the mysterious woman. The situation in New Mexico was presented in Benavides's report as a triumphant vindication of Franciscan missionary efforts. Such a vindication was necessary because the Franciscans had been under fire by other missionary groups, especially the Dominicans, who were accusing the Franciscans of baptizing native peoples en masse without giving them sufficient instruction in the faith beforehand. Dominican Bartolomé de las Casas, for instance, had sarcastically accused the Franciscans of baptizing Indians "in squadrons."[19]

During their conversation Sena told Benavides of a young nun in the town of Ágreda, Sor María de Jesús. She had joined the convent at an early age and became well known as a mystic among her fellow nuns and in the local community. She was reputed to have been seen levitating during her prayers and was one of the many Spanish nuns to whom bilocation was being attributed. Indeed, word was circulating that her bilocation involved preaching the Gospel in the Americas. Bernardino de Sena urged Benavides to visit Sor María at her convent.

Benavides arrived at the convent in April 1631 and interviewed Sor María over a number of days. He became convinced that she was the nun to whom the native peoples of New Mexico had been referring when they said that a person dressed like Sor Luisa had appeared to them. She told him that she had experienced the gift of bilocation from 1620 "to the present year, 1631." Benavides wrote an enthusiastic letter addressed to the missionaries in New Mexico telling them that he had found the mysterious woman. He described Sor María in great detail. He said that she told him that it had been revealed to her that God had told Saint Francis that the native peoples of the Americas would be converted to Catholicism at the mere sight of Franciscans. Benavides included an excerpt of a letter of encouragement from Sor María herself to the New Mexico missionaries. There is, however, no evidence that Benavides's letter containing this excerpt was actually sent or delivered.[20]

---

18. Sholes, *Church and State in New Mexico*, 74.
19. Benavides, *Benavides' Memorial of 1630*, 58–61; Colahan, "María de Jesús de Ágreda," 157; Weber, *The Spanish Frontier in North America*, 99–100. The dispute between Las Casas and the Franciscans was intense. Franciscan missionary Toribio de Motolinía wrote a letter to Carlos V in 1555 harshly criticizing Las Casas. See Lockhart and Otte, *Letters and People of the Spanish Indies*, 219–47.
20. Colahan, *The Visions of Sor María de Ágreda*, 104–11.

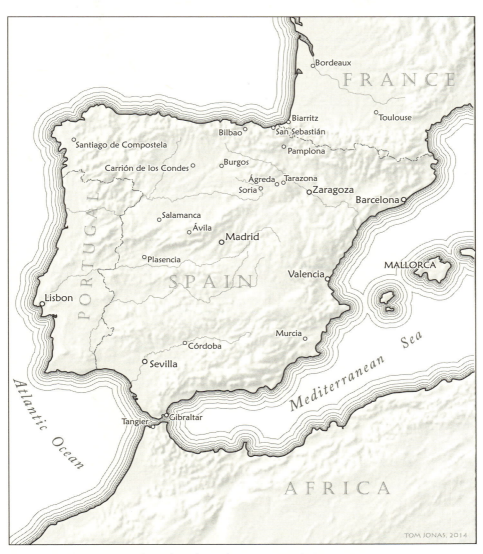

Map 2. The Iberian peninsula in the eighteenth century. *Map by Tom Jonas.*

Benavides went to Rome in 1632 and seems to have stayed there for a few years. He doubtless spent time lobbying for the establishment of a diocese in New Mexico with himself as the bishop. In 1634 he penned a report directed to the pope himself. This report was clearly intended, at least in part, to answer criticisms he had been receiving. For instance, if Sor María had been appearing to the native peoples since 1620, why was there no mention of this by the native peoples to the missionaries until 1629? Benavides stated that the missionaries had indeed asked the Indians that very question. They were told that the Indians never mentioned it because they simply assumed that the missionaries knew all about it. Other parts of the report were clearly Benavides's embellishment of material that he included in his 1630 report. In the 1634 report he stated that the missionaries who arrived from Spain in 1629 told the archbishop in Mexico City that it was common knowledge in Spain that Sor María said she experienced bilocation and preached in New Mexico. The archbishop then told the missionaries to investigate this when they arrived in New Mexico. But there had been no reference to any communication from the archbishop in his 1630 report. The 1631 letter had contained a vague account of some sort of communication from the archbishop to the New Mexico missionaries. Benavides's 1634 document included a reference to a message from the archbishop, but the part he quoted was simply a boilerplate instruction to make sure that the evangelization and conversion of the native peoples was being done according to the proper form required by the Church. Benavides in 1634 also claimed that others, such as Sor Luisa de la Ascensión, also bilocated to New Mexico and preached to the native peoples there. He attributed this story to Sor Luisa's confessor, whom he said was including it in a book he was writing about her. But the confessor, he said, did not allow him to copy it out.[21]

It is not clear whether this report was actually acted upon by anyone in the Vatican. However, the very next year both Sor María and Sor Luisa were visited by interrogators from the Inquisition. Church authorities in Spain were very suspicious of narratives circulating among the people about miracles, for they feared that such popular piety could easily become too exuberant and spin out of institutional control. The group that visited Sor María consisted of six men, two of whom were personally acquainted with her and sympathetic to her. Sor María proved herself to be a formidable and sophisticated interlocutor. The team came away saying that she probably had been overly influenced by Francisco de la Fuente, another Franciscan who claimed to have bilocated to the New World and to have preached to the Indians there. His claim was condemned by the Inquisition in 1632. Sor Luisa, who had a much more extensive group of miracles attributed to

---

21. Benavides, *Fray Alonso de Benavides' Revised Memorial*, 92–96; Colahan, *The Visions of Sor María de Ágreda*, 101–104.

her, was not so fortunate. She was removed from her convent and taken away as a prisoner. Her works were condemned and she died shortly thereafter.[22]

Benavides left Rome and returned to Spain. In 1636 he suddenly headed for Lisbon. The Franciscans let out word in Madrid that he had been appointed bishop of Goa, India. There is no record of his ever having been so appointed or of his ever actually having become a bishop. In fact, Benavides dropped out of sight. Some scholars speculate that he may have died on his way to India. In any event, it is hard to escape the conclusion that his increasingly elaborate story had become an embarrassment for the Franciscans. India was certainly as far away as they could send him from both Europe and New Spain. Perhaps dangling the prospect of a bishopric before him was a way of encouraging him to get on the boat.[23]

Sor María spent the rest of her life as abbess of her convent and rarely spoke of the bilocations. Rather, she devoted herself to composing her life of the Virgin Mary, which was filled with episodes she said had been directly revealed to her by the Virgin. Sor María became very well known in Spain and even engaged in extensive correspondence with King Felipe IV. In 1650 she was again interviewed by the Inquisition as a result of letters she had exchanged, most likely inadvertently, with one of the king's political opponents. In the course of that interview she was once again questioned about the bilocations. She said that she had experienced something like this from 1620 to 1623. This contradicted Benavides's account in his 1630 report that the Indians said she appeared to them as late as 1629. This also contradicted her 1631 letter, in which she said that the bilocations had continued up to that date. In her 1650 discussions with the Inquisition's interrogators she presented herself in 1631 as a young and inexperienced nun who was led into making all sorts of exaggerated statements by Benavides. The interrogators accepted her account. In a letter she composed shortly after her interrogation Sor María said that her confessors, the ones who had originally helped spread the story of her bilocations, were "more well-intentioned than careful." She also stated that Benavides had dramatically exaggerated her account. She maintained that she had had some kind of mystical experiences in the early 1620s, but claimed that she did not know whether she had actually gone to New Mexico in her own body or not.[24]

Sor María's volume *La mística ciudad de Dios* was published not during her lifetime but in 1670, five years after her death. The book contained a long introduction and biography by a former confessor of hers, José Ximénez Samaniego. A section of that introduction, based largely on Benavides's reports, but also

---

22. Colahan, "María de Jesús de Ágreda," 160; Kendrick, *Mary of Ágreda*, 40; Fedewa, *María of Ágreda*, 60.
23. His departure was reported in a letter written by an official in Madrid to the Vatican in 1636. See Benavides, *Fray Alonso de Benavides' Revised Memorial*, 199.
24. These events are treated in Colahan, "María de Jesús de Ágreda" and *The Visions of Sor María de Ágreda*, 115–27.

FIGURE 6. Frontispiece of *La mística ciudad de Dios*, by María de Jesús de Ágreda; illustration by anonymous artist. The work was first published in 1670, five years after the author's death. *Courtesy of the Monasterio de Concepcionistas Franciscanas, Ágreda, Spain.*

containing a section of Sor María's 1650 letter, related the story of her bilocation to New Mexico. The book itself proved very controversial. As a member of the Conceptionist order, a branch of the Franciscans, Sor María was very interested in the notion of the Immaculate Conception, and the biography reflected that concern. Large sections of the beginning of the volume dealt with Mary's experiences in her mother's womb after she had been immaculately conceived. These sections were regarded as highly inappropriate, especially by theologians who did not subscribe to the notion of an Immaculate Conception for the Virgin. In 1674 Sor María's book was investigated by the Inquisition, and in 1681 it was placed on the index of forbidden books. The Habsburgs were able to successfully petition the Vatican so that the condemnation of the volume did not apply to Spain. In 1696 the book was roundly condemned by the faculty at the University of Paris, and in the early part of the seventeenth century it was just as vigorously defended in Spain, especially by the faculty of the University of Salamanca.[25]

Thus, after the 1631 visit by Benavides, Sor María mentioned her bilocations only twice. Both times were in connection with interrogations by the Inquisition. On both occasions she never entirely disavowed those experiences yet successfully downplayed them through a series of artfully evasive answers. But these experiences were by no means the focus of her activities or writing, although her treatment of Mary's life after the crucifixion of Jesus was clearly influenced by her experiences in the 1620s. In the biography, Mary was miraculously transported around the Mediterranean and became a successful evangelist of her son in many different countries. But even here, that focus was secondary, since the volume's fame or infamy rested on the notion of the Immaculate Conception and Sor María's treatment of it.

Bilocation would most likely never have become the primary matter associated with Sor María except for one chance occurrence. When Antonio Llinás visited Europe to seek approval for his idea of colegios apostólicos in the New World, he had to consult with the minister general of the Franciscan order. That person turned out to be none other than José Ximénez Samaniego, Sor María's former confessor and biographer. The fact that someone so identified with Sor María could become the chief Franciscan official in the world was a testament to her great influence in Spain in the seventeenth century. Ximénez Samaniego brought out from the archives Benavides's 1631 letter addressed to the missionaries of New Mexico, which contained Sor María's exhortation to them, and showed the letter to Llinás. Llinás took copies of these letters with him to the New World, and they became well-known to the missionaries at the Colegio de Santa Cruz in Querétaro. Since the letters celebrated Franciscan evangelical triumphs of an earlier

---

25. Ágreda, *Mística ciudad de Dios*, 1:205–13; Rodríguez Cruz and Llamas, "La 'Mística ciudad de Dios' en el ambiente universitario"; Hernández Sánchez-Barba, *Monjas ilustres en la historia de España*, 144–45.

era and demonstrated divine approbation of Franciscan evangelical methods, they were a perfect device to assist Llinás in setting up the colegios apostólicos as institutions that would help the order recover its earlier and successful fervor.[26]

Within a decade missionaries from Querétaro were reporting that native peoples in Texas were telling them that a mysterious woman in blue had long ago appeared to their people. In the 1690s the phenomenon of bilocation itself came to Querétaro. One woman, Francisca de los Angeles, who was closely associated with the Colegio de Santa Cruz and whose spiritual director was one of the friars there, reported that she had been miraculously bilocated to Texas, where she ministered to Indians whose ancestors had earlier contact with Sor María. Francisca said that she herself had even met one very old Indian who had himself been evangelized decades before by Sor María.[27]

The Queretarans publicized what Benavides said about Sor María. As they founded additional colegios apostólicos in Zacatecas and Mexico City, devotion to Sor María spread. In 1730 Benavides's letter was published in Mexico City and then republished in 1747 and around 1760. Anyone who joined the colegios apostólicos in the eighteenth century quickly learned of Sor María's exploits. Sor María also told Benavides that Saint Francis himself had sent two non-Spanish friars to evangelize in the kingdom of Titlas. Since the location of that place was unknown, it opened up an entire range of possible sites on the northern frontier of New Spain where miraculous evangelization might have occurred. Many missionaries were anxious to discover whether these friars or Sor María herself had perhaps worked in areas where they themselves were working. Finally, according to Benavides, Sor María had said that Saint Francis had been assured by God himself that Native Americans would become instantly converted at the sight of Franciscan friars. This statement looked both backward and forward. On the one hand, it served the Franciscans as a defense against the sixteenth-century charge that the order was engaging in mass baptisms of Indians who had not been sufficiently instructed in the faith. On the other hand, Sor María's statement made it possible for any future missionary to regard himself as actively participating in this prophecy. As we shall see, Junípero Serra enthusiastically believed that Sor María's words definitely applied to his own missionary effort.[28]

When Serra arrived at San Fernando, his first request was that he be allowed to live with the novices whose life in the community was the most rigorous and whose youthful fervor he desired to reclaim. That request was denied and

---

26. This story is recounted in a 1690 letter by Querétaro missionary Damián Massanet, found in Bolton, *Spanish Exploration in the Southwest*, 354–55; the Spanish is in Gómez Canedo, *Primeras exploraciones y poblamiento de Texas*, 7–8.
27. Gunnarsdóttir, *Mexican Karismata*, 87–100; Dwyer, "Mystics in Mexico," 210–14; Owens, "Journeys to Dark Lands," 161–69; Colahan, *The Visions of Sor María de Ágreda*, 109.
28. Pérez Villanueva, "Algo más sobre la Inquisición y Sor María de Ágreda," 14–15.

Serra settled into the life of the colegio—a fairly regimented life, with liturgical exercises spread throughout the day, along with conferences on moral theology and the teaching of Christian doctrine. The statutes of the colegios apostólicos also stated that indigenous languages were to be taught. However, the variety of languages on the northern frontier of New Spain and the distances of the mission territory from the colegios did not allow for that particular statute to be generally observed. Life in the colegio must have been difficult for Serra, since he was already an accomplished theologian and teacher.[29]

Sierra Gorda

Serra did not have to bear this difficult life for very long because within six months he and Palóu were dispatched to the colegio's missions in the Sierra Gorda, in the highlands northeast of the city of Querétaro. This area had been inhabited for centuries by people of the Otopame cultural group and had been a zone of transition between the generally sedentary inhabitants of central Mexico and the more nomadic inhabitants of the north. The Pame people themselves were roughly divided into a southern group, in the Sierra Gorda, and a northern group, around the jurisdiction of Villa de Valles.[30] The entire area was a theater of the Chichimeca wars of the sixteenth century. At that time, Augustinian missionaries entered the region and established a few missions and mission stations. But many of these establishments, including one at Xalpa [Jalpan], were destroyed by the Otopame at the end of the 1560s. Franciscan missionaries came into the territory at the beginning of the seventeenth century, and Franciscans from the newly founded colegio apostólico in Querétaro entered the area in the 1680s. For the next fifty years Franciscans, Augustinians, and Dominicans attempted to establish missions and mission stations among the roughly fourteen thousand indigenous inhabitants of the region. Small groups of Jonace and Pame peoples would occasionally agree to enter missions. The Jonaces, whom a local military leader described as "rebels" and "untamed," often left after a short period of time and returned to their traditional living patterns in the countryside and mountains. But a number of the Pame, especially those around Jalpan, tended to appear to be more accommodating to the relatively settled agricultural practices of the missions.[31]

---

29. Rex Galindo, "Propaganda Fide," 175–78, 224–33; González Marmolejo, *Misioneros del desierto*, 177–81; Guest, *Fermín Francisco de Lasuén*, 117; After his time in the Sierra Gorda, Serra served a term as the person responsible for the spiritual formation of the novices at the Colegio de San Fernando: Palóu, *Palóu's Life of Fray Junípero Serra*, 262.

30. Parsons, "El norte-centro de México"; Carrasco Pizana, *Los Otomíes*, 306; Gallardo Arias, *Los pames coloniales*, 18–19, 31.

31. Gallardo Arias, *Los pames coloniales*, 40, 110; Tutino, *Making a New World*, 215.

But as with many indigenous peoples of the Americas, appearances could conceal as much as they revealed. Perceptive missionaries came to understand that local cultures were robust, complex, and resilient. Juan Guadalupe Soriano, the missionary among the Pame who gained the greatest knowledge of their language, remarked in the 1760s, "The more one deals with them, the less one knows about them." After decades of missionary effort he confessed that the Pame were still "inclined to idolatry" and that virtually all of them still followed their own religious leaders and still practiced their traditional dances. At the same time peoples of the region developed their own unique and syncretic form of religion and spirituality. The "cult of Cristo viejo" was a significant example of religious syncretism that arose in the eighteenth century at Xichu, less than fifty miles west of Jalpan.[32]

A group of Franciscans from San Fernando established Mission San José de Vizarrón on the outskirts of the territory in 1740. At around the same time the Fernandinos were establishing this mission, military officer José de Escandón was entrusted with the "pacification" of the region. Escandón represented a new strategy on the part of the colonial government, a strategy that would bring him into conflict with the missionaries. The roots of this new approach dated to the 1720s. At that time, Pedro de Rivera, the military commander of Veracruz, had made an inspection tour of the northern presidios. He wrote a report concluding that the presidios were becoming too expensive to maintain. He also argued that in some of the presidios, soldiers were simply acting as *mayordomos* for the missions and were being forced to perform inappropriate tasks. He wrote that at one presidio "the soldiers do nothing except assist the nearby three missions. Since they are not doing the job of military men, the presidio should be eliminated." As Rivera's report was being circulated and discussed over the next decade, similar accusations were being leveled against the missions from other quarters. Staff members of the Ministerio de Guerra y Hacienda were complaining that the missions were also costing too much, especially considering that under the Patronato Real missionary salaries had to be paid from the treasury. In the 1740s such views were shared by both the viceroy (the first Revillagigedo) and the auditor of the ministry (the Marqués de Altamira.) In Escandón they found the man to carry out a different method of colonization.[33]

32. Pimentel, *Lenguas indígenas de México*, 451–52; Lara Cisneros, "Aculturación religiosa en Sierra Gorda," 61; Lara Cisneros, *El cristianismo en el espejo indígena*, 183–225; Driver and Driver, "Ethnography and Acculturation," 42–43; see also Solís de la Torre, *Bárbaros y ermitaños*, and Jackson, "The Chichimeca Frontier." We thank Professor Robert Jackson for sharing with us a prepublication copy of this essay.
33. Naylor and Polzer, *Pedro de Rivera and the Military Regulations for Northern New Spain*, 158; Osante and Alcaraz Cienfuegos, *Nuevo Santander*, 68; Velázquez, *El marqués de Altamira*, 33–65; Osante, *Testimonio acerca de la causa formada en la colonia del Nuevo Santander*, vi; Osante, *Orígenes del Nuevo Santander*, 146; Mendoza Muñoz, *El conde de Sierra Gorda don José de Escandón*, 97–101; Driver and Driver, "Ethnography and Acculturation," 43; Soustelle, *La familia Otomí-Pame*, 562.

Escandón arrived in Querétaro in 1721 as a low-ranking army officer and gradually established himself as an important figure in the region. His name appears in the public records as both a purchaser and a seller of slaves in the city. He also became the owner of an important textile factory in Querétaro. Escandón undertook military campaigns against the Jonace and other Indians of the Sierra Gorda as early as 1735. His success in these campaigns helped him move up the military ranks, and he became a colonel in 1740. In 1741 he was placed in charge of the Sierra Gorda. Escandón sought to gather into missions the Indians who were willing to be congregated and to attack and to defeat those who were unwilling.

Concerning the first task, he was greatly dissatisfied with the performance of the Augustinian missionaries in the area, such as Father Lucas Cabeza de Vaca at Jalpan, who had not systematically congregated the Indians around the mission. Escandón wanted the Indians to become workers on the haciendas he intended to establish in the area, and he wanted them to learn the fundamentals of ranch and agricultural labor by being forced to work at missions. He looked to the colegios apostólicos, specifically the new Colegio de San Fernando, which had already established a presence at nearby Vizarrón, for assistance in this endeavor, for he knew that these missionaries would try to congregate the Indians at or near the mission complex. In the eighteenth century this had come to be known as the "Texas method," because in the fertile areas of Texas, missionaries from Santa Cruz in Querétaro had been able to congregate the indigenous peoples close to the mission. On the other hand, their colleagues farther south in the deserts of Chihuahua and Sonora were unable to grow sufficient food and had been forced to allow the indigenous peoples there to continue their more nomadic life patterns. Missionary Pedro Pérez de Mezquía, who had worked in Texas two decades earlier, helpfully composed a set of mission regulations that introduced the Texas method into the Sierra Gorda.[34] For the second task, defeating natives who refused to be congregated, Escandón organized expeditions against the Jonace and eventually inflicted a decisive defeat on them at Media Luna in 1748.[35]

Escandón took the mission at Jalpan away from the Augustinians and assigned it to the Colegio de San Fernando. He also told them to establish missions at three other sites he had identified as already populated by Pame settlements. These sites were Landa, Tancoyol, and Concá. Finally, he detached the mission station at Tilaco from the jurisdiction of the mission at Xilitla and placed it under Jalpan,

---

34. Palóu, *Palóu's Life of Fray Junípero Serra*, 265, 488, note 54; Omaechevarría, *Pedro Pérez de Mezquía*, chaps. 3–4 (n.p.); Harrison, "Franciscan Concepts of the Congregated Mission."

35. Osante, *Testimonio acerca de la causa formada en la colonia del Nuevo Santander*, ix; Osante, "Del Cantábrico al Seno Mexicano," 343; Armas Briz and Solís Hernández, *Esclavos negros y mulatos en Querétaro*, 63–64; Mendoza Muñoz, *El conde de Sierra Gorda don José de Escandón*, 234–42; Rea, *Pacificación de los chichimecas de la Sierra Gorda*; Gallardo Arias, *Los pames coloniales*, 81.

thereby assigning it to the Fernandinos as well. In his biography of Serra, Palóu implied that these missions were all new, but the mission at Jalpan and the mission station at Tilaco were already in existence. Escandón forced the Pame living in these areas to congregate near the missions by occasionally sending soldiers out to burn as many indigenous dwellings as they could find in the mountains.[36]

The first few years of the Colegio de San Fernando's experience with the Sierra Gorda missions were quite trying. Originally the colegio did not have enough men to staff the five missions, so priests from the Colegio de Santa Cruz in Querétaro had to fill in. In addition, two severe epidemics ravaged the region in the late 1740s, and four of the Fernandino priests perished in them in 1746–47. The future of the Fernandino mission enterprise in the region did not appear to be very solid.[37]

Yet that fragility was not a concern for Escandón or for the government ministry in Mexico City. He repeatedly stated that he did not foresee an extensive formal mission period for the churches that he was setting up. In 1747 he reported that in a short time the missions could easily be converted into *curatos* or regular parishes. Escandón's plan was that, once the Indians had learned the basics of agriculture and ranching, they would move out of the missions and work as laborers for the settlers. At that point the settler-colonists would become the primary agents of the assimilation of the Indians to the Spanish empire. Since colonists would be attracted by offers of land, the scheme could be carried out at little cost to the treasury.[38]

In the 1740s the Fernandinos were not entirely happy with Escandón's government in the region, but the Colegio de San Fernando did not have the resources to oppose his ideas. In 1742, for example, they denounced the use of some captured Jonace people as involuntary laborers on the haciendas of two regional officials. However, practical considerations forced them to temper their criticisms of his plans for temporary missions: the colegio did not have abundant manpower to send to the area. The four missionary deaths the colegio suffered in the late 1740s put further severe strains on its ability to staff all of the missions, so the colegio had to acquiesce with regard to Escandón's plans. For example, in 1748 Guardian José Ortés de Velasco, who founded the first Fernandino mission in 1740, San José de Vizarrón, agreed that the Sierra Gorda missions would soon be able to be turned into parishes and delivered to the bishop.[39]

This docility stemmed from problems the colegio was experiencing at home. In common with all the colegios apostólicos, San Fernando had three distinct aims, which at times did not sit very well with each other. The most familiar one was to spread the Gospel among the unconverted, specifically the Indians. A second aim

---

36. Gómez Canedo, *Sierra Gorda*, 61, 79, 81–85, 185–92; Palóu, *Palóu's Life of Fray Junípero Serra*, 25, 35; Rex Galindo, "Propaganda Fide," 228.
37. Gómez Canedo, *Sierra Gorda*, 115.
38. Gómez Canedo, *Sierra Gorda*, 81; Velázquez, *El marqués de Altamira*, 59.
39. Gómez Canedo, *Sierra Gorda*, 58, 121, 216.

was to stimulate a renewal of the faith of those who were Catholics by preaching "missions" to them. In fact, San Fernando had been founded as a result of such a "mission" that a group of Queretaran friars preached in Mexico City in 1730–31. The final aim was to engage in pastoral work in the city where the colegio was located.[40]

The first religious who joined the newly established colegio proved to be generally unwilling to engage in missionary activity among the unconverted. At the same time, the priest who went to Spain to obtain the necessary royal and ecclesiastical approvals for the founding of the colegio was unable to recruit any Franciscans there to join the fledgling institution. As a result, the colegio had very few men willing to become missionaries in its first years. Ortés de Velasco wrote in disgust that many friars were too enchanted by life in Mexico City and refused to consider leaving it for extended periods. This situation persisted for decades. When Serra became president of the Alta California missions, he constantly begged the guardian to make sure that these kinds of people were not sent to the missions he was establishing.[41]

The colegio received approval to undertake another recruitment attempt on the Iberian Peninsula in 1739, and this resulted in the arrival of twelve men from Spain in 1742. But no others arrived until the end of the decade. As a result, the colegio found itself forced to agree with Escandón that turning the missions into parishes was the best prospect. This situation dramatically changed when Fray Pedro Pérez de Mezquía's 1749 recruiting trip to Spain proved very successful and was able to attract over thirty new members to the Colegio de San Fernando. Among them were Serra, Palóu, Crespí, and Verger. Reflecting the urgency of the Sierra Gorda situation, Serra and Palóu were both sent to the mountains less than six months after they arrived in Mexico City, even though colegio practice called for new arrivals to spend a year in residence in the capital before being dispatched to the missions.[42]

In 1751, a year after Serra's arrival in Jalpan, Escandón proposed the establishment of a civil settlement, the Villa de Herrera, in the Tancama Valley, slightly south of Jalpan. Soon settlers were complaining to him that they were unable to take full possession of the lands they had been promised because the Indians (supported by the missionaries) were there and would not leave. The settlers were a mixed group of lower-ranking mestizo soldiers and a few officers. But Serra, for whom the only good settler was a distant settler, was upset that they were too close to the mission. So the colegio protested to the authorities in Mexico

---

40. Espinosa, *Crónica de los colegios de propaganda fide de la Nueva España*, xv, 818: Gómez Canedo, "Franciscans in the Americas," 5–45.
41. Gómez Canedo, *Sierra Gorda*, 115; Sáiz Díez, *Los colegios de Propaganda Fide*, 144; see Serra's letter to Juan Andrés, June 12, 1770, later in this volume.
42. On the colegio's efforts to recruit men in Europe, see Beebe and Senkewicz, "Uncertainty on the Mission Frontier," 307.

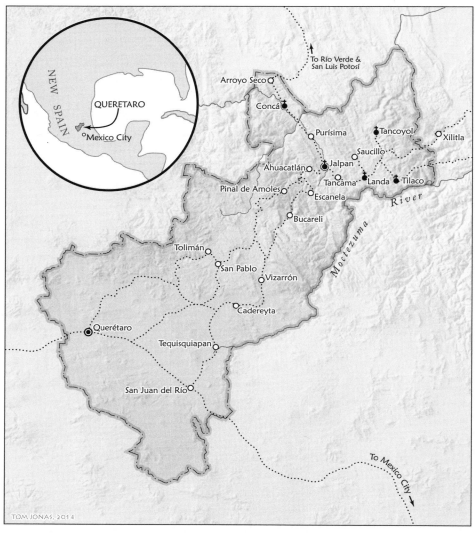

MAP 3. The Sierra Gorda region. Serra was stationed at Jalpan from 1750 to 1758. *Map by Tom Jonas.*

City. A compromise was eventually implemented by military officer Vicente de Posadas in 1754. The settlers were given land around Saucillo, slightly farther away from Jalpan, while the mission itself was allotted its own land in the Tancama Valley. A 1762 Franciscan document still reported with irritation that the Villa de Herrera was "practically right in the middle of the five missions." In the mid-1760s there were approximately eleven hundred families at the five missions.[43]

Unfortunately, we do not know Serra's reaction to this situation because very few Franciscan letters from the Sierra Gorda have survived. Indeed, one of the most frustrating things one encounters when studying the life of Junípero Serra is that, besides the 1749 letter from Veracruz, only one other substantial letter composed by him during his first seventeen years in the New World appears to have survived. That letter relates to his request for the Inquisition to enter the Sierra Gorda at a time during which the missionaries were struggling with José de Escandón. Because of his previous experience with the Inquisition in Mallorca, this was a natural move for him to make after he heard rumors that two women of the area were engaged in some sort of demon worship. He reported that a group of gente de razón "fly through the air at night and are in the habit of meeting in a cave in a hill near a rancho named El Saucillo." This was an area controlled by settlers. Once there, he continued, "they worship and offer sacrifices to the demons who appear in the form of *chivatos* and other things of that sort."[44] Since the Inquisition in New Spain did not technically have jurisdiction over Indians, Serra was at pains to assure the authorities in Mexico City that the leaders of the troubles were not themselves indigenous people.

As we have seen, Serra was convinced that his God and the heavenly court were very interested in his missionary enterprise, to the extent that saints might have helped him on his journey from Veracruz to Mexico. Later on, after he left the Sierra Gorda and was traveling through Mexico, he was convinced that the Holy Family, Jesus, Mary, and Joseph, had appeared to him. The other side of the coin, the belief that the devil was actively trying to thwart his efforts to form a godly society, was as natural for him as it had been for Puritan leader William Bradford in New England a century earlier. So there is no reason to doubt the sincerity of Serra's convictions that the coercive arm of the Church needed to be enlisted in the fight against the demon. Serra assumed that his background

---

43. Gómez Canedo, *Sierra Gorda*, 96–98; Geiger, *Life and Times of Fray Junípero Serra*, 1:127–32; Fray Joseph García, Fray Francisco Palóu, Fray Pedro Pérez de Mezquía, and Fray Junípero Serra, "Estado de las misiones de la Sierra Gorda en 1761," San Fernando de México, 11 January 1762, in Gómez Canedo, *Sierra Gorda*, 240; Gómez Canedo, "Fray Junípero Serra y su noviciado misional en América (1750–1758)," 913; Soustelle, *La familia Otomí-Pame*, 564.
44. In the popular tradition, a chivato was a ghost that represents the demon; it manifests itself as a goat that spits fire through its eyes.

with the Inquisition on Mallorca would make him the logical person to appoint to the position he was requesting, and his assumption proved correct. It is likely that he was also trying to equip himself with additional jurisdictional powers for potential use against the settlers he was finding so troubling.

❋ Report to the Inquisition of the City of Mexico, September 1, 1752

Muy Ilustres Señores Inquisidores Apostólicos,

Fray Junípero Serra, Religious Minor of the Colegio Santo y Apostólico de Propaganda Fide de San Fernando of this Court of Mexico, president of the missions to the infidels, of which the colegio apostólico in the Sierra Madre, commonly known as the Sierra Gorda, is in charge, and missionary minister of the mission of the Holy Apostle Santiago of Xalpan, which is the headquarters of all the missions:

With the veneration I owe to such a high and revered tribunal, I appear before it and inform Vuestra Señoría Muy Ilustre that I have some grave evidence indicating that there are several people in my mission's district and its surroundings, who are *gente de razón*,[45] that is, they are not Indians, who indulge in the most detestable and horrible crimes of sorcery, witchcraft, devil worship, and they have pacts with the devil and others. Inquiry into this matter rests solely with this venerable Holy Tribunal of the Inquisition. If it is necessary to identify one of the people suspected of such crimes, I would specifically name a certain Melchora de los Reyes Acosta, a married *mulata* and a resident of this mission. We, the ministers of this mission, have accusations against her regarding this matter and they appear to be credible. Over the course of the last few days, a Mexican woman named Cayetana, a *ladina*[46] from that mission who is married to a *mulato* named Pérez and lives at the mission, confessed that there is a large group of gente de razón at the mission, that is to say, non-Indians, engaged in these activities (although some Indians also are involved). These gente de razón fly through the air at night and are in the habit of meeting in a cave in a hill near a rancho named El Saucillo. This rancho, which is at the core of these missions, is where they worship and offer sacrifices to the demons who appear in the form of *chivatos* and other things of that sort. Suspected and then accused of committing similar crimes, we have had Cayetana under arrest for a number of days.

Because of these signs and some other evidence that this class of people, who have already been described, that is, non-Indians, have engaged in

---

45. Gente de razón means, literally, "people with the capacity to reason": i.e., any non-Indian.
46. "Ladino" meaning "latinized," referred to indigenous people who were in some fashion, most often linguistically and/or culturally, assimilated to Spanish ways.

such horrible crimes, it is all the more urgent to attack such evil or else this horrible plague will spread among those poor neophytes who are in our charge.

And, finally, because it is my duty, I inform, denounce, and alert this Tribunal of the Faith of everything mentioned above so that it can determine and implement the appropriate measures to take. I certify that the only purpose and motive for my notification and denunciation is the desire to avoid offenses against the Divine Majesty, the fulfillment of my duty, and the greater glory of God.

Colegio Apostólico de San Fernando de Mexico—where I am currently staying before returning to my Mission of Xalpan. September 1, 1752.
Very Holy Tribunal of the Inquisition

In the absence of more extensive letters of Serra from the Sierra Gorda, a reconstruction of his experiences there is very difficult. The only account we have of those years is contained in Palóu's biography. This volume is a very valuable firsthand source for much about Serra and early California. Yet it has often been used uncritically, without an awareness that, like all works of history and biography, it was profoundly influenced by the time in which it was written and by the intentions of its author. Palóu composed the biography in the mid-1780s, when he and the Fernandinos were engaged in what they considered to be a decisive struggle with colonial officials over the proper role of the missions in Spanish colonization. Palóu's account of his and Serra's experiences in the Sierra Gorda was written with that struggle in mind.

Some elements of Palóu's narrative can be verified from other sources. For instance, we know that Serra served as president of the five Sierra Gorda missions for three years, 1751–54. Also, the Sierra Gorda stone churches, with their impressive Baroque façades, were constructed during the 1750s and after. The design and construction were magnificent, and in 2003 they were designated a World Heritage Site by UNESCO.

Other aspects of Palóu's treatment are more questionable. He says, for instance, that Serra quickly learned the Pame language, although Serra himself stated in letters from Alta California that he always had great difficulty in learning indigenous languages. Palóu also stated that Serra wrote a catechism in Pame. It is quite conceivable that Serra composed a short treatise in which he translated some basic prayers into a simple and phonetic version of the Pame language, but anything more elaborate seems unlikely, for the Pame language was not widely studied in Mexico in the middle of the eighteenth century. There seems to have been no instruction in the Pame language at the Colegio de San Fernando, and the earliest extant Pame grammar, which was composed by missionary Juan Guadalupe Soriano, dates from the 1760s, well after Serra had left the Sierra Gorda.[47]

Official Spanish practice regarding what language, indigenous or Castilian, should be employed in the evangelization effort was often confused. The colonial aim of Hispanicizing the native peoples meant that the use of Spanish was officially mandated. Church or state officials intermittently issued various decrees reiterating the official position and requiring that the Indians systematically be taught Spanish. For example, the archbishop of Mexico City issued such a mandate in 1717. But missionaries were more interested in trying to impart what they considered the basis of their faith to the native peoples as quickly as possible. That desire led them to try to acquire the rudiments of the indigenous languages. This strategy was endorsed in the widely employed missionary handbook written by Alonso de la Peña Montenegro, a seventeenth-century archbishop of Quito. Serra and the Fernandinos were familiar with this volume and brought a copy of it to Alta California.[48]

Palóu also stated that Serra baptized a large number of "gentiles" in the Sierra Gorda, although the few surviving pages of baptismal registers from the region during this period indicate that most baptisms were of children who were born at the missions.

In general, Palóu presents an account in which the missionization of the Sierra Gorda was an unbridled success. For example, he says that Serra introduced a number of devotions, especially that of the Immaculate Conception. In addition, the mission population's intense celebration of Holy Week became known far and wide. As Palóu summarized, "There remained not a single pagan in that entire district, for all its inhabitants were baptized by my Venerable Padre and his associates, and civilized, living in towns by the sound of the bell." The missions were also prosperous. The Indians quickly became adept at agriculture and other skills and were even able to engage in commerce by selling some of their wares in neighboring towns. The missions did so well that the Fernandinos were able to deliver them for secularization to the grateful bishop of Mexico City in 1770.

In Palóu's account there was no mention of the population decline the Pame experienced as a result of the mission process.[49] Nor was there any acknowledgment that significant numbers of Pame people resisted the Texas method and fled

---

47. Serra, *Writings*, 1:266–67; Castro, "Lenguas indígenas americanas transmitidas por los franciscanos del siglo 18," 598–99; Aguirre, "La demanda de clérigos 'lenguas' del arzobispado de México, 1700–1749"; Gómez Canedo, *Sierra Gorda*, 128.

48. Gonzalbo, *Historia de la educación en la época colonial*, 191; Peña Montenegro, *Itinerario para párrocos de indios*, 20–27, 30–32, 115–19.

49. Palóu, *Palóu's Life of Fray Junípero Serra*, 24–37; Cruz, *Chichimecas, misioneros, soldados y terratenientes*, 300; Jackson, "The Chichimeca Frontier," 71–77.

the five Fernandino establishments. This flight was sometimes not to the hills but, rather, to missions administered by other religious groups in the surrounding area where the Indians felt they would have more freedom. Indeed, tensions among the various religious groups working in the Sierra Gorda were quite intense, and local native peoples attempted to take advantage of them. The priests at these other missions often refused to send the Indians back, a decision that was supported by the settlers of the area. Fernandinos began to complain about this practice in the early 1740s. More than two decades later, Serra's former student Juan Crespí was still complaining about it when he was working in the Sierra Gorda.[50] Finally, Palóu's volume accorded only a slight mention to soldiers and settlers in the Sierra Gorda and to the tension between them and the missionaries. But as we have seen, such tensions were present from practically the moment Serra and Palóu arrived in the Sierra Gorda. Palóu's account of his and Serra's activities in the Sierra Gorda must be read with an explicit awareness of the major aim of the biography, which was to argue that missions, not presidios or soldiers, and not pueblos and settlers, were the surest way to assimilate the native populations into Spanish society.

When the Colegio de San Fernando was finally able to devote greater manpower to the Sierra Gorda missions, it attempted to resist Escandón's goal of turning the missions into parishes, a goal it had only reluctantly supported in the 1740s. In 1761, for example, some settlers in Escanela, just south of Jalpan, tried to stimulate secularization proceedings. The then-president of the missions, Juan Ramos de Lora, resisted vigorously. The very next year Serra and Palóu joined two other friars in stating that "considerable time, patience, and effort" would be necessary before the missions could be handed over to a bishop. During the 1760s settlers and groups of Pame continued to agitate for secularization. The prospects for secularization received a boost from the appointment of Francisco Antonio Lorenzana as archbishop in 1766. In 1770, saying that it needed to devote all its available manpower to support the missions in the Californias, the colegio accepted the inevitable and agreed to leave the Sierra Gorda.[51]

By this time Escandón had long since left the Sierra Gorda. He was rewarded with the title Conde de Sierra Gorda in 1749 in gratitude for undertaking the

---

50. On the tensions among various religious groups, see the letter of the Augustinian missionary at Jalpan, Lucas Cabeza de Vaca, to Escandón on January 23, 1743, in Ruiz Zavala, *Historia de la provincia agustiniana*, 1:530–32; José Ortes de Velasco to Pedro González de San Miguel, July 12, 1742, Fondo Franciscano, Instituto Nacional de Antropología e Historia. We thank Fr. Francisco Morales, OFM, for sending us a digital copy of this letter. Juan Crespí to Guardián, March 28, 1764, Junípero Serra Collection #75 Santa Bárbara Mission Archive-Library; Cruz, *Chichimecas, misioneros, soldados y terratenientes*, 300; Gómez Canedo, *Sierra Gorda*, 72, 109–11; Solís de la Torre, *Bárbaros y ermitaños*, 132–33; Samperio Gutiérrez, "Las misiones fernandinas de la Sierra Gorda," 100.

51. García et al., "Estado de las misiones," in Gómez Canedo, *Sierra Gorda*, 243. See also Gómez Canedo, *Sierra Gorda*, 120–23.

colonizing task there and for his success in keeping costs down. He was also given the opportunity to colonize Nuevo Santander, the area south of Texas on the Gulf coast of New Spain. There he was able to more fully develop the strategy he had initiated in the Sierra Gorda. Based on his difficulties with the Fernandinos in the Sierra Gorda, he decided to jettison the mission-presidio system in favor of a large number of settlers in pueblos and ranchos. In order for there to be workers on the haciendas he was establishing there, Escandón forcibly uprooted some of the northern Pame and took them with him. Those who survived the brutal trek were forced to work on lands in the new colony. The missions were mostly reduced to simple churches, and the missionaries became little more than chaplains to the settlers, much to the horror of the friars from the Colegio Apostólico de Guadalupe in Zacatecas who staffed the missions. In this strategy Escandón was reflecting Bourbon policy in New Spain, since by this time many missions and Indian parishes in central Mexico had already been secularized.[52]

One result of this method was that settlements were frequently raided by the local Indians whose lands were being taken, and the Indians were attacked in turn by the settlers (who doubled as militia) and soldiers. The authorities declared a sixteenth-century style "war of fire and blood" against the Indians. Captured Indians were often sent to the haciendas of the military leaders or to the textile works in Querétaro, where they labored as virtual slaves. The Indians who resisted had two choices: exile or extermination. By the end of the eighteenth century no more than 1,700 of the approximately 25,000 Indians who had lived in the area at the beginning of the colonization activity were still there.[53] According to one scholar, the legal privileges granted to Escandón in this endeavor were very reminiscent of those granted to sixteenth-century Spanish colonizers. The soldiers who served in his army were also granted various privileges. For example, they were free of the jurisdiction of local authorities, and they often had first claims on the lands that were being emptied of Indians.[54]

The Fernandinos followed all these developments closely, for they believed that diminishing the power of the missions would return New Spain to a very undesirable past. Escandón's policies seemed to them to repeat the exploitation of the native peoples that they believed had marked the first decades of Spanish colonization in the New World. In the narrative of Spanish expansion that was shared by most religious orders, which stemmed from the sixteenth-century sermons

---

52. Chemín Bässler, *Los pames septentrionales de San Luis Potosí*, 68–69; Gallardo Arias, *Los pames coloniales*, 107; Taylor, *Magistrates of the Sacred*, 83–86; Weber, *Bárbaros*, 107–109; Tutino, *Making a New World*, 216–19.
53. Galaviz de Capdevielle, "Descripción y pacificación de la Sierra Gorda," 137; Velázquez, *El marqués de Altamira*, 57; Weber, *The Spanish Frontier in North America*, 194; Francis Guest, "Mission Colonization and Political Control in Spanish California," in Guest, *Hispanic California Revisited*, 87–114.
54. Osante, *Testimonio acerca de la causa formada en la colonia del Nuevo Santander*, x, xxix; Osante, *Orígenes del Nuevo Santander*, 147, 234; Osante and Alcaraz Cienfuegos, *Nuevo Santander*, 82; García Ugarte, *Breve historia de Querétaro*, 102.

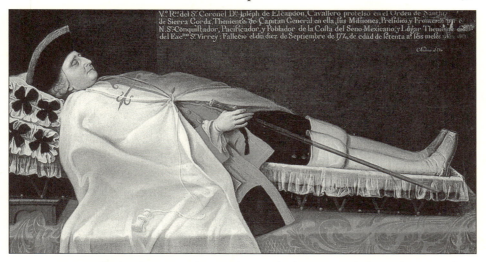

FIGURE 7. *Retrato fúnebre de Don José de Escandón, Conde de Sierra Gorda* (*Funeral Portrait of Don José de Escandón, Conde de Sierra Gorda*), by Andrés de Islas. This work dates from 1770, the year of Escandón's death. *Museo Regional de Querétaro, Querétaro. Instituto Nacional de Antropología e Historia, Mexico City.*

and writings of Antonio de Montesinos and Bartolomé de las Casas, indigenous peoples needed to be grouped into missions to protect them from such oppression. The Fernandinos feared that such a brutal past had sprung to life again.

This was the context of Palóu's biography of Serra. It was written to contest Escandón's vision, which the Fernandinos believed was taking root in Alta California. Palóu created a picture of the Sierra Gorda that would illustrate the superiority of the missionary method over the settler method of converting and assimilating indigenous peoples. The Sierra Gorda chapters of his biography of Serra were meant to argue that missions were indispensable elements of the Spanish colonial project.[55]

Leaving the Sierra Gorda

Serra's departure from Jalpan and the Sierra Gorda was a result of events in faraway Texas. In the 1750s, the Colegios of Santa Cruz in Querétaro and San Fernando in Mexico City agreed to cooperate in the founding of new missions in the Apache territory of Texas. In 1757 the first such mission was established on the banks of the San Sabá River, about 150 miles northwest of San Antonio. A presidio was also established a few miles away. Ironically, few Apaches entered the

---

55. Beebe and Senkewicz, "Constructing California," 21–35.

mission, for they considered it too isolated and too close to Comanche territory. The mission, staffed by one friar from Querétaro and two from San Fernando, was attacked by a large force of Comanches and their allies in March 1758. Two priests, one from each colegio, were killed and the mission was destroyed.[56]

When word of this disaster reached Mexico City, both colegios were ordered to designate replacement missionaries as quickly as possible. Since the order came from the viceroy's office, the authorities at San Fernando decided to name two experienced and veteran missionaries, Serra and Palóu. They were ordered to come to Mexico City immediately to prepare for their departure for Texas. According to Palóu, Serra brought back with him as a trophy "the chief idol which those unhappy Indians had formerly adored as their god." Bringing this object back was a triumphant declaration that traditional practices had been eradicated. However, as we have seen, many Pame continued to flee the missions and engage in their traditional religious practices in the hills.[57]

Serra arrived at San Fernando on September 26, 1758. Three days later he penned this letter to his nephew, Miguel, the son of his sister Juana. Miguel had recently taken his vows as a Capuchin friar, and his uncle took the occasion to congratulate him and urge him to strive for ever-greater adherence to the rules and spirit of the Order. Serra also related what he knew about the destruction of the Texas mission. His information came from Father Miguel Molina, the only priest to survive the Comanche attack, who was now at San Fernando. Serra had known him since 1749, when they both sailed for America on the *Villasota*.[58] Serra reported the death of the two missionaries in a manner consistent with many Christian accounts of martyrdom. They hagiographic tradition was replete with accounts of flowers or crops miraculously sprouting at sites where blood had been shed for the sake of religion. Serra's description of the maize springing up over Father Santiestevan's grave was very much in that vein. He went on to assert, as he did on many occasions during his life, that he was unworthy for "such a great enterprise" as the evangelization of the unbaptized. While part of that was undoubtedly the kind of ritual protestation that was expected of members of religious orders, who self-consciously strove to present themselves as humbly as possible, part of it surely reflected the critical self-knowledge that was so much a part of his personality. The letter clearly indicates that Serra's primary identity was that of an active missionary, ministering among unbaptized and potentially hostile native peoples. This is where he thought his vocation and his God were calling him.

---

56. Hämäläinen, *Comanche Empire*, 59.
57. Geiger, *Life and Times of Fray Junípero Serra*, 1:135–42; Palóu, *Palóu's Life of Fray Junípero Serra*, 34. Geiger suspects that Serra may have brought the idol to Mexico City in 1752, not 1758. See Palóu, *Palóu's Life of Fray Junípero Serra*, 351. On the persistence of traditional ways, see Gallardo Arias, *Los pames coloniales*, 89.
58. Geiger, *Life and Times of Fray Junípero Serra*, 1:63.

❊ Letter to Fray Miguel de Petra, September 29, 1758

Nephew and Brother Fray Miguel de Petra
Dearest one in Jesus, Fray Miguel,

With much consolation in my soul, I received your letter dated February 25 of last year, 1757, in which you give me the worthy and for me very pleasing news that on January 13 of the same year you professed the Rule of Nuestro Padre Seráfico San Francisco at the convent of the Reverendos Padres Capuchinos. I received your letter on September 19 of last year, but am responding over a year later due to the distance and my travels.

I have been away from this Colegio de San Fernando de México for eight years and some months. I just arrived here three days ago and am about to set out on a journey of more than 400 leagues to the lands of the gentiles where we intend to plant our Holy Catholic Faith. I am called to engage in this type of work because of Holy Obedience, which has brought me back here from the missions of the Sierra Gorda where I lived for eight years and some months.

The place where I am going is the province of San Sabá (a name recently given to that land) and the people are called Apaches. However, there are many other tribes bordering the area, all of them gentiles. Three religious from our apostolic institution, Padre Fray Alonso Giraldo Terreros, Padre Fray José de Santistevan, and Padre Fray Miguel Molina, went there last year and personally attended to the mission. The first Padre is from the Colegio de la Santísima Cruz de Querétaro, founded by the Venerable Padre Llinás. The other two are from our Colegio de San Fernando; both of them are my companions. They came from Spain on the same mission as I did.

At dawn on March 16 of this year, when the three of them were together, a large throng of Comanche infidels and Indians from other nations attacked them. When the Indians arrived at the little convent, or rather the humble hut where the religious lived, they pretended they had come as friends, in peace, and said they wanted the Padres to make them Christians. This deceptive behavior allowed the Indians to see for themselves that the Padres were defenseless. As soon as they were certain this was the case, the first person they attacked was Reverendo Padre Presidente Terreros. They shot him with a rifle, then cut off his head and skinned him.

And, in short, they shot Reverendo Padre Molina. With all the confusion no one knows for sure how he survived. He is still alive and just recently was brought to this Colegio where they are treating his injury. He, along with three of the few secular Christians who escaped, is the most reliable witness of the crime.

A number of things or circumstances happened at just the right time, which undoubtedly seemed miraculous, but I cannot relate all of them. However, I will mention that after the barbarians had left the area, the Christians from the nearby presidio went in search of the bodies so they could be buried. Six days later they found the body of Padre Fray José. A very sweet-smelling odor emanated from his body and fresh blood was oozing from his wounds. His head, which was slightly separated from his body, was in the same condition. His body was bound with three cilices with iron barbs. They buried him at that very spot, covering him with dirt. Shortly after, a very lush cluster of maize, which is what you refer to there, and rightly so, as the "wheat of the Indies," sprang up from that very spot. A miracle, so it seems, which as I see it can be interpreted by us as the grain of wheat that lies dead under that ground, promises to bear us much fruit in the harvesting of the souls of those unfortunate people.[59] May it be so. Amen.

So then, in place of my very happy and dear friend, obedience is now sending this wretched sinner, your uncle, along with Padre Lector Fray Francisco Palóu. I am aware of my uselessness and lack of fervor for such a great enterprise. But God is powerful and can make something from nothing at all—actions that are given up for His greater glory.

Commend your uncle, in earnest, to God. For he has always done the same for you since he left you. Tell your parents and my dearest siblings, Miguel and Juana, about my way of life and my good health, thanks be to God, and that I ask them to commend me to God, as I do for them, as well as my friends and enemies. However, you all have the misfortune that my prayers are inadequate, half-hearted, and poor.

I congratulate you a thousand times over on receiving the holy habit and on your solemn profession of such a holy order. Always give thanks to God for such a benefice, for it is greater than we can imagine.

Also, be very grateful to those who have received you into such a well-chosen group and to those who have helped you achieve the standing you have today—especially my dear friend Reverendo Padre Fray Francisco Serra. You are truly in his debt. And, if you should remember me with some affection and respect, you will demonstrate this to me because I am your uncle who has always wanted the best for you. It is my desire (and undoubtedly God's as well, for the beautiful virtue which is gratitude pleases Him so much) that

---

59. A reference to John 12:24.

you show your gratitude to Padre Serra, because you owe much more to him than to me. By thanking him you are thanking me.

The same applies to those who were your teachers and the other religious from Petra. And may there never be a part of you that belittles others as being lesser sons of Nuestro Padre Seráfico San Francisco. For surely that is not to the liking of our Holy Padre nor to God.

Try with all your might and with the grace of God to become a true and perfect Friar Minor. And when it seems to you that you have achieved that goal (if you are fortunate enough to get there) then say with all the sincerity in your heart: *servi inútiles sumus*.[60]

Reflect, also, on the fact that stars fell from the heavens and no less than one-third of them.[61] And so, even though I consider that exemplary convent to be heaven on earth because of the deep religiosity of its inhabitants, do not think that you are secure for that reason. Rather, work on your spiritual health with humility, fear, and trembling.

This Colegio Apostólico de Propaganda Fide de San Fernando where I am living, because of God's great mercy, is the example and source of instruction for these lands. And in the midst of so much good, I am still a fool. Don't you be that way. For the love of God, pray for me.

I beg you to give my humble regards to the Muy Reverendo Padre Guardián, Reverendo Padre Maestro de Novicios, and the other Reverendos Padres of that holy convent. Thank them in my name for all the good things they have done for you and continue to do by receiving you and keeping you in their holy company. And give my best regards to Padres Fray Félix and Fray Bautista de Petra, whom you mention in your letter.

If your superiors give you permission to do so, you could write to Petra or send them this letter, giving my regards to all the Reverendos Padres of Petra, from the Reverendo Padre Guardián to the youngest lay brother; and to the Reverendos Señores Padres of the parish, from top to bottom; especially to dear Dr. Fiol, his brother Antonio, his father and mother, and everyone in the household; also to the entire household of Señor Juan Nicolás, Señor Guillermo Roca, Señor Rafael Moragues (commonly known as Casta), and that of his brother the doctor. And so as not to go on any longer, I beg everyone to commend me to God.

---

60. Luke 17:10: "We are unworthy servants."
61. A popular reference to the defeat of Satan and the fallen angels.

The same applies, especially to your little sisters Juana and Margarita, and above all to your parents. I always pray that God will keep them for many years in His holy love and grace so that we will be together in eternal glory.

Reverendo Padre Fray Guillermo Vicens from Petra died a few days ago in this Santo Colegio after receiving all the Holy Sacraments and with much forbearance, etc. Commend him to God.

The Padre Vicario of this Santo Colegio who is Padre Lector Fray Rafael Verger, Padre Lector Palóu, and Padre Juan Crespí are all in good health, thanks be to God.

Colegio Apostólico de Propaganda Fide de San Fernando de Mexico, September 20, 1758

Humbly asking for your charity,
Your most affectionate brother and servant,
Fray Junípero Serra

Domestic Missions

Serra never went to Texas. The Comanches followed up their attack on the mission with an attack on the presidio during which they killed twenty soldiers. A military expedition was sent to punish the Indians the next year, but after it advanced to the Red River, the Comanches soundly defeated it. Mission San Sabá was not reestablished.[62]

Serra and Palóu spent the next nine years as residents of San Fernando and as itinerant preachers in various regions of Mexico. They were also both elected to a series of offices at the colegio. Palóu served in various administrative positions for six of those nine years. Serra served on the Guardian's council of advisers—the discretorium. He was also master of novices for three years. That position probably did not absorb his energies all that much, since he had only four novices over the time he held the office. By contrast, Serra's own master of novices on Mallorca had supervision of seventeen novices all at once. Serra also spent a considerable amount of time preaching in Mexico City and in other parts of New Spain. He was generally part of a group of friars traveling through specific localities at the invitation of the local bishop and giving domestic missions. These events spanned a number of days and included processions, instruction in doctrine, confessions, and preaching. Although these enterprises were called "missions," their aim was not to convert people. Virtually everyone who came to them was already baptized and, at least formally, members of the Church at

---

62. Hämäläinen, *Comanche Empire*, 60–61.

MAP 4. The known locations where Serra preached domestic missions between 1758 and 1768. *Map by Tom Jonas.*

which the event was held. Rather, the intent was to revivify the devotion and commitment of the local church community.[63]

These domestic missions were often elaborate public spectacles. The missionaries would enter the town in a line, often barefoot and carrying a large cross. They might be accompanied by local religious and civic leaders who would join them in praying the rosary and singing popular religious songs on their way to the principal church of the town. A crowd would gather, and everyone would then march through the town in penitential silence. Back at the church, the missionaries would announce that the mission itself would begin on the following day.

The mission itself might last from a few days to a few weeks. Daily processions, elaborate and emotional sermons elaborating in great detail the sufferings of the damned in hell, and fervent pleas for the faithful to make full and honest confessions dominated the life of the town. The mission would often conclude

---

63. Geiger, *Life and Times of Fray Junípero Serra*, 1:150–75; Palóu, *Palóu's Life of Fray Junípero Serra*, 322. While Serra was stationed at San Fernando, an anonymous devotional work, a series of prayers to Mary under the title of the Immaculate Conception, was published through the colegio in Mexico City. Two nineteenth-century bibliographers later attributed it to Serra. See Weber, *A Marian Novena*.

FIGURE 8. Flagellation processions. *Illustration for a Book: Procession of Monks and Flagellants*, by Giambattista Tiepolo, 1696–1770. Such processions were common in many areas of late medieval Europe. The Elisha Whittelsey Collection, The Elisha Whittelsey Fund, 1959 (59.600.189). *Image copyright:* © The Metropolitan Museum of Art. *Image source: Art Resource*, NY.

with a large silent procession that recalled the mission's opening. However, on this occasion large numbers of those who had been affected by the preaching would join in, barefoot, carrying crosses, wearing crowns of thorns, and smearing ashes on their faces.[64]

Palóu said that Serra participated in these missions in Mexico City and its outskirts, and in the areas of Guadalajara, Puebla, Oaxaca, and Valladolid (Morelia). Serra developed a reputation as an effective preacher. At one point, the bishop of Oaxaca asked him to preach a retreat—a series of sermons over an eight-day period—to the clergy of the diocese. The sermons preached on these domestic missions could be quite emotional. As we have seen, Serra was no stranger to this style of preaching. Palóu recounts that on one occasion in Mexico City, Serra began to scourge himself with a chain in the middle of the sermon.[65]

This action placed Serra within a long tradition of self-flagellation. This practice seems to have originated in monasteries during the early Middle Ages. Participants were expressing a symbolic identification with Christ, who was scourged before he was crucified. The practice was adopted by some members of the laity, especially in Italy, in the thirteenth century. Although opposed by many church authorities,

---

64. The description in the two previous paragraphs is taken from an oral presentation given by Karen Melvin at the conference "Junípero Serra: Context and Representation, 1713–2013" at The Huntington Library, September 20–21, 2013. We are grateful to Professor Melvin for allowing us to use this information here.
65. Palóu, *Palóu's Life of Fray Junípero Serra*, 41–42, 264.

it spread throughout Europe over the next century. The appearance of a good number of flagellant groups was partially a response to the Black Death. These groups also appeared in New Spain, and there, as well as in Europe, a number of clergy would also whip themselves privately as a form of penance. Serra's model, Francisco Solano, was reported to have done so every night. Serra, along with many other men and women members of religious orders of the day, also engaged in this practice. Serra also privately engaged in other forms of physical deprivation. Palóu reported, for instance, that when he was in the mission fields, he refused to wear even the simple sandals worn by Franciscans. Rather, animated by a dialogue between Jesus and his mother Mary in María de Ágreda's *La mística ciudad de Dios*, he insisted on wearing only rough footgear made of hemp.[66]

On other occasions in Serra's preaching, he beat his breast with a large stone to emphasize the necessity of repentance for one's sins. And, to dramatize the punishments of the damned, he would at times singe his skin with a lit taper. Such theatrical extravagances were not uncommon in popular preaching in Spain or the New World. Self-flagellation and other forms of corporal punishment were normal features of the penitential processions that often formed an emotional climax to these domestic missions.[67] Serra may have been more intense than other preachers of missions, but his general approach was widely shared. San Fernando may have had more than its share of this type of preacher, for in 1780 the colegio issued a series of decrees that attempted to rein in its more extravagant pulpit performers.[68]

INQUISITION

In early spring 1766 Serra was nearing the end of a long journey preaching a series of domestic missions. The major venue for the missions was the area of Huasteca, the cultural region in eastern Mexico that had been the center of influence of the Huastec people. According to Palóu, who was a member of this missionary group, it took the party a month to reach the area. The first mission they preached in the region was a failure: many people in the town simply ignored their presence. But shortly after the priests left town an epidemic broke out, and Palóu reported that over sixty people died—all of them people who had refused to attend the mission. Palóu went on to say that as word of this spread through the region, people in the surrounding communities made sure that they attended

---

66. Cohn, *Pursuit of the Millennium*, 127–47; Córdoba y Salinas, *Vida, virtudes, y milagros*, 69; Cruz González, "Landscapes of Conversion," 184; González Marmolejo, *Misioneros del desierto*, 180; Larkin, "Liturgy, Devotion, and Religious Reform," 496–98, 507–11; for a treatment placing flagellation in the Franciscan tradition, see Delio, *Crucified Love*; Palóu, *Palóu's Life of Fray Junípero Serra*, 261.
67. Rex Galindo, "Propaganda Fide," 296–302; Noel, "Missionary Preachers in Spain."
68. Palóu, *Palóu's Life of Fray Junípero Serra*, 236, 274; O'Brien, "'Breve Método.'"

the missions! The missionary group remained in the area for about seven months and then started to head back to Mexico City through the western Huasteca. As they were giving a mission in the town of Aquismón, about fifty miles northeast of the Sierra Gorda region, Serra was approached by Antonio Ladrón de Guevara, a military officer who had been associated with the region since the 1730s. Ladrón de Guevara had been an unsuccessful rival of Escandón in the colonization of Nuevo Santander. He may have been encouraged to approach Serra because of their mutual dislike of Escandón. He may have also come to know Serra when Serra served as a missionary in the Sierra Gorda, for he addressed him as "Padre Presidente" of the missions. He proceeded to ask Serra for a favor.[69]

There was trouble in the town of Valle de Maíz, located in the Ríoverde area about seventy-five miles northwest of Aquismón. A thirty-five-year-old woman, María Dolores de Nava, usually called Pascuala, had been accused of witchcraft. Pascuala was a single mother whose husband had deserted her years earlier. She was also a healer who had learned about local herbs from her mother, who also had been a healer in the community. The proceedings in the case had been somewhat haphazard, and Ladrón de Guevara asked Serra to come and take charge of them.[70]

Ladrón de Guevara wanted Serra involved for a number of reasons. First, he was aware of the Franciscans' long history in the area. They first entered the region, the northern Pamería, in 1617 and founded Mission Nuestra Señora de la Purísima Concepción. Settlers started moving into the region at the end of the 1600s and Valle de Maíz was formally founded in 1735 on lands that the newcomers gradually wrested from mission control. By 1758 the mission was serving over 800 families, of whom 555 were Pame and another 60 were families of "assimilated" Indians. Seventeen families were counted as Spanish and another 207 were "other," most likely mestizos of one caste or another. Indeed, most of the population of the general region was of Indian ancestry, with the next largest group identified in government reports as mulatos, mestizos, and people of African heritage.[71]

By the late 1750s the Inquisition was active in the area as well. A principal object of its concern was Rufino Barragán, a resident of the town. He was originally born Gabriel Fernández in La Mancha, Spain, in 1693. He left his wife and two sons in Spain and went to New Spain around 1715. There he reinvented himself

---

69. Juan Fidel Zorrilla, "Tamaulipas," in Ramírez, *Visión histórica de la Frontera Norte de México*, 170. For the background of Ladrón de Guevara see Hadley, Naylor, and Schuetz-Miller, *The Presidio and Militia on the Northern Frontier of New Spain*, 77–81, and Ladrón de Guevara, *Noticias de los poblados*, xvii–xxiv.
70. Throughout the documents, her first name is spelled as either "Pasquala" or "Pascuala." For consistency, we use "Pascuala." On the mission journey, see Palóu, *Life and Times of Fray Junípero Serra*, 42.
71. Rangel Silva, "Linaje y fortuna," 115–19; Rangel Silva, *Capitanes a guerra*, 67; Rangel Silva, "El discurso de una frontera olvidada," 128–30; López-Velarde López, *Expansión geográfica franciscana*, 117; Gallardo Arias, *Los pames coloniales*, 75.

on the frontier as Rufino Barragán and eventually became one of the richest men in the area of Valle de Maíz. At the end of the 1750s Barragán was denounced as a heretic and a man of loose morals by a group that included army captain José Antonio Ortiz de Zárate. Inquisition investigators from Guadalcázar, some fifty miles to the west, came to Valle de Maíz and opened proceedings. Barragán was accused of a wide range of illicit sexual activities and of holding a variety of heterodox opinions. These included his assertion that sexual activity outside marriage was not a sin, since it was a natural human tendency. He also was reported to have publicly doubted that the 1531 apparition of Nuestra Señora de Guadalupe had ever really occurred. Barragán died in an accident at the end of 1761 before the Inquisition proceedings had been completed.[72]

In the early 1760s tensions appear to have increased between the Pame and others at Mission La Purísima. In 1765 the Pame were removed from that church and placed in a new mission, San José, which was opened on the south side of the town. Ortiz de Zárate, who had initiated proceedings against Rufino Barragán, also held the office of protector of Indians, and he was instrumental in this separation.[73]

Some of these social tensions seem to have been active in the case Serra was being asked to enter. The woman at the center of the case, María Pascuala de Nava, was a *casta* woman, variously identified in the proceedings as a *loba* or a *mulata*, which indicated that she was most likely a dark-skinned woman whose heritage may well have been both Indian and African. One of the accusations against her was that she cavorted with various Pame Indians outside town. And one of the people involved in pushing for action against her was Ortiz de Zárate.

An important reason the local authorities were worried by all of this was that Pascuala was already a controversial figure in the town. In 1759 she and her mother were accused of witchcraft. As the two women were being taken to prison at Guadalcázar, Pascuala escaped and remained at large in Rioverde for about three years. The Inquisition at that time declined to become involved, possibly because it was already engaged in the ongoing investigation of Rufino Barragán. Pascuala returned to Valle de Maíz in 1762, but the stigma of having been once accused of witchcraft clung to her, and many in the town still suspected her. Matters came to a head at the end of 1765. A woman named Dominga de Jesús confronted Pascuala in November. Dominga was suffering from a bronchial condition that had lingered for two years, and she had come to believe that her illness was the result of a spell Pascuala cast on her. When Pascuala's treatments proved ineffective, Dominga denounced her to the chief priest at Mission La Purísima Concepción, Francisco

---

72. Rangel Silva, "Linaje y fortuna," 125–28; Rangel Silva, *Capitanes a guerra*, 150. A few years later, Barragán's son Felipe was accused of saying that the story of the Guadalupe apparition was fabricated by the Spanish to aid the conquest of the Indians. See Rangel Silva, "Herejías y disidencias," 169.
73. Rangel Silva, *Capitanes a guerra*, 130; López-Velarde López, *Expansión geográfica franciscana*, 121.

Núñez. However, he refused to act on her entreaty. But she kept renewing her accusations to Núñez. She made the same complaints to the other priest at the mission, Antonio Salceda, and to the village lieutenant, Melchor de Media Villa y Ascona. Fearing that the situation in the town was spinning out of control, they were forced to consult Ladrón de Guevara.[74]

In some ways the case was a typical eighteenth-century Inquisition case on the northern frontier in New Spain. Witchcraft and sorcery were some of the more common issues investigated by the tribunal in that region. A similar case in the frontier region of Coahuila in 1748 preoccupied the Inquisition authorities in Mexico City for almost a decade. Traditional healers were susceptible of being the objects of such investigation, especially if it was perceived that they were violating long-standing Christian norms. While most traditional healers were not bothered by the Inquisition, those who were perceived to transgress either feminine roles or established morality were closely investigated. Pascuala was certainly one of those transgressors.[75] But the simultaneous involvement of Rufino Barragán in an Inquisition investigation was somewhat less typical. A number of different levels of the social structure of the town were thus involved before the Inquisition, and this no doubt unsettled the region even more. The combination of these factors was probably the basic reason that Ladrón de Guevara was anxious to enlist the services of a veteran *comisario* like Serra in this process.

After almost eight months of travel and preaching, Serra was tired and not at all anxious to get involved. Even though he had been a comisario of the Inquisition in both Mallorca and New Spain, it does not appear that this activity took much of his time or energy in New Spain. The extensive Inquisition records in the Archivo General de la Nación in Mexico City and at The Bancroft Library at Berkeley do not reveal any case besides this one in which he was significantly involved for any length of time. While he was in the Sierra Gorda in 1756 he spent a brief time in Rioverde conducting preliminary interrogations on a case that never resulted in formal Inquisition proceedings. It is entirely possible that he was occasionally asked, as he was traveling throughout New Spain, to apply his experience to various Inquisition-related matters, as Ladrón de Guevara asked him to do at Aquismón, but there is no indication that he ever supervised or spearheaded any case. Palóu did say that Serra "had to labor in many parts and travel many leagues" in fulfilling his duties as Inquisition comisario. However, the primary object of Palóu's book was the group to whom it was dedicated, the Franciscan Province of Mallorca, and as we have seen, the Inquisition had a

---

74. Gallardo Arias, "La transgresión al ideal femenino cristiano," treats the case fully; see especially 87–99. See also Rangel Silva, "Herejías y disidencias," 170.
75. Semboloni, "Cacería de brujas en Coahuila, 1748–1751"; Medina, *Historia del Tribunal del Santo Oficio*, 285–86; Quezada, "The Inquisition's Repression of Curanderos," 52–53.

long and continuing history on that island, so Palóu was probably embellishing Serra's experiences to curry favor with the hometown audience. The existing documentary record indicates that Serra's engagement with the Inquisition in the New World was tangential and intermittent.[76]

Ladrón de Guevara undoubtedly knew that Serra's next mission was scheduled for Villa de Valles, and he told Serra that María Pascuala de Nava could be brought there. Ladrón de Guevara may have also appealed to Serra's knowledge of Pame customs and culture, which he had acquired during his eight years at Jalpan. Serra agreed to participate by interviewing the accuser and the accused during his spare time at Villa de Valles. It appears that Serra agreed to undertake a limited task. He would determine first whether there was a case that should be formally referred to the Inquisition. If he judged that there was a case, he would then obtain statements from the accused and the accuser. These statements were to be recorded in the sworn and notarized form the Inquisition required, for, like many long-lived bureaucratic institutions, over the entire span of its existence the Inquisition in New Spain became increasingly concerned with ensuring that all of its processes and procedures were rigorously observed.[77]

Once he reached Villa de Valles, Serra was briefed by Ladrón de Guevara and probably also gained additional information from the Franciscan priests at the church of Santiago el Mayor, where he was staying. He began the process on April 14. He appointed fellow preacher Juan González Vizcaíno, who had come with him to America in 1749, as notary.

During the next week Serra interacted with two casta women, the leading military officials in the area, and some members of the local clergy. These interactions gave him a deep and firsthand look at the rhythms of life among ordinary people on the northern frontier and into the manner in which the newly arrived Catholicism had become enmeshed with traditional indigenous religious and healing practices among the local people.

Serra first interviewed the accuser, Dominga de Jesús, who related in great detail her attempts to become cured of her illness. She reported that other women in the town initially suggested to her that her sickness was actually a spell cast on her by Pascuala. When she went to Pascuala to get the spell lifted, Pascuala demanded compensation in the form of articles of clothing. Dominga provided them. Pascuala then gave Dominga various herbs and potions, but they had little effect. When the treatment moved to another house, another woman suggested that a representation of a crucifix might help Dominga and protect her from Pascuala, but her cough became worse, so she finally complained to the

---

76. Hackel, *Junípero Serra*, 125–27; Palóu, *Palóu's Life of Fray Junípero Serra*, 43.
77. Mejía González, *Relación de la causa de Juana María*, 39.

local priest. He said he could not do anything: he would need more than a single complaint against Pascuala. The death of another woman, allegedly because of Pascuala, apparently inflamed social tensions in the area, and another priest urged Dominga to forgive Pascuala "for the good of the pueblo" and to go to the local authorities. The authorities brought everyone together. Dominga reported that a search of Pascuala's house revealed a doll. As was the case in many other witchcraft accusations on the northern frontier, Pascuala was believed to have inflicted pain on her victims by manipulating the doll. Pascuala implicated another woman, Agustina Vásquez, but she had fled the pueblo and could not be found. Eventually, after an intense interrogation, Pascuala confessed in the presence of Dominga and the authorities and was jailed.

※ *April 14, 1766*

At this Convent of Santiago in the Villa de los Valles, Custodia of San Salvador of Tampico, on the 14th day of the month of April in the year 1766, I, Fray Junípero Serra of the Order of Friars Minor of Nuestro Padre Seráfico San Francisco, missionary preacher of the Colegio Apostólico de San Fernando de Mexico, Comisario of the Holy Office, have offered to set in motion the inquiries that pertain to the Holy Tribunal. Since here there is no notary appointed by the Holy Office, I designated as my notary (which the same Tribunal has authorized me to do) Padre Predicador Fray Juan González Vizcaíno, of the same order and Colegio Apostólico. He gladly accepted this post and promised under oath to be accurate and confidential, and for the record we both signed this document on the above mentioned day, month, and year.

Fray Junípero Serra	Fray Juan González Vizcaíno
Comisario	Appointed notary

In this Villa de los Valles, on the 14th day of the month of April in the year 1766, in the afternoon, without being summoned there appeared before the Reverendo Padre Comisario of the Holy Office, Fray Junípero Serra, a woman who swore to tell the truth and said her name was Dominga de Jesús. She is dark-skinned, the widow of Juan Luciano Baptista,[78] she is a resident of the pueblo called Valle del Maíz, she is about thirty-five years old. She says that to ease her conscience she is reporting that a little over three years ago

---

78. Throughout the documents, his last name is spelled either as "Baptista" or "Bautista."

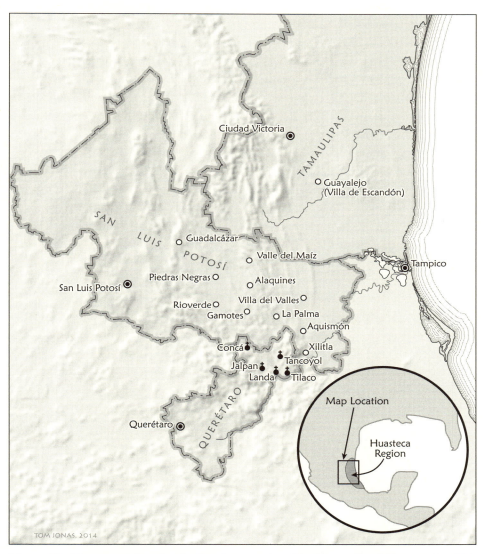

MAP 5. The Huasteca region, showing locations mentioned in the 1766 Inquisition case in which Serra participated. *Map by Tom Jonas.*

she suddenly came down with a continual and bothersome cough, for which she has never been able to determine a natural cause. The cough continued for two years and she was unable to find any remedy known to man. In addition, she developed a hoarseness and tightness in her chest, which was so bad that she could hardly be understood. With great effort she was able to force herself to speak. Various medications and cold remedies were prepared for her, but none had any effect. During that time, a number of people, whom she does not remember, told her on different occasions that what she had was not a natural illness but rather the result of a spell, and that she should stop taking medication.

But the patient did not believe this until a certain day in the month of November of last year, 1765. She is adamant about not remembering the exact day. Agustina Vásquez,[79] a free mulata from the same Valle del Maíz, in the presence of another woman named Victoria, who was married to Alexandro de Nava, told her [Dominga] to go to María Pascuala de Nava, a loba,[80] resident of the same pueblo and married to Andrés Luis, who had been absent for a long time, so that she could cure her. [Vásquez] was very strong in her belief that María Pascuala had cast a spell on Dominga. And she knew that because of the spell, the patient had a sack of worms in her neck and that for the past year she had been praying not to live, but to die. And with this information the accuser went to the house of María Pascuala and she asked her, for the love of God, to cure her. María Pascuala looked at her and, smiling, she said that she could not cure her. The accuser replied that in addition to asking her in the name of God, she would pay her for the cure. To which María Pascuala answered that first she needed for Dominga to give her some petticoats and then she would go to her house to cure her. The patient agreed to this and took the petticoats from her oldest daughter.

The following day she gave them to her when María Pascuala went to the house. The remedy that she applied was Rose of Castile, sugar, and rosemary, which she brewed and gave her to drink. She anointed her and said her illness was pneumonia. In addition to this, she thumped very hard on her chest, which caused the accuser a great deal of pain. She [Dominga] felt as if something had been pulled out from inside her chest. María Pascuala, who was smiling at the pain she [Dominga] felt, assured her that she would be cured. She asked for a shirt, which the patient later took from another one of her daughters, and she gave it to her [María Pascuala]. She apologized for

---

79. Through the documents, her last name is spelled as either "Vásquez" or "Vázquez."
80. A casta designation indicating that her ancestry was both African and Indian.

not being able to give her some white petticoats, which she had also asked for, but the patient did not have any. And thus, in a process that spanned eight days, with treatment occurring every third day, the patient found herself free of the cough and the hoarseness and was very relieved. The treatment on the other days consisted of many herbs, a few of each kind that were boiled and given to the patient to drink. Then she would be anointed and sometimes she [María Pascuala] would blow on her head and the fingers of her hands, and she would put ash on her neck.

After the eight days had passed, she told her [Dominga] that she would not continue to treat her unless she moved to Alexandro de Nava's house, who was María Pascuala's brother, because she did not want the owner of the house where Dominga was living to see her or find out that she was treating her. The accuser moved to Alexandro's house. While Dominga was waiting for María so that she would prepare the medications, Alexandro's wife told the patient that when dealing with witches it was a good idea to place scissors in the form of the cross. As soon as Pascuala arrived, the sister-in-law placed the scissors near her on the floor, which bothered the patient because she was afraid that her *curandera* would become angry. And that is what happened. For without being aware of the scissors, she became very angry, turned around, looked and looked again, found the scissors and closed them, and put them away until now, which is when they were found among her things. She gave the patient a drink, which she said contained a potent medication, in addition to other ingredients that the accuser does not recall. After she drank it, her cough and hoarseness came back stronger than ever and she had so much pain throughout her body that she thought for certain she would die this time. When María Pascuala saw her in such distress, she covered her up with her *rebozo*, for a short time, and this alone was enough to allow her to rest until the night. That is when her cough started up again, as well as the hoarseness. The next day, she also had an upset stomach and other pains.

Seeing herself in such bad shape, she went to complain and denounce María Pascuala before the Reverendo Padre Guardián, or Presidente of that *doctrina*, named Fray Francisco, whose last name she does not recall. She explained to Su Paternidad the reasons why she believed that María Pascuala had cast a spell on her. The Reverendo Padre responded that he could not go forward and form a case or punish her unless there was another complainant or another witness. The accuser responded that there was another sick woman in the pueblo who had experienced something similar. Her name was Juana Morisca, a widow. She had heard her say that María Pascuala had caused her illness. The Reverendo Padre then ordered that Juana Morisca be summoned, and when he asked her about the matter she responded that she had nothing to say against María Pascuala, nor did she have any evidence that she had done anything bad to her. And when the accuser reproached her with what she had previously said to her, she [Juana] persisted in claiming she did not know anything and she had nothing to say against María Pascuala. After Juana died, a woman from her house said she was sure that Juana said what she did because she was hopeful that María Pascuala would cure her, even though it did not turn out this way, since she died. María Pascuala later boasted and confessed before the lieutenant and the two religious at that place that she killed Juana. Even though people stated that there was more alleged evidence regarding María Pascuala's reputation as a witch, and that about six years ago she and her mother had been arrested and taken to the Real de Minas de Guadalcázar based on evidence of such a crime, Su Reverencia did not come to any decision or provide a judgment on this matter because he saw that there was only one formal complaint and accusation by this accuser.

The patient continued to suffer without any relief from her illness. And when María Pascuala found out that the accuser had filed a complaint against her, she went to her [Dominga's] house, which was her brother Alexandro's house, and yelled at her and told her she would no longer treat her. And even though the accuser tried to placate her, she was never able to do so. She returned a few days later, and the same thing happened. Days later (in the midst of which Juana Morisca died), María Pascuala returned and with greater anger she told the accuser that not only did she not want to treat her but she added, "She is going to die just like Juana Morisca died." That response confirmed for the patient that María Pascuala was the cause of her illness, so she went to the preacher of that convent, named Fray Antonio, she does not remember his last name, for him to hear her confession. He urged her to forgive María Pascuala with all her heart, and not because of hate but rather for the good of the pueblo, and to go to the lieutenant and tell him how much she had gone through with María Pascuala. And that is what the accuser did. After the lieutenant had listened to the accuser, he ordered that María Pascuala be put in shackles and brought before him. She responded that she was innocent of all accusations made by Dominga.

The next day the Reverendos Padres Fray Francisco and Fray Antonio gathered at the government building with the lieutenant and brought the accuser and the accused face to face. After arguing back and forth, the accused confessed that it was all true, that she had cast a spell on Dominga and that she had a doll that was the source of the spell. And then, with the directions that María Pascuala herself provided, Fray Antonio and the lieutenant, who was in front with María Pascuala on horseback, went to her house to get the doll. After bringing it back, they had her explain her trickery in the presence of everyone. She said that the doll represented the accuser. And when she removed two small stones that she had placed in the doll's chest, the accuser felt enormous relief in her chest; and when she removed a needle that she had stuck in the doll's head, the accuser also felt relief in her head, as if a thorn that had been causing her great pain had been removed or pulled out. And then they unwound a strand of fiber, one of white silk, and another of white thread from the neck of that same doll. The criminal confessed that the accuser was supposed to die from those ligatures. And after this, the lieutenant asked the prisoner how the patient was supposed to recover. To which the prisoner responded that it was now only necessary to anoint her throat with some fat. The lieutenant ordered the prisoner to anoint her, since she knew how, which is what she did. The accuser felt some relief and then she went home. The prisoner remained in jail. Later, on two different days, not in a row, the accuser repeated her visits to the jail so that María would finish healing her, as the lieutenant had ordered. She prepared some remedies with aguardiente, fat, sugar, and (. . .)[81] that she asked for, which provided some relief, however slight, for the patient. She still had the cough and the headache and neck pain. The hoarseness was worse. On the third visit, in the presence of the lieutenant and a number of other people who were there, María said she could no longer treat her because even though she was doing her part, somebody else was working against her actions and thus renewing the spell. And that person was Agustina Vázquez. This happened recently, just after Holy Week. And in light of what María Pascuala had said, the lieutenant ordered his men to go out and bring back this Agustina person, but up until now she has not appeared. It was learned that a few days before this she had said that they were not going to play with her like they were playing with María Pascuala. And if they tried to arrest her at some point in the future, they would have to eat a lot of salt to succeed. With this the accuser stopped coming to see María Pascuala for remedies and she is not doing well. She is obtaining some medications from respectable people and is trusting in God's will.

And she also says that during the days that she [Dominga] was at the home of María Pascuala's brother, Alexandro de Nava, the accuser overheard María tell her brother: "Alexandro, tell that woman that if she wants to live with

---

81. Illegible word in the manuscript.

you for a few days then she should stop seeing the authorities." Her brother responded by reprimanding her, saying that she did not have the right to speak in this manner, and for her to go out and pull herself together. He did not want to have anything to do with her comings and goings. She also states that on that day, in the presence of the Reverendos Padres Fray Francisco, Fray Antonio, the lieutenant, and others, the doll was brought and examined. As has been stated, two small bags were searched. At the present time the Reverendo Padre Comisario has in his possession the formal inquiries that were sent by the lieutenant. And the prisoner confessed that all of those countless items inside the bags were to be used for killing. She also states that she heard María confess everything else that is written on an unsigned page that he is attaching, which he did. The lieutenant sent it without reading it to her. She does not know that the Reverendo Padre Comisario has such a paper, nor was she questioned about any specific point that is contained therein, because what the accuser says she heard from the mouth of the prisoner is not expressed here. And this is the truth, which she swore to under oath. And after it was read to her she said that it was written correctly, that she did not speak out of hatred. She promised to keep this confidential. And because she did not know how to sign her name, the Reverendo Padre Comisario signed it for her.

Fray Junípero Serra, Comisario

As witnessed by me,
Fray Juan González Vizcaíno,
Appointed Notary

On April 20 Serra brought Dominga back and read the formal statement of the interrogation that the notary, Father Vizcaíno, had prepared. Serra impressed upon her that if she were to proceed, she would become a formal witness in an Inquisition proceeding. He told Dominga she must "swear to it under oath and sign it because what she says now will be used against María Pascuala de Nava." Vizcaíno's account of her interrogation was then read to her word for word. She agreed that it was entirely accurate and promised to keep everything secret.

Dominga formally swore to the truth of the statement in front of Serra, Palóu, and Father Manuel de Arroyo, another priest from San Fernando who was part of the missionary group.

❋ *April 20*

In this Villa de los Valles on the 20th day of the month of April in the year 1766:

Dominga, a dark-skinned woman or loba, widow of Juan Luciano Bautista, resident of the pueblo of Valle del Maíz, appeared before the Reverendo Padre

Comisario Fray Junípero Serra. She said that she is about thirty-five years old. Also present were honest people and religious people, Padre Lector Fray Francisco Palóu and Padre Predicador Fray Manuel de Arroyo, both preachers of the Colegio Apostólico de Propaganda Fide de San Fernando in Mexico. They are sworn to secrecy. The woman took the oath and promised to tell the truth.

—Asked if she remembers having deposed before a judge, against a person, regarding things dealing with our holy faith:

—She said she remembers having testified before the Reverendo Padre Fray Junípero Serra, the judge, against María Pascuala de Nava, a resident of Valle del Maíz. And she recounted in substance what was in the declaration and asked that it be read to her.

—She was told that she is being notified that the Señor Fiscal of the Holy Office is presenting her as a witness *ad perpetuam rei memoriam*[82] in a case against this woman María Pascuala. That she should pay close attention as her statement is being read to her. If there is something that needs to be changed, added, or corrected, she should do so as long as it is the truth. She must swear to it under oath and sign it because what she says now will be used against María Pascuala de Nava.

And what she had stated above was read to her word for word. After the statement was read, Dominga de Jesús said she had heard and understood everything, that those were her words, that she had said what had been read to her, that it was well written and correct, and that she had nothing to change, add, or correct. What was written was the truth. When asked to swear to it, she did, when asked to authenticate it, she did. And if it were necessary, she would again repeat her accusations against María Pascuala de Nava, not out of hatred but rather to ease her conscience. She was instructed to keep everything secret, and she promised to do so. Since she does not know how to sign her name, the Reverendo Padre Comisario and the two religious signed for her.

Fray Junípero Serra, Comisario
Fray Francisco Palóu   Fray Manuel de Arroyo

Serra's next task was to interview Pascuala. Before he did so, he spent some time familiarizing himself with the details of the confession she was said to have given after she had been interrogated by the lieutenant in the presence of the two priests and Dominga a few weeks earlier. Dominga had referred to this document at the end of her statement to Serra. The lieutenant sent the document to Ladrón

---

82. "For the perpetual remembrance of the matter." A legal maxim meaning that her accusation could continue to be used indefinitely into the future.

Figure 9. An inquisitorial interrogation of a woman, drawn by nineteenth-century Mexican artist Constantino Escalante. Serra conducted such an examination of María Pascuala de Nava in Villa de Valles in April 1766. From Luis González Obregón, *D. Guillén de Lampart, La inquisición y la independencia en el siglo XVII* (1908), 217.

de Guevara, who in turn gave it to Serra. The document was a summary, and it did not give any indication of what the interrogation was actually like, or what pressure or torture may have been employed against Pascuala. The document merely recounted what it said was the confession she had made at the end of the interrogation. The carelessness with which the document was put together can be seen in the fact that at times it was written as a third-person report of what Pascuala said and at other times as a first-person account of her words.

In the confession, Pascuala indicated that she had a close relationship with the devil. She said that he appeared to her in the form of a Pame Indian and that they would often engage in carnal acts together. She recounted how the devil had told her that she should kill Dominga and how he had helped her make the doll she used to inflict pain on her victim. She admitted that, at the devil's behest, she had killed another woman in the town and that she and others who were allied with the devil would often go out at night and talk to bats and suck the blood out of small children. The devil also had a number of commands for her which related to the rituals of the Church. He told her not to keep any representations of saints in her house, not to be totally honest with the priest when she went to confession, and not to consume the communion wafer at Mass. The following document is that confession.

One Attachment: April 9

Valle del Maíz, April 9, 1766
Asked name, race, marital status, and residence of the witch
Name: María Pascuala de Nava
Race: loba
Native of the area and resident of the Pueblo del Valle
Marital status: married to Andrés Luis, absent for a long time

Her declaration is as follows: that she made a pact with the Devil a year ago, that the Devil told her that he had already lured her, that the Devil told her that he had already taken hold of her soul and that she was happy. That he was called the "Devil who carried the pall,"[83] that she would see him walking by her side. That he told her to carry herbs to harm the Christians; that she killed someone named Domingo Valtierra by giving him some herbs to drink. That the Devil had ordered her to give them to that man so that he would die and not marry María Pascuala. And that she wanted to get married because the Devil had told her that her husband was dead. But now that the Devil has left her body, she has learned that her husband is alive and is somewhere in the new kingdom of León.[84]

But up until the time she was arrested, the Devil still spent time with her. That he advised her to go off with him, that he would take her to stroll through the mountains, which would be easy for him to do, for what was there for her to do in prison? And that she told him she did not want to go with him; and that he became angry and left. But when the lieutenant came to where I am imprisoned, the Devil had not yet left. He was lodged in my hair in the form of a lizard. And that he told her not to turn her face to look at the people and that she lowered her head. And then the lieutenant came over and asked her why she did not want to look at the people. And he grabbed me by the hair. And then the Devil escaped through the lieutenant's hands because he was afraid of the wax medallion of the Agnus[85] that the lieutenant was wearing around his neck. And that the Devil advised her not to confess

---
83. A shroud, or something in which a corpse is wrapped.
84. Nuevo León, a few hundred miles north.
85. Lamb, a symbol for Christ, the Lamb of God.

to anything that she might be asked. And the Devil told her to kill some lady named Dominga because she was a good singer. And she gave her a good amount of brewed herbs to drink, telling her that they would cure her. And that the Devil ordered her to make an image in the form of a rag doll. That the Devil made it with his hands at the creek where they would always meet. That she would bring the Devil meat and *chancaca*.[86] That she would ask him why he would not eat what she brought him, and that he would become angry when she mentioned God. When she would go out, she would come across him in the form of a Pame Indian, a coyote, ... ,[87] a skunk. And that he told her that the reason she always found him by her side was because he never wanted to let her go, and that he would hug her in the form of a Pame Indian, and that she would sleep with him and engage in carnal acts with him whenever she saw him. And he would tell her not to leave him, that he wanted her to be with him for many years. And that she would respond, telling him to go away and they could be together in a year. And that the Devil would take her at night to Piedras Negras, jurisdiction of Verde, to talk to bats, each one on his own; to wander about to see other Pame Indian women companions, one named Pascuala and the other Gertrudis [. . .][88] de la Cruz. And that they would get together in the mountains, in the creeks. And their Devils were called Guangochudos. And she thought they were going to Mission Gamotes and that of La Palma, all in the form of bats to suck on little children. And that she sucked on two small children who had not been baptized and they died. And that they would return home at dawn. And that she would anoint herself with rosemary mixed with peyote and deer and mountain lion fat. That the Devil would bring these to her and he himself would anoint her. And he also brought bats and she would join up with two other Pame women from the Valle del Maíz, one was Catarina and the other Petrona, both widows, and they too would all get together and go off with the bats. And that these two women's devils were in their petticoats. And that she also got together with another woman, Agustina Vásquez, a gente de razón, and she would go off with her, a native of this area and resident of this pueblo. After they arrested me she disappeared. She [Agustina] is a single woman and her Devil is called Guangachon Queretano, and she also sucked on children. And that the Devil advised her [Agustina Vásquez] to go to the cemetery and get a bone from a dead person so that she could play the *palillos*[89] well and he advised

---

86. Raw, unrefined sugar.
87. Illegible word in the binding of the manuscript.
88. Illegible word in the manuscript.
89. A game played with sticks.

her to carry a small amount of hummingbird, which the Devil had brought her so that men would fall in love with her. And that the Devil ordered her [María Pascuala] to kill a woman named Juana Morisca, by giving her peyote to drink. And that she took Juana Morisca's rosary from her. And that the Devil advised her not to carry any saints nor place them in her house. And he advised her that when she wanted to go to confession, that she confess no more than two or three sins, that was enough. And if she took Communion, she should take it out of her mouth. And that is what she did. She took the Host out of her mouth with a finger and stuck it to a beam that was underneath the Communion rail. And he told her not to pray, that he was the only one she should communicate with. And that the Devil would bring her wine, *pulque*, and *aguamiel*.[90] And she would ask the Devil where he was from and he was say that he was from Hell and the caves. And he would become angry with her because she did not want to go with him to the caves. And that he invited her many times to go to Hell and she said that he would have to take her. This is where the declaration of the witch ends: there are two pouches with her herbs and other items.

The reason for her imprisonment:

It was because of a complaint by Dominga de Jesús, an Indian woman originally from Mission Alaquines and a resident of this pueblo for six years. Wife of Juan Luciano Baptista. I am sending her to appear before Vuestra Merced for it is your jurisdiction, so that she can give her declaration as will another person named Alexandro Nava, who is quoted by the complainant.

When María Pascuala appeared before Serra on April 24, she had shackles around her ankles. Serra's first questions were aimed at forcing her to confess why she was in this condition. With her inferior position clearly established, Serra then asked her why she had been arrested, imprisoned, and sent to him in such a state. She told him that she had been falsely accused of witchcraft by Dominga. She said that when the doll was found in her house, those present immediately accused her of witchcraft, but she insisted that the doll was merely a toy. She insisted that the medication she had given to various people in the town had never harmed anyone. She did acknowledge that the devil sometimes followed her and that he appeared to her in the form of a Pame Indian. But she insisted that he had scared her, that she had told him that she was not interested in his offers, and that she was not in league with him at all. After the questions and answers were concluded, Serra made a point of reading Vizcaíno's notes back to her so that she could be on record that she agreed that the notary's account was accurate.

---

90. Pulque is a thick fermented beverage made from various species of agave. Aguamiel is fermented maguey.

April 22

In the Villa de los Valles, on the 22nd of the month of April, 1766, the Reverendo Padre Comisario Fray Junípero Serra was informed that the accuser (. . . ta)[91] in the above mentioned declaration, and that the Reverendos Padres Fray Francisco and Fray Antonio, the lieutenant from Valle del Maíz, and Alexandro de Nava were absent, and for the record, he ordered that the reason for not summoning them for testimony be explained here. I swear to this,

Fray Juan González Vizcaíno
Appointed Notary

In the Villa de los Valles, on the 24th of the month of April in the year 1766, during the morning a woman, who says her name is María Pascuala de Nava was summoned and appeared before the Reverendo Padre Fray Junípero Serra, Comisario of the Holy Office. She is dark-skinned, married to Andrés Luis, a native and resident of the Valle del Maíz, about thirty years old.

—She was asked by the Reverendo Padre Comisario where she had come from.

—She replied, from the house of the lieutenant of the Villa, named don Manuel.

—And she was asked why she was there.

—She replied that she was under arrest

—And she was asked, who arrested her and who put on the shackles that she had around her feet.

—She said the lieutenant from Valle del Maíz, Don Melchor, along with the *alguacil*[92] and other ministers.

—And she was asked where they arrested her.

—She replied, at home in Valle del Maíz

—And she was then asked how she came to this Villa de los Valles.

—She replied that she was brought here under arrest, that don Melchor had sent her to the Señor Corregidor[93] of this Villa.

—And asked if she knows why they arrested, imprisoned, and sent her here.

—She replied that it was because of stories by a woman named Dominga,

---

91. Illegible word in the manuscript.
92. A constable.
93. A magistrate.

who had accused her falsely before the Reverendo Padre Guardián of the Valle del Maíz and the lieutenant.

—And asked further, what was it that the woman Dominga had said against her before the Reverendo Padre Guardián and the lieutenant.

—She replied that she had given her [Dominga] a remedy for a cough she had but it had gotten worse.

—The Padre Comisario explained to her that this did not seem reason enough to arrest her and place her in jail in irons, as she said they had done; and so in accordance with God and her conscience she should state, if there was another reason for her arrest.

—She replied that in addition to what she had said, the lieutenant went to her house, found some small bags and took them to his house, and when he opened them he found various herbs. And he asked her why so many herbs.

—And this prisoner replied that they were for cures. The lieutenant, don Melchor, answered back that she must be a witch or a sorceress, and that those herbs must be for spells (which this prisoner says is very far from the truth).

—And the Padre Comisario then asked who was present at the lieutenant's house when the small bags were found and searched.

—She replied that Captain don Joseph Antonio, don Phelipe (the one from Laguna Seca), don Miguel Hernández, Antonio Vicencio (the lieutenant's alguacil), Marcos Leonardo (the same lieutenant's minister), and others were there.

—And she was asked if any of the religious from the convent were present when that happened.

—She replied, no. But they came later, first the Padre Ayudante whose name she said is Padre Joseph and then the Padre Guardián whose name is Padre Francisco. They were shown the items in the small bags.

—And she was then asked how they managed to find so many of her things.

—She replied that first they found and removed the small bags. And then they put her on horseback and took her to her home to show them if she had anything else, and she did not show them anything. But after turning her house upside down they found nothing more than a doll, which was her daughter's toy. And they began to tell her it must be witchcraft and that the doll was probably dressed like Dominga, whom she had made sick, which she says is so far from the truth.

—And she was then asked what else happened with the lieutenant after they returned from her house with the doll they had found.

—She replied that there, in front of the two religious and the other assistants she mentioned, the lieutenant began to say that she was a witch and without doubt she was possessed by the Devil, and that the doll was probably some sort of witchcraft, and other similar things. And she remained quiet. The only thing she said was that there was a good God out there and that she did not owe God anything. They accused her of other things, that she had used herbs and witchcraft to kill some man named Domingo Valtierra and some woman named Juana de los Reyes. She said that she had prepared medications for them and that she had not done them any harm at all.

—She was then asked by the Reverendo Padre Comisario if prior to Dominga's appearing before the Reverendos Padres and the lieutenant to lodge a complaint, had she had any fights with her or had she threatened to kill her or do her any harm.

—She replied that she had not uttered a word to her, nor did she even know her.

—She was then asked by the Padre Comisario if in fact she has had some pact with the Devil or communication with him.

—She replied that it is true that the Devil appeared to her at times in the form of a Pame Indian. At other times in the form of a dog, a coyote, other times like a white or mangy cat, a turkey, other times like an owl, a hawk, a lizard, a snake. Other times in the form of a centurion on top of a black horse with an embroidered saddle, and he was very handsome. And that she always was running away from his body.

—And she was then asked by the Padre Comisario how she knew that those Pames, the dog, etc. were the Devil.

—She replied that it was because they were following her and this scared her. And she knew that he was coming for her; that she saw him a number of times but others who were close by did not see him. And sometimes he would speak to her, not only in the form of a Pame Indian but also in the form of an animal. And once, when he appeared in the form of a Pame Indian, she asked him his name. The Devil responded that it was Mantillón.[94]

—She was then asked by the Padre Comisario, what the Devil would say to her and what she would answer.

—She replied that he asked for her soul and that he persuaded her to never abandon her evil way of being, and that he would give her clothes and anything else she needed to survive. And that other souls had pleased him in this way and that she should also give him what he asked for. And that she always responded, no. And that she did not want his clothes nor to be taken care of by him.

---

94. A rogue, rascal, trickster, etc.

—She was then asked if she had learned or performed any sort of spells or witchcraft.

—She replied, no. And that this is the truth, which she said under oath. After reading the statement to her she said it was correctly written, that she did not have anything more to declare or add. And because she did not know how to sign her name, the Reverendo Padre Comisario signed it for her, after which she said "*vale.*"[95]

Fray Junípero Serra, Comisario

As witnessed by me,
Fray Juan González Vizcaíno,
Appointed Notary

After his interrogation of María Pascuala, Serra knew that his next move would be to confront her with the document reporting her confession. So he called Ladrón de Guevara before him to vouch for the legitimacy of the document. Then he called Lieutenant Media Villa y Ascona to certify that the contents of the document accurately represented what she had said in his presence on April 9. Ladrón de Guevara also told Serra that Agustina Vásquez, who had been mentioned in connection with Pascuala, had recently been found in the town of Guayalejo in Nuevo Santander.

※ *April 25*

In the Villa de los Valles, on the 25th day of the month of April 1766, the Reverendo Padre Comisario Fray Junípero Serra summoned Señor don Antonio Ladrón de Guevara, the corregidor of this villa and its jurisdiction. After he swore to tell the truth, he was asked if he recognized a document composed of two sheets of paper with no signature, and he states it was prepared in the Valle del Maíz on the 13th of April of this year. The document contains a declaration given there by María Pascuala de Nava regarding crimes she has perpetrated, which fall under the auspices of the Holy Office of Inquisition.

—He [Ladrón de Guevara] replied that he knew it well, since don Melchor de Media Villa y Ascona, his lieutenant in the Valle del Maíz, had sent it to Su Señoría[96] with a letter attached stating that the document was the declaration given by María Pascuala de Nava, a mulata and a witch. She was sent at the same time so that Su Señoría could begin the legal proceedings, as the person in authority who had access to a Comisario of the Holy Office, which is what Su Señoría did. He sent the Reverendo Padre Comisario the document, along with the prisoner and the accuser.

---
95. "God be with you" or "Farewell" in Latin.
96. Su Señoría refers to Ladrón de Guevara.

—He was then asked by the Padre Comisario if he had in his possession that letter, in which the aforementioned was stated.

—He replied that he thought he did and he immediately looked through his papers. But as hard as he looked, the letter could not be found.

—He was then asked by the Padre Comisario how it could be proved that that declaration was actually what that woman María Pascuala had said in her own words. (Su Señoría offered to speak with the lieutenant about the contents of that document and if his version corresponded with what was supposedly written, he would have him swear to that. Then, everyone who was present at the time of the declaration would be brought together.) This was carried out right away and the Reverendo Padre Comisario was grateful. He [Ladrón de Guevara] also showed the Reverendo Padre Comisario a subsequent letter by the same lieutenant, dated April 13, in which he informs him that he received news that Agustina Vásquez, who had fled from the Valle del Maíz, and according to that confession is a witch like María Pascuala, can be found in the Nueva Colonia de Santander, in the Pueblo of Guayalejo, also known as the Villa de Escandón. She is at a brother's house. His name is Joseph Vásquez. The Señor Corregidor added that what he has stated is the truth under the oath he has taken. After it was read to him he said that it was well written and he did not say anything out of hatred. He promised to keep this confidential and signed his name.

Don Antonio Ladrón de Guevara   As witnessed by me,
Fray Juan González Vizcaíno

April 26

In the Villa de los Valles on the 26th day of the month of April of the year 1766, note that the unsigned document consists of two pages, from start to finish, and it conveys the declaration given by María Pascuala de Nava in the pueblo of Valle del Maíz, regarding the crimes that are described herein. According to what the Señor Corregidor don Antonio Ladrón de Guevara stated, the declaration was given in the presence of his lieutenant, don Melchor de Media Villa y Ascona, who is quoted numerous times in these formal proceedings, and this declaration is indispensable for understanding María Pascuala de Nava's last declaration and confession. The Reverendo Padre Comisario said to add this first declaration and confession to the other proceedings. This is how Su Señoría prepared, arranged, and sent everything. And the person who signs below swears that this is true.

Fray Juan González Vizcaíno,
Appointed Notary

On the afternoon of April 26, Serra summoned María Pascuala once again. His task was simple. Now that he had verified that the document contained what she had actually said, he wanted to get it into the official record. He first impressed upon her the solemnity of the occasion in a manner that was calculated to intimidate her. Then he read her the confession, sentence by sentence, and asked her if she had indeed said what was in each sentence. She admitted that she had, but she refused to admit that she had ever desecrated the communion wafer at Mass. And she insisted that the document represented the past, not the present. The document, she maintained, did not describe her current state.

✳ April 26

In the Villa de los Valles in the afternoon of the 26th day of the month of April in the year 1766, María Pascuala de Nava, a dark-skinned woman who is a resident of the Valle del Maíz, was taken for the second time from where she was being held prisoner to appear before the Reverendo Padre Comisario Fray Junípero Serra. She swore to tell the truth with regard to what she would be asked by the Reverendo Padre Comisario, which were the points contained in the declaration that was taken in the afternoon on the 23rd of this same month and year, as is noted in these formal proceedings. The Reverendo Padre Comisario read them to her, one by one. The prisoner replied that she was being asked to confirm and swear that the same things were true, but with regard to the matter in question, being the Christian that she is, she never could have committed what she is charged with doing, which is being a witch, nor had she done any harm to anybody.

The Reverendo Padre Comisario told her to think about whether she had declared under oath, on a particular day and at some other place, that she had committed one or more crimes that fall under the auspices of the Holy Office of the Inquisition, for which she is being questioned now. If she were to deny them now, while under oath, she would be guilty of perjury. The detestable nature of that crime was explained to her. To which she replied that she had never declared, anywhere, that she had committed such crimes. She added that, in truth, she had never done anything like those crimes because she is a Christian.

Then the Reverendo Padre Comisario told her to pay attention and listen to him read a certain document that he had in his possession, and for her to remember if at some point in time she had said or declared something that is contained in that document. After María Pascuala de Nava replied that she was paying attention, the Reverendo Padre Comisario began to read word for word, in a deliberate and clear manner, the document that is attached to these formal proceedings. And it is the document that is quoted as such in the accusation by Dominga de Jesús and in the statements of the Señor Corregidor don Antonio Ladrón de Guevara. The title of the document, which contains the place, time of the declaration, is omitted. The Reverendo Padre Comisario began to read in the following manner: "Declaration of María Pascuala de Nava. It states: She made a pact with the Devil." And from this point on he continued reading without adding or omitting a single word until he got to the end.

—After reading the first clause the Reverendo Padre Comisario asked the prisoner if she could hear him and if she understood.

—To which she replied that she had heard him just fine and understood.

—Then the Reverendo Padre Comisario asked if it were true that she had declared at some point in the past what had been read to her.

—She replied that it was true, that was how she had declared and confessed before the lieutenant of the Valle del Maíz and other people who were there and named in her first declaration. And that it was also true that it had happened like she stated and how it is written. But now, that was no longer true. And she replied in the same way after the Reverendo Padre Comisario read each clause of the document to her and asked her the same questions after each one, if she had heard him, if she had declared that, and if she had done that. And she only paused for a moment, first to deny and then to confess, on points dealing with whether she had engaged in carnal acts with the Devil, flying up high with the bats, and having sucked on the two children who were not baptized. And with regard to the point that she took the Blessed Host from her mouth and stuck it on a beam [under the Communion rail], she said that she did it. But her excuse was that after having taken Communion, she felt the need to spit out phlegm from her mouth.

At the end she added that this is the truth based on the oath she had taken. And that she used to do those things but now she does not act in that way at all. After the document was read to her, she said that it was well written and that she had nothing more to add or declare. And since she did not know how to sign her name, the Reverendo Padre Comisario signed it for her.

Fray Junípero Serra, Comisario

As witnessed by me,
Fray Juan González Vizcaíno,
Appointed Notary

Serra departed Villa de Valles shortly thereafter and headed south. At Mission Nuestra Señora de la Luz at Tancoyol, one of the five Sierra Gorda missions he had administered in the 1750s, he gathered all the documents together and composed two cover letters for the documents on May 1 and May 6.

❋ May 1

When I was in the Pueblo of Aquismón preaching a mission, the corregidor of the Villa del Valles informed me that he was there because his lieutenant from the Valle del Maíz had written to him saying that he was going to arrest a witch who had caused the death of a poor woman, as well as other wicked acts. I told him that since I was about ready to go with my companions to the Villa de Valles to preach a mission, he should order his lieutenant to send the woman there, along with the accuser and any witnesses who had information about her crimes. It was carried out in that manner. The record of the inquiries I was able to conduct while occupied with preaching the mission are on their way. The lieutenant said that he had sent Alexandro de Nava, but when I looked for him he had already returned to the Valle del Maíz. Since the criminal had already been arrested, I ordered that she remain there in the custody of the Holy Tribunal so that she would not escape as her companion Agustina Vázquez had done. I am already on my way to that court because we have finished our ministries. And, if more specific information on the matter is needed, I can provide that later, so as not to cause any delays. I continue to pray that God keep Vuestros Señores many years in His holy love and grace. From Mission Nuestra Señora de la Luz de Tancoyol. May 1, 1766

Your devoted comisario capellán and humble servant kisses the hand of Vuestros Señores
Fray Junípero Serra

❋ May 6

At this mission, Nuestra Señora de la Luz de Tancoyol in the Sierra Gorda, on the sixth day of the month of May in the year 1766.

Fray Junípero Serra, the Reverendo Padre Comisario of the Holy Office, bears in mind that other information related to the content of these formal inquiries might be able to be obtained, but this would necessitate considerable travel and much time. However, Su Señoría demands that he return to the Colegio Apostólico de San Fernando in Mexico, which he is required to do because of Holy Obedience. The formal inquiries are contained in seventeen single sheets, four quarter sheets, the rest are numbered. All of the pages have been stitched together, wrapped, and sealed and sent to the Muy Ilustres Señores of the Holy Office so that they may determine how best to proceed. That is how he prepared, arranged, and sent the materials. As evidence that he has proceeded in a faithful and legal manner, he certifies that [Fray Juan González Vizcaíno] signed this in his presence.

Fray Junípero Serra	Fray Juan Gonzalez Vizcaíno
Comisario	Appointed Notary

A few weeks later, Serra and Palóu, by this time back at the colegio in Mexico City, were informed that Miguel José Pereli, a priest based in Tampamolon, about fifteen miles east of Aquismón, had asked to be appointed comisario to continue the investigation. Pereli had extensive experience as an ecclesiastical judge for the missions of the Huasteca and the Pamería, and he most likely saw the unfinished case as a way to obtain a promotion. He told the Inquisition that he had met Serra, who lamented the lack of any Inquisition comisario for the vast Huasteca region. He asked Serra if he thought that he might be able to obtain such a position and said Serra encouraged him to apply. (Pereli did not indicate when this conversation occurred, or whether it happened before or after Serra became involved with the María Pascuala case.) Serra and Palóu vouched for Pereli. He was intelligent and studious, they said, and could do the job well. Pereli was appointed at the end of June. He arrived in Valla de Maíz at the end of September and proceeded to interview Dominga de Jesús and more than a score of other residents of the area.[97]

Pereli did not interview María Pascuala, This was probably because by that time she had been moved to Mexico City. Perhaps because she had escaped from incarceration in the region earlier, she was sent to the capital and jailed in the basement of the Inquisition building. It is not clear who requested or arranged for this transfer or when she actually was removed from the area. Pereli concluded his investigation during the second week of October and forwarded the material on to the Inquisition offices in Mexico City. That body reached a decision on December 11 that María Pascuala de Nava was a genuine witch who had made a pact with the devil. The verdict basically repeated the words of the confession that she made at the beginning of April, before Serra even became involved in her case.

That same evening, around six o'clock, prison guards and a nurse discovered María Pascuala hunched over and unconscious in her cell. The report in the

---

97. Pereli's request, Serra and Palóu's assessment of him, and his formal appointment are contained in the document "Solicitud y nombramiento del Br. D. José Miguel Pereli, cura por S.M. en el partido de Santiago de Tampamolon, para comisario del Santo Oficio en el dicho partido," This is originally from the Archivo General de la Nación in Mexico City, Inquisición, tomo 1166, exp. 1. A copy is at the Santa Bárbara Mission Archive-Library, Junípero Serra Collection, doc. 79.

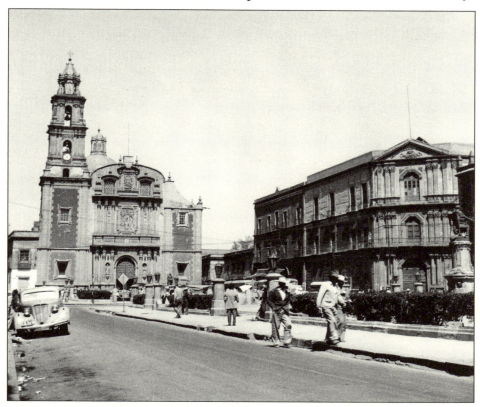

FIGURE 10. Mid-twentieth-century photo of the Church of Santo Domingo, Mexico City. The building that had been the headquarters of the Inquisition is to the church's right. Photograph by Fr. Maynard Geiger, OFM. *Courtesy of the Santa Bárbara Mission Archive-Library.*

Inquisition file said vaguely that she had suffered a "grave accident." The prison doctor was called but was unable to revive her. A priest administered conditional absolution to her and gave her the last sacrament of Extreme Unction. She died at about 12:45 in the morning. She was wrapped in a blanket and carried on the shoulders of an Indian to the Convent of Santo Domingo, which was next door. She was secretly buried there.

Pereli remained in the area as comisario for another four years and resumed the investigation of the Barragán family, especially of Rufino's son Felipe. The social tensions that had contributed to the case of María Pascuala persisted in the region, for at least two other women were accused of similar offenses in the 1780s.[98]

---

98. Rangel Silva, "Linaje y fortuna," 157–60; Gallardo Arias, *Los pames coloniales,* 79, 100.

The few weeks Serra spent involved in this Inquisition interrogation confirmed a number of the perceptions he had previously acquired when he was a missionary in the Sierra Gorda. The fact that a wealthy Spaniard such as Rufino Barragán, whose family was in the process of acquiring a number of extensive ranches in the area, held heterodox views confirmed Serra's belief that settlers in a mission area were an enormous hindrance to the successful evangelization of the native peoples. That a number of Barragán's views were related to sexual behavior solidified Serra's concerns that unsupervised settlers might use their powerful positions to take tremendous advantage of native women.

Also, the fact that the devil assumed the form of various Pame Indians who were living outside the mission system strengthened his belief that successful evangelization demanded a very substantial rejection by native peoples of their traditional lifeways. The locations where Pascuala said she assumed the form of a bat to suck on little children—Piedras Negras, San Felipe de Gamotes, and La Palma—were remote outposts far removed from both Villa de Maíz and Villa de Valles. They were closer to Rioverde, to which she had escaped in the late 1750s. The fact that Pame Indians living at Mission San José, the Indian parish, tended not to appear in the narratives of Dominga and María Pascuala made Serra believe even more strongly that separation between indigenous peoples and others in the area was an important factor in preserving the gains of missionization.[99]

Finally, what Serra heard from Dominga and Pascuala opened up for him a window into the rhythms of daily life in a typical remote village on the frontier of New Spain. He witnessed firsthand the amalgamation of Christian and indigenous folkways that animated the lives of many of the people in Valle de Maíz. He saw that the fabric of these people's existence was neither entirely Christian nor entirely non-Christian, but a shifting mixture of the two perspectives. He undoubtedly left Villa de Valles convinced that should he ever become a missionary among non-Christian peoples, he would have to take a hard line against Spaniards and other settlers, but that his approach to the indigenous peoples themselves would have to be flexible and provisional if it were to have any chance of succeeding. The interrogations he conducted revealed many aspects of the popular religiosity that was so prevalent in rural areas of New Spain in the eighteenth century. When Junípero Serra came to Alta California a few years later, he was well aware, probably much more so than all of the soldiers and officials who accompanied him, of the full range of indigenous traditional spiritual practices.

---

99. The Indians at San José became involved in the case during Pereli's later interrogations.

CHAPTER 3

Baja California

Junípero Serra spent exactly fifteen months in Baja California. He stepped ashore at Loreto on April 1, 1768. On July 1, 1769, he arrived at what he called "the famous and desired port of San Diego." These fifteen months are not as well known as other periods in Serra's career, yet the time spent in Baja California was crucial in his own development. It was in Baja California, specifically during his journey to San Diego, that Serra had his first extensive contacts with native peoples who had not been baptized. It was only then that he felt he was finally and for the first time becoming a true missionary. What Serra observed of the native peoples of the Baja California peninsula and the way in which he and his fellow missionaries reacted to those peoples set the course for much of the indigenous/missionary interaction that was to occur in Alta California after 1769.

Serra's appointment to Baja California happened abruptly. In July 1767 he was preaching a mission at Ixmiquilpan, about halfway between Mexico City and his former missions in the Sierra Gorda. He received an order to return to the Colegio de San Fernando immediately. When he arrived there on July 12, he discovered that the Jesuits had been expelled from New Spain, that the viceregal authorities had decided that San Fernando would take over the Jesuit missions on the remote peninsula called California, that he had been appointed as the leader of the missionaries assigned to California, and that he would be leaving for his new post in a matter of days. Eight other Franciscans at San Fernando, including Palóu, were assigned to join Serra in this new missionary endeavor. They were supplemented by five missionaries currently working in the Sierra Gorda. This group included Juan Crespí and Fermín Francisco de Lasuén. By mid-August, Serra and the group from San Fernando were at Tepic awaiting passage to the peninsula.[1]

Serra was very excited by the chance to assume control of the seventeen missions the Jesuits founded between 1697 and 1767 in the southern two-thirds of

---

1. Geiger, *Life and Times of Fray Junípero Serra*, 1:182–90.

Figure 11. Map of Baja California. This rendition appeared in the first written history of California, Miguel Venegas's *Noticia de la California*, published in Madrid in 1757. *Courtesy of The Bancroft Library, University of California, Berkeley.* BANC MSS M-M 1733.

the peninsula that is now called Baja California. Like most people in New Spain, he knew little about the peninsula, but he was most likely quite aware that the Jesuits had managed to attain a considerable degree of control over the military and that Baja California had not attracted a large number of civilian settlers. In other words, the balance of power was reversed from that in the Sierra Gorda. Another aspect of Baja California that attracted Serra was that the Jesuits had been in the process of expanding their chain of missions northward. There was every reason for him to hope that he would be able to continue the expansion. He anticipated that for the first time in his missionary career he would have the opportunity to come into significant contact with large numbers of unbaptized Indians, an opportunity that had eluded him in the Sierra Gorda and on his domestic preaching journeys. Thus Baja California offered him the possibility of finally engaging in missionary activity among large numbers of native people who had not been baptized. This was the prospect that had fired his desire to become a missionary in the first place and yet, seventeen years after he landed in the New World, he had never been able to do this.

This state of affairs explains an odd occurrence that happened while Serra and the Fernandinos were at Tepic in Nayarit. There were other Franciscans in the city as well, one group from the Colegio Apostólico de Santa Cruz in Querétaro and the other from the Province of Jalisco. Both of these groups were bound for the former Jesuit missions in Sonora, where Jesuits had waged hard struggles against settlers and soldiers for decades. Serra himself was at the port of San Blas inspecting the vessel that was slated to take him and his colleagues across the Gulf of California to the Baja California peninsula.[2]

Suddenly, the viceroy ordered that the assignments were to be changed. The Jaliscans were to go to Baja California and the Fernandinos were to go to Sonora. The reason given was that since the Fernandinos and the Queretarans were from apostolic colleges, they would probably be able to work better together in Sonora. The Jaliscans, coming from another type of Franciscan institution, the province, wondered whether they would be able to work with the Queretarans on the mainland and argued that everything would be better if they were allowed to work separately in Baja California.

Serra was furious and fired off a letter to the Colegio de San Fernando. The letter made it clear that for Serra the major attraction of California was the presence of unbaptized people near the expanding Jesuit missions. The Sonora missions, on the other hand, were similar to those of the Sierra Gorda in an important way: the Indians there were already evangelized and large groups of

---

2. Palóu, *Historical Memoirs of New California*, 1:13–16; Palóu, *Recopilación de noticias*, 17; Gómez Canedo, *Evangelización, cultura y promoción social* , 621–22.

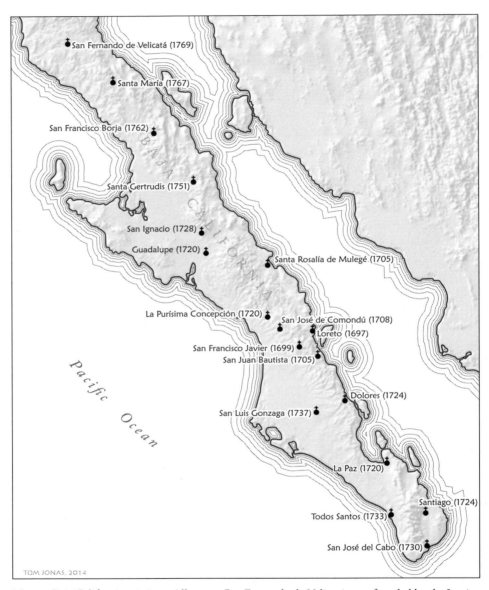

Map 6. Baja California missions. All except San Fernando de Velicatá were founded by the Jesuits. *Map by Tom Jonas.*

unbaptized people were not available, since the area to the north of the missions was controlled by hostile Apaches. As the experience of San Sabá in 1758 had demonstrated, missionization in the far North was a risky enterprise. So Serra told the college authorities that he was sending Palóu and Miguel de la Campa to Guadalajara to try to find the visitor general and lobby to have the order changed.

✻ *Letter to the Colegio de San Fernando, October 17, 1767*

Muy Reverendo Padre Guardián y Venerable Discretorio del Colegio Apostólico de San Fernando de Mexico

Vuestras Paternidades are already aware of the inordinate amount of pain and suffering that the sudden change in the missions has caused my religious companions from this Colegio Apostólico, for they wrote to the Venerable Discretorio during my absence.

My distress was having to retrace my steps for twenty leagues on a wretched road, after I had already boarded the ship, to then find my dear brothers in such a state of sadness. The commanders and officers of the militia were very upset and were speaking in a horrible manner. The Padres from the Colegio de la Santa Cruz in Querétaro were filled with bitterness seeing their reputation dragged through the mud after it was made known throughout the region that, since nobody could live in peace with them, the missionaries from the Colegio de San Fernando have been removed from California. I leave this matter to the higher wisdom of Vuestras Paternidades.

The Reverendos Padres from Querétaro have tried to salvage their honor by means of the documents they are attaching to my letter to Vuestras Paternidades. Duplicates are being sent to our Muy Reverendo Padre Comisario General and another full set to the Colegio de Santa Cruz.

The *coronel comandante*, the treasurer, and all of the officers offered to provide us with documents attesting to the great importance of our presence in California and how these new measures would set back our efforts. I refused to accept these measures and will try to calm their uneasiness. The Señor Gobernador of California, Don Gaspar de Portolá, explained to everyone how bad he felt, but in the end we are left without the Californias, without infidels, and possibly without missions.

Since our experience has shown us how long it takes for letters to arrive here, I am sending Padres Palóu and Campa to Guadalajara. And if the spirit should move them to go to that Santo Colegio, I give them permission to do so. In fact, I am begging them strongly to go. They can then explain in detail the points we have communicated so that the Venerable Discretorio might take into consideration our situation and religious commitment and take the necessary steps for the greater good of those thousands of infidels in California who are at the door waiting for Holy Baptism, which, from what we have been told, does not happen in Sonora. There it is necessary to travel many leagues through unpopulated areas to meet up with even one infidel. May this be settled conclusively.

The Padres from the Province of Jalisco could be given the area of Chinipa, which contains twelve missions founded by the Jesuit Padres and is independent of Sonora. The area appears to be free of danger from infidels.

May God Our Father enlighten Vuestras Paternidades so that you can determine how best to proceed for the greater good of the souls, the glory of God, the honor of the Apostolic Institution, and the consolation of these your subjects, who continue praying.

May God keep you in His Holy Grace many years.

From this residence of Santa Cruz de Tepic, October 17, 1767
Your dearest servant and subject kisses the hand of Vuestras Paternidades,
Fray Junípero Serra

The efforts of Palóu and Campa were successful. They met Visitador General José de Gálvez in Guanajuato on November 1. He agreed with them and gave them a letter to take to the viceroy in Mexico City. They arrived there on November 9, and the viceroy rescinded the new orders a few days later. We suspect that the impetus for the proposed change in destinations was Manuel de Ocio, a Baja California entrepreneur who had long quarreled with the Jesuits about the Jesuits' significant control over the few settlers in Baja California. Ocio owned property in Guadalajara, and his son had just married into a prosperous Guadalajara family. Ocio may well have hoped that Franciscans from the Guadalajara region might be more amenable to allowing settlers greater influence than yet another missionary group headquartered in Mexico City, as the Jesuits had been. But Serra's strong reaction to the proposal indicated that Baja California had a particular attraction for him. With missionaries dominant over settlers it was the reverse image of the Sierra Gorda.[3]

In March, as the Franciscans were preparing to depart for San Blas to board a vessel that had recently arrived there with the expelled Jesuits, Serra wrote the viceroy directly to thank him for his intervention. This communication is the first extant letter that Serra directed toward the viceroy in Mexico City. Many more such letters would follow, and this channel of communication would eventually cause Serra great difficulties with his Franciscan brethren.[4]

---

3. Crosby, *Antigua California*, 362–63.
4. For the actual expulsion of the Jesuits from Baja California, see Bernabéu Albert, *Expulsados del infierno*, 82–126. The ultimate destinations of the other groups of Franciscans can be found in Osante, "Los problemas de la administración franciscana," 280–81, and Torre Curiel, *Twilight of the Mission Frontier*, 191, 199.

FIGURE 12. Portrait of Gaspar de Portolá from the municipal building in Lérida, Spain. Portolá was the first governor of the Californias. He returned to Mexico City in 1770, served as governor of Puebla for eight years, and eventually returned to Spain, where he died in 1784. From F. Boneu Companys, *Gaspar de Portolá: Explorer and Founder of California*, frontispiece.

※ *Letter to the Viceroy, March 2, 1768*

Hail Jesus, Mary, and Joseph
Excelentísimo Señor Virrey

Señor: The religious of the Colegio Apostólico de San Fernando of this court of Mexico, designated by Vuestra Excelencia to go to the missions of California, which previously were administered by the Jesuit Padres, after a long stay of close to seven months in this pueblo of Tepic waiting for a vessel and orders for our desired departure, now (thanks be to God) feel great consolation. We are about to leave for the port of San Blas. We leave this pueblo tomorrow. As soon as we arrive there, we will board the ship called *La Concepción*, which recently came from California with the Padres of the Compañía.[5]

We were upset to see two vessels, which were amply suited for our needs, namely *El Príncipe* and the above-mentioned *La Concepción*, already spoken for by these men to take them to other destinations, with no hope of taking us anytime soon on our voyage. But with the arrival of the new commander, Don Manuel de Rivera, we have achieved some consolation. For he has been able to recognize that, without causing the least bit of delay to what remains of the expedition from Sonora, the spiritual expedition from California could be quickly assisted. And because I have no doubt that some persuasive recommendation from Vuestra Excelencia must have had a major influence on this new decision, I thank Vuestra Excelencia most humbly, in my name and in that of all my Religious.

All sixteen of us, who with great pleasure are going to carry out the apostolic ministry on that peninsula, offer ourselves once again to Vuestra Excelencia as your most humble chaplains. And as president, although unworthy, of those Religious, I recognize that I am the most indebted and must not neglect to give Vuestra Excelencia this good news. And thus, I take this opportunity to offer myself, with the greatest of pleasure, to fulfill any precepts you would be kind enough to ask me to do, while I continue to pray.

May the Lord our God keep you healthy and in His Holy Grace many years.

From this residence of Santa Cruz de Tepic, March 2, 1768
Excelentísimo Señor, your dearest servant and chaplain who venerates and loves, kisses the feet of Vuestra Excelencia,
Fray Junípero Serra

---

5. Jesuits, i.e., Society of Jesus. In Spanish the order was called the Company (Compañía) of Jesus.

When Serra came to Baja California, the Spanish had already been there for decades. They established a permanent presence there in 1697 under the auspices of the Jesuits, who ironically were led into the peninsula by an Italian priest named Giovanni (Juan) María Salvatierra. The Jesuits established seventeen missions in Baja California, from San José del Cabo at the southern tip of the peninsula to Santa María Cabujakaamung, some 600 miles north. The 1,100-mile-long Baja California peninsula was home to perhaps forty thousand people at the end of the seventeenth century. These people were divided into three large ethnic groups—the Pericú at the southern tip, the Guaycura to their north, and the Cochimí, who occupied nearly the remaining half of the peninsula. At the extreme north, spreading from the Colorado Delta area to the Pacific, were some groups of Yuman-speaking people, including the Kumeyaay.[6]

Given the extreme remoteness of Baja California from the rest of New Spain, the Jesuits had been able to extract concessions from the colonial officials in Mexico City in exchange for their willingness to establish an imperial presence there. The Jesuits agreed to finance the operations themselves through an endowment they raised called the Pious Fund. In return they received extensive powers over the peninsula's affairs. For example, they were able to appoint the peninsula's military commander. In the absence of a governor, the Jesuit superior was de facto the highest authority in the region. While the Jesuits had to surrender some of their power after a revolt of the Pericú people at the southern end of the peninsula in 1734, they retained considerable control until their expulsion.

When the Franciscans arrived the peninsula was suffering from a series of natural disasters, including four years of drought and a plague of locusts. Mission registers counted 7,149 baptized natives at the missions. Serra set himself up at the old Jesuit headquarters, Mission Nuestra Señora de Loreto Conchó, then assigned priests to staff the missions and undertook a brief trip to the north to reconnoiter the landscape.[7]

In May at a meeting convened by Visitador General José de Gálvez at the western Mexican port of San Blas, plans were drawn up for the initial colonization of Alta California. Gálvez himself arrived in Baja California on July 5 and remained there for eleven months. He was the highest-ranking Spanish official ever to visit either Baja or Alta California. He was a midlevel official at the royal court when at the conclusion of the Seven Years' War King Carlos III decided to attempt to strengthen the Spanish military presence in the colonies. The king

---

6. General information on Baja California comes from Mathes, *Land of Calafia*. For the Jesuit period, the definitive volume is Crosby, *Antigua California*. Dunne, *Black Robes in Lower California*, while older, contains good information on the Jesuits. Vernon, *Las Misiones Antiguas* and Mathes, *Las misiones de Baja California*, contain important information on each mission establishment.

7. Crosby, *Gateway to Alta California*, 13–14; Palóu, *Historical Memoirs of New California*, 1:31; Geiger, *Life and Times of Fray Junípero Serra*, 1:191–99.

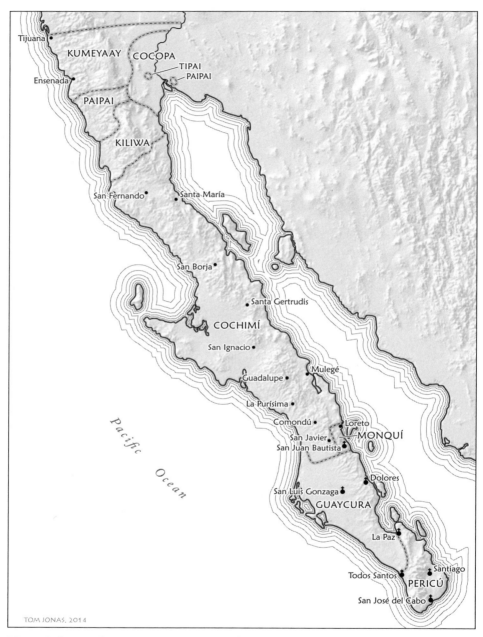

MAP 7. Indigenous linguistic groups in Baja California. *Map by Tom Jonas.*

also wanted to reform the colonial administration and increase the revenues from America, which had been declining for over a century. The government decided to appoint a *visitador general* who would travel to New Spain. This official was given wide powers to effect these measures. After the initial appointee died at sea en route to America, Gálvez was appointed to the post.[8]

Gálvez, like his sovereign, was a man of the Enlightenment. He believed that the imposition of rational reforms on what he regarded as chaotic colonial situations would result in a more efficient and profitable empire. When he arrived in Mexico City he found the viceroy, Joaquín de Montserrat, Marqués de Cruillas, insufficiently attentive to his dictates. Cruillas was quickly removed, and his successor, Carlos Francisco de Croix, was specifically instructed to defer to the visitador general. Gálvez attended to matters relating to the establishment of a government tobacco monopoly and the reforms of the customs service at Veracruz before turning his attention to the northern frontier. He drew up plans for intensifying military operations against the native peoples and for strengthening the military presence on the northwestern frontier. He decided to go personally to Baja California and direct preparations for the move northward.[9] In planning this expedition Gálvez sought to avoid giving too much power to any one group. He did not want to replace the Jesuits with another powerful religious order, for he believed that the Jesuits had accumulated too much power in the northern frontier regions such as Sonora and Baja California. Gálvez therefore determined to limit the potential sway of the missionary group going to Alta California. On the other hand, since he was interested, as a Bourbon reformer, in increasing the authority of the state, he did not want to give as much authority to individual colonizers as Escandón had received in Nuevo Santander. Thus Gálvez believed that a strong military presence in Alta California would be best. He also probably hoped that the presence of so many Catalán volunteers in the expedition would help relations between the military and the missionaries, who were led by a Catalán-speaking Mallorcan.[10]

Gálvez brought his vision of enlightened despotism with him to Baja California. He promulgated a sweeping and unrealistic series of plans for the peninsula, involving trade fairs, improved mining, Indian towns, and other measures that he thought would bring prosperity to Baja California. He quickly judged that the traditional lifeways of the Baja California Indians were inimical to the progress he envisioned. Therefore, in his view, those lifeways had to change. Since the sixteenth century Indians had been forcibly removed from their homes to other locations

---

8. Pietschma, "Consideraciones en torno," 347–48.
9. Priestley, *José de Gálvez*, 170–71.
10. Osante, "Presencia misional," 114.

in New Spain according to the calculations of colonial officials. Sometimes they were moved so they could be compelled to labor in the mines. Indeed, along the northern frontier in the seventeenth and eighteenth centuries, missionaries were constantly criticizing miners for their harsh treatment of these Indians. At other times Indians were moved from central Mexico northward to serve as willing or unwilling role models for other Indians whose land was being appropriated. Gálvez brought this long-standing tradition and this strategy to Baja California.[11]

He perceived that the missions at the southern end of the peninsula had good agricultural prospects and was disappointed that they had become depopulated. Therefore, he decided to consolidate the remaining Pericú at Mission Santiago, which entailed moving a number of them from Todos Santos to that mission. That would free Todos Santos to receive a large number of Guaycura neophytes from two missions farther north, Dolores and San Luis Gonzaga. The Jesuits had never attempted to congregate large numbers of Guaycura people at those two missions given the arid nature of the landscape. Instead, the vast majority of indigenous peoples generally remained after baptism in their traditional villages at some distance from the mission. Moving to Todos Santos therefore would have entailed a double move—to a new territory and into a different social unit, the mission village. Gálvez realized there could be problems with this move and envisioned a larger-than-normal contingent of soldiers for Todos Santos. Palóu reported that the Guaycura who were forced to relocate engaged in various forms of resistance at their new mission and that the move was not a success. Of the 800 people who were relocated, only 170 remained at the mission three years later. While some undoubtedly fled, many died from diseases they contracted at the new location. Gálvez also ordered forty-four people to move from Mission San Javier to Loreto in order to increase the population there. According to Palóu, who remained in Baja California until 1773, all of Gálvez's edicts about Indian relocation were resisted in one fashion or another by the native peoples, and the ill feelings created by these moves caused the missionaries great problems. But the closure of Missions Dolores and San Luis Gonzaga did have the effect of freeing up missionary personnel for the voyage to San Diego.[12]

Technically, Gaspar de Portolá, a Spanish soldier who had been detached from the army fighting the indigenous peoples in Sonora and appointed the first governor of California, was the preeminent Spanish official in Baja California.

---

11. Río, "Utopia in Baja California"; Gonzalbo, *Historia de la educación en la época colonial*, 178; Almada, *Breve historia de Sonora*, 79–82.
12. Crosby, *Doomed to Fail*, 8–9; Palóu, *Historical Memoirs of New California*, 1:39–41, 166–68; Crosby, *Antigua California*, 388; Palóu, *Cartas desde la península de California*, 88–89, 423–33; Rodríguez Tomp, *Cautivos de Dios*, 185, 206; Guest, *Fermín Francisco de Lasuén*, 43; see also León Velazco, "Conflictos de poder en la California misional (1768–1775)."

FIGURE 13. José de Gálvez. Gálvez was one of the most important Spanish colonial officials of the late eighteenth century. He served as visitor general of New Spain (1764–72) and minister of the Indies (1775–87). Private collection. *Courtesy of Dr. Iris Engstrand, University of San Diego.*

FIGURE 14. Autographs of some of the men of the Portolá expedition. *Courtesy of Harry W. Crosby.*

To emphasize his authority over Portolá, Gálvez chose not to live at the Presidio of Loreto, where the residence of the governor was located. He lodged instead at the Real de Santa Ana, headquarters of the independent entrepreneur Manuel de Ocio, who had more or less successfully managed to assert his independence from Jesuit control. To win favor with the missionaries, Gálvez issued a decree ending the authority of the commissioners who had been appointed by Portolá to supervise the missions after the departure of the Jesuits. He thus handed the management of the missions' temporal affairs to the Franciscans. Serra, who had initiated a correspondence with Gálvez soon after the visitador general had landed, met him personally at Santa Ana at the end of October. Serra was enthusiastic about going north and agreed with Gálvez that Franciscans would accompany the expedition and establish missions at the two great harbors that had been discovered by previous explorers—San Diego and Monterey. After the meeting Serra toured the southern missions and heard from the priest at Todos Santos of the unhappiness of the eight hundred Guaycura who were forced to relocate there. According to Palóu, Serra communicated this sentiment to Gálvez.[13]

Serra had already decided on missionaries for the various stages of the colonization journey, which consisted of land and sea components. Fernando Parrón, who had been stationed at Loreto, was appointed to sail on the first vessel, the *San Carlos*. Serra hurried to La Paz to bless the vessel and its chaplain and crew before their departure. Juan González Vizcaíno, who sailed to the New World with Serra in 1749 and served as Serra's notary in the 1766 inquisition case, joined Francisco Gómez on the second vessel, the *Concepción*. Gómez was the missionary freed to join the expedition by the closing of Mission Dolores, where he had been serving. Juan Crespí, Serra's former student in Mallorca who had been at Mission La Purísima, was assigned to accompany the first overland journey that was to be led by Fernando de Rivera y Moncada, commander of the presidio at Loreto. Serra was slated to accompany Gaspar de Portolá on the second overland expedition that would follow the trail blazed by the first.

Rivera y Moncada left Loreto at the end of September 1768 and headed north. He stopped at the missions along the way and requisitioned items and livestock he thought would be necessary for the Monterey expedition. Rivera y Moncada chose Velicatá as his staging point. He and the Jesuits had already determined that this site would be suitable for the next northern mission. The expedition departed from Velicatá on March 24, 1769, and arrived at San Diego on May 14.[14]

---

13. Palóu, *Historical Memoirs of New California*, 1:47.
14. Geiger, *Franciscan Missionaries*, 51–55, 109–10, 121.

Loreto to San Diego

Serra kept an extensive diary of his own journey from Baja California to San Diego. This document is the longest text composed by Serra that has survived. We do not know very much about the circumstances of its creation. If Serra composed in the same general fashion as other Franciscan diarists of the period, he probably jotted down a series of notes as he was going along. When there was a lull in the expedition's progress and after reaching his final destination, he most likely organized the notes into diary form. He probably put together an almost-final version of the complete diary in San Diego while the Portolá party was engaged in its fruitless search for Monterey during summer and fall 1769. Fray Juan González Vizcaíno took a copy of what Serra had completed back to Mexico City in February 1770. Palóu found a complete copy of the diary among Serra's papers after Serra's death and took that copy with him back to Mexico City. This was probably the copy that Father Maynard Geiger discovered in the Archivo General de la Nación in Mexico City in 1945. A copy of this version is now at the Santa Barbara Mission Archive-Library, and this is the copy we used.[15]

Serra always hoped that the diary of Juan Crespí would be the major diary of the journey from Baja California to Alta California, since Crespí had accompanied Portolá from San Diego to San Francisco Bay and back in 1769. However, Serra became frustrated with Crespí's delays in completing a final version of his diary and thought his former student was including too much extraneous material in his account. Serra's original intention was for Crespí's diary to circulate and attract a wide readership, which in turn would attract new missionaries to California. Letters and accounts from Catholic missionaries all over the world, especially from Jesuits, were circulating widely in eighteenth-century Europe. Thirty-four volumes of Jesuit missionary letters from around the world were published in France between 1702 and 1776 under the general title *Lettres édifiantes et curieuses écrites des missions étrangères*. Sixteen volumes were translated into Spanish and published as *Cartas edificantes y curiosas de algunos misioneros jesuitas* between 1753 and 1756. Serra wanted the tone of Crespí's account to be one of zealous enthusiasm, which might fire the imagination of the young religious who would read it. But Crespí insisted on writing what he thought was a more complete record, including detailed descriptions of both the landscape and the native peoples the expedition encountered. When Serra tried in 1771 to convince Crespí to rid the diary of what Serra considered "trivia and repetitions," Crespí became annoyed and asked Serra if he wanted him to tell what had actually happened or not. Serra sighed and let Crespí continue. But he continued to be frustrated that Alta California diaries and letters were not well known in Europe.

---

15. Serra, *Writings*, 1:238.

One of his last requests to Palóu was that he try to arrange for the publication of the Crespí diary.¹⁶

The type of tone Serra desired was seen in Francisco Palóu's 1774 diary account of his voyage with Fernando de Rivera y Moncada to reconnoiter San Francisco Bay. In this document Palóu took every opportunity to interpret polite indigenous hospitality as an enthusiastic desire for an extension of the missions. In the southern Santa Clara Valley, near present-day Gilroy, he wrote of a group of Indians the expedition encountered: "We stayed with them a little while and they showed great friendliness toward us. I made the sign of the cross on every one that came up, and not one resisted, being very attentive to the ceremony, as though they understood it." A few days later, on the San Francisco peninsula, he intensified the same theme when describing the expedition's encounter with another group: "I thanked them and told them that we were going very early in the morning, but that afterward we would return to live with them, to teach them what was necessary to be saved. They showed signs of being well pleased and said they would all get together and build their houses." A few days later, in San Francisco: "I told them . . . that I would return to live with them, which it seems they understood, for they appeared to be very happy about it." Finally, on the way back to Monterey, they met another group: "We took our leave of them, at which they seemed to be quite sad."¹⁷

Serra struck something of this tone in his 1769 diary. The document describes his excitement at meeting unbaptized Indians, his overly optimistic assessment that they were eager, and his increasingly unbridled enthusiasm at the missionary success he was certain awaited him. And the tone was genuine, for the original intended audience of this diary was limited. He was writing for his fellow Franciscans at the colegio, and he probably expected that the diary would also come into the hands of the visitador general who had organized the expedition. In this chapter we present those parts of the diary that throw light on his developing religious identity as a missionary and on his interaction with a large number of unbaptized native peoples he was encountering for the first time in his life.

※ *Diary of the expedition of Padre Junípero Serra from Loreto to San Diego from March 28 to July 1, 1769*

Hail Jesus, Mary, Joseph

Diary of the expedition to the ports of San Diego and Monterey for the greater glory of God and the conversion of the infidels to our Holy Catholic faith. After visiting the missions of the south where I met with the

---
16. Crespí, *A Description of Distant Roads*, 84.
17. Palóu, *Historical Memoirs of New California*, 3:258, 266, 292.

Ilustrísimo Señor Don José de Gálvez of His Majesty's Chamber Council, Visitador General of New Spain and principal director of these conquests, with whom I conversed at length about this expedition, I set out from my mission and the Royal Presidio of Loreto in California on March 28, 1769, the third day after the Feast of the Resurrection.

Note 1[18]

On January 6 of this same year, finding myself at the port of La Paz with Su Ilustrísima Señor Visitador General, I blessed the packet boat named *San Carlos*. Aboard ship I sang the Mass and blessed the royal standards. The litany and other prayers to Our Lady were sung. Su Ilustrísima gave a passionate speech that invigorated the spirits of all who would be sailing on that vessel to the ports of San Diego and Monterey. They boarded the night of [January] 9 and set sail on the 10th. Don Vicente Vila, a celebrated pilot in European waters, was selected commander of the sea expedition. Don Miguel Costansó was the engineer. The leader of the troop was Don Pedro Fages, lieutenant of the company of volunteers. I appointed Padre Predicador Fray Fernando Parrón missionary of the expedition and later missionary to the infidels. He had been my companion in Loreto from the time we had arrived in California. Everyone was exceedingly happy when they left on January 10.

Note 2

On February 15, when I had already returned to Loreto, the same blessing of the vessel and of the royal standards was performed at Cabo San Lucas on the second packet boat, the *San Antonio*, also known as *El Príncipe*, which immediately set out for the same ports. On board were Padres Predicadores Fray Juan González Vizcaíno and Fray Francisco Gómez, whose goal was the same as that of the other missionaries. Vizcaíno had recently arrived from Mexico and Gómez had been a minister at the Misión de la Pasión,[19] which had been suppressed by order of Su Ilustrísima. The Indians from that mission were moved to Mission Todos Santos. And with this the maritime or naval expedition was set in motion.

Note 3

Su Ilustrísima decided that for the land expedition, Don Fernando de Rivera y Moncada, the capitán of the company of this peninsula, should begin to

---

18. The four notes at the beginning of the diary refer to the four successful stages of the expedition, two by sea and two by land. There was supposed to be a fifth stage, a supply ship, but it became disabled and did not participate in the expedition. It sank the next year. Bancroft, *History of California*, 1:123–24.
19. La Pasión was the shorthand method of referring to Mission Nuestra Señora de los Dolores.

Figure 15. Contemporary rendition of the *San Carlos* by artist Raymond Aker. This vessel was part of the Portolá expedition. In 1775 it became the first Spanish ship to enter San Francisco Bay. *Courtesy of the Raymond Aker Family.*

arrange everything that the horses and pack mules would need for the journey, as well as all the food and provisions. He is the same person who was here during the time of the Jesuit Padres. Rivera y Moncada was to travel to all of the missions and deliver the order from Su Ilustrísima to the Padres misioneros who already had control over the mission temporalities. For the successful completion of these endeavors and so that Rivera y Moncada could then begin the land journey, at the request of His Majesty, on September 28, 1768, I sang a Mass of intercession at Loreto in honor of San José, who was chosen as the patron saint of both the land and the sea expeditions. Two days later, Rivera y Moncada left Loreto and headed to Mission San Javier to begin his process of removing whatever pleased his fancy from what was available at that mission and at the others.

That is exactly what he did. And even though it was done with a rather heavy hand, they suffered through it for God and for the king. Rivera y

Moncada spent three days at this place called Velicatá, which is now a new mission, so his animals could have enough time to rest. He then left with twenty-five soldiers, three mule drivers, a sufficient number of Indians on foot, and all the provisions he deemed necessary. He also took Padre Predicador Fray Juan Crespí with him to serve as priest and missionary for that portion of the expedition. Until then, Crespí had been the minister of Mission La Purísima Concepción de Cadegomó. May God protect them along the way so that their journey will end happily.

Note 4

In order to complete the land expedition, at the beginning of the month of March, Su Ilustrísima ordered that the governor and commander of this peninsula, Don Gaspar de Portolá, set out with the rest of the missionaries who had been appointed, the rest of the soldiers, and the provisions and other necessary items for such an arduous and large-scale expedition. Portolá would be the commander-in-chief of both portions of the land expedition. The governor obeyed the order and left his Royal Presidio of Loreto on March 9 with his retinue. Even though I was always eager to join this expedition, I was not able to leave so quickly. I was determined and promised to do so as soon as possible (as I later did). In the meantime, I gave Padre Predicador Fray Miguel de la Campa the assignment of accompanying the travelers. He was the minister at Mission San Ignacio. As soon as the travelers arrived at his mission, he joined them. He traveled with the expedition until they reached Mission Santa María de los Angeles at the edge of the frontier. They had to stay there for quite some time waiting for the provisions that were supposed to arrive by ship at the Bay of San Luis Gonzaga, which was close to that last mission. They then spent time getting the pack train ready and making other preparations until I arrived there to join up with their group, as I shall recount later.

Serra chose to leave Loreto on the Tuesday after Easter. As was so often the case with him, the date was not accidental. In 1749 he left his ancestral village of Petra on the exact same day in the Catholic liturgical calendar. At that time he thought he was journeying to become a missionary among the unbaptized. But events had disappointed him, as he had spent two decades working among people who had already received that sacrament. Now, exactly twenty years later, he believed he was finally undertaking the journey on which he thought he had been embarking in 1749—a journey that would enable him to work among those who had not been baptized.

Serra's first stop was Mission San Javier, staffed by Francisco Palóu, who would soon be moving to Loreto as chief administrator of the Baja California missions. There was one item of business that had to be taken care of immediately. When Portolá had passed through San Javier on his way to Velicatá a few weeks earlier, he had told Palóu that he was concerned about the poor condition of Serra's leg (it had grown worse during the trip Serra made to the southern missions after his meeting with Gálvez). Portolá believed that Serra's condition might slow the progress of the expedition. He asked Palóu to try and convince Serra not to make the journey and allow Palóu to go in his place. Palóu agreed, although he undoubtedly knew that Serra would vigorously refuse such a request. Palóu made the request and Serra of course refused to consider it. After that, the two of them got down to business.

Serra spent three days at San Javier, mainly briefing Palóu on the issues he would be facing after Serra left. Palóu offered Serra some additional provisions for his journey, provisions he sorely needed. Serra's departure was very emotional. He and Palóu had known each other for almost thirty years, and they had no idea if they would ever see one another again. Serra certainly hoped they would. According to Palóu, Serra's words of farewell were "Goodbye until we meet in Monterey, where I hope we shall see each other in order to labor in that vineyard of the Lord." Palóu was less certain. His farewell was simply, "Until we meet in eternity."

March 28, the third day after the feast of the Resurrection of Our Lord Jesus Christ. After celebrating all of the services of Holy Week with the utmost solemnity and devotion possible, I sang Mass on Easter, and preached my farewell sermon exactly one year to the day, according to the ecclesiastical calendar, from when I had preached my first sermon taking spiritual possession of that mission and church. The following two days I celebrated Mass in honor of Nuestra Señora de Loreto, asking that she protect us during such a difficult journey on foot. I left after saying Mass. My first day's journey ended at Mission San Francisco Javier de Biaundó. Nothing happened along the way worth mentioning. Since the route and the terrain are well known, I do not need to comment on them. The same applies to the rest of the old missions along the way.

March 29, 30, and 31. I lingered at the mission for a variety of reasons. The most important reason for stopping was to see the mission's minister, Padre Lector Fray Francisco Palóu, Comisario of the Holy Office, with whom I share a special and longtime friendship. He was elected by our colegio to succeed me as president of these missions if I were to die or be away for a prolonged period of time. This last circumstance was the second important reason for stopping here. We needed to discuss and agree on the measures he

FIGURE 16. View of Mission San Francisco Javier de Viggé-Biaundó from the south slope of the arroyo, 1967. When the Franciscans arrived in Baja California in 1768, Serra assigned Palóu to this church, which was the closest mission to Serra's headquarters at Loreto. *Photograph by Harry W. Crosby. Courtesy of Mandeville Special Collections Library, University of California, San Diego.*

would have to undertake to maintain the stability of these missions during my absence. And the measures would have to be clearly defined and put into place by the time Su Ilustrísima Señor Visitador General arrived in Loreto, which was expected at any time. The third, and for me the most important reason for stopping, was to express my gratitude. The fact is that the only provisions I took from my mission in Loreto for such a long journey were a loaf of bread and a piece of cheese. During the year I was there I had no say with regard to temporal matters. I was treated as a mere guest of the Señor Real Comisario, who lavished me with crumbs. When I left, his generosity toward me did not exceed what I have described. However, Reverendo Padre Palóu more than made up for this insult. He generously provided me with food, clothing for my own use, and other amenities for my journey. I could

FIGURE 17. Mission Nuestra Señora de Loreto Conchó, 1750. Founded in 1697 by the Jesuits, it served as their missionary headquarters, and thus as the administrative center of Baja California during the entire colonial period. From Rafael Espinosa, "Viaje a Loreto y San Javier en la Baja California," in *La ilustración mexicana*, 1851, 376–80.

not bring myself to reflect upon whether I should take all that he had given me or consider leaving any of it behind, for being the sinner that I am, I am still attached to my creature comforts. May God reward such charity.

Serra left early on the morning of April 1 and arrived at the next mission, San José de Comondú, a bit before noon. The resident minister, Father Antonio Martínez, who had come to America on the same expedition as Serra and had worked with him in the Sierra Gorda, was not there. He was looking after the mission that had been vacated by Juan Crespí, who had gone to participate in the Rivera-led leg of the Portolá expedition. Fortunately, Martínez left provisions for Serra, so he was able to celebrate Mass for the congregation on April 2. Serra remained at San José de Comondú for a few days and then headed off to the next mission, La Purísima.

April 1. I said goodbye with great sorrow to the Padre, someone I have known and loved since he was a youth. I set out at dawn and began walking to the next mission, San José de Comondú, which is more than twelve leagues away. I arrived at about eleven o'clock that same morning, which shows how early I had gotten up. Padre Predicador Fray Antonio Martínez, who was and still is the Padre Ministro at the mission, was not there. However, I was not lacking in provisions because my dear friend had left everything prepared for me in case I arrived while he was gone. He had gone to Mission La Purísima and was in charge of that mission due to the absence of its minister, Padre Predicador Fray Juan Crespí, who had left on the first leg of the expedition, as has already been mentioned. Fray Martínez is an old friend of mine, from the time we met in the city of Cádiz to travel to our colegio. Later he was my fellow missionary in the Sierra Gorda.[20]

April 2. Since it was Low Sunday[21] I sang the Mass and preached to the people from the pueblo or mission, who would have heard neither if I had left. Since I also heard a number of confessions, the time I spent there was put to good use.

April 3. This was also a feast day. We celebrated the Annunciation of Our Lady. This year it fell on Holy Saturday.[22] I did the same things today. I sang the Mass, preached, and heard confessions. The Padre misionero, who had been notified that I was already at his mission, arrived during the morning.

April 4. We spent part of yesterday and all of today arranging some of my equipment that could not be attended to at San Javier. In the meantime, the mule drivers, who were not in a good mood because they did not have any blankets, ropes, or fodder for their animals, made adjustments to their loads. Everything was resolved due to the kind generosity of the Reverendo Padre, who repeatedly told me to check and see if there was anything else there that he could offer us. May God reward him.

April 5. I set out for Mission La Purísima accompanied by Reverendo Padre Martínez.[23] We arrived that same morning without incident. As I have indicated, Padre Predicador Fray Juan Crespí had been the first and only minister of our order at that mission. He is another dear friend of mine whom I have known since he was a youth. Before he set out, he left a number of things

---

20. An outbreak of measles later in 1769 would reduce the population of San José de Comondú by 40 percent. See Rodríguez Tomp, *Cautivos de Dios*, 202.
21. The Sunday after Easter.
22. The feast was normally celebrated on March 25.
23. He was the missionary who had arrived the day before.

prepared for me to take on my journey. Don Francisco María de Castro, the *mayordomo* and a soldier of the escort at that mission, was entrusted with delivering the items to me and giving me free access to anything else I might need. We were welcomed by this honorable soldier with the provisions and by painted Indians who had been sent to dance for us with all the solemnity that is possible in places such as this.[24]

April 6. Today and part of yesterday were spent arranging what the mules would be carrying. Among the items were four loads of cookies that had been prepared for the religious to enjoy during the expedition, by order of the Señor Capitán[25] and the careful attention of the Padre. Other provisions included flour, pinole,[26] figs, raisins, and other items that would help make the journey easier. Everything was arranged well by the Padre who, as already has been said, was in charge of Mission San José. My traveling companions and I ended up with many more provisions than I could have dreamed of or imagined. Blessed be God.

On his way to the next mission, Guadalupe, Serra met about ten Indian families. They communicated to him that they were from Mission Guadalupe, but since food was scarce at the mission the resident priest there, Juan Sancho, had told them they had to go out to the hills and find food for themselves. His encounter with them left a deep impression on him, for the devotional song they sang for him convinced him that Christianity had taken root among these people. This filled him with hope for the project he was undertaking farther north. On the other hand, his perception that the Indians were unable to feed themselves after close to half a century of mission life increased his sense that the missionaries' responsibility for the welfare of their flock was going to be a very deep and profound one. Serra did not record who else was with him during this encounter. He only remarked that the pack train was not there because it had been delayed. Therefore, it is not entirely clear what the quality of communication between him and the native people actually was on this occasion, and what they actually told or tried to tell him. But whatever did happen, Serra chose to interpret it as a sign of hope for the future and in a way that increased the importance of the role of the missionary in providing for the livelihood of converted Indians.

---

24. Castro had been appointed comisionado of the mission by Portolá. After the management of mission affairs was given to the Franciscans he stayed on as mayordomo. Serra's unsolicited tribute to him was at odds with the official Fernandino position that the comisionados had ravaged the missions. Serra's remarks here reflected the reality that the comisionados generally did a fine job under extremely difficult circumstances and shows that the Fernandinos were aware of that reality. See Crosby, *Doomed to Fail*, 16–17.
25. The Capitán was Rivera y Moncada.
26. Pinole is parched corn, ground and mixed with sugar and water for a drink. It also refers to the ground seeds of other plants.

FIGURE 18. One of the several agricultural plots developed at Mission San José de Comondú, 1967. Serra passed through here on his way to San Diego in 1769. *Photograph by Harry W. Crosby. Courtesy of Mandeville Special Collections Library, University of California, San Diego.*

April 7. After saying goodbye to the Reverendo Padre from San José, who was staying at the mission a bit longer before returning to his own mission, I set out very early in the morning for the next mission, Guadalupe. I walked all day, only stopping briefly at noon to have a bite to eat and rest for a while. As night was falling, I arrived at the spot called El Cardón, where I slept under the stars. There I met about ten Indian families—men, women, boys, and girls. When I asked them why they were there, they told me with great sadness that they were from Mission Guadalupe. They were not from any of the *rancherías* but rather from the mission village. Because there was not enough food, the Padre had been forced to send them back to the mountains to look for food. Since they were not accustomed to doing this, they were not having much success. It was very hard on them, especially seeing their children suffer and hearing them cry. I felt very sorry for them. It was most unfortunate that the pack train had been delayed and would not arrive there that night, but the Indians were not left without aid. A pot of good *atole*[27] was made for the women and children from some corn that was in a pouch. The process was repeated and the second pot of atole was given to the men, which was of some consolation to them. They were even happier when I told them to go back to their mission because the Padre would be receiving corn by sea on the canoe from Mulegé, by order of Su Ilustrísima Señor Visitador General. I went to lie down and rest and the Indians went off to pray together. They ended by singing a tender hymn about the love of God. The Indians from that mission are reputed to have a talent for singing sweetly. Their reputation is well deserved, for the time I spent listening to them was of great consolation to me.

April 8. I left that place and after a laborious trek through those hills I arrived at around noon at the pueblo of San Miguel, which is a *visita*[28] of that mission. I encountered the same or a greater number of Indians from that mission village. They related the same thing that the other Indians had told me. They were given the same remedy and left alone. A few of them followed me that afternoon when I left for Mission Guadalupe. It was already night when I arrived at the mission, and I was extremely tired. I had arrived again at the farthest point of a journey that I had ever made before in California.

Serra arrived at Mission Guadalupe late on Saturday night, April 8. He remained there until April 14, spending most of his time catching up on correspondence.

---

27. Atole is a cooked mixture of water and ground, dried grains; a staple mission food.
28. A station attached to a mission, which a priest would occasionally visit to administer the sacraments.

The priest of the mission, Juan Sancho, who had been a student of Serra's in Mallorca, gave him a fifteen-year-old boy to be his servant for the rest of the journey. The boy's name was Juan Evangelista Benno. He was named after Benno Ducrue, the Jesuit who had baptized him. Father Juan Ignacio Gastón, the minister of Mission Santa Rosalía de Mulegé, came to bid Serra farewell. Gastón came to the New World with Serra in 1749 and they worked together in the Sierra Gorda. Serra, Sancho, and Gastón spent a considerable amount of time together, not knowing if they would ever see each other again.

> *April 9.* Since it was Sunday, I said Mass and rested, which I really needed to do. The long stretch between the last mission and this one is about thirty leagues. This was the first portion of the journey in which the mules were carrying full loads, and it took them three more days to get here. After arriving, the animals needed to rest and recover their strength. I also had to stop on the 10th, 11th, 12th, and 13th. I used the time to write about a number of matters that were still pending and to respond to various letters. During this time Padre Lector Fray Juan Sancho, a Master of Arts and former professor of philosophy and, later, former lector of theology in his native country, now minister of that mission, graciously helped me find ways to make my trip more comfortable. Because others had told him, he was aware that of all the animals that had passed by here on their way to Monterey, none were as wretched as the ones that had been assigned to me. He therefore rounded up all the animals from his mission so they could transport all the loads as far as the next mission. And that is what happened. This allowed my animals to travel unburdened and rest during the next four days of the journey. It turns out that this favor was very necessary. Even though the animals were not carrying loads, one of them had to be left behind halfway along the route, and another was left at the next mission. The favor extended to us was greater than one might think, if one takes into account that the few animals that were left at that mission after it had been heavily plundered by the captain were old and practically useless. As has been said, the Padre was in dire need of food, and even though he knew he could obtain some at La Purísima, he did not dare send the mules for fear that the trip would finish them off completely.
>
> In addition to the other favors the Padre offered, the one I appreciated the most was his providing me with a young, ladino, Indian page to help me.[29] The boy, who is fifteen years old, knows how to assist at Mass, he can read, and he can serve in many other ways. The Padre provided him with a change

---

29. The boy's Spanish name was Juan Evangelista Benno, and he died at San Diego in February 1770. Serra, *Writings*, 4:343.

of clothing, a leather jacket, boots, etc. He also outfitted him with everything he would need to ride on horseback, such as a saddle, saddlebags, and so forth. The Padre gave him one of the mules that he himself would ride, which made me very happy. The boy and his parents viewed this as a stroke of good fortune, and this pleased everyone. It just so happens that I have known this Reverendo Padre since the days when he was a young, secular student. May God bless him.

April 10. The Padre Ministro of Mission Santa Rosalía de Mulegé came here today to bid me farewell. His mission is situated near the beach along the coast of the Gulf of California and is the only mission not along the route of my journey. This Padre, Fray Juan Ignacio Gastón, was one of the missionary recruits who came with me from Spain. Later, he was my fellow missionary in the Sierra Gorda. I have always been especially fond of him and I am indebted to him. The three of us spent today and the days that followed consoling one another, knowing that we most likely will not see one another again until we meet in Heaven, and that our efforts are for the greater glory of God. Each of us, wherever we may be, will work to win many souls for His Most Holy Majesty. May it be so. Amen.

On April 13 Gastón returned to Mulegé, and then Serra and Sancho together made an inventory of the items at the mission in order to determine what that institution might be able to contribute to the new missions of Alta California. They decided to send some items to Loreto, from where they could eventually be shipped north. On April 14 Serra left Guadalupe for the next mission, San Ignacio. The journey was longer than a day. He caught up with some mule drivers who had left Guadalupe a day before he had, and that night he slept in the open fields.

Serra arrived at Mission San Ignacio early the next morning, April 15. He was received in a very ceremonial fashion by the resident missionary, Juan León de Medinaveitia. The next day, Sunday, April 16, was a Franciscan feast day and Serra rested at San Ignacio. He remained at the mission an additional day to talk with Fray Juan León, who had recently arrived at San Ignacio. León had asked Serra to be reassigned from a lonely and frustrating stint at the northernmost mission, Santa María. Serra undoubtedly comforted him but also probably took the opportunity to size up his ability to continue as a missionary.

April 15. I got an early start and arrived at Mission San Ignacio at around nine o'clock in the morning or maybe a bit later. Last night, the new Padre Ministro of that mission, Padre Predicador Fray Juan León de Medinaveitia, sent dinner to me at the place where I slept. And this morning he came to greet me about a league away from the mission. After we greeted one another, we chatted for a while and walked together, but then he went on ahead of me. Vested in surplice, stole, and cope, the Padre and his Indians received me at the door of the church through which we entered to give thanks to God and praise Him for the gifts He had bestowed upon us.

Serra left San Ignacio on April 18. He traveled for two days and reached the outskirts of Mission Santa Gertrudis. At that mission he met a very lonely and depressed missionary, Dionisio Basterra. The two of them had preached domestic missions together for a number of months in 1763 and 1764 in Puebla and Oaxaca, and this was their first meeting in a year. It was an emotional encounter, and Serra stayed at Santa Gertrudis for six days.

While there he became personally involved in Gálvez's plan to shift Indian populations among various missions. Some of the people at Santa Gertrudis were slated to be removed south to the missions of La Purísima and San José de Comondú. The people resisted that move and indicated that they would end their affiliation with the mission rather than move south. Four months earlier the priest at the nearby mission of San Borja, Fermín Francisco de Lasuén, had reported similar resistance among the people of that mission to Gálvez, and the visitor general had rescinded the order relating to San Borja.[30]

Serra undoubtedly knew of this situation, yet he and Basterra spent a good amount of time going around and urging the Indians to accept the move. He stated in his diary that Gálvez's plan was "very much to my liking." He clearly implied that the Indians were persuaded to move. But he never precisely said that. Rather, he merely stated that things were "in good order."

It is hard to imagine Serra going against what he knew was the opinion of his resident missionaries on this score. In fact, the Santa Gertrudis Indians continued to refuse to move, and Serra had to have known that this would be the most likely outcome. The important thing was that any colonial official in Mexico City who read the diary would learn that Serra had supported the policies of the visitador general.

Basterra's loneliness points to an important aspect of mission life that persisted beyond Serra's own death. Much of the historiography of Alta California has emphasized the tension between the missionaries and the soldiers. That tension was indeed present. But there was another side to the story that is indicated by Basterra's anguish at not having anybody else to converse with. Although

---

30. Lasuén, *Writings*, 1:17–20.

FIGURE 19. *Mules and Indian Boy*, 1816, by Louis Choris. The Indian boy Juan Evangelista Benno, who was entrusted to Serra at Guadalupe in Baja California, was fifteen years old. *Courtesy of The Bancroft Library, University of California, Berkeley.* BANC PIC 1963.002: 1313-FR.

FIGURE 20. El Camino Real midway between Mission Nuestro Señor San Ignacio de Kadakaamán and Santa Gertrudis de Cadacamán, 1967. Serra traveled this path in April 1769. *Photograph by Harry W. Crosby. Courtesy of Mandeville Special Collections Library, University of California, San Diego.*

missionaries and the lower-ranking corporals and soldiers who constituted the mission escort had different roles at the missions, their shared language created a unique bond. Their relationships were most often recorded in the documentary sources when they were in conflict, such as at San Diego in 1773 or Santa Inés in 1824. But in the normal day-to-day workings of any mission, their relationships were undoubtedly more cooperative than confrontational, for they provided each other with a kind of companionship that no one else at the mission complex could provide. In addition, the frontier background of the typical California soldier gave him a set of ranching skills that were sorely needed at the missions. Gaspar de Portolá noticed this soon after he arrived in Baja California. He wrote to the viceroy that the Baja California leather-jacket soldier was "more cowboy than soldier."[31] The frequent presence of soldiers in the mission registers as witnesses to various sacraments is an important indication of how closely priests and soldiers relied on each other.

> *April 20.* I started out very early in the morning and passed by El Rosario shortly after the break of day. When I arrived that morning at Mission Santa Gertrudis, the Indians came out to greet me at the entrance with dancing and joyous gestures. Waiting for me at the door of the church was the Padre Ministro of the mission, Padre Predicador Fray Dionisio Basterra. He was donned with his cope and accompanied by acolytes, carrying a cross, candles, a censer, and holy water. I venerated the holy cross in his hands and incensed it. I sprinkled the people with holy water and we entered the church to give thanks to God, as we should, for all that He has given us.
>
> As soon as the Padre had removed the sacred vestments, we hugged one another for the first time and our eyes filled with tears (my eyes still fill with tears as I write this). We were so overcome that we were unable to speak until we had paid due tribute to this natural human emotion.
>
> The Padre had been deeply depressed for many days because he felt so isolated. Even though there were many Indians in the mission, there were no soldiers or servants (the Capitán had taken them from him for the expedition), not even an interpreter to help him. He had expressed his frustration to me in numerous letters, asking me for help, which I was not able to give, no matter how much I wanted to do so. I tried by every means possible, not just with conciliatory letters but also by speaking to Su Ilustrísima Señor Visitador General, writing to the captain, and speaking with the governor, but it was all to no avail. Through none of these channels was I able to obtain

---

31. Portolá to Croix, March 22, 1768, Archivo General de la Nación, Mexico City, Californias, vol. 76, ex. 14. We thank Lucila León Velazco for bringing this reference to our attention.

a soldier for the escort, with whom the Padre could communicate, which would have been of some relief and comfort to him. Su Ilustrísima told me that the escort had been removed against his express order but that the captain would reinstate it, and if not, then the governor would do it. I wrote back to Su Ilustrísima about this and his reply to me was that he needed soldiers for himself, therefore the governor should replace the escort. I spoke with the governor and when he passed by the Padre's mission, the Padre forcefully explained the situation to the governor while being as courteous as possible. The governor responded that not only could he not provide him with an escort but that he was intent on removing the escort from the next mission, San Borja, which always had at least three soldiers. Taking all of this into consideration, together with the affection I have felt for this young religious since he began his apostolic ministry of missions among the faithful (as my companion on the long pilgrimage along the coast of Oaxaca, navigating the Los Miges river, preaching in the city of Antequera and on our way back to Mexico along the *camino real*), explains the wave of emotion that overcame us when we saw one another again a little more than a year after bidding each other farewell in Loreto.

Heeding his pleas, I remained there for the next five days to give him as much encouragement as possible. The time was not spent idly. We were busy bringing the rancherías[32] together to propose Su Ilustrísima Señor Visitador General's plan. The plan, which was very much to my liking, was that a good number of families, even if it were two hundred, would move to Mission La Purísima de Cadegomó and take up residence there. There are few people at that mission and more than enough food, water, and land upon which they can plant crops for themselves and for the community. And above all, they would be guaranteed three meals a day and appropriate clothing, all of which they always lacked at their mission. Or, perhaps it would be better to say that the lack of food was due to the rugged terrain and the lack or scarcity of land for planting. Those days were spent explaining the plan, answering questions, proposing solutions, and waiting for others who could not arrive as quickly because their rancherías were situated farther away in the mountains. When I left, everything was in good order and the Padre felt consoled.

Serra spent the next two days traveling to Mission San Borja.

---

32. An Indian village or settlement. The Spanish usually used the term to refer to non-Christian Indians. It is now a common term in English for small communities of Alta California Indians.

Figure 21. Mission Santa Gertrudis de Cadacamán. Serra spent a week here in April 1769. Photograph by Fr. Maynard Geiger, OFM. *Courtesy of the Santa Bárbara Mission Archive-Library.*

FIGURE 22. El Cajón, the road Serra termed "tortuous." *Photograph by Harry W. Crosby. Courtesy of Mandeville Special Collections Library, University of California, San Diego.*

April 28. I arrived at Mission San Francisco de Borja in the morning and was received by its minister, Padre Fray Fermín Francisco Lasuén, with the same solemnity as the previous Padre had offered. Even though I was very anxious to be with the members of the expedition who were at the next mission, the special affection I felt for this venerable minister kept me here for the next two days, which for me was very gratifying because of his friendly nature.

April 29. We spent this day discussing matters related to the expedition and the gentile territory. He asked me repeatedly to allow him to join us, seeing that there was so much work to be done at that mission and at the next one. For quite some time the Padre had been filling in during the absence of the mission's own minister.

April 30. Sunday. At the request of the Padre, during the High Mass that I celebrated I preached to those poor neophytes. The Lord inspired my words, as He had done the Sunday before at Mission Santa Gertrudis, where I preached at the request of its Padre Ministro.

Serra spent the next four days traveling to Mission Santa María.

May 5. I set out early along a tortuous road they call El Cajón. I arrived at Mission Santa María de los Angeles around eight-thirty in the morning. There I met with the Señor Gobernador and Padre Fray Miguel de la Campa. Part of the retinue had already gone ahead to Velicatá to water and feed the animals, where there was plenty of grass, unlike here, where there was none. We were so happy to see one another together again, ready to embark on our new pilgrimage to a deserted land populated only by a great number of gentile infidels.

May 6. While the corn and other provisions for this expedition that had arrived in the canoe from San Javier were being brought up from the beach of San Luis Gonzaga (which took about four days to do), the equipment and provisions for the mules were being prepared. In the meantime, Padre Campa, the Señor Gobernador and I, accompanied by the soldier Salgado, who was a member of the escort at that mission, inspected the water supply and the land that had been sown, which would be suitable for planting. We discussed the suitability of the area in terms of pasture and water for the animals and everything else that a mission would need. The area did not seem as bad to us as it had been described. In fact, from what I had been told, I arrived with the intention of moving the mission from this place. But now that I had seen the area with my own eyes, I was totally convinced of just the opposite. And that is what I wrote to Su Ilustrísima Señor Visitador General and to Padre Lector Palóu, who would be in charge of it as president of the missions during my absence.

May 7. Sunday. I said High Mass and preached to those poor neophytes, the poorest I had seen. In the afternoon I went in search of a new route to the beach of San Luis. We found one that was half as long as the one that we had been using up until now. Even though it is a rough trail that crosses rocky hills, the other one is worse because it is longer. Halfway along the trail there is a beautiful watering spot that was unknown until now. There is plenty of grass for the animals to eat along the way. Because we were intrigued by the clever way the Indians caught a beautiful antelope there, we named the spot and the watering hole El Berrendo. I had the idea that the water might be suitable for irrigation, but I saw that it was not possible because there is no flat land at all in that area. Therefore, that spot can only serve as a place to water and pasture the animals. But as we were wandering about we passed by a creek about one-quarter league away from the mission. I will speak of this later.

Serra and the others remained at Santa María for a few days waiting for a pack train as Portolá attended to various details. On the morning of May 11 they set out for Velicatá, the final staging area for the expedition. Since Santa María was the northernmost mission that the Jesuits had established, they were now entering the territory of the Indians who had never been missionized. Serra's excitement at being in "gentile" territory began to mount. Serra used the term "gentile" fairly consistently when he referred to unbaptized Indians. This term derived from the Christian scriptures, especially the writings of Saint Paul, who referred to himself as an apostle to the gentiles (Romans 11:13). At that time the term immediately referred to non-Jewish people. Paul's use of it related to debates in primitive Christianity about whether the fledgling Jesus movement ought to be a movement within Judaism or apart from it. Over time the term came to apply to those who were the object of evangelical activity, as non-Jews were for Paul. This term, and to a lesser extent another religiously derived term, "infidels" (literally, "those without the faith"), were Serra's terms of choice when referring to the non-Christian native peoples of the Californias. He usually avoided another set of words that were common in eighteenth-century Spanish discourse when referring to Indians outside the orbit of empire. These terms included *bárbaros* (barbarians), *salvajes* (savages), and *indios bravos* (wild Indians). In his choice of words, as in so much else, Serra's primary frame of reference was religious.[33]

> *May 12.* We arrived at the place called Pozo de Agua Dulce. Along the way we saw some small rancherías of gentiles and fresh footprints, but nobody, young or old, allowed themselves to be seen by us. Their reticence thwarted the hopes I had of seeing them, of speaking to them, and of cherishing them.

> *May 13.* We also saw a number of small huts and gentile footprints, but no one appeared. This entire stretch of land is much poorer than the other areas of the Californias in terms of providing for the meager sustenance of its inhabitants. From Santa María up to this point, I did not see even one *pitahaya* tree, neither sweet nor sour, only a *cardón* cactus every so often, and an occasional *garambullo*. Most are *cirios*, trees that are totally useless, even for burning.[34]

---

33. Weber, *Bárbaros*, 15–16, 282; Jiménez, "El bárbaro," 369, 391.
34. Technically speaking, the pitahaya and the cirio are not trees but types of cactus. Garambullo is called the "Old Man Cactus," or *Myrtillocactus geometrizans*.

FIGURE 23. Mission San Fernando Rey de España de Velicatá around the turn of the twentieth century. This was the first mission Serra founded. Photograph by G. W. Hendry. *Courtesy of Edward Vernon.*

May 14. Sunday. Pentecost. Early in the morning, one of the small huts that had been erected by members in the first group of the expedition was cleaned and prepared for celebrating Mass. We were told that this very hut had served as a chapel on February 22, the feast day of Santa Margarita de Cortona. This is when Padre Predicador Fray Fermín Lasuén said the first Mass in Velicatá. He came from Santa María to give communion to the Capitán and the soldiers and to hear their confessions so that they could fulfill their Easter duty[35] and prepare for the expedition. It is said that this was the first Mass celebrated in this place. Even though the Jesuit Padre Linck had been there, as stated in his diary, the soldiers who accompanied him said he did not celebrate Mass there.

An altar was prepared in that hut. The soldiers put on their leather jackets and carried their weapons and shields. And with all of the purity of holy poverty I celebrated Mass on that great day. I was comforted knowing that this was the first of many Masses that would continue to be celebrated regularly at the new Mission San Fernando, founded on that day. The soldiers fired their arms repeatedly, which added to the solemnity of the celebration. This

---

35. Catholics were required to go to confession and receive communion at least once during the Easter season.

time, the smoke of gunpowder took the place of burning incense, since we did not have any with us. Since there were no other candles than the one that was burning, which was a small end of a candle I had found, and the candle that belonged to the Padre, only one Mass was said that day. The Padre and the soldiers assisted at Mass in fulfillment of their obligation. We then sang the third version of the *Veni Creator Spiritus*.[36] The gathering was made up of ourselves, the soldiers, and the Indian neophytes who were accompanying us. Not a single gentile appeared. Perhaps they were frightened by the loud noise from the firearms.

Serra and Fray Miguel de la Campa spent the rest of the day scouting the terrain and noting the location of sources of water. The following day was quite emotional because Serra encountered, for the first time in his life, a group of unbaptized and unmissionized Indians. Serra reported that he was overcome by intense feeling. In his diary he employed images of the Garden of Eden in the book of Genesis, indicating his belief that the missionary activity on which he was about to embark involved turning the clock back and re-creating the world anew. This encounter contained two elements that would characterize many of the interactions between the native and Spanish people on this journey. First, Serra remarked that the Spanish had no stomach for the food the native people offered them. On a number of occasions during the journey, the reverse was also discovered to be true, for the native people had no stomach for the food the Europeans offered (for instance, June 8, 10, 26, and 27). Second, the first speech Serra gave to the Cochimí who approached him urged them to respect the property of others, especially the cattle of the mission. He would remark on many other occasions before he arrived at San Diego how the native people would seek to appropriate the possessions of the Spanish. This was especially true, he thought, of the Kumeyaay (for instance, June 26 and 27). Also, Serra began to realize on this journey the intensity of the gap that separated the indigenous and Spanish/Catholic worldviews. As a Catholic missionary and loyal Spaniard, Serra never doubted for an instant that his worldview was objectively superior to the indigenous worldviews. But this trip helped him begin to grasp that an effective missionary strategy would have to acknowledge the existence of the spaces between the various cultures. A successful strategy would have to be tentative and provisional, and its results would be gradual.

---

36. The Spanish we have translated as "third version" is *de tercera*. According to Professor Craig Russell, this may well refer to a unique musical arrangement of this hymn which was reserved for special occasions. Since this was the first mission that Serra had ever founded, this day was a deeply extraordinary one for him. We thank Professor Russell for his generous assistance in helping us understand this part of Serra's diary.

May 15. Since candles had already arrived on the pack train, the two priests and I celebrated Mass in succession. For me, it was a day of great consolation. Soon after the Masses were said, while I was quiet with my thoughts in the small hut that was my dwelling place, they alerted me that the gentiles were approaching and that they were close. I praised God, kissed the ground, and gave thanks to Our Lord for granting me this opportunity to be among the gentiles in their land, after longing for this for so many years. I quickly went out and there I saw twelve gentiles, all of them grown men, with the exception of one boy who was about ten years old and the other who was about sixteen years old. I saw what I could hardly believe when I would read about it or when I would be told about it, which was that the gentiles were totally naked, like Adam in paradise before the fall. That is how they went about and that is how they presented themselves to us. We interacted with them for quite some time and not once did they show any sign of embarrassment seeing that we were clothed and they were not. I placed my hands on the head of each gentile, one at a time, as a sign of affection. I filled both of their hands with overripe figs, which they immediately began to eat. We received a gift from them and with signs we showed them how much we appreciated it. The gift was a net full of roasted mescal and four beautiful fish, which were more than medium size. Unfortunately, the poor people had not thought to clean the fish beforehand or even to salt them, so the cook said the fish were not any good. Padre Campa also gave them his raisins, the Señor Gobernador gave them tobacco leaves, and all the soldiers received them warmly and gave them food to eat. With the help of the interpreter, I let them know that a Padre was already there, in that very spot, and his name was Padre Miguel. I told them that they and other people they know should come and visit him. They also should let it be known that there is no reason for fear or mistrust. The Padre would be their friend and those men, the soldiers who were standing next to the Padre, would be very good to them and would cause them no harm. I told them that if they were in need, they should not steal the cattle that were grazing in the fields but rather come and ask the Padre and he would always give them what he could. It seems that they understood very well what I had explained and they made signs to that effect, all of which led me to believe that it would not be long before they allowed themselves to be gathered together in the apostolic and evangelical net. And this is what happened, as I shall explain later. According to the Señor Gobernador, the person who came with them as their chief held that position by acclaim or

Figure 24. Cattle in the *tinaja* at Rancho del Zorrillo, 1980. As Serra went north, he was careful to note the location of sources of water, which would be indispensable for future missions. *Photograph by Harry W. Crosby. Courtesy of Mandeville Special Collections Library, University of California, San Diego.*

will of his people, but from this day forward, he was officially appointing him chief in the name of the king.

That same afternoon, although I was sad to have to leave the Indians and their new minister who would be staying there, I set out with the Señor Gobernador and his retinue. After traveling for three hours or so, we stopped at a spot halfway between the mission and our next stop. There was some grass for the animals, but no water.

May 16. After three more hours of travel we arrived at the place called San Juan de Dios. It is a pleasant spot with plenty of water and pasture, willows, tule, and a bright sky. Sergeant Don Francisco Ortega and some soldiers were here for a number of days with many of the animals that would be following us along the road. This was a perfect spot for the animals to rest and recover. It was a day of joy because all of us who were going to travel together on the expedition were finally together, except for a few Indians from San Borja who did not arrive until two days later. In order to reach this creek and this spot, it is necessary to travel down a very steep hill. But since the path is well trodden, it does not pose any real difficulties.

As Portolá had feared, Serra's leg now began to cause him great pain. Serra began to worry that he would have to be carried on a stretcher, and he was not sure the governor would let him continue. But the next day he received word from Velicatá that cheered him up greatly. The Indians there were seeking baptism. He interpreted this news in the context of the stories Llinás had brought to the Americas about Sor María de Jesús de Ágreda. The possibility that Serra himself might now be participating in the fulfillment of Sor María's words thrilled him. A few months shy of his fifty-sixth birthday, he felt that he had finally encountered his life's true purpose. Yet there was another level to all of this activity that Serra only dimly understood. The Jesuits had established a presence in the territory of the northern Cochimí by 1762, when they founded Mission San Francisco de Borja. They solidified that presence five years later, with the establishment of Mission Santa María de los Angeles de Cabujakaamung. As Serra noted in his diary, Jesuit explorer Wenceslaus Linck had visited Velicatá itself in 1766. Linck stated that the indigenous people there, after some hesitation, welcomed them and shared some seeds with them. Linck baptized an infant girl, who soon died. A day later he baptized an old man and placed a cross around his neck. According to Linck, the man promised that he would never remove it. It appears that this group of people had already decided on their own, three years before Serra met them, that they would seek to accommodate themselves in some fashion to the newcomers.[37]

> *May 17.* I said Mass there even though I was already having a hard time standing because my left foot was very inflamed. I have been suffering for over a year now. Now the wounds are inflamed and the swelling has gone halfway up my leg. This is why I was lying in bed during the time we stayed here. I feared that before long I would have to follow behind the expedition on a stretcher. In the meantime, the Señor Gobernador and his people went about arranging the loads and determining the shortcuts. They also allowed the animals that had arrived last time to rest and recover in this place, which provided what was needed.
>
> *May 18.* We continued to stay here. I was not able to celebrate Mass due to what I have already described. However, I took great comfort from the letter

---

37. Linck, *Linck's Diary*, 58–59; Lazcano Sahagún, *La primera entrada*, 205; Sales, *Observations on California*, 63; Crosby, *Antigua California*, 191, 348–49.

I received from Velicatá, in which the Padre from that mission informed me that the same gentile chief whom I had seen and warmly received, along with eleven of his people, had already gone to the mission with a larger number of men, women, boys, and girls—a total of forty-four people. They all asked to be baptized. On that very same day they began to receive instruction. I was overjoyed and wrote back to the Padre, congratulating him a thousand times over. Because the chief was such an important person, I begged the Padre to baptize him first and to give him the name Francisco in honor of Nuestro Padre Seráfico. I piously believe that such a happy event has come to pass as fulfillment of the promise that the Lord Our God made to him during these last days which, according to what the Venerable Madre María de Jesús de Ágreda affirms, at the mere sight of his sons, the gentiles will convert to our Holy Catholic Faith. And I believe that it is worth mentioning that once this chief from Velicatá becomes a Christian, he, his family, and his ranchería deserve to always be treated well, because from the moment the Spaniards set foot on his land, he began to visit them, give them gifts, and serve them. He was able to interact with them and gained their trust. This is what he did with the first group of our expedition. Sergeant Ortega and some soldiers arrived after the first group had left and before we had arrived. Some Indians immediately came to welcome them, and the chief arrived three days later. He explained that he would have come sooner but he was very far away on the opposite coast. When his people informed him of the arrival of the Spaniards, he immediately headed back, traveling as fast as he could for two days and one night to arrive as quickly as possible. The chief gave Ortega two *tercios* of mezcal. He also offered to send some of his people out to fish and to help in any way they could. He treated us in the same way that I have described. And above all, he asked to be the first person of such a large group to receive Holy Baptism. And he promised to bring more people. May God make him a saint. Amen.

May 19. I awoke feeling much better and celebrated Mass. The rest of the day was spent arranging things for our departure so we could head out the next day. The Indians from Mission San Borja arrived. They were to follow behind us, together with the Indians from Missions Santa Gertrudis and Santa María who were already here.

Because of rain and threatening clouds, the expedition did not travel on May 20.

FIGURE 25. This woodcut of Sor María de Jesús de Ágreda preaching to the Indians was done in Mexico in 1730 to accompany the publication of Benavides's letter of 1631. *Courtesy Catholic Archives of Texas, Austin.*

May 21. Sunday and feast of the Holy Trinity. After I celebrated Mass, for which everyone was present, I spoke briefly about the need for all of us to conduct ourselves properly during the journey. I emphasized that the main objective was the greater honor and glory of God. I blessed them in the name of the Father, and of the Son, and of the Holy Ghost, whose trinity of persons in unity of divine nature we were celebrating on that day. And in the name of God, three in one, everything was in order and we began our march. We left this place and headed in a westerly direction. But before long, we encountered a high mountain that forced us to change course and head north. We followed this path and from the top of a hill they pointed out to us a large number of gentiles who had caught sight of us from the right side of a spot down below. Even though two neophytes went down to offer them our friendship, they went away, leaving behind a bow and a good handful of arrows that our neophytes brought back to us. I very much admired the skillful craftsmanship of their flints and the variety of vivid colors used to paint the shafts.

We followed a river with trees, pasture, and water. After traveling for three hours or so, the Indian guides said that it was necessary to stop because we would have to travel very far to find any more water. Later we discovered that this was not the case, but in the meantime we had to stay there.

At the place where we stopped we came upon an old gentile man. He was as naked as the rest. We treated him kindly and gave him some food to eat. He told us that many of his people lived nearby. He said that awhile ago a Padre passed by there with many people. Based on his description, the Padre probably was a Jesuit. When the other Indians saw them, they fled, as they did now. He, however, would never flee. It was obvious that this old man was not intimidated by anybody. While he was conversing with us, he squatted down in front of the whole group and quickly began to relieve himself, unencumbered by having to remove any clothes since he was not wearing any. After he finished, he continued conversing with us just as calm as can be and just as relieved. The interpreters asked him if he wanted to become a Christian and he said yes. When they asked him when, he said, "Now," and since the Padre was already there, he could baptize him that afternoon. They told him that first he needed to be taught the law of God. He responded that they should teach it to him. And so the interpreter began to give him religious instruction, spending most of the afternoon on it. The old man was very eager to learn. A messenger had traveled with us up to this point. He was supposed to return to Velicatá the next day, and did so. I arranged for the old man to go with the messenger so that as soon as he had finished his religious instruction, the Padre could baptize him. I do not know how it all ended, but I do know that the good old man was happy and would surely tell his people how well we had treated him.

Serra spent the early morning of May 22 writing letters that were carried back by a courier. He set out at eight o'clock in the morning and spent an uneventful day on the trail. He ended his diary account that day by writing, "We saw footprints made by gentiles, but did not see the actual people."

> *May 23.* We continued our journey. We left the river and headed toward the mountains that would take us to the opposite coast. According to my calculations, we traveled four and one-half hours today. We spent more than half the time going up and down a rocky and difficult road. The rest of the time was spent traveling through some flat plains. There were clear indications that the first group of the expedition had stopped here, so we did the same thing. Seeing that there was no water, we dug a hole in the ground and the animals drank from it. A short while later we learned that we could have avoided all that work because a league or so away we found running water and good pasture. We named this large area "Santiago" since this was the feast day celebrating when Santiago appeared to the Spaniards and offered to help them.[38]

The next day and a half was spent traveling. By this time the group was about fifty miles from Velicatá. On the afternoon of May 25 they spotted some Indians and tried to make contact. That effort was unsuccessful, but the next day the Baja California Indians on the expedition were able to bring one Indian into the camp. Serra ended his narrative of the events by saying that the expedition gave the man many gifts so that he would tell his people "how kindly we had treated him." But this individual had been brought into camp tied up with rope, and he was resisting so vigorously that he had to be dragged along the ground, which tore up his thighs and knees. Finally, he was forced to kneel before Serra. Even though no one really understood his language, the Spanish thought he was confessing to planning an attack on them. So they made a show of graciously forgiving him, although it is not at all clear how he interpreted their gestures and signs. It is hard to imagine that, when he got back to his people, his central message to them revolved around the kindness of the strangers.

> *May 25.* Shortly after, our attention was drawn to a very tall and leafy tree, something we had not seen outside the missions. As I got closer to the tree, I

---

38. Saint James was said to have appeared to help on May 23, 844, at the legendary battle of Clavijo.

saw that it was a poplar. I was quite struck by this, so we decided to call this place "El Alamo Solo."[39] From this point on, the terrain began to be more pleasing, with a number of tall and leafy trees (but not as leafy as the poplar.) The branches and leaves of these trees are similar to a cypress. There were other trees of the same height and different types of flowers. It seemed as if we were in a different land. This afternoon, three gentiles appeared on a small hill that we could see from where we had stopped. We sent two Indians from our group to go and invite the gentiles to come down because we were their friends. But as soon as the gentiles saw them approach, they fled and nothing else happened.

May 26. We stayed here because it was an excellent place for the animals to rest and recover their strength. Over the last few days they had been overworked. Two gentiles appeared at the same hill and they were watching us closely. Our Indians were better prepared today than yesterday and went after the gentiles with caution so they would not escape. However, one gentile did slip through their hands, but they were able to tie up the other one tightly with a rope halter. It was necessary to do this because he continued to fight to keep them from bringing him to us. He put up such a hard fight that they had to drag him along the ground, which tore up his thighs and knees very badly. But they were finally able to bring him back. They brought him before me, and after making him kneel, I placed my hands on his head and prayed the Gospel of San Juan. I made the sign of the cross and untied him. He was extremely frightened and very upset. We took him to the Señor Gobernador's tent to try and raise his spirits. He was a robust young man, probably about twenty years old. When he was asked what his name was, he said "Axajui." The men wanted to know what that word meant in his language, but it was too much to ask to try and find a linguist among these people, so they decided that "Axajui" was his name and that was the end of it.

We placed overly ripe figs, meat, and tortillas in front of our Axajui so that he would eat. He ate some, but only a little at a time, since he was so upset. He grabbed a fistful of dirt and brought it up to his mouth, saying, "Pinole." We wondered how he knew about pinole. We gave him a jug of powdered pinole and he ate some of it. He did not seem to like it. Another jug of pinole was prepared for him, but this time it was mixed with water. He ate it all up. All his talking seemed to be his way of trying to apologize for having spied on us from the top of the small hill both yesterday and today. By admitting this

---

39. The Lone Poplar.

venial sin he committed a mortal one. He said that his chief had sent him to spy on us. The chief and his ranchería, along with four other rancherías that would join his, were all in agreement that they would hide behind some rocks and wait for us to head back out on our journey. Then they would come out and kill the Padre and his group, even if it was a large number of people. We forgave him his murderous intentions and gave him many gifts so he could go back and tell his people how kindly we had treated him and also say what we had asked him to do, which was for all of them to come and meet us. Nobody came, even though we did see a few of them on that same hill. He was naked like the rest of them. All he had were his bow and arrows, which we returned to him. His long hair was tied back with a small cord made of blue wool. It was nicely made. We could not imagine where it came from.

The expedition traveled the next day to a place called La Cieneguilla. Here they left Linck's path, for from this spot the Jesuit had headed east toward the San Felipe desert. The Portolá expedition, following the path of Rivera y Moncada, headed north. After they departed from La Cieneguilla the expedition left the territory of the Cochimí and entered the land of the Kiliwa people. The expedition noted that the clothing worn by the people they were now encountering, especially the women, differed from that of the Indians they had previously met. It was more modest by their standards. As the expedition continued north, Serra's enthusiasm, which had burst forth at Velicatá, persisted. On May 28, they had two encounters with different groups of Indians. The first one, at La Cieneguilla, was very difficult and involved gunfire. The Indians tried to block their way, and two soldiers had to fire their weapons to get them to disperse. However, the second encounter, about seven miles past La Cieneguilla, was viewed by Serra as a much friendlier encounter. This group produced a staged battle in front of the Spaniards and then insisted that they would accompany the expedition out of their territory. Serra interpreted these actions simply as entertainment and friendliness, although they were likely fraught with much greater meaning than he realized. But Serra persisted in his growing enthusiasm. Indeed, he believed that God had sent him the second group of Indians so that his spirits would not flag.[40] And on the very next day, when a large group of native people tried to obstruct the progress of the expedition, Serra similarly interpreted their actions as motivated by happiness and their shouts as enthusiastic greetings. He believed the people were saying how much they would welcome a mission among them. Portolá and the soldiers saw things differently and once again had to fire a warning shot to get the group to disperse. And, for the rest of the time

---

40. Lazcano Sahagún, *Diario de fray Junípero Serra*, 71–72, note 60; Crosby, *Gateway to Alta California*, 69.

the expedition was in Kiliwa territory, it encountered very few Indians. Serra's enthusiasm does not appear to have been shared by the Indians themselves or by his military companions on the expedition.

> *May 28.* Sunday. Before we left, some gentiles approached us. These were the same gentiles that the soldiers, who were keeping watch over the animals, had seen. Nearby they had about twelve small huts, which were placed close together. Our neophytes immediately set out to bring them back to us. A huge shouting match erupted between the gentiles and the neophytes. Several times the gentiles threatened to attack the neophytes no matter how much our Indians spoke about peace. In the end, they brought them back, but the gentiles were so angry that there was no way to calm them down. It was time to say Mass. The soldiers formed a circle to hear Mass and placed the gentiles in the middle of the circle for the duration of the Mass. After Mass had ended, another large number of gentiles arrived and the shouting continued. The first group, which consisted of four gentiles, was given food before and after Mass. They all took out their pipes and began to smoke. After we told them they could leave on good terms, they joined the others and soon there were more than forty of them. There was no way to quiet them down or separate them. According to our interpreters, the gentiles were saying that we should not go on ahead but rather go back and that they wanted to fight. We spent a long and difficult time trying to get them to leave peacefully, but it was to no avail. We feared that there would be blood shed. The Señor Gobernador ordered four soldiers, armed and mounted on horseback, to line up as a means of forcing the Indians to retreat. They refused to leave, even with this tactic. One soldier then fired a shot into the air, and shortly after, another soldier did the same. The Indians then began to flee, and our men loaded up the pack train so we could continue on our journey.
>
> We left at ten o'clock in the morning. We traveled for four hours during the hottest time of the day, and the trip was unbearable. A half an hour or less after leaving, we went down to a river where there was much vegetation but no water. It was situated in a beautiful plain about a quarter of a league wide and more than two leagues long. The soil was good. The first portion of the plain has good soil, but the second portion is composed of rather fine sand. In the area with good soil, one can see much vegetation that starts from the base of the hills and heads toward the opposite coast. One of our neophytes told us that there was plenty of water there. If that is the case, we all deemed this beautiful place the site for a mission, Santa Humiliana. After that,

the mountains get closer together. We followed a dry riverbed between the mountains and arrived at a place with running water and good pasture, which the animals were able to enjoy.

It seems that the gentiles from that morning wanted to prove that what Axajui had said on May 26 was true, not only what was said but also what was done. For when we left the place where we had stopped today, the gentiles were following us through the hills of the opposite coast. During the whole day's journey we saw a large throng of them following us continuously through the hills. But for them to catch up with us meant that they had to go down to the plain, which I have already described. Since this plain was wide, we were in no apparent danger. But the situation changed when the mountains were closer together and we had to travel through a narrow pass. That is when all the soldiers put on their leather jackets. They and the mule drivers were armed and ready to fight. Everyone kept their eyes peeled but the enemy never appeared. We suspected that these Indians might be from the Bay of San Quintín. Admiral Cabrera Bueno describes these Indians in his *Navegación especulativa y práctica*, part 5, chapter 4, as being warlike and daring.[41] The Bay of San Quintín is located at 32 degrees on the opposite coast. But in the end, we did not see these Indians again.

In order to temper the distress we had experienced with the Indians, God quickly sent us other Indians who behaved very differently. About a league away from our stopping place, twelve new gentiles joined our group. They were very pleasant. They said they would show us how to get to the place where we were going to stop. And that is what they did. Their behavior was quite discreet, for as soon as we arrived, they retired to a hillside nearby and sat there motionless. It seems they did not want to hamper the process of unloading the pack train. As soon as we were finished, I had my page and an interpreter take them a gift of figs and meat along with a message inviting them to come and greet us without fear, for we were their friends. They responded with gestures of appreciation but indicated that they would not be able to come and see us until they had received the gift they wanted to give to us. They had already requested it from their ranchería, which was nearby. It so happened that after we had eaten and rested, the Indians came down to where we were with their nets filled with cooked mezcals[42] and with their

---

41. José González Cabrera Bueno's *Navegación especulativa, y práctica* was published in Manila in 1734. The descriptions of California in this volume were generally taken from the accounts of Vizcaíno's chief pilot, Francisco de Bolaños.
42. A Náhuatl word that means "cooked agave."

weapons, which they placed on the ground. They began to explain to us how they used each of the weapons in battle. They acted out the parts of attacker and victim so cleverly and vividly, which kept us quite entertained for a good while. We did not need the interpreters to explain what the Indians wanted to tell us in this regard. Up to this point, there were no women at all among the gentiles. I had not seen any gentile women, and for the moment, I did not wish to see any. But two women appeared during these festivities. They were chattering away inanely as women are known to do. When I saw that they were modestly covered up, which was comparable to the modesty displayed by the Christian women at the missions, I was not bothered by their arrival. They said that the youngest woman was the wife of the chief who was there. She was carrying the gift on her head, which was something I had never seen before. It was a large torte made of dough that was filled with thick fibers. When I started to place my hands on her head, she put the torte in my hands. Then she and her husband began to explain to me how to eat it. The older woman also shouted when she spoke, even more so than the others. The chief and his companions continued with the explanation. We were all so engrossed in what was being said that we did not notice that the women had left. It was not until a short while later, when we inquired where they were so we could return the favor, that we realized they had already left. May God bless them. We gave the chief a gift for his wife. Everyone else also received a gift. We said they could now leave and they obediently and happily did so. But they said they wanted to continue traveling with us and follow us as friends.

May 29. We left this place and traveled for three full hours. It was a hard journey up and down steep grades. The hillsides, all composed of soil, were steep and difficult. We finally were able to get down to the plain. It was well worth the effort because it was an excellent spot, unlike any other we had seen until now.

At the beginning of today's journey, we found in a small plain the huts belonging to our gentile friends from yesterday afternoon. The huts were very well constructed, just like those we have frequently seen during these last few days of traveling. And from the hillside that paralleled the plain, our Indian friends from yesterday, accompanied by even more Indians, careened down upon us, fulfilling the promise they had made to accompany us. Their actions were similar to those of yesterday. They were running, shouting, and gleefully crossing in front of our path. Since the road was in poor condition and narrow, the Indians were creating an uproar and doing more harm than good. The animals were frightened and were in danger of falling off a cliff. The Indians were told to quiet down and that we were pleased with their gestures of friendship, which they reinforced by bringing more mescals for the neophytes who were on foot. But with all the ruckus, they paid no attention and understood nothing of what we were saying, so nothing changed. The situation went from bad to worse, especially the condition of the road. We summoned their chief and explained the situation to him. He tried to quiet them down and bring them all together, but he was only partially successful. Finally, the Señor Gobernador, who had gone on ahead, turned back. He exerted his influence. But seeing that it was to no avail, he found it necessary to fire his shotgun into the air in the direction of the Indians, who became frightened and stopped. That put an end to the racket. I feared, however, that this radical action would leave the Indians doubting the sincerity of our love for them. Their love for us was confirmed when three gentiles appeared before us shortly after we had arrived at this place. They came unarmed, with only a pipe in their hands. They told us that a messenger from the last place where we had stopped had come to tell them that we came in peace and for them to welcome us because we were good people. And that is what they did. May God make these Indians, and the others we met, Christians as quickly as possible. I firmly believe this would be the case if a mission were to be established here right away because this place is ripe for it.

May 30 was the feast of San Fernando, patron of the colegio apostólico in Mexico City and of the mission Serra had just founded in Velicatá. He reported that he said Mass that morning "with much consolation."

May 30. There are more poplars and trees of all sorts here than in any mission. The land is flat. There is green pasture and water running on the surface of the land. Some plots of land are soaked in water; some look like wheat fields amid tall green grass; others look like some type of bean field. And if one did not know any better, one would think this was a mission that has developed as the result of many years of work. The lush foliage of this place forms a semi-circle, and there is a rock-ribbed hill in the middle on which the mission or pueblo could be built. There it would be protected from the dampness and would have a panoramic view of that beautiful area. If it is possible for the mission at Velicatá to keep the name San Fernando, separate from Santa María, then I would be happy for this place to be called San Pedro Regalado. But for now, I will only name this place San Fernando, whose feast day is today. May it be God's will that we see this place populated soon.

When it is time to move the cattle currently kept at Velicatá and intended for the new missions, if they arrive at this place alive, they could stay here and take time to regain their strength before moving on.

The march on May 31 traversed a series of hills. Serra recounted meeting a group of Indians, the first they had seen in a couple of days. But this encounter was exceptional, for they met no more Indians while they went through Kiliwa territory. Most likely, the two consecutive days (May 28 and 29) of Spanish gunfire suppressed the willingness of these people to meet the expedition.

> *May 31.* We stopped at a small, high plain that offered us at its edge an abundance of water and grass where the animals were able to wander and feed. In the middle of the afternoon, some gentiles appeared. Two arrived first and then up to eleven. They were very gentle and humble. We welcomed them warmly and gave them food to eat. And when they took out their roughly made pipes, we gave them tobacco. After a good while they left, very happy. And I praised God for allowing me to encounter such humble creatures for whom there appear to be no obstacles that would prevent them from receiving the light of the Holy Gospel.

The expedition marched steadily during the first five days of June without encountering any native peoples. On June 2 they came across the grave of Manuel Valladares, an Indian from Mission San Ignacio who had died during the Rivera y Moncada expedition. The grave had been disturbed, so they gathered what bones they could and performed a reburial. Toward the end of this series of marches, they entered Pai-Pai territory. On June 6, an Indian came into their camp and told them that the first group of the expedition had come this way and that the expedition was camped farther north at a spot close to the ocean. This was true, for the two vessels had arrived at San Diego in April and the first leg of the land party had reached there in the middle of May. Serra also understood the Indian to report that the priests in San Diego were already baptizing people. That was not accurate, but his willingness to credit it demonstrated the depth of his faith that California's native people were anxious for Christianity. The news energized Serra, although its major significance, underappreciated at the time, was in indicating the effectiveness of the communication networks among the native peoples of northern Baja California.

> *June 6.* Shortly after we arrived, we noticed that a few gentiles were on a small hill nearby keeping an eye on us. Then one of them started to come toward us, leaving the rest behind to keep watch. We received him with much

affection and gave him a gift. He stayed with us all afternoon and night. He told us that the first group of the expedition had come this way and that some of the Indians from here had accompanied the expedition as it continued on. He said that the group was now camped at a spot close to the ocean.[43] At that place the Padre was handing out rosaries and clothing to the Indians and was pouring water on their heads. The Indians from that place had sent messengers to the Indians here, to see if they wanted to take part in any of this. This news was of great consolation to me and to the others as well. We asked him how far that place was from here and he said it was still far away. May God allow us to arrive there. Amen.

Even though today I am praying on the eighth day after the feast of San Fernando, who seems to have wanted to spread out his blessings over these eight days, we have named this place "Los Santos Gorgomienses" among whom San Norberto has two sons and Nuestro Padre San Francisco has eleven.[44]

On June 7 the expedition remained where it was to give the animals some rest.

June 8. Today three gentiles came to see us without being invited. They were unarmed, which was a great sign that they have confidence in our friendship. But we have not been able to persuade them to eat any of the food we have put before them. Nor were we able to get any information we wanted from them regarding the route ahead and how to proceed.

They left on the morning of June 9 and marched for four hours. On June 10, they encountered a man they called "The Dancer." Serra told the story in a whimsical, almost bemused fashion: the man said that he had to dance around the food he was offered before he could eat it, and then, after they had placed some food in the center, he widened his circle of dancing and even began to dance around their provisions and animals. Was he planning to eat everything the expedition had? And then, after having done all of this, he inexplicably left. Maybe someone had inadvertently said something untoward to him, Serra thought.

But on April 16, in this same territory, the first leg of the expedition had captured an old man who said he was some sort of shaman. José Cañizares, who was on that first leg of the expedition and kept his own diary, described him as "arrogant," and said that his actions disgusted the members of the expedition. Another man with him became so angry that "he yanked out bits of his hair." Juan

---
43. The Rivera y Moncada expedition had arrived at San Diego on May 14.
44. "The Holy Martyrs of Gorkum." This was a group of nineteen Dutch Catholic clergy who were executed on July 9, 1572, in the town of Gorkum in Holland.

Crespí stated that he did not know "how this [old] man might be distinguished from the ugliest demon ever depicted . . . for a single glance at his face with its bands of white, yellow, and red paint was enough to horrify one." Since the Baja California Indians accompanying the expedition did not understand the man, communication proved impossible. Rivera sent him away with some beads and ribbons, and he and those with him "left well pleased." The Spanish thought that the gifts of beads were establishing a generalized reciprocity with the Indians. It is not clear that the native people shared this understanding.[45]

Such sketchy descriptions make it difficult to ascertain what actually occurred, let alone its significance to the native peoples involved. It seems reasonably clear, however, that the Spanish had captured and insulted one of the group's leading figures, and it is doubtful that they actually "left well pleased." There is no reason to assume that the old man who visited Serra was the same person who had been captured by Rivera, but it seems that, whoever he was, the object of his dancing was perhaps to purify the land that had been contaminated by this new group of interlopers, to engage in a ritual that would protect the people from them, or to inflict some kind of damage upon them. For the Pai-Pai as for many other indigenous groups in the Californias, song and dance were an integral part of the way in which the core identity of the group was expressed. Whatever the man was doing, he was hardly dancing for food.[46]

> *June 9.* In terms of water, I only know that it can be found in a few places. What we have drunk in this area is very good. Of the two days that we spent in the last place, if we had spent one of those days here, we would have had the opportunity to see what type of irrigation these watering places could offer. But since there is no time to examine this, those who come to found the mission will see this copious field of gentiles. It seems that the only thing needed is workers, since all signs indicate they are ready for reaping. *Rogate ergo Dómium mesis,* etc.[47] In the language of the gentiles, this place is called Matiropi. We named it Santa Margarita.
>
> *June 10.* During the morning, while preparations were under way for our departure, one of the gentiles who allowed themselves to be seen from a small hill nearby approached us with a club in one hand and a rattle in the other. After welcoming him with much affection, we tried to get him to eat without

---

45. Cañizares, "Putting a Lid on California," 268–69; Crespí, *A Description of Distant Roads,* 211; O'Neil, "The Spanish Use of Glass Beads as Pacification Gifts."
46. Owen, Walstrom, and Michelsen, "Musical Culture and Ethnic Solidarity."
47. The Latin text means "Pray therefore the Lord of the harvest." It is found in Matthew 9:38 and Luke 10:2. In both cases Jesus says, "The harvest is plentiful but the laborers are few. Pray therefore the Lord of the harvest to send out workers into the harvest."

being afraid. It is a long story how we tried everything imaginable to get him to eat. First we would eat some of what we had given him so he would not be afraid, but it was to no avail. He did swallow a few gulps of pinole as if forced to do so and then vomited it all up. He finally explained his behavior, saying that he was the dancer of that region and that he could not eat anything until he had performed a ceremonial dance around the food. He said that if we wanted to give him something, we should put it on the ground and allow him to do his dance. Then he would eat. We gave him permission and freedom to proceed. He then began to dance and sing around the offerings. While this was going on, a soldier would come with a piece of tortilla, sugar, or meat and try to put it in the Indian's mouth, but he always resisted, making signs that they should put the food on the pile so he could dance around it. The pile of food seemed small to the Indian, so after asking us for permission he danced around all of our provisions and animals. It seemed he was preparing himself to eat everything we had brought. After that he was very happy and said he was no longer afraid. He ate and began to answer very frankly the questions from our interpreters. He told us we were four and one-half days away from arriving in San Diego. There we would find the other Padre and his people who days previously had passed through this area whose name I mentioned above [Matiropi]. He told us that if we wanted, he could accompany us up to that place [San Diego]. And, if it suited him, he would stay there, and if not, he would return to this area, but under the condition that we allow him to dance along the entire route. We were very pleased to agree to his terms and I had high hopes of baptizing him there [San Diego]. From that point on we referred to him only as Baylón, saving the name Pascual for the day of his holy baptism.[48] But all was lost. When we were ready to leave this place, someone from our group said something to him, which he misunderstood. He ran off to the hill as if he were a deer, leaving everything we had given him behind, except for the club and rattle he had brought.

The expedition continued north for the next five days without encountering any other local inhabitants. But a number of the Baja California Indians on the expedition decided to leave on June 14. Serra's response was a generous assessment of their unsung contributions to the expedition.

June 14. We got up early because we really needed to find water. After traveling for two hours we arrived at the first watering place where the animals

---

48. Saint Pascal Baylón was a sixteenth-century Franciscan mystic. *Baylón* (*bailón*) means "dancer," and Serra was making a play on words here.

(Left) FIGURE 26. "Women and Men of California," from Miguel Venegas, *Noticia de la California* (1757). *Courtesy of The Bancroft Library, University of California, Berkeley.* BANC MSS M-M 1733.

(Right) FIGURE 27. "The Manner of Caring for the Sick in California" and "Sorcerers of California," from Miguel Venegas, *Noticia de la California* (1757). Serra encountered a good number of indigenous folkways and cultural manifestations as he went north through Baja California, but he was not always able to understand their full significance. *Courtesy of The Bancroft Library, University of California, Berkeley.* BANC MSS M-M 1733.

were able to quench their intense thirst to their heart's delight. The road wound through continuous canyons and hillsides of pure soil, like all the hills we have seen, not only today but everywhere we have been. There are so many that we have lost count. Shortly before arriving at our stopping place, one of our mule drivers happened upon a silver mine that everyone says is very rich. May it bring them good fortune. In addition to water, this place abounds with beautiful pasture and plentiful shade from the abundance of trees—enough for a fine ranch. We called this place San Basilio.

We talked about heading on to our next stopping place today since it was supposed to be close by, but we thought it over carefully and decided to stay here all day so the animals could rest. After midday and after everyone had eaten, nine of the Indians who had accompanied us up to this point abruptly deserted us. Six of them were from Mission San Borja and the other three were from Santa María de los Angeles. We realized they were missing in the middle of the afternoon and sent men out to find them. But no trace of them was to be found. We questioned the Indians who had remained as to what would have prompted such unexpected behavior from the others, considering that we gave them food, treated them well, and they had always appeared to be happy. The Indians responded that they did not know. They could only surmise that since we were getting close to San Diego, the others may have feared that they would be forced to stay there without the possibility of returning to their missions. May God bless them, not only for how well they have served us but also for how much we will miss them in the future. We only have five Indians left from Santa Gertrudis, three from San Borja, two from Santa María, and two boys who ride their mules and act as mule drivers of the pack. May God keep them safe and free from all harm. Amen.

On June 15 the expedition marched for only an hour or so and stopped to inspect various sources of water. As Serra and José Francisco de Ortega went off by themselves to inspect some springs, they encountered a group of Indians who appeared to be hostile to their presence. Serra, although he was skeptical about the consequences of allowing the Indians to think they could successfully order the Spanish around, convinced Ortega that in this circumstance discretion was the better part of valor. So they turned back.

June 15. On our way to inspect the third source of water, we saw some gentile women. We pretended that we had not even seen them and went on ahead without speaking to them. As we got closer to the end of the plain that ends at a hill, a group of armed gentiles appeared on top of the hill. One of the gentiles started screeching at the top of his lungs. His actions seemed to be telling us to turn back. We gestured and shouted for them to come down to us, but it was to no avail. If we had proceeded forward, we would have found ourselves under their feet. The sergeant who accompanied me had already put on his leather jacket and was ready to fight. He asked me if we should continue on or turn back. I feared this was not the time to break off relations with these poor people and cause any sort of trouble. I believed, although with great difficulty, that it would be best to allow them to be victorious on this battlefield. That is why we did not have a good look at the source of the water supply, which is the only thing we were looking for. The mere sight of the soldiers, who later went there on horseback, scared off any gentiles in those hills who might start shrieking. The soldiers tell me they saw many bushes of the Rose of Castile, an abundance of water, and thousands of other lovely things. Thanks be to God.

The expedition rested on June 16, but a scout party brought back some Indian artifacts, which Serra judged to be well constructed and comparable to the workmanship of central Mexico. As had previously been the case, Serra's enthusiasm for the native peoples he was encountering was mirrored in his enthusiasm for their material culture.

> *June 16.* They have found piles of delicious seeds that the gentiles eat, which I have tried and find very tasty; a large and very strong tray made of clay and woven grass, and other small pieces of fine broken earthenware that were very smooth and delicate, similar to what is found in Guadalajara. But the gentiles have not allowed themselves to be seen.

After a day of marching, on June 17 two more Baja California mission Indians left. Serra made a point of emphasizing how dependent the expedition was upon the consistent and unpaid labor of these Indians.

> *June 18.* We left after eating. As we were leaving, two of the three Indians from San Borja who, as I said on June 14, had remained with us, ran away without our knowing why. Little by little, companions who are more necessary to us than some people may think are drifting away from us. Only someone who sees the situation firsthand can attest to how hard they work and how little they are fed without receiving a salary.

The expedition was now entering the land of the southern Kumeyaay people. On June 19, a series of hills and creeks made progress difficult.

> *June 19.* On today's journey, one of the Señor Gobernador's servants, a Genoese cook, showed the strength of his sword by thrusting it through the

hindquarters of a she-ass because the animal had the audacity to cut in front of the cook when he was riding, thus slowing him down. The she-ass died at the cook's feet. The Señor Gobernador was convinced a crime had been committed based on the statements of eyewitnesses and the confession of the man who committed the "burricide." The governor fired the cook and ordered that he be stripped of his weapons. He sentenced him to following the expedition on foot and fined him forty pesos, which is four times the value of the animal. A mare gave birth to a pretty little mule here. Since the young animal would not be able to keep up with the pack train, it was given to the Indians, who quickly slaughtered it. They cooked the pieces over an open fire and then began to feast on the fresh and tender meat. May they benefit from it.

The expedition was now at Ensenada de Todos Santos, site of the modern Mexican city of Ensenada. They were now among the Kumeyaay, whose territory stretched from slightly south of where the expedition was to north of San Diego. The Kumeyaay had developed a sophisticated and effective communication system. It is extremely likely that every Indian group they encountered for the rest of the journey knew some days in advance that they were approaching.[49]

Serra's enthusiasm for the native peoples he encountered between here and San Diego was generally quite high, for he interpreted their behavior as indicating that they were friendly and anxious for the Gospel. But the situation was not so simple. These people had behaved very differently when the first leg of the expedition passed through their territory seven weeks before the second leg did. For instance, Serra was rhapsodic about the native peoples he encountered on June 23 around Punta de San Miguel just outside Ensenada. But when the first expedition had been in that vicinity on May 4, the native peoples were hostile. Cañizares reported:

> While we were in the mountains during the afternoon, we saw nineteen natives who were shouting at us from a hill. They were armed with bows and arrows, and this put us on our guard. The Capitán deployed the men, in case anything should happen, but the natives went away, and we made camp and erected a barricade. The watch was doubled in case of danger.

On the next day he added, "In the afternoon some Indians appeared on the same hill. They were armed as on the day before and they indicated a desire to fight and then withdrew."[50]

---

49. Rodríguez Tomp, *Cautivos de Dios*, 193; Lazcano Sahagún, *Pa-tai*, 96.
50. Cañizares, "Putting a Lid on California," 349.

June 23. We left this place and turned toward a row of hills that form this side of the cove. After less than an hour of traveling we found ourselves back at the edge of the ocean. We followed the shore for the rest of our journey, which lasted about three and one-half hours. The road is good, flat, and firm until it meets up with a hill that ends in the ocean itself. At the foot of the hill there is a very green area with a number of pools of good, sweet water. We spent the night here.

A large ranchería of gentiles lives right here. The time we have spent with them has been most pleasurable. Their beautiful physique, comportment, friendliness, and happiness have won all our hearts. They presented us with fish and clams. They went out in their small canoes to fish just for us. They danced in their own way for us and told us to sleep here for two nights. When we would say things to them in Spanish, they would repeat what we said very clearly. In short, all of the gentiles have pleased me, but these gentiles in particular have captured my heart. The only thing that has caused them great fear and amazement are the mules. When the gentiles are in our midst, they feel very secure. But if they see the mules approaching, they all tremble and shout "mula, mula" (since they had heard us call the animals by that name) and want to run off until somebody gets up to shoo the animals away. This spot does not appear to have any other use than that of serving as a ranchería, therefore, for the record we shall call it the Ranchería de San Juan. The women cover themselves up discreetly, but the men are naked, like all the other men. They carry their quivers, which are usually painted, on their shoulders. Most of them wear on their head a type of crown made of otter skin or some other fine fur. Their hair is cut in the shape of a short wig and is covered with white mud—all done very cleanly. May God grant them such cleanliness of the soul. Amen.

June 24 offered another example of the different ways in which the local people reacted to the two expeditions. Serra found the people so friendly that he thought they wanted him to stay with them. But the first expedition, passing through the same area on May 7, had reported hostility and a distinct lack of friendliness. Crespí wrote about a "good-sized throng" of people who approached the expedition and "shouted at us a great deal": "All of them naked, heavily armed, with their large quivers on their backs and bows and arrows in their hands, and all went running along the crests of the hill in view alongside of us; and they kept following us in this way nearly the whole day's march with loud shouting and hubbub." Cañizares added that the native peoples shot at least one arrow toward the expedition's animals, "so we kept our weapons handy until they went away."[51]

---

51. Cañizares, "Putting a Lid on California," 350; Crespí, *A Description of Distant Roads*, 233.

Also, by this time Serra knew he was nearing San Diego. So he gave considerable thought to the nature of the landscape through which they were passing. He was increasingly on the lookout for possible mission sites: locations that combined a large number of native people, good water, and land where European-style agriculture might flourish.

June 24. Feast day of the Holy Precursor, San Juan. After Mass, the soldiers and the gentiles began to banter and swap small pieces of white cloth, which the gentiles really want, for a few baskets of fresh fish. The gentiles were quite astute when it came to exchanging goods. If the piece of cloth was small, then the fish they gave in return would be equally small. There was no use arguing the point or trying to barter. If the piece of cloth was double the size, they would double the amount of fish. After we bid farewell to these good people, we continued on our way. . . .

We slept under the protection of a sprawling oak tree. Here we did not have the California advantage of being free from fleas. We were covered with them and also with some ticks. We met many gentiles along the way. When we would pass by a ranchería, they would all come out to greet us, without being asked to do so. After arriving, gentiles from another ranchería near where we stopped would come to see us. These gentiles and the ones we met along the route were as friendly as those we had met previously. When I asked them, among other questions, if they wanted me to stay with them there, they said they did. It pained me terribly to have to leave so many gentle souls.

June 25. After Mass and other matters that needed attention, we continued our journey along a very difficult road. Most of the time we could see the ocean. Today's trek lasted three and one-half hours. We found the valley where we would be stopping, but the path down to it was very long and extremely steep. It seemed as if we were sliding down the hill instead of walking. The soil was not tamped down—it was basically dust and all the animals would get stuck. We finally made it down the hill and stopped at the lower part of a verdant plain. It looks like a mission that has already been established, not only for the beauty of the place but also because of the many gentile huts that are scattered around the area. There is a great deal of vegetation on the land, much water, and many trees. In the middle of this place there is a very large pool, from which an estuary flows to the ocean. The ocean can be seen through a pass formed by the hills in front. The beach appears to be about two leagues away. Much of the ground is filled with sedge and tule. There are many climbing vines among the willows. From the north side a canyon begins to form. It then branches off in various directions according to the location of the hills. The canyon is filled with large trees. Everyone felt this was an excellent site for another mission. I named it San Juan de Capistrano.

Along the way we saw hares, rabbits, and herds of antelope. But we saw even greater numbers of poor, lost sheep, that is, so many gentiles of both sexes and of every age. They do not run away from us as did the gentiles whom we met at the beginning. Instead, they stay close to us along the road, as well as when we arrive at a stopping place. They act as if they had known us and interacted with us their entire lives. This is why I do not have the heart to leave them like that, so I invited them all to go with us to San Diego. May God help bring them there. Or may He send ministers who can guide them to Heaven in their own fertile and blessed land, which they have already been given.

June 26. We pressed on and the first thing we were faced with was a very steep hill. This was followed by long stretches of flat lands, but they were so high that it seemed as if all of the very high hills we could see in every direction were beneath our feet. We saw low ridges, steep slopes, and ravines. After five hours, the length of today's trek, we saw that we had to go down an incline that was so steep, practically a sheer drop, that just looking at it set our teeth on edge. Everyone dismounted. Half walking, half crawling, falling and getting up, we made it down to the valley, which was no less verdant than the previous one. And it is close to the ocean along a rugged coast. A bit farther up, there is a cove where the waves come in and break gently.

This is also a beautiful spot. However, because the land is so untamed, it would take an enormous amount of work to make the land suitable for agriculture. The tules and sedge alone cover large areas of land, not to mention the large groves of trees. A large part of the land is filled with green reeds, willows, and many other plants I do not recognize. The vegetation is so tall that one would not be able to see a man on horseback, even if he were to raise his arms high in the air. Because there was so much vegetation, we were not able to examine this place well. We did, however, find a good watering hole for the animals and some water for the men.

Aside from that, we only examined the area near the ocean where there are a number of large pools of water. Some of the pools are salty, others are brackish, and some have sweet, good water. If this place is going to be settled, bringing water down to the area from up above is going to be very costly. There is no doubt that water can be found there. Everything in this place is so green because of the pools of fresh water and the tule swamps higher up.

This place has a small flat hill that is quite large and very well suited for the establishment of the pueblo. It is away from the dampness, and there is plenty of water close by for irrigation.

We named this beautiful place San Francisco Solano trusting that with the support of this Holy Apostle of the Spanish Indies, the many gentile Indians who have gathered here with us will be led to the pale of the Church. It seems to me that even though we have seen many Indians, we have not seen so many gathered together in one place as we have here. And as to their friendly nature, I cannot find the appropriate words to describe it. In addition to the countless number of men, a large group of women and children sat around me in a circle. One of the women wanted me to hold the infant she was nursing. I held him in my arms for a while, so wishing that I could baptize him, but I then returned the child to his mother. I make the sign of the cross and bless each of them. I have them say "Jesus and Mary." I give them what I am able to give and cherish them in the best way I can. We manage to get by like this since there is no other work we can do at the present time. A person must use some caution when with these poor souls because they cannot be trusted. They have an intense longing or craving for articles of clothing or any sort of bauble they imagine they could use to adorn themselves. Food is not that appealing to them. They are fat, so it seems they have enough. The majority of them are tall and would be useful to the Señor Gobernador as grenadiers. But they are capable of flying off the handle, as they say, over a small piece of cloth or some rag, and do not give a damn about anybody. When I give them something to eat, they usually tell me with very clear gestures that they do not want that. Instead, they want me to give them my holy habit and grab me by the sleeve. If I had given the habit to all who requested it, I already would have a large community of gentile friars. What I would like to instill firmly in their hearts is the *Induimini Dominum Jesum Christum*.[52] May the most generous Lord and Padre who clothes the little birds with feathers, the mountains with grass, etc. Amen.

On June 27, the expedition was just south of Rosarito. Serra reported that the people offered him and Portolá some very fine-tasting fish and some spices in a basket. They had a meeting with a number of people who were quite friendly and who dealt with the Spanish with an air of familiarity. Serra gave a man his glasses, which were passed around from hand to hand and returned to him only with difficulty.

---

52. "Clothe yourself with the Lord Jesus Christ" (Romans 13:14).

Six weeks earlier Crespí had reported a much more aggressive approach by the indigenous people. The Indians refused to share their fish unless the Spanish bartered for it. The leader of the group was "rummaging through our entire camp," and spurs and blankets were stolen. In all, Crespí summarized, the Indians were "great thieves."[53]

On the whole, the Kumeyaay demonstrated considerably more public friendliness to the second leg of the expedition than they did to the first. Because of their communication system, every leader who interacted with Portolá and Serra knew that the first expedition had arrived at San Diego and that it had demonstrated no sign of leaving. This new expedition was most likely destined to reinforce that first outpost. The Kumeyaay had no reason to believe that this second expedition would be the last incursion into their territory. The situation therefore called for caution and an appearance of friendliness while the indigenous people tried to decide how most effectively to deal with the newcomers, whose numbers were increasing. Serra also noted that the Kumeyaay women would come into the camp and move freely around all the Spanish livestock and possessions. He was puzzled by this. But the Kumeyaay had undoubtedly come to realize that the entirely male Spanish groups they were encountering did not regard women as significant actors in military, political, or religious affairs. Since the Spanish basically thought of them as dim-witted nuisances, they were the perfect people to spy out the strengths and weaknesses of the Spanish encampment. But, carried away by his own enthusiasm for the missionary task on which he was embarking, Serra interpreted their behavior much as he had interpreted the behavior of the northern Cochimí he had met at Velicatá at the beginning of the expedition. Serra remained absolutely convinced that the unbaptized people of California were eager to receive the Gospel. On June 30 Ortega warned Serra that there was another side to the indigenous demeanor, but this admonition fell on deaf ears.

> *June 27.* We set out very early because our sergeant had already warned us that today's trek would be a long one. All of the gentiles were present when we left, and they followed us along the road, both men and women. We traveled along the seashore. Even though the ground was level, there were just as many ravines or gullies as on dry land. These were probably formed by the water that runs off from the nearby hills and ends up in the ocean. For me, this was one of the hardest journeys we have had. It lasted more than six hours. Along the road I have described, besides the place I mentioned that has an estuary, we saw that the land was covered with many fine mescals, which we had not seen for a long time. I do not think the mescals are

---

53. Crespí, *A Description of Distant Roads*, 245.

of much interest to these gentiles because there is an abundance of fish and other food. At this place and also at the previous three, there is an abundance of good *nopales* and *tunas*,[54] which we saw very little of before. We also saw far out in the ocean two and sometimes four or five tule balsas, which are small Indian canoes used by the gentile fishermen. The first time we saw one was on June 21 at the place called Visitación de Nuestra Señora, but it was beached on shore.

Along the route today the gentiles gave us reason to fear they might be plotting something. They followed us in great numbers and acted in a friendly manner toward us, but they would engage in skirmishes after which they would divide up into two groups, one on each side of the road. And since they were always armed with bow and arrow, it was possible for them to attack in some fashion. But at the same time, they would leave their women with us. The women would wander in and out among the mules, soldiers, and mule drivers. There was no way of keeping them away or containing them because they would respond with cackling laughter and just continue running around like deer. During all of this there would not be a single gentile man in sight, but then all of a sudden a throng of them would appear shrieking as they do. In the end, the men and women would tire and then we would continue on our journey. These gentiles and those from the last two stopping places either were not afraid of the mules or quickly lost their fear of the animals.

We finally arrived at the stopping place, which is a valley that is neither very large nor very small. A good-sized creek runs through it among the tules. The entire valley and its surrounding hillsides are richly covered with good grass. The valley is close to the ocean and it is a beautiful place. We named it San Benvenuto.

We had barely arrived when two gentiles from a large ranchería nearby came to greet us, after which one of them ran off and quickly returned with a large piece of grilled fish artfully arranged on some greens. The Señor Gobernador and I tasted the fish. It was very good. We continued eating. At the same time the man presented us with a cup-shaped basket they made from grasses. In these parts they call them *coras*. It was filled with a large amount of a powdery substance, which at first glance looked like dark soil to me. Seeing that we did not seem to appreciate the powder, the gentile put the basket

---

54. *Nopal* cactus is commonly referred to in English as "prickly pear," "Indian fig," or "Barbary fig." There are two principal fresh food crops derived from the Nopal *Opuntia ficus-indica* cactus. One is the nopalitos, the cactus pads or leaves, and the other is the tuna, or the "prickly pear" fruit.

up to our noses so we could smell it. The fragrance was so pleasing, and it tasted like a mixture of ground spices. We then sprinkled some of the powder on the fish, which gave it the flavor of cloves and pepper.

After a while, more and more gentiles—men, women, and children—gathered together with us. There were so many that I could not count them. Their friendliness transformed into a comfortable form of familiarity. If we placed our hand on their head or back as a gesture of affection, they would do the same to us. If they saw that we were seated, they would sit down and cozy up next to us with the hope that we would give them anything they asked for. They were not pleased with mere trifles. They would ask me for my habit and the governor for his leather jacket, waistcoat, breeches, and anything else he was wearing. They would do this to everybody. They pestered me quite a bit to give them my spectacles. The actions of one of the gentiles led me to believe that he just wanted to borrow the spectacles so he could see what they were. So I handed them to him. God knows how hard it was for me to get them back because he ran away with them. Finally, after much difficulty, I got them back, but only after the women, and anybody else who wanted to, had handled them. The only thing they refused was food.

In the afternoon we could see in the distance that the two gentiles were returning. One of them was wearing a blue shirt, which was something new. Up to this point we had not seen any gentiles wearing a stitch of clothing. We anxiously awaited his arrival, because all signs indicated to us that he was bringing good news. And that is what happened. He told us he had come from San Diego, where they had given him that outfit. The reason it took him two days to get here was because he had stopped to do some fishing. He explained everything to us, but much of what he told us seemed implausible, for example, that the two boats and many Padres were there. What pleased us most was when he said he had met the sergeant and his companion on the road. As I mentioned before, the sergeant had gone on ahead to scout out stopping places with ample water so we could plan our daily treks. The gentile said that the sergeant probably had been in San Diego since yesterday, which was the case.

June 28. We remained here so the animals could rest. Around mid-morning we were told that many people on horseback had been spotted heading our way. Sergeant Ortega arrived soon after with ten more soldiers from the first group of the expedition. Señor Capitán Rivera had ordered them to come from the port of San Diego to meet the Señor Gobernador and his retinue.

They brought fresh animals and letters for me from the two Padres, Fray Juan Crespí and Fray Fernando Parrón. We were very happy. We found out what had happened to the boats and how and why both of the boats were there, as well as news about the four Padres, and everything else that had transpired. This news invigorated us and made us that much more anxious to arrive at our destination.

June 29. Early in the morning, the Señor Gobernador, his servant, and eight soldiers quickly started out ahead of us to reach the port of San Diego on that same day. I said Mass on this day of celebration for those who stayed behind. Quite a few gentiles paid close attention to the Mass. In the afternoon we traveled for two and one-half hours with the assistance of two guides who had come from San Diego. We traveled along the edge of the shore. The only trouble we had was with a number of ravines, similar to what we had experienced the day before, but there were not as many. We stopped near a gentile ranchería located on a beautiful plateau that looks like an island. It is surrounded by a ravine except for the area where the ocean washes up.

As soon as the gentiles saw us, they came over and begged us to go and stay at the plateau near their huts. But it seemed to us that it would be better to set up camp on the other side of the ravine, where there is another flat area large enough to accommodate us. Later they all came to visit us there. They were very happy and did not bother us at all. Among these gentiles was the man with the shirt from the last stopping place. He told us that his home was there and that he had only left in order to give us the news. But now he was as naked as the rest. This place within the ravine and next to the ranchería has a medium-sized spring of good, sweet water from which the gentiles drink. Even though our animals could have drunk from there, we did not allow it since they had already had enough to drink that day, and also because we did not want to contaminate in any way the watering place of these poor gentiles. High mountains rise on each side of this place, on the side where we are camped as well as where the Indians live. The manner in which we are enclosed is why I named this place "La Cárcel de San Pedro," whose feast day we celebrated today.[55]

June 30. We left in the morning, and the first thing we had to do was cross the ravine and climb up the opposite hill. After going up and down several times, a very long stretch of flat land appeared before us, on which we would

---

55. "The Jail of St. Peter" refers to Peter's imprisonment by King Herod and his miraculous release that is recounted in Acts 12.

travel with the hills to the right of us. Our entire day's journey, which lasted four and one-half hours, was along this flat terrain. But there were so many ravines that we had to cross. We could not avoid a single one of them or even change direction because they all originated from the interior of the mountain range. Even though I prayed as I crossed all of them and tried to resign myself to the situation, etc., I could feel my chest tighten because of the ever-present danger in each ravine. No sooner had we gotten out of one ravine then we found ourselves faced with another one, with no reprieve. I once asked the guides how many more ravines we had to cross, and they responded that there were still many more. And that was true, as we were to find out. Just as all things in this world come to an end, so did the ravines. After traveling for a little over three hours, we arrived at a ranchería populated by many gentiles. We were inclined to stop there because we were so tired, but the sergeant informed us that these gentiles were insolent. They liked the clothing the sergeant was wearing and tried to obtain it by tempting the sergeant and his companion Cota with women and encouraging them to sleep there. When the sergeant and Cota resisted, they found themselves in grave danger and were forced to give the gentiles any loose articles of cloth they had, such as napkins, handkerchiefs, etc. Because of that situation, as well as wanting to arrive in San Diego as rested as possible, we forged ahead the following day, with the intention of stopping at another ranchería a few leagues away. They said there was enough water at that place. However, it was very inferior in quantity and quality to the water supply that belonged to those troublesome gentiles we had left behind. But since the road was flat and the guides already knew how to get to the port by the way the wind was blowing, we headed straight for it, leaving the beaten track behind and to our right. After traveling for about an hour we found a beautiful creek of good water flowing through the verdant pasture land. We stopped there instead of going on to the next ranchería. This was the third time the sergeant had traveled this route. But neither he nor the others who, counting this trip, had passed by here five times had ever seen this spot. We felt this would be a wonderful place for good-sized mission that we would call San Pablo. It is a very large plain. It seems to me that it is about one league, more or less, from the ocean. The animals were able to travel easily through the area. And we had no other care in the world than our strong desires to arrive at the port of San Diego and embrace everyone who was waiting there for us with open arms. All that was left was this last day's journey.

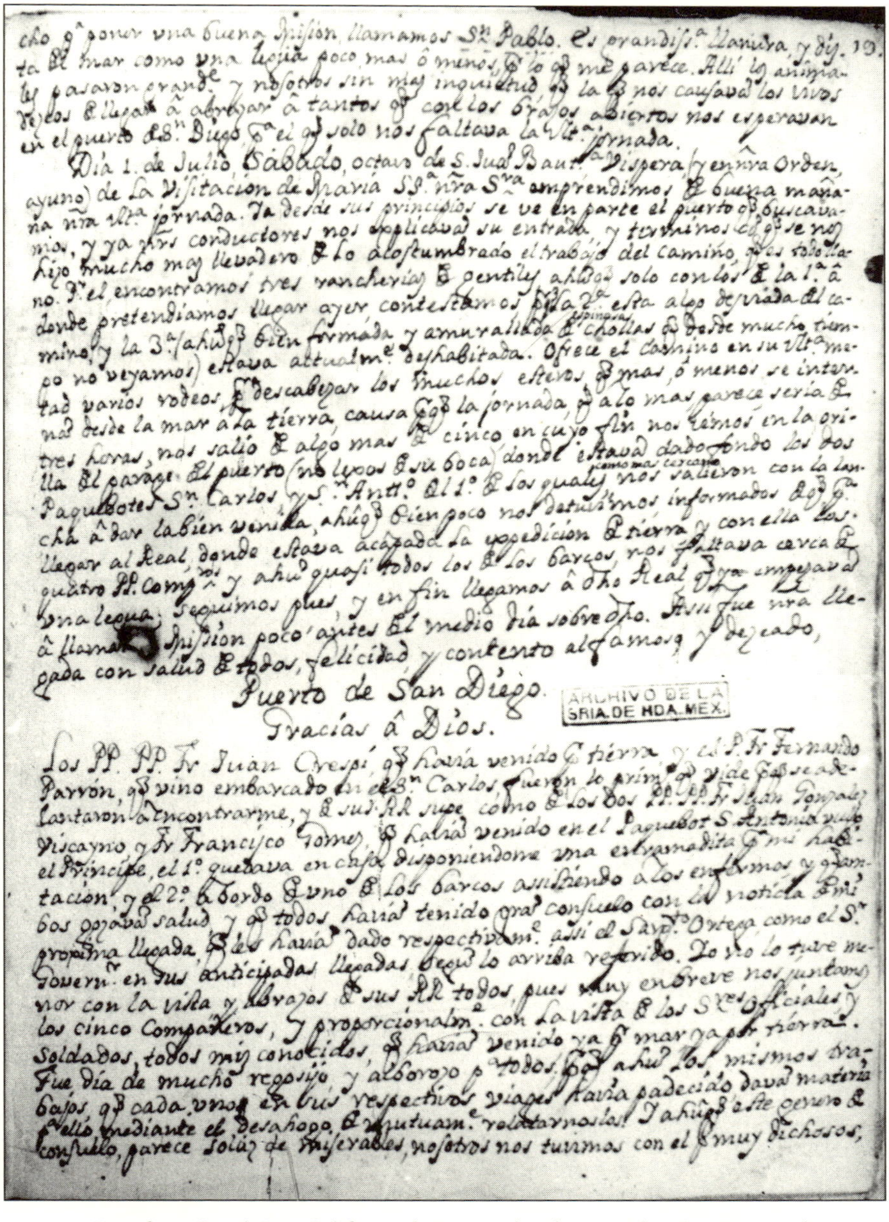

FIGURE 28. Page from Serra's Baja California diary recording his arrival in San Diego, July 1, 1769. In the middle of the page he emphasized the phrase "Puerto de San Diego, Gracias a Dios" (Port of San Diego, Thanks be to God). *Courtesy of the Santa Bárbara Mission Archive-Library.*

July 1. Saturday, the eve of the eighth day after the feast day of San Juan Bautista. In our order it is the feast of the Visitation of Nuestra Señora María Santísima. We began our last day's journey very early in the morning. We can already see where the port we were looking for begins. Because our guides had already informed us about the entrance to the port and its boundaries, our journey along this road, which was totally flat, was much easier than what we were accustomed to. Along the way we came upon three gentile rancherías, but we only interacted with those from the first one, which is where we had intended on stopping yesterday. The second ranchería is a bit out of the way, and the third one (although it was well developed and surrounded by a wall of thorny *chollas*,[56] which we had not seen for quite some time) was now uninhabited. The last half of the road twists and turns to avoid the many estuaries that more or less go into the land from the sea. This is why our journey lasted more than five hours when it should have been no more than three. At the end of the road we found ourselves at the edge of the shore of the port, not far from its mouth, where the two packet boats, the *San Carlos* and the *San Antonio*, were anchored. People came over on a skiff from the first boat, which was closer, to welcome us. We did not stay long because we had been informed that we were still about a league away from where the members of the land expedition were camped, along with the four Padres and almost everyone from the boats. We therefore continued on. Shortly before noon we finally arrived at the campsite that they already were beginning to call a mission. This was how we arrived at the famous and desired port of San Diego with everyone in good health, happy, and content. Thanks be to God.

---

56. Chollas are a genus of cylindrically stemmed cacti.

CHAPTER 4

San Diego and Monterey

When Portolá and his leg of the expedition crew reached San Diego on July 1, he quickly conferred with the senior officers at the scene. He discovered that the naval voyages had not gone nearly as well as the land journeys had. The *San Antonio* left Cabo San Lucas on February 15 and arrived at San Diego on April 11, more than a month before Rivera y Moncada's land expedition crew arrived. Many of its men were sick from scurvy. The captain of the *San Antonio*, the Mallorcan Juan Pérez, was puzzled that the *San Carlos* was nowhere to be seen even though it had left La Paz a month earlier than his vessel. Pérez thus ordered his men to remain on board the *San Antonio*. Under these circumstances his orders called for him to remain at San Diego for twenty days and then proceed to Monterey. The *San Carlos*, captained by Vicente Vila, arrived two days before the *San Antonio* was slated to leave. Its voyage had also been very trying, and the many sick men on board were relocated to the beach. Pedro Prat, the surgeon on hand, did what he could. The area was reasonably well populated. Fages estimated that there were at least eight indigenous settlements in the vicinity. The Spanish survived because the Kumeyaay were willing to provide them with game and food in exchange for cloth. But through it all, men continued to die.

When Rivera y Moncada arrived in the middle of May he prevailed upon Fages to move the camp a bit farther inland closer to fresh water and the village of Cosoy, but men still continued to die. By the time the Portolá party arrived, only one sailor from the *San Carlos* had survived, so Portolá decided to send the *San Antonio* back to San Blas for more supplies.

Two days after arriving in San Diego, Serra wrote to Palóu. He first summarized what happened to the two vessels on the basis of information he received from Fathers Parrón, Vizcaíno, and Gómez. Then he described his own journey. The tone of his letter was quite similar to that of his diary: his enthusiasm for the land he had entered and the people he met along the way was evident.

❋ *Letter to Francisco Palóu, July 3, 1769*

Hail Jesus, Mary, Joseph!
Reverendo Padre Lector and Presidente Fray Francisco Palóu
My dearest friend and Señor:

I will be delighted to learn that Vuestra Reverencia finds himself in good health and working with much consolation and happiness in the reorganization of that new Mission of Loreto and of the others. And that the new ministers who will provide assistance will arrive as soon as possible so that everything may be settled in good order, as a consolation for everyone.

I, thanks be to God, arrived the day before yesterday, July 1, at this port of San Diego. It is truly beautiful and deservedly famous. Here I caught up with those who had left before I did, by sea and by land, except for the dead.

Our companions, Padres Crespí, Vizcaíno, Parrón, and Gómez are here with me. Everyone is well, thanks be to God. The two ships are here. The *San Carlos* has no sailors because they all died from scurvy. Only one sailor survived, as well as a cook.

Don Juan Pérez, our fellow countryman from the shores of Palma, is the Captain of the *San Antonio*, also known as *El Príncipe*. Even though it left a month and a half after the other ship, it arrived here twenty days ahead of it. The *San Carlos* arrived when the *San Antonio* was about ready to leave for Monterey. The crew of the *San Antonio* stayed to help the crew of the *San Carlos*, but they became ill as well and eight people died. In the end it was decided that the *San Antonio* should leave here and return to San Blas and bring back sailors for itself and the *San Carlos*. And then they both will set sail. We shall see what shape the packet boat *San José* is in when it arrives. And if all is well, the last ship in will be the first to leave.

Two factors caused the delay of the *San Carlos*.

First, the poor condition of the barrels. They were surprised to discover that water was leaking out of them. With what was left in four barrels, they were unable to fill one. Therefore, they had to quickly head for land to obtain water. But what they found was from a bad location and of poor quality, and as a result, the men began to get sick.

The second was a misconception held by all, including Su Ilustrísima, which was that this port was between 33 and 34 degrees of latitude from the pole. Some authorities say it is 33 and others say it is 34. Capitán Vila and the other captain were given strict orders to sail out at sea as far as the 34th degree of latitude and then head toward land in search of the port. The truth of the matter is that this port is no higher than 32 degrees and 34 minutes, according to the observations made by these men. Thus, they went very far beyond this port and when they looked for it they could not find it. That is why their voyage was longer. With the men already sick, the weather getting colder, and the bad water, the situation was so dire that if they had not found the port right away, everyone would have died. They were so weak they were unable to lower the launch into the ocean to let water out or do anything with the rigging.

Padre Fray Fernando worked hard taking care of the sick men and even though he was very thin when he arrived, his health was not impaired and he is now fine. But now that he is well, I do not want him to embark again. He is very happy remaining here.

I am taking this opportunity to write at length to Su Ilustrísima, to the colegio, and to our Padre Comisario General. And that is why I am somewhat tired. If it had not been that Capitán Pérez had the courtesy to wait, seeing that I was so busy writing, I believe he would have gone and I could not have finished writing everything I wanted to say.

With regard to Padre Fray Juan Crespí's journey with the captain, he tells me that he is writing to Vuestra Reverencia and the letter will arrive on this same boat, therefore, I have no need to say anything further.

As for me, the journey has been a truly happy one, with no particular weakening or change in my health. I left the frontier with a very bad foot and leg, but God took care of me and each day I felt better. I continued my daily journeys as if I nothing were wrong with me. At the present time, the foot is as healthy as the other one, but from the ankle up to the middle of my leg it is like the foot was before. It is a wound but it is not swollen nor does it hurt, although it does itch at times. In the end, it is nothing to worry about.

I never had to go without food or other necessities; neither did the Indian neophytes who came with us, who all arrived healthy and fat. I kept a diary which I will send to Vuestra Reverencia the first chance I get. The missions, along the stretch of land we have seen, will all be very good because there is good land and a good water supply. The land here and in the area much in the distance is not rocky or full of thorns. Yes, there are plenty of mountains, and big ones too, but they are of pure soil. The roads are both good and bad, although more so the latter, but it is nothing major. Halfway on our journey, or just before that, the arroyos and valleys begin to be lined with trees. There are good grapevines which grow well and in some places they are laden with grapes. By various arroyos along the way and at the place where we are now, in addition to the grapevines, there are different types of Roses of Castile.

In short, this land is a beautiful land and it is very different than the land of Antigua California.

As I wrote to Vuestra Reverencia, from when we left San Juan de Dios on May 21 until July 1 when we arrived here, we were on the road every day, with the exception of about eight days, interspersed here and there to rest the animals. The longest day's journey was six hours, and we only had two that were that long; the others were four, four and a half, three, two, or one and a half hours long, as described in the diary. The pace was that of a pack train. One can infer that once the roads are laid out and improved, time can be saved by avoiding many leagues of useless detours. It is not very far. I believe that after these improvements are made, the trip would take the Padres about twelve days. Even now, the soldiers are saying that traveling at an easy pace, they would be able to reach the frontier of Velicatá in much less time.

There are great numbers of gentiles, and all those who are on the west coast, through which we came from the Bay of Todos Santos, as it is called on the maps and charts, live very comfortably. They eat various types of seeds and fish they catch from their tule boats shaped like canoes. In these canoes they can go quite far out to sea. They are very friendly and all the males, both adults and children, go about naked. The women and young girls, are decently covered up, even the baby girls. They would come out to greet us like this on the roads, as well as where we would set up camp. They treated us with such familiarity and trust, as if they had known us all their lives. We tried to give them something to eat, but they always would say they did not want that. What they wanted were clothes. The soldiers and mule drivers would swap clothing for fish, which was the only thing the Indians would take in exchange. All along the road you see hares, rabbits, some deer and many antelope.

The governor tells me he wants to continue the land expedition, accompanied by the captain, in the next three or four days. He says he will leave us with eight leather-jacket soldiers of the escort and several sick Catalans, so that if they recover they might be of service. The mission has not been founded, but as soon as they leave, I will put my hand to it.

My friend, our fellow countryman, the captain, just came in to tell me that he cannot wait any longer without getting himself into trouble. So it is here where I must conclude by saying that these Padres send their best to Vuestra Reverencia. We are well and happy. My regards to Padre Martínez and the rest of the Padres to whom I had intended to write, but I am unable to. I will do so at the first opportunity. I am addressing this letter to Padre Ramos because our fellow countryman tells me that he will be going that far south. That way he can read it and then forward it to Vuestra Reverencia.

May God protect your life and health many years

From this Port and projected new Mission of San Diego in California of the North, July 3, 1769
Your most affectionate brother and servant kisses the hand of Vuestra Reverencia,
Fray Junípero Serra

After Portolá sent the *San Antonio* south for supplies, he immediately turned his attention to fulfilling the second part of his mission—the occupation of Monterey. He proceeded to divide the supplies and equipment between the group that was to head to Monterey and the smaller group that was to remain at San Diego. On July 14 Portolá and his expedition headed north. This expedition once again included Fathers Crespí and Gómez. Serra formally founded Mission San Diego de Alcalá two days later on July 16, the feast of the Exaltation of the Holy Cross. The date was also the anniversary of a famous Christian victory over the Moors at Navas de Tolosa in 1212. The ceremony was an abbreviated version of what had occurred at Velicatá on May 14. But since there was a very small number of able-bodied soldiers present and supplies were tight, there was undoubtedly considerably less celebratory firing of arms. All in all, it was probably a fairly Spartan ceremony.

The San Diego encampment was guarded by eight *soldados de cuera* (leatherjacket soldiers) under the command of Corporal Mariano Carrillo. Fourteen Catalán volunteers completed the military complement even though they were ill. Serra and the two other priests, Vizcaíno and Parrón, attended to the fledgling mission. In addition, eight Baja California Indians were at the camp. Included in this group of Indians were Juan Evangelista Benno, who had been entrusted to Serra by Father Sancho at Guadalupe, and Sebastián Taraval from Santa Gertrudis. Taraval would later escape from Mission San Gabriel and serve as Anza's guide in 1774. A number of others were also on hand, including Serra's muleteer, José María Vergerano. Ten people remained on board the *San Carlos*.[1]

A number of Kumeyaay visited the camp after the departure of Portolá. They most likely wanted to scout out the situation now that one of the vessels and a majority of the soldiers were gone. Their visits presented Serra with his first

---

1. The information on personnel comes from Harry W. Crosby, who is writing a biography of a Baja California soldier, Xavier Aguilar, one of the men on the Portolá expedition. Information on the state of the San Diego encampment shortly after the arrival of the first parties is taken from Engstrand, "Pedro Fages and Miguel Costansó," 1–11.

opportunity to introduce nonbaptized people to Christianity at a mission he had founded. He wanted to let them "taste and see that the Lord is good," as he had preached twenty-five years earlier in Mallorca. Serra was deeply frustrated that he was unable to communicate with the Kumeyaay, but it was not possible because the Baja California Indians did not know the local language. In any event, the Kumeyaay, who had been in more or less constant contact with the Spanish for over two months, had their own agenda. Skirmishes apparently took place in the vicinity of the fortified camp on August 13 and 14. On the morning of August 15 the mission encampment was attacked. José María Vergerano was killed and three others were wounded, including Father Vizcaíno. An undetermined number of Kumeyaay were also killed.[2]

Contact between the indigenous people and the newcomers at the camp continued over the next few months. At one point Serra believed he had communicated sufficiently with a young Indian boy to make him understand that he would like to baptize an infant. According to Palóu, a group of Indians brought an infant to Serra, who began the ritual by dressing the infant in a baptismal gown. But the other Indians quickly snatched the infant away and thus Serra's attempt was thwarted.[3]

This episode underlined a fundamental difficulty that affected the Alta California mission enterprise during Serra's lifetime. The garrison at San Diego consisted of a handful of priests, Baja California soldiers, native peoples from Baja California, and Catalán soldiers. None of them understood the language of the people in whose land they were encamped. The form of communication between these newcomers and the Kumeyaay most likely consisted of signs, gestures, and a gradual exchange of basic words. It is reasonable to assume that the Baja California natives and soldiers proved more adept at this than the Spanish priests and Catalán soldiers. However, it is impossible to imagine that the native peoples would have become remotely conversant with the worldview that underlay the notion of baptism after just a few months of rudimentary exchange. Therefore, it is really impossible to say why the baby was initially presented to Serra for baptism.

Believing that they had been unable to find Monterey, Portolá and his frustrated party returned from the north on January 24. Since neither the third supply ship, the *San José*, nor the *San Antonio* had arrived, Portolá sent Rivera y Moncada and a group of soldiers back to Baja California for supplies. The wounded Vizcaíno accompanied them and never returned to Alta California. He spent the next fifteen years giving domestic missions in Mexico and returned

---

2. Most accounts speak only of the attack on August 15, but Serra said that he had been in danger from the Kumeyaay on three separate occasions, August 13–15. See Serra, *Writings*, 1:158–59.
3. Palóu, *Palóu's Life of Fray Junípero Serra*, 78.

to Spain in 1784. The men at the camp settled in as best they could. As supplies began to run short, sickness affected a number of the Baja California Indians, who were probably not given the same amount of supplies as the soldiers and priests. On the trail these Indians were expected to forage for their own supplies, and a similar situation probably occurred at the camp. Juan Evangelista Benno, the Indian youth from Mission Guadalupe, died in February. A few days later two other Indians from Mission Santa María also died.[4]

By the beginning of March supplies were running low for everyone. Portolá told Serra that if a supply ship did not arrive by March 19, which was the feast of San José (the religious patron of the entire enterprise), the presidio and mission at San Diego would have to be abandoned. However, Serra hoped to be able to remain at San Diego even if Portolá abandoned it, and he tried to convince the captain of the *San Carlos* to stay in the harbor. Whether Portolá would have allowed that or not is unknown, for the situation never became that grave. Serra and the other priests began a novena—a nine-day period of intense prayer. The *San Antonio* was sighted on March 19, the last day of the novena. It had reached San Blas at the end of July and picked up fresh supplies.

San Diego to Monterey

After the *San Antonio* landed at San Diego on March 23, the men at the camp spent several weeks unloading it. Portolá prepared for another trip north, this time by both land and sea. Serra left Fathers Gómez and Parrón in charge at San Diego and boarded the *San Antonio*, which left for Monterey on April 16. The land expedition, headed once again by Portolá, departed the next day and arrived at Monterey and recognized it on May 24. The *San Antonio* entered Monterey Bay on May 31, and the people on the ship recognized it as well. The presidio and mission were founded a few days later, on Sunday, June 3, the feast of Pentecost.

The concepts of "presidio" and "mission" had deep roots in the centuries-long expansion of Spanish rule in the Americas. The word "presidio," meaning a garrison or a fortified establishment, entered the Spanish language from Latin in the sixteenth century, and it referred to Spain's forts in Morocco. Both the word and the institution it described were quickly put to use in northern New Spain. After silver was discovered in the late 1540s in Zacatecas, three hundred miles northwest of Mexico City, a rush of miners descended on the region. The indigenous peoples of the area were much less sedentary than the more urbanized people of central Mexico, and they quickly began to prey upon the convoys that

---

4. Crosby, *Gateway to Alta California*, 69; Geiger, *Franciscan Missionaries*, 121; Geiger, *Life and Times of Fray Junípero Serra*, 1:228–44; Serra, *Writings*, 4:342.

carried supplies north and silver south. The government established a series of presidios along the caravan routes to guard the miners and settlers and also to serve as bases for mobile expeditions against the Indians. During the frontier wars of the seventeenth century, a number of these forts were constructed. As we have seen, Pedro de Rivera undertook an inspection tour in the 1720s, and he visited twenty-three of the existing twenty-four presidios. The only one he omitted was Loreto in Baja California. His tour led to the promulgation of a 1729 report, which helped to lay the groundwork for Escandón's policy of de-emphasizing the ongoing role of missions in the colonization effort. Over the next few decades, more presidios were founded, while others were allowed to languish and die. As part of the Bourbon reforms, the Marqués de Rubí undertook another inspection tour of the presidios in 1766, and his recommendations were embodied in a new set of regulations issued in 1772.[5]

None of the presidios was grandly constructed. They consisted of enclosed adobe quadrangles and sometimes included towers at one or more of the corners. The soldiers were often part-time soldiers and part-time colonists, while the commanders tended to be ranchers or merchants who sought to use their positions to further their commercial endeavors. As would be the case at Monterey, a number of these presidios later became the nuclei of civilian settlements.

The origins of what would become the mission system in California stretched back to the very beginnings of the Spanish presence in the New World. In the 1490s, the Spanish adapted the Castilian institution of the *encomienda* to define their relationships with the peoples of the islands they were claiming as their own. In Reconquista Spain, Christian warriors were given jurisdiction over the people who lived in the areas they had taken from the Moors. In return for protection, the people were "entrusted" (the Spanish word is *encomendar*) to the knight and had to give over a certain amount of the labor to him. In the Caribbean, the Indians were forced to labor for the conquistador. The labor, often searching for gold, tended to be extremely brutal. As we have seen, criticism of this system was soon voiced, and the critiques made their way to the court. In 1512, Spain promulgated the Laws of Burgos, which attempted to rein in the worst abuses of the encomienda system, but the system survived and took root in Mexico after the conquest by Cortés. Protests against it continued. In 1542, Spain promulgated the New Laws, which abolished Indian slavery, prohibited the holding of encomiendas by public institutions and by the clergy, forbade new encomiendas, and provided that already existing encomiendas could not be

---

5. The role of the presidios and missions in the growth of New Spain has generated an enormous historiography. Weber's *The Spanish Frontier in North America* offers an excellent summary of these developments, especially as they affected the far north.

passed from one generation to the next. This last provision would have destroyed the system in one generation if it had gone into effect, but massive resistance on the part of the *encomenderos* in America prevented that. The Crown drastically weakened the New Laws and allowed the encomienda arrangements to continue. The institution was gradually modified and lost its central place in the continuing Spanish conquest, but it was not formally abolished until the eighteenth century.

As a reaction to the brutality and persistence of the encomienda, Las Casas and other religious advocated establishing separate areas for the Indians in which they could be protected from the worst abuses of the system. In 1516, Las Casas pushed through the court a proposal that would have abolished the encomiendas and set up autonomous Indian villages, each governed by an indigenous cacique assisted by a priest and a secular administrator. This proposal was never implemented, but the idea of gathering the Indians into their own villages and separating them from the Spanish population persisted. In the Caribbean, in fact, "congregating" the Indians into towns or "reducing" them into compact population centers also appealed to the secular authorities, since the catastrophic population decline was making it more difficult to organize the scattered survivors into work parties. Clustering the Indians into tight settlements was also consistent with Iberian municipal tradition, so the move appealed to royal authorities who were charged with hispanicizing the indigenous peoples.

In central Mexico, many of the Indians already lived in more or less compact communities. As each locality was brought under Spanish control, a church was constructed, sometimes on an earlier indigenous ceremonial site. These sixteenth-century churches combined European elements with spaces for outdoor ceremonies that also accommodated indigenous religious traditions.

A tug of war for control often ensued between the clergy, especially the members of the religious orders, such as the Franciscans, Dominicans, and Augustinians, and the conquistadors. As the conquest expanded, religious authorities took more of the lead, trying to congregate the more scattered Indians on their own and create a religious space separate from the area of the encomienda and *repartimiento*. The Mexican bishops called for such steps in 1537, and as the effort took hold to create such *congregaciones* or *reducciones*, as they were called, they became essential to Spanish expansion in New Spain.

These efforts became even more important as the frontier moved northward, where subduing the indigenous peoples proved to be no easy task. As early as 1541, widespread resistance, the Mixton Revolt, broke out near Guadalajara. North of Zacatecas the situation was even more unsettled as the mobile Chichimecas proved adept at avoiding stationary Spanish positions and inflicting considerable damage on both the military and the silver trade. By the 1580s, it was clear that a new strategy had to be adopted. At the same time, the religious orders were anxious to evangelize the northern Indians. Thus the government adopted the policy of establishing new reducciones, which along the northern frontier were more frequently termed missions, in order to bring the semi-nomadic Indians of the northern areas under Spanish sway and introduce them into the Spanish way of life. The Franciscans and the newly arrived Jesuits were both quite active in the north. The Franciscans evangelized extensively as far north as New Mexico, while the Jesuits worked in the northwest.

The large atrium that was a characteristic feature of the monastery churches of central Mexico gradually expanded as the missions moved farther north, until the atrium was turned into a mission cloister, which sometimes entirely enclosed and embraced a large complex of shops, storehouses, dormitories, and offices, as well as a church. The missions also controlled extensive lands, where the Indians were supposed to be taught agriculture and ranching. As the mission system spread, however, the religious authorities found themselves mirroring, to some extent, the secular encomenderos whose excesses had partially led to the establishment of the missions in the first place: the missions relied of necessity on force or the threat of force. The indigenous laborers at the missions were generally treated much less brutally than indigenous laborers in encomiendas, haciendas, and mining enterprises elsewhere in New Spain; however, their labor was still coerced.

There never was one unified and standard mission system in the Americas. Missions evolved over time, and regional variations abounded. In some cases large numbers of Indians lived at the mission site, but in other instances it proved impossible or unfeasible to gather large numbers into a stable community near the church complex. In some localities, like seventeenth-century New Mexico, Indians whose lifestyle was already sedentary were congregated at the missions, but it proved much more difficult to entice nomadic groups in the same region to settle there.

The colonial government that established the missions intended for them to be temporary institutions. The Indians were to learn the Spanish religion, language, and way of life, and then after a period of ten years or so, the church was to be turned into a regular parish (a process known as "secularization"). The mission lands were to be divided among the Indians, who would then take their places in society as Spanish and Catholic farmers and ranchers. As Enlightenment ideas gradually spread from Europe and Bourbon Spain into eighteenth-century New Spain, the missions began to be viewed with a more critical eye. Their frank paternalism did not sit well with new ideas about liberty and equality. The slow pace of secularization led to criticism that the missionaries were keeping the Indians too separated from the Spanish settlers and in a kind of perpetual servitude in order to preserve their own privileges, riches, and land.

By the mid-eighteenth century, the mission system in the north was already on the defensive in significant parts of New Spain. Some missions were beginning to accommodate themselves to the rising criticism by allowing greater contact between the mission Indians and the settlers.

Nine days after the presidio and the mission were founded at Monterey, Serra described the events in a letter to the guardian. Since Monterey was projected to be the major establishment in Alta California, the founding ceremonies for both institutions were elaborate and highly ritualized. They chose the site that was supposed to be the location at which Mass was celebrated when the Vizcaíno expedition visited Monterey in 1602. Parties from the campsite at Carmel and the ship in the harbor converged. Serra intoned the solemn hymns and assisted in raising and planting a cross in the ground. The flags of León and Castilla were raised and saluted. The ground was blessed and Mass was sung in a solemn manner. Then Portolá and his entourage marked off an area and performed the formal ceremony of taking possession.

A few days later the initial location for the presidio and mission were determined, and the place did not satisfy Serra. He was troubled by the fact that it was too far away from the Indian settlements in the area. He had learned from Crespí that the Carmel River, where the land party had initially camped, was closer to indigenous villages. He quickly concluded that the mission might be better located there. Serra's initial reason for questioning Monterey as a place for a mission was not the infertility of the land or the proximity of the soldiers—two reasons commonly adduced to explain his desire to move from Monterey. Rather, the basic reason was that Monterey was far away from existing native villages. Serra wanted the mission to be close to the existing settlements so that people could easily visit the mission, where they could "taste and see."

✳ *Serra to Juan Andrés, June 12, 1770*

We left that port [San Diego] on the 16th of the same month [April], since neither God nor the wind let us leave on Easter, which, to my delight, allowed us to sanctify the feast day.

The voyage was somewhat difficult and it lasted for many days. Each day, instead of getting closer to Monterey, we would be farther away from what we were looking for. The voyage ended up lasting exactly a month and a half. On May 31 we entered and dropped anchor in our contested port. There was no doubt that in essence and circumstance this was the same unchanged spot where our Spanish ancestors dropped anchor in 1603. It is very fitting and proper to entirely erase from the record that this port did not exist, as has been printed in reports from the last land expedition.

The same night we arrived we learned that the land expedition had arrived eight days earlier and that they were camped two leagues away near the Carmel River. The next day Padre Crespí came to visit us with the officers of the expedition. A feeling of great consolation was mutually felt by all.

At this gathering I set the date—Sunday the 3rd, the Feast of Pentecost—for the celebration of the first Mass and the erection in this land of the standard—the Most Holy Cross. We all were in agreement.

The day arrived. A chapel and altar were set up next to the same little ravine and oak tree, all close to the beach, where it is said the first Mass was celebrated at the beginning of the last century. Those who had come by sea and those who came by land arrived at the spot at the same time. We in the launch were singing the divine praises while those on land were singing in their hearts.[6]

When we arrived we were welcomed by the ringing of the bells hanging from the oak tree. Everything needed had been arranged. Having donned my alb and stole, we all knelt before the altar and I intoned the hymn *Veni Creator Spiritus*, after which the Holy Spirit was invoked to aid us in all that we were going to do, and then I blessed the salt and the water. We all then headed toward a large cross that had been placed on the ground. Together, we raised the cross. I sang the blessing, we planted the cross in the ground, and we all venerated it with the tenderness of our hearts. I sprinkled the surrounding area with holy water. After the standard of the King of Heaven had been raised, the same was done for those of Our Catholic Monarch. As each flag was unfurled, we rejoiced at the top of our lungs: *Viva la Fe, Viva el Rey*,[7] accompanied by the ringing of bells, rifle shots, and the firing of cannons from the ship.

Then, at the foot of the cross, we buried the only person who had died aboard ship on this second expedition—a sailor who was a caulker.

When this was concluded I began the sung Mass. The sermon followed the Gospel. And it all was greatly accompanied by salvos from the cannons. When Mass was finished, I removed my chasuble. Then, standing before the beautiful image of Nuestra Señora that was on the altar, we all sang the *Salve Regina* in Spanish. The Ilustrísimo Señor Visitador General had allowed us to use this image for the celebration, with the expressed provision that we return it to him afterward. I will do so as soon as the ship sets sail.

---

6. Song was a very important part of the evangelization efforts for Serra. However, according to Palóu, Serra was not a very good singer himself. See Palóu, *Palóu's Life of Fray Junípero Serra*, 44, 262.

7. Long live the Faith, Long live the King!

And as a way of concluding, I stood and intoned the *Te Deum Laudamus*. We sang it slowly and solemnly to the end, with responses and prayers to the Santísima Trinidad; to Nuestra Señora; to the Santísimo San José, the patron of our expedition; to San Carlos, who is the patron of this port, presidio, and mission; and then the prayer of thanksgiving.

May all these prayers of thanksgiving be given to God. As I was offering my prayers of thanksgiving (having already removed the sacred vestments) for that day's Mass, the officers performed the formal ritual of taking possession of the land in the name of His Catholic Majesty. The royal flag was again unfurled and waved, grasses were pulled from the ground, and stones were moved about, in addition to other ceremonial acts prescribed by law. Everything was accompanied by cheers, bell ringing, gun shots, etc. In addition, we all ate together on the beach and then strolled along the beach in the evening until those from the land expedition returned to their Carmel and we to the ship. Thus ended the celebration.[8]

A few days later that expedition moved to a beautiful plain within a rifle shot from the beach. That is where the presidio is being laid out, the mission in its shadow. Thus, our dear colegio can count on adding another new mission. This one is called San Carlos de Monterey, per order of the Ilustrísimo Señor Visitador General in honor of Our Catholic Monarch and of the Excelentísimo Señor Virrey—both named Carlos. And do not forget these two poor ministers of yours. Commend us to God. Give us direction, for we are your most humble subjects, and be assured that at the slightest insinuation from Vuestra Reverencia, I will quickly and happily go as near or as far, or remain in place for as long as I live. Also, do not forget to help us with our physical needs by using the alms that have been designated as our *sínodo* by the Ilustrísimo Señor Visitador General. He told me it amounts to 700 pesos and is to be collected in Mexico by the *síndico* of this holy colegio.

There is no ranchería at all in the vicinity of this port. Because of this, if we see that they are determined to accept our holy faith, we need to recognize the special difficulty they will have in taking up residence here. It might be necessary to leave the presidio here and, with a few soldiers of the escort, move the mission close to the Carmel River, two short leagues to the south. It is a truly splendid location, capable of producing abundant crops because of the plentiful and excellent land and water. However, we will not speak about this issue until we have more people here and after first consulting with

---

8. This ceremony of taking possession of new land was a standard part of the civil rituals of the Spanish Empire. See Seed, *Ceremonies of Possession*, 69–99.

the holy colegio and the officials in Mexico City who can order the troops to agree to cooperate in the move.

I have not received a single letter from the land of the Christians since a year ago May. I do not know if the mission has arrived from Spain, nor anything else of that sort that may have happened during that period of time in Mexico or in Christian California. And so, provided that there are ministers available, I am requesting two. This would give us a total of six, which is the number necessary for the three missions. But they must not be men who grimace when there is work to be done or men who become restless as soon as they arrive and are then anxious to return to the colegio.

As everyone knows, those who come willing to make a sacrifice for such a holy endeavor will experience hardships. For, even though I have no reason to shed tears over them, those that I have experienced, or am experiencing now, are not easy to speak about. It should be expected that there will be hardships in these remote areas, and they will be harder to tolerate if they fall upon someone who does not want to be lacking anything. However, I do not believe that anyone who is coming here is like that.

Monterey

The founding of the mission put Serra in high spirits. June 14 was the feast day of Corpus Christi, which was celebrated in Mexico City with elaborate pageantry. Serra organized a Corpus Christi procession at Monterey and enthusiastically reported to Gálvez that the Monterey celebration would not have been out of place in the capital.[9]

His immediate and overriding concern continued to be what it had been since the location for the mission had been determined—how to get closer to the local native peoples. Less than a month after his arrival, Serra expressed frustration in a note to a nun in Spain regarding the inevitable necessities involved in getting himself and his fellow Franciscans organized in these new surroundings.

❊ Serra to Sister Antonia Valladolid, June 30, 1770

Here I am, having just arrived, with so much to do building a small house of wooden poles in which to live. It will also serve as a place to store food or to store the items for the church, the house, and the supplies that were brought on the ship. It will also serve as a church where we can say Mass. All of these inconveniences are inevitable in the beginning stages.

---

9. Serra, *Writings*, 1:182–91. On the development of the feast of Corpus Christi and the centrality of its celebration in Spanish popular piety, see Ruiz, *A King Travels*, 264–92. On Corpus Christi processions in New Spain, see Schroeder and Poole, *Religion in New Spain*, 7.

> I have barely been able to find time to meet the gentiles who live at some distance from here, even though they have come to see us a number of times. They very humbly and generously have given us some of their food.

In 1770 the Rumsen people who lived near Carmel numbered approximately five hundred. They lived in five distinct villages, some of which may have been year-round residences, while others were occupied on a more seasonal basis. The indigenous population of the Monterey region as a whole was approximately twenty-eight hundred.[10]

As we noted in the previous section, Serra investigated the surrounding settlements and began to wonder if he was in the right place. But even in the face of this difficulty he began to attempt to reach out to the local native communities. A letter he wrote to José de Gálvez at the beginning of July described one friendly exchange.

❋ *Serra to José de Gálvez, July 2, 1770*

> By way of two good Indians I sent, I received word today from the gentiles who live at a distance from here that they are busy harvesting. But in four days they will come and leave their small children with me. And they sent me a bit of fresh deer meat. May God bless them.

The first baptism at Mission San Carlos occurred on December 26, 1770. Serra baptized a five-year-old boy from the nearby village of Achasta, located somewhere on the north side of the Carmel River. This baptism was followed by additional baptisms a day later when he administered the sacrament to two more boys from Achasta. All of the baptisms that occurred at Mission San Carlos over the first few years of its existence were of young children. The oldest was a girl whom the missionaries estimated to be eleven years old. This practice of baptizing young children followed a long-standing missionary custom. Missionaries believed that younger children would more easily assimilate into Spanish ways, that they would adopt the rituals and trappings of Catholicism more quickly, and, most importantly, that they would be able to learn Spanish in a relatively short time. The missionaries hoped that once the baptized boys learned Spanish and grew into young men they would be able to serve as ambassadors between the mission and their own families and communities in their home villages.[11]

---

10. Mujal, "Out of the Apocalypse to Alta California," 356; Hackel, *Children of Coyote*, 22; Breschini and Haversat, "Rumsen Seasonality and Population Dynamics."

11. Unless otherwise indicated, all baptismal data comes from the Early California Population Project at The Huntington Library, at http://www.huntington.org/Information/ECPPmain.htm. The eleven-year-old child was a girl from Achasta, who was given the name María Candelaria, San Carlos baptism 00012. On the use of children in the evangelization strategies, see Gómez Canedo, "Aspectos característicos," 445–50.

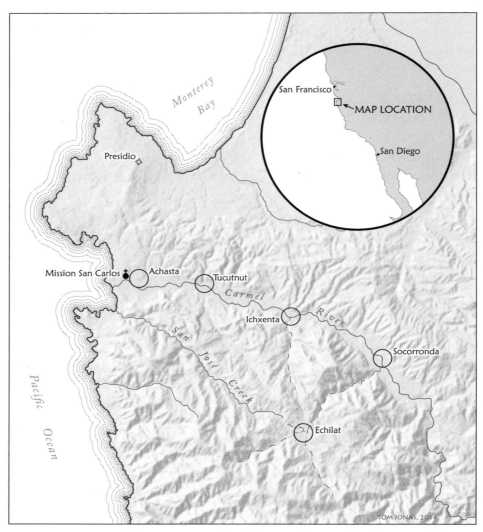

MAP 8. Rumsen village locations in the Monterey Bay region from research by Randall Milliken, 2014. Courtesy of Randall Milliken. *Map by Tom Jonas.*

However, there was another side to the story. The fact that the young children would be able to learn the language of the newcomers more quickly was undoubtedly one of the reasons that indigenous villages throughout California often presented children for baptism first. Many California Indians along the coast, where the missions were founded, had long-standing trade relations with groups that spoke a different language, so they were quite familiar with the mechanics of language acquisition. The village leaders no doubt expected that the children would be able to learn more about the ways of the Spanish because of their ability to pick up the language more quickly. During the first decade of the seventeenth century the main chief of the Powhatan Indians along the James River in Virginia adopted such a strategy with one of his daughters—Mataoka, nicknamed Pocahontas. The indigenous peoples of California were faced with a similar situation and adopted similar tactics in dealing with those who had suddenly settled on their land.[12]

Even before Serra moved the mission to the banks of the Carmel River, he started to lay the foundations for what he hoped would be a vibrant native Christian community in the Monterey Bay region. He began on March 19, 1771. This was the feast day of San José, the patron saint of the overland expedition. It was also exactly one year to the day when the relief ship *San Antonio* was seen at San Diego just as Gaspar de Portolá was about to order the abandonment of Alta California. Serra loved anniversaries, so he used that day to lay the symbolic foundation of his hoped-for new community at Carmel by baptizing three boys. One nine-year-old boy, to whom he gave the name Juan Evangelista José, was from Achasta. The name was undoubtedly meant to commemorate Juan Evangelista Benno, the boy from Mission Guadalupe in Baja California who died at San Diego in February 1770. A second boy, Fernando José, slightly younger than Juan Evangelista, hailed from Tucutnut, which was located farther up the Carmel River. A third boy, six years of age, whom he christened Diego José, was from Ichxenta, a village in the vicinity of San José Creek near Point Lobos. Even before Mission San Carlos Borromeo was established at Carmel, Serra was already envisioning a new multivillage Rumsen community as its congregation.[13]

By the middle of 1771 Serra very much believed that this strategy was proving to be successful. He reported that four of the boys who had been baptized, including two who were baptized on March 19, 1771, were becoming very adept at understanding Spanish, and he hoped that before long they would be able to begin to speak the language. He reported enthusiastically to the viceroy.

---

12. Laverty, "Recognizing Indians," 84; Laverty, "The Ohlone/Costanoan-Esselen Nation of Monterey," 43; Golla, *California Indian Languages*, 6; Townsend, *Pocahontas and the Powhatan Dilemma*.
13. San Carlos baptisms 00015–00017.

❋ *Serra to Francisco Carlos de Croix, June 18, 1771*
> And through the mercy of God in the Highest, in the short time we have been working here, we have already performed twenty baptisms. And of these twenty, four are slightly older boys who, in addition to knowing how to pray well, are making good progress learning the Spanish language. And with them as my teachers, I am doing the best I can to learn their language. In San Diego, the number of baptisms is somewhat less but there is greater progress in terms of the Spanish language. Two young adult males who were baptized are already serving as interpreters for the gentiles and as teachers for the Padres. So I hope that by awakening the fervor in many areas, by means of ten new missions, in addition to these and that of San Buenaventura, we will see before long vast new dominions incorporated into the fellowship of Our Holy Mother Church and part of the Spanish Crown.

Two days later, he elaborated on the possibilities he saw.

❋ *Serra to Rafael Verger, June 22, 1769*
> The gentiles from this area continue to be as gentle as they were when we encountered them. By knowing the language or having an interpreter, it seems that with the grace of God there will be little left to overcome. And in order to use every means possible, seeing that these dear new Christians have taken such a liking to the ship, I am thinking of having one of them travel on the ship. For during the year it will take to travel, stay, and return, I believe that he will have turned into a fine Spaniard. We shall see if this happens and how it all turns out, because according to what I am told, there are gentiles who would like to try this.

A year later, Serra reported that two of the boys, eight-year-old Buenaventura and ten-year-old Fernando, had become especially enamored of the ship in the harbor. He was expecting that they would be allowed to go out on the ship the next time it set sail. He thought this would be a tremendous opportunity for the boys to be able to assimilate and to master Spanish.

❋ *Serra to Francisco Palóu, June 22, 1771*
> The gentiles continue to be as gentle as they naturally are with nothing different to report. I have performed twenty baptisms and if I had known their language, I believe that almost everything would have been completed with the grace of God. Four older boys, Francisco, Buenaventura, Fernando, and Diego, are making some progress in terms of understanding Spanish, but

FIGURE 29. Serra's record of the baptism of Bernardino de Jesús, December 26, 1770. This was the first baptism Serra performed in Alta California, and he gave the child the same Spanish name as that of the patron of the church in which he had attended grammar school in Petra. *Courtesy of Rev. Carl Faria, Diocese of Monterey, in California Archives.*

they do not speak it. But we have a plan to get them to speak. Two of the boys, Buenaventura and Fernando, who are about eight and ten years old respectively, will get to travel on the ship, since they have become so fascinated by it. The captain will be in charge of the first boy [Buenaventura] and the quartermaster will have the second boy [Fernando] with the condition that, without fail, they must be on the ship when it returns. Our hope is that they will have turned into fine Spaniards by the time they return.

But the catastrophic indigenous death rate that was to become so pronounced a feature of mission life was already beginning to take root at Carmel. Of the four boys Serra mentioned, only one, Francisco, would outlive Serra. Diego died in 1774, Fernando in 1780, and Buenaventura in 1781. From December 1770 through December 1771 Serra baptized twenty-three Rumsen people. He performed two more baptisms in 1772, but both of those were of infants who were already near death.

Serra was certainly aware that death was a constant presence at Mission San Carlos. Part of this was no doubt due to the fact that parents would sometimes present ill children for baptism when their own traditional healing methods could not cure them. But native people would also die from having contracted

FIGURE 30. Reception of visiting Frenchman La Pérouse at Mission San Carlos in Carmel in 1786, two years after Serra's death. Unenthusiastic native people are lined up for the formal reception of the visiting Frenchman La Pérouse. Father Lasuén awaits the visitor in the doorway of the church. This work was copied at the mission by Malaspina expedition artist José Cardero from a now lost original done by La Pérouse expedition member Gaspar de Vancy. *Courtesy of the Museo Naval, Madrid.* MS 1723-1.

imported diseases for which their bodies had not acquired immunity. Serra would consistently interpret death in the way in which his faith taught him: for someone who was baptized, death was an entry into eternal life. In 1772, for instance, he wrote, "The fact is that hardships or not, there are many souls from Monterey, San Antonio, and San Diego now in Heaven." Serra himself did not have to confront the enormity of the suffering that would be experienced by the native peoples of California, a suffering that replicated the experiences of other indigenous peoples in the Americas who lived under Spanish, English, or U.S. rule. While Serra was alive, over a thousand people, mostly Indians, were baptized at Carmel and less than two hundred died at the mission. But the ratio of births and baptisms to deaths inexorably changed after Serra's time. By 1820 Serra's successor Mariano Payeras was acknowledging, "Every thoughtful missionary has noted that while the gentiles procreate easily and are healthy and robust (though errant) in the wilds, in spite of hunger, nakedness, and living outdoors like beasts, as soon as they commit themselves to a sociable and Christian life, they become extremely feeble, lose weight, get sick, and die. This plague affects the women particularly, especially those who have recently become pregnant."[14]

The overwhelming majority of the children baptized at Mission San Carlos through 1772 came from the nearby village of Achasta. It was not until 1773 that the mission began to attract numbers of people from farther away, from villages such as Tucutnut. The willingness of these more distant people to consider entering the missions may well have been at least a partial result of the Spanish animals ranging farther into the Carmel Valley for grazing. By eating the native grasses and trampling the native plants, the animals were also making the preservation of the traditional way of life at these places more difficult.[15]

Serra continued to be as enthusiastic as he was when he first arrived. Even the rote repetition of Spanish religious phrases by various Indians thrilled him.

※ *Serra to Rafael Verger, August 8, 1772*

What I am really saying is that (with the grace of God) we will soon have interpreters and the gentiles are as docile, friendly, and tranquil now as when we arrived. One can be at a distance of many leagues and the only greetings you will hear them say are "Love God! Hail Jesus, Mary, and Joseph! Holy Cross!" And when they sigh, they say "Oh, Jesus!" and similar expressions.

Serra's enthusiasm at what he took to be a very successful beginning of Christianity in the Monterey Bay area was probably responsible, at least in part, for his extravagant behavior in the summer of 1771 when he went to found Mission San Antonio. The founding of this mission became possible when ten additional missionaries arrived at Monterey on May 21, 1771. Two months later Serra took two of the newly arrived priests, Miguel Pieras and Buenaventura Sitjar, and, with seven soldiers, a few sailors, and some of the Indians who had come up from Baja California, headed out to found the new mission, San Antonio. According to Palóu, when the party reached the spot on which a temporary mission might be established, a bell was hung from an oak tree and Serra began to ring the bell vigorously. Palóu related that he started to cry out, "Come, gentiles, come to the Holy Church and receive the faith of Jesus Christ." When a nonplused Pieras asked him what he was doing, Serra said he hoped that this bell might be heard throughout the whole world and cited Sor María de Jesús de Ágreda

---

14. San Carlos death records 00018, 00156, and 00209. By the time Serra died on August 28, 1784, 1,014 people had been baptized at Mission San Carlos and 172 burials had been performed there. Payeras, *Writings*, 225.
15. Hackel, *Children of Coyote*, 77.

as justification. One suspects that Pieras might well have been wondering at this point if he had made a mistake coming so far to place himself under the jurisdiction of this individual! Even Palóu admitted that Serra was "almost beside himself" with excitement on this location. Palóu also said that when he was passing through San Antonio in 1773, the two priests told him that a very old indigenous woman reported that her parents told her that a man dressed like the missionaries visited these people long before. Palóu related this account to the statement of Sor María in 1631 that Saint Francis, from Heaven, sent two friars to the New World to preach the Gospel. Palóu was convinced that one of them had reached San Antonio. It is likely that Serra believed this as well. The story served to place Serra, full of enthusiasm as he was, in a tradition both heroic and miraculous. The enthusiasm with which he founded Mission San Antonio was informed by his belief that he was engaged in a journey directly aided by Heaven.[16]

16. Palóu, *Palóu's Life of Fray Junípero Serra*, 110–14, 290.

PLATE A. Allegory of the Llullian doctrine from a fourteenth-century manuscript, the *Breviculum*. In this drawing Ramón Llull says that the ladder of the intellect can be ascended only if it rests on the tower of faith. Serra used the same image of a ladder to represent the missions he founded in Alta California. *Breviculum Codex. Miniature. Baden Memorial Library, Karlsruhe, Germany. Photograph by Prisma/UIG via Getty Images.*

Plate B. *Brother Junípero and the Beggar*, ca. 1646, by Bartolomé Esteban Murillo. The artist's painting of a famous episode from the life of Brother Junípero, in which he gives his cloak to a beggar. *Courtesy of the Louvre, Paris, France. R.F. 1964-1. Photograph by Erich Lessing/Art Resource, N.Y.*

PLATE C. *Fray Juan Duns Escoto*. Anonymous. An eighteenth-century depiction of John Duns Scotus. *Courtesy of the Museo Nacional del Virreinato, Tepotzotlán, Mexico, and the Instituto Nacional de Antropología e Historia, Mexico City. Inv. 10-89281.*

PLATE D. *María de Jesús de Ágreda* at the age of twenty. Anonymous. According to Sor María, her bilocations occurred while she was in her twenties. *Courtesy of the Museo Nacional del Virreinato, Tepotzotlán, Mexico, and the Instituto Nacional de Antropología e Historia, Mexico City. Inv. 10-92127.*

PLATES E & F. *Rendition of a Chichimeco*, 1711, and *Rendition of a Chichimeca*, 1711, by Manuel Arellano. "Chichimeca" was a derogatory Náhuatl term applied by the peoples of central Mexico to various seminomadic groups to the north of them. The Spanish retained the term, sometimes shortening it to "Meca." The indigenous groups among whom Serra worked in the Sierra Gorda, including the Pame and the Jonace, were sometimes referred to as "Chichimecas." *Courtesy of the Museo de América, Madrid. Inv. 2000/05/01 and 2000/05/02.*

PLATE G. Friars preaching. This illumination from the eighteenth-century work *Crónica de la Provincia de los Santos Apóstoles S. Pedro y S. Pablo de Michoacán*, by Fray Pablo de Beaumont, illustrates the missionaries' belief in the nearness of the devil, seen in the two panels on the left, and the salvation offered by their preaching, exemplified by the two panels on the right. *Courtesy of the Granger Collection, New York.*

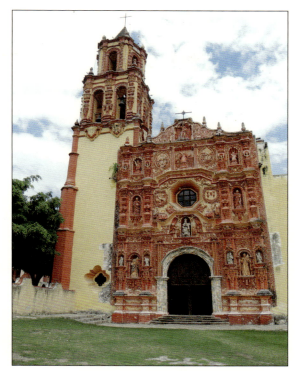

Plates H & I. Missions Santa María del Agua de Landa *(right)* and San Miguel Concá *(below)* were founded by the Colegio de San Fernando on sites chosen by José de Escandón. *Photographs by and courtesy of Robert Michels and Stephanie Daffer.*

(Left) PLATE J. Mission Santiago de Jalpan, a much older mission, was the church administered by Serra and Palóu in the 1750s. *Photograph by and courtesy of Robert Michels and Stephanie Daffer.*

(Below) PLATE K. Mission Nuestra Señora de la Luz de Tancoyol. This mission was in existence when the Fernandinos arrived in the Sierra Gorda, and it was assigned to them by Escandón. In 1766 Serra completed his Inquisition reports at this mission. *Photograph by and courtesy of Robert Michels and Stephanie Daffer.*

CHAPTER 5

Journey to Mexico City

Within a very short time after establishing his presence in Monterey, Serra became embroiled in a series of conflicts with the military commander, Pedro Fages. These conflicts set the pattern for Serra's relationships with every military and political leader he dealt with in Alta California for the rest of his life. This particular conflict with Fages would eventually lead him to Mexico City and an audience with the viceroy.

Pedro Fages was born in Catalonia in 1734. He joined the military and served in Portugal toward the end of the Seven Years War. Then he and his unit returned to Andalucía. When a group of Catalán volunteers was formed in 1767 to go to the New World as part of a campaign against the Indians of the northern frontier of New Spain, Fages joined. He was promoted to the rank of lieutenant and was made second-in-command to Agustín Callis. Fages took part in a few skirmishes in the campaign against the Seri Indians, but he and a group of his volunteers were soon dispatched to Baja California to be part of the movement to colonize Alta California. He and his men arrived in Baja California in the middle of October 1768. They were aboard the *San Carlos* when it left La Paz on January 11, 1769. The voyage was long and difficult, and they arrived in San Diego 110 days after leaving La Paz. The second ship, the *San Antonio*, had already arrived. By this time scurvy had so ravaged both crews that only six of Fages's volunteers were fit for duty.[1]

Fages was part of the Portolá expedition that left San Diego in July to search for Monterey. He was also part of the subsequent land expedition led by Portolá that found the Monterey site the following spring. After establishing the presidio, Portolá returned to Baja California and ultimately to Mexico City. He left Fages as military commander of New California. When he assumed command, Fages had only twelve Catalán volunteers and seven leather-jacket soldiers under him. He

---

1. Biographical data on Fages comes from Rodríguez-Sala, *Los gobernadores de las Californias, 1767–1804*, and Nuttall, "Pedro Fages and the Advance of the Northern Frontier of New Spain, 1767–1782."

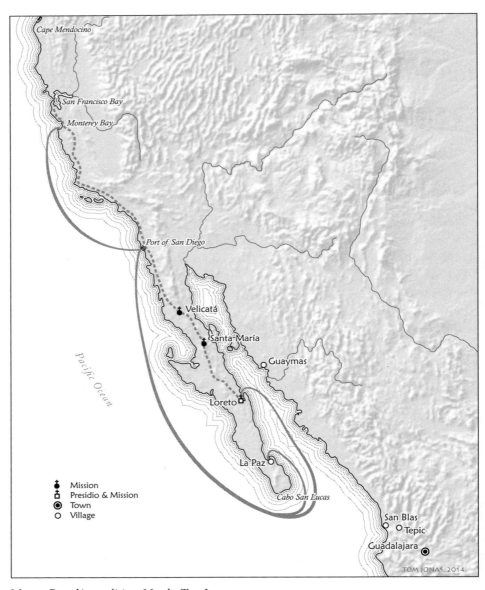

MAP 9. Portolá expedition. *Map by Tom Jonas.*

quickly began to experience the difficulties that would plague his tenure as military commander. For one thing, the relationships between him and the leather-jacket soldiers from Baja California began to deteriorate. This deterioration was underscored by Fernando de Rivera y Moncada's refusal, when he returned from Baja California with additional soldiers in 1770, to bring the soldiers to Monterey. Rather, Rivera y Moncada and his men stayed in San Diego. He apparently was irked that Fages rather than himself had been appointed as military commander, and he asked for permission to retire from service. When that permission was granted in early 1772, he left San Diego. However, Rivera y Moncada was not the only leather-jacket soldier who disliked Fages. Corporal Mariano Carrillo, who had stayed with Serra at San Diego in 1769 while Portolá went north, complained that Fages gave special favors to his personal servant and muleteer, Juan Antonio Coronel, at the expense of Carrillo and his fellow soldiers.[2]

Some of the leather-jacket frontier soldiers also felt that Fages favored his own Catalán volunteers. However, the Cataláns also had trouble with him and complained about how he treated them. The issues revolved around workload and rations. Since no one else was available, the soldiers had to become the main construction workers on the presidio. Many resented the demanding work schedule Fages imposed on them. In addition, Fages himself tended to be arrogant and dismissive of the concerns of the men who served under him.[3]

Serra had his own issues with Fages and was able to use the commander's mounting difficulties with his own troops to his advantage. Gálvez's original instructions had called for the establishment of three missions—San Diego, Monterey, and one at an undetermined location somewhere between the two. Serra quickly became convinced that this third mission should be placed near the Santa Bárbara Channel. Influenced by Juan Crespí's description of the area and its people, Serra quickly became convinced that the Chumash of the region were essential to the evangelization of Alta California. He suggested that he and Crespí could separate, with one of them remaining at Monterey and the other going to San Buenaventura, which is what the Channel mission would be called. In Serra's mind the most important thing was to start this third mission as soon as possible. But Fages disagreed. He had only nineteen soldiers available to him. He had also been through Chumash territory three times and feared the difficulties that establishing a mission in a densely populated area would entail.[4]

A situation such as this invited conflict, and neither man possessed the temperament that might have enabled them to mitigate their differences. Serra's experiences

---

2. Erickson, "Violence and Manhood," 211–12.
3. Sánchez, *Spanish Bluecoats*, 63–66.
4. Serra, *Writings*, 1:163, 173.

with the Cochimí in Baja California, with the Kumeyaay between Ensenada and San Diego, and with the Rumsen at Monterey Bay had convinced him that the peoples of the Californias, and especially of Alta California, were ready and anxious for the Gospel and that he was on the cusp of a tremendous missionary accomplishment. So he was propelled by a single-minded intensity. This was part of his nature, and even those who knew him best could find it off-putting. His close friend Palóu admitted that Serra could be driven by a desire to found too many missions much too quickly. Rafael Verger, a former colleague of Serra's at the university in Palma who became guardian at the Colegio de San Fernando, wrote diplomatically about the need to "restrain" Serra's "ardent zeal." As for Fages, the Monterey garrison was his first command, and he did not understand the difference between commanding respect from his men and earning that respect from them. He would eventually develop into a capable commander, but that was in the future. Also, as a military officer, Fages regarded the Indians as potential adversaries, and that led him (and his successors Fernando de Rivera y Moncada and Felipe de Neve) to a more cautious approach toward California's native peoples than Serra wanted.[5]

Serra was absolutely convinced that the early successes he believed he had experienced at San Carlos and San Antonio presaged a bright future for the conversion of Alta California. Even in the midst of a food shortage in 1772 his optimism did not wane. If there was any problem with evangelization, he said, it related to language difficulties. He characteristically attempted to shoulder much of the blame himself.

❋ *Serra to Francisco Palóu, August 18, 1772*

All the ministers are complaining about the vexations, the hardships, and the setbacks we have to endure. But nobody wishes or plans to leave his mission. The fact is that hardships or not, there are many souls from Monterey, San Antonio, and San Diego now in Heaven. At the present time, I am unaware of the situation at San Gabriel. There are a good number of Christians who praise God, whose holy name is on the lips of these very gentiles more frequently than on the lips of the many Christians. And even though some anticipate that the gentle sheep, which all of them are, will some day turn into tigers and lions, that is quite possible, if God permits it. But we have almost three years of experience with those from Monterey and two years with those from San Antonio, and each day they improve.

And above all, regarding the promise God made in these final days to Nuestro Padre San Francisco (as the Madre Seráfica María de Jesús [de Ágreda] says) that just by seeing his sons the gentiles will convert to our

---

5. Palóu, *Cartas desde la península de California*, 179; Geiger, *Life and Times of Fray Junípero Serra*, 1:268.

Figure 31. Pedro Fages. Detail from Mariano Guerrero's painting of Serra receiving Viaticum. *Courtesy of the Museo Nacional de Historia, Castillo de Chapultepec, and the Instituto Nacional de Antropología e Historia, Mexico City.*

Holy Catholic faith; it seems to me that I can already see it and appreciate it. Because if all the gentiles here are not already Christians, it is my understanding that it is due to lack of the language. This difficulty is not new to me. I always imagined that my sins made me very unworthy of receiving this grace. In lands like these, where one would not expect to find an interpreter or a teacher who could help us understand these people, it will be necessary to let some time go by until someone from here can learn Spanish.

This was the context in which Serra and Fages argued, and they argued about everything. The specifics were less important than the underlying tension. Serra believed that Fages was needlessly inhibiting the growth of the mission system. Fages believed that Serra was undermining his authority, especially as more and more soldiers began to share with the priests their dislike of his command style. One of their first recorded arguments was about lanterns. When a batch of lanterns was discovered on a ship, Serra said they could be put to great use in the church, while Fages insisted they were intended for the ships. Over the next two years they argued about mules, workers, and soldiers at the missions; rations; the location of the door at the priests' residence at Monterey; possession of various keys; and seemingly about anything else that arose.[6]

---

6. Serra, *Writings*, 1:184–87; Geiger, *Life and Times of Fray Junípero Serra*, 1:279.

As Fages's treatment of his soldiers became more brusque, desertions began to increase. It irked the commander tremendously that the only people who seemed to be able to convince the deserters to return were the priests. He became greatly annoyed at the deals the priests arranged with deserters. In 1771, for instance, Father Antonio Paterna convinced a group of deserters to return to San Diego with the promise that they could be stationed at the mission rather than at the presidio. Fages was enraged at what he considered Paterna's undercutting of his own authority and refused to honor the agreement. A month later another group deserted and Fages had to enlist another missionary, Father Francisco Dumetz, to convince them to return.[7]

The most substantial issues between Fages and Serra concerned Mission San Gabriel. The mission was founded in September 1771, and its early months were marked by tensions between it and the native peoples of the area. The various missionary accounts offer different reasons for the troubles. The best-known account was offered by Palóu in his biography of Serra. According to this version, the mission was founded as a result of an almost miraculously calming effect a painting of Nuestra Señora de los Dolores had on a group of warlike and hostile Indians. The painting completely erased the hostility of the Indians who "came, time and again, to visit the friars." In the face of such a promising beginning, a soldier raped the wife of a local chief who then organized a force to attack the soldier. But the attack was unsuccessful and the soldier managed to kill the chief.[8]

A different version was offered by Serra in 1773. In his telling, the local people were delighted that a mission was placed among them and worked very hard (harder than the soldiers, he added!) in the construction of the primitive complex. They visited the mission constantly. The women were especially taken with the painting of the Virgin that the Fathers had put in the church. The women often left offerings in front of the picture. But Fages ordered the soldiers not to allow more than five Indians in the mission at one time. Then a soldier who was supposed to be looking after the cattle killed the chief, cut off his head, and brought it back to the mission as a trophy. Fages used the pretext of the disturbances at San Gabriel to order an increase in the mission guard, which meant that no soldiers were available to staff the projected mission along the Santa Bárbara Channel. The soldiers at San Gabriel, commanded by a useless corporal, became increasingly unruly and would go out into the fields and lasso Indian women so they could rape them.[9]

A third version came from the pen of Pedro Cambón, one of the priests at San Gabriel. Cambón related a story about a group of native people confronting the

---
7. Geiger, *Life and Times of Fray Junípero Serra*, 1:341, 345.
8. Palóu, *Palóu's Life of Fray Junípero Serra*, 119.
9. Serra, *Writings*, 1:358–63.

soldiers and priests as they were about to cross a river, and he said that the priests unfurled the painting of Mary. But his account said that the incident happened in the middle of August, more than three weeks before the mission was actually founded. Cambón's prose was also less dramatic and sensational than Palóu's later version. Cambón was more interested in what happened after the mission was founded. He stated that many Indians were visiting the mission, that they would bring local seeds to the missionaries, and that sometimes they would leave their children there for instruction. Fages was concerned about this and ordered the number of Indians who had access to the mission at any one time restricted to four or five. At that point, some Indians tried to break in and rob the compound. By the beginning of October, the mission itself had been attacked three times, and a series of skirmishes ensued. In one encounter, a group of Indians attacked two soldiers who were attending the cattle, and in the melee one of the soldiers shot and killed the chief, whose name was Fomear. His head was left on a pole in the field as a lesson to his compatriots. Fages arrived a few days later with two priests and some soldiers on his way to establish Mission San Buenaventura. When he was informed about what was happening, Fages decided that military resources needed to be concentrated at San Gabriel and that San Buenaventura could not be established immediately.[10]

Cambón's version, which dates from 1772, seems most plausible. Serra's version, found in his memorandum to the viceroy in 1773, is rooted in one aspect of Cambón's story, which is that Fages and the soldiers at San Gabriel were suspicious that so many Indians wanted to visit the mission so soon after its founding. Mission San Gabriel was located in a much more populated area than the regions in which the three previous missions—San Diego, San Carlos, and San Antonio—were founded. None of the soldiers at San Gabriel had ever been posted to a garrison where they were so thoroughly surrounded by so many non-Christian native peoples, and they did not know what to expect. Thus, from their perspective, restricting access to the mission was perhaps a reasonable precaution. The native peoples, however, did not regard that restriction as a hospitable act, especially with some of their own children inside. In such a situation tensions would inevitably increase, but the version put forth by Serra, and later embellished by Palóu, enabled him to place the blame for the trouble at San Gabriel on two specific individuals—Fages and one sinful and lustful soldier.

---

10. Geiger, *Life and Times of Fray Junípero Serra*, 1:304–307. Cambón's letter was summarized by Verger in a report to the viceroy. Verger's report is document 292 in the Junípero Serra Collection at the Santa Bárbara Mission Archive-Library. His summary of Cambón's report begins on page 41. In his English rendition of parts of the report, Thomas Workman Temple exaggerated and overdramatized Cambon's description to make it more consistent with Palóu's later account. Temple's version may be found in Weber, *The Pride of the Missions*, 4–5.

FIGURE 32. *Mission San Luis Obispo* as drawn by Edward Vischer. Serra founded this mission in 1772 when he and Pedro Fages were en route to San Diego. *Courtesy of The Bancroft Library, University of California, Berkeley.* BANC PIC 19xx.039.10-ALB.

Serra never mentioned the story of the painting that rendered the Indians peaceful at initial contact. Given his desire to publicize any account that might indicate divine intervention in his mission project, he certainly would have emphasized this story had he known about it and thought that the incident played a significant role in the founding of the mission. Instead, in a report to the viceroy he simply stated that the Indian women were very attracted to a painting of the Virgin that they found in the church. The reason for the attraction related to the important presence of a commanding woman figure in local Gabrielino religion. This attraction, along with Cambón's account, was most likely the kernel of the story Palóu later embellished in the biography. Palóu's account of the first year at San Gabriel in his *New California*, composed in the 1770s, was broadly consonant with Cambón's account and does not mention the role of the painting in the Indians' allowing the founding of the mission.[11]

---

11. Serra, *Writings*, 1:358–59; Sandos, *Converting California*, 8–9; Palóu, *Historical Memoirs of New California*, 2:321–28.

The outcome was that, because of the trouble at San Gabriel, Fages ordered that San Buenaventura not be founded. The commander was probably quite pleased to issue this order, for he knew how much Serra wanted to expand the number of missions. But the order soured his relationship with Serra beyond repair.

In 1772 the supply ships that arrived in August were unable to make it all the way to Monterey. Since the food situation in Monterey was getting desperate, Serra and Fages decided to journey to San Diego together. On the way south, Serra established Mission San Luis Obispo in an area where Fages had temporarily alleviated the food shortage through a series of bear hunts earlier in the year. Farther along they reconnoitered a site in the Santa Bárbara Channel area for Mission San Buenaventura. Then Serra was able to visit San Gabriel for the first time. When they finally arrived in San Diego, matters came to a head between them. Serra said that the new mission they would be founding on their way back would require at least twenty soldiers because the area was so heavily populated. He also issued a series of demands: for example, explicit agreements about the authority of the priests at the mission should be drawn up, the mission should be given a dozen mules, and soldiers should not be taken away from the mission to be employed as mail couriers. Fages replied that many of Serra's demands were unreasonable. "It is not possible to give what one does not have," he said, referring to mules and muleteers. Indeed, Fages had already been begging the governor of Las Californias, Felipe de Barri, for more mules, but his requests were denied. But Serra replied that he could not establish a new mission under such circumstances.[12]

Jurisdictional conflicts between soldiers and governors, on the one hand, and missionaries, on the other hand, were more than two centuries old by the 1770s. They were a staple of Spanish expansion into the northern frontier. As we have seen, they were a constant part of life in New Mexico in the early seventeenth century. What gave these conflicts a special bite in California was not that the military officers Serra dealt with were that much different from any other officers on the northern frontier. Rather, it was that Serra was quite different from many other missionaries. By this time he was in his mid-fifties, but he felt that he was just beginning his missionary career. His advancing age, of which he was well aware, meant that he did not have much time to delay, and the optimism he had acquired in Baja California, San Diego, and Monterey made him deeply believe that there was absolutely no reason to delay. This impatience, which grew in him from 1769 on, could make him a difficult colleague on the colonial frontier.

So Serra convened a meeting of the missionaries in San Diego and raised a possibility he first suggested in a letter written before he even set out for San Diego.

---

12. Geiger, *Life and Times of Fray Junípero Serra*, 1:327–37; León Velazco, "Los soldados de Baja California," 214.

Serra proposed that someone needed to go to Mexico City and appeal directly to the viceroy. As he undoubtedly expected, the other priests said he would be the perfect person to undertake this mission. So he and his Indian servant Juan Evangelista left San Diego aboard one of the supply ships and sailed to San Blas.

It was not an easy journey. After landing they traveled overland to Guadalajara and arrived there sick. When they recovered they proceeded to Querétaro, where Serra fell ill once more. But he recovered, and he and Juan Evangelista arrived at the Colegio de San Fernando at the beginning of February 1773. Serra spent a good part of the journey drafting a memorandum to the newly appointed viceroy, Antonio María Bucareli y Ursúa. When Serra arrived, he showed the draft to the guardian, Rafael Verger, a fellow Mallorcan.

Bucareli, a native of Seville, Spain, was a military officer who was appointed governor of Cuba in 1766 as part of the Bourbon effort to increase Spanish military effectiveness in the New World. He already had a reputation of being friendly to missionaries. Many of the expelled Jesuits passed through Havana in 1767 and 1768, and Bucareli was reported to have treated them considerately and humanely while they were in his city.[13]

Further, shortly after he arrived in Mexico City to assume his new office, Bucareli asked Verger to draft a set of guidelines that might be used in the establishment of missions along the northern frontier. Verger responded by composing a document calling for a "new method" of missionary practice. This new method was actually an older one, for it involved making the early eighteenth-century Texas method of congregating the native peoples in fixed locations adjacent to the mission church the normative method. The Fernandinos had employed this method in the Sierra Gorda. Verger called for a "mixed government" in which the missionaries would congregate the Indians and be responsible for all the spiritual and temporal affairs of the mission complex.[14]

Verger based his recommendations on a 1770 report that the Colegio de San Fernando had sent to Bucareli's predecessor, Viceroy Carlos Francisco de Croix. In that report the colegio vigorously argued that the alleged despoiling of mission herds and property by the Baja California comisionados, who had been placed in charge of the missions between the Jesuits' departure and the Franciscans' arrival, had conclusively demonstrated that the success of the mission enterprise depended on the missionaries' being able to exercise control over all mission temporalities.[15]

Verger may have employed the term "new method" because he was aware that a proposal to restrict missionary jurisdiction to spiritual matters was circulating

---

13. Alegre, *Historia de la Compañía de Jesús en Nueva España*, 3:302.
14. Tapia Méndez, "Fray Rafael José Verger y Suau," 972; Ponç i Fullana, *Fr. Rafael Josep Verger i Suau*, 100–101.
15. Colegio de San Fernando, *Representación al virrey para el reforme de las misiones*, 8–9.

Journey to Mexico City

in official circles. This "new method" was being formulated by Fiscal José de Areche, a follower of Gálvez.[16]

Serra obtained an audience with the viceroy at the beginning of March. When Bucareli asked him at the end of the meeting to put his thoughts in writing, Serra was more than prepared. He had already consulted with Verger and knew that Bucareli was favorably inclined toward missions.[17]

Serra began his memorandum to the viceroy by using the same strategies he had employed as a teacher and preacher in Mallorca. He attempted to establish a rapport between himself and his audience. In his memorandum he started not with the missions themselves but, rather, with the connection between Mexico and California as experienced in the supply chain and proceeded to articulate a set of fairly straightforward problems which the viceroy could immediately deal with. Serra was also at pains to indicate to the viceroy that he himself had personal experience with a number of these items. He said, for instance, that he himself had been on the new frigate and therefore knew what kind of cargo it would be able to carry.[18]

With this introduction completed, Serra plunged into his main points. The memorandum contained two main sections. The first dealt with the question of authority, and the second revolved around the temporal needs of the missions. The section on authority contained two parts. First, Serra engaged the basic question of military authority in the Californias. He asked the viceroy to remove Fages from office and to replace him with Sergeant José Francisco de Ortega, with whom Serra became acquainted in Baja California and who accompanied him on the second land leg of the Portolá expedition. Second, Serra considered the issue of authority within the missions themselves. Here his major concern was to assert the authority of the missionaries over everyone within the mission compound, specifically the Indians and the soldiers. He argued that the priests should have exclusive control over the treatment of the Indians in the mission. This control should extend, he continued, to the decision of whether and how to punish them. The only exception he would allow was for capital cases.

In the second section of the memorandum Serra took up various issues related to the physical component of the missions. He insisted that the missions needed more laborers, that livestock herds needed to be increased, and that other Indians, especially from Baja California, should be brought to the missions to serve as role models for the Alta California indigenous people. In this regard he was especially concerned that at least some of the Baja California Indians who would

---
16. Weber, *Bárbaros*, 102–104, 309, note 95.
17. Geiger, *Life and Times of Fray Junípero Serra*, 1:348–58.
18. The memorandum is in Serra, *Writings*, 1:294–327.

be brought to Alta California should be married. He said he had heard that the native peoples of Alta California did not believe marriage was allowed among Christian Indians, and so he thought the Baja California Indians might serve as convincing examples that such was not the case. He also argued that each mission should have one soldier present who would be chosen by the missionary and report directly to him. The soldier would function as a type of mayordomo. Serra also said the missions needed blacksmiths and carpenters. Little escaped his attention. He stated, for instance, that the bells sent to the missions should not be manufactured in San Blas because he had seen those bells and they were significantly inferior to bells cast in Mexico City. He spoke about the need for more liturgical vestments. He said he was very concerned that the mail sent to the missionaries should be delivered directly to the missionaries and not routed to them through the presidios or the military.

Serra concluded the memorandum with a series of requests relating to the soldiers. He asked that five Catalán soldiers be allowed to leave Alta California. He also requested special treatment for soldiers who married Indian women. To deal with the frequent desertions from military posts in Alta California, he urged amnesty for those deserters who might return. These requests allowed him to end the memorandum by reminding the viceroy of Pedro Fages's faults. Serra had already argued that Fages was principally responsible for the bad morale of the soldiers in Alta California. He concluded the memorandum with a request that the viceroy send him a copy of any orders he might issue concerning these recommendations. Serra then went on to request that the viceroy also send him a copy of all orders that might be sent to the Alta California military in the future. This extraordinary request would have made Serra an equal to the military commander of the region. It was never approved by the government.

Over the next few months the viceroy's office considered Serra's proposals. Serra did not merely sit and wait for a response, however. When he heard that a decision had been made to close the port of San Blas, he penned a report to the viceroy urging that the port remain open. Serra's position carried the day.[19] Bucareli and his council formally agreed to a number of Serra's requests on May 6, and Serra was informed of this a week later. But the council balked at committing itself to supplying one hundred soldiers for Alta California, the number Serra had stated was essential. The council instead asked for a report on the missions to justify the request. Serra responded by reducing his estimate from one hundred to eighty, which he had probably learned was the number favored by Juan José Echeveste, an official who was drawing up a formal set of

---

19. Serra, *Writings*, 1:330–43; Thurman, *Naval Department of San Blas*, 108–12.

Figure 33. *Antonio María de Bucareli y Ursúa, Viceroy of New Spain, 1771–79.* Anonymous. *Courtesy of the Museo Nacional del Virreinato, Tepotzotlán, Mexico, and the Instituto Nacional de Antropología e Historia, Mexico City. Inv. 10-54049.*

regulations to implement the council's decisions. But Serra insisted that the new number was the absolute minimum. He acknowledged that there were far fewer soldiers in Baja California. However, in his estimation, Baja California was not a good model. Since there were so many more non-Christian Indians in Alta California than there were on the Baja California peninsula, he said, the military presence needed to be stronger in the new mission region. In the same letter he also offered a capsule summary of the founding and early development of the five Alta California missions.[20] Three days after receiving Serra's letter, Bucareli approved Echeveste's regulations.[21]

---

20. Serra, *Writings*, 1:344–73.
21. The regulation, usually called the Echeveste Reglamento, and its accompanying documents are in Palóu, *Historical Memoirs of New California*, 3:58–100; the Spanish can be found in Palóu, *Recopilación de noticias*, 1:653–74.

In early June, Serra forwarded directly to the viceroy's office the complaints of some soldiers regarding Fages's treatment of them. A week later he wrote the viceroy to thank him for taking favorable action on a number of the items in the March memorandum. He listed items on which action had not yet been taken and repeated his request that he be given copies of orders sent to the Alta California military authorities.[22]

Overall, Serra gained most of what he requested, especially concerning an affirmation of the primary authority of the priests over the Indians at the missions. Fages was removed, but Serra's idea of appointing Ortega as his replacement was rejected. Instead, the viceroy made the logical decision to appoint as military commander the only other available military officer with experience in Alta California, Fernando de Rivera y Moncada.

A month before he left Mexico City, Serra wrote a letter to his nephew Miguel. When Verger had been on a recruiting mission for the colegio a few years earlier, he had encountered Serra's nephew on Ibiza, and the nephew had complained that his uncle had not answered any of the letters he had sent to America. So Serra recounted what he had been doing for the past four years, and expressed disappointment that all the details involved in establishing institutions during his first few years in Alta California had not allowed him to work at "what we truly desire."

By this time Miguel had become well known in Mallorca as a mathematician and architect. He was very involved in the reconstruction of the Capuchin residence outside the city walls and had traveled to Madrid, where he successfully lobbied for government funding for the project. Serra may have known some of this, but he responded in a relatively ungracious way. He said that he had already written one long letter to Miguel a few years ago, and he berated his nephew for expecting more. He urged him to make the pastoral work of preaching and hearing confessions the center of his life.

But Miguel chose a different path. He became very involved in the Enlightenment-oriented Sociedad Económica de Amigos del País when a branch of it was founded in Mallorca in the late 1770s. He also wrote a treatise on mathematics. If there was any further correspondence between him and his uncle in California, none has survived. In any event, the emotional distance Serra created between himself and his close family members may have made it virtually impossible for him to understand or appreciate the tight family and kinship ties that animated and structured the clan-based indigenous societies to whom he was attempting to minister in California.[23]

---

22. Serra, *Writings*, 1:374–87.
23. Tous Meliá, *Palma a través de la cartografía*, 145–46; Cantarellas Camps, "La institucionalización de la enseñanza artística en Mallorca," 288; Campaner y Fuertes, *Cronicon Mayoricense*, 577.

✳ *Letter to Miguel de Petra, August 4, 1773*
Padre Predicador Fray Miguel de Petra,
My dearest nephew, brother, and Señor:

My reason for not having answered the various letters I received from Vuestra Reverencia is not due to a lack of affection. When I left my dear country, I had to get used to the idea that I was not just leaving physically. I could have corresponded with a number of people by means of letters, for Vuestra Reverencia knows that I am not lacking friends and acquaintances in and out of the religious life. But, if I constantly had to keep present in my memory what I had left behind, then why did I leave at all? I already wrote to Vuestra Reverencia at length after you took your vows. Vuestra Reverencia already received news about me from Padre Lector Verger, who is currently our guardian.

I received the letter from Vuestra Reverencia while I was among the gentiles, more than 300 leagues from all of Christendom. There is where I must live, and there is where I wait for God, that is, my death. When that time comes, there will be someone from our Province who will communicate the news so that I will be commended to God, and Vuestra Reverencia will know. So, what more could one ask for? Since Vuestra Reverencia lives among saints, I do not believe you are in need of my advice, which is the only reason my letters would be of any use to you.

Let us make good use of the time so that our efforts conform with the vocation to which we were called by God. Let us work toward our spiritual health with fear and trembling and with fervent charity and zeal for the spiritual health of our brothers who will follow us. And may this all be for the glory of our great God.

With this thought in mind, I was extremely pleased to learn that Vuestra Reverencia was preaching a mission in Ibiza, when Padre Comisario Verger passed through there. What Vuestra Reverencia can bring to this apostolic ministry, with the blessing of your prelates, preaching with words and by example, and hearing confessions with love and patience, seems to me to be a productive use of your time, and time well spent.

Even though I lack fervor and am wretched and useless, each day during the holy sacrifice of the Mass, I remember my very dear and only sister Juana, your mother, and her children, and most especially my Capuchin. I will hope that everyone will do the same for me so that the Lord will assist me when I am faced with dangerous situations among naked and barbarous people. Let that be the extent of our mutual correspondence, and the rest is up to God.

And to give you some indication as to where I am, Vuestra Reverencia should look at a map of America. You will see on the coast of the South Sea, incorrectly called the Pacific Ocean, the peninsula of California. I was there for one year as Presidente of the missions in that area. Those missions were founded by the Jesuit Padres who were later expelled. Keep going up north along the same coast and right before it says "Cape Mendocino" you will see on some maps the name "Port of Monterey." Well, that is where your uncle lives among those poor people.

I went there with the first Christians in 1770. There I sang the first Mass, and I was in the company of Padre Predicador Fray Juan Crespí up until the end of last August, which is when I left to come to this colegio to try to procure from the Excelentísimo Señor Virrey the necessary measures to ensure the permanence and growth of that new Christendom as well as the new establishments that have been founded and those yet to come.

Su Excelencia has been attentive to everything (thanks be to God) and he has granted all of my requests, which I hope (with Divine help) will ensure a wide and speedy propagation of the Holy Faith and an increase in the dominions of our Catholic king.

We extended the boundaries of Christianity in California with the founding of a new mission, which I named San Fernando de Velicatá. In these remote lands five missions have already been founded. They are Monterey, administered by Padre Crespí and me; San Antonio de Padua, twenty-five leagues away, to which I assigned as ministers Padres Fray Miguel Pieras and Fray Buenaventura Sitjar; San Luis Obispo, another twenty-five leagues away, to which I assigned two religious from the province of Cataluña, Padre Juncosa and Padre Cavaller; San Gabriel, more than seventy leagues to the south toward California, in which I placed someone from the province of Los Angeles and another from the province of Andalucía; and finally, San Diego, which is the closest to California, although it is more than one hundred leagues away. I assigned Padre Fray Francisco Dumetz and Padre Fray Luis Jayme as ministers there.

Everyone works with determination and successfully in their respective assignments. I left Padre Palóu as Presidente of California when I left there in 1769. And I have not seen him since. But now that those old missions that used to belong to the Jesuits are being turned over to the Dominicans, Padre Lector Palóu will come with others to join me in founding the missions of San Buenaventura, Santa Clara, and that of Nuestro Padre San Francisco. I already have the ornaments, sacred vessels, other church-related items, and other necessities there.

The number of Christians in those lands where the name of Jesus Christ had never been uttered is not very large, even though there are a few in each of the missions. We have been busy constructing our humble dwellings and small churches, training some boys to be interpreters, and attending to other essential matters, all of which has not allowed us to work at what we truly desire.

Now that things are on a somewhat firm foundation, and that, per my request, Su Excelencia has approved various measures that were seriously lacking, with God's help the fruit of our labors, such as they are, will prove to be a bountiful harvest. I say "such as they are" because if I were to describe our labors to the people of your country, these labors might seem like something very grand, when in fact, if seen up close they are not that significant.

Thanks be to God, I have been in good health in that distant land, even though it is very cold there, our dwellings are not comfortable, and there are shortages of food. But this trip to Mexico has taken a heavy toll on my health. At the end of a backbreaking journey I arrived in the city of Guadalajara, burning up with fever. After a few days I was told to receive the last rites. I was in grave danger for many days. After the persistent fever broke, it turned into a tertian fever.[24] I continued traveling while suffering from this fever. I arrived at the city of Querétaro, again in such a weakened state that they told me to receive the last rites. I recovered rather quickly and finally arrived at this holy colegio on February 6 of this year.

I remained in a very weakened state for quite some time due to my lack of appetite. But now, blessed be God, I have recovered my health and finished the business that I came here to do. I am ready to take to the road and return to that vineyard of the Lord.

When I was sick in Querétaro, Padre Predicador Fray Alejandro Llanera attended to me with exceptional care and devotion. But shortly after I arrived here, we received news that he had died from a raging fever.[25] He died after receiving all the sacraments and the assistance of that holy community. The patience and resignation of the dying man was a great example that all of us should follow. I beg Vuestra Reverencia to commend him to God.

From the mission field to which I return, only once a year do we have the opportunity to receive letters from this colegio and to write to it. And if those

---

24. A fever recurring in three-day cycles (every second day); applied to the type of fever caused by certain forms of malarial parasites. See Miller-Keane and Keane, *Encyclopedia and Dictionary of Medicine, Nursing, and Allied Health.*
25. The word Serra uses is *tabardillo*, which often means typhoid fever.

here receive one letter from us at the end of the year, is it any wonder that we are slow in writing to other parts of the world? In any event, if the Lord Our God grants me safe passage back, I may be able to send news that I have arrived, as well as any other news worthy of note.

In the meantime, I send the deepest affection that a brother can have to your mother, my dearest sister, to my niece, and to all our relatives; and to my esteemed Dr. Onofre Verd and to my other pupils, friends, and acquaintances, most especially to the Señor Rector de Selva, Dr. Jayme Font; and lastly, to everyone, with the hope that they will commend me to God so that His Majesty in His infinite mercy will see fit to make me a worthy minister of His Divine Word and grant me a holy death.

From this Colegio Apostólico de Propaganda Fide de San Fernando, Mexico, August 4, 1773
Your dear uncle, brother, and servant kisses the hand of Vuestra Reverencia, Fray Junípero Serra

CHAPTER 6

Return to Carmel

Serra left Mexico City around the middle of September and traveled through Guadalajara and Tepic to San Blas. There he boarded the *Santiago*, which was slated to undertake a voyage of exploration along the California coast north of Monterey. The ship left San Blas on January 25 and arrived in San Diego on March 14. During the voyage one of the passengers died and was buried at sea. Serra remarked that for all of the time he had been traveling aboard ships, this was the first burial at sea he had ever witnessed.[1]

When Serra arrived, the San Diego mission was located inside the presidio. The church building was constructed of logs and had a tule roof. The residence for the three priests currently working there was made of wood and adobe. The rest of the presidio complex consisted of soldiers' barracks and a warehouse. The walls surrounding the fort contained two cannons, one pointed at the harbor and the other at the village of Cosoy. By the end of 1773 there had been eighty-three baptisms of both children and adults. A few weeks after he arrived at San Diego he wrote to the guardian. The tone of his letter indicated that he was returning to Alta California in high spirits and that his optimism about converting native Californians continued unabated. After his successful encounter with the viceroy, Serra was convinced that the principal obstacle to the successful evangelization of California—that is, the intransigence of Fages—had been removed. While he was far from happy about the appointment of Rivera y Moncada, he believed that the favorable rulings he obtained in Mexico City and the supplies he managed to gather for the missions (which the *Santiago* was going to drop off at Monterey on its way north) would give the missions a solid and lasting foundation for the successful evangelization of Alta California.[2]

---
1. Serra, *Writings*, 2:34.
2. Palóu, *Historical Memoirs of New California*, 3:215.

❋ *Serra to Fr. Guardian, March 31, 1774*

> With regard to spiritual matters, the Indians from all the missions continue to be as gentle and docile as ever, with no evidence to the contrary at any mission. At this mission, San Diego, there have been several baptisms since I left, but the increase in the number of Christians has been slow. When I left, this mission had the largest number of baptisms, but now several others have surpassed it.

A week later he wrote to the viceroy in the same spirit.

❋ *Serra to Antonio María de Bucareli y Ursúa, April 5, 1774*

> For now, and it is hearsay, I can say that there is nothing new to report in terms of the docility and gentleness of the Indians, Christians as well as gentiles. And crops have been planted at all of the missions, based on what is more or less possible at each one. At Mission San Gabriel, 110 fanegas of corn and some beans were harvested last year. When we arrived here [San Diego] I saw that these crops are being used to provide food for both missions as well as the escort at each one. At all of the missions the wheat has sprouted, and if the harvest is good, we will no longer have to rely as much on the assistance from the ships.

Serra left San Diego on April 6. After a stop at San Gabriel he continued north. On April 27 he met Juan Bautista de Anza, who led the first overland journey from northern Mexico to Alta California. In his diary Anza recorded that Serra was very anxious to speak with him. "He [Serra] begged me several times to stop with him so that he might learn about my journey," he wrote. "I yielded to his request and remained with him for the rest of the day and for the night." Serra was very anxious to hear about the possibility of establishing a permanent land route between Alta California and the rest of New Spain. Ironically, Anza had been guided on his trek to Alta California by Sebastián Taraval, whom Serra remembered from the Portolá expedition and his first stay in San Diego during 1769–70. Taraval escaped from Mission San Gabriel in 1773. Father Francisco Garcés, a missionary from Querétaro who was accompanying Anza, informed Serra about Taraval's role as guide to Anza. However, Taraval was not with Anza when Serra met him.[3]

Shortly before arriving at Monterey, Serra recorded a long conversation with Juan Evangelista, who was with him during the entire trip to Mexico City. What Serra wrote down as one conversation was probably his distillation of various

---

3. Serra, *Writings*, 2:43; Bolton, *Anza's California Expeditions*, 2:223.

conversations he had with Juan over a series of months. Serra reported that he probed his young Indian companion about the nature of the spiritual beliefs of the Ohlone around the Monterey Bay area. In doing so he was searching for ways in which those beliefs might open a door to the preaching of the Christian Gospel.

He asked the boy about the cross left by the 1769 Portolá expedition to Monterey. Juan reported that the Indians had been initially afraid of the cross, to which they gave the name *porpor*, or poplar tree.[4] They had left a number of offerings on it and at its foot, in an attempt to render it benevolent. Indeed, in Ohlone religion, offerings were often attached to poles, so the placement of the cross by the Spanish had unwittingly connected to an aspect of the local culture. Juan Evangelista also said that the cross seemed to change its size and appearance as the Indians viewed it. He reported further that the original arrival of the Portolá expedition in the Monterey Bay area had been accompanied by a favorable omen, the appearance of a group of beautiful birds.

Serra and the other missionaries had little idea of the rich narrative tradition, involving actors such as Fox, Hummingbird, Hawk, and Coyote, that expressed the Ohlone view of the world.[5] But Serra's experiences during the 1766 Inquisition case gave him a firsthand view of the ways in which indigenous and Christian religious concepts could be closely intertwined. This exchange is one of the few hints we are provided in all Serra's writings of how he and other missionaries attempted to use traditional beliefs as springboards for their own preaching. This long-standing method of Christian evangelization was very consistent with the method he had used in preaching his 1744 sermons at the Convento de Santa Clara in Mallorca. There, as now at Monterey Bay, Serra thought that beginning with people's own experiences was the best way to preach the Christian Gospel. He may have attempted this even in San Diego in 1769 and 1770. For instance, there were some superficial similarities between Kumeyaay and Christian practices, such as indigenous bird songs and Christian chants, as well as native talismans and Spanish medallions of saints. Serra may have noticed these similarities while he was there. Serra indicated that he intended to undertake a systematic study of Indian beliefs. If he ever got around to that task, the results have unfortunately not survived.[6]

We have already seen many times how Serra's interpretation of the native peoples was greatly influenced by the standards and categories of European secular and religious thought. Like most other Europeans, Serra understood the native peoples of the Americas through the analytical categories and religious concepts of his own culture. Juan Evangelista's answer to Serra's questions indicated that

---
4. Heizer, *California Indian Linguistic Records*, 18.
5. Ortiz, "Chocheño and Rumsen Narratives," 142.
6. Connolly Miskwish, "The Changing Economy of the Kumeyaay," 273–74.

a similar process was at work in California's indigenous communities. He said, for instance, that the people initially understood the Spanish to be from the underworld, and speculated that they were the spirits of ancestors who had died long ago. Much as Europeans were doing, California's native peoples interpreted the newcomers through the narratives and traditions they were familiar with.

The following document is an account that Serra prepared of his conversation with Juan Evangelista.

✳︎ *Memorandum, June 22, 1774*

On the trip to Mexico, the Padre Presidente took a recently baptized Indian from this Mission of Monterey with him. Upon their return, as they were getting closer to the Indian's native land, the Padre was instructing him on how he should explain to his people what he had seen.

And to this end, he asked him if when he and his people saw the Padres, the officers, and the soldiers, if they had ever imagined that there was such a land where everybody wore clothes, etc.?

He said no, that they believed all lands to be like theirs. And with respect to the soldiers and the Padres, after they had taken a long, hard look at them, they believed them to be the sons of the mules that were carrying them.

The Padre replied that, according to that belief, they probably imagined there were lands where mules give birth to men and make *cotones*[7] and clothing?

He said no, but rather the elders said they had come out from under the ground and that they were the souls (in their way of understanding) of the old gentiles from that area who had reappeared in that manner. However, he now recognized that none of that was true and he would tell them so.

He later asked him why, when our people returned to the area near Monterey where we had planted two crosses when we first arrived, we found that the gentiles had hung strings of sardines and pieces of deer meat on the arms of the cross and had thrown many broken arrows at the foot of the cross?

He responded that they did that so the cross, which they called porpor, would not be angry with them. He explained why they were afraid, by saying that the *chupadores*[8] and dancers who go about at night, would see the cross rise up to the heavens every night. And the cross was not dark like a tree trunk but rather very bright and beautiful. That is why they had so much respect for it and would present it with as much food as they could as gifts.

---

7. Woolen shirt or blouse worn by neophytes.
8. "Sucking doctors."

The Padre decided to look further into these statements, for if they were true, they would be invaluable. After he arrived at Carmel he discovered that not only was the statement regarding the main cross that had been planted on the beach near the port, which was unknown at that time, true, but it was also true in terms of the crosses on the rosaries that our men and the Padres wore around their necks.

He says, and the interpreter that the Padres have at that mission, a Californio Indian[9] who from when he was a child learned the Spanish language well and is very intelligent, affirms, that everyone who could see our men from afar said they saw on our men's chests a cross as large as the one on the beach. It was very bright and they were so amazed that something so large could be carried. But as our men got closer to them, the cross began to appear smaller and smaller. And when our men were right in front of them, the Indians saw the actual size of the cross on each person's rosary as well as the size of the Holy Christ on the Padres' chests.

He adds that since then, they have viewed the cross as something very good and they also have great respect for our people. When they saw our people coming through the fields they also saw a large number of beautiful birds of various colors, which they had never seen before, come down from the sky and hover in the air in front of our men, singing. It was as if the birds had come to welcome and introduce those new guests to this land. This experience made them even more inclined to be receptive to us.

Other information of that nature, as well as that dealing with their ancient religion and customs will be discussed later, after conducting a thorough and accurate investigation. The door is open for such work thanks to the interpreters, which we were lacking before. With the knowledge and help of the interpreters, the religious missionaries are beginning to learn the various languages. And I say various, because of the five missions that have been founded, and of those we expect to found soon, there are not even two missions where the same language is spoken.

Serra arrived back at Carmel on May 11 in high spirits because the long-awaited supply ship had arrived two days before. Less than two weeks after Serra's arrival Fernando de Rivera y Moncada arrived to take over as military commander.

Two months after Serra arrived in Monterey he composed a long letter to the authorities at the Colegio de San Fernando. The communication clearly indicated that Serra felt himself in a very strong position and wanted to press his advantage

---

9. An Indian from Baja California.

as much as he could. He believed that his successful interviews with the viceroy increased his clout at the colegio itself. Indeed, in the second paragraph of this letter he somewhat gratuitously reminded the people at San Fernando of his successful relationship with the viceroy. He would discover two years later that this special relationship irritated some members of the colegio. He also reminded the colegio, perhaps undiplomatically, that Alta California was currently the colegio's only missionary field. The implication was that the California missions ought to be at the center of the colegio's concerns. The letter also demonstrated that he had faced considerable criticism at San Fernando for what at least some of the religious there judged to be his too hectic pace in attempting to establish additional missions. He rebutted that criticism by arguing that if he had waited until all of the formal conditions necessary for the founding of missions were met, that is, according to what some people at San Fernando believed he should do, he simply would not have been able to found missions in California. Had that been allowed to occur, he went on, the colegio would have left itself open to serious criticisms about its inability to live up to its own ideals in New Spain, and its "honor" in religious circles would have been dramatically harmed.

The letter also demonstrated that Serra wasted no time in attempting to press his advantage with Rivera y Moncada. At their first meeting Rivera y Moncada assured Serra that he was going to govern Alta California in a different manner from Fages. But Serra quickly discovered that the commander shared many of Fages's military judgments about the number of troops that were needed to support the establishment of missions. Rivera y Moncada himself was proving, as Serra feared he would, too cautious in his support of increasing the number of missions. Serra found this deeply frustrating. After his successes in Mexico City, he was in no mood to compromise with the commander. He also indicated that he would press Rivera y Moncada as vigorously as he had pressed Fages over the perceived moral irregularities in the conduct of the soldiers. Serra stated that he had already pressed the commander on a range of issues relating to the missions. Where in the past he criticized Fages for being too distant from his soldiers, he now criticized Rivera y Moncada for being too close to his men, especially to Baja California men who had been with him for years, such as the Carrillo brothers and their nephew. He also thought that he could do a better job assigning soldiers to various locations in California than the commander was doing. He was also deeply irritated that he, who had walked the corridors of power in the capital, was having to fight an obscure frontier commander on a matter as mundane as the allocation of mules. Serra said that he regarded Rivera y Moncada's assertion that Echeveste agreed with him with deep skepticism. He was also very upset by the suggestion that the Alta California missionaries were commandeering livestock that were more needed in Baja California.

This long letter deals with many topics and indicates the wide range of issues Serra was concerned about. The letter also provides a good illustration of the number of issues that were pressing in at him from all sides. A feeling of being hemmed in permeates the letter. And that beleaguered sense would remain in Serra for the rest of his time in California. Already in this letter, irritants and potential roadblocks seemed to be growing. He was angry that mules destined for Alta California were being delayed or commandeered by officials in Baja California. He was interested in maintaining good relations with officials at San Blas. He was upset that cattle were being held by the military and not being distributed among the missions. He was frustrated that rations for those working at the missions were being held back.

Serra concluded the letter with a slightly modified version of his report about his conversations with Juan Evangelista. In this revised account he added that the missionaries had learned of the Indians' belief in evil spirits. He said that they called them *muur*, a version of the local indigenous word *mur*, which meant "night" or "darkness." Serra speculated that they were similar to the demons of Christian thought and that this might provide a good gateway for the introduction of some Christian concepts. He thought he and the other missionaries had already made some progress in relating this particular indigenous belief to the Christian belief in devils and in hell. He added that from initial indications it appeared that Juan Evangelista was having a very positive effect on the local indigenous people, and he thought his own progress at Carmel indicated that God himself was directing his efforts.

This exchange between Serra and Juan Evangelista pointed to a deeper dynamic characterizing the encounter between the Spanish missionaries and the native peoples of California. While the missionaries were always on the lookout for aspects of the local culture that they thought might serve as a bridge for the introduction of Christianity, their ignorance of the local languages, especially at the beginning of the encounters, made that difficult. So they had to resort to using Spanish words to express key concepts of their religious view. For instance, in the Monterey area, the missionaries tried to adapt the *Catecismo breve*, which was put together in 1644 on the northern Mexican frontier by Jesuit missionary Bartolomé Castaño, to the local situation. In 1776 Font reported that this catechism was recited in Spanish at all of the Alta California missions. However, by 1790, many of the words had been put into the local language. For instance, the 1790 Rumsen version of the catechism shows that by then the word *sirre*, which meant "intestines" or "liver"—basically the "insides" of the body—was being used to express the Christian concept of "soul." That decision, and others like it, was made not by the missionaries, but by the local people in consultation with local translators, who were most likely other native people from Baja or Alta California. But when a local word was used to express a Christian concept that was new to the people, it did not shed its older and more traditional connotations. We do not know exactly what those connotations were, but we may be sure that they were significantly different than the connotations surrounding the immaterial and immortal soul, which was a staple of medieval Christianity.[10]

At other points in the 1790 catechism, the priests would simply retain a Spanish word if they thought it expressed something too different from indigenous concepts, or if the local community was unable to come up with an agreed-upon equivalent. So, for instance, they used the Spanish word *Dios* for God. But the simple use of the Spanish term did not significantly affect the dynamics of translation. Thus the catechism answer to the question "Where is God" was "In Heaven, on the earth, and in all things." This came out in Rumsen as "Sky, land, all thing(s)."

But sky and land already had a rich context in the stories and tales of the group, so this Dios, whoever else he may have been, would have to have been the kind of entity who fit into the ideas current in the indigenous community of what happened in the sky and into their experience of their land and their ground. When the Rumsen and the other inhabitants of native Alta California talked of this Dios, they would inevitably bestow on him attributes that were consonant with their own folkways and traditions. The nineteenth-century Luiseño Pablo Tac, when he was studying for the priesthood in Rome, translated the Spanish word *Dios* into his own language as *Chanichñich*, the central deity in the religious world of the Luiseño people. As the most recent scholarly investigation of Tac observes, "The thought and practices surrounding *Chanichñich* persisted alongside Catholicism and often imparted new meaning to it." Indeed, the more missionaries learned of the native languages and worldviews, the more they tended to realize that theological constructs based on the linguistic conventions of medieval Latin and other Romance languages often did not sit comfortably with the conventions of other languages. One Jesuit missionary working among the Huron people in the seventeenth century expressed the difficulty of translating what the missionaries regarded as a simple Christian prayer into an indigenous language: "A relative noun for them always includes the meaning of one of the three persons of the possessive pronoun, so that they cannot say simply father, son, master, servant, but are obliged to say one of these three: my father, your father, his or

---

10. Font, *With Anza to California*, 180; Heizer, *California Indian Linguistic Records*, 18; Kroeber, *The Chumash and Costanoan Languages*, 244; Shaul, "Two Mission Indian (Ohlone/Costanoan) Catechisms," 35.

her father. To facilitate the task of translating prayers, I have designated one of their nouns to stand for the word 'Father,' but we nevertheless find it impossible to get them to say properly in their language, 'In the name of the Father, and of the Son, and of the Holy Ghost.'" Religious ideas were always filtered through indigenous concepts and notions, and the Christianity that emerged in the Americas might be quite different from seventeenth- or eighteenth-century European Christianity. This is certainly what happened in Alta California.[11]

※ *Letter to the Guardian and Council of the Colegio de San Fernando, July 18, 1774*

Muy Reverendo Padre Guardián y Discretos del Apostólico Colegio de San Fernando

Muy Reverendos Padres and my dear Señores:

I am hoping, as is proper, that Vuestras Paternidades will pay particular attention to the condition, provisions, and needs of the only missions of that apostolic and holy colegio, for in large part the progress of these missions depends on your decision. This seems to be the appropriate time for me to provide you with some information. I am hoping to send more information as the opportunity and occasion present themselves.

First, I assume that based on my request, Vuestras Paternidades are already fully informed of the measures that the current Excelentísimo Señor Virrey recently took. Or you can inform yourselves whenever and however you choose, since an exact copy of my memoranda and his responses and decrees have been left at the holy colegio in the hands of the Reverend Father Guardián.

Now I am adding that the measures pertaining to the Department of San Blas have already been put into place well by Don Francisco Hijosa, the comisario there. I expect that he will persevere in working on our behalf. Should the need arise, or if we have to request a special favor for which his influence is needed, it is good to know that in addition to the friends he has inside the colegio, he is close friends with the Señor Correo Mayor Don Domingo Antonio López and the Señor de Lotería Real, in whose home he was living.[12] I do not know his name. It will be to our benefit to be on friendly terms with the Comisario of San Blas, but we do not want to ask him to do anything at all that would burden his conscience. Nor do we want him to disobey the orders from his superiors, not one iota. I would never attempt to pit one against the other.

---

11. Shaul, "Two Mission Indian (Ohlone/Costanoan) Catechisms," 29; Haas, *Pablo Tac, Indigenous Scholar*, 21–22; Greer, "Conversion and Identity," 182.
12. The officials were the postmaster and the local head of the Royal Lottery, which began in New Spain in 1771.

I already wrote to the Reverendo Padre Guardián (whose name I still do not know) from the port of San Diego. I told him that after boarding the new frigate in San Blas, on January 24, we set sail the next day, the 25th. I landed at the port of San Diego on March 14. Padre Mugártegui was sick and stayed at the mission, so Padre Fray Gregorio Amurrió was appointed the ship's chaplain, in his place, from that point on to Monterey. Those two missions now had sufficient provisions to last them until the ship, *El Príncipe*, which was at San Blas loading up supplies, arrived. On April 6 that frigate left San Diego for Monterey, and on the same day I left for the same place, but on land.

At each mission I found the religious to be in good health. They gave me an earful regarding how much they had suffered because of the long delay in the ship's arrival, as well as the offensive behavior of the soldiers. But in spite of all that, I marveled at the progress they all had made, both spiritually and temporally. I distributed chocolate, which they had not tasted for many months, and flour, which they immediately used to make bread. Every mission had an oven except for San Antonio. With these items and the good news I shared, all of their past sorrows turned into pleasures. Blessed be God.

I stayed a few days at each mission to examine the fields that had been planted. And at a number of places I performed some baptisms. All the travails I had endured were worth the effort when I saw how happy all my brothers were.

On May 11 I arrived at the presidio of Monterey and later at this mission, which is a mile from the presidio. The frigate had arrived two days earlier, on the 9th. I found everyone to be in a good mood. Nobody showed me a sour face, thanks be to God. They all confessed that not only were the hard times over, but also the dread of having to suffer this way on a regular basis in the future.

This year the missions have received, apart from the provisions from this holy colegio, alms from Our Sovereign the King, which amounted to the freight charges being paid for out of the extra funds from the sínodos.[13] And everything arrived undamaged. Vuestras Paternidades can see this on the list, in my handwriting, that I am including with this letter. In addition, all the missions have an adequate amount of crops that they will be able to harvest. And from here on out they have the means of expanding their planting

---

13. Annual stipends paid to the missionaries by the government of New Spain. In Alta California these stipends were financed from the Pious Fund, the endowment originally established by the Jesuits in the eighteenth century to support the Baja California missions.

of crops in excellent soil. Without forgetting that "God is above all," it seems to us that the prediction mentioned above is based on prudent assumptions.

With what has been said, I hope that the minds of those who so rashly reputed the founding of these missions on the basis that it was being done without the necessary provisions, will be consoled.

It seems to me that if we, the religious of San Fernando, had turned our backs on establishing a presence here while the secular officials were moving forward, there would have been little honor in this for our colegio. And if they had been founded with all the conveniences one could ask for, our credibility would not be as it is now. Moreover, if we had waited for those conditions, the missions would never have been founded. Nor have I read about enterprises of this type that have not had to pay the price of hardships and danger in order to succeed.

And above all, if the naysayers still believe that this was a mistake, they should console themselves with the *rectum ab errore*.[14] At the present time, with a slight increase in the number of cattle so they can eat meat, and with the mules they have requested, these missions have no reason to be envious of those in [Antigua] California. And they are not an inheritance from any other religious order, but rather the work of the Colegio de San Fernando. In a short time, the four yet-to-be-founded missions between Monterey and San Diego will have the same level of success. It is extremely important that they be founded as quickly as possible before speaking about the port of San Francisco or taking a step beyond Monterey.

And so, not only for that reason but for others as well, I beg that Vuestras Paternidades strongly persuade Su Excelencia to allow the four missions to be established. And that they be located at places deemed appropriate by me, which is what the former Excelentísimo ordered done with the first missions, so as to guard against disputes with the officer who can situate the presidios where he pleases.

As is already known, two of the missions are to be named San Buenaventura and Santa Clara. If Su Excelencia does not assign names to the other two, as was done with the first missions, the Venerable Discretorio should assign the names.

Even though Padres Usón, Juncosa, and Prestamero are returning to that holy colegio, there are enough religious here for the four new missions. When these four missions are established, if one travels from San Diego to

---

14. "The right things resulted from a mistake."

FIGURES 34 AND 35. Two views of Mission San Carlos in 1791, drawn from different vantage points by José Cardero. *Top image courtesy of the Museo Naval, Madrid.* AMN 1723 (4). *Bottom image courtesy of The Bancroft Library, University of California, Berkeley.* BANC PIC 1963.002: 1309 FR.

Monterey at a good pace, every third day it will be possible to spend the night with people and thus ensure the peace in the area.

If the new officer had been as imprudent as me, perhaps the two missions would already have been founded when Su Excelencia was informed. But aware of his opinions, I have little confidence that we will go forward.

I do not want to complain yet, but I am afraid that I will have to do so at some point, and it will only be because I have no other recourse. I am consoled by the fact that I did not request him, nor was I mistaken about him.

In spite of this, in terms of having peace and being able to make progress, there is a tremendous difference in how we carry out our ministry now and in times past. He assured me of this and it is not a small consolation. Thanks be to God.

With regard to what may transpire some day with that situation, I will write to that Venerable Discretorio and to no one else, as with the other mission-related matters so that nothing said will be kept hidden from the Discretorio. I am enclosing an accurate copy of my response to two letters I received from Su Excelencia that came on this last ship. I will do the same in the future unless Vuestras Paternidades order me to do something else.

And if you specifically want to know what I am alluding to when I say, "If I could only instill in the officer's mind my wishes, etc.," the following will spell out more clearly what I have said above:

I proposed to him the founding of Mission San Buenaventura. Both worlds[15] have been mistaken for years believing that this is an old mission, when it has not even been born yet.

I calculated in the following manner the number of soldiers needed for this mission, without any detriment to the other missions or the presidios:

The Reglamento allows for twenty-six soldiers at the Presidio of San Diego: twenty-two soldiers, two corporals, one sergeant, and one lieutenant. And Mission San Diego is permitted six soldiers: five soldiers and a corporal. At the present time, Mission San Diego and the presidio are one entity, and they will be so for the foreseeable future, therefore, the six men at the mission are six too many.

Of the six they allow me for Carmel, take three away, for with the remaining three and the other people I have here, I am as well defended as possible.

Let us put the nine soldiers together and establish a new mission. And let us give some of these extra religious something to do. If nine soldiers are not enough for that mission, then three or four more from the twenty-six at the Presidio of San Diego can be added, since Su Excelencia has given permission and there is even an order to this effect. We are not lacking soldiers. There is enough food to eat. I can provide, without harm to anyone, one hundred fanegas of grain. All that would be needed is the loan of some mules to transport it.

That was what I proposed and it is probably good that Vuestras Paternidades are aware of it. But the response was negative on the grounds that even

---
15. Mexico City and Madrid.

if he is given one hundred more men for the presidios, the same problem will still exist. That the Indians might revolt, who is going to deny that?

There is peace in this land and the manner in which we have spent the last four full years here, with the purpose of spreading Christianity throughout the entire area, with fewer people and at less expense than what is incurred by others who are faced with insolent, warlike, and restless Indians—that this is not viewed as some sort of progress, I do not approve or agree.

The Señor Capitán says that he convinced Señor Echeveste regarding this matter, but he did not have the support of the president.

I am saying, "with no more trouble than that of lending as many mules as he can spare." Because that is what it is, nothing small.

Mission San Antonio is only twenty-five leagues away. The few mules it has, added to those from this mission, are transporting their supplies and provisions. And we will keep transporting so that before the rains come, the mission will have everything. But the same will not be possible at Mission San Luis, which is fifty leagues away. The Padre there has written that if they want to take fifty fanegas of corn in exchange for beads, he will happily make that exchange. And I think he would be just as happy to give one hundred fanegas, because he says that it is much easier to sustain his people on the pinole that he can obtain from the gentiles in exchange for the beads than with the two hundred fanegas of corn he has in Monterey. His mules have come only once. And when I was waiting for them to come a second time, so we could add the mules we have here to the pack, I was informed they cannot return for a long time because they are in such bad shape.

While I was faced with this problem, I learned that by the tenth of this month, one of the king's large pack trains was about to head out to San Diego, with no loads, to assist with the unloading of the ship and then head to [Antigua] California to pick up the families who have been waiting there. However, the ship was still here and we kept looking at it for days to come. For me, this news helped me see my way out of this difficulty. Since they would have to pass by San Luis on their way, the pack train could take them the almost twenty loads of flour that are left here.

I wrote to the captain and explained to him, in earnest and with the utmost humility, how urgent was our need. I had Padre Dumetz act as the courier so that my request would have more impact.

But the response was negative. Because the ship might arrive soon, if the mules took the load to San Luis, the trip would take longer and this would cause a delay of a number of days. Therefore, he decided that only ten *tercios*

FIGURE 36. *Church, Mission, and Ruins of Mission San Antonio de Padua* as drawn by Edward Vischer. Serra founded this mission in 1771 with great and theatrical enthusiasm. *Courtesy of The Bancroft Library, University of California, Berkeley.* BANC PIC 19XX.039:7-ALB.

of corn should be taken to that mission for the escort. And that is what was done. The pack train left, but not right away. He took the corn for the soldiers at San Luis, but he did not take anything, not a single grain, for the Padres or the "children" of the mission, not even a speck of flour, which I had asked him to take since it was easier to transport.

This matter pertaining to the lack of mules at the missions was what I tried hardest to impress upon Su Excelencia in writing and in conversation. I finally said, and more than once, that they should transport one hundred mules from the other coast. The only cost to the Real Hacienda would be that of bringing the mules to Monterey and turning them over to me for the missions. And the missions would pay the cost of the purchase out of the ministers' sínodo.

I later learned that Su Excelencia had given orders to that effect in Sonora and in San Blas, so that one hundred mules would be sent to [Antigua] California and then to Monterey. Fifty were sent when Don Fernando sailed, and the ship later returned for the other fifty. When Don Fernando and the first mules arrived, the governor of California said that even though Señor

Corvalán was sending them, and said they were for Monterey, he had not received orders, and with that the mules remained stranded there.

When the others arrive, which should have happened by now, the governor of California can then give the order to send them, or at least let them move forward. He also needs to send another order to this captain stating that the animals are for the missions. If not, we will not receive any of them.

I would be happy if the animals were paid for by the missions, but only after they have been delivered. We would not want a repeat of what happened to the cattle, mules, and mares—all paid for—that are still in [Antigua] California. They cost us money. However, we do not hold out much hope of obtaining them.

Vuestras Paternidades will easily be able to find out by means of the palace if the one hundred mules in question are, or are not intended for the mission. If none or only some are for us, then we must be patient.

If we are not able to obtain from [Antigua] California, what was stipulated in the concordat, what was purchased, or those forty-some loads of items that had belonged to the religious and thus will be useful at these missions, which were purchased from the royal warehouses and paid for by the síndico[16] with money, then again we must be patient.

But I must request that they take pity on those two religious who are there looking after those loads and hearing, perhaps, what the first religious who were expelled never heard.

What I am saying is that for the natural defense of the honor of that holy colegio, Padre Palóu's papers are here at the house. In these papers not one detail is left unexplained or fact unproven regarding what happened or the state in which everything was left. Padre Campa, who is here, is also well informed on the matter.

Vuestras Paternidades, for the love of God, find a way to get rid of this shame that is on our holy habit and institution. Or tell me if I must remove those poor religious from that area. And may the Señor Gobernador and the others who are still there have the pleasure of keeping the forty loads and opening them up and recognizing the miserable rags that belonged to the religious. And let them comment on each one, where it might have come from, etc. For as you at the holy colegio already have discovered, from the very beginning they have stopped at no less. And for what other reason are those loads still being detained up to this very day?

---

16. A public attorney or advocate/representative of a mission. Among Franciscans, the síndico was the person, usually a non-Franciscan, who managed the order's funds, for the upkeep of its institutions, including its missions. See Palóu, *Palóu's Life of Fray Junípero Serra*, 349, note 30.

But returning to these missions, and what we now have in our hands (I am writing this letter in dribs and drabs because I get very tired) based on my experience, I am realizing more each day that we will make very little progress if we have to depend on the captain for anything—not even the issues that were resolved by the junta and ordered by Su Excelencia to be observed.

Yesterday, the 16th of the current month, I went to the Royal Presidio to discuss a few issues with him.

The first was the concubinage of the leather-jacket soldiers, for which there is no apparent remedy. With regard to this I just received letters from San Luis confirming that, among others, the corporal of that escort is involved, and even worse, the corporal at San Antonio. He [the captain] listens, very reluctantly, to the idea of transferring these soldiers. And the Padres are already writing to me about their fears that things will get worse before they get better because the captain is so biased when it comes to his soldiers. We shall see where this all ends.

The second issue had to do with the cows from Santa Clara and San Francisco that the Real Junta and Su Excelencia ordered be delivered to me. Fages was going to turn them over to me, or at least he said he was, in light of the original document that I showed him regarding the decision. Don Fernando came and said that it was up to him to do this since he was already here.

They went back and forth about who was supposed to carry out that order. It did not matter at all to me if it were one or the other. I ran into Don Fernando and he told me to wait until he was not busy. I was a man destined to wait. And when I finally went to meet with him, the ship had apparently already left. And now I find myself in this predicament, which is that he is not going to hand anything over to me. He has already documented this in his diary, stating that he has sent the inventory of the cows to Su Excelencia and is waiting for a new order from Su Excelencia telling him which cows he has to turn over. And when I told him that we should come to some sort of agreement to avoid more ultimatums, he cut me off and said that it was already written down in his diary and there was nothing he could do about it. And I have learned of this when I am so short of time, therefore all I can do is report briefly on it to Vuestras Paternidades.

Another point of discussion was regarding the soldier mayordomo whom they refer to as the missionary. In my memorandum to Su Excelencia I explained the importance of this position. When Don Fernando arrived, the missions had such a position. Finally, after I had left, Señor Fages had agreed to it. And Don Fernando now prohibits it. I did not find out about this until our last meeting.

He told the soldier mayordomo at San Antonio (Don Fernando himself told me this, and not somebody else) that at the mission he was to do everything that the other soldiers did, such as sentry duty, taking care of the horses, and escort duty. And if he made some sort of arrangement with the Padres to help them plant the crops, help with the mules, or similar things, the captain should not find out about it. Since it is impossible to do something without the captain finding out, he was basically telling him not to do it.

At San Luis, they did not have a soldier mayordomo because Señor Fages had just dismissed the man from that position at the request of the Padres, because this man, who was both a corporal and a mayordomo, publicly engaged in concubinage. Don Fernando arrived and immediately appointed him corporal at San Luis. I quickly went and complained, saying that this soldier used to be a corporal at San Antonio and they dismissed him because of his scandalous concubinage. And then, after being placed at San Luis, his behavior was even worse, and that is why they had just dismissed him from there. The captain told me that because he had not known about this, he was going to send him to San Luis, but now he would not.

I arrived at the mission and quickly found out that the captain had sent him to San Antonio as a corporal. The mere sight of this man distressed the Padres, but we will have to put up with this until things change.

With regard to the rations for the people who work at the missions, and even for those at the presidio, there is already such a change. What Su Excelencia ordered was cut in half by the Comisario of San Blas. Hunger is once again an issue, even though the corn is stacked in the middle of the patio because there is not enough room in the granary. The soldiers themselves have told him that they used to eat better during times of hunger than now when there is an abundance of food. With regard to this issue, I am planning on writing to Su Excelencia. I do not want these poor people, whom I have brought here and who see that I am aware of everything, to say that I have deceived them. And if it is going to be this way for four or five years, then that is no way to live.

And this would not be a problem if the people could obtain some food by paying for it from their salary, but if they ask for more corn on credit, their request is flatly denied.

We have received an abundance of ham. For people whose rations consist entirely of corn and beans, and not much of either one, and no meat or lard, or anything else, they would pay any price for a bit of ham. But their request is flatly denied.

My Mexican blacksmiths are practically naked, and they have already paid back the money they were given in advance. And they have not managed to acquire breeches, pots, ladles, frying pans, or *metates*.[17] In terms of what is available, it is either feast or famine. These families have to make tortillas and cook their beans with metates and pots they have borrowed from the mission.

The captain only eats with two soldiers from the Carrillo family, who are the uncles of the "favorite" who is now the corporal at San Antonio. He does not interact with Don Juan Soler or with anybody else.[18]

On the feast of San Fernando we had as guests of honor the naval officers and those from the presidio, with the exception of Don Fernando. On the feast of Corpus Christi, considering the fact that we do not have many resources, the procession and the altars were worthy of what one would have seen in large cities. And the meal that followed was not bad. Don Fernando was the only one who did not attend the festivities. To ask if we invited him would be unnecessary. For, in terms of events such as these and everything else, for that matter, we have always paid him every courtesy in keeping with his position. We choose to err on the side of too many invitations instead of not enough, which is how we also operated with the former captain.

Now, and for some time to come, you will see if I had grounds for loathing this individual. For even though I am not a soothsayer, with my experience, such as it is, with this type of character, I was not expecting anything else, nor do I believe that I was deceived in any way. If all of this were to be compared with what I said at the little house in the garden in the presence of the Señor Inquisidor Mayor, Señor Echeveste—and I do not know if Señor Meave, Padre Lector Ximenes, and others were there—you would see if it is as I have said, and I did predict correctly.

I now feel obligated to put everything down on paper—record the responses and provide a report in a timely fashion. This is a heavy cross for me to bear, when I thought I had finally managed to work with some periods of rest. But it is unavoidable, since when one is in charge he must discharge. The man in question writes down in his diary everything that happens. He says that he has orders to do this from Su Excelencia. And if at one time

---

17. A curved stone, in the shape of an inclined plane, resting on three feet, used for grinding corn, etc.
18. The Carrillos were brothers Mariano and Guillermo and the cousin was Mariano Verdugo. All had been members of the Portolá expedition. Soler was in charge of the warehouse at the Monterey presidio.

or another we propose to discuss something that happened in the past, his response is "It is already noted in the diary."

And that was the whole solution to the problem regarding the cattle from Missions San Francisco and Santa Clara. And it seemed to him that his reasons for rejecting a decision that Su Excelencia and the entire junta had made were quite sufficient. And in order to explain the reasons for the ranting and raving that will inevitably start up in the future, it seems to me that the above mentioned practice is necessary, unless Vuestras Paternidades think otherwise. You will determine if it is advisable to leave everything as it is for the time being, or state our position again so as not to have to endure years of that type of situation or worse. With regard to this matter, I must say that all the religious are becoming more and more discouraged. The extra religious are asking, "What are we doing here, since one can already see that with this man a new mission will never be founded?" Those who are busy ask, "What progress will we make in terms of spiritual matters if the problem of concubinage is not treated with the appropriate solution that was furnished by Su Excelencia? And what progress will we make in terms of temporal matters if we cannot have a man who will supervise the work, the animals, and the dealings of the mission?"

It seems that their complaints are justified. Today the missions are filled with provisions, thanks be to God and to Su Excelencia, but if we consume it all and do not progress with the resources we have purchased up until now, what will happen later?

In spite of everything, I hope that God, in one way or another, will continue the work He began. For with each day there appears new evidence that demonstrates that from the beginning, His Divine Majesty had control of this enterprise.

As I was getting closer to these lands with my Juan Evangelista, I was considering how he might be able to explain to his relatives a portion of how very much he had seen. I wanted to give him some guidance in doing this, so I asked him if he and his people, after seeing the Padres and the soldiers, imagined that there might be lands totally inhabited by these types of people, who wore clothing, were Christians, etc. He said no, that the elders said they had come from below the earth, and (as he explained) they were the souls of their ancestors, the old gentiles, who had reappeared in that guise. But he now saw that it was all a lie and he would tell that to his people.

Later, when I was talking to him about the Christian symbol that he had seen everywhere, that is, the Holy Cross, I asked him why was it that on the cross that the first expedition had planted near the beach at Monterey, when we returned we found that the gentiles had hung strings of sardines, pieces of deer meat, and feathers on the arms of the cross. And there were many broken arrows at the foot of the cross. He responded that they did that as a means of keeping the cross from getting angry with them, for they were very afraid of the cross. He explained the reason for their fear was that the chupadores and dancers who normally roam about at night, would see the cross rise up to the heavens every night. The cross was not dark like wood, but rather bright, beautiful, and shiny like the sun.

He also said it seemed to everyone that the cross was a very good thing. They respected it very much, even though they did not know why. This information made me exceedingly happy, and I intended to look into this matter with great detail upon arrival. And that is what I did. Not only did I find that everyone confirmed what he had said, but I also learned that there was even more reaction with regard to the crucifixes the Padres wore on their chests and the crosses on the soldiers' rosaries.

The Indians say that when our people appeared on land, they could see on their chests crosses as large as the one our people later planted on the beach. And they were in awe as to how the men could carry something so large and so resplendent. Those who had the courage to approach our men saw that the closer they got, the smaller the crosses became. And when they were right in front of one another, the Indians were able to see the actual size of the cross and what it really was. They said this allowed them to allay their fears and feel affection toward our people, especially when they saw that no harm came to them when our men approached them. On the contrary, our men would treat them kindly and give them presents.

Another thing also helped them respect our men. According to the Indians, on a number of occasions they saw a very large flock of beautiful small birds of various colors come down from the sky. They had never seen them before. It seemed as if the birds were flying down to meet our men and welcome them. As soon as the birds would find them, they would accompany the men for a good while.

According to the Indians' explanation, there was nothing these poor people knew better than that demons do exist, that they are bad, and that they are their enemies, which is what a Christian should know. The Indians call their demons Muur. They are now happy to find out that the demons' home is in Hell and that God is punishing them. With God's help, I will carefully gather information about the wicked behavior the demons engaged in with the Indians, and other things. I should point out that the aforementioned stories are just from this area around Monterey. I have heard other versions from other missions, as well as from here. I hope these stories do not remain untold.

There is a good deal of evidence demonstrating that God's blessing is extensive and plentiful.

The manner in which the seeds have been sown is known to God. And we all marvel at how the crops are growing.

I have just received letters from San Luis saying they have harvested half the wheat and they hope it will be no less than two hundred fanegas. With regard to the corn, it is as much as they could hope for.

At San Gabriel, they will harvest no less.

At San Antonio, they are also harvesting, and it does not look bad. The corn is excellent.

Here, we obtained twenty fanegas from less than three almudes of barley. Today I began to harvest the wheat, from the three and one-half fanegas that were sown. Everything has grown well and I have never seen such healthy corn.

The gentiles from all parts are starting to come closer. Yesterday some gentiles from the mountains sent word for us to go with mules to pick up some meat. They sent four bear thighs and an entire deer. Today and tomorrow our people will be treated to this.

It appears that with what the boy has told them about his time in Mexico and the fact that they have seen so many women arrive, they have finally understood why we came here. We did not need them for anything; we have only come for their well-being.

This is what the volunteer soldiers who were married said when they saw Juan:

"Now our women will surely believe that there is another world and that we could have gotten married elsewhere."

In the end, I hope that because of the prayers of this holy community and those of other holy people, who throughout the world are praying for the conversion of the infidels, thousands will be incorporated into the fellowship of our Holy Church. I beg you, for the love of God, to help us with the necessary measures that lead to this holy purpose, by asking Su Excelencia to decree what must come from there, and arranging a plan for the most careful possible transport of supplies.

We live amid an infinite number of naked people. If we purchase clothing haphazardly, hoping to clothe one hundred people, we will not have enough for twenty. That clothing made in Querétaro should be purchased in Mexico does not seem to make much sense. And what with some perseverance could be obtained in Mexico for ten pesos but ends up costing fifteen due to sheer laziness—that is not progress.

When I was at the colegio I suggested something to this effect to the former Reverendo Padre Guardián. And he told me it was true that a lot of money was wasted, as if it were being thrown down the drain. He said they do not want a religious to become attached to that. They, whoever they are, who do not want this and can get away with saying this, can be no other than the members of that Venerable Discretorio. Vuestras Paternidades, consider, for God's sake, if you want to do this in the future so that the work of this Colegio Apostólico can move forward and its workers can toil with greater consolation.

A few weeks after he wrote the previous letter to the Colegio de San Fernando, Serra wrote directly to the viceroy. He painted a very optimistic picture of the spread of Christianity in Alta California, saying that he was in the process of creating a new area of "Christendom" on the northern frontier of New Spain. He reported that a group of native peoples who lived farther away, the Esselen, were begging for a mission to be established among them, and he described the origin of the place-name "Soledad." And he believed that closer to home things were progressing very well. Particularly significant was the picture Serra painted of an episode on the beach. He reported that just as the harvesting of the mission crops was beginning a very large number of sardines appeared offshore. Since the native people needed to begin to gather them immediately, an arrangement was worked out whereby they agreed to work at the mission in the morning so long as they could engage in the traditional fishing and harvesting of the sardines in the afternoon. This arrangement lasted for a few weeks, and Serra ended his account with a bucolic scene of the Rumsen gathering in family groups on the beach roasting and eating birds.

This portrayal of native peoples gradually learning the techniques of European agriculture, of a mission work schedule divided evenly between imported and traditional occupations, of Europeans appreciating the skill of native California fishermen, and of priests appreciatively watching a Rumsen community gathering may well have been an idealized one. However, it contained a strong vision of the kind of Christian community Serra thought he was in the process of creating in Alta California. In describing this scene, Serra used the Spanish phrase *bello teatro*, which was probably an allusion to the well-known 1698 work by Fray Agustín Vetancurt, *Teatro mexicano*. He was thus consciously placing his own efforts in Alta California in the heroic Franciscan tradition of missionary accomplishments in the New World. In his mind such promising scenes could be replicated up and down the coast if only obstructionist leaders like Rivera y Moncada as well as overly cautious friars at San Fernando would get out of his way and cooperate.

Serra to Antonio María de Bucareli y Ursúa, August 24, 1774

Seeing how one hundred boys and girls of about the same age pray and answer all the questions about Christian doctrine by themselves; how they sing; the way they are dressed in cotton cloth and striped wool; how happily they play; and how they cling to the Padre as if they had always known him—this is a tender sight to behold and one for which God should be praised.

It seems that based on the information from the little Indian boy, whom Vuestra Excelencia warmly received, and the fact that the women they saw arriving on both ships looked like and spoke the same language as the men, they finally believe there are other lands and that we have not come here seeking riches but rather to work on their behalf. And that is what a number of them have said. "Now we believe," they say. "Now we do."

Each day they leave the very remote rancherías nestled in the dense vegetation of the mountains. At the present time, there are some who seem to come from Eslen, also known as La Soledad, a place halfway along the route (a distance of about twelve leagues) between this mission and Mission San Antonio. They make it very clear that they would be pleased to have Padres on their land. They see the church, which is clean; abundant cornfields; many children; and other people like themselves but who are clothed and who sing and who have plenty to eat even though they work. All of this, together with the way Our Lord God touches their souls—who can doubt that He will win their hearts?

This is now the second time they have come. Shortly before this, one of the Padres from this mission, who had gone to Mission San Antonio on some business, told me upon his return that the Indians from La Soledad asked him to give the "Padre Viejo" their regards. I do not know nor did I want to ask how they had expressed themselves, but when they arrived a few days later, they kept stroking my shoulder with their hands, repeating, "Padre Viejo, Padre Viejo." And yes, they are telling the truth—I am old, so what can I do about it, Vuestra Excelencia?

I have traveled through their land a number of times and have seen many gentiles of all ages living there, as well as in the many rancherías they have in the surrounding area. They are all so pleasant. They often have followed after me, young and old alike, shouting at the top of their lungs, "Love God, Padre. Long live Jesús."

Once they become familiar with that expression they take hold of it and do not let it go. Either because they know it pleases us to hear that expression or, without knowing why, it has made an impression on them, it is the first thing you hear them say when they see one of our own. And after that, they ask for something. They used to ask for beads, but now it is tobacco.

The origin of the name "Soledad" came about as follows: Three years ago, when I was returning from founding Mission San Antonio, I spent the night at that place. When we arrived there in the afternoon, a few gentiles approached us and gave us some seeds they had prepared for us to eat. I accepted them and gave them some glass beads. I was welcoming them when they asked me, by way of signs, if I wanted some women who were nearby to approach. When they were given permission, two women came over. Neither before nor after have I seen other women like them.

Only in terms of their clothing were they like gentile Indians. I asked one of them, who had given me a present, what her name was, since that was something I knew how to say in their language. It seemed to me that she responded, "Soledad." I was amazed and turning to those who had accompanied me, I said, "May I present to you, María de la Soledad." And without further ado, that is the name everyone uses. Oh, Señor, these poor people have had enough solitude. Vuestra Excelencia will decide how to proceed. I am very ready to keep them company. And including this area, we had twenty-five leagues of continuous Christendom....

[...] The new Christians of this mission, adults, who with the example of the few laborers that I have been able to obtain up to this point, are beginning to work harder at their jobs. Some with hoes in hand, break up the ground to widen the area for sowing, others dig in the garden, others make adobe bricks, while others use saws. During these last weeks, everyone has been involved with the wheat harvest, hauling the sacks to the granary and doing whatever else they are told to do.

The harvesting began on July 18. It had to be prolonged until August 11 because as soon as the harvesting began, so many sardines appeared on the beach near the mission that we found it necessary to harvest wheat until noon and then gather sardines in the afternoon. This arrangement lasted for twenty consecutive days. Besides the sardines that so many people ate during that time (even people who came from remote areas ate sardines) and what we and our people ate fresh, we were left with the fish that was given to us. This consists of twenty barrels packed full of salted sardines. At first we had more, but as the fish began to settle in the barrels, three barrels full would become two.

Ten barrels were prepared for some other people, but seeing that we were running out of barrels and salt, it occurred to us to open up the sardines, debone them, and set them out to dry in the sun, which is how the gentiles

FIGURE 37. *Indian Woman from Monterey*, 1791, by José Cardero. She is attired in the traditional garb that the missionaries sought to replace. *Courtesy of the Museo de América, Madrid. Inv. 02284.*

who live in the Santa Bárbara Channel do it. We give away the sardines that we have dried in this manner to anybody who asks for them.

After two weeks of meatless meals, the following Sunday the Indians took a break from eating sardines and went out as a group to look for the nests that fish-eating birds build between the rocks. They pulled out large numbers of young birds that were the size of a large hen. They spent that Sunday camped out on the beach of Carmel, divided up into countless little groups, each with its own fire upon which they roasted the birds, and then they ate. I went with two other Padres to see the gathering. It was a period of contentment, a beautiful setting.

[. . .] With regard to the garden, I said, and say again that it is bountiful. It has many vegetables. And I do have to confess that we have a bed of tobacco plants, because of what I mentioned about the gentiles from Soledad. On this last long walk from San Diego up to here, without exception, I always heard the Indians say, "Love God, Padre" and then "Chuqui, chuqui." And since it seemed to them that I did not understand them, they would say loud and clear, "Tobacco, Padre." Since I do not use it, I did not have any with me.

After his return from Mexico City, Serra was tightly focused on expanding the scope of the mission enterprise, a focus that manifested itself in some very unlikely places or situations—such as at a farewell Mass. After supplies were unloaded from the *Santiago* at Monterey in 1774, the ship sailed north on a voyage of exploration. But before it set sail, Serra preached the sermon at the farewell Mass and told all of the people present that the entire reason for the northern explorations was the conversion of some gentiles. Those who heard Serra's sermon knew this was not the case. It was evident that the sermon itself indicated how all-consuming the advancement of the mission system had become for him and how consistently he was trying to impose his own narrative framework on events in Alta California.[19]

Some events seemed to be bearing out his hopes for conversion of gentiles. Soon after Serra returned to Monterey, Tatlun, the chief of the village of Ichxenta, presented his four-year-old son for baptism. Serra was so pleased by this that he gave the boy the Christian name Junípero. Roughly a year later the chief and his wife were themselves baptized. Serra named the chief Antonio María de Bucareli and his wife María Antonia de Ursúa, for the viceroy and his wife. Serra was delighted that the influence of the mission was spreading farther and farther into the Rumsen territory and deeper into Rumsen society.[20]

---

19. Serra, *Writings*, 2:60–61; for the voyage, see Rodríguez-Sala, *De San Blas hasta la Alta California*, 11–33.
20. San Carlos baptisms 00176, 00358, and 00359.

He was aware of difficulties that attended his efforts, but tended to interpret them with the most positive theological slant he could employ. For example, he was conscious of the fact that many young children at the mission were dying and he generally alluded to this when reporting the sudden spread of some disease or other condition. At the end of August 1774 he reported several deaths.

> *Serra to the Guardian and Discretorium of the Colegio de San Fernando, August 31, 1774*
>
> Two weeks ago, over the course of a few days, eleven infants from this mission ascended to Heaven, one after the other. And there were days when two would die and when three would die. And several adults also died. Some were baptized at the point of death and others had been baptized before. The illness that was taking them ceased. It was dysentery.

The deaths of these young children was a grisly symbol of the way in which the presence of Spanish people and institutions in Rumsen territory was dramatically affecting the lifeways of the local indigenous people.

By the middle of the summer of 1775 the relationship between Serra and Rivera y Moncada, which was never strong in the first place, was deteriorating significantly. In the last months of 1774 and the initial months of 1775 Serra expressed irritation with the commander in letters to both the guardian at the Colegio de San Fernando and the viceroy. In January 1775 Serra repeated to the guardian his complaint that there was no rationale for the commander to keep twenty soldiers at the San Diego presidio when six soldiers were already at the mission. He acknowledged that the commander said the soldiers were there to prevent an uprising of the Indians, but Serra said they could be better employed elsewhere. Serra was more diplomatic when writing to the viceroy. He merely expressed disappointment that in the eighteen months since he had returned from Mexico City, he had been unable to establish even one little cell for a single monk.[21]

In July 1775 Serra received word from the viceroy that a presidio and two missions were to be founded near San Francisco. He was gratified by this news. He wrote back and strongly encouraged the viceroy to make sure that these two new missions were adequately supplied during their first few years of their development. Serra also indicated that he intended to send some Baja California Indians to those missions. That same month, when he heard that there were conversations in Mexico about establishing two missions along the Colorado River, he immediately wrote to the guardian and said that at least one of those missions should be under the jurisdiction of the Colegio de San Fernando. That would,

---

21. Serra, *Writings*, 2:168–71, 174–77, 196–97, 207.

of course, have placed it under Serra's own jurisdiction! In August, when Rivera y Moncada was at Carmel, Serra dropped any pretense at subtlety and told him directly that he was keeping too many soldiers at the San Diego presidio. The commander merely replied that he would give the matter some thought.[22]

A few days later, on August 12, 1775, Serra and fellow missionary José Murguía went to the presidio to discuss new missions. Rivera y Moncada told them that six soldiers would be sufficient for one new mission. Serra had received a copy of a letter from the viceroy, and he and the other missionaries had mistakenly read in it the number thirteen (*trece*) instead of the number six (*seis*). So Serra challenged the commander and accused him of not accurately carrying out the viceroy's commands. Serra became so agitated that he banged the table with his hand. The exchange ended when the commander, who generally maintained his calm, showed Serra his copy of the letter, which clearly said "six." Serra was mortified. According to Lasuén, who was present, Rivera y Moncada remained calm and composed throughout the exchange.[23]

---

22. Serra, *Writings*, 2:262–67, 292–93; Geiger, *Life and Times of Fray Junípero Serra*, 2:36.
23. Serra, *Writings*, 2:384–91; Lasuén, *Writings*, 1:57; Rivera y Moncada, *Diario del capitán comandante Fernando de Rivera y Moncada*, 1:168–69. Serra was able to joke about this, saying that it was embarrassing for someone whose formal academic title was Lector ("Reader") to make such a mistake.

Plate L. Escudo or shield of the Mexican Inquisition. Serra was appointed as a comisario of this Inquisition in 1752. *Courtesy of the Museo Nacional del Virreinato, Tepotzotlán, Mexico, and the Instituto Nacional de Antropología e Historia, Mexico City.* Inv. 10-53997.

Plate M. The kind of Agnus Dei (Lamb of God) medallion that María Pascuala de Nava said that the lieutenant in Valle de Maíz was wearing. She said this medallion frightened the devil. *Courtesy of Haus zum Dolder, Dr. Edmund Müller Collection, Beromünster, Switzerland.*

PLATE N. *Rendition of a Mulata*, 1711, by Manuel Arellano. In the Spanish casta system, a mulato(a) was the offspring of a union between a Spaniard and an Indian. In colonial Latin America, mulato(a) could also mean an individual of mixed African and Indian ancestry. In remote and frontier areas, these categories were never so fixed as the formal system implied. Collection of Jan and Frederick Mayer, Denver. *Courtesy of the Denver Art Museum.*

PLATE O. *De chino cambujo e india, loba*, 1763, by Miguel Cabrera. The term *chino* refers to the offspring of a union between an African and an Indian. The adjective *cambujo* means dark-skinned. María Pascuala de Nava, accused of witchcraft in 1766, was variously identified as a loba and a mulata. *Courtesy of Album / Art Resource, New York.*

PLATE P. Jaguar warrior. Izmiquilpan church mural series, Hidalgo, Mexico. This depiction of a traditional figure in a Catholic church building affords a good example of the syncretism between native and imported Christian worldviews that permeated much of indigenous Catholicism in colonial New Spain. *Photograph courtesy of Dr. Robert H. Jackson, Mexico City.*

(Top) Plate Q. Mission Santiago. "Santiago or the mission named after Saint Joseph in California which I almost completed." Watercolor by Jesuit Fr. Ignacio Tirsch, sj. This painting and others by Fr. Tirsch were done shortly before the expulsion of the Jesuits from Baja California. *Courtesy of the National Library of the Czech Republic, XVI B18 2050 EX0009R.*

(Bottom) Plate R. Farm at Mission Santiago. "This is my little farm which I received as a bequest from the Mission of Santiago, located three miles on the way to San José del Cabo." Watercolor by Fr. Ignacio Tirsch, sj. *Courtesy of the National Library of the Czech Republic, XVI B18 2050 EX0006R.*

(Top) PLATE S. Killing a deer. "How two California Indians killed a deer with arrows, how they skinned it in the field and [prepared it for roasting], etc." Watercolor by Fr. Ignacio Tirsch, sj. *Courtesy of the National Library of the Czech Republic, XVI B18 2050 EX0031R.*

(Bottom) PLATE T. California Indian woman. "A California Indian woman carrying green seed pulp, and a California Mayordomo like those who came from Spain." Fr. Ignacio Tirsch, sj. *Courtesy of the National Library of the Czech Republic, XVI B18 2050 EX0033R.*

(*Above*) PLATE U. *Indians of California* (*Indiens de la Californie*), by Alexandre-Jean Noël. Only sixteen years old at the time, Noël was a member of a Spanish-French scientific expedition that journeyed to Baja California to observe the Transit of Venus from just outside San José del Cabo in 1769. *Courtesy of the Musée du Louvre, Paris, France. Cabinet des Dessins, Inv. No. 31471.* © RMN-Grand Palais / Art Resource, New York.

(*Opposite*) PLATES V & W. Plants of Baja California. Father Ignacio Tirsch produced a number of paintings of the plant life in Baja California and was careful to identify precisely as many of them as he could. A considerable number of the plants and vegetation in these two illustrations were sighted and recorded by Serra and Juan Crespí in their Baja California diaries. *Courtesy of the National Library of the Czech Republic, XVI B18 2050 EX0001R and XVI B18 2050 EX0002R.*

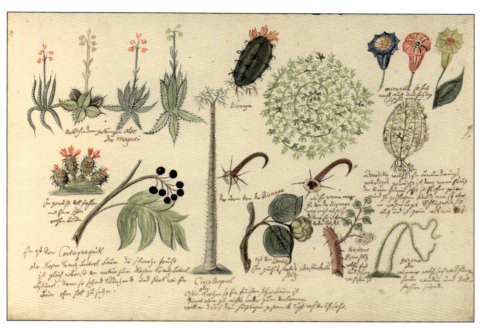

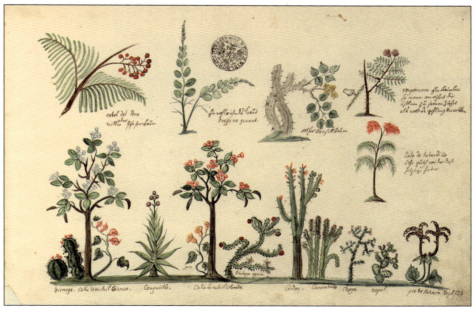

(Top) Plate X. Heathens coming out of the wilderness. "Out of the wilderness a heathen and his wife are coming with their daughters and son to the Mission to be converted." Watercolor by Fr. Ignacio Tirsch, sj. The placement of the church on a hill was a graphic illustration of the missionary conviction that Christianity offered the native peoples a superior way of life. *Courtesy of the National Library of the Czech Republic, XVI B18 2050 0030R.*

(Bottom) Plate Y. *Soldado de cuera*, by Raymundo Murillo. A Spanish cavalry soldier equipped for duty along the northern frontier of New Spain at the beginning of the nineteenth century. The numbered elements of his equipment include (1) leather jacket; (2) saddle tree; (3) musket; (4) saddlebags; (5) lance; (6) pistols; (7) shield; (8) boots and spurs; (9) wooden stirrups; and (10) cartridge belt. Most soldiers Serra met on the remote frontiers of New Spain were not so fully equipped. *Courtesy of the Ministerio de Educación, Cultura y Deporte, Archivo General de Indias, MP Uniformes 81, Soldado de Cuera.*

CHAPTER 7

Serra-Rivera Correspondence

Fernando de Rivera y Moncada kept a diary for at least part of the time that he was military commander of Alta California. Portions of that diary have survived, and they enable us to reconstruct some of the dynamics of the exchange between him and Serra in a way that is not possible with the exchanges between Serra and the other two military commanders with whom he had dealings, namely Fages and Neve. This exchange gives a close view of the multitude of issues on which the president of the missions and the military commander of Alta California were engaged on a daily basis. And this exchange is unique, for it is the only instance we have in Serra's writings that enables us to witness the day-to-day quality of his interactions with another person. As we have already seen, most of Serra's letters were written to individuals hundreds or thousands of miles distant, and he knew that his correspondents would not receive his words for many months. And many times he was responding in his letters to documents composed a year or more in the past. But he and Rivera were only a few miles distant from each other, and their letters were delivered to each other by couriers, sometimes on the same day they were composed. This series of letters thus offers a unique glimpse, not only into Serra's daily concerns, but into the interactions between two important and powerful figures in Spanish Alta California.

Fernando de Rivera y Moncada was born in Compostela, New Spain, in 1724. His father, Cristóbal de Rivera y Mendoza, was a local magistrate and a member of the town council. His mother, Josefa Ramona de Moncada y de la Peña, was Cristóbal's second wife. She also had family connections in Compostela and in Guadalajara.[1]

Since the early eighteenth century significant connections had existed between Compostela and Baja California. A number of presidio soldiers at Loreto came from there. This connection stemmed from the fact that a leading figure in the

---

1. This biographical information is taken from Crosby, *Antigua California*.

area of Compostela, the Conde de Miravalle, was a benefactor of the Jesuits and was able to steer young men to service in the Jesuit missions on the Baja California peninsula. Rivera y Moncada was one such young man. He joined the military in 1741 and served in the southern branch of the Loreto presidio detachment. In the late 1740s he saw some action in military engagements against the Uchití, a group of southern Guaycura people. In 1751, on the recommendation of the local Jesuit leader, Miguel del Barco, Rivera y Moncada was appointed commander of the presidio at Loreto. He was twenty-six years old at the time. Rivera was appointed even though two other soldiers, a lieutenant and a sergeant, outranked him. The Jesuits chose not to appoint either the lieutenant or the sergeant because both of these men were related by marriage to Manuel de Ocio, with whom the Jesuits had a tumultuous and hostile relationship. Barco was stationed at Mission San Javier outside Loreto and may have come to know Rivera y Moncada in the 1740s. In addition, the relatively high standing of Rivera y Moncada's family in Compostela most likely ensured his acceptance among many of the enlisted soldiers.

Rivera y Moncada more than justified the Jesuits' trust in him. He proved to be a zealous and capable explorer whose knowledge of the peninsula helped the Jesuits expand their mission frontier to the north. He accompanied and sometimes led expeditions with Fernando Consag in the 1750s and Wenceslao Linck in the 1760s. His post as the senior military leader in an area in which there were no other colonial officials also endowed him with certain judicial responsibilities. His legal rulings consistently favored the Jesuits against Ocio and others.

When Gaspar de Portolá arrived at San José del Cabo on November 30, 1767, Rivera y Moncada happened to be in the area, and a few days later he met the new governor. Portolá's primary orders were to expel the Jesuits. He then appointed commissioners to administer the temporal affairs of the missions. These commissioners were often the soldiers who were already serving at the missions as mayordomos. Thus Rivera y Moncada knew them all.

When José de Gálvez arrived in Baja California to organize the expedition northward, he decided he needed to win the favor of the missionaries, so he gave the management of the mission property to the new priests—the Franciscans from the Colegio de San Fernando. Once Gálvez realized that the Baja California missions were actually in very poor condition, he was faced with something of a dilemma. He wanted those missions to supply the expedition to the north, so he had to represent the poverty of the missions as only a temporary state of affairs. Otherwise, he could not make the case that these missions could afford to contribute various goods to the northern expedition while still continuing to function as missions themselves. To accomplish this he concocted a fiction that the poverty of the missions was the result of the greed of the commissioners whom Portolá had placed over them. These commissioners, the story went, had despoiled the missions. With the commissioners gone, the prosperity of the missions would return. The Franciscans went along with the account that Gálvez put forth. A version of it appears in Palóu's *Historical Memoirs of New California*. In that volume the story is used as an object lesson to drive home the point that only missionaries could be trusted with the mission's physical possessions. Thanks to the research of Harry Crosby, we know the identities of these commissioners. Not one of them ever enriched himself with mission plunder. The missionaries' acceptance of the story of their alleged greed was probably something that made Rivera y Moncada begin to distrust the leader of the new missionary group—Junípero Serra.[2]

As an accomplished soldier and experienced explorer, Rivera y Moncada was the obvious choice to lead the first leg of the overland journey to San Diego. Indeed, it is difficult to imagine anyone else in Baja California who could have performed this task.[3] During that journey he and a few other scouts normally moved out ahead of the main body of the expedition. He generally followed an inland route and avoided the coast, which earlier experiences had suggested to him might well prove to be impassable. When the expedition reached San Diego, it encountered two boats, many sick and dying men, and a makeshift camp and hospital close to the shore. Rivera y Moncada immediately moved the camp closer to the river at a site near what would eventually be the San Diego presidio. He accompanied Portolá on his unsuccessful journey to find Monterey. The scouting duties on that journey were given to Sergeant José Francisco de Ortega, who had performed those duties for Portolá on the second leg of the land expedition. This may have irritated Rivera y Moncada, especially since he and Ortega had not been on the best of terms in Baja California. Indeed, Ortega had once represented Ocio at a hearing before Rivera y Moncada. During the Portolá expedition's final attempt to locate Monterey after its return from San Francisco Bay, Rivera y Moncada was sent out on a last desperate scouting expedition that was not successful. At a conference at the Point of Pines in December, Rivera y Moncada expressed his deep frustration with the journey.[4] When the expedition returned to San Diego at the end of January 1770, Portolá sent Rivera y Moncada and a group of soldiers to Baja California to obtain cattle.

He reached Velicatá by the beginning of March, gathered some soldiers and cattle, and was back in San Diego by July. There he learned that the supply ship had arrived in March, that Monterey had been founded, that Portolá had left, and that Fages was in command. Not desiring to serve under Fages, he remained

---

2. Palóu, *Historical Memoirs of New California*, 1:32–37; Crosby, *Gateway to Alta California*, 13–14, 38–41; Crosby, *Doomed to Fail*.
3. Crespí, *A Description of Distant Roads*, 53.
4. Beebe and Senkewicz, *Lands of Promise and Despair*, 133–35.

in San Diego. He then wrote to the viceroy requesting that he be relieved of all of his responsibilities for the expedition to the north and that he be allowed to retire. The request was granted, and Rivera y Moncada left San Diego on April 26, 1771. After some time in Loreto, he departed Baja California on January 15, 1772.[5]

He appears to have spent the next year and a half in Guadalajara, where he was able to purchase a small ranch; he also spent time in Mexico City. He married María Teresa Dávalos y Padrón in 1755 and they had four children. One of their children eventually was ordained a priest. Rivera y Moncada seems to have been in Mexico City when Serra visited there in 1773. After the viceroy decided not to accede to Serra's request to name Ortega as military commander of Alta California, he sent Echeveste and some other officials to the Colegio de San Fernando. They met with Serra and floated Rivera y Moncada's name as a replacement for Fages. Serra strongly objected, but Rivera y Moncada was nevertheless appointed. He traveled to Sinaloa to recruit an additional group of soldiers and families for Alta California and was able to gather fifty-one people. The group arrived in Loreto in March 1774. They then marched north and reached Monterey on May 23. Rivera y Moncada assumed command two days later.[6]

The Correspondence

The first two letters dealt with the local Indian groups and pointed to the ways in which the presence of a presidio and missions in Ohlone territory was already beginning to affect the lifeways of the local indigenous people.

The first letter centered on an incident involving an Indian muleteer by the name of Simón Carpio, who was probably from Loreto in Baja California. A trusted local Indian named Cipriano caught Carpio having sexual intercourse with a baptized woman named María Victoria near the Carmel River. Cipriano was also from Baja California—from the Guadalupe visita of Mission San Francisco Borja. It is believed that he probably came with the original land parties. If this is true, he was the only Indian from San Francisco Borja who had not left the expedition before they reached San Diego. Cipriano was a key figure in the early years of Mission San Carlos. He was the groom in the second marriage performed there. In November 1772 he married a woman from Achasta, the ranchería closest to the mission. Because he hailed from Baja California, Serra

---

5. Fernando de Rivera y Moncada to Carlos Francisco de Croix, May 8, 1771, in Herbert Eugene Bolton Papers, The Bancroft Library, C-B 840, carton 9, folder 14, item 95. We thank Harry Crosby for sharing this reference with us; Palóu, *Cartas desde la península de California*, 205.
6. Rivera y Moncada, *Diario del capitán comandante Fernando de Rivera y Moncada*, 1:xxii; Font, *With Anza to California*, 255; Serra letter to Guardian and Members of the Discretorium of the Colegio Apostólico de San Fernando, July 18, 1774, earlier in this volume; Bancroft, *History of California*, 1:218, 225. Rivera was aware at the time of Serra's opposition. See Font, *With Anza to California*, 255.

and the early missionaries were hoping that Cipriano and the other Baja California Indians would become valuable emissaries and intermediaries between the missionaries and the Ohlone people.[7]

Rivera y Moncada reported in his diary that Simón Carpio was put in stocks at the presidio and that at first he denied having sexual relations with María Victoria. The next day the commander went to the mission to question María Victoria, who also denied that she had sexual relations with Carpio. Rivera y Moncada stated that he thought this whole affair was probably related to an episode that took place six weeks earlier (the previous December) at Mission San Antonio, when another Baja California Indian was sent to the presidio and sentenced to twenty-five lashes for having sexual relations with a married Indian woman at Mission San Antonio. Rivera y Moncada interpreted the situation as follows: Cipriano was not morally concerned about the affair by the river. He was simply involved in a dispute among Indians who had come from Baja California. If this indeed was the case, then Cipriano's tactic worked, because Simón Carpio was whipped as a punishment. María Victoria eventually married another man from Achasta in January 1776.[8]

> Señor Capitán Comandante Don Fernando
> My dear Señor,
>
> During today's siesta, at about two o'clock in the afternoon, Simón Carpio, the Indian muleteer, was caught fornicating at the river with a Christian woman from this mission. She is commonly known as "Gil's mother," since she has a son by that name. We were waiting for him so the corporal could arrest him, and then we see that he is heading toward the presidio. I beg Vuestra Merced to arrest him and we will punish him here, so it will serve as an example.
>
> Cipriano, who is an eyewitness, can relate all of the details. And we have the woman here, under lock and key.
>
> May God keep Vuestra Merced many years.
>
> Carmel, Sunday, January 22, 1775, etc.
> Fray Junípero Serra

The next letter concerned a group of native peoples with whom Serra had occasionally interacted since 1771—the Esselen. As we have seen, he first came

---

7. The identification of the woman is in Hackel, *Children of Coyote*, 203–204; Mathes, *Las misiones de Baja California*, 113; San Carlos marriage 00002; Crespí, *A Description of Distant Roads*, 220–21. The identification of Carpio as from Loreto is based on the presence of a large Indian family in the area of that name. We thank Harry Crosby for sharing this information with us.
8. Rivera y Moncada, *Diario del capitán comandante Fernando de Rivera y Moncada*, 1:84, 102; San Carlos marriage 00070.

FIGURE 38. *Indian Man from Monterey*, 1791, by José Cardero. The bow and arrow in his hands were generally used for hunting game and could also serve as a formidable weapon against Spanish soldiers. Courtesy of the Museo de América, Madrid. Inv. 02283.

into contact with the Esselen on his return from founding Mission San Antonio. People from this group had visited Mission San Carlos at least twice since then. In this letter Serra recounted the visit of an older Esselen man to Mission San Carlos. The man said that his village was being threatened by enemies. The possibility of a potential conflict in the general area of their home territory alarmed the Indians living close to the mission, so Serra decided to visit the area himself. In May 1775 he personally journeyed to a location he called Xasauan, about ten leagues from Carmel. There he baptized a chief named Pach-hepas, whom he identified as the captain of the Esselen territory. Over the next three years more than thirty people from the same immediate area as well as about ten more from additional Esselen villages were baptized.[9]

Since there had long been ill feeling between the Esselen and the Rumsen, the enemy to whom the old man referred was most likely Rumsen. Indeed, it appears that, when the Esselen joined the mission, they and the Rumsen who were there

---

9. San Carlos baptism 00350; Breschini and Haversat, *The Esselen Indians of the Big Sur Country*, 176–81.

lived apart from each other and maintained separate identities within the mission complex. And indeed, tensions between the mission and some indigenous people of the area persisted. At the end of 1775 and the beginning of 1776, rumors swirled through the area that a group of people living about twenty miles away were preparing to attack the compound.[10]

> Señor Capitán Don Fernando de Rivera y Moncada
> My dear Señor,
>
> An old gentile man arrived at this mission last night. He said that he was sent by the Esselen because the people from that ranchería are afraid to venture out in search of food. They are hoping that we can go there and escort them here, where they will feel safer. He added that their enemies were saying that they were already well aware of the condition of the ranchería at night. And after having spent many days busily making arrows, they said they would come at night. They would first burn the buildings and then attack the people. This news alarmed the Christians and catechumens so much that they have not been able to calm down at all tonight.
>
> I am providing Vuestra Merced with this information so you may act as you see fit.
>
> May God, Our Lord, keep you many years, etc.
>
> The Mission, February 27, 1775.
> Fray Junípero Serra

The next two letters concerned supplies for the Monterey area. The mules to which Serra had referred in his July 18, 1774, letter to the guardian had finally arrived. A hundred had been gathered in Sonora. Eleven of them had died in route to Baja California. By the time they had been driven to San Diego, they only numbered fifty-nine. Serra informed the commander that in his judgment all of these mules should be designated for the missions. Serra stated that this group of mules was undoubtedly part of the one hundred mules the viceroy promised Serra when he was in Mexico City.

Rivera y Moncada's response was calculated to let Serra know that he, not the missionary, would decide on the allocation of mules. The commander probably took great pleasure in telling Serra that when the mules reached San Diego, Presidio Commander José Francisco de Ortega decided to keep a dozen mules for

---

10. Breschini and Haversat, *The Esselen Indians of the Big Sur Country*, 180; Ginn, "Creating Community in Spanish California," 53–58; Cutter, *California in 1792*, 149; Palóu, *Palóu's Life of Fray Junípero Serra*, 285–86; Serra, *Writings*, 4:266–67; Fages, *A Historical, Political, and Natural Description of California*, 64.

himself. Rivera y Moncada knew that Ortega and Serra had a close relationship and that Serra had recommended him for the position of military commander of Alta California. Rivera y Moncada informed Serra that Ortega kept the mules because he knew that was what Rivera y Moncada would have ordered him to do.

When the remainder of the mules reached Monterey, the commander took what he needed and said he would be happy to give the rest to the missions. At the end of the letter Rivera y Moncada reminded Serra of an uncomfortable truth: the survival and livelihood of the missions depended on the presidios. The relationship between missionaries and soldiers was always very contentious, and Serra did not like being reminded that in a fundamental sense the viability of his enterprise rested on the availability of military personnel.

> Señor Capitán Comandante Don Fernando Rivera y Moncada
> My dear Señor,
> Vuestra Merced knows, and you already knew about it in Mexico when I was there attending to matters concerning these missions, that I informed the Excelentísimo Señor Virrey about the lack of mules at these missions. I asked that one hundred be brought here to us and that they be paid for from our funds. I was informed that Su Excelencia had given the order that my request be fulfilled and that we would receive the hundred mules.
> I recommended to our colegio, and have repeated that recommendation in writing from here, that they not interfere with the payment of these mules by our síndico, if Su Excelencia is in agreement, because the mules are important to us.
> Based on what I have stated, in addition to other reasons, I believe that the one hundred mules Señor Corvalán sent to the Señor Gobernador of the Californias, don Phelipe Barry, with word that they were for Monterey, and which are the ones Vuestra Merced has just received, are the mules allotted to these missions. However, I am not certain, but it is probable at the very least, that it is not the exact number of mules. For when the Excelentísimo Señor gave the order to round up and send that number of mules, such a herd had not been requested by the officer (who was at that time the commander) for the royal presidios or for the soldiers.
> The above is consistent with the letter I received from the new governor of the Californias, don Phelipe Neve, dated at Loreto, March 7 of this year, which arrived in the latest mail. In the letter he tells me that he has orders from the Excelentísimo Señor Virrey to reimburse these missions for nine mules, four horses, and two mares, which two benefactors had donated on

behalf of these missions but which were used for other purposes by the then-comisario of Loreto. He then added: "Su Excelencia has also informed me of the request for the one hundred mules, which has been verified by my predecessor Don Phelipe Barry, and for thirty *chichigua*[11] cows respectively, etc."

Therefore, it seems to me that if the issue regarding the hundred mules had nothing to do with these missions, then there was no reason to write to me about it and to include it with other issues that were undoubtedly mission-related.

In spite of everything, I awaited the arrival of the boat so I could discuss the matter with Vuestra Merced and thus be able to present a direct, clear, and compelling case that the livestock belongs to the missions. And even though I found out that Vuestra Merced had already ordered that part of the herd be delivered to the presidio of San Diego, and that you were considering distributing the rest among the soldiers, I did not say a word. And I would not have said anything if Vuestra Merced had not asked me about it face to face, as you did last Saturday.

My answer then is the same as what I am putting down in writing, which is what Vuestra Merced asked me to do.

Vuestra Merced, see if my arguments, together with the fact that you have no evidence to the contrary, as you yourself told me, are strong enough to prove that the mules belong to these missions and not to those royal presidios. And do whatever God inspires you to do, since I have nothing more to say.

My wish is that God Our Lord keep you in perfect health and in His holy grace many years.

From this the Mission of San Carlos in Monterey, [commonly known as Carmel], June 20, 1775
Your dear friend and chaplain kisses the hand of Vuestra Merced,
Fray Junípero Serra

I sent this letter the following day with Ignacio Juvera, the servant.
It is about the issue regarding the mules, which presently remains the same except for what I recount in my other letters.

---

11. A *chichigua* is a female animal that is nursing her young.

Muy Reverendo Padre Presidente Fray Junípero Serra
My dearest Señor,

I received Vuestra Reverencia's letter yesterday and I am glad that you continue to be in good health. I now turn to the content of your letter. With regard to what I discussed with Vuestra Reverencia and what you now have written to me about, I must apologize for going into so much detail. In short, I have written to don Felipe Barry in Mexico, and to Gobernador don Felipe Neve about the matter regarding the mules and whether I was mistaken in my hope that those presidios would keep some of the animals for their own benefit or whether the phrase "new establishments" was in reference to the missions. The lieutenant at San Diego, don Francisco Ortega, informs me that fifty-nine mules arrived there and they kept twelve of them. That action was taken in anticipation of the order he expected me to give. The shortage of animals at that presidio is not remedied with these twelve mules, but at least they represent a partial solution.

Forty-seven mules have arrived here. From that number, I have decided to keep sixteen of them here, and send the remaining thirty-one to Vuestra Reverencia. I will say the same thing about this presidio as I did about the one in San Diego. There is a very real and persistent need to keep a part of the herd here. If I could go anywhere at all, there is no doubt that I would swoop down on a large hacienda and seize enough mules for the quartermasters at those presidios. I am so convinced of this that if I were now to receive an order from the Excelentísimo Señor Virrey, I would proceed with the same amount of restraint as I have outlined here for Vuestra Reverencia and I would report my decision to Su Excelencia.

If Vuestra Reverencia would like to name or send someone to receive the mules, keep in mind that Vuestra Reverencia has the larger number, which includes the two small males. Believe me, Vuestra Reverencia, for there to be missions, it is necessary to have presidios. And just because there are soldiers afoot does not mean that place can be called a presidio.

May God keep Vuestra Reverencia many years.

Monterey, June 22, 1775, etc.
Fernando de Rivera y Moncada

The next four letters indicate the ways in which the most routine of activities, such as unloading a boat, could cause friction between Serra and Rivera y Moncada. When the supply ship *San Carlos* arrived at Monterey, Rivera y Moncada informed Serra that the captain of the vessel requested that some Indians be sent to unload the cargo. The *San Carlos* had experienced a rough voyage—it left San Blas on March 16 and arrived in Monterey on June 27. The commanding officer, Juan Bautista de Ayala, was actually just a lieutenant who had assumed command when the captain became unable to remain in charge of the vessel.[12]

Serra responded that it was proving difficult to get the Indians to do the type of work the mission required. Thus he was very reluctant to put additional burdens on them when he was still in the process of trying to instill in them the habits of work that European-style agriculture would entail. As we have seen, his preferred approach was to attempt to attract the native peoples into the rhythms of mission life in a gradual fashion, and he felt that he was the best judge of the appropriate pace of that effort. Besides, the Indians were needed to work in the fields, for the crops were already picked and needed to be brought in immediately. Serra suggested to Rivera y Moncada that there were plenty of people at the presidio, including soldiers, who would be able to unload the cargo. He also appealed to the digest of Spanish colonial laws that set limits on the amount of work that could be demanded of recently converted Indians. Serra also told the commander that in his opinion, the unloading of cargo was a more urgent task than what the commander was requiring his soldiers to do, specifically the construction of an additional dwelling at the presidio.

These particular letters do not indicate who actually finally unloaded the cargo. Rivera y Moncada's diary simply reported that the cargo was unloaded and taken from the beach on July 7–9. In the end, the soldiers probably did the work. But the exchange indicates that in Serra's judgment there was no issue so small that it could not be used to assert what he deemed the legitimate privileges of the missionaries and, in his mind, to protect the Indians from exploitation. Serra's letters point out what he believed was a crucial distinction. For him, a former teacher of Scholastic philosophy and Scotistic theology, distinctions were necessary to apprehend the truth. Therefore, on the one hand, the work the Indians were being asked to do as members of mission communities was legitimate and did not involve exploiting them. But on the other hand, the attempt of others, especially the military, to employ Indian labor was illegitimate, for this scenario was a virtual reenactment of the cruel treatment of the Indians in the early days of the Spanish empire. Rivera y Moncada's seemingly temperate requests were reminiscent of the behavior of the conquistadors whom Bartolomé de las Casas had so vigorously denounced. In addition, Serra's experiences with Escandón had convinced him that such behavior might well reappear in the present. He genuinely believed that to accede to even the most inconsequential of these approaches would be to open the door to continued exploitation of the native peoples.

---

12. Bancroft, *History of California*, 1:241.

As part of this exchange Rivera y Moncada thanked Serra for allowing Father Fermín Francisco de Lasuén, whom he had known in Baja California, to serve as chaplain at the presidio. When the commander stopped at Mission San Gabriel on his way to Monterey in 1774, he asked Lasuén to serve in this capacity. He did not believe this would cause any strain on the mission, since he noticed that Lasuén was an extra missionary at Mission San Gabriel. Lasuén agreed to relocate to the Monterey presidio, where he would at least have a ministry to the soldiers and their families. At first Serra refused to allow this, however, because he was afraid of setting the precedent that missionaries would be expected to staff the presidios even if there were not enough of them to have two priests stationed at each mission. The commander continued making the request and Serra continued refusing, but finally, and very reluctantly, he gave in. Lasuén then moved into the Monterey presidio. Serra never accepted this arrangement, and Lasuén complained of Serra's "coldness and aloofness" toward him while he was at the presidio.[13]

> Muy Reverendo Padre Presidente Fray Junípero Serra
> My dear Señor,
> Don Juan de Ayala, the captain of the *San Carlos*, has told me to write a short note to Vuestra Reverencia asking you for six or eight strong Indians to help him unload the boat because a number of sailors have become ill. The captain will provide them with food.
> The Reverendo Padre Fermín has arrived; I am grateful to Vuestra Reverencia for this favor, and I pray to Our Lord that He keep Vuestra Merced many years.
>
> Monterey, July 5, 1775, etc.
> Fernando Rivera y Moncada

> Señor Capitán Don Fernando de Rivera y Moncada
> My dear Señor,
> Last night I received the note written by Vuestra Merced on behalf of Don Juan Ayala, captain of the packet boat the *San Carlos*, who voiced this request to you. He is asking for strong Indians to help unload the boat and offers to provide them with food while they work.
> Vuestra Merced may respond to the Señor Capitán, to whom I send my regards, that prescinding from what Su Majestad ordered in terms of the

---

13. Guest, *Fermín Francisco de Lasuén*, 77–82.

FIGURE 39. *View of Monterey Presidio*, 1791, by José Cardero. The presidio remained in the spot chosen by Portolá in 1770, while Serra moved the mission to the banks of the Carmel River in 1771. *Courtesy of The Bancroft Library, University of California, Berkeley.* HN000971.

work of the recently converted Indians, I am being presented with a very delicate situation. The work the Indians do here is their own work. Even though they are never asked to work without receiving food and clothing in return, they are so wary that at times from a group of fifty, we are lucky to get even a dozen who are willing to work. We find ourselves without firewood to cook the pozole for them, even though it is easy to find because there is so much of it. We are tolerating this and are carefully trying to encourage them so that little by little they will learn.

When the sailors can no longer do the unloading themselves, there are people closer by who have a greater stake in this and can do a better job. I will not go on any longer. It seems to me that what has been said should be enough of a response for the captain.

I hope to have many Indians who are strong in the faith. As for those who are physically strong enough to carry packs or unload boats, according to what I have read in the royal decrees of the *Recopilación de Indias*, we must not put pressure on those who have recently been converted, especially those who for the most part (speaking about the older ones) have not been Christians for even one year, etc.

Mission of San Carlos of Monterey, July 6, 1775, etc.
Fray Junípero Serra

[After copying the letter into his diary, Rivera y Moncada noted the following]:
In a postscript, he adds that today they are beginning to harvest the barley that is dry and falling off.

Muy Reverendo Padre Presidente Fray Junípero Serra
My dear Señor,

    I am informing Vuestra Reverencia that when the *carreta* and the saddled mules went to the beach to haul the cargo, they could not find it. The corporal I stationed at the beach came to inform me on behalf of the captain that if no Indians come, there is no cargo because his men will not go into the water. After receiving last night's note, I thought it best to share this information with Vuestra Reverencia. I hope that Vuestra Reverencia will not find it strange that I cannot make up for this shortage of workmen. For, if there is cargo, my soldiers have to transport it here and then unload the sacks so they can be returned. If they do not do this, I will assign them to work on the house. As soon as I was informed, I ordered the men to unsaddle the mules, go cut some wood, and haul it back. Even though there is much work left to do on the house and it is already in use, don Juan de Ayala wants to designate a section of the house for those who are ill.

    May God keep Vuestra Reverencia many years.

Monterey, July 6, 1775, etc.
Don Fernando de Rivera y Moncada

Señor Capitán Comandante Don Fernando de Rivera y Moncada
My dear Señor,

    After sending a soldier from this escort with my response to the note from Vuestra Merced that I received last night, in which you asked me to provide strong Indians to unload the packet boat *San Carlos* that is anchored in this port, I have now received another note from Vuestra Merced, dated today, insisting on the same request. You include the message from the Señor Capitán, Don Juan de Ayala, which says if no Indians come, there is no cargo, because his men will not go into the water.

I shall respond exactly how I did this morning to your note. I will not begin to judge or question why Vuestra Merced does not assign your own people to do the work and give those sailors the opportunity to rest as their captain has requested. However, I will say, if there is enough reason to continue working on a house, and that work could easily be interrupted, while cargo is on the beach waiting to be handled, is there not even more reason to attend to the difficult task of storing the harvest in the granary, especially since it is so dry that it is crumbling in their hands? And this is food for them to eat. There are seven hundred fanegas of corn left to unload, yet there is not a single grain for the Indians. This would be the case even if these Indians were not such recently converted Christians who are accorded certain privileges by royal decrees.

I wish Vuestra Merced perfect health. May God, Our Lord, keep you many years in His holy grace.

From this Mission of San Carlos of Monterey, July 6, 1775, etc.
Fray Junípero Serra

The next two letters concern the matter of servants at the missions and underscore the extent to which Serra depended on Rivera y Moncada for granting rations to the mission servants. In this particular case it appears that the commander had no problem with extending rations to the two servants for whom Serra requested them. But the necessity of having to ask was undoubtedly irksome to Serra.

Señor Capitán Comandante Don Fernando de Rivera y Moncada
My dear Señor,

I wrote a note yesterday to Comisario Don Juan Soler to inform him that two servants of this mission left their positions. One of them was the sailor Mariano Basilio, who returned to seafaring; the other was the young man Ignacio Olvera, who moved away from here because he wanted to return to his own people. Foreseeing this, I spoke to the ship's captain a few days ago, trying to see if one or more men could be left to take their place, as stipulated by the May 12, 1773, ruling of the Excelentísimo Señor Virrey and the Real Junta of May 12, 1773. I encountered some difficulty on the part of the officer. And on the other hand, a man who came to offer himself for the job was ill and not of much use. For over a year now, no one who has worked here has exceeded or even equaled the quality of work that two young men, Diego Olvera and Conrado Toledo,[14] performed in the fields. Until now, they have worked for whatever recompense the mission could give them. Since it also happened this way with Ignacio Olivera at the beginning, I concluded that there was no one better than Diego and Conrado to fill the two vacant positions. But they are unhappy because they are not earning any salary whatsoever. And for that reason, one of them in particular has given us a number of indications that he wants to leave this land. If Vuestra Merced does not see any drawbacks that I have overlooked, I ask that beginning today, you order that they be given rations. And beginning tomorrow, they should start earning a salary.

I wish Vuestra Merced perfect health. And may God, Our Lord, keep you many years in His holy grace.

From this Mission of San Carlos of Monterey. July 14, 1775, etc.
Fray Junípero Serra

Muy Reverendo Padre Presidente Fray Junípero Serra
My dear Señor,
After I received Vuestra Reverencia's letter, the two young men, Diego and Conrado, are now recognized by the warehouse as being servants of the mission. Based on what Vuestra Reverencia has written with regard to them, I will thus instruct Don Juan Soler to put them under his authority, create an account for them in his record book, and administer rations to them.

May God keep Your Reverence many years,

Monterey, July 15, 1775, etc.
Fernando de Rivera y Moncada

The next two letters deal with an issue that was of great importance to Serra—the availability of soldiers to recapture baptized Indians who had fled from the missions. As a child of the Mallorcan Inquisition, which as we have seen was suspicious of the unsupervised behavior of new Christians, Serra was quite concerned that the Indians not be given the opportunity to resume their former sacred practices. He was especially worried about this occurring in the traditional locations where those dances, chants, and rituals had been carried on for generations.

In one sense Serra's concern was justified, for many baptized California Indians

---

14. Conrado de Toledo came to Alta California with Serra from Mexico in 1774. He previously worked at Jalpan. See Geiger, *Life and Times of Fray Junípero Serra*, 1:414.

continued to practice their native rituals for years after they had accepted baptism. At Mission San Francisco, for example, baptized Ohlone people would often leave the mission for important life events, such as giving birth and preparing for death. Further, many used the rituals of the Catholic sacraments of baptism and matrimony in ways that strengthened traditional clan affiliations. Serra therefore was correct in his judgment that traditional religion was alive and well even in the lives of those who had been baptized. But it could not have been otherwise. California non-Christian peoples did exactly what every other non-Christian group has ever done when confronted with Christian missionaries—they integrated what they found attractive into their own spirituality and worldviews and interpreted Christianity through the prism of their own traditional beliefs. This notion of how indigenous peoples related to Christianity is well understood now, and it has been studied and documented by scholars from a number of disciplines. But it was also intuited very perceptively by a number of early-modern Christian missionaries such as sixteenth-century Franciscans in central Mexico and seventeenth-century Jesuits in China. Serra, however, found it difficult to adopt this perspective. Perhaps this was a downside of his training in philosophy and theology, in that he may have become too comfortable with abstractions, too ready to see nuanced issues only in black and white.[15]

However, some California missionaries who did follow him were less influenced by the Mallorcan Inquisition and more influenced by a developing appreciation of some types of tolerance in the Iberian Atlantic world. Thus these missionaries were more nuanced in their approaches. The Ohlone people who were depicted in a painting by Georg Heinrich von Langsdorff as they danced at Mission San José in 1806, or the Petaluma people whom Louis Choris portrayed as dancing in the plaza of Mission Dolores a decade later, engaged in these activities with at least the tacit approval of the resident missionary. When Auguste Duhaut-Cilly visited Mission San Luis Rey in 1827, he witnessed a native dance there and remarked of the Indians, "Although they may all be Christians, they retain many of their former beliefs, which the padres, as a matter of policy, pretend not to notice." Try as he might, however, it was very difficult for Junípero Serra ever to pretend not to notice anything![16]

---

15. Newell, *Constructing Lives at Mission San Francisco*, chaps. 4–6; Eire, "The Concept of Popular Religion," 9.
16. Schwartz, *All Can Be Saved*; Duhaut-Cilly and Frugé, *A Voyage to California, the Sandwich Islands and around the World in the Years 1826–1829*, 119. Serra's comment that he was responsible for the souls of the Indians at a very high tribunal indicated that he held to a fairly strict interpretation of the medieval maxim "extra eclesiam nulla salus" (outside the Church there is no salvation). But that strict interpretation was beginning to be challenged by some of Serra's contemporaries. Pedro Font, for instance, accompanied Anza through the lands of more unbaptized native peoples than he had ever seen before. This made him wonder in the pages of his diary how a just God could condemn to hell untold numbers of people who had never even heard of Him. Font, *With Anza to California*, 138–42.

FIGURE 40. *Indians Dancing at Mission San José*. German naturalist Georg Heinrich von Langsdorff (1773–1850), traveling with a Russian expedition, created this depiction of Indians from Mission San José in 1806. Wearing paint for a formal dance ceremony, they were most likely celebrating having survived the severe measles epidemic that had just ravaged the mission's native community. *Courtesy of The Bancroft Library, University of California, Berkeley.* BANC PIC 1963.002:1023-FR.

Rivera y Moncada responded to Serra's appeal for soldiers by appealing to the limited resources at his disposal. He said there was already a sufficient number of soldiers at the missions to enable Serra to organize such an expedition against those who had fled. He also told Serra that he had not issued any order stating that soldiers at the mission should not stay out all night. Such an order would have made an expedition to recover fugitives impossible, and Serra clearly thought it had been issued. This information had been given to Serra by the corporal of the mission escort, Marcelino Bravo. He had been recruited by Gálvez from San Luis Potosí in 1768, so he was not one of the veteran Baja California soldiers with whom Rivera y Moncada maintained a close relationship. Perhaps the real

FIGURE 41. *Mission San Luis Rey*, drawn by Frenchman Auguste Duhaut-Cilly, who visited the mission in 1827. This drawing affords a good view of the indigenous dwellings that surrounded virtually every mission founded in Alta California. *Courtesy of The Bancroft Library, University of California, Berkeley. G440.B48 Vault v. 1 opp. p. 215.*

reason was that Bravo did not want to go out in pursuit of these fugitives and told Serra he was ordered not to do so. Rivera y Moncada simply told Serra to have the corporal show him the actual order because he was positive that no such order truly existed.

In reality, the argument was not really about the order but, rather, about the appropriate role of the military. For Serra, the missions were the preeminent institutions in Alta California, and the military's primary responsibilities should be to serve the missions' interests. Rivera dramatically disagreed.

> Señor Comandante Don Fernando
> My dear Señor,
> Late yesterday, Padre Predicador Fray Fermín Lasuén related Vuestra Merced's message to me saying that you had not responded to a letter I sent you eight days ago, in which I asked for an escort of soldiers to go out and bring back some of the new Christians of this mission who had fled and gone back to the gentiles, because you were too busy and not because of ill will.

The message was that Vuestra Merced could not spare any soldiers because you have so few. I responded by asking the Padre to extend my greetings and kind regards to Vuestra Merced and if this message was meant to be your response, then that was enough, and there was no need to go to any more trouble.

Now, my dearest Señor, I must inform Vuestra Merced that these lost sheep are in my charge. I am responsible for them, not at the Court of Public Accounts in México, but rather at another court, which is much higher than that one. Therefore, with regard to the proposed matter, do not be surprised, Vuestra Merced, if I happen to refuse something because it is inopportune.

I did not ask Vuestra Merced to provide soldiers who were specifically from that presidio. But, according to Vuestra Merced's order, the soldiers at the mission cannot spend the night away from the mission. And now, if they are to be away for the entire day, it seems that they have been instructed to inform Vuestra Merced beforehand, based on what I noticed in the case of the Indian woman who had been shot with arrows. Therefore, to avoid running the risk of receiving a resounding no, I presented you with my request days before I wanted the soldiers to go out. If Vuestra Merced had determined that four of the six soldiers stationed here could go, we would have managed for the duration of the expedition with the remaining two. And even better if Vuestra Merced could have sent us two retired soldiers to stand guard at night. But if neither solution is possible, the only thing left is patience.

I do not know how anyone who views this theater from afar can believe that a mission with an escort of six soldiers and a presidio a league away cannot be provided with four or five soldiers to go after and bring back eight or ten fugitive neophytes. But those of us who are actually here do not have to be convinced of this, because we are witnessing it.

I am forced to explain my feelings of distress to Vuestra Merced, because after Padre Fray Fermín told me of your decision late yesterday, this morning I received the news that one of the women who has run away with her son-in-law, an Indian commonly known as Pólvora, is either dead or dying.

I ordered Padre Dumetz to go out there, and two soldiers from here accompanied him. If she or any of the other deserters die without anyone there to say the name of Jesus, I do not want to be responsible for having failed to do something. And this is the only reason why I am now writing to Vuestra Merced. If I have not explained myself as diplomatically as I had hoped, it is simply due to the anguish I feel when I think about those poor people, who, after having become Christians, are now in such evident danger of eternal damnation.

I wish Your Grace perfect health and every happiness. I always pray that God, Our Lord will keep you many years in His holy love and grace.

From this Mission of San Carlos of Monterey, July 20, 1775, etc.
Fray Junípero Serra

Muy Reverendo Padre Fray Junípero Serra
My dear Señor,
I received Vuestra Reverencia's letter with the same date as this response.
I respond:
If I sent the message to Vuestra Reverencia by means of the Reverendo Padre Fray Fermín, it was because I cannot send the escort since I have no more than three soldiers on hand (not counting the four guards) because the rest are ill. And now the boat is here, which means I have to send them there, in addition to other duties. Why does Vuestra Reverencia, in your letter, ignore these fundamental facts, for they are the reason it is impossible for me to do as you ask? What will they say in México if they read your letter? And I might add, even though Vuestra Reverencia already knows about it, that a number of days ago I sent the sergeant and eight soldiers with two prisoners to San Diego.

From Vuestra Reverencia's same letter, I have come to the conclusion that I have a greater obligation to the lost sheep, for whatever the results may be, in addition to reporting to God, I will also have to report to Mexico.

If Vuestra Reverencia was not asking me for soldiers from this presidio, and you could complete the task with the soldiers of that escort, then why did you not do so? If it was because of an order that I had given the corporal that they not venture out during the entire day, Vuestra Reverencia, please ask the corporal to show you that order and have him deliver it to me himself. If I had given such an order, how is it that two soldiers are now accompanying Father Dumetz? Therefore, either the corporal does not have such an order, or he is informing me about things only when he feels like it. Vuestra Reverencia should review the letter I wrote to you when you turned to me to inform me about the corporal. In that letter I conveyed the instructions I gave to the corporal and told you about the letter I sent him. And Vuestra

Reverencia acknowledged this. You will see what I told him and whether he had an order or not.

    May God keep Vuestra Reverencia many years.

Monterey, July 20 of 1775
Fernando de Rivera y Moncada

This next letter is a request that Serra go to the presidio to sign a document in accordance with an article in the Echeveste Reglamento.[17] Serra undoubtedly complied. The letter points to the many purely administrative tasks that consumed much of Serra's time in his role as mission president.

Muy Reverendo Padre Presidente Fray Junípero Serra
My dear Señor,
    I am notifying Vuestra Reverencia that Don Juan de Ayala, captain of the *San Carlos*, signed his certification today in fulfillment of Article 13 of the Reglamento. Vuestra Reverencia, if you would be so good as to stop by the presidio this afternoon to sign your certification.
    May God keep Vuestra Reverencia many years.

Monterey, July 21, 1775
Don Fernando de Rivera y Moncada

This next letter indicates that Serra did in fact have a range of other options for bringing back those Indians who decided they did not want to remain in the missions. He reported that he sent eleven adults, most likely baptized Indians under the command of Cipriano, to chase after some Indians who refused to return. This expedition managed to recover nine neophytes. Serra sent four whom he regarded as ringleaders to Rivera y Moncada at the presidio. Three of the four were baptized in 1773. Serra reported that they had deserted a number of times since then. The fourth person, Ildefonso, was baptized slightly over a year earlier, but Serra judged that he was a potential ringleader and therefore wanted him punished in the same fashion as the first three.

Two of the men were from Achasta, and two were from Tucutnut. The fact that one operation had been organized by people from two distinct rancherías may have been one of the things that particularly alarmed Serra about this episode. His explicit recommendation was two or three rounds of whipping (probably twenty-five lashes for each round) at the presidio and a month's imprisonment there. His justification was that it would be a good lesson for them and would also offer spiritual benefit to everyone else in the mission community. There is no

---

17. The regulation is in Palóu, *Historical Memoirs of New California*, 3:74.

reason to doubt that Serra sincerely thought of himself as the type of just father and honest physician he had preached about in Mallorca thirty years earlier.

> Señor Capitán Comandante Don Fernando de Rivera y Moncada
> My dear Señor,
>
> Last Friday, I sent eleven adults to the mountains with a young man named Cipriano in search of my lost sheep. Last night they brought back to me nine neophytes from this mission. I am sending four of them to Vuestra Merced. They are: Cristóbal, Carlos, Gerónimo, and Ildefonso, all married to women who remain here at the ranchería.[18] The first three have deserted a number of times, and after receiving a number of punishments, they show no signs of having changed their ways. The fourth one has only deserted once, because he is a new Christian. This single desertion, however, has been a lengthy one, and his attitude gives rise to the suspicion that he could be a leader among the discontented. That leaves only one deserter, whose situation is similar to that of the first three. When I finally catch him, he can take the place of the fourth.
>
> I am sending them to you for punishment—a period of time in exile and two or three rounds of whipping, which Vuestra Merced can order to be applied on different days per your orders. This should be a good lesson for them as well as for the others, and it will be of spiritual benefit for everyone, which is the goal of our efforts. If Vuestra Merced does not have shackles on hand, if you let us know, they can be sent from here. I believe their punishment should last a month.
>
> I wish Your Grace excellent health. May God, Our Lord, keep you many years in His holy grace.
>
> Mission of San Carlos, July 31, 1775, etc.
> Fray Junípero Serra

The following three letters were written a few days after Serra and Rivera y Moncada had their dramatic August 12, 1775, confrontation about the number of soldiers—thirteen or six—that should be assigned to new missions. These letters concerned the distribution of supplies, but this time the supplies were cattle. The tone of correspondence between Serra and the commander was proper and correct. These letters indicate that even in the midst of intense disagreement it was possible for relationships between military and missionaries to be carried on in a more or less civil fashion.

---

18. Cristóbal (SC baptism 00122) and Carlos (SC baptism 00079) were from Achasta. Gerónimo (SC baptism 00120) and Ildefonso (SC baptism 00303) were from Tucutnut.

Muy Reverendo Padre Presidente Fray Junípero Serra
My dear Señor,

The inventory of cattle, down to the last number, is as follows:

> 55 pregnant cows
> 24 calves, going on two years old
> 7 small bulls of the same age
> 4 breeding bulls
> 2 steers
> 27 young female cows, branded with our brand
> 23 small bulls with the same brand
> Add 3 small bulls and 1 steer that the frigate took
> 1 that was killed when the *Príncipe* arrived
> Another that was given to the *Príncipe* on its departure

Given that the Excelentísimo Señor Virrey is already thinking about establishing the Mission of San Francisco, I have decided to give you the two allotments of cattle that were at this presidio for when the missions of San Francisco and Santa Clara were to be established. Delivery:

Of 55 cows, I give Vuestra Reverencia 37
Of 24 calves, I give Vuestra Reverencia 16.
Of 7 small bulls, I give you 2, and 2 steers that have already been castrated, for a total of 4
Of 4 large bulls, 2
Of 27 breeding cows, 18
Of 23 yearling male calves, 15
Total: 92 head.

I have heard that Don Pedro Fages gave the Reverendo Padre Fray Francisco Palóu four castrated bulls for the [mission] of San Francisco. That being so, as Vuestra Reverencia will notice, they are not part of the inventory. However, I hope that Vuestra Reverencia will remember that the missions of San Luis and San Gabriel are owed three or four steers. I said three or four because I was told that Capitán Don Juan Bautista took a cow from the river as payment for one of the three he was given.

May God keep Vuestra Reverencia many years.

Monterey, August 16, 1774.
Fernando Rivera y Moncada

Señor Capitán Comandante Don Fernando de Rivera y Moncada
My dear Señor,

The corporal of this mission delivered Vuestra Merced's notice that the departure of the mail for San Diego is imminent, as well as the departure of Padre Fray Fermín Lasuén, who is to establish the Mission of San Juan Capistrano, which Vuestra Merced and I agreed upon. I ask Vuestra Merced—barring any obstacles—to send me a total of seven female and male mules. Three of these mules should be from the ones that arrived already broken and able to pull the plow at the new mission that is being built. These mules, plus the ones the two Padres allocated for that mission, to be on the safe side, will amount to the same number of mules normally given to supply the missions at their founding.

Another matter: according to past practice regarding these missions, and in view of what the Excelentísimo Señor told me, I wrote to Vuestra Merced on December 15 regarding the new missions of San Francisco. And I asked you to contribute the necessary assistance and provisions, to the extent that is possible, for their establishment. I would like for Vuestra Merced to tell me if you can send the following items to that mission[19] from either the warehouse here or the warehouse in San Diego:

> Six tercios of wheatmeal[20] for the priests;
> Four tercios of unsifted flour;
> Three tercios of beans;
> One tercio of rice;
> Twenty-five fanegas of corn.

As to any additional items the Padres and Indians will need to survive the year, as well as any other items they will need at the beginning, I will try to have the missions provide them. The missions will follow the orders and make sure that everything is ready and in good order.

If we could be given a few extra days to issue these orders and make sure that everything is done in an appropriate way, I would be very grateful to Vuestra Merced, whose life I ask that God keep many years in His holy grace.

Mission of San Carlos, August 16, 1775
Fray Junípero Serra

---

19. San Juan Capistrano.
20. Brown flour is intermediate between white flour and wholemeal flour.

Muy Reverendo Padre Presidente Fray Junípero Serra
My dear Señor,

Regarding the letter I received from Vuestra Reverencia yesterday, my response is that I am handing over to you seven mules: three males and two tame females from the group that has recently arrived; and also from that group, an untamed male and a female that arrived previously.

From this presidio, I will assign you four tercios of wheatmeal (two of which are unsifted), three fanegas of beans, one tercio of rice, and twenty-five fanegas of corn. I will write to Don Rafael so that they can be distributed at San Diego.

May God keep Vuestra Reverencia many years.

Monterey, August 17, 1775, etc.
Fernando de Rivera y Moncada

P.S. Regarding what Vuestra Reverencia tells me about giving a few more days of extra time, my response is that they will not leave tomorrow as I had first decided, but rather on the 21st, but no later.

In this next letter Rivera y Moncada said that he was going to send a group of soldiers to San Francisco since he had not heard anything about the *San Carlos*, which left Monterey on July 24 to explore San Francisco Bay. The *San Carlos* actually spent over forty days off Angel Island in San Francisco Bay. Rivera y Moncada was simply notifying Serra as a courtesy in case he wanted to send a message to Father Vicente de Santa María, the priest on board. The *San Carlos* returned to Monterey on September 24.[21]

Muy Reverendo Padre Presidente Fray Junípero Serra
My dear Señor,

I am informing Vuestra Reverencia of my decision to have a group of soldiers leave for San Francisco by tomorrow afternoon. I would like some news about the *San Carlos*. They will be there until October 1 and then will return here. I wanted to let Vuestra Reverencia know about this in case there is something you need.

May God keep Vuestra Reverencia many years.

Monterey, September 13, 1775, etc.
Fernando de Rivera y Moncada

These next two letters about servants contain a routine request. Two men who were on board the *Santiago*, which had recently returned from a voyage of

---

21. Bancroft, *History of California*, 1:246.

exploration to the north, asked for permission to stay at the missions as servants. Serra asked that they be given rations, and there is no indication that this request caused any difficulty.

> Señor Capitán Comandante Don Fernando de Rivera y Moncada
> My dear Señor,
> A sailor named Josef Pío Quinto Zúñiga came yesterday, with the permission of his captain, Don Bruno Hezeta, to ask to stay as a servant in one of the missions. For the time being he will be at San Antonio. I ask Vuestra Merced to have him register in the book at the warehouse and that he be given his ration starting today.
> I wish Vuestra Merced health and may God keep you many years.
>
> From this, your Mission of San Carlos, September 16, 1775, etc.
> Fray Junípero Serra

> Señor Capitán Comandante Don Fernando de Rivera y Moncada,
> My dear Señor,
> Regarding the porter's weekly trek for rations and what is allotted to Mission San Antonio, there is no longer a need to bring rations for the servant named Ruelas. I ask Vuestra Merced to have the young sailor Pedro Josef Romero register in the book of occupations and in the book at the warehouse. He has received permission from his captain, Don Bruno de Hezeta, to become a servant at Mission San Antonio. His ration should be given to him as of today.
> I wish that God, Our Lord, keep Vuestra Merced many years.
>
> From this, your Mission of San Carlos, October 14, 1775, etc.
> Fray Junípero Serra

This next letter is a routine request that Rivera y Moncada supply certain information to the authorities in Mexico City so that the finances of the missions can be attended to. This letter underscores that the missions were funded by the state. Much of the funding came from the Pious Fund, the endowment created by the Jesuits in the early eighteenth century and administered by the government. The missionaries' salaries were generally used to buy supplies for the missions, such as liturgical vestments, paintings, statues, various implements that could not be produced in Alta California, and Spanish-style clothing for the Indians. Since the Franciscan understanding of their vow of poverty prohibited them from handling money themselves, the accounting work was done by the síndico, a lay employee of the colegio in Mexico City.

> Señor Capitán Comandante Don Fernando de Rivera y Moncada.
> My dear Señor:
>
> So that the payment of sínodos allowed to the religious who administer these missions of Monterey and those under its jurisdiction is not neglected, we need to produce the certification and testimony, which according to custom and decree is usually presented to the appropriate royal officials. These officials are responsible for presenting these documents to the principal officer or judge of the territory to demonstrate that the missionaries reside and work in their respective missions. I am appealing to you, Vuestra Merced, as capitán comandante of these new establishments from San Diego to Monterey, as well as those that will be added, to be so kind as to declare and certify that these five missions have been established and administered within this territory by missionaries of the Seraphic Order from the Colegio Apostólico de San Fernando de México, of the Propaganda Fide. They are:
>
> > Mission San Diego
> > Mission San Gabriel
> > Mission San Luis Obispo
> > Mission San Antonio de Padua, and
> > Mission San Carlos de Monterey
>
> What needs to be stated is:
>
> If at least two ministers have served at each mission during all of last year and are still there at the present time. And, if these ministers were occupied during that time, and are still occupied with the conversion of the infidels to our Holy Catholic Faith, with the education and instruction of the new converts, and with the administration of their respective missions, both spiritually and temporally; in a word, that the missionaries have been, and continue to be, engaged in their apostolic ministry.
>
> With respect to the other three that are about to be founded, according to the orders of the Excelentísimo Señor Virrey el Bailío Frey[22] Don Antonio María Bucareli y Ursúa, namely:
>
> The Mission of Nuestro Padre San Francisco, in his port
> The second mission in the general vicinity which does not yet have a name
> The Mission of San Juan Capistrano

---

22. El Bailío is a knight commander of the Order of Malta.

Two religious for each of the first two missions are here and have been here for quite some time. They have been given their assignments and are ready to begin. With regard to the third mission, two religious, one from Monterey and the other from San Luis Obispo, set out at the end of August with the necessary provisions, an escort, mules, etc.

And, finally, even after providing ministers for all the missions in the manner described above, there are still a number of missionaries available. We ask that Su Excelencia command by decree that they be allowed to establish other missions. If Su Excelencia wishes to know the exact number of religious priests from that colegio who reside at these missions, our names, and where each of us works and lives, Vuestra Merced can list the information as follows, which is accurate as of today.

At Mission San Carlos:
  Padre Fray Junípero Serra, President
  Padre Lector Fray Francisco Palóu,
  Padre Predicador Fray José Antonio Murguía,
  Padre Predicador Fray Juan Crespí,
  Padre Predicador Fray Francisco Dumetz, and
  Padre Predicador Fray Tomás de la Peña.

At Mission San Antonio:
  Padre Predicador Fray Miguel Pieras,
  Padre Predicador Fray Buenaventura Sitjar, and
  Padre Predicador Pedro Benito Cambón.

At Mission San Luis Obispo:
  Padre Predicador Fray José Cavaller,
  Padre Predicador Fray Juan Figuer, and
  Padre Lector Fray Pablo Mugártegui.

At Mission San Gabriel:
  Padre Predicador Fray Antonio Cruzado,
  Padre Predicador Fray Antonio Paterna, and
  Padre Predicador Fray Miguel Sánchez.

At Mission San Diego:
  Padre Lector Fray Luis Jayme, and
  Padre Predicador Fray Vicente Fuster, and in the matters relating to

San Juan Capistrano:
  Padre Predicador Fray Fermín Francisco Lasuén, and
  Padre Predicador Fray Gregorio de Amurrió.

Those who will be going to the two missions of the port of San Francisco are mentioned above and listed in their present place of residence. For the first mission, they are the already mentioned Padres Palóu and Cambón.

And for the second mission, Fathers Murguía and Peña, also mentioned above.

For the time being, this is all that I request of Vuestra Merced.

I continue to ask that God keep you many years in health and in His divine grace.

From this Mission of San Carlos de Monterey, October 14, 1775
Your dear friend and devoted servant kisses the hand of Vuestra Merced,
Fray Junípero Serra

This next series of letters offers a dramatic indication of the ways in which the issues that were the subject of some of the earlier letters, such as servants and rations, could expose tensions that were simmering very close to the surface. Rivera y Moncada wrote two letters to Serra on October 23. Both letters dealt with servants, specifically with their salaries and their rations. The letters were short and somewhat curt.

In his first letter the commander quoted the reglamento and gave it a narrow interpretation on the issue of how long mission servants would be eligible to receive their salaries. He probably received a great deal of satisfaction from that tactic, for he knew that Serra had been very involved in drawing up the reglamento. The idea of using this document to restrict the influence of the missions appealed to the commander. In the second letter he dealt with rations and took the opportunity to raise the issue of whether or not the missions would be able to support the presidios if there were a shortage of corn. He threatened to stop distributing rations to the mission servants unless Serra gave a positive response to this question.

Serra responded at typical great length to both of these letters. Concerning the salaries of the servants, he contested the commander's interpretation of the reglamento. He told him that he would be wasting his time if he appealed to the viceroy when the matter was so clearly, in Serra's view, spelled out in the reglamento itself, in the legal opinion of the fiscal, and in the decrees of the junta Bucareli had convened in 1773 after Serra's visit. On the issue of rations, Serra criticized the estimate of the amount of rations available. However, he did not criticize Rivera y Moncada directly. Instead he directed his comments at warehouse keeper Juan Soler. He included elements of a conversation between Rivera y Moncada and Hezeta, which had apparently been reported to him by Hezeta or a member of the *Santiago*'s crew. His argument was that the commander was incorrect in maintaining that any shortage of rations existed. Thus there should not be any problem with the ability of the presidio to distribute these rations to the mission servants. And, while he was on the general topic of supplies, he could not resist bringing up once again his overall irritation about the situation with the mules.

Rivera y Moncada responded to Serra's letters the next day. He dismissed each of Serra's detailed arguments in a sentence. He also insisted that there was no need for him to go into great detail about the rationing situation and what the warehouse did or did not contain. There was no reason, he said, for Serra to be notified about all of this. In fact, he added, Serra was the one who was deficient in the matter of providing notifications. For instance, Serra did not always notify him when Indians fled from the missions. The implication was that the location of the Indians was much more urgent for the well-being of the province than the types of items in the warehouse. The commander pointed out that Serra was at greater fault for not keeping him more closely informed about the status of the Indians at the missions. In addition, he used this letter as an opportunity to assert his authority over Serra, saying that as military commander of the area he had every right to take mules and servants and letter satchels from the mission if he needed them for matters of military necessity. He ended by saying that he expected no questions or quarrels or grief from Serra about this.

After sending this response, Rivera y Moncada received another letter from Serra. Both of Serra's letters from the day before were extremely long and closely argued. The necessity of composing them had taken a toll on Serra, and the tone of the letter reflected that—it was angry and intemperate. Serra said he hoped that God would forgive Rivera y Moncada for all of the work he just made Serra do in responding to these two letters. This was especially difficult, he continued, because there were so many other things that were going on and he did not appreciate having to drop everything just to respond to these questions from the commander.

Rivera y Moncada was ready and fired off his own angry letter to Serra in which he criticized Serra for not ensuring that the presidio soldiers were given access to the sacraments and rituals of the church. He was referring to the fact that Serra had moved Lasuén out of the presidio in August and sent him south to help found the projected new mission at San Juan Capistrano. Serra did not send a replacement for Lasuén even though, with the arrival of the group of Franciscans from Baja California in late 1773, there was a surplus of priests at Carmel. At the conclusion of the letter, Rivera y Moncada took great pleasure in throwing Serra's earlier reference to the Court of Accounting in Mexico City right back at him.

After this angry exchange Serra composed a formal reply to the commander's response to his two initial letters. In this he stepped back from the mutual recriminations and most recent exchanges. He acknowledged that Rivera y Moncada had the authority to requisition mules and servants and leather satchels from the mission in the case of military necessity. Serra assured him that there would not be any problem whatsoever with this. However, he could not resist ending the letter with yet another request for additional mules.

> Muy Reverendo Padre Presidente Fray Junípero Serra
> My dear Señor,
> Vuestra Reverencia asked the Señor Excelentísimo for servant boys for the missions and Su Excelencia granted this request per Real Junta. These seem to be the same servants referred to in the second and third articles of the Reglamento. Based on this understanding, I would like to propose the following to Vuestra Reverencia:
> The Reglamento was put into effect in the year 1774 and we are now in the year 1775. Servants would be given salaries for two years and rations for five. Therefore, it seems that the salary ends this year, unless one is to understand that each new servant will be given a salary for two years. Because of that uncertainty and the fact that five missions were established when this favor was granted, I cannot presume to decide if this policy should also be extended to the missions that are yet to be established.[23]
> If Vuestra Reverencia would appeal directly to the Señor Excelentísimo, he will advise us on how to proceed. In this manner I am certain we will be able to proceed without any doubts. Vuestra Reverencia can be certain that in these matters I recognize the limits of my authority. I am, and will be, very pleased to see the missions receive assistance as well as any progress they make.
> May God keep Vuestra Reverencia many years.
> Monterey, October 23, 1775, etc.
> Fernando de Rivera y Moncada

> Muy Reverendo Padre Presidente Fray Junípero Serra
> My dear Señor,
> What happened last year was that about 600 fanegas of corn were received and the families did not begin to use it until they arrived here in late November. There was no double ration for anyone. In fact, I felt it would be best, as

---

23. Palóu included the relevant passage of the Reglamento in *New California*, 3:82.

a precaution in case of a possible shortage, to reduce the ration for the single men by half an *almud*. If I had not done that, the *San Carlos* would have found us without any corn. Now, in Don Juan Soler's response, which I am forwarding to you, Vuestra Reverencia will be able to see that the allotment of corn received this year was not up to last year's amount. And that is why I propose the following to Vuestra Reverencia. Since the six servants at Mission Carmel, the five at Mission San Antonio, and the two at Mission San Luis all receive weekly rations from this warehouse amounting to four fanegas and half an almud—and I do not know if we will be able to continue with this same distribution—I am asking Vuestra Reverencia if the missions could help the presidio if there is a shortage of corn. Unfortunately, if that cannot be done, it is clear from the warehouse keeper's statement that there will not be enough corn to continue rationing it to the servants and that practice will cease. I hope this communication can be of use to Vuestra Reverencia in your appeal to Su Excelencia, whom we hope, because of his well-known piety, will decree that the missions be granted the equivalent amount of rations that they give their servants.

   May God keep Vuestra Reverencia many years.

Monterey, October 23, 1775, etc.
Fernando de Rivera y Moncada

Señor Capitán Don Fernando de Rivera y Moncada.
My very dear Señor,
   Last night the surgeon Don Joseph Dávila personally delivered to me two official letters from you, bundled together and dated the 23rd of this month. Both letters dealt with matters regarding the servants in these missions.
   One letter was about the problems with their salaries, and the other about the problems with their rations. I will render my answers in the same manner as Vuestra Merced did in your proposals. In this letter I will respond first to the issue of their salaries and then I will address the matter regarding their rations in a separate letter.
   In the first letter, Vuestra Merced explains to me that Vuestra Merced and I should have recourse to Su Excelencia so that he can clarify the two points in question that Vuestra Merced is hesitant to resolve regarding the servants' salaries. You are certain that by doing this we will be able to proceed without

any doubts. I am in complete agreement that this is the most appropriate and indisputable way to clear up all our uncertainties.

But at the same time, it seems to me that since Su Excelencia is continuously surrounded by the many tasks that governing such an expansive kingdom entails, we should not add to those tasks by seeking his advice on matters such as these. Once the letter is on its way, we might regret having sent it and say, "The issue I was unclear about is specifically and expressly addressed right here in the Reglamento."

Let us see, now, if the two points for which Vuestra Merced has questions are of this kind.

The first is if the time limit of two years for the salary for those to whom it has been granted should be calculated from the time the Reglamento came into effect, which was January 1, 1774, or from the time the employees began their work here.

Well, Señor, it seems to me that the Reglamento clearly favors the second option and not the first. The Reglamento says that on every voyage of the frigate, they should encourage those who are coming to bring their wives, and they will be eligible to earn the two years of salary and rations. Since the frigate only comes once a year, what reward or pay will those who come at the end of the second year receive? How could they earn a salary here if they were in their own homes last year and perhaps had never even heard yet of Monterey? Therefore, if the Reglamento states that those who come with their wives will be given a salary for two years and rations for five, it is clear that the two years were not meant to start on the first day of last year but rather on the date that each family begins its service. Nobody knew about such a Reglamento here because it did not arrive until May. But if Vuestra Merced still thinks we should consult Su Excelencia, even after taking these reflections into consideration, then let us do so quickly.

And this gives me the opportunity to comment on what Vuestra Merced said about the young servant boys I requested for the missions. I made my request of the Excelentísimo Señor, and Su Excelencia granted my request per Real Junta. They appear to be the same ones referred to in the second and third articles of the Reglamento from which Vuestra Merced inferred that at the end of their second year their salary should cease. This can be understood as being in effect either from the date the Reglamento began or from the time the servants began working. In terms of the single men who have come as sailors and have the option of returning home at the end of one year, we are then faced with having to find others to replace them, which means that the two years of salary and five years of rations are not intended for them. However, it does apply to the families, man and wife, who come as settlers and intend to establish themselves here. The article numbers in the Reglamento that Vuestra Merced cites indicate that distinction, although there is some ambiguity.

In Number Two, there is no mention of settlers or women; neither does it mention the two years of salary, etc. And in Number Three, in which women and settlers are mentioned, it also mentions the terms of salary and rations. The person who makes this distinction even more clearly is the Señor Fiscal de Su Majestad, who clarifies Señor Echeveste's proposal. He goes on to the second point that mentioned the workers, but there is no mention of a distribution of time, and he says the following: "In Number Three, he explains the usefulness of free transportation for the people who will bring their wives or family. The only cost is rations for five years and salary for two years."

From all of this it seems clear that the terms are meant for families, as described above, and not for the single young men who enlisted as sailors and can stay for as long as they like. Nor does it refer to those who support themselves by simply working as servants, for they do not have the time or the ability to work for themselves to save something for when the term of their salary and rations has ended. This is why I say that the servants who are mentioned in those particular articles of the Reglamento are in part the ones I asked for and who were given to me, but in part they are not, for neither in my memorandum nor in the response I was given (under point number 12) is there any mention of families or of a specific period of time for salaries and rations.

It seems that everything points in this direction. The Reglamento was not drawn up to change the decision of the preceding Real Junta, nor would the Caballero Echeveste have the intention of doing so after the junta had rendered its decision. Therefore, when we find the junta cited in the Reglamento, we should turn to it if there are any uncertainties. And based on what we find there, we should clarify the Reglamento if that needs to be done.

With regard to our case, let us proceed in that manner. I believe we will overcome the difficulty we are having. It seems to me that Vuestra Merced should do this in the case of the soldier Manuel Butrón, who is asking to be relieved because he is old and tired.

Vuestra Merced asked him—if he spoke truthfully—what he would do if he was no longer a soldier and how he would support himself. You told him he could not be a servant at this mission because it already had the maximum number.

What I am now saying is that the Reglamento does not specify a number. It simply says, "Those whom you want." The Señor Fiscal repeats the same thing. Therefore, why would Butrón not be able to become a servant at the mission just because there are six here already? I am saying this merely to clarify the regulation by the junta based on which I requested six servants at each mission. Since the response corresponds with the manner in which I made the request, it is our understanding that we are allowed six under the terms of this article. And we understand the "However many you want" of the decree to refer to the families who come in earnest as settlers. But as of today, we do not have even one such family. Nor do I believe it will be easy to recruit such people under the conditions Vuestra Merced has told me he believes are essential, for the reasons I have already explained to you.

The second uncertainty that Vuestra Merced is hesitant to resolve is whether the current practice of granting six workers to each of the five missions is to be extended to the missions we are in the process of establishing. In my humble opinion, it seems to me that this issue is also resolved in the Reglamento.

In that same second article that Vuestra Merced cites, it says: "For now, leave the missions on the same footing as the five that have been erected . . . and until such a time, etc., shall be given what is required by any other mission that may be founded."

Then it goes on to talk about the workers and the families, etc., without excluding from that benefit the mission that was to be founded, which has turned out to be San Juan Capistrano. And for those missions that will follow, the solution can be deduced logically. For if the current Señor Excelentísimo granted the missions the benefit of having servants to help advance the missions that had been established by Su Excelentísimo's predecessor, missions that had already made some progress, then how can it be doubted that the same gentleman, who happily governs, would not favor the missions that are to be his personal project at least as much, if not more than the other missions, especially since, at the present time, these new missions consist of nothing more than the land created by God on which they can be established.

And with this I have expressed my opinion regarding the two uncertainties that Vuestra Merced presented to me.

If, in spite of what I have said, Vuestra Merced still believes that we should consult Su Excelencia, I am most happy to oblige. I will submit my interpretation for correction, without fail, so that his evaluation of what is proper for founding or not founding missions can enlighten me for the future.

I wish and continue to pray that God, Our Lord, keep Vuestra Merced many years in His divine grace.

From this your Mission of San Carlos of Monterey, October 24, 1775. Your faithful and devoted chaplain kisses the hand of Vuestra Merced, Fray Junípero Serra

Señor Capitán Comandante Don Fernando Rivera y Moncada
My very dear Señor,

I have just responded to Vuestra Merced's official letter regarding the issue of the salaries of the servants at these missions. In this letter, I will respond to Vuestra Merced's other letter, which was included under the same cover, with regard to the issue of their rations, or of the difficulties that Vuestra Merced has encountered in supplying them in accordance with what the Excelentísimo Señor Virrey and the Real Junta have ordered.

Vuestra Merced is essentially telling me that you have asked or ordered the warehouse keeper, Don Juan Soler, to state how much corn is available to be rationed. He answered that it amounted to 295 fanegas and 11 almudes, and that a careful count indicates that it would only last until the end of next February.

Because of this, Vuestra Merced is asking me if the missions would be able to supply the presidio if there were a shortage of corn. You add that if this cannot be done, it is evident from Don Juan Soler's statement that there is not enough corn to supply rations to the young men who are servants of these missions. This would force Vuestra Merced to suspend the rationing. And that your official letter should be used in my appeal to the Excelentísimo Señor Virrey.

I confess, Señor Capitán, with the sincerity of a friend and of a religious (although a bad one), that, even after considering all the good arguments you were so happy to concoct, I do not believe that your official letter or your decision are well-grounded. And therefore, Vuestra Merced, for the love of God, without becoming angry, please take my objections into consideration.

First: If Don Juan Soler had known why he was being questioned, he could have added in his statement that more than fifty fanegas of wheat were harvested this year in the king's cornfield. With that amount of corn on hand, I heard Vuestra Merced say that you had written or were writing to Su Excelencia stating that the warehouse would provide rations for this year without excluding the servants of these missions.

Second: He could have said that if more corn was consumed last year than what has arrived this year, it was because the significant quantity of fine flour that was brought to the royal warehouses by the frigate has not been used, or has been barely used. He could have also specified the amount in the warehouse today and compared last year's amount to this year's. Then, after adding it all up, he could have calculated how much longer the rations will last, especially since distributing flour instead of corn has become more frequent during the last years.

Third: He could have mentioned that there is another substitute for corn, which is hardtack. The warehouse has some left over from last year, and the captain of the frigate, Don Bruno de Hezeta, put forty *quintales* of it in the warehouse this year. It is evident that he has more, which he can offer. And he might be able to give them even more, if they want it and ask for it. We also know that hardtack has often been used instead of corn, especially on expeditions.

Fourth: He could have stated (seeing that there is talk of eliminating the rations altogether or suspending them for a few people) the quantity of beans in the warehouse, which is no small amount, since Vuestra Merced recently offered Capitán Don Bruno (when he was planning on repeating his expedition northward) eighty fanegas of beans. And you assured him that you would not need the beans for rations throughout the year. The same applies for all the other food items in the warehouse. Even though they may not be plentiful, all the items are food and rations.

Fifth: Before attempting to take away the rations or to appeal to the missions, he might have considered that this year the warehouse in San Diego received 700 fanegas of corn and not one grain less. Before they were measured, there was still some left for the poor. Knowing this, Vuestra Merced confided to Capitán Don Bruno, who was planning on spending the winter in San Diego, that there would be no difficulty in supplying him with corn at that location.

And so if they could help Don Bruno, who no longer needs help, then why can't they help us or help that Royal Presidio if such a need should occur? Even though that presidio is far away, I am an eyewitness to the fact that when that escort and mission were in need, they were helped from here. And, vice versa, I have seen help arrive here from there.

The double rations that Vuestra Merced mentions to me as a new burden were three, as far as I know. But now they will only be two. Neither the three, nor the two, have increased the expenses of corn for Vuestra Merced. On the contrary, you have managed to save on expenses. Instead of the half almud that has been allotted to the wife, they have been given seven pounds of flour instead, such as it is. Therefore, the double rations consist of the combination of the flour and the beans.

I will now address the question Vuestra Merced has asked me, which is: "If there is not enough corn, will the missions be able to assist the presidios?"

If you had said: "Lacking provisions for rationing, be it corn, flour, hardtack, or wheat," your question would have been more precise.

And my response to your question is:

In such a case (which I hope to God does not happen), the missions will do what they have done many times, which is, to provide the troops with whatever they need for their sustenance, from whatever the mission has.

Vuestra Merced knows, and so do many others, that in the past, when the escorts at San Diego, San Gabriel, San Luis, and San Antonio needed food, the Padres at each of those missions, at the slightest hint from Capitán Fages, would kill cattle for the troops, and not for themselves, so that the troops would have food to eat. The same was done for Don Juan de Anza's expedition.

Vuestra Merced knows that in the year we arrived in these lands for the second time, the escort at San Gabriel and in part, that at San Diego, as well as the escorts at the two missions, all ate from the 110 fanegas of corn that were harvested at Mission San Gabriel, which was the first harvest ever heard of in these lands.

And, finally, it so happens that every day the escorts at Missions San Luis and San Antonio run out of provisions because the pack train that delivers the supplies is delayed. Every time this happens, the missions come to their assistance and give them rations.

In this regard I heard Vuestra Merced say, when talking about the abovementioned soldiers: "They always tell me how grateful they are to the Padres."

This mission and the one from San Antonio have offered their mules to transport the provisions for the escorts of San Antonio and San Luis. They are willing to bear this inconvenience, and are allowing Vuestra Merced to keep their forty-five mules should Vuestra Merced need them. These mules were given to these missions by Su Excelencia, which I have on record in the letter from the Reverendo Padre Guardián of our colegio, which came on the frigate. Vuestra Merced also has a letter from Su Excelencia, which deals with the same point, in which he tells you to hand the mules over to me. In the nearly two months that have passed, I have neither asked for the mules nor have I even hinted about this matter to Vuestra Merced, since I thought that it would be more appropriate for Vuestra Merced to give me this news personally.

Finally, my dearest Señor, the missions have done and will continue to do all they can on behalf of the presidio and the troops, whenever the need arises.

Thus, in conclusion:

Vuestra Merced knows how much the missions have harvested and how much they have, since we do not hide what we have from anyone. Vuestra Merced knows how it is used and that we do not sell it or throw it away. Instead, we use it as carefully and as economically as we can. I have no way of knowing what position the missions will be in when the presidio does not have supplies for rations. But I do know that whatever the case may be, the missions will continue to be generous with the presidio so that the troops have food to eat, even if it should be necessary to send away most or all of the new Christians for a period of time, since they are able to find food for themselves in the mountains or on the beach, which is what they used to do not so many years ago.

This is what will be done, with the grace of God. If this promise does not suffice to keep Vuestra Merced from taking the rations away from the servants of the missions, then do as you please, as I continue to pray that,

God, Our Lord, keep Vuestra Merced in His divine grace and in perfect health many years.

From this Mission of San Carlos of Monterey, October 24, 1775
Your faithful and loving chaplain kisses the hand of Vuestra Merced,
Fray Junípero Serra

Muy Reverendo Padre Presidente Fray Junípero Serra
My dear Señor,
Today I received two letters from Vuestra Reverencia dated yesterday, October 24, in response to the letters I sent to Vuestra Reverencia. I shall respond to one, because the other requires more time.

Corn is what is commonly rationed at the present time. Don Juan Soler responded in accordance to what he was asked; that there is flour and some wheat. I had no intention of hiding this from Vuestra Reverencia and the proof is that I did not ask Vuestra Reverencia for corn to ration to the people of the presidio once theirs ran out. It is true that there are about 300 fanegas of beans, and if the consumption of it does not increase, I think it will last about two years. I did not request the hardtack with the purpose of using it for the presidio rations. Instead, I want to have it available for the journeys and other undertakings that may occur. I certainly did not intend to use them as rations for the young servants. It is true that Don Bruno de Hezeta has offered me forty quintales more. Since Vuestra Reverencia has mentioned it, if you believe that the hardtack can be used as rations for the servants at the missions, I will request it immediately. Vuestra Reverencia should notify me to avoid a major problem, which is what would happen if the recently converted Christians were allowed to leave the mission. Living in the mountains and interacting with the gentiles would put them in danger of perdition.

In response to the matter of the mules, if Vuestra Reverencia had wanted me to discuss this with you, you could have told me so. I omitted this detail, believing that the matter had been settled in the letter dated June 22. If you reread it, you will find complete answers to everything you believe was unanswered. The only difference is that in the letter you cite, I offered to hand over thirty-one mules, but when the time came I gave you thirty-three. I have given an accounting of the distribution of those mules to the Excelentísimo Señor. I am awaiting new orders to do things differently. I would like to add that the number of mules the presidio has received is forty-four and not forty-five.

There is no doubt that seven hundred fanegas of corn arrived at the warehouse in San Diego. There is also no doubt that I do not have mules to transport the corn if I needed it. So if Vuestra Reverencia would like to send your servants with mules from the missions, I will supply them with an order that they be given a portion of the surplus. But if that is not the case and Vuestra Reverencia would like to keep receiving rations from this warehouse, you can be certain that when the time comes, I will avail myself of the missions' mules, some of the missions' servants, and saddlebags, which the warehouse does not have and which are necessary for such long trips to keep from losing provisions along the way.

I will notify you ahead of time if such a case arises to avoid problems, quarrels, or disapproval. If Vuestra Reverencia takes into consideration how very carefully you look after the well-being of the mission servants, then you will realize that I, too, have every reason to make sure that the soldiers are not lacking anything, especially since they are so necessary for the missions. With regard to the mules the two missions have offered to provide for transporting provisions to the escorts, I would be happy if, in the future, the missions use them for their servants. I will make do with the old and sickly mules for everything else.

May God keep Vuestra Reverencia many years.

Monterey, October 25, 1775, etc.
Fernando de Rivera y Moncada

Señor Capitán Comandante Don Fernando
My very dear Señor,

May God forgive Vuestra Merced for what you have given me to do with your two very brief letters, right when the mail or the boats are about to leave and I have to attend to other important matters. But if my work is to be of some value, then completing it will serve as some consolation.

I already can see, and Vuestra Merced will see as well, that we are both fulfilling our responsibilities.

May God, Our Lord, grant us His grace so that we will not have the slightest clash of wills.

May His Divine Majesty keep Vuestra Merced in His holy grace many years.

From this your Mission of San Carlos, October 25, 1775,
Fray Junípero Serra

Muy Reverendo Padre Presidente Fray Junípero Serra
My dear Señor,

Vuestra Reverencia tells me that, may God forgive me for what I have given you to do with two very brief letters, etc.

I am of such a different opinion that I even hope for glory, for I do what I can, I am solely attentive to my duty, and I try to anticipate what might happen. I will say this simply and directly: Vuestra Reverencia tells me what I have not done, what I am doing, and what I am saying. What you are not telling me is what I am actually thinking, because I believe you cannot penetrate my thoughts. I shall then start at the beginning.

May God forgive Vuestra Reverencia for the doctrine the children are not learning and for the upbringing they are not receiving.

May God forgive Vuestra Reverencia for the sermons and Masses which we, young and old, have not heard.

May God forgive Vuestra Reverencia for the confessions that perhaps will stop being heard here because Vuestra Reverencia has taken Padre Fermín away from us. This is certainly something to fear because it concerns the salvation of our fellow man, and only God knows if this may be due to the Padre having been removed from here. This was done without offering the slightest excuse such as there not being enough Padres, when in fact there are more than enough of them. Will the Court of Public Accounts in Mexico not notice this, as Vuestra Reverencia wrote to me on a certain occasion?

We should put these disputes behind us and restore our former relationship so that friendship and trust can grow.

May Our Lord keep Vuestra Reverencia in His glory many years.

Monterey, October 26, 1775, etc.
Fernando de Rivera y Moncada

Señor Capitán Comandante Don Fernando de Rivera y Moncada
My dear Señor,

From the letter I just received from Vuestra Merced with yesterday's date (the 25th of this month), I believe there are two points that require my response, since the rest of the letter is a response to my earlier letter.

The first point is: Do I think that the servants of these missions could be given hardtack as rations? For if that is the case, more could be requested. The other point is: Do I want the servants to continue receiving rations from that warehouse? You inform me that if it is necessary to turn to San Diego for assistance, Vuestra Merced will avail yourself of the missions' mules, some young men from the missions, and saddlebags. And you state that you would inform me ahead of time so that there would be no problems, quarrels, or disapproval.

To the first point, I am saying that I want the servants at the missions to be treated like the ones at the Royal Presidio in issues regarding rations, since they all serve the same master. When the rest are given hardtack, whether it is because they are going on an expedition or because that is what Vuestra Merced wishes, then give these servants hardtack as well, which, as I was saying, would help save corn.

As for the second point, I do not know why Vuestra Merced is hesitant to accept the offer I made in my earlier letter regarding the missions helping the presidio in whatever way we can when the presidio is in need, unless availing yourself of our help is in some way unauthorized, which is something I cannot foresee. The saddlebags were all sent by our colegio and paid for from our funds. For Vuestra Merced to say that you will avail yourself of them without making a specific request is not something that will cause problems, either now or in the future. I reiterate the offer I already made, and the same applies to the mules and the servants. The missions will agree to help with anything when Vuestra Merced deems it necessary to go there to collect provisions for rations for the presidio and for the servants. With regard to the mules, the Señor Gobernador of California wrote to me that he had sent eighty-five. The missions have received a total of forty mules on two different occasions. Therefore, I request the remaining forty-five. If there are not more than forty-four, then patience is required.

May God, Our Lord, keep Vuestra Merced in His holy grace many years.

Mission of San Carlos of Monterey, October 26, 1775, etc.
Fray Junípero Serra

The final letter in this correspondence dates from July 1776, more than six months after the previous exchanges. Serra took the opportunity of a discussion about mail service to make an argument for more missions. This letter contains one of the most thorough statements Serra ever made about the missions being placed at a certain distance from each other for the ease and facility of travelers. This was not a new theme for him. As early as February 1770, while he was still at San Diego, he was envisioning a "range" (cordillera) of missions between Velicatá and San Diego. In other letters he spoke of a group of missions filling in the gaps between various missions. In 1771, for instance, he spoke of putting three missions between San Luis Obispo and San Buenaventura, even though that latter mission had not yet been established. He told the guardian at the Colegio de San Fernando that this would make it possible for missionaries coming to Alta California to be able to sleep every third day in a mission that belonged to San Fernando. He brought up the issue of a postal service in a letter to the viceroy in

August 1774. He said that missions located about twenty-five leagues apart from each other would make it possible to deliver mail every two months. In another letter to the viceroy five months later he said that four additional missions would improve communication between the missions and the presidios.[24]

This letter and others like it in the Serra correspondence have given rise to the notion that one of the primary purposes of the missions was to facilitate travel. One still reads in many places that the California missions were deliberately set a day's journey apart from each other so that they could function as convenient way stations for various travelers along the El Camino Real. This was not Serra's objective. The notion that the missions could be employed as stops for travelers was an argument that Serra developed because he thought this argument would further his principal objective, which was the establishment of more missions. A wonderful aspect of this argument was that it was infinitely adaptable. If Serra were writing to his missionary superior in Mexico City, then the travelers would be missionaries. If he were writing to the viceroy, then the travelers would be soldiers. If the issue were mail service, then the travelers would be couriers. As we have seen, Serra's principal objective was to found an increasing number of missions. He was roundly criticized for that, not only by military personnel and colonial officials but even by fellow missionaries. The "rest-for-travelers" argument was simply one argument among many that he employed in the service of his principal objective. And no argument was too far-fetched. At one point he suggested to a fellow Franciscan from Mallorca that since there were twelve Franciscan friaries on Mallorca and Menorca, there ought to be twelve missions in California![25]

Providing rest for travelers was never the principal object of the missions. Their locations in relation to each other was never a primary concern for Serra. In this next letter to Rivera y Moncada, Serra specifically said the principal objective of the missions was the propagation of the faith. That remained his consistent objective. The notion about a "chain" of missions deliberately placed a day or so apart from each other was something that became popular in the early twentieth century through the efforts of the Automobile Club of Southern California. This was never Serra's intention. In fact, he did not use the word "chain" to describe the cluster of missions he was founding. The word he employed was *escala*—ladder or stairway—a form of the word *escalera*, which he used in 1744 to describe his five sermons to the nuns at the Convento de Santa Clara in Palma. The term had the same meaning for Serra in California as it had thirty years before in Palma. The escalera was a way for people to grow closer to and ascend to the Divine.

24. Serra, *Writings*, 1:156, 216, 2:142,196.
25. Serra, *Writings*, 4:192.

Junípero Serra cared very much about what he thought was the relation of the people in the missions to his God, and he cared very little about the relationship of the missions' location to each other.

> Señor Capitán Comandante Don Fernando de Rivera y Moncada
> My dear Señor,
>
> I received with great pleasure Vuestra Merced's letter dated the 24th of this month. Enclosed was a copy of a letter from the Excelentísimo Señor Virrey dated February 14 of this year. The letter dealt with establishing a monthly mail service from these new establishments to those of Antigua California and from there to the Court of Mexico. Insofar as the missions are concerned, if the project can be carried out, I think it would be quite helpful, as Su Excelencia has stated.
>
> The Excelentísimo Señor has ordered Vuestra Merced to discuss this matter with me and to let him know what we decide and agree upon. We have already had discussions on this matter on a number of occasions.
> We have examined the distances, the unpopulated areas, and other difficulties connected with this project. Since Vuestra Merced has proposed to me in writing the conditions you have taken upon yourself to include in your report to Su Excelencia, all that I can do is offer something to accompany Vuestra Merced's report, should Su Excelencia wish to see my ideas in writing as well. This is what I have to say:
>
> It seems to me that if the Excelentísimo Señor would be happy for the time being with dispatching a courier on the first day of the month from this Presidio of San Diego to the frontier of Antigua California, the courier should leave, whether or not he has letters from Monterey or San Francisco, so that they can at least have frequent communication from these parts. They would receive letters from farther north whenever they could be sent from there.
> I do not believe this would cause any great difficulty, since those who have experience say that a courier can travel this distance in three or four days. But I do agree with Vuestra Merced regarding the difficulties you mention in your letter in terms of traveling monthly from the port or fort of San Francisco. However, there is a sure way to alleviate many of the most troubling problems; in fact, there is a way to eliminate all of them, which is to put into effect something that I have wanted to do for a long time.
>
> The potential for accomplishing what I have wanted was always great, and now it is even greater, which is to complete, between the Presidio of San Diego and the Presidio of Monterey, a ladder of missions about twenty-five

leagues apart from each other. The principal objective is the propagation of the holy faith, but the project would also offer comfort to travelers and contribute to more peaceful relations with the indigenous nations along the route. To accomplish this, all that needs to be done is: reestablish San Juan Capistrano, found San Buenaventura on the site that was designated for it right from the beginning, and found just one more mission, La Purísima Concepción, near the point of that name at the upper end of the Santa Bárbara Channel.

Just by taking these steps, couriers traveling from Monterey to San Diego could sleep every night in Christian pueblos and in places that are well defended. Thus, as the couriers travel back and forth, they would not have to leave their tired animals within reach of the gentiles and risk losing them. Nor would they be vulnerable to outbreaks of hostilities with those gentiles. It is easy to imagine the many advantages to be gained by this.

But if these measures are not taken, I am afraid of what will happen when our people travel frequently through that troublesome yet very convenient Santa Bárbara Channel.

Nevertheless, I do not want my opinion to stand in the way, in the slightest, of Su Excelencia's plans and good intentions. Taking Vuestra Merced's report into consideration, he will decide, as always, what is best and most appropriate.

May God keep Vuestra Merced, etc.

Presidio of San Diego, July 27, 1776
Kisses the hand, etc.
Fray Junípero Serra

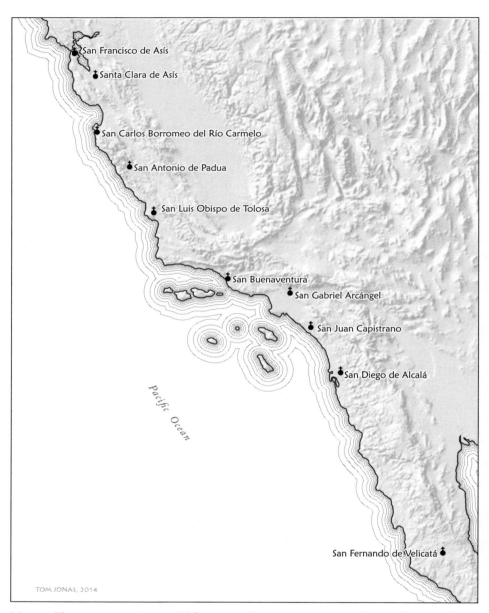

Map 10. The ten missions in Las Californias established during the presidency of Junípero Serra. *Map by Tom Jonas.*

CHAPTER 8

San Diego

Serra's world changed dramatically and permanently on the night of December 13, 1775. That evening Fernando de Rivera y Moncada personally rode from the Monterey presidio to Mission San Carlos at Carmel. He told Serra that he had just received news that Mission San Diego was destroyed on November 5 in a coordinated attack by a large group of Kumeyaay Indians and that one of the missionaries there, Father Luis Jayme, had been killed. The commander gave Serra a letter from Father Vicente Fuster, the surviving missionary at San Diego, which gave details of the attack. Serra reported the details in a letter he wrote to the viceroy two days later.

The destruction of Mission San Diego affected Serra on many different levels, and these levels found their way into his letter to the viceroy. First, since he was usually focused on the future, Serra was extremely concerned about the prospects for additional missions in Alta California. For when word of the destruction of San Diego reached San Juan Capistrano, the commander there ordered that the mission be abandoned, so the priests and soldiers at that site returned to the San Diego Presidio. In Serra's mind, this was uncomfortably similar to what had happened at San Sabá in 1758. As we have seen, although there were plans to reestablish the mission at San Sabá after its destruction, those plans were never carried out. Serra was afraid that the attack might decisively end his dream of further growth of the mission "ladder." He feared that the destruction of Mission San Diego would mean that officials in Mexico City would come to share Rivera y Moncada's opinion that more soldiers were needed at the presidios, but not at any additional missions. His concern that the commander's narrative of events in Alta California might become the dominant one was heightened by Rivera y Moncada's refusal to let Serra accompany him to San Diego. Finally, the killing of Father Jayme forced Serra to make explicit his opinion about what he thought should happen after a missionary was killed by Indians. He put the matter in very personal terms and explicitly requested what he called "moderate punishment" for any Indians who might kill him or any other missionary in the future. Serra maintained this position for the rest of his life and found that it often collided with military opinion about the punishment of rebellious Indians.

In his letter to Serra, Fuster described the condition of Jayme's body when it was discovered. He said that the priest "was disfigured from head to foot." Fuster added, "He was stripped completely of all his clothing, even to his undergarments around his middle," and "his face was one great bruise from the clubbing and stoning it had suffered." The manner in which Father Jayme was physically attacked was surely not accidental. It indicated that the Kumeyaay who killed him were directing their blows at the religious worldview he encapsulated. Jayme's most distinctive feature, his religious garb, was stripped from him as his attackers symbolically rejected the mission's demands that they be clothed in European fashion. Further, for most native people in the Americas, Christianity was above all a verbal religion. This religion resided in the words the priests spoke in the church, in the prayers and songs the neophytes were taught, and in the answers they were instructed to memorize as they learned the catechism. The disfigurement of Father Jayme's face was an attack on his mouth—the source of the religion the Kumeyaay were rejecting. The sixteenth-century Franciscan writer Gerónimo de Mendieta recorded an instance in which native people specifically attacked the lips and teeth of a priest they killed. The beating of Father Jayme was most likely in the same vein.[1]

The destruction of San Diego dramatically and decisively altered Serra's experiences in Alta California. His optimism had proven to be naive, his enthusiasm had proven to be unfounded, and his criticism of the military commander's placement of soldiers had proven to be reckless. For the rest of his life, Serra was never in so strong a position as he had been in California before the San Diego uprising.

❋ Letter to Antonio María de Bucareli y Ursúa, December 15, 1775

Long Live Jesus, Mary, Joseph

Muy Venerado Señor mío Excelentísimo,

Being as we are in the valley of tears, not all news and events can be favorable. And so, I cannot avoid reporting to Vuestra Excelencia the tragic news I have just received regarding the total destruction of Mission San Diego and the death of Padre Lector Fray Luis Jayme (the main priest of the two religious ministers there) at the hands of the gentiles and Christian neophytes who rebelled. It happened on November 5 at about one or two o'clock in the

---
1. Ahern, "Martyrs and Idols," 284.

morning. According to what I have been told, gentiles from forty rancherías joined together and, after ransacking the church, set fire to it. And then they proceeded to the granary, the Padres' house, the soldiers' guardhouse, and the rest of the buildings.

They killed a carpenter from Guadalajara and a blacksmith from Tepic. They shot with arrows four soldiers—the only ones who were guarding the mission. And even though two of them were badly wounded, they now are completely recovered.

The other religious, named Padre Fray Vicente Fuster, apart from being frightened, was only injured on his shoulder, which was hit by a rock. He was in pain for a few days. Immediately after that sad night, he headed for the presidio with the few people who were still alive. The Christian Indians who had remained loyal carried the dead and gravely injured on their shoulders. He has written to me from the presidio asking me to tell him what he should do.

I received this news day before yesterday at nine o'clock in the evening. Capitán Comandante Don Fernando came to inform me in person and also brought letters.

Yesterday, most of the morning was spent in vigil for the dead, a sung Mass, and prayers for the soul of the deceased Padre. Since the afternoon was taken up with Don Fernando's second visit and his departure, all I had time to do was finish reading the letters. He told us that he was leaving this afternoon, and I suggested to him that a religious accompany him. He responded that he was in quite a hurry and would not be stopping, not even at the missions along the way. I asked him if later they could provide an escort for a religious to go there. He said no, because there were few soldiers left.

That being said, my idea of going down there to help reestablish the two missions that were lost with one blow, namely San Diego and San Juan Capistrano, was thwarted. And seeing that I do not have any time left to write to the three Padres who are there to give them some instructions, nor do I know how much attention the officials would pay to what I said since they have already started the formal judicial proceedings, I leave it in God's hands. In the human sphere, the only refuge I have is the authority and protection of Vuestra Excelencia. I most earnestly implore you to order most rigorously the very quick reestablishment of those two missions on their exact same sites before the time of the rebellion at San Diego, if in effect this has not already been done by the time Vuestra Excelencia's orders arrive.

The reason San Juan Capistrano was lost is as follows: After spending many days becoming very familiar with the surrounding area, regarding which I have a long diary consisting of seven sheets of paper provided by the missionary at that new mission, the mission was founded on October 30, the eighth day of the Saint's feast, at the spot deemed most suitable and with the appropriate ceremonies. The site was blessed, the first Mass was sung, the holy standard of the cross was raised, etc., and with this, that new pueblo of Christianity was considered as having been founded and dedicated with the name of that saint. It is twenty-three leagues from San Diego and nineteen from San Gabriel de los Temblores, next to the Camino Real, and thus a very convenient stopping place along that route.

Since that day, the Padres and a few [Baja] California Indians and other servants, with some help from the soldiers, had begun the task of constructing those first humble structures that mark the beginning of such an enterprise. They continued working until November 7. That afternoon, mail arrived from San Diego for the lieutenant of that presidio, who was present for the new founding to provide encouragement. He was informed of what happened on the 5th and the tragic news of the death of the Padre, etc. Based on this information, the officer decided that all the soldiers must go to the presidio of San Diego and that the new settlement should be abandoned. And that was done with much sadness on the part of the two Padres who had founded the mission and who had been warmly received and regaled with many tokens of affection by the gentiles of that area.

That is how two missions were lost. Each in its own way looked very promising.

May God's Holy Will be done. And again, I beg Vuestra Excelencia to rectify this situation, for the love of God.

With regard to the loss of San Diego, a number of thoughts have occurred to me. But since complaining about what happened in the past does not change anything, I will let it all go. But I will again suggest to Vuestra Excelencia what I mentioned in a previous letter, which is, with conquests of this nature, the place where soldiers are most important is at the missions. In many places presidios might be very beneficial and very necessary, but from here I can only comment on what I see.

Mission San Diego is about two leagues from the presidio, but it is situated in such a way that by day, everything that goes on at the mission can be seen from the presidio. And the gunshot that is fired each morning to signal the changing of the guard can usually be heard at the mission. And while the entire mission was ablaze, with flames shooting high into the sky from one or two in the morning until dawn, and gunshots being fired during that entire time, those at the presidio did not see or hear anything. They say it was because of the way the wind was blowing.

And with just two men who were firing shots during that entire time, many lives that would have been lost without that defense were saved. But after the Padre has been killed, the mission has burned down, and its many, beautiful ornaments, sacred vessels, images, and baptismal, marriage, and burial records have been destroyed, along with the furnishings for the sacristy, the house, and the farm implements, it is now that the forces from the two presidios are joining together to set things right.

Since the circumstances surrounding this tragedy are so similar to what happened at Mission San Sabá (to where I was assigned, having been called from the Sierra Gorda for that purpose, I was ready to set out from our colegio as quickly as possible), God willing, the results will not be the same. Before reestablishing the mission, they wanted the presidios to join together to apprehend the guilty parties responsible for the burning of the mission and the death of the Padres, and punish them. The Indians they were pursuing rose up again and were further enraged. I ended up not going to that mission. Up to this day I do not know if the mission has been reestablished or not.

The soldiers are there in the presidio and the Indians are back to their gentile way of being.

Señor Excelentísimo: One of the most important things I requested of the Ilustrísimo Visitador General at the beginning of these conquests was that, if the Indians were to kill me, whether they be gentiles or Christians, they should be forgiven. And I request the same of Vuestra Excelencia. And I was negligent in not requesting this sooner. Seeing a formal decree from Vuestra Excelencia regarding this matter would be of great consolation to me during the time the Lord Our God sees fit to add to my advanced years of life. It would also be a consolation to the other religious who are here now and those who will come in the future.

It is only right that, for as long as the missionary is alive, the soldiers should guard and watch over him as God would guard the apple of his eye.[2] And I will not refuse such a favor for myself. But if they have already killed the missionary, what are we going to gain with military campaigns?

I am saying, so that others are not killed, guard them better than you guarded the deceased. And let the murderer live so he can be saved, which is

---
2. Deuteronomy 32:10.

the purpose of our coming here and the reason for forgiving him. Help him to understand, with some moderate punishment, that he is being pardoned in accordance with our law, which orders us to forgive offenses and to prepare him, not for his death, but for eternal life.

Señor Excelentísimo, Vuestra Excelencia, please forgive me for I have already overstepped, who knows to what extent?

Vuestra Excelencia will see the details of the entire event in the officers' reports.

The statements include some unfortunate news from the Colorado River. What is known for certain is that Señor Anza has not appeared and we do not know what may have happened to him.

I have no time to say anything further. And I beg Vuestra Excelencia to forgive the mistakes and lack of tact, for this letter was written in a great hurry.

May God keep Vuestra Excelencia many years. My wishes are that He extend your fervent rule on behalf of these souls. And may He continue to keep you evermore in His holy grace.

From this Mission, San Carlos de Monterey, which is totally dependent on Vuestra Excelencia, December 15, 1775.

Señor Excelentísimo,
Your most affectionate and humble servant and chaplain who loves you dearly, kisses the hand of Vuestra Excelencia,
Fray Junípero Serra

For a few years after the Kumeyaay attack, San Diego was at the center of Serra's concerns. We do not know as much as we would like about the early history of Mission San Diego. The original baptismal register was destroyed in the uprising in 1775, and Serra reconstructed it as best he could when he was at San Diego in 1776. The priest who performed many of the earliest baptisms, Father Fernando Parrón, was not available because he left California and returned to Mexico in 1771. We do know that, as at Monterey, the local inhabitants related that the first appearance of the Spaniards in San Diego Bay was accompanied by a series of omens—an eclipse of the sun and an earthquake.[3] These omens were more threatening than those at Monterey.

There were no baptisms for at least a year and a half after the founding of San Diego. As was the case at Mission San Carlos, the earliest baptisms came from

---

3. Geiger, *Franciscan Missionaries*, 182; Sandos and Sandos, "Chisli, Canuch, and Junípero Serra," 56; Serra, *Writings*, 1:364–67.

the Indian settlement that was the closest to the mission site, the settlement of Cosoy. The Spanish called Cosoy the "Ranchería de San Diego." At some point in 1771 one of the leaders of Cosoy, named Chisli, presented his three-year-old son for baptism. The child was given the name Francisco Antonio, and his baptism was soon followed by those of both of his parents and of Chisli's brother Canuch. Chisli was given the name Carlos, and Canuch was given the name Francisco.[4]

The beginning years of Mission San Diego were difficult. Since the area's topography was similar to that of Baja California, the Texas method favored by the missionaries from the Colegio de San Fernando proved to be impossible. The more desert-type landscape afforded little possibility for the successful development of European-style agriculture. Accordingly, many of the one hundred or so baptized Kumeyaay continued to reside in their own villages and came to the mission for various religious functions. The Kumeyaay were thus able to maintain some of their traditional lifeways during this time. People often lived in different village locations for the summer and winter and actively managed their natural environment. Since their management did not involve the regular plowed fields of Europe, the Spanish were unaware of the degree of activity in which the Kumeyaay were engaged. They also maintained active trading relationships with neighboring peoples. The spiritual world of the Kumeyaay people was richly developed and expressed in a variety of songs, dances, and other ceremonies. Access to this spiritual world was facilitated by shamans.[5]

San Diego was similar to other missions in one important respect. The priests soon began to complain that the soldiers at the mission and the nearby presidio systematically abused the native women. When Serra went to Mexico City at the end of 1772, he took with him a long letter from one of the resident missionaries at San Diego, Luis Jayme, in which the priest denounced this behavior, which he said was widespread. Serra renewed this criticism in a letter to the viceroy shortly after his return from Mexico City.[6]

Partially to move the mission away from the soldiers and partially to seek out a spot in which agriculture might be able to flourish more successfully, the local priests moved the mission away from the presidio in August 1774. It was transferred roughly four miles, to a location on the banks of the San Diego River near the village of Nipaguay. In the middle of 1775 a large number of Kumeyaay people from villages south of the river converted and accepted baptism. The

---

4. On the location of Cosoy, see La Rose, "Political Geography and Colonialism in Mission Valley, San Diego"; San Diego baptisms 00001, 00032, 00035, 00036.
5. Carrico, *Strangers in a Stolen Land*, 10–21; Gamble and Zepeda, "Social Differentiation and Exchange among the Kumeyaay Indians," 73; Connolly Miskwish, "The Changing Economy of the Kumeyaay," 273; Waterman, "The Religious Practices of the Diegueño Indians"; Lazcano Sahagún, *Pa-tai*, 98–105.
6. Jayme, "Soldiers and Indians," in Beebe and Senkewicz, *Lands of Promise and Despair*, 155–61.

missionaries were delighted at this turn of events, for it seemed to them to be a confirmation of their wisdom in moving the mission. However, at least some of the newly baptized were most likely attracted by the possibility of being allowed to reconnoiter the mission from the inside after they had become formal members of the Church. The new converts maintained their contacts at their home settlements. Also, the leadership patterns at those villages did not change, village leaders continued to interact with each other regularly, and villages maintained their traditional autonomy: these factors made coordinated action easier to plan.[7]

On October 2, Carlos and Francisco left the mission with the permission of Fathers Jayme and Fuster, but they did not return. Presidio Commander José Francisco de Ortega sent a party of a dozen soldiers out to get them on October 11, but the search was unsuccessful. On October 19 Ortega himself left San Diego with twelve soldiers and Father Lasuén to supervise the foundation of a new mission at San Juan Capistrano. Soon increasing numbers of mission Indians were visiting the mission. A large number came in on the night of Saturday, November 4. At around half-past one that morning the mission was attacked and burned. Father Jayme was killed, and his severely mutilated body was not found until a few days later.[8]

Ortega returned to the mission on November 8 and quickly began an investigation. He soon arrested four Indians. Two of them, Diego Rivera and José María Rivera, were young men who served as pages and interpreters at the mission. Two others, Miguel and Ignacio, were known to be friends of Carlos and Francisco, generally regarded as important leaders of the uprising. Unsurprisingly, the testimony of the two interpreters implicated both Carlos and Francisco. A few days after Ortega questioned them, they were both released. Various other possible leaders of the attack were captured, and Ortega's treatment of the prisoners seems to have become increasingly harsh.[9]

When word of the destruction of Mission San Diego reached Monterey, Rivera y Moncada immediately headed south. On January 4, 1776, while he was at Mission San Gabriel, he met Juan Bautista de Anza, who had just arrived with a large group of colonists whom he had recruited in northern Mexico to found and populate a presidio at San Francisco and a pueblo at San José. Anza agreed

---

7. Geiger, *Life and Times of Fray Junípero Serra*, 2:58; in reconstructing the baptismal records, Serra estimated that over one hundred people were baptized in August 1775. See San Diego baptisms 00172–00276; Shipek, "Kumeyaay Socio-political Structure."
8. Palóu, *Historical Memoirs of New California*, 4:62; José Francisco de Ortega to Juan Bautista de Anza, November 30, 1775, in *Archive of California*, The Bancroft Library, C-A 15:1–2; Geiger, *Life and Times of Fray Junípero Serra*, 2:61–65.
9. The closest study of the investigation is Saunt, "'My Medicine Is Punishment.'" The two men were named Rivera because Fernando de Rivera y Moncada had been the godfather at their baptisms. The baptisms took place while Rivera y Moncada was at San Diego awaiting permission to retire from the service. See San Diego baptisms 00008 and 00009; Rivera y Moncada, *Diario*, 2:445.

FIGURE 42. *How California Indians Fight*, 1791, by Tomás de Suría. A composite scene that depicts three Ohlone with bows and arrows defending a village against a mounted incursion. *Courtesy of the Museo Naval, Madrid. Inv. MS 1726-47.*

to leave most of them at San Gabriel and proceed with Rivera y Moncada to San Diego. They both arrived there on January 11.[10]

Soon after their arrival Diego was rearrested on suspicion of planning to leave the mission to join Carlos, Francisco, and the other leaders of the uprising in the vicinity. Diego received fifty lashes but refused to confess to all of these charges.[11]

Over the following weeks, the relationship between Rivera y Moncada and Anza deteriorated significantly. Anza's orders were to proceed north for the founding of the new presidio and the pueblo. Rivera y Moncada, on the other hand, thought the situation at San Diego continued to be too volatile and dangerous and therefore wanted Anza to remain in the south with his own soldiers. Since Anza agreed that it would be foolish to proceed north during the rainy season, he remained at San Diego for approximately a month. During this time he became increasingly frustrated with what he regarded as Rivera y Moncada's overly slow, methodical, and cautious approach to trying to track down the conspirators. He finally left San Diego on February 9.[12]

10. Font, *With Anza to California*, 187.
11. Saunt, "'My Medicine Is Punishment,'" 691–92.
12. Font, *With Anza to California*, 49–57.

Rivera y Moncada organized a series of sorties into the interior in an attempt to capture the leaders of the uprising. All the sorties were unsuccessful. On March 16, Father Fuster found Carlos at the presidio hiding in a warehouse that was being used as a temporary church. It is unclear whether Carlos went there deliberately, knowing that it had been converted into a church and hoping to talk with one of the priests, or whether he was there accidentally. In any event, Fuster informed Rivera y Moncada that Carlos was in the church and that he could not be seized because of the tradition of sanctuary. The commander ignored Fuster's remarks about sanctuary and immediately entered the church/warehouse and arrested Carlos. The priests on the scene declared Rivera y Moncada excommunicated from the Church because of this violation of sanctuary. Rivera y Moncada was in many ways a very religious man and traveled to Monterey to appeal to Serra. He was deeply agitated by this turn of events and acted somewhat brusquely and bizarrely when he encountered Anza just south of Monterey. At Carmel, Serra met Rivera y Moncada and refused explicitly to overrule the judgment of the San Diego missionaries. But with Anza and his soldiers on their way out of Alta California, Serra knew that he was losing a powerful ally in his struggle against Rivera y Moncada and realized that he could not push that man too far. Therefore, a face-saving arrangement was worked out. Rivera y Moncada returned to San Diego, took Carlos to the warehouse, and released him to Father Fuster. The priest escorted Carlos out of the warehouse and turned him over to Rivera y Moncada, who then sent him back to jail.[13]

A month later Francisco was captured by soldiers on one of the sorties the commander had ordered. Rivera y Moncada spent the summer months interrogating the brothers as well as a few other prisoners he had captured. Serra himself arrived in San Diego to supervise the rebuilding of the mission on July 11.

One of the Indians the soldiers captured was named Naguasajo. He was interrogated on August 13 and, according to Palóu, was visited in prison by Serra shortly thereafter. Serra tried to get him to accept baptism, but he refused. The next morning Naguasajo was found dead in his cell from an apparent suicide. Palóu asserted that this man had been one of the ringleaders of the attack on the fledgling mission in 1769 and that his suicide on August 15 was fitting symmetry, since the original attack took place on August 15, 1769. Serra did not allude to any of this in his extant correspondence. At least thirteen Kumeyaay men remained in prison through the spring of 1777, but as Serra wished, they were eventually all released.[14]

---

13. Geiger, *Life and Times of Fray Junípero Serra*, 2:88–98; Lasuén, *Writings*, 1:64.
14. Saunt, "'My Medicine Is Punishment,'" 697; Palóu, *Palóu's Life of Fray Junípero Serra*, 79; Serra, *Writings*, 3:252–53.

Rivera y Moncada made the decision to exile the prisoners to San Blas. Serra very much objected to this. He reiterated what he had said to the viceroy about the treatment of rebellious Indians when he first heard of the death of Father Jayme. He told Rivera y Moncada that the viceroy had agreed with his assessment. He also told Rivera y Moncada that shipping the prisoners off into exile would greatly upset the local people and perhaps even spark another rebellion. In a long letter to the commander dated October 5, Serra was able to use correspondence between himself and the viceroy to argue for leniency.

✳ *Letter to Fernando de Rivera y Moncada, October 5, 1776*

Señor Capitán Comandante Don Fernando de Rivera y Moncada.
My dear Señor,

When I saw that the forces of the presidios of Monterey and San Diego had joined together as if to rectify the already irreparable death of the Padre and the rest of the destruction done to Mission San Diego or, that is to say, to teach the guilty ones a lesson and to repress the enemy forces, I feared that this course of action could cause defiance and lead to greater damage, such as what happened in a similar case that I mentioned to Su Excelencia. Therefore, I explained to the Excelentísimo Señor that what I wanted was for the Padres who were still alive to be protected as if we were the apple of God's eye, which was most appropriate. But the deceased Padre should be allowed to enjoy God's grace. And the evildoers should be forgiven after giving them a moderate punishment for their offense, which would show them that we practice the laws we teach them about returning good for evil and of forgiving one's enemies.

Undoubtedly moved by his inherent kindness, which many have already experienced, and not by the reasons I gave him, Su Excelencia responded to this proposal on April 3 of this year in this way:

"In view of the prudent Christian reflections that Vuestra Reverencia offers, I believe that it is more fitting to try to attract the rebel neophytes than to punish them. My response to Vuestra Reverencia is that I have decided to send an order this very day to Comandante Don Fernando de Rivera y Moncada to take this approach, since it offers a better way for the pacification of the Indians and the tranquility of their souls. Indeed, this amiable and good treatment will also advance the reduction of the neighboring gentiles, who no doubt expected to be punished and have their ranchería destroyed because of their actions."

This is where the words of the Señor Excelentísimo end.

Following what I had formulated and proposed to Vuestra Merced face-to-face, the best way to carry out Su Excelencia's orders is to quickly and vehemently capture the majority of the murderers who are still missing as well as the commander of the enemy force and anybody else Vuestra Merced knows was involved or has a special standing among them. They should be grouped with the rest of the prisoners and, by means of an interpreter, should be told clearly and vigorously that what they have done is a great evil for which they deserve a severe punishment. The interpreter should then impress upon them the great power that our Rey and Señor possesses to finish them off, which is what they deserve. They should also see that new soldiers have arrived and there are many more who might still come. But even though the Señor Rey is very powerful, he is also very much a Christian and feels sorry for them.

I am not saying that they should then be immediately released. Rather, once assured that their lives have been spared, they should be sentenced to time in prison and receive punishments based on the severity of their crimes.

I am convinced that Su Excelencia would be pleased with this plan and agree that it corresponds to the holy objectives that the Señor Excelentísimo supports, with the promise that they will be realized. From what I understand, these objectives are different from the ones that Vuestra Merced has proposed to carry out with the prisoners whom you have kept in shackles and in the stocks for so long.

Vuestra Merced had made up your mind how you would proceed long before Su Excelencia had made his decision. You planned to put the prisoners, just as they are, on a ship and send them off to San Blas so that Su Excelencia could decide the best course of action to take with them. We all know this is true because we heard the words come out of Vuestra Merced's mouth. And you also had informed Su Excelencia of your decision.

If the people here were to see the prisoners shipped off in such a manner and suddenly disappear from this land, Vuestra Merced has always thought this would be a critical situation that would expose us to the danger of a new uprising. That is why Vuestra Merced decided not to move away from here with the twelve soldiers you have with you from the department of Monterey, to undertake the founding of the missions of San Francisco. That is why they have not been founded and are not presently being founded. Everyone knows the reason you are staying here, even though it may not be the only reason, just as everyone knows that you are determined to ship off the prisoners. I am not surprised by anything you have said on other occasions, or by any of your resolutions or decrees. But I am surprised that Vuestra Merced continues to hold firm to your line of thinking (according to what I have been told) even in the face of an expressed command by Su Excelencia.

Under the present circumstances, I would like to remind Vuestra Merced of the following considerations, and I shall do so now. First, if Vuestra Merced ships off the prisoners in this fashion, the objectives established by Su Excelencia would not be met. These are "pacification and tranquility of the spirit," and perhaps also "that the gentiles in the area will come into the mission after seeing that they are treated amiably and well."

What type of "pacification of the spirit" would one achieve by shipping them off? For those left behind, it would be tantamount to seeing them hanged. What "tranquility of the spirit" would result from an action that Vuestra Merced fears will upset people who are finally calm and peaceful and cause them to take up arms and initiate hostilities again? The only thing it would do would be to prove that your staying here and increasing the number of troops in San Diego was not pointless.

It seems that another consideration could be added: if the punishment the prisoners were going to receive before Su Excelencia made a judgment on this were still to be applied, then his orders would be in vain and rendered ineffectual.

At the end of the Señor Excelentísimo's letter, which I have just cited, after laying out various directives, the first of which we have just discussed, he concludes by saying:

"I make everything available to Vuestra Reverencia for your satisfaction and to assist you in the hope that Vuestra Reverencia will continue to implement my measures."

To offer what little help I can provide so that the very pious directive given to Vuestra Merced from Su Excelencia is carried out effectively, I am begging you to not ship off the prisoners. Instead, let the proceedings be carried out in the manner I have outlined above or in some other fashion that Vuestra Merced deems appropriate. But let them be carried out with the benevolence that Su Excelencia has demonstrated. I am confident that, just as the Excelentísimo Señor was kind enough to listen to my plea, Vuestra Merced will also respond in a similar manner, for the terms that I am requesting do not conflict with the terms that Su Excelencia has explained to Vuestra Merced.

I continue to pray that God, Our Lord, keep Vuestra Merced in good health and in His grace many years.

The Mission and Royal Presidio of San Diego, October 5, 1776
Kissing Vuestra Merced's hand, etc.
Fray Junípero Serra

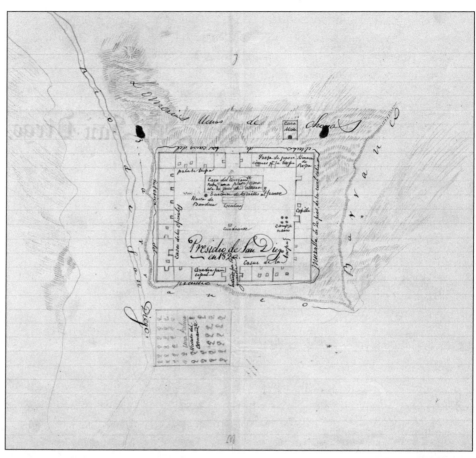

FIGURE 43. The Presidio of San Diego in 1820 as drawn by Mariano Guadalupe Vallejo. The presidio remained in the general vicinity chosen by Fernando de Rivera y Moncada in 1769, but the mission was moved farther inland in 1774. *Courtesy of The Bancroft Library, University of California, Berkeley.* BANC MSS 77/37 folder 3:3.

Serra's letter to Rivera had its intended effect, and the Indians were pardoned and released, but rumors of additional attacks continued to swirl through the San Diego region in 1777 and 1778. In spring 1778, Mariano Carrillo captured four alleged rebel leaders at the village of Pa'mu, and they were brought to the presidio and imprisoned. One died there. The other three were sentenced to death.[15] Serra wrote Lasuén to explain how the situation should be handled.

※ *Serra to Lasuén, April 22, 1778*

I have just received the letters from Vuestra Reverencia. But before confirming with the Señor Gobernador, I will respond briefly to your first letter (just in case the mail will be going out soon) by saying that I feel very sorry for those poor souls who have been sentenced, even though I really doubt the sentence will be carried out. But if it does happen, I believe that Vuestra Reverencia should administer solemn baptism to them in that very prison on the evening before. That way they will not be without benefit of the many prayers that are ordered by our pious Mother the Holy Church. And the time that is left before the execution, or right up to that moment, should be spent engaging the person in acts of faith, etc., fervent prayer, and exhortations to bear that heavy burden with patience, and any other measure that will help them prepare for a good death.

The death sentence was eventually lifted by the governor.[16] Serra asked that the prisoners be set free and that the priests be given a very visible role in their release. In this way he hoped to render them more receptive to the priests in the future.

※ *Serra to Lasuén, April 25–26, 1780*

Today I have written requesting that the three gentiles at that presidio be set free. And in his nonwritten response, sent by way of Padre Dumetz, he blames the lieutenant for not releasing them as soon as they were pardoned. But they will be released.

I would appreciate it if they were not simply released to go off, but rather that they were made to appear before the Padres of San Juan Capistrano first. Then, after the Padres have given them a lecture, they can be released. In this manner the possibility of their conversion would seem more promising. But, since we have no say in the matter, if what has been proposed cannot be done, Vuestra Reverencia can exchange one favor for another. (Quid pro quo.)[17]

---

15. Geiger, *Life and Times of Fray Junípero Serra*, 2:118; Serra, *Writings*, 3:177; Carrico, *Strangers in a Stolen Land*, 38.
16. Geiger, *Life and Times of Fray Junípero Serra*, 2:167.
17. See also Engelhardt, *San Diego Mission*, 96–98.

The situation in the area continued tense. Three years later Ortega continued to complain to the governor that the indigenous people in the San Diego area were still dangerous and insolent. He also said that the people from Pa'mu refused to come into the mission for church services, since they believed that the soldiers would kill them. Lasuén begged Serra to try to get the number of soldiers at the mission increased.[18]

While in San Diego, Serra quarreled with Rivera y Moncada over the pace of the mission's reconstruction. Serra asked the commander to have the soldiers assist with the rebuilding tasks. The commander, however, thought the situation in the San Diego region was still much too dangerous and did not favor the immediate reconstruction of the mission at a site miles away from the presidio. Accordingly, he refused to make the soldiers available. He also eventually forbade a group of sailors recruited by Serra to help in the reconstruction of the church. Serra left San Diego at the end of October. The mission church at San Diego was not rebuilt until 1780.[19]

Serra refounded Mission San Juan Capistrano on November 1 and reached Carmel on January 15, 1777. But the disappointment of San Diego stayed with him all the way home. When he arrived at Carmel, his description of the situation there was uncharacteristically downbeat for a moment, although he quickly recovered his hopes for the future.

※ *Serra to Pangua, February 26, 1777*
> The gentiles have drawn back farther and we are gathering few in our net, but it is not because of a lack of gentiles in the surrounding areas. This mission has 442 baptisms. We should be able to baptize that many or more from one and probably no more than two rancherías in this area. And these are not the only rancherías that surround us.

In the midst of these tensions and disagreements, Serra was convinced that his policy of leniency toward the organizers of the uprising was bearing fruit. In April 1778 he expressed great satisfaction at the increased number of baptisms at San Diego and thanked Lasuén for gathering the remains of Father Luis Jayme in the new church, which was under construction.[20]

※ *Serra to Lasuén, April 6, 1778*
> I offer Vuestra Reverencia and Padre Fray Juan my heartfelt appreciation for transferring the remains of my dearly departed Padre Fray Luis to the

---

18. Carrico, *Strangers in a Stolen Land*, 39; Serra, *Writings*, 3:204–205; Temple, "Two Letters from Sergeant José Francisco Ortega," 124–25.
19. Geiger, *Life and Times of Fray Junípero Serra*, 2:99–108; Engelhardt, *San Diego Mission*, 106.
20. Serra, *Writings*, 3:179.

mission where he gave up his life for the Lord Our God and can now await the resurrection of the body.

In October 1778 he happily reported that both Carlos and Francisco, whom he termed "models," were among those to whom he administered the sacrament of confirmation. The first to receive the sacrament on that occasion was the interpreter Diego, who died three days later.[21] Serra also rejoiced that three Indians whom he said had been in the group that killed Father Jayme had also received the sacrament. He described the scene in a letter to Viceroy Bucareli.

❋ *Serra to Bucareli y Úrsua, October 4, 1778*

In order to share this blessing with all the missions, I came to this one. Only here, because they are so poor, do the neophytes live widespread in their own rancherías. They come only on Sundays, and not on a regular basis, which is precisely why administering confirmation will be a much slower process. Up until today, there have been close to three hundred confirmations, and there are about that many still left to do. When that is finished, with the grace of God I will begin my overland trek of 210 leagues, a distance calculated from this port up to the port of Nuestro Padre San Francisco, with necessary stops along the way at each of the missions. My stay at each mission will be brief, since they all have their respective Christians who gather together at the sound of the bell.

I do not want to forget to share a bit of news, which I believe will please Vuestra Excelencia, just as it has given me great consolation. Vuestra Excelencia already knows from past reports that those who placed their sacrilegious hands on the body of Padre Lector Fray Luis and killed him in such a cruel manner were five in number—three Christians and two gentiles.

On the eve of the feast day of San Miguel, after having prepared them as well as possible and after selecting a godfather to my liking, I confirmed three Christians named Bernardino, the captain from Matamó, Dimas Chiulchicup, and Nicolás Supelpex. Of the two gentiles, I learned that one had already died a Christian and his name was Fernando. The one gentile who is left has not appeared. May God bring him to us for His greater glory.

Since I had to start my confirmations here, as I did, on the feast day of the Apóstol San Mateo, even though Lieutenant Ortega's children were here to receive that sacrament as well as those of the warehouse guard, I made sure that the first one to be confirmed was an Indian named Diego. From the beginning he had been faithful and was very special to me. He betrayed my

---

21. San Diego burial record 00042.

trust by participating in the revolt, and he was one of the prisoners who they said deserved the death sentence. Because he was so sick, he had to be carried to the church, and I confirmed him first. Three days later, after receiving the other sacraments and attended to by me and the two other Padres, he went to Heaven to reveal his new being. The following day I sang Mass with his body laid out.

Since he had become quite Spanish, it touched me deeply to hear how he was preparing himself for his death. The two brothers who were the ringleaders of the uprising behave with such loyalty that the Padres trust them the most. They have already been confirmed.

Thus Serra's response to the uprising was broadly consonant with his earlier attitudes. He consistently called for leniency for captured Indians who had participated in the rebellion. When he visited San Diego and took personal charge of the effort to regather the mission community and rebuild the ruined mission structure, he did all he could to rekindle the optimism that was such an important part of his outlook before the uprising. So the administration of the sacrament of confirmation to a number of Indians who had participated in the rebellion became a crucial part of the narrative of redemption he was constructing.

Around this time the paths of Francisco and Carlos appear to have diverged, at least on the surface. Serra and Lasuén arranged for Francisco to be elected alcalde, and he spent the rest of his life as an active and apparently loyal member of the mission. Carlos, on the other hand, became involved with activities that were hostile to the Spanish presence. In 1779 he was associated with a movement to foment another uprising. Governor Felipe de Neve had him arrested and whipped. Neve wanted to sentence Carlos to work as a deck hand on the supply ship for the rest of his life. Serra expressed his objection in this letter to Lasuén.

❈ Serra to Lasuén, January 12, 1780

I am greatly saddened by Carlos and Bernardino's continued insolence because I am especially fond of them and wish for the salvation of their souls. And to that end, I would not be upset if, for however many punishments they are to be given, their sentence could be commuted to life in prison or being placed in the stocks every day. For it would be easier for them to have a good death there. Is it not possible that by keeping them in prison for a good amount of time and with the help of interpreters, explaining to them about the eternal life to come, and commending them to God, that they would repent and reform? Could they not be made to understand that they are still alive because we insisted upon it and took the steps to make it happen even though they deserved a cruel death for what they did in the past? But for the sake of God we set them free so they could lead better lives, etc. But, Vuestra Reverencia must have told them that, and much more, many times. Therefore, I have nothing more to say on the topic, except that I ask you to give them my regards since they are like members of my family.

Neve relented and sentenced Carlos and two others to imprisonment. They were held at the presidio in San Diego for three years. Serra kept urging Lasuén to stay in touch with him.

※ *Serra to Lasuén, April 24–25, 1780*
I have not spoken about Carlos and his companions. When the opportunities present themselves, and if it seems there is some hope of their changing their ways, perhaps Vuestra Reverencia could appeal to them again and something might be gained from all of this. If Vuestra Reverencia could please let me know if they were already in custody when the pardon was announced, because in reality, I do not know.

In 1782, over Serra's objections, Neve exiled Carlos to Loreto in Baja California. Carlos eventually returned to San Diego after Serra's successor, Lasuén, successfully appealed to the new governor, Pedro Fages, for leniency in 1785. On his return he once again tried to foment an uprising. Fages then permanently exiled him to Mission San Carlos. He died in Monterey in 1809.[22]

The two contemporary scholars who have studied Carlos and Francisco most closely have observed that it is impossible to discern whether or not Francisco was actually as committed a mission Indian as he appeared to be. Indeed, it is entirely plausible that Carlos and Francisco were working in tandem, at least in 1779. It may well be that Francisco remained as a kind of spy within the mission system while his older brother Carlos assumed the responsibility of trying to organize the Indians in the surrounding area for another uprising such as the one in 1775. In this matter as with so much else that concerns the Indians, who were the overwhelming majority of people in California during this period, we shall never know all of the details.[23]

Serra remained keenly aware of the potential for rebellion in San Diego. Indeed, after he heard about the 1781 Colorado River battle in which the Quechán Indians killed Francisco de Rivera y Moncada, a number of the Spanish soldiers, and four missionaries, including Francisco Garcés, Serra wrote to Lasuén at San Diego and told him that he must make sure this episode did not give the Indians at San Diego any ideas about rebelling again.

22. Serra, *Writings*, 4:136–41; Lasuén, *Writings*, 1:93–94; San Carlos burial record 01844.
23. Sandos and Sandos, "Chisli, Canuch, and Junípero Serra," 70–74.

❋ *Serra to Lasuén, December 8, 1781*

> Your Diegueños are undoubtedly aware of the bravery of the Indians of the Colorado. But tell them to wait a bit so they can find out if those Indians end up faring as well as they did with their revolt. They are content as long as they are tranquil. But otherwise, they would pay the price for what they did both then and now.

The southern Kumeyaay, between San Diego and Ensenada, were never pacified during Serra's lifetime. Their eastern neighbors, such as the Quechán and Mojave peoples, remained independent and out of colonial control for the entire Spanish and Mexican eras.[24]

On the whole, when we examine the fashion in which a number of Kumeyaay people (those who had participated in the uprising and those who had not) responded to the reestablishment of Spanish control, we are left with a picture of great ambiguity regarding the native peoples' view of the mission community. Members of some families seem to go in opposite directions, with some people rejoining the community and others staying apart from it. Such behavior most likely indicates that the native peoples were hedging their bets and that families were trying to position themselves with one foot in the mission and the other foot in their traditional communities. On the whole, it seems that Serra's optimism that the mission community was reestablishing itself was considerably premature.

---

24. Lazcano Sahagún, *Pa-tai*, 124; Zappia, "The Interior World," 74–172.

CHAPTER 9

A Series of Setbacks

Serra experienced a series of setbacks in the years after the San Diego uprising. First, when Felipe de Neve was appointed governor of Las Californias, he moved the capital from Loreto in Baja California to Monterey in Alta California. Serra's initial good feelings toward Neve (he thought Neve would support the immediate establishment of missions in the Chumash area around Santa Bárbara) quickly soured as he realized that Neve represented a new and hostile point of view concerning the placement of civil settlements alongside the missions, the nature of the missions themselves, and the authority of indigenous officials within the mission communities.

Second, the Spanish government, under Gálvez's leadership, approved the formation of the Provincias Internas, which separated the northern frontier from the jurisdiction of the viceroy and placed the Provincias Internas under the control of a commander general based in Sonora. This move had the effect of cutting Serra off from the viceroy's office in Mexico City, from which he had received such great benefits in 1773. Serra's relationship with the first commander general was never warm or close.

Third, when Serra received permission from the Vatican to administer the sacrament of confirmation, a permission often given to the head missionary in a region where no resident bishop existed, Neve insisted on seeing the original countersigned document before he would allow Serra to administer the sacrament. A voluminous correspondence ensued, in which Serra was forced to expend enormous time and energy (as Neve intended) defending his ability to administer the sacrament.

Finally, when Juan Bautista de Anza met Serra in 1776, he handed him a letter from the Franciscan head of the Colegio de San Fernando, Serra's missionary headquarters in Mexico City. The letter, an obvious response to a series of complaints about Serra's leadership that had been sent by Franciscans in Alta California to Mexico City, severely limited Serra's powers as president of the missions.

A New Governor

Felipe de Neve was appointed governor of Las Californias in 1775. Later that year, at the urging of Gálvez, the Spanish government moved the capital of Las Californias from Loreto in Baja California to Monterey in Alta California. Neve was instructed to take up residence in Monterey. Rivera y Moncada, on the other hand, was assigned to Loreto and given the new title of lieutenant governor of Las Californias. Neve left Baja California at the end of 1776 and arrived in Monterey on February 3, 1777. Rivera y Moncada left exactly one month later.

Neve was born in 1727 in Andalucía, Spain. He joined the military at a young age and was commissioned a lieutenant in 1749. He arrived in the New World as part of the first wave of Spaniards sent across the ocean to implement a series of administrative changes that came to be called the Bourbon Reforms. One reason the government of King Carlos III felt impelled to introduce significant changes in the empire was Spain's poor showing in the Seven Years' War. In particular, the British capture of both Havana and Manila in 1762 dramatized the shortcomings of Spanish military abilities, so in 1764 the captain general of Andalucía, Juan de Villalba y Angulo, was appointed inspector general of the army of New Spain. He arrived at Veracruz in November of that year and immediately began to disband a number of military units and organize others to replace them. One such new unit was the Provincial Regiment of Querétaro. Neve was assigned to this unit shortly after his arrival in New Spain and soon became its commander. He was then assigned to organize another new unit, the Provincial Regiment of Michoacán, but popular resistance in the area prevented the unit's immediate formation. When the Jesuits were ordered expelled from New Spain in 1767, Neve was assigned to Zacatecas, where he arrested the resident Jesuits, sent them to Veracruz, and took charge of their property. He remained in Zacatecas until 1774, when he was appointed by Bucareli to succeed Felipe de Barri as governor of Las Californias.[1]

Neve's experiences in New Spain before coming to Las Californias meant that he was a direct participant in two of the central developments in the empire during the last third of the eighteenth century. Those developments were, first, the insertion of royal institutions and power more directly into colonial society and, second, the relative decline in influence of the Church. The military was given a series of legal privileges in New Spain that generally placed military officers outside of the conventional civil and legal jurisdictions. Similar arrangements occurred in other vice royalties, such as New Granada and Peru. Also, the Church saw its influence diminish in mission areas, as the military was given the

---

1. Biographical information on Neve comes from Beilharz, *Felipe de Neve*, and Rodríguez-Sala, *Los gobernadores de las Californias, 1767–1804*. See also McAlister, *The "Fuero Militar" in New Spain*, 3–4, 94–95, and Archer, *The Army in Bourbon Mexico*, 10.

task of spearheading the establishment of colonial control over native peoples outside the imperial orbit. As we have seen in the case of Escandón and Nuevo Santander, significant numbers of settlers were increasingly being regarded as a necessary part of the colonial process. This happened not only in New Spain but also in other parts of the empire, such as New Granada. Therefore, when Neve arrived in Monterey he brought to Alta California a perspective on the relationship between the military and missionaries that was not going to please Serra. He was also a much more accomplished and experienced administrator than Fages or Rivera y Moncada had been.[2]

Happy to be rid of Rivera y Moncada, Serra greeted Neve's appointment with hope and anticipation. Serra was especially delighted when at one of their first meetings Neve seemed quite receptive to the notion of opening new missions in the Santa Bárbara Channel area. Serra wrote to Bucareli with a summary of this meeting.

> *Serra to Antonio María de Bucareli y Ursúa, March 1, 1777*
>
> But it has been very comforting to me to hear the Señor Gobernador say that after he traveled through this same territory and saw the native peoples, he has deemed their conversion to our Holy Catholic faith to be of utmost importance. This can be accomplished by constructing a fort or a presidio in the middle of the Santa Bárbara Channel area, where ships could call. There would be a mission nearby as well as one mission at each end of the channel—San Buenaventura at one end and another at Point Concepción. The fort at Santa Bárbara would defend the area. And there would be a notable increase in the number of Christians and subjects of the crown. The fort would also provide a very important service, which would be a greater sense of security for those traveling from one new establishment to another. Because the Señor Gobernador's plan is literally so in keeping with my long-standing aspirations, when I heard it, I realized once more, in the midst of my joy, that reason and truth resemble one another.

But Serra quickly changed his mind about the new governor. In November 1777 Neve supervised the founding of Alta California's first pueblo, San José de Guadalupe, located directly across the Guadalupe River from the lands of Mission Santa Clara. With the arrival of a formal pueblo, the full range of colonial institutions—presidio, mission, and pueblo—took root in Alta California.

Like the presidio and the mission, the pueblo had deep roots in Spanish colonial history. The Iberian municipal tradition stretched back to the days of the Roman empire and was strengthened during the Reconquista. The conquistadors

---

2. McAlister, *The "Fuero Militar" in New Spain*, 1–21; Kuethe, *Military Reform and Society in New Granada*, 133–44.

brought this strong urban tradition with them across the sea. By 1575 the Spanish had established over two hundred distinct municipalities in the Americas. As much as possible, they were laid out around a central plaza, with land for houses (*solares*) distributed in a fashion that was meant to be more or less symmetrical and orderly. Plots of arable land for agriculture (*suertes*) outside the urban area were also distributed.[3]

Cities and towns were founded in New Spain from the beginning of the conquest. As the frontier went north, towns were often in the vanguard. Guadalajara was established in 1532, Zacatecas in 1546, Durango in 1563, and Santa Fe in 1610. By the time Spanish development of the Californias was well under way in the eighteenth century, towns were a normal part of frontier life, and settlements existed as far north and west as present-day Arizona, at Tucson, Tubac, and Yuma. Although a considerable number of Spaniards also lived in and around the presidios, the towns were a crucial component of frontier life.

These pueblos were, above all, frontier towns. Northwestern Mexico, then as now, could be a harsh and difficult land. A number of these towns had originated as mining camps, but minerals did not exist either in abundance or in locations that made them easily extractable. And the Sonora Desert was not the most hospitable place to grow crops or raise cattle. Composed of former soldiers, miners, colonists, Indians, and their families, the frontier towns were more often gritty and dusty pockets than the stable and secure foundations of Spanish prosperity they were intended to be. But they still pointed to the ultimate aim of colonization, which was to transform the land and its people into productive parts of the Spanish empire; for all their imperfection, they were symbols of the society into which New Spain was designed to evolve.

For Serra the emergence of this institution in Alta California and its location so close to a mission reminded him of the trouble he and the other Fernandinos had with the civil settlements fostered by Escandón very near the Sierra Gorda missions. And it underscored a fundamental dilemma at the very root of the missionary experience in New Spain: The missionaries, as we have seen, genuinely believed they were protecting the native peoples from exploitation by unscrupulous and potentially cruel settlers. But in the actual working-out of Spanish expansion in eighteenth-century New Spain, the practical function of the missions was to prepare the indigenous population for the arrival of settlers by teaching them skills that would make them useful and assimilated ranch hands. Missionaries attempted to prevent themselves from having to acknowledge this by prolonging the mission experience well beyond the limited time period during

---

3. The historiography on the role of the pueblo in New Spain is immense. The essays on municipal development in Guest, *Hispanic California Revisited*, afford an excellent overview of the great variety of scholarship on this topic.

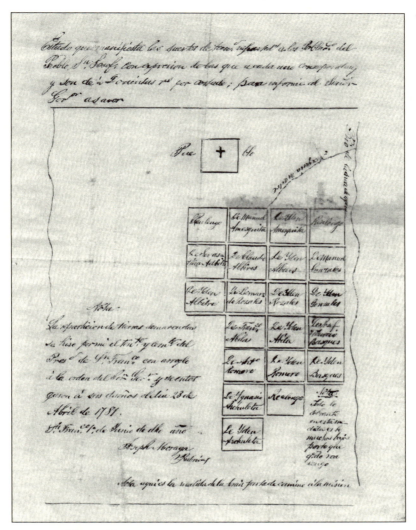

FIGURE 44. Map of the Pueblo de San José, 1781, by Joseph Moraga, showing the distribution of land to the early settlers.
(top): Report that shows the plots of land distributed to the settlers of the Pueblo of San José, with the designation as to who owns each plot and the homes that flank one another; this is so that the Señor Gobernador will be informed.
(bottom left): The distribution of the demarcated lands was done by me, the lieutenant and commander of the Presidio of San Francisco in accordance with the order from the Señor Gobernador, and they were submitted for his consideration on April 23, 1781.
San Francisco, June 1 of the same year. Joseph Moraga (Rubric).
(right side): Water that branches off from the main river.
(bottom right): All of the land that remains has not yet been allotted.
(bottom center): Note: Here is the way to head out to the bay along the road to the mission. *Courtesy of History San José.*

which the missions were supposed to exist. But they could do this only by insisting that the native peoples were not yet ready for independence and assimilation. In doing so, they opened themselves to two complementary criticisms: that they were ineffective in realizing their own goals and that they were selfishly holding on to their own power. The arrival of settlers brought all these tensions to the surface, and Serra did not like this situation at all. He objected to the existence of this new civil settlement and in the following letter described a meeting that he had with the new governor about this development.

> ❋ *Serra to Antonio María de Bucareli y Ursúa, June 30, 1778*
>
> In private conversations I had with the Señor Gobernador, I only discussed the manner in which the pueblos of Spaniards have begun to be established, which, in my opinion, did not seem to be the best thing to do. The purported reason for the pueblos was that they would provide people who would stock the royal warehouses with provisions so that the stability of these possessions would not depend on the arrival of the ships. However, instead of supporting those pueblos, this would be better achieved by increasing and fostering the missions, which would also help in terms of spiritual advancement. And that is what will happen.
>
> I imagined that settlers who demonstrate propriety, although few in number for the time being, could be assigned to the missions until more promising times. But everything I said served no other purpose than to express my feelings on the topic, for it fell on deaf ears.

In addition, Serra quickly discovered that Neve was no more willing than Fages or Rivera y Moncada had been to follow Serra's recommendations about the placement of soldiers at the various missions. In fact, the situation seemed even worse. Whereas the two former military commanders had disagreed with Serra about the number of soldiers needed to establish a new mission, Neve disagreed with Serra about the number of troops needed to staff existing missions. In 1778, when the missionaries at San Diego were concerned about the possibility of additional uprisings in the vicinity, Serra requested that more troops be placed at that mission. Neve blithely responded that flogging the Indians ought to take care of the problem. But Serra retorted that even that would require additional soldiers. He feared that if the soldiers whipped the Indians more, the Indians would then take it out on the priests, with the potential result of another uprising and more dead missionaries. Serra knew that coercion and force were indispensable elements of the mission system in New Spain. But he appears to have favored an environment in which the threat of force would render actual force unnecessary. Again, he saw himself as a strict but just parent. If parents articulated clear rules of behavior for their children, and if the children knew they would be punished for disobeying those rules, then they would follow them. And the children would gradually come to understand and appreciate the wisdom of the rules. When Serra recounted to Lasuén his meeting with Neve, he reported that the result was unsatisfactory.

❊ *Serra to Fermín Francisco de Lasuén, July 10, 1778*

> I kept insisting on this point but the answer was always that there were few troops at the presidio and he could not spare any. For if he offered a certain number of soldiers to one place and other soldiers to another place, there would be none left for the presidios, and the mission is safe with the measures that are in place. Frankly, that reason will always remain the same, no matter how many soldiers there are.
>
> I told him, as Vuestra Reverencia has said, that everyone is aware of the temperament of those Indians. To which he responded: "Well, flog them."
>
> "Well, even for that we need troops in order to carry it out without fear. Vuestra Merced, give the Padres some assistance." To which he responded, "They can do without it, there is no reason for it, things being as they are."
>
> "But Señor, (I said in conclusion) I am very happy and satisfied with the Padres. I see them in such distress. If there is no way to better reassure them, I will have to give them permission to return to the presidio if they feel they need to do so."
>
> I felt that his response to me was not something I deserved from Su Señoría: "Well, if they do that, it is not going to bother me at all. And if they want more soldiers for the escort, have them appeal to the viceroy. And if he should ask me if these soldiers are necessary, I will tell him what I think."
>
> That is what I have gotten in return for my obsequiousness and all the recommendations from a viceroy—all this in response to a humble and well-intentioned proposal that was offered with as many honey-coated words as would fit in my mouth.
>
> Believe me, if you will, Vuestra Reverencia. For all the rough patches I have had to endure and those yet to come, nothing has been as bitter as this.

In fact, Neve was not even willing to agree with Serra about the nature of the religious establishments of Alta California. The following letter contains Serra's account of a series of meetings Neve had at the Monterey presidio with the priests who were celebrating Mass there.

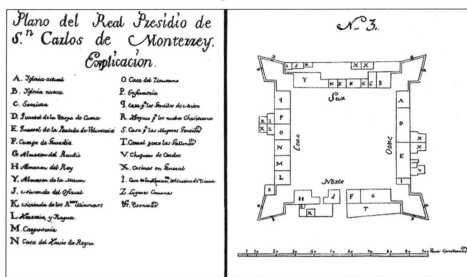

Figure 45. Plan of the Royal Presidio of San Carlos of Monterey prepared by Miguel Costansó around 1770. The letters are: A. present; B. new church; C. sacristy; D. quarters for the leather-jacket troops; E. quarters for the volunteer troops; F. guard room; G. presidio warehouse; H. king's warehouse; Y. mission warehouse; J. officers' dwelling; K. missionaries' dwelling; L. blacksmith shop and forge; M. carpenter's shop; N. house for the pack train drivers; O. surgeon's house; P. infirmary; Q. house for the visiting gentiles; R. hospital for the new Christians; S. house for the gentile women; T. chicken yard; V. pigpen; X. common kitchens; I. storage room for farming implements; Z. privies; Vr. embrasures. *Courtesy of Rev. Carl Faria, Diocese of Monterey, in California Archives.*

✳︎ *Serra to the Guardian and Discretorium of the Colegio de San Fernando, August 13, 1778*

Since that friendly meeting, it seems that the word "missions" and the issue of confirmations have become repugnant to him. That being said, the following Sunday when Padre Dumetz went to say Mass, as he was leaving he said: "I am going back to the mission." Su Señoría replied: "Mission? Where is there a mission?" The Padre responded: "Over that hill." To which that Señor replied: "That is a doctrina, not a mission!"

On another Sunday, when Padre Crespí went, the same thing happened. The Padre said the word "mission" and Su Señoría corrected him, saying, "Doctrina, doctrina."

FIGURE 46. *Plaza of the Presidio of Monterey*, 1791, by José Cardero. The chapel in which Fr. Lasuén ministered to the presidio personnel in the mid-1770s is at the center. *Courtesy of The Bancroft Library, University of California, Berkeley.* HN001334.

And when the Padre added that he wanted to return right away to attend the confirmations that were being celebrated that Sunday, the Señor asked him, "Well, and what authority does the Padre have to confirm?"

Should one be surprised by such a question considering everything that happened before?

The Padre responded: "The patent from the Prefect of the Missions, as well as a decree and instructions from Rome, give him the authority to confirm. And he, if anyone, should know."

He replied: "But he is lacking permission from the bishop of Guadalajara, because at every Mass, Vuestras Reverencias say, 'Antistitem nostrum Antonium,' which is what I used to say."[4]

This is the situation with which we are faced. And I continue to administer that holy sacrament.

---

4. In one standard prayer of the Mass, the priest named the bishop under whose jurisdiction the liturgy was being celebrated. The bishop of Guadalajara was Antonio Alcalde y Barriga.

Neve was insisting on an important point in these exchanges, arguing that the religious establishments in Alta California were not missions but doctrinas. The term "doctrina" referred to Indian parishes that were established by various religious orders in the sixteenth century under the overall jurisdiction of a bishop in the diocese. As we have seen earlier, the church serving the Pame people in Villa de Valles in 1766 was called a doctrina. As a result of two royal decrees in the middle of the eighteenth century, a number of the doctrinas in central Mexico had been secularized, which meant that they were taken away from the members of the religious orders and turned over to diocesan priests who worked directly under a bishop. Neve also specifically said he thought Alta California was part of the diocese of Guadalajara, since the missionaries always prayed for "our Bishop Antonio" in the course of the Masses that Neve had heard.[5]

Neve's position was a direct challenge to the religious authority of the Franciscans in Alta California. He was claiming that the religious situation in Alta California was similar to the religious situation in other parts of New Spain. If the Franciscans were not administering formal missions, then they were only in charge of temporary parishes that were in the process of being taken away from religious orders like theirs. The implication was that Franciscan rule in California was destined to be brief. The reference to a bishop was Neve's way of telling Serra that his authority was already limited.

These challenges of the new governor made Serra less optimistic about the future than he previously had been. In another letter, he admitted that even at Carmel the missionary enterprise was not going as well as he had hoped. Indeed, one of the Indians to whom he had been closest, his Mexico City companion Juan Evangelista, had recently died. Thus the mission was bereft of the most potentially effective bridge between the indigenous and Spanish worlds. The death of Tatlun, the chief of Ichxenta whom Serra baptized as Antonio María de Bucareli, also removed a potential mediator between indigenous and Spanish cultures.[6]

One of the clear implications of Neve's remarks about the missions was the notion that the priests were more concerned about themselves than about the welfare of the Indians. Serra bristled at this implication, and this letter to Neve expressed his anger.

❊ Serra to Felipe de Neve, April 18, 1780

If our request for the advancement of the missions and for the equitable payment of what is due them appears to be excessive, one must keep in mind that this was achieved through the toil of many poor and wretched Indians. And

---

5. Melvin, *Building Colonial Cities of God*, 2, 55.
6. Serra, *Writings*, 3:246–47.

if advocating effectively on their behalf has the appearance of greed, many saints who have come before us and who have surpassed us, will not be free from that accusation. If the clothing and provisions requested are to stave off hunger and cover the Indians' nudity, doing so should appear as an act of charity. And that being so, it should not be harshly criticized as being excessive, since the charity of God Himself is praised as such.

We work for the good of these poor people, without harming others and without duplicity, of which, it seems, some have accused us.

In the same letter Serra implied that while Neve may have had the ear of Teodoro de Croix, commander general of the Provincias Internas, he himself was not without friends in high places. He related that he had dealt personally with Gálvez, who was now minister of the Indies. Gálvez, he told Neve, would let me know beforehand when he was planning to do something, and that was an example you might consider following!

Another matter that irritated Serra about Neve was his air of confidence—he knew the workings of the Spanish bureaucracy and even the Church bureaucracy better than Serra did. Once when they were discussing a letter from the viceroy, Neve told Serra that all such official communications had to be taken with a grain of salt. He explained that the document they were reading was actually written by a scribe who was trying to make sure he accurately transcribed the viceroy's major thoughts while not offending any other official. That is why, Neve told Serra, these documents do not really have a straightforward meaning. They should be approached as if they were from the oracle at Delphi, whose pronouncements were notorious in antiquity for being susceptible to multiple interpretations. Such an approach made it impossible for Serra to use letters from the viceroy against Neve with the same force he was able to employ when he quoted them to Rivera y Moncada.[7]

On another occasion Neve told Serra not to be so concerned about what he called fornication among the soldiers. Everyone knows about it, he claimed. According to Serra, Neve said that officials in Madrid tolerated such behavior and that the Church officials in Rome were aware of it and merely turned a blind eye to it. However, Serra was hardly swayed by such arguments. He was a Scotist, which meant that acts of the will and free choices were the basic elements in defining a person.[8]

Serra continued to be very upset at what he regarded as the disastrous implications of Neve's policy. When word reached Alta California of the destruction of two missions along the Colorado River in 1781, Serra and the Fernandinos ascribed the rebellious behavior of the local indigenous people to the fact that the missionaries,

---

7. Serra, *Writings*, 3:344–45.
8. Serra, *Writings*, 4:63.

who were from Querétaro, were employing a new method of missionization that contained approaches similar to Neve's. They were not employing the tried-and-true Texas method so favored by the Colegio de San Fernando. Serra thought it was tragically ironic that such a mistake had cost the life of Fernando de Rivera y Moncada, who had been, in his words, so cautious in dealing with Indians.[9]

The controversy over the ecclesiastical nature of the Franciscan establishments in Alta California persisted for a number of years. In April 1782 Serra told Croix that if he and Neve really insisted that the California religious institutions were doctrinas rather than missions, then the Franciscans from the Colegio de San Fernando would have to leave. After all, he said, we are missionaries, not priests who run doctrinas.[10] This was a significant threat, since Croix, Neve, and most importantly the viceregal authorities in Mexico City knew that it would be virtually impossible to replace the Fernandinos. Serra did not live to see it, but by the end of the 1780s this argument had won the day. The missions developed substantially along the lines Serra had envisioned, with two priests generally in attendance and the mission lands extending for miles outward from the church. The priests were in charge of all the spiritual and temporal affairs of the entire establishment, and at least on paper they had virtually unchecked authority over the Indians.

Provincias Internas

On June 20, 1778, Serra received a letter from Viceroy Bucareli dated January 14, 1778. The viceroy informed Serra that the government in Madrid had altered the administrative structure of New Spain. The northern frontier was being detached from the viceroyalty and formed into an entity called the Provincias Internas. This entity, which included Las Californias, Texas, New Mexico, Sonora, Sinaloa, and a few other provinces, would be led by a commander general. Teodoro de Croix, nephew of the viceroy who had preceded Bucareli, was appointed to this new position. Gálvez had conceived this reorganization when he was visitor general in New Spain, as a means of strengthening frontier defenses, and implemented it when he was appointed minister of the Indies in 1775.[11]

Serra was crushed by this turn of events, for it meant that the relationship with Bucareli, which had been so important to him and had in his opinion increased his authority with both the military authorities and the Colegio de San Fernando, was over. All affairs relating to Alta California would now be administered by the commander general headquartered in Arispe, Sonora.

---

9. Serra, *Writings*, 4:103.
10. Serra, *Writings*, 4:122–23.
11. Navarro García, *Don José de Gálvez y la comandancia general*, 157–60, 275.

Serra told Bucareli that it was completely impossible for him to describe how bad he felt about this, so he would adopt the tactic of the Roman orator Cicero and simply pass over this matter in silence. But silence did not come naturally to Junípero Serra, and two months later he poured out his disappointment and frustrations with Neve in his first letter to Croix. Those frustrations revolved around two issues. The establishment of the pueblo of San José and the probability of another pueblo in the southern part of Alta California threatened to bring more settlers into the region. His experiences in the Sierra Gorda had convinced him that settlers and missions could not coexist. He was also frustrated that the long-delayed mission on the Santa Bárbara Channel had still not come into existence.

※ *Serra to Teodoro de Croix, August 22, 1778*

And indeed, Señor, as I now reflect on how very much the Excelentísimo Señor the current viceroy, has favored, valued, and increased [the number] of these new establishments, despite all of this and much to our chagrin, Su Excelencia's and my desire to establish and populate missions along the very important span of territory of the Santa Bárbara Channel that is teeming with gentiles, still remains to be done. As soon as Vuestra Señoría's most excellent uncle received the news that we were now established in this port of Monterey, he wrote to me. In this first letter, which I was honored to receive from him, he informed me that his primary objective was to convert and christianize the Santa Bárbara Channel area without having the Indians from the islands move to the mainland. Each group would be evangelized where they were living. As I reflect on the circumstances involved, I must piously state that Divine Providence in its holy intentions has reserved this great undertaking for the zeal of Vuestra Señoría as the blood relative of that most excellent first founder of this new Christian territory.

Everything described is all still waiting to be done. On the first printed document[12] that was given to the public to announce the successful conquest of Monterey and the establishment of the presidio and mission, it was stated that the plan was to build Mission San Buenaventura at the place where the channel begins, which is next to the pueblo of Asunta. It still has not been founded because of the difficulty in forming a larger escort, which always has been deemed necessary for that site, more so than for the other establishment....

I am not saying that my wishes to see all of them become Christians should be taken into account because of this. Undoubtedly, Vuestra Señoría will

---

12. This document was printed in Mexico City on August 16, 1770. Palóu included it in his biography. Palóu, *Palóu's Life of Fray Junípero Serra*, 98–100.

have greater reasons for employing your holy zeal in this service to the king, our lord (may God favor him), and for giving the Lord Our God such glory.

With regard to the eight missions that have already been founded, I do not speak about requests for help but rather will wait for an opportune time to refer to my last letter, which Vuestra Señoría tells me he has received.

With respect to the good treatment of the neophytes, Señor, they are our children, for nobody else has engendered them in Christ. And so we look upon them as a father looks upon his children. For that reason we requested and with great consolation obtained a general pardon for those who set fire to Mission San Diego and most cruelly took the life of the main minister, Reverendo Padre Lector Fray Luis Jayme. They all live at the mission and are respected and looked after by the religious there.

We also have a very special assignment from our holy Colegio de San Fernando regarding the same matter. I trust in the Lord Our God that the very prudent warning from Vuestra Señoría, coupled with the aforementioned circumstances, will keep Vuestra Señoría from having to experience any trouble with regard to this issue. But I cannot fail to recognize that as human beings, we make mistakes. May God grant us success in all we do. Amen.

It is my understanding that the annual report of the state and progress of these missions, which up until now we prepared and sent to the Excelentísimo Señor Virrey, should from here on out be sent to Vuestra Señoría. But the report that is due deals with this past year, 1777, at the end of which we sent Vuestra Señoría information about all or almost all of the items that are part of the annual report, including the census, a description of the land, and other information. Therefore, it seemed to me and to the Señor Gobernador that we could be saved the trouble of having to prepare the report for 1777 and prepare a report for the current year when it ends. I hope that Vuestra Señoría will approve of this.

Finally, Señor, with regard to my brief reflections, which Vuestra Señoría has kindly allowed me to offer, I can only say that at the moment, I have gone over in my mind many times the new idea of establishing pueblos of Spaniards or mulatos among the gentiles instead of adding more missions. And I have not be able to come up with or conceive of any advantage at all, either temporal or spiritual, but rather many disadvantages.

The Señor Gobernador already knows how I feel and when I was asked to sign the document in which Su Señoría strongly advocates this idea as a means of bringing prosperity to these lands, I had to catch my breath for a moment, and then asked: "Can it really be true, Señor, that I have to sign this?"

To which he responded that it was only Su Señoría who was speaking, and that I was only an observer. And with that answer, I signed it.

Having shared this information, I can now feel at ease. And I would be happy if, in addition to Vuestra Señoría, my Venerado Ilustrísimo Señor Don José de Gálvez were also informed.

All right, establish those pueblos, if that is what the superiors decree, and stop building missions. But let it be known that I will end as I began, expressing nothing more than what seems fair and appropriate to be based on the wisdom that Our Lord God has seen fit to bestow upon me.

Missions, Señor, missions are what this territory needs. They will provide the territory not only with what is most important, that is, the light of the Holy Gospel, but also with food for the missions themselves and for the royal presidios, which is better than what these pueblos without priests can do, among other things that they cannot provide.

I maintain that settlements populated by fine Spanish citizens who are models of good behavior can be established only after the gentiles who are scattered across the territory have become Christians and have been brought together in their respective reducciones or missions. That is when there will be plenty of valuable uncultivated and uninhabited lands or possessions of the Crown. But for now, this is very repugnant to me for various reasons.

But I beg Vuestra Señoría to not interpret what I have expressed as a form of opposition. That is not the case; rather, as I have already stated, I am expressing my opinion, which I subject along with my entire being to the precepts and the slightest words of advice from Vuestra Señoría.

The Neve Reglamento

The Spanish government, most likely driven by the opinion of Gálvez, was never satisfied with the 1774 Echeveste Reglamento. A royal order of March 1775 decreed that a new reglamento for Las Californias be drawn up. In 1777 Neve, at Croix's request, composed a long memorandum about points he thought should be included in the new memorandum. Croix was quite pleased with Neve's effort and ordered him to condense his memorandum into a practical regulation. Neve completed this task on June 1, 1779. After approval at various levels the Neve Reglamento was put into effect on October 24, 1781.[13]

Most of the reglamento was concerned with reducing the costs of the California government and with promoting the internal development of the province. The

---

13. Beilharz, *Felipe de Neve*, 85–96; Neve, *Reglamento para el gobierno de la provincia de Californias, 1781*, 19–31. The Spanish text of the Reglamento is Document 3 at the end of this book. An English translation may be found in Nunis, *The Founding Documents of Los Angeles*, 72–109.

area of greatest concern to Serra was the last section, the one that dealt with missions, which Neve referred to by the earlier term "reducciones." Neve said that after the establishment of reducciones that were already planned along the Santa Bárbara Channel, the new establishments should shift from being constructed along a north-south direction to an east-west direction, thus allowing them to move into the interior of California. He decreed that all future reducciones would be limited to one priest in residence as a means of freeing up missionaries for this expansion. The same situation would gradually take place at the older reducciones. As missionaries retired or died, only one missionary would be allowed at each institution.

Serra regarded this as a deliberate attempt to weaken the power of the missionaries in California. He urged the colegio to lobby as vigorously as it could for the repeal of that part of the reglamento. This lobbying effort was eventually successful, and that part of the reglamento did not go into effect.

Indigenous Officials

One reason behind Neve's provisions about missions in his reglamento was that he and others in New Spain and on the Spanish mainland genuinely believed that the mission system was not succeeding in one of its primary tasks—the assimilation of the native peoples into the Spanish way of life. In this view he was very much associated with the policy view that had earlier animated Escandón and other officials who argued that this task of assimilation was being hindered rather than advanced by the existing mission system. To this end Neve ordered at the end of 1778 that the Christian Indians at the missions begin to be exposed to a form of self-government. He decreed that elections be held at each mission. Two *alcaldes* (a combination executive and judicial official) and two *regidores* (council members) would be chosen by the mission Indians, and then these indigenous officials would be formally invested in office.[14]

For Serra, this decree struck at the heart of missionaries' control over the native peoples. During the first months of 1779 he struggled to find a way to deal with this new decree. He shared the result of his deliberations with Lasuén, who was now at San Diego, in a letter at the end of March. The letter was an agonized one. Serra admitted that he was so upset that even news of the approval of plans to establish missions on the Santa Bárbara Channel, which he had so ardently desired for so long, could not cheer him up. Serra described an unpleasant encounter he had had with the governor right before he began to say Mass. He was so agitated that he, a man who had spent his entire life dealing with

---

14. Beilharz, *Felipe de Neve*, 64–66; Geiger, *Life and Times of Fray Junípero Serra*, 2:244–54.

words, could not find the right expressions as he was trying to compose a reply to Neve. After a fitful series of attempts to get some sleep, and crying out to God for help, he found consolation in a scripture verse whose sudden presence in his mind he took as an answer to his prayers. Serra told Lasuén that he believed the missionaries would be able to manipulate the elections and assure the election of alcaldes and regidores who looked favorably on the maintenance of priestly control over significant aspects of indigenous activity. He urged Lasuén to enlist the assistance of Presidio Commander José Francisco de Ortega in this effort.

❋ *Serra to Fermín Francisco de Lasuén, March 29, 1779*

[. . .] I do not consider the "misfortune" of that mission, if that is the term used to describe "difficulties," to be as bad as the "misfortune" I always seem to face with every step I take to help the mission.

I have not been able to forget the response I received when I insisted on more soldiers, based on what Vuestras Reverencias determined we needed at that time.

Now I have cried out for rations and for the suspension of those elections. And yesterday, Palm Sunday, I celebrated Mass at the presidio. Before Mass we had a brief conversation and he said something to me that was so far from the truth that I could not restrain myself and I shouted at him, saying, "Nobody has ever said such a thing to me because there has never been cause for them to speak to me that way."

He replied, with a snicker, that he also was a logical man, giving me to understand that what he told me was not actually expressed but rather inferred.

I responded that his logic was very sloppy because such an inference did not exist nor was it anywhere close. And that was that.

He told me very sarcastically not to get upset, that we would just keep this between the two of us.

I told him that even if one person knew about this, it would be one too many for my liking.

The dispute finally ended, and that is how I prepared for Mass on such a solemn day. I stood before the altar for quite some time trying to calm myself down. I said Mass. I then had a short conversation about routine matters, and then came here to sing the Passion with my companions who were waiting for me. The bickering had to do with the alcaldes.

The rest of the day I felt distressed and could not seem to let go of this issue. I kept pondering a thousand times over how best to proceed. Even though I had already spoken to that Señor about this and many other things,

I began to write a letter to him with the intention of including the letters from Vuestra Reverencia and Padre Fray Juan, in which you both requested permission to step down in case the aforementioned elections were held.

As soon as I would finish writing a sentence, I would see something wrong with it, so I would then stop, think, and rethink it. I attributed this to the fact that I was so upset. After struggling with this poor letter up until close to midnight, I took out a clean sheet of paper to see if I could get a fresh start. I then began to write a letter to Padre Sánchez, and it was a long one. I finished the letter, sealed and addressed it, and put it aside. I then started to ruminate about this issue again, and the same thing happened to me as before.

At that point I realized that it was getting very late and if I did not lie down for awhile (even though I was not at all sleepy) I would be useless for the entire day today. I therefore decided to lie down, dressed as I was. And as soon as I entered the bedroom, I thought I could lie down and let my thoughts soar to loftier heights. But I found myself so incapable of doing this that I burst forth with, "What is this all about, Señor?"

And it seems that a voice deep from within me responded with great intensity: *Prudentes sicut serpentes, et simplices sicut columbae*.[15]

I fell asleep and woke up at the usual time to pray the Liturgy of the Hours.[16] And immediately afterward I sang a Mass of thanksgiving in honor of the birth of a daughter named María Luisa, born to the Señor Príncipe of Asturias. Vuestras Reverencias may wish to do the same, but without mentioning the president.

And so I have been thinking that we should do what the gentleman requests, but in such a way that will not cause the slightest change for the Indians or in the routine Vuestras Reverencias have in place.

Let Francisco be the first alcalde. He already has the staff and coat, so the only thing to do is change the name. Another alcalde could be the chief of one of the rancherías, the ones that come to the mission every fifteen days. And the two regidores, who do not carry a staff—one could be from one ranchería and the other from a different one. It does not matter if the regidor is a captain or not, though it would be better if he were. The issue can be handled in this manner without any fanfare.

---

15. Matthew 10:16. The full verse: "I am sending you out like sheep among wolves. Therefore be as shrewd as serpents and as innocent as doves."
16. The set of prayers and readings from scripture and the Church Fathers that clergy were mandated to perform each day. This is sometimes also called the Divine Office.

A Series of Setbacks

The way in which the Señor Teniente explains the responsibilities of the position to them at the time he installs them into office is what will help the most. Without disobeying to the slightest degree the instructions from his superior officer, for the love of God as well as for my sake and for that of Vuestras Reverencias, ask the lieutenant not to let the Indians have a less favorable opinion of the Padres than they have had up until now. The document that is to be used in conferring these positions can be as strongly worded as you like, since Vuestras Reverencias are the only ones who will receive it and read it.

I am trusting in God that in this way, the difficulties that I am almost morally certain would have occurred during a different time will not come to pass. The gentleman seems to think he is clever. But with God's help and in the interest of His cause, the following could prove true: *sed et serpens era callidior*.[17] And when this phrase is linked with that of the dove, which is verified in the Holy Gospel, what more could we want?

Of the two unsealed letters that Vuestras Reverencias sent me so I could hand over the one I judged to be the best, as soon as I read the letter I immediately knew it was the right one. I then sealed it so I could hand it over. But after I read the second letter, I started to have some doubts. And since I would be the courier on that very day, I took both letters with me because I was very unsure of which one to hand over. In the end, I told him you had sent me the second letter like that, unsealed, so I could be informed. This should not have caused any upset. But later, seeing how offended he was by a letter of mine, for no reason whatsoever, I started to wonder if it was really worth the effort to quarrel with such creatures or merely be pleasant to them. But in the end, it would have been better to do that.

With regard to the rations, he said, "It is true that they are owed to the mission, but right now we find ourselves at a time when the lieutenant has written stating that he has put the troops on half rations."

"Well," I told him, "don't they have any flour there?"

He replied, "There is nothing. They have run out of everything in San Diego. I do not know how they manage."

His attitude with regard to the missions and their ministers is starting to manifest itself. The confirmations I administer cause him considerable annoyance. And other things specific to this mission provide beautiful opportunities to prove oneself patient. May God grant it to us. *Consolamini, consolamini, dicit Dominus Deus noster*.[18]

---

17. Genesis 3:1: the "serpent was more shrewd."
18. Isaiah 40:1: "Be comforted, be comforted my people, says the Lord Our God."

> The news that has arrived in the latest mail would have made me dance with joy under other circumstances. But with what I see happening now, I can anticipate what might happen in the future. And the only thing that seems to increase is my anxiety. What arrived is news of the decision to found a presidio and three missions as quickly as possible in the Santa Bárbara Channel. And as soon as the mail arrives in Loreto, Don Fernando is supposed to sail to the other coast to assemble troops and animals.
>
> The three missions: San Buenaventura has a site; La Purísima Concepción near Point Concepción; and Santa Bárbara in the middle, near the presidio, but we do not know its name. I have already expressed some doubts, and the solutions offered are of little satisfaction to me. If I cannot resolve this now, I hope to send my opinions via ship to our colegio. That way all loose ends can be tied up before sending the religious. But in the midst of everything, I am happy because giving birth to children has its painful moments. We all have laments: but when speaking about these missions, one could say, "Miscebatur lamentatio matrum et ad coelum transibat oblatio parvulorum."[19]
>
> I am deeply saddened by the hardships and deaths of those gentiles due to hunger. If only there had been a granary at San Diego as there is at San Gabriel, to provide them with food and acquire them for Heaven. I am trusting in God that you will have a good harvest this year and thus things will change for the better at the mission and your burdens will be lightened.
>
> Now, with the water flowing, the mission must be a very beautiful sight to behold. May God allow this to continue. According to what I read in the report I received, which pleased me very much, the ditch was repaired. May it be suitable for irrigation. And as soon as these issues have passed, I will see how and when the credits your mission has run up with the royal warehouse can be paid.

A few months later in another letter to Lasuén, Serra admitted that the new Indian officers were a mixed lot. While some were proving amenable to the missionary desires, others were showing unwelcome signs of independence.

❈ Serra to Fermín Francisco de Lasuén, August 16, 1779

> Regarding the matter of the alcaldes, I have exhausted my imagination. I never took this to be a mere formality. And I soon saw here that it was not

---

19. "The lamentations of the mothers were mixed together and the offering of the little ones ascended to Heaven." This is from a commentary by Saint Augustine on the Feast of the Holy Innocents. See Engelhardt, *Missions and Missionaries*, 2:340.

the case. But this situation is impossible to remedy or correct and still maintain uniformity at all the missions.

Some were simply very pleased, and they have told him they were getting along well with them. However, the Padre from San Luis, who was one of their biggest supporters, now says that the only one who is of any use is the regidor. But the alcalde has taken advantage of his authority to engage in wrongdoing. Because the alcaldes were praised excessively, they began to consider themselves gentlemen. The alcalde here, has not removed his cotón,[20] blanket, and breechclout. And he has also complained about this to Su Señoría. Since he cannot obtain anything from the presidio, this is all he has. Each day he becomes less and less useful.

From all that has been said, it seemed to me that the situation with the alcaldes has nothing to do with what Vuestra Reverencia fears, which is that the old Indians of that mission will be forced to work at the presidio. The response Vuestras Reverencias provided to the document delivered by the lieutenant, which will end up in Su Señoría's hands, is, in my opinion, sufficient for the time being. Let him digest that bitter pill for now.

Slightly over a year after Neve announced his policy of Indian elections, Serra composed a long and emotional letter to the governor in which he denounced what he regarded as a perilous new state of affairs that the elections had ushered in. He was most concerned about the weakening of clerical control over the baptized Indians. He was also concerned that the missionaries' ability to mandate and supervise physical punishment for the Indians, which he judged to be absolutely necessary for the maintenance of good order, was being undermined by Neve's policy. He launched into a long defense about the necessity and propriety of flogging and whipping Indians who were judged recalcitrant.

Serra was also quite concerned that some of the new Indian officials were engaged in behavior that was inconsistent with the conduct he was trying to instill in them. He objected to the persistence of traditional sexual practices exhibited by one of the alcaldes, Baltasar. Serra admitted that a good number of the male Christian Indians at the mission had a "gentile wife" in their village in addition to their "Christian wife" at the mission. Therefore, to put one of these people in a position of authority, he protested, undermined the attempts of the missionaries to replace native culture with Catholic moral norms. Serra also complained about Nicolás, the San Gabriel alcalde, who, he said, was arranging liaisons between soldiers and various Indian women. Again, he repeated, Neve's system was putting the wrong kind of Indians in power.

---

20. Shirt or blouse worn by neophytes.

According to Serra, Neve's policy was a complete failure. From Serra's point of view, his judgment would prove correct, for in 1780, after the death of his mission wife and child, Baltasar abandoned San Carlos and relocated to the Big Sur area. And the year after Serra's death, Nicolás joined the female indigenous leader Toypurina to organize a plot to attack Mission San Gabriel. While protesting his willingness to follow Neve's orders completely, at the end of the letter Serra basically threw up his hands and said nothing could be done as long as Neve continued his policy.[21]

Serra's reactions to Neve's innovations combined two different aspects of his background. First, the Inquisition-based suspicion of what new Christians were doing when they were outside the supervision of Church authorities led him to view any weakening of perceived Church authority among the neophytes as an invitation to backsliding. As we have seen, his experiences in Mexico, especially what he heard during the Inquisition proceedings in Villa de Valles in 1766, had exposed him to a wide variety of ways in which non-Christian forms of spirituality could thrive in nominally Christian communities. His early experience at San Carlos suggests that he accepted the notion that conversion would be a gradual process that might include a period of syncretism and amalgamation of distinct worldviews. But he was unwilling to have people who openly engaged in non-Christian practices placed in leadership positions. What he thought was happening among the chuetas of Mallorca taught him that the gradual (and, for him, normal) process of conversion could easily be hijacked by those who had no interest in actually becoming Christians. He was determined that such a process not take root in Alta California.

Second, his belief in the potentially salvation-bringing effects of punishment led him consistently to approve flogging, a very common eighteenth-century form of punishment for a variety of offenses, and a punishment that was regarded by colonial military officials as particularly suitable for native peoples. As we have seen, Neve himself urged Serra to have Indians flogged, and after the San Diego uprising the officer in charge at the San Diego presidio consistently used extensive flogging as a means of obtaining confessions from Kumeyaay suspects.

The thrust of Serra's argument was that the priests needed the authority to order the flogging of any Indian, even an Indian alcalde. He insisted that at least some of the native people would understand such missionary behavior in terms he articulated in his third sermon at the Convento de Santa Clara in Mallorca in 1744. In his view, these Indians would eventually understand that the priests were like loving parents trying to help their children. He seemed unaware that the child-rearing practices of most Alta California Indians did not involve this sort of corporal punishment. In fact, when missionaries commented on the way in which

---

21. Beebe and Senkewicz, "Revolt at Mission San Gabriel"; Hackel, "Sources of Rebellion," 652.

California Indians raised their children, they criticized them for being too lenient. Missionaries a few decades after Serra's death criticized the native Californians for showing an "extravagant love" for their children and criticized Indian parents for refusing to "chastise them."[22] It is therefore difficult to see how indigenous Californians could have interpreted flogging in the sense Serra intended.

Serra also justified flogging by appealing to some stories that were current in the religious narrative of the Americas. He cited a tradition relating to Hernán Cortés that originated in Franciscan circles. According to a story popular in religious writings in New Spain, in Texcoco an Indian was flogged for missing Mass. This caused anger in the local community, and Cortés arranged with the priests to be late for the next Mass himself and allow himself to be whipped for this offense. The story says that in this way the Indians were taught that religious edicts were to be obeyed by all, and they were not being singled out for punishment. The story appeared in works by the Franciscan writer Agustín Vetancurt and the Jesuit writer Andrés Cavo.[23] Further, for Serra and those religious who practiced self-flagellation, flogging was similar to what they did to themselves, but the whips used for flogging were considerably more substantial and painful than the instruments religious used to discipline themselves.

✳ Letter to Felipe de Neve, January 7, 1780

Señor Coronel and Gobernador, don Felipe de Neve
My dear Señor:

I have read with great interest and appreciation Vuestra Señoría's letter, dated the 5th of this month and received by me during the afternoon of that same day. I would first like to assure you, with all sincerity, that I very much wish to please Vuestra Señoría, as has always been the case, when it comes to matters which in my estimation are not adverse to the progress (especially spiritual progress) of these missions, of which I am in charge.

My response to the main point of your letter is:

First: I now understand, as I did not before, that Vuestra Señoría is aware of the ineptitude of those poor new Christians to conduct the elections on their own of the officials who will replace those whose terms have expired. Vuestra Señoría believes he can guarantee the success of these elections by placing the matter in the hands of the missionaries at each mission.

---

22. This critique of indigenous child rearing appears most fully in the missionaries' responses to question 4 of the 1812 *Interrogatorio*: "Do they love their wives and children? What sort of education do they give their children? And do they urge them on to agriculture and mechanical arts?" See Geiger and Meighan, *As the Padres Saw Them*, 23–27 (quote on 25).
23. See Vetancurt, *Teatro mexicano*, 3:6–7; Cavo, *Historia de México*, 183; Cruz González, "Landscapes of Conversion," 145. We thank Cristina Cruz González for leading us to the Vetancurt reference.

Even though Vuestra Señoría parenthetically says that you had suggested such a thing, I have no memory of it. But I do remember mentioning to Vuestra Señoría on several occasions that I felt they were incapable of governing under the conditions specified by Vuestra Señoría. You always tried to encourage and convince me that they would do a good job, that they would patrol the ranchería at night, that they would bring people to pray and to work, and that this would take some of the burden off of us. Since this is much more difficult to implement than the election of new alcaldes, it should not be surprising that I do not have a clear idea of what Vuestra Señoría is now talking about.

I suppose that Vuestra Señoría's good intentions are what led you to have such high expectations. And because we have already seen them thwarted, it therefore seemed to me that since you trust us completely to make sure the elections are successful, you should also trust us to train, reprimand, and guide those who are elected. And then perhaps the new ones would be better than their predecessors.

But above all, my understanding is that with only three members remaining of the original four whose terms have expired, Vuestra Señoría still wants to hold the elections. And you are asking us to provide guidance to make up for their shortcomings. Well, the elections will be held with the grace of God, as soon as possible.

Currently, both of them are sick in bed in their homes, therefore neither last Sunday nor on Epiphany were they able to attend Mass. I will try to encourage them to come or have them brought to the church. I am willing to do this solely as a means of pleasing Vuestra Señoría and not because my point of view has changed with regard to what I expressed in my last letter. Measures were not taken to apprehend the alcalde Baltazar and his cohorts prior to the elections that were held, and I believe this, as well as the other statements Vuestra Señoría quotes in your letter, to be prejudicial.

Vuestra Señoría's main point in your response to me is that just because the former alcalde was bad does not mean the new ones will be bad. In an academic sense, I admit you are correct, but in a moral sense, it seems to me that nobody can deny that scandals which are not stopped or punished usually have unfortunate consequences. And this is especially bad among simple and ignorant people.

During the time Baltazar held the office of alcalde, from the moment he was aware of his privileges and that he was exempt from punishment by the Padres, he did whatever he pleased.[24] He had a son by one of his

---

24. Baltazar, from Ichxenta was estimated to be forty years old when he was baptized in 1775 at Mission San Carlos. San Carlos baptismal record 00268.

sisters-in-law; he beat a Baja California Indian because he had obeyed an order the Padre had given him, as I reported to Vuestra Señoría at the time. All this in addition to neglecting the responsibilities of his position. And now everyone sees or recognizes the manner in which this deserter and adulterer operates. He sends word to the people here and personally interacts with those who have permission to leave the mission. This is all done as a means of increasing his number of cohorts in the mountains, by adding new Indian deserters from this mission.

This is the current state of affairs. If we want to see some greatly needed improvement in the behavior of these people, there can be no doubt that with the newly elected officials, today an Indian will flee because he was punished or scolded. On another day, another Indian will flee because he has friends outside the mission. They are leaving little by little, filing out of the mission to join the enemies, just as I said. This situation is just as I have described it. In my opinion, we would have been able to rid ourselves of those problems in our midst if the arrest had been made and if that group of rebels had been punished.

And even if this meant only putting a stop to the offenses they are committing against God, the majority of them have a gentile woman as well as a Christian wife whom they have left at the mission. (We were told this by an Indian who just arrived from the mountains, and thanks to him the whole pueblo probably already knows about it.) This is the greatest difficulty we face in trying to convert those gentiles to Christianity, be they men or women. It seems to me that this problem merits immediate attention so that a solution can be found as quickly as possible.

In your letter Vuestra Señoría shows great respect (may God bless you) for the religious of these missions. You add: "With the elections or appointments of a new republic, His Majesty's plans for this area will have been carried out. And with time, under our guidance these natives will become useful subjects of Church and State."

That is our wish, Señor, and we hope to see it realized, not through any effort or labor of our own but rather through the help and grace of God. It is Our Divine Majesty who deserves all the glory for bringing this to fruition in the former missions of the Sierra Gorda. His Majesty (may God keep him) saw fit to entrust these missions to our Colegio Apostólico de San Fernando. Everyone in the kingdom knew of our work, as did the Court. And of the religious who toiled there for many years, today there are seven working in these new Christian areas. But those of us who were there know that whenever some Indians would flee and a religious wanted to go after them (both scenarios happened frequently), there was never anyone there to render it difficult, and there was always somebody to escort them. For in that region, the soldiers were strictly militiamen who did not receive a salary.

As far as reprimanding the Indians is concerned, even though we made quite an effort to treat the governors, alcaldes, and fiscales[25] with respect, when it seemed to us that they deserved to be punished, they would be flogged or put in the stocks, based on the seriousness of the crime. Therefore, the alcaldes were very careful to fulfill the responsibilities of their respective positions. I have traveled throughout the kingdom and have seen this technique used everywhere. Based on my experience, officials such as these do follow the orders given by their missionaries or parish priests. Therefore, I believe this technique should be employed everywhere. On one occasion, when I was in Acayucán, a very largo pueblo in the diocese of Oaxaca, I was an eyewitness to the punishment meted out to the Indian governor at the door of the church. Also present were the priest, the principal vicar, and four other vicars. They all were the type of priest one wishes to have in every parish in the kingdom. And I was there with two companions preaching a mission. The alcalde mayor, who was there to keep an eye on things, normally would have handed the staff of authority over to the Indian governor, but there was no hint of any dispute with regard to the punishment. I have no doubt the same thing happens in many places.

The spiritual Padres' flogging of their children, the Indians, appears to be a practice as old as the conquest of these kingdoms and so common that not even the saints disagreed with it. And the first Padres who came here were known to be saints.

In the biography of the solemnly canonized San Francisco Solano, one reads that the saint had a special God-given talent for taming the ferocious nature of the most barbarous Indians. He could do this by his mere presence and loving words. This was especially evident in terms of the way of life at his mission in the province of Tucumán, Perú. It is recounted in his biography that when the Indians did not follow the orders they had been given, he would order the fiscales to punish them.

And since the alcaldes are also the missionaries' children, and therefore under the Padres' care, they are no less in need of the Padres' training, reprimands, and upbringing. I know of no law, nor can there be any reason why they should be exempt.

And it is true that when the renowned Hernando Cortés allowed himself, or, rather, made the Padres flog him in front of the Indians, he did not do this

---

25. The fiscal was a native officeholder whose duties involved seeing that Indians attended church services.

to merely set an example for those who did not carry the staff of authority. He did it to set an example for everybody. For no matter how high-ranking any Indian might be, they could never reach the level of this man who was being humbled in this manner.

For these and other reasons, it has always seemed strange to me that Vuestra Señoría would consider it a personal snub that my fellow missionaries here would order the flogging of a recently converted Indian at this mission, who happens to be the alcalde. And it seems strange that Vuestra Señoría should equate this practice with other bad habits the Padres from San Fernando passed on to the Reverendos Padres Dominicos of Antigua California. Without a doubt, our people were conducting themselves based on what they knew from before. And undoubtedly, therein lies the explanation.

And I have no doubt that with regard to the punishment we are discussing, there probably have been some irregularities and excesses on the part of some Padres. We all run this risk. But this applies equally to the children who are not alcaldes. In terms of one group and another, the trust they have in us is based on the fact that when we came here, none of them were Christians. And we have given them birth in Christ. We have all come here and remained here for the sole purpose of their well-being and salvation. And I believe everyone realizes we love them.

But now, Señor, if what has been said is of no value, then we at this mission should not be trusted with disciplining the alcaldes, since it is obvious that Vuestra Señoría can make up for our shortcomings. But what can be done at a mission like San Gabriel, which is forty leagues away from the closest presidio? What about San Luis Obispo, which is fifty leagues away from this, its closest presidio?

They have written to me from San Gabriel that the Padres of that mission investigated and have proof that their alcalde, Nicolás, provided women to however many soldiers asked for them. So as not to punish him themselves, or order that he be punished, the Padres turned him over to the corporal, who indeed punished him. But later they were informed that Vuestra Señoría disapproved of this action and stated that the corporal cannot carry out such a punishment. He is only allowed to apprehend the alcalde in the event of an uprising or a death, and he must then send word.

That being the case, even if the alcalde is scandalously living in sin, is a thief and a tyrant, beats people, and responds to the Padres or soldiers in a cocky manner, we will have to put up with it, since neither the Padres nor the corporal are allowed to whip him.

At Mission San Luis, their alcalde took another man's woman and fled with her. They were away from the mission for quite some time before he was caught. The Padre at San Luis acted in the same manner as the Padre at San Gabriel—he handed the Indian over to the corporal, who punished him ever so lightly. The corporal himself acknowledged that the punishment did not fit the crime. But seeing that the Padre did not say a word, he let him go.

I have not heard how this case turned out. But the corporal at San Luis probably received the same instructions as the one at San Gabriel. Therefore, if the Padre is not aware of this and requests the same punishment in the future, his request will be refused.

It seems that Mission San Antonio is the only place that has not had problems with its alcalde and regidor. But men being men, we do not know what tomorrow will bring.

I cannot bear to speak about San Diego, for they have complained a great deal about the alcaldes. But they are fortunate to have the presidio nearby. May God help them.

And so my only request of Vuestra Señoría is that you be so kind as to tell me what instructions I should give the Padres of Missions San Luis and San Gabriel. With regard to the rest, I trust in God that everything will be resolved, and above all, I shall act in accordance with His holy will. And I shall let your wishes be known as a means of honoring Vuestra Señoría.

May the Lord Our God keep Vuestra Señoría's life and health in His holy grace many years.

From Vuestra Señoría's Mission, San Carlos de Monterey, January 7, 1780. Your most loving servant and chaplain kisses the hand of Vuestra Señoría, Fray Junípero Serra

By the end of April 1870 Serra was feeling slightly better about the alcalde situation.

Serra to Lasuén, April 25–26, 1780

With regard to the alcaldes, since they will allow us to manage them as we see fit, I no longer foresee as many problems. And it is possible that they will leave us in peace. With the bitter pill he has in his body, which he is yet to digest, and the fact that I am still waiting for a response and instructions from him: *qui tacet*,[26] etc., I have therefore already written to San Luis and San Gabriel telling them to give them what they deserve.

---

26. "Qui tacet consentire" means "Silence gives consent."

Confirmation

Serra's background as an academic meant that he was familiar with formal bureaucracies, and on occasion he was able to hold his own with Neve. For instance, one set of disagreements revolved around the mission inventories that Neve asked to be forwarded to him so he could use them in preparing his reports to Croix. According to Neve, Serra agreed to do this "directly" (*en derechura*). But then it turned out that Serra had meant "directly" not in the sense of "right away," but in the sense that he would send the material "straight" to the viceroy.[27] As was typical in the Spanish empire, this dispute generated an enormous correspondence at various levels of the colonial bureaucracy. When Serra was finally ordered by Croix to turn the material over to the governor, Serra gamely protested that he had never really been explicitly ordered to hand over the inventories, and thus the implication in Croix's order that he had not complied with legitimate orders was erroneous. He said he would be happy to obey. However, the documents he would need in order to comply with this order had already been sent to Mexico City. And, he was sorry to have to add, there was also a serious shortage of paper in the missions. Thus he was not sure if he had anything to write the reports on! He insisted, however implausibly, that he was anxious to fulfill these orders and would do so just as soon as humanly possible.[28]

A similar situation occurred around the sacrament of confirmation. This sacrament, a follow-up to baptism, was normally administered by a bishop. However, in remote areas such as a mission territory where a bishop did not reside, the Vatican often delegated the authority to administer this sacrament to the chief missionary of the area. The Jesuits received such authority in Baja California. The Franciscans in Alta California routinely applied for this privilege for themselves in the early 1770s. The Vatican granted this request in 1774. As was the case in the Spanish empire, the Vatican document was sent to Madrid, where it was countersigned by the Council of the Indies. This document was then forwarded to Mexico City. In 1778 the colegio sent Serra a document telling him that everything had been approved and he was authorized to administer the sacrament of confirmation. He soon started doing so at various missions. When Neve found out, he demanded to see the document entitling Serra to administer confirmations. Relying on a bureaucratic procedure that was put in place in 1777, Neve claimed that he needed to see the original and countersigned document sent from Madrid to Mexico City, not the document sent to Serra by his superiors in Mexico City. Neve said that as chief authority in the area he was required to add his own signature. This document was, of course, at the colegio in Mexico City. The normal voluminous correspondence again ensued.

---

27. Beilharz, *Felipe de Neve*, 176 n. 12.
28. Beilharz, *Felipe de Neve*, 49–55; Serra, *Writings*, 3:125–35.

At one point Serra received an escort of soldiers to convey him to San Francisco, on the express condition that he not administer confirmation there. He accepted that condition, but once he arrived there, he proceeded to administer the sacrament. Neve and Croix were extremely upset. Serra was then specifically ordered by Croix to completely cease administering confirmation and to turn over to Neve the document he received from the colegio. Neve would then send it to Croix's headquarters in Sonora for inspection. Serra had anticipated this request and replied that he had already sent those documents on to Mexico City so that they could be sent from there to Sonora. He disingenuously claimed that he did this so that the documents could get to Sonora faster! The colegio and the viceroy ultimately negotiated a solution to this impasse which Croix accepted. Serra received permission to resume confirmations in 1781.[29]

Serra was animated in this confirmation controversy by a desire to assert what he regarded as legitimate prerogatives of the Church against the interference of the state. But we believe another factor was also in play. Ever since the San Diego uprising, Serra found his work becoming more and more purely administrative. "I spend half my life at a writing desk," he complained even before the Kumeyaay uprising in 1775. That situation only got worse after San Diego. The quarrels he had with Rivera y Moncada about reconstructing Mission San Diego, the necessity to defend himself from charges leveled by his own colegio, and Neve's extremely effective ability to frustrate him meant that he was spending an increasing amount of his time on administrative tasks. A few months later, he lamented that he was "more of a writer than a missionary."[30] As a result, he had less time to give to the project that had originally drawn him to the Americas and Las Californias—the preaching of the Gospel to the indigenous people. Serra found that his increasing administrative tasks were beginning to weigh on him. Life as president was proving to have the same pitfalls for him as his former life as a college professor. He was feeling that he was getting farther and farther away from his identity as a priest. As a Scotist, he believed that living relationships were indispensable to the well-lived life. As we have seen, in his teaching and preaching he had always tried to establish these relationships with his audiences.

The ability to administer confirmation gave Serra a reason to travel to all the missions that were founded under his presidency and establish a direct relationship with virtually all of the native peoples who were baptized at those places. He took on that opportunity with a vengeance. When he first received the document from the Colegio de San Fernando, he quickly started confirming at Mission San Carlos at the end of June 1778. By the third week of August he had confirmed over 180

---

29. Beilharz, *Felipe de Neve*, 55–61; Geiger, *Life and Times of Fray Junípero Serra*, 2:159–70.
30. Serra, *Writings*, 2:320–21, 394–95.

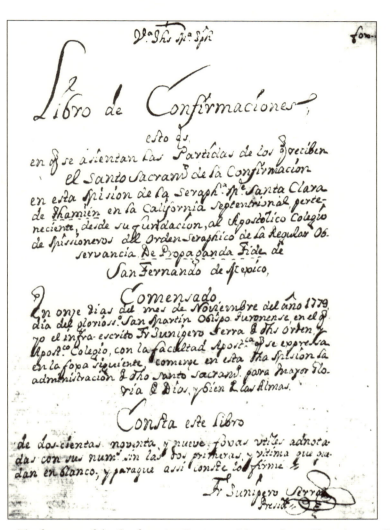

FIGURE 47. The first page of the Confirmation Register at Mission Santa Clara. Against Governor Neve's wishes, Serra administered the sacrament there in 1779. *Courtesy of the Santa Clara University Archives.*

people. Serra sailed south in September and engaged in a series of major confirmation events at San Diego, San Juan Capistrano, San Gabriel, San Luis Obispo, and San Antonio. By the time he was specifically ordered to cease administering the sacrament, Serra had confirmed 2,455 people.[31] The overwhelming majority of these confirmations were of baptized native people. Confirmation gave Serra the ability to act as a priest and to engage in direct sacramental ministry. It was probably more important to him than to any person who received the sacrament.

Reprimand

At the same time Serra was dealing with the difficulties that followed the Kumeyaay revolt in San Diego and also trying to thwart Neve's designs, he encountered a series of troublesome issues relating to his religious identities. These issues surfaced explicitly on March 11, 1776, when Juan Bautista de Anza handed him a letter from the guardian of the Colegio de San Fernando, Francisco Pangua. The letter had been written over a year earlier, on February 7, 1775. It concerned the conduct of missionaries in Alta California, and it severely limited Serra's powers. Serra was explicitly forbidden to move priests from one mission to another except under severely restricted circumstances. He was forbidden to take items that had been assigned to one mission and give them to another mission. All of the missionaries were urged to treat the soldiers stationed at the missions with moderation and prudence. Most explicitly, Serra was forbidden in very emphatic language to engage in communication with any royal officials, and that included the viceroy. Stated in the letter was that all communication with these officials was to be channeled through the colegio. The reason was made very clear in the guardian's cover letter to Serra: the colegio was tired of Serra's bypassing the normal chain of authority and of his asking royal officials for more new missions, which the colegio did not think it would be able to support. Serra could be tone-deaf on this issue. At one point he told Gálvez that he could use a hundred additional missionaries in Alta California. When this remark reached the colegio, its leaders were horrified, for they could not come close to supplying even a fraction of that number. The colegio authorities generally felt that there should be roughly two to three people in Mexico City for each missionary in the field. In 1772, for instance, there were seventy-one people at the Colegio de San Fernando and forty-three in the missions of Baja California and Alta California. So if Serra had one hundred missionaries, they would need at least two hundred people at San Fernando. They believed that figure was totally unrealistic. Serra undoubtedly thought that with the colegio's renunciation of the missions in the Sierra Gorda and Baja California

---

31. Geiger, *Life and Times of Fray Junípero Serra*, 2:217.

it could well afford to send more people, and that the ratio of people in Mexico City to people in the missions was getting too high. For example, in 1776 there were seventy-one men in the colegio and eighteen in Alta California.[32]

The letter clearly reflected complaints about Serra's conduct that had reached the authorities at San Fernando. Some of the complaints may have come from soldiers or other officials in Alta California. However, a considerable number of these complaints had to originate from the missionaries themselves. Serra suspected that many complaints came from the missionaries at San Luis Obispo.

That mission, which Serra had established in 1772, had a rocky start. The site decided on for the mission was not near any existing native village, but given the topography and the location of the creeks the mission needed, it was the best that Serra could do. The priest whom Serra left in charge when he departed only a day after the founding was thirty-two-year-old José Cavaller, who had never worked in a mission before. He arrived in Alta California in 1771 and was stationed at Mission San Carlos in Monterey while he awaited his assignment. When Serra moved the mission to Carmel, Cavaller and another priest, Domingo Juncosa, remained in Monterey as chaplains to the presidio. Cavaller went with Serra to San Luis Obispo, but Juncosa remained at Monterey and did not arrive at San Luis Obispo until the end of 1772 or the beginning of 1773. By the time he arrived there, one baptism had taken place, a sick boy of eight or nine years who died a few days after receiving the sacrament.[33]

Juncosa had a tough time at San Luis Obispo. He did not get along with the soldiers, and there had been only twelve total baptisms by the time Francisco Palóu stopped there in November 1773 on his way to Carmel. Palóu quickly moved Juncosa from San Luis Obispo and placed him at San Antonio. In his place he stationed José Murguía, a veteran of the Sierra Gorda and Baja California missions. Palóu noted that the native peoples were not affiliating with the missions at a very rapid pace. He attributed this to the abundance of natural resources in the area. The people of the area, he said, "harvest an abundance of very nutritious wild seeds, and have game, such as deer and rabbits, and the beach Indians catch large quantities of fish. For this reason, it will not be easy to induce them to live at the mission."[34]

At some point in early 1774, Murguía and Juncosa switched places, with Murguía going to San Antonio and Juncosa returning to San Luis Obispo. In the

---

32. A translation of Pangua's letter is in Serra, *Writings*, 2:459–63; Serra's responses are in Serra, *Writings*, 2:422–43, 3:40–71; Geiger, *Life and Times of Fray Junípero Serra*, 2:120–32. See also Chauvet, *La iglesia de San Fernando de México*, 42–43; Geiger, "Internal Organization," 4; Ocaranza, *Capítulos de la historia franciscana*, 319–21.
33. Geiger, *Franciscan Missionaries*, 47–49, 134–35, 162–64; San Luis Obispo baptismal record no. 1.
34. Palóu, *Historical Memoirs of New California*, 3:222–23.

spring of 1774, the mission planted its first substantial crops, with the labor of some Baja California Indians—four husbands and wives and five young men—whom Palóu had brought with him and left there.[35]

In the midst of Cavaller's adjustment to these rapid changes of Franciscan personnel and the arrival of thirteen new people from Baja California, Serra arrived at the beginning of May on his way back to Carmel from Mexico City. Bubbling with enthusiasm at the success of his mission to the capital, he told Cavaller that he had procured a great painting of the mission's patron and that it would only cost the mission eighteen pesos. This was probably the last thing Cavaller wanted to hear, and he expressed his disapproval so strongly that Serra did not even get a chance to unwrap the painting and show it to Cavaller.

A few months later, Serra heard from Cavaller that the harvest was going well, and he wrote back suggesting that Cavaller might want to lay aside a part of the harvest so that it would be available to help the new mission of San Francisco when it started. Cavaller never responded to Serra's request. With this as background, Serra became especially irritated when he heard that Cavaller had offered to sell corn to Anza's soldiers when they passed through San Luis Obispo at the beginning of March 1776 on their way to Monterey, and he wrote Cavaller a letter of reprimand.[36]

His fellow Franciscans had been critical of some aspects of Serra's leadership for a considerable time. Palóu criticized Serra in a letter to Verger in 1771. Verger, who preceded Pangua as guardian and who prized organization and systematic activity more than Serra did, wrote to a colonial official in that same year that the Alta California enterprise "had been undertaken without that preparation, maturity, and caution that have always been employed in similar circumstances." Verger said he thought it would take "a miracle" for it to succeed.[37]

Pangua's letter also contained other orders that did not affect Serra directly but reflected poorly on his management of the missions as Padre Presidente. For instance, all missionaries were instructed to be absolutely certain they did not baptize any child over the age of eight in the same way they baptized infants. The point was that children who had reached the "age of reason" at eight years were required to be formally instructed about Catholicism before baptism. Children who had not yet reached that age did not require such instruction. Accordingly, missionaries would be able to perform more baptisms more quickly if they were very flexible in their interpretation of whether or not a particular child had

---

35. San Antonio baptismal record 174 (the year was 1774, not 1773); San Luis Obispo baptismal records nos. 43–44.
36. Geiger, *Life and Times of Fray Junípero Serra*, 1:414, 2:124–25; Serra, *Writings*, 2:429.
37. Palóu, *Cartas desde la península de California*, 179; Geiger, "Fray Rafael Verger," 207; Gómez Canedo, *Evangelización, cultura y promoción social*, 703, 714.

reached the required age. The implication was that the Alta California missionaries, by treating older children as if they were younger, could do more baptisms than normal and were thus artificially inflating the number of baptisms they performed. Also, missionaries were forbidden to carry arms when they traveled. And if they were returning to Mexico City from Alta California, they were instructed to take the most expeditious and least expensive route, which was by sea from San Diego or Monterey, rather than travel overland through Baja California or Sonora, which would prolong the journey and be more expensive. While the document did not imply that Serra himself had done any of these things, the letter was a clear indication that the authorities at the Colegio de San Fernando judged that the California missions were poorly managed. The guardian also required Serra to send this letter to each mission. The senior missionary at each institution would then sign the original and make a copy of it to be kept on file at that mission. After that process was completed, Serra was instructed to send the original to the colegio.

Serra composed a long response to the document and gave it to Anza to carry back to Mexico City. He said that he had not changed the assignments of any missionaries since he returned from Mexico City. With respect to the one missionary he had shifted from San Diego to San Carlos, he only said, "I know why I brought him to this mission." Serra attributed a good number of the issues about mission property to misunderstandings on the part of some of the missionaries, especially those at San Luis Obispo. He protested that he had been as fair as he possibly could be when distributing goods that arrived in Alta California destined for the missions in general to the individual institutions that he judged needed them the most.

Serra said he would obey the instruction not to communicate directly with various officials. He told the guardian that he had recently received a letter asking for some information about Alta California from Juan José Echeveste, the official who wrote the regulations that implemented the viceroy's favorable verdict on Serra's 1773 memorandum. But he said he would not respond to that letter, since, as he put it, he would rather be impolite than disobedient. The message was clear—Serra was telling the authorities at San Fernando that he thought he had a better relationship with the colonial officials than they did. To force Serra not to respond to an official request would be to insult the official making the request. In that case, the colegio would suffer.

After a few months Serra returned to this subject in another letter to the guardian dated October 7, 1776. In this communication he raised once again the question that most directly bothered him: the prohibition against communicating with colonial officials. Serra was particularly irked that he had heard that when Anza was passing through San Luis Obispo on his way back to Mexico, one of the priests there, undoubtedly Cavaller, told the commander, apparently with great satisfaction, that Serra was forbidden to communicate with colonial officials. Serra was afraid that if this prohibition became widely known it would tremendously undermine his potential authority with any official or military officer sent to Alta California. What should I do when I get a letter from the viceroy? he asked. Should I just send it back to him unopened? I did not even have to do that when I received letters from Escandón in the Sierra Gorda. The implication was clear: he thought that in addition to undermining his own authority, the prohibition would bring harm to the colegio itself.[38]

He also protested against the prohibition of moving priests from one mission to another. He laid out a series of situations in which missionary work might suffer because of disagreements or incompatibility between the two priests at a particular mission. He then asked for a reconsideration of that policy as well.

The extant correspondence does not indicate whether or not the colegio specifically responded to these requests. However, as Serra well knew, the long distance between Alta California and Mexico City and the fact that the guardian and his council were limited to three-year terms meant that in the practical order, Serra was in a strong position. While he did not formally disobey any of the orders, he managed to arrange things so that his own channels of communication with officials in Mexico City and his own authority in the eyes of the colonial officers in California were preserved.

---

38. While Anza was at San Luis Obispo, Father Pedro Cambón arrived from Carmel to deliver a letter from Serra to Anza. Cambón probably told Cavaller of the reprimand Serra had received from the colegio. Pedro Font reported that Cavaller was in great spirits during Anza's stay at the mission. See Font, *With Anza to California*, 358.

PLATE Z. *Cómo los misioneros cruzan los ríos* (*How Missionaries Cross Rivers*), by Fr. Florián Paucke, SJ. This drawing by a Jesuit working in South America in the eighteenth century shows missionaries being transported by Indians in a manner similar to how Serra described his experience near Santa Bárbara in December 1776. *Courtesy of the Archive Library of the Cistercian Abbey, Zwettl, Austria.*

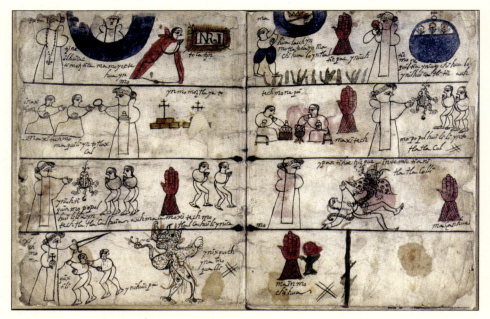

(Above) Plate aa. *Lord's Prayer in hieroglyphics. Christian missionaries used a variety of oral and visual methods to introduce their religion to indigenous peoples. This seventeenth-century pictograph employed Christian and Náhuatl symbolic and linguistic forms to convey the Lord's Prayer. Serra hoped that his conversations with Juan Evangelista would enable California missionaries to devise similar catechetical devices. From the Doctrina Cristiana, Egerton* ms *2898, fol. 1b. Museum Number: Am1962.03.213. © Trustees of the British Museum.*

(Opposite, top) Plate bb. *Mission San Gabriel in 1832, by Ferdinand Deppe. A series of disputes about the proper management of this mission during its first years resulted in serious tensions between Serra and military commander Pedro Fages. Courtesy of the Santa Bárbara Mission Archive-Library.*

(Opposite, bottom) Plate cc. *La Dolorosa (Our Lady of Sorrows). This is the painting whose subject struck many of the native peoples in the San Gabriel region as being similar to an important female figure in their own religion. Courtesy of the Braun Research Library, Autry National Center, Los Angeles. Photo 3.P.2.*

(Above) PLATE DD. *Mission San Carlos Borromeo del Río Carmelo, ca. 1899, by Edwin Deakin. This painting captures the isolation of the mission during the late nineteenth century. Courtesy of the Santa Bárbara Mission Archive-Library.*

(Right) PLATE EE. *The Flagellation of Hernán Cortés by Franciscan Friars. Seventeenth century. Ozumba Portería, Mexico. Serra used this story as a way of justifying the punishment of flogging for Indians who violated mission norms. Courtesy of Dr. Cristina Cruz González, Oklahoma State University.*

PLATE FF. Pictograph from Burro Flats in the Simi Hills, Los Angeles County. The Burro Flats rock art site has been attributed to Ventureño Chumash shamans. *Courtesy of Kathleen Conti, Director of Museum Programs, Research, and Resources for the Santa Ynez Band of Chumash Indians.*

(Opposite) PLATE GG. Pleito Creek: Chumash painted shelter facing east and Chumash painted shelter detail. *Photographs by and courtesy of Rick Bury.*

(Above) PLATE HH. *Santa Bárbara Presidio Chapel, 1855,* by James Madison Alden. After the founding of the Santa Bárbara Presidio in 1782, Serra assumed that a mission would immediately follow. But Neve refused to allow that, and Serra left the Santa Bárbara area very depressed and angry. *Courtesy of the Santa Bárbara Mission Archive-Library.*

PLATE II. *Junípero Serra recibe el Viático* (*Junípero Serra Receives the Viaticum*), 1785. This painting of Serra receiving Holy Communion shortly before his death, the "Viaticum," was done by Mexico City artist Mariano Guerrero. It was based on the description of the event contained in a letter by Francisco Palóu to the Colegio de San Fernando. *Courtesy of the Museo Nacional de Historia, Castillo de Chapultepec, and the Instituto Nacional de Antropología e Historia, Mexico City.*

CHAPTER 10

Mission among the Chumash

In the spring of 1779 Serra received word that Croix had approved the establishment of a presidio and three missions along the Santa Bárbara Channel. Coming in the midst of so many problems, this news was gratifying for him. The establishment of a mission beachhead along the channel had been a preoccupation of Serra's since 1770.

Indeed, a mere week and a half after the founding of Mission San Carlos, he said in a letter to Palóu that his next task would be "to establish the mission of San Buenaventura along the Santa Bárbara Channel. It is a section of greater value than San Diego or Monterey, or of the entire territory thus far discovered." In a letter written to the guardian of the Colegio de San Fernando the day before, Serra described the Santa Bárbara Channel as "full of a huge number (*numerísimos*) of formal pueblos, and a most wonderful (*provehidísma*) land." The two superlatives joined so closely together testified to the tremendous enthusiasm he developed at the prospect of evangelizing the area. At one point he told Portolá that he would be willing to remain alone at San Carlos if the other missionaries could be sent to the Santa Bárbara Channel.[1]

Where did Serra get this notion of Santa Bárbara's importance? Clearly it came from talking to his former student and fellow Mallorcan Juan Crespí, who accompanied the overland expedition from San Diego to San Francisco Bay in 1769. This expedition passed through Chumash territory twice during its journey, and Crespí interacted with many of the inhabitants.

Two aspects of Chumash society stood out in Crespí's mind: the character of the people and the orderly structure of their villages. He reported that the Chumash were quite hospitable to the expedition that was passing through their territory. He interpreted this hospitality as an indication that a concerted missionary effort might be richly rewarded. In a letter to José de Gálvez, Crespí

---

1. Serra, *Writings*, 1:178–79, 172–73; Geiger, "Spreading the News," 403.

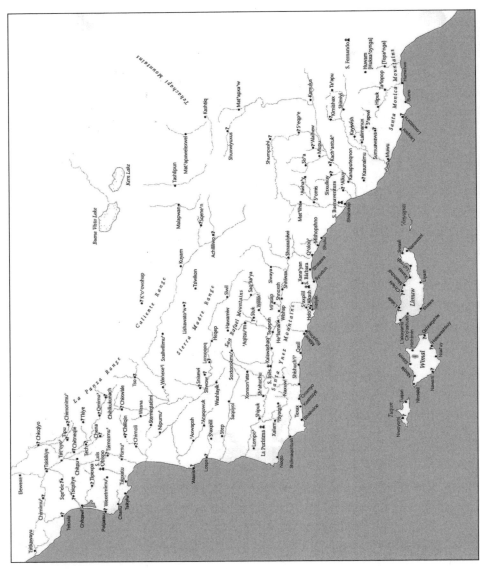

MAP 11. As Serra knew, the Chumash region was one of the most heavily populated along the Alta California coast. This map, based on the extensive research of John Johnson of the Santa Barbara Museum of Natural History, reconstructs Chumash settlements along the central coast area as they existed at the time of the Spanish incursion. *Courtesy of the Santa Barbara Museum of Natural History and the Archaeology and Ethnography Program of the National Park Service.*

reported that the Chumash would make a great point of approaching the expedition's two priests and would try to engage them in conversation "in an extremely friendly way." Crespí often commented on the affability and good humor of the native people he met. They greeted us, he wrote, "with uproar and laughter," creating a picture of a group that could hardly contain itself at the sight of the Spanish. Crespí described the people as "very gentle and friendly" and "very good people." Even Pedro Fages was affected by Crespí's enthusiasm. Fages was not a person to whom the words "mission" and "conversion" came easily, but he did write that "the docility and good disposition of the Indians give good reason for entertaining a moral certainty of their reduction as soon as the word of God is preached to them."[2]

Crespí was also very taken by the spatial arrangements of the Chumash settlements, especially how orderly they were. When he first reached Shisholop, which he called Asunción, he referred to it by the normal term "ranchería." But in an early revision of his journal, he called it the first "formal pueblo" on the channel. A bit later at Mishopshno, Crespí saw "thirty-eight very large round grass-roofed houses... some of them so large inside that they hold a vast number of families." Pedro Fages explicitly referred to this village as a "pueblo." When the expedition reached Syuxtun, the place that was to become Santa Bárbara, Crespí noted that "there is a very large number of gentiles at this spot; the villages we have been encountering are becoming larger every day.... These gentiles lived gathered into formal pueblos."[3]

The manner in which the Chumash lived in these well-laid-out pueblos also impressed Crespí. The expedition's soldiers gave the village of Mishopshno the name "The Carpenter's Shop" (La Carpintería), because they witnessed a *tomol* being constructed there. Crespí had already been impressed with these vessels: "Some canoes are quite long, about eight yards.... Two or three Indians with two or three paddles travel in each and when they wish, they make them go so that they seem to be flying through the water." He also noted the musical instruments the people had made. More than once he referred to the flutes and pipes as "very well-carved." He also noticed that a number of Chumash were very interested in the way his wooden rosary was carved. Crespí continually referred to the importance of music and dance in the lives of the people.[4]

Iberians long associated being engaged in domestic manufacturing and living in orderly pueblos with civilization and culture. Crespí, Serra, and Fages were saying that in their judgment the Chumash had already advanced considerably

---

2. Crespí, *A Description of Distant Roads*, 61, 414, 390; Fages, *A Historical, Political, and Natural Description of California*, 26.
3. Crespí, *A Description of Distant Roads*, 388, 406, 422; Fages, *A Historical, Political, and Natural Description of California*, 26.
4. Crespí, *A Description of Distant Roads*, 61, 403, 406, 422.

Mission among the Chumash

FIGURE 48. Chumash artifacts. *(Opposite, clockwise from top)* Olivella shell bead-making kit, Santa Rosa Island; serpentine bowl inlaid with olivella shell beads, unprovenanced Santa Barbara County, Phelan Collection. Chumash basket collected by navigator on whaling ship *Equator*, about 1819. *(Above)* Abalone and bone fishhooks from Santa Cruz Island. All photographs by George H. Huey. *Courtesy of the Santa Bárbara Museum of Natural History.*

toward that European model. For centuries a basic Christian missionary strategy had been to attempt to convert non-Christian societies by enticing the society's leaders to affiliate with the Church.[5] Serra quickly came to believe that the Chumash were the societal leaders of indigenous Alta California. For the rest of his life the Chumash were a primary object of his missionary concern.

Even during the mid-1770s, when much attention was being directed at the San Francisco Bay area and the rebuilding of San Diego, the Santa Bárbara Channel remained at the forefront of Serra's concerns. As we have seen, his original enthusiasm for Neve stemmed from his belief that the governor favored missions at Santa Bárbara.

For Serra the greatest validation of these opinions about the Chumash occurred in the incident with which we began this volume, his encounter with a friendly group of Chumash in December 1776. He reported the incident to the viceroy a few months later.

❋ *Serra to Antonio María de Bucareli y Ursúa, March 1, 1777*

On this, my third and most recent land journey along the Santa Bárbara Channel, strong winds, heavy rains, much mud, and rough, high seas did not

---

5. Fletcher, *The Barbarian Conversion*, 97–129.

allow us to set foot on the beach, which would have made for a shorter and easier walk. By their actions, those poor gentiles proved themselves worthy of receiving all that is good, which has taken so long to reach them. In the midst of my half-heartedness, tears came to my eyes when I saw how eager they were to help me. Since I could not travel on foot or on horseback, with one person on each side, they took hold of my arms and carried me over the muddy hills. I was not able to repay them for their efforts and their act of compassion, nor do I think I will ever be able to repay them as I would hope to do. When I was able to sing, a large number of them would happily join in and accompany me. When we stopped, I blessed those who had helped me and then a second group came over and asked me to bless them as well. A number of them accompanied us for many days. And for me, this served to deepen the compassion I have felt for them for quite some time.

But the Chumash region remained dangerous. The next year, writing to the Guardian about making another trip through the Channel area, Serra expressed both fear and determination.

❉ Serra to Rafael Verger, August 19, 1778

In addition, the way in which the Señor Gobernador has galvanized my resolve, the small undertaking of walking a span of more than two hundred leagues among gentiles with risks to my life, as well as other dangers I may encounter upon my return, will help keep me humble.

The idea of traveling through the Santa Bárbara Channel again causes my weakened flesh to tremble. But some day, the holy colegio will deem it more honorable to have martyrs there instead of missions. The truth is that I have always found the poor gentiles to be very loving. The greatest danger occurs when an unjust act on the part of the soldiers incites the gentiles, which has happened. Danger is always present at every turn. However, each journey through areas that are heavily populated by gentiles has been without incident. If this is not attributed to a miracle, then it is due to a very special form of Divine Providence.

He elaborated on this theme in another letter a few days later.

❉ Serra to Teodoro de Croix, August 22, 1778

I have sailed to these islands three different times and have had the pleasure of seeing some of their inhabitants. They would approach us in their canoes. Some would come aboard our boat. Their very pleasing behavior, their features, and their disposition made it that much more painful for me to see them lacking the light of the Holy Gospel.

On other occasions I have traveled along the coast of the mainland among thousands of its inhabitants. I have always found them to be very loving. One time, when the ground was so muddy (because shortly before it had rained heavily), since I could not travel on foot or on horseback, with one person on each side, they took hold of my arms and carried me a great distance until they could set me down on firmer ground.

Even though the Santa Bárbara establishments had been approved in 1779, they were not started until 1782. At the end of March of that year, Neve and Serra left San Gabriel together and headed for San Buenaventura. One day into the journey Neve was called back to Mission San Gabriel to confer with Pedro Fages about events along the Colorado River. Fages had just arrived at the mission.

Fages's reappearance in California did not surprise Serra. His removal from the position of military commander of Alta California did not put an end to his military career. It was quite the opposite. When word reached Madrid that Bucareli had removed Fages, the minister of the Indies, Julián de Arriaga asked José de Gálvez for his opinion. At that time, Gálvez was a counselor to the Council of the Indies. Gálvez responded that he strongly opposed Bucareli's move. At the very least, he said, the viceroy should have involved Fages's immediate superior, Governor of Las Californias Felipe de Barri, in the decision. Gálvez said that Fages was a very capable officer and, in his judgment, a better officer than Rivera y Moncada. Thus he should be appointed to an important position, such as commander of one of the frontier presidios.[6]

Fages himself spent the months after he arrived back in Mexico City composing an important report on California. When it was completed he was appointed commander of the Second Company of Catalán Volunteers in Guadalajara. In 1778 Fages and the Catalán volunteers were posted to the Real de los Alamos in Sonora, where they served in campaigns against the Seri Indians. Later that year Fages was appointed commander of the Santa Cruz Presidio in Sonora. In 1781 he was made commander of the presidio at El Pitic. When the Quechán rebellion occurred in July of that year, Fages was placed in charge of a military expedition to the Colorado River. José Antonio Romeu replaced Fages as commander of the expedition in early 1782, and Fages was instructed to go to California and convey orders to Neve about his participation in putting down the rebellion. He arrived in Alta California at Mission San Gabriel on March 26.[7]

---

6. Guest, *Fermín Francisco de Lasuén*, 79; Nuttall, "Light Cast upon Shadows," 254. Palóu, who had no way of knowing what Gálvez had said, thought that Fages had been given another command because Serra had written him a letter of recommendation: Palóu, *Palóu's Life of Fray Junípero Serra*, 272.
7. Rodríguez-Sala, *Los gobernadores de las Californias, 1767–1804*, 224–27.

FIGURE 49. *Mission San Buenaventura*, 1856, by Henry Ford Miller. Begun in 1782, it was the last mission Serra was able to found. *Courtesy of The Bancroft Library, University of California, Berkeley,* BANC PIC 1905.00006-B.

After Neve's departure for San Gabriel, Serra was allowed to continue toward San Buenaventura. Some soldiers went with him, while others were assigned to return to San Gabriel with Neve. Serra could not resist recording what he said was the reaction of the soldiers who were chosen to accompany him: "Those who were chosen to go with us for the founding were dancing with delight, not so much because of their devotion to the saint but more so because of their lack of devotion to another master."[8] Thus San Buenaventura was founded without Neve's presence. The senior military officer in attendance was Serra's old friend José Francisco de Ortega. The instructions in Neve's reglamento about new missions were not implemented, and Serra was able to proceed under the older system. He established Mission San Buenaventura at Shisholop in 1782 (on the spot he had reconnoitered ten years earlier). Serra described in two different letters, extracted below, the behavior of the local population as a final confirmation of his deep hopes for them.

❊ Serra to Francisco Pangua, July 17, 1782

We arrived at the site and carefully inspected it again. We prepared what was necessary, and on Easter Sunday (the day of the Resurrection of Our Lord

---

8. Serra to Francisco Pangua, July 17, 1782.

Jesus Christ), much to the delight of all who were present, the mission was founded with all of the customary ceremonial acts associated with such a solemn and glorious event.

A sheep was killed for us and for the officials to eat. A young bull from the Señor Gobernador's herd was killed for the rest of the people. The owner of the animals was not happy about the situation, but it was too late for him to do anything about it after the fact. There was nobody whom he could punish because they said I was to blame, which was true if blame were to be placed on anybody. I must tell you right away that the gentiles from the surrounding area showed us, by means of gestures, how pleased they were. And the site is excellent. It is the same one that was chosen ten years ago.

Serra to Fermín Francisco de Lasuén, March 31, 1782

Since the Lord Our God, by means of his creatures, has pushed us farther away, when I thought we would be getting closer, I found it necessary to spend Holy Week in gentile territory. Today He has been kind enough to grant me the consolation, after many years of longing, of witnessing the founding of the Holy Mission of Nuestro Seráfico Doctor San Buenaventura. And the same thing can be said of this founding as of the canonization of the saint: *Quo tardius, eo solemnius*.[9]

This took place on Easter Sunday. Present were all the officers, troops, and families who were assigned to this mission as well as to the presidio and Mission Santa Bárbara. Indians from La Asumpta, the ranchería nearby, were there with great pleasure. With all due formality, by means of interpreters, we asked them for their approval for our new establishment.

The blessing of the site and of a large cross, a sung Mass, a sermon, the formal taking possession of the land in name of the king, and the Te Deum—all were done in a very solemn manner. And as the saying goes, Vuestra Reverencia has another servant to whom you can give orders. But now, due to the recent events at the Colorado River, the other foundings will be suspended. If nothing changes, everyone will remain here with their provisions, etc., and I hope something will be accomplished here that could not be achieved easily elsewhere.

For Serra it was important that this first mission in the vicinity was being established with what he regarded as the permission of the local people. He believed that he had established a personal relationship with them as they carried

---

9. "The more slowly, the more solemnly."

him through the rain and mud in December 1776. He considered the establishment of San Buenaventura as the deepening of that bond. Even though he knew next to nothing about the deep spiritual tradition of the Chumash people, he believed their permission both gave a promise of future success and indicated that the people themselves were already advancing on the road to progress. In his mind, that is what made the Chumash so central for the evangelization of Alta California.

At the conclusion of his consultations with Fages, Neve went to San Buenaventura. He let matters stand there, but he was not about to countenance the establishment of what he considered another old-fashioned mission. The expedition then proceeded to Santa Bárbara, where the presidio was established. Serra assumed that a mission would soon follow. He described his first two weeks at Santa Bárbara enthusiastically in this letter to Teodoro de Croix.

※ *Serra to Teodoro de Croix, April 28, 1782*

So that this letter will not get longer and longer, I bring it to a close with the good news that on the 15th of this month I arrived at this place on the Santa Bárbara Channel (where I am now) with the Señor Gobernador and his troops. We spent considerable time deliberating on which site would be most appropriate for the founding and then discussed the other preparations. The following Sunday, which was the third Sunday after Easter and the feast day of the patron saint the Most Holy Patriarch San José, this mission-presidio (for now, they are one entity) of the Blessed Virgin and Martyr Santa Bárbara was founded with all of the customary formality surrounding the placement and blessing of the tall cross, the blessing of the ground, and the first Mass and sermon.

May God allow us to see the mission-presidio grow with increasing numbers of Christians as we now see it surrounded and frequently visited by so many gentiles.

He offered additional details in another letter the next day.

※ *Serra to Fermín Francisco de Lasuén, April 29, 1782*

On the feast day of San José, we raised the cross and blessed it. The ground was blessed, the first Mass was celebrated (with a sermon), and the mission-presidio of Santa Bárbara, Virgen y Mártir, was founded in the land of Yamnonalit. I was alone and I still am alone, and that is why it was a low Mass. Instead of the Te Deum, we sang the Alabado, which is equivalent to the Laudamus. May God bless this place. Amen.

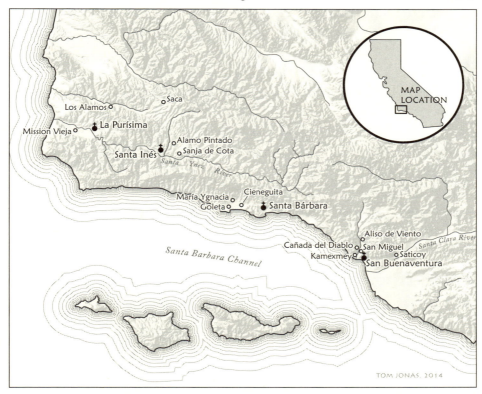

MAP 12. Spanish and indigenous communities of the Santa Bárbara region in the nineteenth century. In comparison with map 11, the large number of Chumash communities had been greatly reduced. *Map by Tom Jonas.*

He signed his first letters from there as being from the "Mission-Presidio of Santa Bárbara."[10] However, after a bit more time Neve made it crystal clear that the mission would not be founded, so Serra left for Carmel. He was bitter. After so many years of hardships and frustrations, he felt that the establishment of San Buenaventura meant that he had finally found his footing again. That made Neve's refusal to allow the founding of the mission at Santa Bárbara even more irritating to Serra. San Buenaventura was the last mission Serra founded, but the whole experience left a very sour taste in his mouth.

---

10. Serra, *Writings*, 4:123, 134, 141.

✳ *Serra to Francisco Pangua, July 17, 1782*

On the same day that I left, the 15th, the Señor Gobernador and I arrived at the site that Su Señoría had chosen for the presidio of Santa Bárbara. In my humble opinion, this site is not good for a presidio or for a mission.

I am not in the mood to describe the calamity surrounding the founding of the mission, and what I saw and heard during the three weeks that I stayed at the site. I witnessed the Señor Gobernador acting as a missionary. He said that we do not have the expertise for this, and he promised Father Cambón that he would provide him with a method for how to be a missionary.

Neve was referring to what he did at San Gabriel in 1781. To prepare for the founding of Los Angeles he engaged in systematic diplomacy with the Tongva people, especially those in the village of Yabit or Yangna. During the spring of that year the governor was the godfather at the baptisms of a dozen Tongva, most of whom were given "de Neve" as part of their Christian names. Two were even called Felipe and Felipa.[11] So at Santa Bárbara, Neve was telling Serra that in his opinion what he accomplished at San Gabriel provided a model for future conversions. California natives would be attracted to the Gospel through contact with soldiers and settlers, not necessarily with missionaries. Neve had a way of getting under Serra's skin, and he knew it. He undoubtedly intended to irritate Serra with his comment regarding how happy he would be to teach the Franciscans how to be real missionaries. He succeeded.

---

11. San Gabriel baptisms 00589, 00634–00641, 00726, and 00732–00733.

CHAPTER 11

Final Years

Serra's last years were extremely trying ones for him. Palóu remembered, "Two years before he died, he was dismayed that the conquest was going so slowly, and that those who should have given him every encouragement and support did just the opposite, retarding and even hurting the missions in both a spiritual and temporal way." For, in addition to the difficulties he experienced in trying to found a number of missions along the Santa Bárbara Channel, he dealt with what seemed to be a continuous series of political, religious, and personal problems.[1]

Politics

On September 4, 1782, Neve and Fages both received word that Neve had been appointed inspector general, the second-highest position in the Provincias Internas. The next year Neve was appointed comandante general of the Provincias Internas, replacing Croix, who was promoted to the position of viceroy of Peru and entrusted with the difficult task of dealing with the aftermath of the Tupac Amarú rebellion. Neve, however, died a year and a half after assuming his new position.[2]

Neve's successor as governor was Pedro Fages. This appointment brought Serra full circle. Even though he had written a somewhat gracious letter of recommendation for Fages when he left Alta California in 1774, both men knew that Serra was responsible for Fages's removal as military commander of Alta California in 1773. Neve and Fages had spent a good amount of time together over the recent months. In the hurried instructions that Neve left for Fages before taking their leave of one another, Neve said that the two of them had talked extensively about the governor's relations with the president of the missions, and he urged Fages "to follow the same procedure I have used" regarding relations with Serra and the missionaries.[3]

---
1. Palóu, *Palóu's Life of Fray Junípero Serra*, 266.
2. Campbell, *Military and Society in Colonial Peru*, 154.
3. Beilharz, *Felipe de Neve*, 171.

We do not know much about the actual relationship between Fages and Serra during the almost two years that Fages was governor while Serra was still alive. However, in 1783 Fages wrote Neve two letters in which he expressed negative opinions of various activities in which Serra was engaged. It is reasonable to assume that the hostility between the two men persisted, although relations may have been civil on the surface.[4]

Religion

Rome also contributed to Serra's religious anxieties. In 1779 the Vatican created the diocese of Sonora, which consisted of Sonora, Sinaloa, and both Californias. The next year a Franciscan from the colegio at Querétaro, Antonio de los Reyes, was appointed bishop. Reyes proposed to organize his diocese into four *custodias*, that is, incipient Franciscan provinces. Members of these custodias were to be recruited from various Franciscan institutions in Spain and America. Under this plan, Alta California would be reorganized as the Custodia de San Gabriel and would be jointly staffed by Franciscans from the Province of Michoacán and the Colegio de San Fernando. The custodia arrangement would have ended the unique relationship between the colegios apostólicos and the mission territories. In addition, priests were to be recruited from a variety of locations and were to be responsible directly to a custodian and, through him, to a bishop. The preeminent role that the Colegio de San Fernando had played in Alta California would have ended.[5]

Reyes's plan for his diocese was as impractical as the plans Gálvez proposed for Baja California in 1768. The custodia arrangement never even came close to being implemented due to lack of manpower and the lack of agreement from the colegios that were currently providing the personnel for the new diocese. The idea was formally dropped in the late 1780s.

For Serra even the prospect of such an arrangement was difficult to stomach. It would have meant that the future of the missions he spent so much energy in founding was to be taken away from him and his successors and directed by someone who, in his judgment, had little understanding of the practicalities of life in Alta California. It did not help that as Reyes was proposing the custodia arrangement, he also criticized in various documents the work of the colegios apostólicos on the northern frontier. For Serra the potential custodia arrangement was an ecclesiastical version of the Provincias Internas. The custodias threatened to disrupt long-standing relationships and throw the future of his mission

---

4. Geiger, *Life and Times of Fray Junípero Serra*, 2:330.
5. García, "América en la legislación general," 675–89.

enterprise into radical doubt. While this arrangement never really took hold, and disintegrated after Serra's death, its possibility was an enormous concern for him.[6]

Also, rumors were circulating that the Franciscans were going to be expelled from Alta California, just as the Jesuits had been expelled from Baja California. Although nothing came of these rumors, they caused Serra great anxiety during his last year of life. Along with the possibility of this new arrangement, rumors began to circulate that perhaps Reyes would want the Dominicans who were currently in Baja California to take over the missions in Alta California. Like the custodia arrangement, this idea never came to pass but it certainly increased Serra's level of anxiety. In the twilight of his life he was facing challenges that in his opinion had the potential to undermine what he had accomplished in California.[7]

Fellow Missionaries

Also, things were not going well with his fellow religious. Some were depressed, some were upset with him, and some, his oldest companions, were dying. Serra was not the only Franciscan in Alta California who experienced crises related to religious values and institutions. In the midst of his correspondence with Lasuén about the alcalde election issue, Serra wrote another letter to San Diego. This was a more personal letter to the other missionary there, Juan Figuer, who had written Serra a few weeks earlier apparently in a state of despondency and depression about his work at San Diego. Figuer was from Aragón and had come to the New World in 1770. He was first stationed in Baja California and was sent to Alta California at the end of 1772 to staff the projected mission of San Buenaventura. When Fages refused to allow the establishment of that mission, Figuer was sent first to San Gabriel and then to San Luis Obispo. He was assigned to San Diego in 1777 and would remain there until his death at the age of forty-two in 1784. The difficulties involved in rebuilding the church, coping with the constant possibility of additional Kumeyaay attacks, and dealing with Neve's insistence on the installation of Indian alcaldes took a toll on Figuer, and he told Serra that he wished to leave California and return to the colegio in Mexico City. Serra assured Figuer that other missions in Alta California were experiencing similar difficulties, and he pointed to recent flooding at Santa Clara as an example. He encouraged Figuer not to let himself be so overwhelmed by his problems that he would be unable to appreciate the successes San Diego had realized since he and Lasuén had arrived there.

The tone of Serra's letter was one of understanding and patience as he urged Figuer to persist in his efforts. That Serra was able to write such a tender and

---

6. Stagg, *The First Bishop of Sonora*, 72–88.
7. Geiger, *Life and Times of Fray Junípero Serra*, 2:367–74.

heartfelt letter undoubtedly stemmed from the fact that over the past few years he himself had experienced great spells of despondency and uncertainty about the future of the missionary enterprise in Alta California.

❋ Serra to Juan Figuer, March 30, 1779

When I placed Vuestra Reverencia's letter of March 8 in front of me to answer it, the first thing that came to mind was a story I read years ago in a Spanish anthology.

One of our communities had begun matins,[8] and shortly after they began, a friar went over to the guardian and said, "Padre, may I have permission to retire to my cell because I find that my heart is not in this." The prelate responded, "Brother, for God's sake stay in your place. I can assure you that if every person in the choir whose heart was not in it were to leave, there would be no matins, because everybody would leave. And I would be the first one to go."

This anecdote should not be taken literally, but rather as a metaphor, for I believe it is quite analogous to our case. Vuestra Reverencia tells me that up until now, staying at that mission has been unbearable for you. And if the new positions are ushered in, this will be intolerable for you. For that reason you seek permission to retire to your cell.

With regard to the second point, as of yet Vuestra Reverencia has no experience. And perhaps (I am trusting in God) with what I have said about the matter in my letter to my dear Padre Lasuén, there will be no difficulty whatsoever. What is currently distressing to Vuestra Reverencia are the shortages at that mission, the problems with the presidio, and the fear of an Indian uprising.

It is true that with regard to the presidio, there is no comparison between what you are experiencing and what is happening here [Monterey], in San Francisco, or in Santa Clara with its neighboring pueblo. On that particular point I can assure Vuestra Reverencia that everything ends up like that, to say the least.

A few days ago the Señor Gobernador was talking to me about the new presidio that is going to be founded in the Santa Bárbara Channel area. I told him that my greatest concern had to do with the religious who were to be assigned to the mission in that vicinity that was named for the saint. I assumed, of course, that the annoyances, insolence, and scandalous behavior of the troops would be the same (if not worse) as what has been experienced

---

8. A part of the Divine Office, prayed at night.

at the other missions situated close to a presidio. This mission, San Carlos, is at the top of the list. In terms of the new government, the fears you have are quite similar to what has become a reality here at this mission.

In terms of shortages of food and other necessities, not only am I aware of the situation and recognize that San Diego is by far the worst, but I have also spoken and written about it to the colegio, the Señor Virrey, the governor, and anybody else I could talk to about these missions. I also acknowledge that the temporal work conducted by those training for the ministry cannot compare to what is being done at San Diego. Undoubtedly, Vuestra Reverencia must have heard the following question bandied about: "Which is harder—to feel like eating when you have nothing to eat, or to have a lot to eat when you do not feel like eating?"

That is the situation faced by Santa Clara and San Francisco. When they had nothing to eat, they blamed the shortage of food for their not being able to perform the wonders of conversion and baptism. And now that they have food, there is nobody to eat it. And at Santa Clara, in addition to that, the river they idolized (*ut ita dicam*)[9] has flooded, which forced Padre Peña to flee with the children, taking whatever effects they could, to a place called El Roblar, which is one-fourth of a league away. Padre Murguía has remained behind at the muddied site, which he did not think was so bad, in order to avoid having to stretch the limited provisions. The people in the pueblo, whom they serve all year long, have refused to provide them with an escort.

He resorted to asking the Señor Gobernador for the escort. He tells me that even if they do not provide him with one, he will stay there alone. They only have one chalice, and if one person is saying Mass, the other person is without a chalice. Poor Peña, he is constructing his huts there; and the worst thing is that they are convinced and have acknowledged that it is necessary to change the mission site. But they still do not have a location.

That fact is that there are difficulties everywhere, be they great or small. And your mission, which has more than its share, does have an element of success that is unequaled by any other mission, which is the many souls it has added and continues to add to the fellowship of Our Holy Mother Church. Because it completely slipped my mind to say this in my letter to Padre Lasuén, who informed me about the number of newly baptized, I must now extend a thousand congratulations to both of you. In addition to this, while dealing with your own poverty, you earned a wealth of merits when you assisted those poor starving people who were in dire need of food. Your

---

9. As I would call it.

actions distinguish you from others who have full granaries, which is what Christ, Our Life, said to the widow who came and tossed in two small copper coins, that were worth a penny.

And so, my friend, we shall continue with our matins until the final prayer, *Sacrosanctae*,[10] when we will pray that He who sends or allows these hardships will also provide us with as much patience as is needed. Where does the ox that does not plow go? He goes to the butcher. Perhaps some who left for similar reasons would now happily resume the work they gave up back then because it frustrated them. Or at least it would have been better for them if they had not left.

If I were to speak about the beauty of hardships it would not be a proof of my ability to speak with authority or eloquently on this topic, because much has been written about it. All that is needed is to read a bit from San Buenaventura's book or library on the crucified Christ.[11] But I will repeat what another has said: "*Predicatoribus non est praedicandum*, etc."[12]

But seeing how successful you have been in winning souls for God, is it possible that you would want to turn back and slow down this enterprise without showing any concern for who best could take your place, or concern for what is gained and what is lost, and to just leave things as they are?

I have belabored this point because Vuestra Reverencia has informed me that this is the third time you have asked me for permission to retire, and for the same reason. I have come to the conclusion that if what I have said has *no impact*, then: *Salvetur sacro-sancta libertas!*[13]

Our laws do not put Vuestra Reverencia under any obligation to do more. Vuestra Reverencia, see if you recognize some part of yourself in this saying by San Pablo: *Charitas Dei urget nos*.[14] You may not be bound by justice, but you are by charity.

Vuestra Reverencia, for the love of God, stay and work with those poor people for as long as God gives you strength. He will not fail to help you with His holy grace. After you reflect on this in a very calm and mature manner, please let me know what you have decided to do. Rest assured that you are speaking with someone who thinks highly of you and whose only desire is for your well-being and consolation. I pray that God keep Vuestra Reverencia many years in good health and in His holy grace.

---

10. A prayer usually said at the conclusion of any part of the Divine Office, such as matins.
11. San Buenaventura had a great devotion to Christ crucified. See Delio, *Crucified Love*.
12. One should not preach to preachers.
13. May your most holy freedom be preserved.
14. The love of Christ urges us on (2 Corinthians 5:14).

The Padres who are my companions want to be remembered to you with deep affection.

From this mission, San Carlos de Monterey, March 30, 1779.
Your dear friend and servant kisses the hand of Vuestra Reverencia,
Fray Junípero Serra

Even the successful founding of San Buenaventura presented Serra with some thorny issues relating to his religious community. Staffing the mission proved no easy matter. In 1781 the Colegio de San Fernando decided to suspend sending men to Alta California as a protest against Neve's reglamento.[15] As a result, when Serra was allowed to start San Buenaventura he did not have fresh missionaries to assign to it and thus had to scour around. He was not happy with the result and wrote Pangua to complain.

✳ *Serra to Francisco Pangua, July 17, 1782*

I was hoping that with the new priests, the spiritual and temporal nature of the mission would have developed very much to my expectations. They have not arrived, and I have had to assign others there since there were no new priests. I had hoped for much gentler men. *Sit nomen Domini benedictum.*[16]

The two men whom Serra unwillingly sent to San Buenaventura were Francisco Dumetz and Vicente de Santa María. Dumetz arrived in California in 1771 and was sent to San Diego. The very next year Serra removed him from there. He reported to the guardian, "I found by letters I received that it was advisable to move Padre Dumetz to another mission." Serra never said why. Serra assigned Dumetz to Mission San Carlos but never really involved him very much in the affairs of the mission. Dumetz was usually given auxiliary tasks such as saying Mass at the presidio or going to Baja California to pick up various items and bring them north.[17]

Santa María came to Alta California as a ship chaplain in 1775 aboard the *San Carlos* when it entered San Francisco Bay. He returned to California the next year, and Serra asked him to staff San Diego during the reconstruction after the Kumeyaay revolt. The following letter presents Serra's account of the priest's response.

✳ *Serra to Francisco Pangua, February 26, 1777*

I went to his [Santa María's] room with Padre Fuster, and put before him the plan that he should be a companion of the Padre and minister of that mission

---
15. Geiger, *Life and Times of Fray Junípero Serra*, 2:292.
16. Blessed be the name of the Lord (Psalm 113:2).
17. Geiger, *Franciscan Missionaries*, 66–68; Serra, *Writings*, 1:253, 2:427.

[San Diego]. He got so red in the face, as if I had insulted him. He answered that he regretted that he had been asked at so late a date; that he could have gone to San Francisco and continued on with his chaplaincy . . . that all his belongings were in San Gabriel, and that he was handed a mission that nobody else had any use for. . . . Seeing that he did not yield an inch, I left him and went on with my work. The Padre refused to speak to me anymore.

Santa María ended up at San Francisco, where Francisco Palóu agreed to have him, even though Serra called him "superfluous" and "difficult to manage."[18] Serra was not happy with having to put Dumetz and Santa María at San Buenaventura. When two new missionaries did arrive in 1783, Serra assigned them to San Buenaventura in place of the two who were there. Both Dumetz and Santa María wrote to Mexico City protesting this move. In a letter to the guardian, Serra just threw up his hands.

※ *Serra to Juan Sancho, October 27, 1783*

I know very well that the two priests from San Buenaventura have written to you. They are speculating about the damage to their reputation and are distressed that they might be moved. But if Padre Dumetz is to remain here, I have already said that I will not be responsible for that mission or for whatever that priest feels like spending. Nor will I answer the complaints that will arise from the other missions when those other two priests take charge of them, whether those missions like it or not.

As it turned out, Dumetz and Santa María remained together at San Buenaventura for fifteen years. In fact, Santa María remained there until his death in 1806. Dumetz served at San Fernando Rey and San Gabriel until his passing in 1811.

Personal losses compounded Serra's concerns about the state of his religious community. At the end of 1781 Juan Crespí fell ill.

※ *Serra to Francisco Pangua, July 17, 1782*

Padre Fray Juan admitted that he was very tired. And with each day the tightening in his chest got worse, as did the swelling of his feet, which kept moving up his legs, despite all the remedies from the *Florilegeum*[19] that could be applied. Before Christmas he had to be confined to his bed. After

---

18. Serra, *Writings*, 3:317.
19. In general, this term referred to early modern anthologies of botanical illustrations of plants used in cooking and medicine. The volume to which Serra was referring was probably *Florilegio medicinal de todas las enfermedades*, a 1712 volume by Juan de Esteynefer, a Jesuit missionary in northern New Spain.

receiving the Holy Sacraments of Penance, Viaticum, and Extreme Unction, on January 1 of this year, at about six o'clock in the morning, he surrendered his soul to its creator. We buried him the following day.

On January 2, 1782, Serra sadly placed the following notation in the Carmel burial register.

> On January 2, 1782, in the church of this mission, San Carlos de Monterey, I performed the ecclesiastical burial of the body of Padre Predicador Fray Juan Crespí near the high altar on the Gospel side. This was preceded by a vigil and a Requiem Mass, sung with the body present, with all of the rituals that our manual prescribes for the burial of religious.
>
> Fray Crespí was the minister of this mission since its founding, as noted on the front page of this burial record book, as well as in other administrative record books. He was a son of the Holy Province of Mallorca. He longed to convert the infidels and left Mallorca in the year 1749, with an official letter granting him permission to join the Propaganda Fide missionaries at the Colegio Apostólico de San Fernando in Mexico. He arrived there at the beginning of the following year.
>
> He died at about six o'clock in the morning on January 1, the Feast of the Circumcision of Christ and of the Sweet Name of Jesus, after receiving the Holy Sacraments of Penance, the Eucharist, and Extreme Unction and in the presence of his companions from the same province. His death was that of a true religious. He was sixty years and ten months old to the day. He lived as a religious for forty-four years, minus three days. And he worked as a missionary among the infidels of the Sierra Gorda, California, and Monterey for thirty years. And so that it will be on record, I, who was his former professor and in the end, his companion of many years, sign this burial record.
>
> Fray Junípero Serra

In the midst of these difficulties Serra took refuge by undertaking a long confirmation journey in 1783. As we suggested earlier, for him the administration of the sacrament of confirmation was a way of getting out from under various administrative duties and circumstances that he could find suffocating at times. The custodia threat was one such circumstance. Also, the permission to administer confirmation was granted by the Vatican in 1774 for a ten-year period—it was due to expire on July 10, 1784. This confirmation journey would be Serra's last, and he desperately wanted to make it.

He started by administering confirmations at Carmel in June 1783. Then he set sail to Santa Bárbara, from where he traveled overland to San Buenaventura for more confirmations. He then sailed on to San Diego, where he remained for a month. Next he went to San Juan Capistrano, where he confirmed 221 people in a grueling three-day stint. Then he traveled to San Gabriel. By this time Serra's health was poor, and he remained there for three weeks, during which he confirmed another 233 people. He then headed north and confirmed once again at San Buenaventura, San Luis Obispo, and San Antonio. Arriving at Carmel in December he engaged in a final round of confirmations.[20]

This was an extremely tiring journey for Serra. Confirmation was a major liturgical event at each mission, and virtually the entire community would participate. In this journey Serra personally encountered the overwhelming majority of all the baptized indigenous people in Alta California. These people were the reason he left his homeland. Seeing these people undoubtedly provided Serra with an emotional validation of the choice he made to go to the Americas thirty-five years earlier.

Final Report

When he returned to Carmel at the end of this tiring confirmation journey, he supervised the completion of a long report on the history of Mission San Carlos. It was signed by him and the other priest in residence, Matías Antonio Noriega. Since Noriega had only been at San Carlos for two years, the report was basically the work of Serra. It represented his final and retrospective assessment of what he and his fellow missionaries had accomplished during the thirteen years they had lived in the Monterey Bay region.

The report began with a year-by-year narrative of the gradual growth of the mission complex. The climax of the document was the final section, which summarized the year 1783. Here Serra reflected on how he had been able to place Mission San Carlos on a solid footing in the face of constant obstacles. Most of the report concentrated on the material culture of the mission, such as the amount of crops harvested, methods of clearing and irrigating the lands, the pace of building construction, and the amount of livestock at the mission's disposal. Serra also spent a good amount of time on the economics of mission administration. His consistent point was that the mission surplus was directed toward the benefit of the soldiers at the presidio. He insisted that the mission had paid its full share of the contribution the government requested to support Spain's war against England. (Spain was an ally of the United States during the American Revolution. Serra, however, never referred to the British colonies on the Atlantic

---

20. Geiger, *Life and Times of Fray Junípero Serra*, 2:337.

coast of North America. Rather, he always spoke of Spain's conflict against England.) Given the contributions the missions were making to the welfare of the province, he resented that they were being charged for mail delivery. Finally he insisted, as many of his successors would do over the next half century, that whatever funds the missions might have left over from all of this work ought to be consistently targeted to the welfare of the indigenous converts at the missions.

The thoroughness with which he was able to describe the material and spiritual culture of the mission must have been deeply satisfying to him, but he did not sentimentalize it. He proudly painted a picture of many native people living and working at San Carlos, yet was specifically aware that other indigenous people were not happy at the mission and continued to leave it.

Report on the Mission

The Year 1783

This can be considered the happiest year for the mission because the number of baptisms was 175 and the number of marriages was 36.

The seeds that were sown amounted to 84 fanegas and 8 almuds. This included 1½ fanegas of wheat, ½ a fanega of corn, and 2 almuds of beans which were sown for the Baja California Indians who settled here and were married at this mission.

The harvest, minus what belonged to these Indians, which was 47 fanegas, as well as some of the crops that were given to the people, such as a portion of the barley crop which they could reap for themselves, and about 20 fanegas of wheat from the threshing of the chaff, that was stored in the mission granary amounted to 2,613½ fanegas. The measure of barley was 670 fanegas, 835 of wheat, and according to our calculations only 200 fanegas are kept with the spikes covering the kernels. According to our calculations there were 971 fanegas of both types of corn, 63 fanegas of chick-peas, 4 fanegas of lentils, and 53 fanegas of various types of beans.

Of the seeds of new Christianity that have been sown at this mission, we have sustained and continue to sustain without any shortages, as of today, 614 living persons, although some are in the habit of going off on their own for a period of time. We have supplied the *habilitado* of the Royal Presidio of San Carlos with 130 fanegas of corn because that is all they asked for, and also 30 fanegas of beans. The *alférez habilitado* requested a ration of two types of grain for the escort of this mission. There have been no further distributions of any consequence, therefore, in our sound judgment, of the two principal grains, wheat and corn, about half of the harvest still remains.

The cost of the food supplied to the presidio has already been paid for in cloth with which the Indians who worked the fields now clothe themselves. But even with that, it still distresses us to see so much nudity among them.

We no longer acquire any clothing from the soldiers like we used to, not even from those who are in debt to us, no matter how small it may be. At some missions there is already quite enough sheep's wool to cover nakedness. But up until now it has not been of any help to us here because so many sheep are stolen. For more than three years our stock of sheep and goats has not exceeded 200 head. And what we do get from shearing the few sheep we have is of little value.

And so, as of today, the state of this mission in terms of spiritual labors, consists of the following:

Baptisms	1006
Confirmations at the same mission	936
And since in some way what is accomplished at all of the other missions also pertains to this missions, it is noted in passing that their number, as of today, is	5307
Marriages at this mission	259
Burials	356

The number of Christian families, all living under the bell and eating as a community, as well as widowers, single men, and children of both sexes, is not included here because it is recorded on the enclosed census. They pray twice a day with the priest in the church. More than 120 make their confession in Spanish, and many who have died would do so equally well. Others do the best they can. They do all types of work at the mission. They tend the herds and groom the animals and work as shepherds, milkers, diggers, gardeners, carpenters, and field laborers. They water and harvest the crops. They work as blacksmiths and sacristans, and any other jobs for which they can be of service and which will have a positive impact on their physical and spiritual well-being.

The work of cleaning the fields every year, sometimes two or three times, is considerable because it is very fertile land. Whenever new land is cleared, it is exhausting work. All in all there is enough cleared land that is ready for planting more than 100 fanegas of wheat, which is parceled into areas for wheat, barley, vegetables, and corn. Each year something new is added.

It took seven months' of work to take water from the river to irrigate the fields, as mentioned above. Added to that was the work involved in channeling the water to the lagoon, which is right next to the mission residence. The lagoon would be dry some years, but now it is always filled, which is a great convenience for the mission as well as being pleasing. Because the water is channeled into the lagoon, salmon have begun to appear there, so now we have that fish at home.

The palisade of timbers that was placed around the sown land to protect it proved to be inadequate because the timbers are stolen for firewood. Therefore we dug a defensive wall or circular ditch, thousands of varas long. It took two years to complete, but even that is not enough to prevent losses each year.

Some sections of the land that has been prepared for planting were entangled not only with large grasses and dense bushes but also with large trees, willows, alders, etc., but it has been worth the effort. There is also a large, walled garden with abundant vegetables and some fruit.

During the first years we worked hard on the church and other buildings, which were palisade structures with flat earthen roofs to minimize the fire danger. But no matter what we did, the roofs always leaked like a sieve. That, in addition to the humidity, caused everything to rot, so we decided to build with adobe. And that is what all the buildings are made of today, for example:

An adobe church, forty varas long by eight varas wide, with a thatched roof.

Idem: three rooms made of adobe, which are the living quarters for the three priests. One room is larger and has its own bedroom. Flat earthen floor and a thatched roof.

Idem: a granary, about 20 varas long with various compartments for grains, a *tepanco*,[21] and a thatched roof.

Idem: another granary, 30 varas long with its portico, four windows with grillwork made from beams, flat earthen floor, and a thatched roof on top.

Idem: another adobe house, 30 varas long, divided for now into three rooms—one serves as an office; the one at the opposite end is the bedroom for the girls; and the one in the middle is a large sitting room with two barred windows and doors. The room is whitewashed and clean and serves as lodging for the ships' officers and for other gatherings. It is ready to be divided into two rooms, and the two doors already have their hinges attached.

Idem: another adobe building with an earthen roof and with its roof and key that serves as a forge on which the blacksmith works. It has a corridor and a window.

---

21. A porch.

Idem: next to this building is another, which we call the carpenter shop. It has a room with a door and key (in addition to the main door) to better safeguard the tools. It has two windows with bars and doors.

Idem: another building next to the ones just mentioned where the women do grinding, they make cheese, and other items are kept there.

Idem: another building, more spacious than the others, where the Mexican blacksmith's family lives for now.

Idem: four other adobe buildings that serve as a storage room for shotguns, storage for firewood, a kitchen, and a henhouse.

There is also an adequate adobe corral with sections for sheep and goats and next to this a separate pen for pigs. The corrals for horses and cattle, with their respective stud and bull pens, are all palisades. When repairs are needed, it involves quite a bit of work.

The total number of livestock, small and large, as of today is:

Cattle	500
Sheep and goats, about half of each species	220
Mules, draft and riding	018
Horses, tame and broken	020
Four herds of mares, with their colts	090
and among them are two young mules from when we had a donkey	
An old she-donkey, they say she is pregnant	001
Pigs that can be found	025

With regard to the other aspects of the state of the mission, when the ships arrive with the supplies from Mexico, we usually find out if we have enough money or if we owe something from our sínodos. The ship has not arrived yet so we do not have that information.

We do not know if the mission owes anything here, but some unknown or forgotten debt could appear, as some have in the past.

This mission paid Lieutenant Ortega eighteen pesos for a tent that he obtained on credit from the royal warehouse for the Padre Presidente to use while he was at Mission San Buenaventura for the founding of the new presidio of Santa Bárbara. He did not think such a debt existed until they came to collect.

This mission recently paid fifteen pesos as a donation for the war, which ended more than a year ago, based on a sinister report that was given to the *Comandancia General*, which stated that after the lists had been prepared, the Padre Presidente lowered the numbers to account for some Indians who had run away from the mission. It did not happen that way. When the lists were prepared, some had been in the state of apostasy for two and even three years. The only reason this was mentioned was so they would go and bring them back to the mission for me.

After the lists were prepared it did not occur to us to lower the numbers at all or even mention those who had run away or who had died. But in the end we paid the other fifteen pesos, and thus the total donation amounted to more than one hundred pesos, which is what they recently requested. At the beginning of the year, when the Señor Gobernador showed me these reports, inventories, and census lists for the missions which would be sent to the Comandancia General, I responded that I would be happy to take care of this, since the Reverendo Padre Guardián of our holy colegio had also ordered me to do this.

But it had to be under the condition that we would not have to pay the postage for the sealed documents and letters that would accompany them. For, if a letter I had just received from the Señor Comandante General, which had fewer pages than any of these reports would have, came with a note stating that it cost 11 reales to send, how much would all of those papers cost us?

His response to me was yes, there would be no fee. In fact, the alférez always encouraged me to accept the letters, saying that, even though there was a number written down, that number was for other accounts, and I did not have to pay it. Knowing that, I could proceed with the peace of mind and certainty that I would not have to pay for the sealed document that came from San Gabriel entitled "Reports, Inventories, and Census from Mission San Gabriel" even though attached was a note stating that it cost 20 reales. I kept that note, just in case I might need it.

That being said, a few days ago we received a bill from the quartermaster:

"Idem: 29 pesos, 2 reales for letters sent to the mission." They charged us and collected. There was nothing more we could do except hope that some other unexpected debt, of which I have no knowledge, does not appear.

What we usually receive annually, which is purchased with the money collected in Mexico by our sínodos, is already known. After paying for our clothing, chocolate, wine, candles for Mass, and some other small object for the church, the rest is used for the benefit of the Indians, most of it on clothing to cover them up. And it seems to us, this is all that needs to be said with regard to this matter.

If there is any other information needed regarding the administration and state of the mission, you may question us directly with the assurance that we have nothing to hide from you. Because God is benevolent, we do not abhor the light. What has been stated here is true, and for the record, we, the ministers of this mission, sign this document, July 1, 1784.

Fray Junípero Serra
Fray Matías Antonio de Santa Catalina Noriega

At the end of April 1784 Serra went to Santa Clara to participate in the dedication ceremony for the new church. His old compatriot José Murguía had supervised the construction. The church was not quite ready, so he administered some confirmations there and then went to San Francisco, where he confirmed again. While Serra was at San Francisco, Murguía died. His death was as difficult for Serra as the death of Crespí had been three years earlier. Murguía was already ministering in the Sierra Gorda when Serra arrived there in 1750, and he was one of the priests who accompanied Serra to Baja California. He then came with Palóu to Alta California in 1773 and stayed at Mission San Carlos with Serra for three years. Murguía was one of the two founders of Mission Santa Clara in 1777. Serra wrote a personal letter to all of the California missionaries about his death.

※ *Letter to the Ministers of San Carlos and other missions, May 11, 1784*

Muy Reverendos Padres Ministros of the following missions, San Carlos, San Antonio, San Luis Obispo, San Buenaventura, San Gabriel, San Juan Capistrano, San Diego
Dearest Padres who are my companions,

May the peace and grace of our Lord Jesus Christ be with Vuestras Reverencias. Amen.

I am obliged out of duty and brotherly love to share some news with Vuestras Reverencias, which will be especially sad for everyone. On this very day, at a quarter past nine in the morning, at the mission of Nuestra Madre Seráfica Santa Clara, Our Lord God deemed this the moment to receive for Himself the soul of Reverendo Padre Predicador Fray José Antonio de Murguía, who had received the Holy Sacraments of Penance, Eucharist, and Extreme Unction. Padres Fray Francisco Palóu and his cominister, Fray Tomás de la Peña, were present. He died in the manner of a true religious and of a devoted son of Nuestro Padre Seráfico San Francisco.

I left Mission Santa Clara on the 4th of this month to come here [San Francisco]. On the previous day, Padre Murguía had taken to his bed because he had a fever, which was thought to have been caused by indigestion. The fever persisted and got worse in the days that followed. When it was apparent

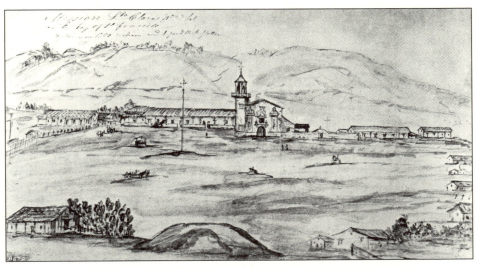

FIGURE 50. *Mission Santa Clara 39° 20' Lat. on the Bay of St. Francisco Containing 1500 Indians and a Good Stock of Cattle.* Sketched in 1842 by Gustavus M. Waseurtz af Sandels. This building dates from the 1820s. It was constructed after the complex where Serra and Palóu spent some emotional days together in 1784 was destroyed by an earthquake in 1818. *Courtesy of the Santa Clara University Archives. General Photograph Collection, Box 15, f. MSC Sketches. Sandels-MSC-1.jpg.*

that he had typhoid fever, his assistant notified me. I then asked Padre Palóu to go to the mission. He traveled as fast as he could and was able to be present when Padre Murguía received the sacraments and when he died.

May God keep him in His holy glory. Amen. We must do our part to help him achieve eternal rest as soon as possible. Therefore, Vuestras Reverencias, I instruct each and every one of you to pray the suffrages[22] as quickly as possible. We mutually agreed, from the outset, that each priest would say twenty Masses. And at each mission, one of these Masses should be a sung Mass with a vigil. Therefore, as soon as each mission receives this letter, I implore you to waste no time in forwarding it to the next mission. And I request that the Reverendos Padres of San Diego, forward this letter to the Reverendo Padre Guardián of our Santo Colegio de San Fernando, when the first opportunity to do so presents itself. In the meantime, I will make a point of writing to them about the situation.

---

22. Suffrages were Masses and prayers offered on behalf of the dead.

FIGURE 51. *Mission San Francisco de Asís* by Henry Chapman Ford. Palóu was one of the founders of this mission in 1776. Courtesy of The Bancroft Library, University of California, Berkeley. BANC PIC 1963.002:0918.22-ffALB.

May God keep Vuestras Reverencias many years in good health and in His holy grace.

Mission of Nuestro Padre Seráfico San Francisco. May 11, 1784.
Your dear brother, companion, and servant kisses the hand of Vuestras Reverencias,
Fray Junípero Serra.

P.S. If anybody at San Gabriel or San Diego knows where the Reverendo Padre Presidente of Sonora is living, they can add this to the heading of the letter and send it, and hope for the best. God be with you.

Final Months

The death of Murguía and a growing sense that his own life was nearing its conclusion, combined with all of the administrative difficulties he was experiencing, contributed to Serra's anxiety about the future of the missions he had founded. The news he was receiving from the Colegio de San Fernando deepened his concern. The colegio was not in good shape. A recruiting expedition to Spain in

1774 was not able to fill its quota, and no other recruitment trip occurred until 1784. Letters from the colegio at the time constantly bemoaned the lack of young religious among its members. In addition, official Franciscan visitors to the colegio in 1774 and 1780 pointed out a number of deficiencies in the observance of religious life at the colegio. Serra, who had always been worried that the colegio might send people to California who were not suited for the rigors of mission life, began to wonder if the colegio was ever going to be able to send enough hardy missionaries to California to continue his work.[23]

In a 1783 letter to the Colegio de San Fernando, Serra consoled the guardian about the deaths and defections at the colegio and expressed the hope that somehow or other the colegio might experience a revival of the primitive zeal that animated Antonio Llinás, the founder of the colegios apostólicos. And in June 1784 he lamented that the "spirit of novelty" was becoming too prevalent among his religious brethren in Mexico City. Serra originally came to the New World in search of personal and institutional renewal. That letter, composed so close to the end of his life, was not written by a man who believed his search had been uniformly successful.[24]

When Serra arrived at Santa Clara on the last stop of his confirmation journey, he was tired. Palóu, who had hurried to Santa Clara from San Francisco when word reached there of Murguía's illness, was still there. Palóu related what happened:

※ *Palóu's Account of His Meeting with Serra*

> Even though I was thinking about going back to my mission, Su Paternidad stopped me from leaving. He said he wanted to prepare for his death, in case we would not see one another again, for he was already feeble and he probably did not have much time left to live. He spent several days in spiritual exercises and made a general confession, or repeated the one he had made at other times. He shed many tears, and I no fewer. I was upset that this might be the last time we would see one another. And, we would not be able to die together as we had hoped, or at least that the last one to die would be there to assist the one who died first. Seeing that Su Paternidad was going back to his mission as I was to mine, it would not be very easy to assist him because the distance between the two missions was forty-two leagues and that entire area was populated by gentiles. But the Father of Mercies and the God of all

---

23. On the difficulties at San Fernando, see Beebe and Senkewicz, "Uncertainty on the Mission Frontier," 307–11; Serra's concerns were heightened by his experiences trying to staff San Buenaventura, but they were long-standing. See his letter to Juan Andrés, June 12, 1770, earlier in this volume; Borges Morán, *El envío de misioneros a América*, 518–21.

24. Serra, *Writings*, 4:194–95, 252–53.

Consolation wanted to afford me this solace, which I will speak about in the next chapter.

His last days at Santa Clara were spent preparing himself for death. He also was engaged in the holy exercise of baptizing some who had gathered there. (He had always longed to do this and never tired of it.) And he confirmed the neophytes who had not received this holy sacrament. Because some were ill and could not come to the church, Su Paternidad went to their ranchería and confirmed them in their homes so they would not be deprived of this benefit. He did not leave one single Christian without the sacrament of confirmation. On the very day he administered the last confirmations, he headed back to his mission in Monterey, leaving me with that feeling of great sadness which is a result of filial love.[25]

Death

At the end of July 1784 Fages sent Serra word that the establishment of a mission at Santa Bárbara had been approved. Fages asked Serra how they should go about this task. This was exactly what Neve had not allowed Serra himself to do in 1782, and Serra's response to Fages indicated that he had not forgotten that.

※ *Serra to Pedro Fages, July 31, 1784*

My response is that Vuestra Señoría and everyone else are fully aware of my viewpoint regarding the founding of that mission as well as others for the sake of extending the reach of our Holy Catholic faith. How many souls from Montecito and other gentile places, in whose midst we live, would already be in Heaven if my viewpoint had been embraced?

Serra never thought he would be the one to found that mission, since he was growing ever weaker. A few weeks after Serra wrote Fages, he asked Palóu to come to Carmel. The vessel *San Carlos* was at San Francisco, but Palóu did not want to wait for it, so he went over land.

Palóu found Serra tremendously weakened and suffering from congestion in his chest. He might temporarily recover during religious services in the primitive adobe church, but he was clearly declining. When the *San Carlos* arrived at Monterey, the surgeon on board was unable to provide any relief. Palóu sent word to the missionaries at San Antonio and San Luis Obispo that they should come quickly, but they were not able to arrive in time. On August 27 Serra asked Palóu for the Viaticum, traditionally the final reception of Holy Communion before

---

25. Palóu, *Relación histórica del Venerable Padre Fray Junípero Serra*, chap. 57 (translation by the authors).

death. Serra insisted that this ritual be administered in the church, rather than in his own room. That evening Palóu administered the last rites to his longtime friend and teacher.

The next morning the captain of the *San Carlos* came to pay his last respects. This was José Cañizares, who in 1769 had been with Rivera y Moncada and Crespí on the first leg of the Portolá expedition. He had also served as chief pilot on the *San Carlos* when it made its entry into San Francisco Bay in 1775. Serra tried to put him at ease with a little joke about his imminent death. A crowd from the ship and mission had gathered in the parlor of the priests' residence, and Palóu led them in some final prayers and then sprinkled Serra's room with holy water. But Serra began to become agitated and fearful. So Palóu led the group in some additional prayers and this calmed Serra. After taking some broth, he was led back to his own room and lay down. When Palóu returned to the room a few hours later, he found that Serra had already died.

Palóu then described the community's reaction to Serra's death in the traditional way that hagiographic Christian accounts of the death of a holy person had been formulated for centuries. Grieving members of the community paid their respects to his remains, and so many people wanted to do so that the church needed to be kept open all night. In addition, the stricken members of the deceased's congregation wished to possess any memento of their departed leader they could obtain, including parts of his clothes and even fringes of his hair. Palóu was adamant that they could not call these items "relics," since that term was reserved for those whose lives had been formally judged to be holy by the appropriate church authorities.

❋ Palóu, "Exemplary Death of Venerable Padre Junípero"

As I read the letter from the Reverendo Padre Presidente in which he told me to go to Monterey, even though he did not say I should go right away, I decided to travel by land, seeing that the ship would be slow in leaving. I arrived at his Mission San Carlos on August 18. I found Su Paternidad very weak physically, and his chest was extremely congested, yet he was up and about. He did not let his condition keep him from going to church in the afternoon to recite the catechism and say prayers with the neophytes. He concluded the devotions with the tender and pious "Canto de los Versos,"[26] composed by the Venerable Padre Margil in honor of the Assumption of Our Lady, whose octave we were celebrating. When I heard him sing, his voice sounded as strong as ever, and I mentioned this to a soldier who was talking to me: "The Padre Presidente does

---

26. A song in thirteen verses composed by Margil in honor of the Assumption of Mary.

not seem to be so ill." The soldier, who had known him since 1769, replied, "Padre, appearances are deceiving. He is ill. When it comes to praying and singing, this holy Padre is always strong, but he is dying."

The following day, August 19, he told me he was feeling very sluggish and therefore asked me to sing the Mass for the most holy patriarch San José, something that was done every month. And I did as he asked. However, Su Paternidad did not fail to sing in the choir with the neophytes or recite the Our Father seven times, in addition to the other usual prayers. In the afternoon he was there to pray and sing the "Versos de la Virgen" and the next day, which was Friday, as always, he prayed the Stations of the Cross in the church with everyone present.

We took our time discussing the issues for which he had summoned me, while we waited for the ship to arrive. But I kept fearing that the time of his death was quickly approaching, because whenever I would enter his small room, or cell made of adobe, I would find him very withdrawn within himself. His companion told me that he had been this way since the day his authority to confirm had expired. As I said, this was the same ship that had anchored at these establishments. Five days after I arrived in Monterey, the packet-boat anchored in that port. The royal surgeon immediately went to the mission to visit the Reverendo Padre Presidente. The surgeon found his breathing to be so labored that he prescribed the application of hot poultices to draw out the fluid that had accumulated in his chest. The Padre told him he could apply as many of these remedies as he wished. The surgeon did so, but the poultices only served to inflict more pain in that weary body. One never heard him utter the slightest complaint with regard to this powerful remedy or the pain he was suffering. It was as if this misfortune had not befallen him. He was always up and about, as if he were healthy. When some cloth that came on the ship was brought to the mission, with his own hands he started to cut the cloth in pieces and distribute it to the neophytes so they could cover up their nakedness.

August 25: He told me he was sorry the Padres from Missions San Antonio and San Luis had not come and said, "It is possible that the letters I wrote to them were somehow delayed." I immediately sent word to the presidio and someone brought the letters back, saying they had forgotten to send them. As soon as I saw the content of the letters, in which he was inviting them to come and bid him a final farewell, I sent a courier to deliver these letters. I included a message of my own saying they should come right away. I feared our dear Prelate would not be with us much longer because he had deteriorated so much. As soon as they received the letters, the Padres set out, but they did not arrive in time. They were only able to attend his burial. The Padre from San Luis arrived three days later because that mission is fifty leagues away. He was only able to attend the *honores*[27] that were held on the seventh day, I will explain later.

August 26: When he got up, he was even weaker. And he told me he had a bad night. Therefore, he wanted to prepare himself for whatever God had planned for him. He spent the entire day alone, quiet with his thoughts, and did not permit any distractions whatsoever. That night he made his general confession to me shedding many tears, yet with such mental clarity that it was as if he were well. Once this was concluded, and after a short period of reflection, he drank a cup of broth and then went to lie down. He did not want anybody to stay in his small room with him.

On August 27, at dawn, I went in to visit him and found him with his breviary in his hand, for it was customary for him to begin matins before dawn. And whenever he was on the road, he would begin at dawn. I asked him how he had spent the night and he replied, "The same." Nevertheless, he wanted me to consecrate a Host and have it ready. He would let me know when he would be ready to receive it. That is what I did. After Mass, I went back to inform him. He told me he wanted to receive the Most Holy Viaticum and that he would go to the church to do so. I told him there was no need for that. His small cell could be adorned in the best possible manner so that the Divine Majesty could come and visit him. His response was no. He wanted to receive Him in church because he was still able to walk and there was no reason for the Lord to come to him. I had to acquiesce and fulfill his holy wishes. He walked on his own to the church, which is more than 100 varas away. He was accompanied by the presidio commander, who came to the ceremony with some of the soldiers, who were joined there by those of the mission. All of the Indians from the pueblo or the mission exhibited much tenderness and devotion as they accompanied the devout, ill Padre to the church.

When Su Paternidad reached the steps of the sanctuary, he knelt before a small table that had been prepared for the ceremony. I came out of the sacristy vested. When I arrived at the altar, as soon as I prepared the incense to begin the devotional ceremony, the fervent servant of God intoned the verse *Tantum ergo Sacramentum* with tears in his eyes. His voice was as strong and as resonant as when he was well. I administered the Holy Viaticum to

---

27. Requiem services.

him with all the formalities of this rite. When this very devotional ceremony was over, one which I had never experienced under these circumstances, Su Paternidad remained in the same kneeling position as he gave thanks to God. When he finished, he returned to his small cell. Everyone accompanied him. Some were crying out of devotion and tenderness, others out of pain and sorrow because they feared the loss of their dear Padre. He remained alone in his small cell, seated on the dining table chair, quiet in his thoughts. Seeing him so deep in thought, I did not allow anyone to go in and speak to him.

When I saw that the carpenter from the presidio was about to go in, I stopped him. He said the Padre had called for him to come and make the coffin in which he would be buried, and he wanted to ask him how he wanted it made. I was moved by this but did not let him enter to speak with the Padre. Instead, I told him to make the same type of coffin as the one he made for Padre Crespí. The Venerable Padre spent the entire day seated on the chair in utter silence and deep in thought. He partook of nothing more than a bit of broth and did not take to his bed to rest.

During the night he felt much worse and asked me to bring the holy oils to anoint him. He received this Holy Sacrament seated on an *equipal*, a modest chair made of reeds.[28] He prayed the Litany of the Saints with us, and also the penitential psalms. He was awake all night, most of it spent kneeling with his chest resting on the boards of his bed. I told him he should lie down for awhile. He responded that he felt more relief by staying in that position. There were other times when he would be seated on the floor, leaning back and supported in the lap of the neophytes. The small cell was filled with neophytes all night long. The great love they felt for the Padre who had given them birth in the Lord is what drew them here. Seeing him in such a weakened state, cradled in the arms of the Indians, I asked the surgeon for his opinion on the Padre's condition. He responded (it seemed to him that the situation was very grave): "It seems to me that this blessed Padre wants to die on the floor."

I then entered and asked the Padre if he wanted absolution and the application of the plenary indulgence. He said yes and prepared himself and got down on his knees to receive the plenary absolution. I also applied the plenary indulgence of the Order, which was of great consolation to him. He spent the entire night in the manner described. When he awakened on August 28, the feast day of the Doctor of the Church, San Agustín, he seemed better and had less chest congestion, even though he did not sleep at all that night nor did he have anything to eat. He spent the morning seated

---

28. For a picture of an equipal from northern Mexico, see Fontana, Faubert, and Burns, *The Other Southwest*, 47.

FIGURE 52. Serra seated on the *equipal* as Palóu blesses him on August 28, 1784. Painted in Mallorca by Fr. Andrés Caymari in 1790. *Courtesy of the Biblioteca Nacional de España.*

on the reed armchair that was placed next to the bed. His bed consisted of several hard, roughhewn boards covered by a blanket, which did a better job of hiding the boards than it did of creating a comfortable place to rest. He would not even put a sheepskin on the bed, as was customary at the colegio. And on the road, he would do the same thing. He would place a blanket and pillow on the ground and lie down on top of it for his necessary rest. He would always sleep embracing a cross that he placed on his chest. This cross was about a foot long. He had carried it with him since he was in the novitiate at the colegio, and he was never without it. During his travels he always carried it, along with the blanket and pillow. Wherever he stopped and also at his mission, he would place the cross on the pillow as soon as he would get out of bed. And that is where the cross was on this occasion when he refused to take to his bed, during the night or during the morning of the day he would deliver his soul to the Creator.

At about ten o'clock in the morning on the feast day of San Agustín, the officers from the frigate came to visit him—Capitán and Comandante Don José Cañizares, whom Su Paternidad knew very well, ever since the first expedition in 1769—and the Royal Chaplain, don Cristóbal Díaz, whom he had also met in this port in 1779. He gave them an extraordinary welcome by ordering the solemn ringing of the bells in their honor. He stood up and warmly embraced them, as if he were not ill, and engaged in the customary formalities of respect that a religious would afford such officers. After they sat down, Su Paternidad returned to his equipal. They had not seen one another since 1779. They told the Padre all about their voyages to Peru.

After listening to their stories, he said: "Well, Señores, after so much time that has passed since we last saw one another, and after all of your travels, I thank you for coming to this port from so far away to throw a bit of earth on top of me." When the men, and everyone else who was present heard this, we were all surprised. There he was, seated on his small chair made of reeds, answering every question, his mind as sharp as ever. As they tried to hold back the tears, which they could not control, they told him: "No, Padre, we trust in God that He will make you well so you can continue the conquest." The Servant of God (who, if he did not have a revelation regarding the hour of his death, at the very least had to say that he expected it would be soon) told them: "Yes, yes, do me that favor and show me some compassion by tossing a bit of earth on me, for which I would be most grateful." He then looked me straight in the eye and said: "For now, I wish to be buried in the church, very close to Padre Fray Juan Crespí, because when the stone church is built, they will toss me wherever they want."

When my tears finally eased enough so I could respond to him, I said: "Padre Presidente, if God sees fit to call you to Himself, what Vuestra Paternidad has requested will be done. And in that case, because of the love and great affection you have always had for me, when you find yourself in the presence of the Most Holy Trinity, I ask Vuestra Paternidad to adore it in my name. And do not forget about me or forget to pray for everyone who lives at these missions, especially for those here present." He replied: "I promise, if the Lord in His infinite mercy grants me this eternal happiness, which I do not deserve because of my sins, I will pray for everyone and for the reducción of the many gentiles I leave behind without conversion."

It was not very long before he asked me to sprinkle his small room with holy water, which I did. I asked him if he was in any pain and he said no, but he wanted this to be done so there would be no pain. He was profoundly silent. Then, all of a sudden, he became very frightened and said: "A great fear has swept over me, I am very scared. Read me the 'Commendation of the Soul' and speak loud enough so I can hear it." I did as he asked. The above-mentioned gentlemen from the ship, as well as the Padre's companion Padre Matías Noriega, the surgeon, and others from the ship and the mission were present. I read the "Commendation of the Soul" to him. Seated on his equipal or reed chair, the Venerable Padre responded as if he were well, which deeply touched all of us.

As soon as I had finished, he joyfully exclaimed: "Thanks be to God, thanks be to God, I am no longer afraid, so let us go outside." We all went to a small outside room with Su Paternidad. When we noticed this change, we were both surprised and happy, all at the same time. The ship captain said: "Padre Presidente, Vuestra Paternidad now sees what my devoted San Antonio is able to do. I have asked him to make you well and I expect that he will. And you will still be able to embark on more journeys for the good of the poor Indians." The Venerable Padre responded not with words but rather with a little chuckle, which made it very clear to us that he did not expect this to happen, nor did he believe he would recover.

He sat down on the chair by the table, picked up his *diurnal*,[29] and began to pray. As soon as he was finished, I told him it was already past one o'clock in the afternoon and asked him if he would like to have a cup of broth. He said yes and took it. After giving thanks, he said: "Well, we must now rest." He walked on his own to the small room where he had his bed, which was more like a bench. After taking off only his mantle, he lay down on the boards that

---

29. A book that contained part of the Divine Office.

were covered with the blanket and his holy cross, as described above, so he could rest. We all thought he was going to sleep, since he had not slept at all during the entire night. The gentlemen went out to eat. I was a bit worried, so a short time later I returned to his room and went over to his bed to see if he was sleeping. I found him exactly as we had left him just a short while before, but now he was asleep in the Lord. He showed no signs of having struggled. The only evidence of death was that his breathing had stopped, but it really did seem like he was sleeping. We piously believe that he went to sleep in the Lord a little before two o'clock in the afternoon on the feast day of San Agustín in the year 1784, and that he would be receiving his heavenly reward for his apostolic labors.

His life of toilsome work ended when he was seventy years, nine months, and four days old. He was a layperson for sixteen years, nine months, and twenty-one days. He was a religious for fifty-three years, eleven months, and thirteen days, of which he spent thirty-five years and thirteen days as an apostolic missionary. During this time he performed the glorious deeds that we have already seen, in which his merits were greater than his accomplishments. His life was one of continuous activity. He was always occupied in virtuous and holy work and in extraordinary heroic deeds—all for the greater glory of God and the salvation of souls. And for someone who worked with such zeal for these souls, how much harder would he work for the salvation of his own soul? There is much I could say about this, but it requires more time and must be done calmly. If God grants me this, and if it is His most holy will, I shall not fail to write something about his heroic virtues, which will serve to edify by example.

As soon as I came to terms with the fact we were now orphans, deprived of the pleasant company of our venerated Prelate, who was not sleeping but who had actually died, I ordered the neophytes who were there to ring the bells twice to announce his death. As soon as the bells were rung, the entire pueblo gathered together and wept over the death of their beloved Padre who had given them birth in the Lord. They loved him more than if he had been their natural father. They all wanted to see him in order to ease the sorrow that had taken hold of their hearts and be able to express it with tears. The throng of people, Indians as well as soldiers and sailors, was so large that it was necessary to close the door in order to place Su Paternidad in the coffin he had ordered made the previous day. The only thing we had to do to shroud him was to take off his sandals (which the captain of the packet-boat and the Padre Chaplain received as a memento). He remained in the shroud he was

(Above) FIGURE 53. Serra's silk burial stole. *Courtesy of Carmel Mission Basilica.*

(Right) FIGURE 54. The cross with which Serra was buried, the "Cruz de Caravaca." The origins of the design of this cross were rooted in the Spanish Reconquista. This particular cross contained nine relics, at least two of which were related to the Mallorcan Ramón Llull. *Courtesy of Carmel Mission Basilica.*

FIGURE 55. Ceremonial opening of Fr. Serra's tomb in 1882. Photograph by Charles Pierce. *This item is reproduced by permission of The Huntington Library, San Marino, California. 609 HEH Pierce, box 23 image 3683.*

wearing when he died, namely the habit, cowl, and cord, but no tunic underneath. Six days before he died, he sent the two tunics he used when traveling to be washed, along with a change of underwear. He did not want to wear the tunics. Instead, he preferred to die wearing only the habit, cowl, and cord.

After the venerable cadaver had been placed in the coffin, surrounded by six burning candles, the door to the cell was opened. Waiting there were the sad neophyte children with their bouquets of colorful wildflowers to adorn the body of their deceased Venerable Padre. The body remained in the cell until nightfall. A steady stream of people went in and out of the cell, praying to him and touching his venerable hands and face with rosaries and medals. Without mincing words they would call him "Padre Santo," "Padre Bendito," and other affectionate names that stemmed from the love they felt for him and from the heroic virtues they had seen in him during his life.

At nightfall we took him to the church in a procession that included the pueblo of neophytes and the soldiers and sailors who had remained behind. The coffin was placed on a table surrounded by six burning candles. The ceremony ended with a response. They asked me to keep the church open so they could stand vigil and pray the Rosary for the soul of the deceased. They would change shifts throughout the night and thus maintain continuous prayer. I agreed to this and had two soldiers remain as guards to prevent any pious indiscretion or theft. Everyone longed to have even the tiniest object that had been touched by the deceased. This was especially true of the sailors and the soldiers, because they had known him better and had a high opinion of the virtue and sanctity of the deceased Venerable Padre. Those who had dealings with him at sea and on land kept asking me for some small object that he had used. Even though I promised them I would take care of their request after the burial, this did not keep them from overstepping bounds by cutting off pieces of his habit from areas down below where it would not be noticed. They even cut some fringes of hair from around his tonsure, and the guard could do nothing about it. Or perhaps he had agreed to it and was an active participant in this pious theft. Everyone longed to have something that belonged to the deceased to remember him by. They held him in such high esteem that they called these mementoes "relics." I tried to correct them and explain it to them.[30]

---

30. Palóu, *Relación histórica del Venerable Padre Fray Junípero Serra*, chap. 58 (translation by authors).

Conclusion

Junípero Serra was an eighteenth-century man whose fundamental angle of vision pointed toward the past. In Mallorca he studied and taught a form of medieval Scholastic philosophy and theology that relied on the work of a thirteenth-century Franciscan scholar. His decision to go to the New World stemmed from a desire to recover for himself what he regarded as the more pure spiritual dedication of his earlier days. He was associated for sixteen years in Mexico City with an institution, the apostolic college, which attempted to recover for the Franciscan missionary enterprise the more pure spiritual dedication of its earlier days. He worked in three missionary fields, and in each of them he was convinced that he was carrying on a strategy that had been developed in the sixteenth century to protect indigenous peoples. In the Sierra Gorda and in Alta California he encountered officials whom he believed were attempting to bring back to life the colonial strategies that had oppressed those indigenous peoples for centuries. He believed that ranchers and settlers on the northern frontier of New Spain would treat the Indians just as brutally as sixteenth-century encomenderos had done in the Caribbean and on the Mexican mainland.

All of this made sense to Junípero Serra because the world in which he lived and worked resembled in many ways the worlds from which he drew inspiration. Most young Franciscans in Europe and America still studied Scholasticism. Serra worked in a Spanish empire that was almost three centuries old. When Serra spoke to the viceroy of New Spain in 1773, he spoke to the direct successor of the first occupant of that office, who had been appointed in 1535. The peoples among whom Serra labored in the Americas were organized in relatively compact family and clan groups. Their culture was oral rather than written. Spanish soldiers, priests, and settlers had been encountering such people in New Spain since the 1540s. Junípero Serra believed that he was engaging in a set of activities that had been undertaken for centuries, and he was basically correct.

He had no way of knowing that he was living near the end of an era. After his death, the worlds that had inspired and sustained him changed dramatically. Ships tell the story. Boats had always been a terribly important part of Serra's and California's life while he served as president of the missions. His correspondence and Palóu's biography are filled with the comings and goings of various Spanish supply and exploration vessels. They were the lifeblood of California. Yet less than two decades after Serra's death, a different kind of vessel began appearing on the California coast. Ships from England and the United States began to call, first periodically and, over time, with increasing regularity. Also, after 1810 the Spanish vessels that filled Serra's correspondence and Palóu's pages vanished from the coast, as colonial officials in Mexico City had to divert resources as they struggled to deal with the Hidalgo insurgency and its aftermath.

These changes had two results. The first was that California became involved in global trade in a different way than it had been previously, and it became an important source of goods prized in other parts of the globe. The skin of the sea otter was in great demand in Asia. Eventually cattle became the predominant engine of wealth, as California became an important source of tallow for Hawaii and hides for the United States. At the same time, in the absence of regular supplies from New Spain, California had to become much more self-sufficient. The best-organized economic units in the province, the entities that were best able to take advantage of the new situation, were the missions. They grew rapidly. As it became increasingly clear that native populations at most missions were not reproducing themselves, the missions reached farther and farther out to bring in new laborers so that the production levels could be maintained. By the 1810s and 1820s foreign visitors were describing them as large-scale agricultural enterprises.

In this new environment, California was dominated by the very type of people Serra feared most: ranchers. But here the ranchers were missionaries. Junípero Serra initiated an enterprise that evolved in ways he could never have imagined. His "ladder" of missions became something else. In 1801 Serra's successor Lasuén bristled when colonial officials called the group of missions a "system."[1] But the officials were correct, for the mission compounds were experiencing fundamental changes. Ironically, the missions in Alta California in the nineteenth century ended up doing there exactly what José de Escandón had wanted the Fernandino missions to do in the Sierra Gorda in the 1740s. The major social role the missions played was to train the indigenous people who managed to survive to be experienced and knowledgeable ranch hands.

This was not Junípero Serra's intention, and we have no way of knowing what he would have thought of these changes. Most likely he would have approved

---

1. Lasuén, *Writings*, 2:212.

Figure 56. Mission San Carlos Borromeo (1949), as seen through the eyes of Manuel Mallafré Sunyer, a Catalonian master stonemason (*maestro de obras*). This photograph was taken exactly two hundred years after Junípero Serra left Mallorca. *From the authors' family collection.*

of some of them, opposed some, and been ambivalent about others. The California mission enterprise he started acquired a life of its own, and the people involved in it—native peoples, soldiers, Spanish and Mexican officials, settlers, even missionaries—attempted to react to the changing circumstances of their own eras, not to ask themselves what lessons Serra's life might teach them. That was appropriate, for Serra's struggle was his own. His attempt to live out his religious ideals as a missionary among the peoples of America gave his own life its deepest meaning. He profoundly believed that encounters with missionaries would prove more advantageous to eighteenth-century indigenous peoples than the other possibilities that he thought were realistically available to them, specifically domination by soldiers or settlers. In the New Spain of the mid-eighteenth century, this belief was quite reasonable.

APPENDIX

Four Sermons

First Sermon: Of the Sweetness of God in His Divine Calls: "Taste and see that the Lord is good," Psalm 33

What a difference there is between a temperament that is harsh, stern, and severe, and a disposition that is mild, loving, sweet, and gentle.[1] The harsh temperament rides roughshod over everything, causes trouble everywhere, and usually ruins everything. The mild disposition, on the other hand, arranges everything peacefully, softens everything, and attracts everyone with its tenderness. The harsh temperament stirs up reasons or excuses for disorder; the mild disposition dismisses any tricks that might be put forward to exempt itself from the law of fairness. It believes that when a monarch treats his subjects with kindness, it is a definite mistake not to esteem him in a fashion consistent with the greatness of his rank.

This sort of kindness was shown by that notable King of Aragón Alfonso. When his nobles said he was being too indulgent, he told them, "I would greatly prefer to win over many people with my mercy than to lose even a few by being severe or harsh."

The magnanimity of our Lord and God consists in the boundless extent of this benevolent condition. He is complete mercy, complete love, and complete tenderness toward men, even toward the most ungrateful sinners. Truly God's justice is as boundless as His mercy, but when His mercy is spreading continuously, so that it covers all the earth (*The earth is full of the mercy of the Lord*),[2] then the justice wielded by His right hand is not active (*Your right hand is full of justice*).[3]

The Lord wishes all people to attain the ends for which He compassionately created us. He yearns that we might believe that He is the way, the truth, and

---
1. The current numbering of the Psalms is slightly different than the one Serra employed, which was based on the Septuagint. The verse to which he refers here is now numbered Psalm 34:8. All references to the Psalms in the notes are given in the current numbering. However, when Serra employed a numerical reference in his text, that usage is retained in the text, and the current numbering is given in a note.
2. Psalm 33:5.
3. Psalm 48:10.

the life and that we might advance toward the salvation He wills for us (*He wills everyone to be saved and to come to a knowledge of the truth*).[4] For that reason He extends the golden bonds of His goodwill and love to entice us and unite us to himself (*I led them with bonds of love*).[5]

This type of goodwill is so much a part of the Lord that the apostles, when they had enough experience with Him to begin to be able to understand Him, were amazed to see a tiny sliver of His justice when He cursed the barren fig tree (*The disciples were amazed*).[6] They were not amazed to see Him cure the blind, the sick, the deaf, the crippled, or the lepers. They were not amazed to see Him raise Lazarus or the daughter of the synagogue official from the dead. However, they were surprised to see Him make a fig tree wither. Witnessing Him showing mercy to men was completely normal, but seeing such sternness toward an inanimate creature was extraordinary. For such goodwill is so much a part of the very nature of the Lord.

During this holy season of Lent, I myself do not have the ability to persuade men to abandon the love of worldly and mortal things or to convince those who are bound and imprisoned by their sins to free themselves and follow the path of virtue, which is also the path to heavenly glory. In order that they might make the Lord the object of their affection and love, I have determined simply to remind them of the gentle goodwill of our God. The Lord, who so values this kindness, will not cease helping me to make it more evident and to extol it among those who are listening to me.

And if the Lord judges that the loving bonds of His love are the best way to attract people to himself (*I led them with cords of human kindness*),[7] the best way to win all my listeners for heaven will be to have them consider how sweet and gentle the Lord is and to prompt them to taste His sweetness and gentleness. The Father of the Church, Saint Augustine, says this: "The love of temporal things is not extinguished except by the sweetness of eternal things." Therefore, I have chosen as the theme of all these sermons the words of Psalm 33, in which the Psalmist King tells us, "Above all, the Lord is gentle." He invites us to taste and experience that as He says to us, *Taste and see that the Lord is good.*

Anyone who has tasted the sweetness of the Lord just once regards as empty all of this life's pleasures and delights, if they even deserve to be called these. Thus Hugo Cardenal writes, "Whoever tastes the gentle sweetness of God finds his carnal desires withering away."[8] Whoever tastes this divine sweetness finds that

---

4. 1 Timothy 2:4.
5. Hosea 11:4.
6. Matthew 21:20.
7. Hosea 11:4.
8. Hugo Cardenal was a thirteenth-century French Dominican and scripture scholar.

it makes him more gentle, more calm, more nurturing, and much more strong. "God's rich sweetness overflows. It nourishes, it strengthens, it defends, and it fortifies," says the authority whom I have just cited.

Those who do not know anything about this sweetness and do not taste it do not have any appetite for it. But someone who has tried it just once discovers that he has an increasing appetite for it, for he finds it very soothing. As the Lord himself says, "Those who eat of me will hunger for more, and those who drink of me will thirst for more."[9] Thus the Psalmist, in the words of my theme, invites us to taste it before fully committing ourselves to it. *Taste and see*.

In a similar fashion Saint Peter the Apostle says in his first letter that we long for the sweetness of the Lord just like small children long for sweet nectar from the breasts of their mothers, *Like newborn infants, long for the pure, spiritual milk*. Then He immediately adds, *If indeed you have tasted that the Lord is good*.[10] It is as if he were saying, I exhort you to this if you have already tasted how sweet the Lord is. But if not, it would be useless to urge you to desire it.

Do not think, Christian, that the statement about the Lord being sweet and gentle is true of Him only in His glory with the blessed ones. It refers to the Lord in everything, with everyone, and at all times. That is why David, in Psalm 30, terms the divine gentleness abundant: "Oh, how abundant is your goodness, Lord."[11] The Lord is sweet and gentle in the words with which He calls us to His love, as Saint Peter the Apostle said: *You have the words of eternal life*.[12] He is gentle in the law He orders us to observe, as He himself said through Saint Matthew: *For my yoke is easy*.[13] He is gentle even in the sufferings He sends us, as David states: *Your rod and your staff comfort me*.[14] He is gentle in the mercy with which He generously pardons us, as we read in Psalm 102: *As a father has compassion on his children*.[15] And finally, He is gentle in the delights of the glory with which He rewards His own at the end of their lives, as Psalm 35 says: *You give them to drink from the river of your delights*.[16] Don Ricardo de San Lorenzo summarizes all of this: *Taste and see. Sweet in His word; sweet in His yoke; sweet in His scourging; sweet in the forgiveness of sins; and, in the end, sweetest of all in the bestowal of His rewards*.[17]

In these five rungs of the ladder of divine gentleness we have been given, I have the design of the five evenings of this Lent. I will name the ladder rung by

---

9. Sirach 24:21.
10. 1 Peter 2:2–3.
11. Psalms 31:19.
12. John 6:68.
13. Matthew 11:30.
14. Psalms 23:4.
15. Psalms 103:13.
16. Psalms 36:8.
17. Ricardo de San Lorenzo was a thirteenth-century Franciscan.

rung. Through the order of these rungs the Lord desires to elevate all of us to His glory, as Saint Augustine says: "He has not ceased to call you, or neglected to strengthen you when called, or ceased to perfect you when strengthened, or neglected to crown you when perfected."[18]

This ladder is a gift to us. Today it is time for us to ascend the first rung: to taste and attend to the gentleness of the divine voice with which the Lord calls us to His love and to the disregard of everything connected with this life. These voices are without a doubt entirely sweet and gentle, *gentle in His word*, because all His words are words of eternal life: *You have the words of eternal life*.

Today I wish to know how to offer worthy praise of these divine voices with which the Lord calls everyone. I wish to know how to entice us all during this Lent with the divine sweetness so that these sermons might be for the greater honor and glory of God and for the greater spiritual benefit of our souls. That is the only aim I have as I speak here and the only aim the word of God ought to have. So I ask the Lord to grant us the gentleness of His divine grace. Therefore I set as our intercessor the ever-immaculate Queen Mary and say with the Angel, *Hail Mary*.

Taste and See

The most convincing sign that a father loves his son, or a king loves his vassal, or a master loves his servant is to demonstrate his favor with loving and sweet words even when the son or vassal or servant does not deserve that favor because of his misdeeds. The power of this sign increases as the distance between the high position of the superior and the low estate of the subject increases. It becomes even more powerful if we consider the case of a subject able to rise from his tomb and serve and obey his master.

We have proof of this in what happened between Christ in His majesty and Lazarus. Since Christ was truly King of Kings, it was fitting to His position to summon Lazarus in this way: *Lazarus, come forth*. When they heard this, all the bystanders understood how much He loved him: *See how much He loved him!* At the same time, the loving voice with which the Lord called Lazarus had such an effect on him that he came out immediately from the tomb to obey Him: *The dead man came out*.[19]

The Lord calls all of us with loving voices when we leave behind not only our faults but the bad habits and situations in our lives which lead to these faults, and love Him alone. As a proof of His tremendous devotion to us, He tells us that He is standing at our door and calling us: *I am standing at the door, knocking*.[20]

---

18. Augustine of Hippo, *Expositions on the Book of Psalms*, 6 vols., ed. John Henry Parker (London: F. and J. Rivington, 1853), 5:39.
19. John 11:43, 36, 44.
20. Revelation 3:20.

When he considered this, the holy Doctor Saint Bonaventure burst forth in these angelic words of his own: "Oh, the great and indescribable devotion of our God! He calls the one who is unwilling to return to Him so that he can return. And, to enable him to return, He calls again and again." Let us attend, then, to these voices and let us observe how sweet and gentle our Lord shows himself in them: *Taste and see; gentle in the word with which He calls us.*

Scripture tells us that the Lord calls us in two ways, with interior and exterior voices. He speaks to us himself with interior voices in our hearts. He also speaks with exterior voices to our ears, through His ministers. We need to attend to both types of gentle voices. And this is the first rung on the spiritual ladder we have been given, the ladder of His glory.

The Interior Voices of God to Man's Heart

First, the Lord calls us by speaking to us in the vast interior spaces of our heart. He does this so that we can put aside our affection for fleeting things and give all our heart to the Lord himself. He speaks to us with a great, sweet, and gentle tone with which a father might address his favorite child. So we see that the Lord, through the prophet Hosea, refers to the many faults and sins which the house of Israel—a symbol of the sinful soul—has committed. This grieves Him, but He nevertheless speaks to them in this fashion: *Therefore, I will now allure her, and bring her into the wilderness, and speak tenderly to her.*[21] That is, therefore I will provide gifts and sweets—*I will allure her*. I will spare her the vicissitudes of the world, I will speak to her heart: *I will speak tenderly*. Oh, the indescribable goodwill of the Lord! "Oh, the indescribable devotion of our God!"[22] Who has ever seen a more loving proof of a father's concern for a favorite son? But tell me, Lord—what words of love will you speak to the heart of that ungrateful soul? The common phrase explains it: *I will flatter her so that she might turn to me*. I, says the Lord, will give her a thousand praises. I will speak to her with the greatest sweetness in telling her simply to turn to me, *So that she might turn to me*.

Oh Christian soul! See how the Lord behaves with you. He admonishes you to put everything relating to this life out of your mind, so that you can hear more directly the voices with which He speaks to your heart. And even though you might make yourself deaf to His approaches, He will not stop constantly addressing you in your heart, so that you might turn to Him. "He calls the one who is unwilling to return to Him so that he can return." Do not make yourself deaf to such soft voices. Get ready beforehand and prepare yourself to hear them sooner. When you do hear them, respond lovingly to such goodwill. As San Mauricio

---

21. Hosea 2:14.
22. Cf. 2 Corinthians 9:15.

says, "Hearken to the invitation of your Savior; listen to the voice of salvation with which He is addressing you!"[23]

Oh Christians! If we really knew how to taste this sweetness, if we knew how to value the Lord's compassion, we would disdain our temporal interests, our cares, and the worldly tastes which are now keeping our affections imprisoned and making our hearts lukewarm. On one occasion the Jews, scandalized by a point of doctrine which Christ in His grandeur was preaching to them, left Him in a humiliating way. The Lord turned to His apostles and said to them, *Do you also wish to go away?* Do you also want to leave? Saint Peter the apostle answered Him, *Lord, to whom can we go? You have the words of eternal life.*[24] Lord, to whom shall we go? Your words are so sweet, words of eternal life. The Lord is constantly speaking similar words to us in our hearts. May He find us completely ready to respond.

But let us pay attention to what the word *therefore* refers in the phrase I quoted from the prophet Hosea: *Therefore I will allure her*. Lord, why do you behave so graciously to this soul? If we look at the beginning of this chapter, we find nothing in this soul but faults and ingratitude. So, Lord, is this what spurs you to such graciousness in speaking to the heart in such a gentle way? Why "therefore"? Here is the truth, Christians. From us there is nothing except ingratitude. From the Lord, everything stems from His infinite mercy. That is why the verse says, *Therefore, etc., because I am merciful*.

So, Christians, listen to what the Lord says through Isaiah: *Remember this in your heart, you transgressors.*[25] I beg you to reflect for a moment on what is occurring in your heart. It is completely clothed in earthly emotions, and it is full of impatience, anger, and other faults. But the same heart also contains the opposite, since the Supreme Maker fashioned it in the shape of a pyramid. He placed its widest part on the top so that it might be a wider field to the reception of heavenly matters. The other section, located on the bottom, has less space for things of the earth to leave their mark. But in your own hearts, earthly matters are too many to count, while heavenly influences hardly exist.

Remember this in your heart, and there you will find the Lord, who was knocking on the door and calling: *I will speak to his heart*. I beg you to let Him in. Do this simply because, in His infinite mercy, He loves you. *Remember this in your heart*. Because if you know how to taste the sweet voices of the Lord, you will assure yourself of a more rational life and you will resist the voices with which your enemy wants to corrupt you over and over again.

---

23. Saint Maurus was an early disciple of Saint Benedict.
24. John 6:67–68.
25. Isaiah 46:8.

In this Sunday's gospel, Saint Matthew relates to us that the spirit of the tempter approached Christ to convince him to turn some stones into bread: *Command these stones to become loaves of bread.* But the Lord responded in these words: *Man does not live by bread alone, but by every word that comes from the mouth of God.*[26] That is, begone, begone you evil spirit, because man does not live only by bread. Instead he lives principally by the word of God. And what did Christ mean by this? To understand this, let us recall that man consists of an inferior or sentient part, which he shares with the irrational creatures, and a superior or rational part, which he shares with the angels: *To think with the angels.*

Bread is what sustains the inferior part. But the sustenance of the superior part, that which is necessary to preserve man's better life, consists of the divine voice with which the Lord speaks to the heart, which enables the heart to turn to Him. Just as bread does not give life to the inferior part unless it is chewed and digested, so even less will man be able to live the life of the soul without pondering the divine words which the Lord speaks to his heart: *Remember this in your heart, you transgressors.* Return to the heart, because there these voices of the Lord will assist and sustain us with a very gentle gift. For God himself said that those who savor His voice would never encounter death: *Whoever keeps my word will never taste death.*[27]

Let us say, then, with the Psalmist King, *I will hear what the Lord God will speak to me.*[28] I will listen to what my God and Lord says within me. I know that there will be only greater and greater peace and goodwill for those who know how to turn to Him in their heart: *Because He will speak peace to those who turn to Him in their heart.*[29]

Better yet, let us all say with the boy Samuel, *Speak, Lord, for your servant is listening.*[30] Speak, Lord, for your servant is listening with a contrite heart and with great pleasure. Dearest Christian, may what Saint Lawrence Justin says come to pass: "When one is called by the breath of heaven, let him without delay renounce his vices and evil habits."[31]

On the other hand, may it not happen that anyone could cause the loving complaints which the Lord makes through Job: *I call to my servant but he gives me no answer. I myself must plead with him.*[32] Is it possible, says the Lord, that I have called and continue calling my servant over and over again with my own voice

---

26. Luke 4:4, based on Deuteronomy 8:3.
27. John 8:52.
28. Psalm 85:8.
29. Psalm 85:8.
30. 1 Samuel 3:10.
31. Saint Lawrence Justinian was a fifteenth-century Augustinian who composed a series of ascetical writings.
32. Job 19:16.

and he has never answered me? *He gives me no answer.* But Lord, if someone has shown himself so ungrateful and disobedient toward you, would you still keep calling that servant of yours? Indeed, yes, Christians, so filled with goodwill, so gentle is the Lord in the words He directs to men!

I do not know if, at the beginning of the world, the Lord created man on the sixth day, when He had already created all the other creatures, so that these creatures would provide an example for man to obey the voice of God without hesitation. For these creatures obeyed that voice even when they did not exist: *For He spoke and it came to be; He ordered from nothing.*[33] And Saint Paul wrote, *He calls into existence the things that do not exist.*[34] Once they were created, they also obeyed Him with reverence, according to Baruch: *He sends forth the light and it goes; He called it and it obeyed Him trembling.*[35] Following, then, this example and attracted by the Lord's great goodwill, let us obey His interior voices, for such gentleness well deserves it. *Taste and see. Gentle in word. He calls in an interior way.*

Exterior Voices of God to Man

In the second place, the Lord calls us with exterior voices, through His ministers. This is no less an argument of His goodwill. The Lord sees that men are so worn out by their engagement with things of the senses that they have difficulty perceiving the spiritual voices with which He himself speaks to the heart. So He places His words in the mouth of His ministers so that He can call them to live according to His holy and divine law through their senses, that is, their ears. But, at the same time, so that the real or supposed ineptitude of the minister does not diminish his listeners' appreciation of the word of God, the Lord himself is saying to His ministers, *He who hears you, hears me; he who rejects you, rejects me.*[36] Whoever listens to you reverently is also listening to me; and whoever scorns you scorns me. This is an important doctrine. Whoever the minister who speaks the word of God might be, to scorn the minister is to scorn God himself. I am not the one saying this. A Lapide or Oleastro are not the ones saying this. This comes from the mouth of the Lord Himself.[37]

To emphasize the reverence with which we ought to listen to the voices that God sends us through His ministers, let us recall what is said about San Antonio de Padua. Once when men refused to listen to him, he went and preached to the fish, who did listen to him. Also, it is said of Venerable Bede that, when he was blind, they took him to preach to a bunch of rocks, telling him they were men.

---

33. Psalm 33:9.
34. Romans 4:17.
35. Baruch 3:33.
36. Luke 10:16.
37. Cornelius a Lapide was a seventeenth-century Flemish Jesuit and scripture scholar. Gerónimo de Oleastro was a sixteenth-century Dominican and scripture scholar.

He concluded his sermon with the words, "May we all meet again in the heavenly glory," and the rocks responded, "Amen!"

Saint Bernard of Siena tells us the same thing with these words: *Brothers and sisters, which do you think is more important, the body of Christ or the word of God?* He himself answered, *If you want to tell the truth, you should answer in this way: that the word of God is due no less respect than the body of Christ.* Oh Christian, learn this teaching! There is no Christian, however barbarous he might be, who, upon being shown the body of Christ, would not reverence it and repent. Then do the same whenever you hear the word of God.

The sacred scriptures are full of testimonies that show us how pleased the Lord is when we listen to the voices of the ministers He sends us. They also speak of the prizes, the sweetness, and the gifts the Lord promises to those who diligently listen to and obey these voices. On the other hand, they also speak of the punishments deserved by those who do not listen to these voices, or those who listen to them but quickly forget them. The same applies to those who do not put them into practice by improving their lives and fulfilling the obligations of their state. In the final analysis, these are the voices of God Himself who calls us with great reverence and sweetness. Test this out in your own experience and you will certainly see it. *Taste and see. Gentle in word. He calls in an exterior way.*

As a confirmation of what these voices can do—both the interior ones in the heart and the exterior ones that come into the ear—remember what happened with Saint Margaret of Cortona—specifically, to be brief, her conversion and subsequent life. Christians, let us follow the example of this saint. Let us not become attached to the things of this life. As Saint Peter Chrysologus says, *The one who grasps after this earthly dwelling when he is called to the heavenly kingdom demonstrates a very limited mind.*

Finally, with complete submission, let us say to the Lord, with Saint Augustine, Father of the Church, "Lord, up until now you have been calling us. Now we are calling you, we yearn for you. We have heard you, Lord, now listen to us." From the depths of our soul, with a contrite and heavy heart, we say to you, because you are who you are, we are sorry.

Second Sermon: Of the Sweetness of God in His Divine Law

A common error and a common saying are both in circulation these days. They are opposite of each other and conflict with each other. The error is entirely wrong, while the saying has a solid element of truth in it.

We can ask anyone at all if, when he leaves this miserable life, he wishes to go and enjoy God in His glory. He will surely respond yes. If we go on to ask why this person is not keeping the holy and divine law down to the smallest detail, since this is the only way to gain what he says he wants, as the Lord says—*If you want to enter into life, keep the Commandments*[38]—the man will respond that he definitely does desire this, but it is very difficult. And that is the common error.

At the same time one often hears the same people say that it is harder to be bad than good. They say that it is tougher and more arduous to live a faulty and sinful life or a life not based on the holy and divine law than it is to live a perfect and holy life. That is the common saying. It contains a basic truth that is often repeated but rarely believed.

According to the design I put before you in my first sermon, today I have to refute the common error, that is, to try to make the case that the yoke of the holy and divine law is very light, easy, and soft. In other words, that the Lord is benign, loving, and soft in the holy law which he places before us with great love: *Taste and see that the Lord is good. He is gentle in the yoke of the law which He lovingly places upon us.* Indeed, Christ himself says the same thing through Saint Matthew, *My yoke is easy and my burden is light.*[39] The yoke of my law is gentle and very light. This is a grand demonstration of the goodwill of the Lord, of His love toward us, and of how much He wishes that we willingly carry this yoke.

The scribes and Pharisees, who were a depraved and perverse people, *a depraved and perverse generation*,[40] as Christ called them, placed heavy and unbearable laws on people which they completely refused to carry out themselves: *They tie up heavy burdens and place them on men's shoulders, but they themselves are unwilling to lift a finger to move them.*[41]

But the Lord has a completely opposite attitude. He cannot do anything except grant us a law that is pure and holy, *the immaculate law of the Lord*, exceedingly easy and soft, *it is sweet and light*, and he fulfilled it in every detail: *I have not come to abolish the law, but to fulfill it.*[42]

But now it seems to me that I am hearing my listeners offer this objection: how can he say that the divine law is sweet and gentle and that the road to heaven is easy? Experience shows us that the opposite is true. Christ Himself, through Saint Matthew, says, *For the gate is narrow, and the road is hard.*[43] The door and the road that lead to the glory of eternal life are narrow.

I hope to be able to answer this objection convincingly and in a way that will console my listeners. It is true that the Lord said that the door and gate were narrow. But He did not say that it is a difficult and burdensome matter to enter that door

---

38. Matthew 19:17.
39. Matthew 11:30.
40. Matthew 17:17.
41. Matthew 23:4.
42. Matthew 5:17.
43. Matthew 7:14.

and to walk down that road. For this simply consists in learning and observing His holy and divine law. And the Lord himself says that His law is gentle and sweet. The Holy Spirit says the same thing in various places, through the mouth of David.

But we can even go beyond the answer I have just offered. We ourselves can very easily fill out and broaden the divine law as much as we want. For the Father Saint Augustine comments on the psalmist's words, *By the word of your lips, I have avoided hard ways.*[44] He says, *The roads of the Lord are narrow or difficult for those who fear them, but for those who love the Lord, those roads are gentle and soft.* And Saint Gregory the Pope writes that the path of the Lord or of His law seems narrow at its beginning to those who are only barely animated by the love of God and divine matters: "The path is narrow for those who are beginning on it, but for those who are living well, it is wide. For them, due to God's love, even persecution is pleasing." This is true because love softens everything: *Love makes everything as soft as a trifle.* Therefore the Psalmist King said, I followed your divine laws with great love and because of that my experience with them was like going through a wide and spacious path: *I shall walk in liberty, for I have sought your precepts.*[45]

All of this is what the Divine Wisdom is saying in Proverbs. God, speaking to the soul, says, I will conduct you through the road of perfection, the road of my law. Once you have entered it, you will find it not narrow, but wide and soft. *I have led you in the paths of uprightness; when we walk your step will not be hampered.*[46] Commenting on this text, Dr. Rabano observes, *What begins as very narrow becomes, through the passage of time and the delights of inexhaustible sweetness, very enjoyable.*[47]

See here, Christians, how that objection you offered is resolved. See here a doctrine which ought to offer tremendous consolation to all. The path of the holy and divine law should not be called narrow, because it is not. It only seems that way when you look at it from a distance, and have not actually undertaken it. "When one is in stupor, simply taking food is a burden for a long time, but afterward it becomes delightful," as Hugo Cardenal says.

That path seems difficult to you because you don't yet have the kind of love you ought to have for the Lord and for divine matters. As the Venerable Father Saint Jerome says, "There is nothing more easy than love." Thus when there is love, the divine law and the road of glory turn out to be extremely easy.

For more confirmation of the saying *taste and see*, try out the path of the Lord. Taste it and you will see that it is completely soft and sweet. Love is the first

---

44. Psalms 17:4.
45. Psalms 119:45.
46. Proverbs 4:11.
47. Rabanus Maurus was a ninth-century Benedictine monk who wrote a series of commentaries on scripture.

commandment of the holy law of God, and, as Saint Jerome says, the whole law consists in loving. So then how can the whole law not be gentle as soon as you get into the habit of living in the purest observance of it? *Taste and see.* This is what I have to accomplish in you today, Christian soul, assisted, as we both are, by divine grace. So let us beg for the intercession of the most immaculate Queen of Heaven and say with the angel, *Hail Mary*.

Taste and See

The easier it is to observe the laws and ordinances of a prince or sovereign, the more blameworthy is a subject who transgresses them. For the goodwill of the prince and the gentleness of his law render invalid any excuses aimed at lessening the blame of the offender. The holy Fathers of the Church have often investigated the reason for which the Lord, who is so benign and gentle, so patient and merciful, punished our first parents so harshly for a sin which seems of such small consequence. Our Lord punished horribly the sin of the bad angel who wanted to ascend to the throne of divinity: *I will raise my throne above the stars of heaven, I will make myself like the Most High*.[48] This seems quite just, since that was the height of presumption and a great sin. It is also understandable that God would punish the sin of Nimrod and those other giants who tried to construct the tower of Babel and thus storm heaven. But it is not easy to understand why God punished our first parents and all their descendants with eternal exile from Paradise and with a host of miseries they suffered and we still suffer for taking a bite of a fruit from a tree.

The doctor Saint Augustine has an acute response to this difficulty: *The smaller you consider the sin of our first parents, the greater you make their guilt, since, if God had demanded something more difficult, it would not seem that significant a fault not to fulfill the command of the Lord.* God had set them up as masters of all of Paradise, where they could eat every kind of fruit. He merely set aside one tree whose fruit he ordered them not to touch. So the divine commandment was actually quite easy to fulfill. Thus for them to transgress it was a very serious fault. So the Lord's punishment of them was completely fair.

Today, Christians, I want to show you that the law that the Lord has enjoined upon us is gentle and very easy to observe. *The Lord is gentle, gentle in the yoke He imposes.* I want to show you that the more you understand the law, the easier it is to observe it with complete fidelity and to embark upon a good and holy life. I want to show you that disobedience to the law renders you worthy of great punishment. The yoke of the holy and divine law is gentle for two reasons: first

---

48. Isaiah 14:13–14.

its intrinsic nature, and second, due because of various extrinsic circumstances. I invite you, then, with the psalmist, to taste its sweetness. This is the second rung of the mystical and wonderful ladder to glory.

Its Intrinsic Gentleness

First, the yoke of the divine and holy law is gentle due to its own nature. This is because, with the Lord's never-failing assistance and grace, it does not order us to do anything which is not easy to do. It does not tire us out, especially in comparison to living without a concern for that law. Remember the passage from Saint Matthew to which I have already referred. Christ tells those who are living a life filled with difficult tasks, Come to me, you who are carrying a heavy burden on your shoulders, for I want to give you rest and take away your burden. *Come to me, all you who are weary and are carrying heavy burdens, and I will give you rest.*[49] Christian! To whom do you think the Lord is speaking in this passage? Do you think He is speaking to those who are carrying his holy law on their shoulders so that he can relieve them of that and give them the refreshment of his glory? Hardly! Right before, He summons those whom he is calling here and warns them to observe His holy and divine law: *Take my yoke upon you.*

Then why does He say that they are troubled by a heavy burden? Hugo says that it is because these people are those who live a life that does not conform to their obligations: *They are burdened with the burden of their sins.* Thus, living in a way that does not conform to what God orders is a difficult and heavy task. But living according to the law and the Lord is a gentle and easy matter. Those who fulfill the law of God are the ones to whom Christ in His majesty is speaking: *I will refresh you.* So put out of your mind that old error. Discard it as soon as possible so that you will not have to do so when you will not be able to garner any benefit from doing so.

Listen to the confessions of the disillusioned, of those who, without merit and without fruit, lament that they maintained that error during their lives: *We took our fill of the paths of lawlessness and we journeyed through the trackless deserts.*[50] Those wretched peoples are saying, We have led a wearying life and have taken many heavy and difficult steps. And I ask them, Tell me, gentleman, isn't it true that you lived according to your own tastes? Didn't you give yourselves free rein to have what people usually call a "good life"? And they are forced to reply, You are correct. We now understand that that life was actually very difficult and burdensome. *We took our fill.* Christians! It is not too late for us to realize the truth. Beginning right now, let us be entirely animated by a love of the Lord. Let

---

49. Matthew 11:28.
50. Wisdom 5:7.

us begin to live a holy life, and let each one of us be conformed to the obligations of his state of life.

Sustain me with flowers, refresh me with apples, for I am faint with love. In chapter 2, verse 5 of the Song of Songs, the Holy Spirit is asking insistently that she be sustained and comforted with flowers and apples because she has grown faint with love. But what relief can flowers and apples give her when she is swooning in love? And what flowers and apples would those be? The Chaldean Paraphrase explains it clearly: *Sustain me in the words of the law, through which the world becomes gentle. Place it upon my neck, for they are as sweet and as pleasurable as the apples of paradise.*[51] For the spouse, these flowers and apples are the commands of the divine law of her husband. She is completely given over to his love: *You whom my soul loves; I am faint with love.*[52] She judges that there is nothing sweeter, more wonderful, or more gentle than to take upon her shoulders the divine law of God, that is, to carry it out exactly. You who are the beloved of the best divine spouse, Jesus Christ, say to Him in the voice of the song: *I am faint with love; sustain me with the words of the law, place it upon my neck.* Let the holy and divine law come over us, since it is in itself truly sweet and gentle.

And to all Christians everywhere, *Taste and see.* Look at the Psalmist King. See how he loves the Lord and His holy law: *I loved your law.*[53] See how he regards the law: *Your commandment is exceedingly broad.*[54] O Lord, how full, how extensive, how spacious is your law! And take note of what God Himself is saying to you in Deuteronomy 30:11: *This commandment that I am commanding you today is not too hard for you, nor it is too far away. It is not in heaven that you should say, Who will go up into heaven for us?* What I am commanding you, my son, is not anything beyond what you can do. It is not far away, so that you would have to undertake a long journey to reach it. Just the opposite. As Saint Paul says, *The word is near you, on your lips and in your heart.*[55] What I am commanding you is near; it is in your mouth and your heart. In sum, how easy, how sweet, how gentle it is!

And if David said that, and God Himself said the same of the old law, what might God be saying in our own times, with the law of grace? How can the gentleness of the two laws even be compared? The old law contained 613 precepts. In our law, as you know, that number was reduced to ten, and really only to one—the law of love. That was what Saint Gregory was saying: *Everything really only involves one commandment, since whatever is commanded is linked to love.* The old

---

51. The Chaldean Paraphrase was a second-century Targum, an Aramaic translation and commentary on scripture. In 1515 Cardinal Ximénez de Cisneros included parts of it in the Alcalá Bible, and through that it became known in the Spanish world.
52. Song of Songs 1:7, 2:5.
53. Psalm 119:97.
54. Psalm 119:96.
55. Romans 10:8.

law did not have the outpouring of grace that our law has in the sacraments. So if the old rule was, according to God's own word, very gentle, how gentle might we expect the present law to be?

You might still say that it is hard to observe the Lord's holy law and follow the heavenly path, for the penances involved make you shudder. But this is a trick. Do you know what the Venerable Father Saint Bernard says: *Many people see the wounds we have, but they do not see balms we also have.* Those who gaze at the heavenly path from afar can accurately see the penances involved, but they are unable to see the consolations. A penance that you see in the examples of the Saints appears to be large, but you do not notice the interior comfort in which they live as a gift from the Lord.

And really, my Christians, even if the only thing you might receive were a tranquil conscience, which characterizes the lives of good and just people, what is in this life more gracious, sweet, and gentle?

The Prophet King says that the tranquil conscience is so gracious that it is a glory in itself: *This is our glory, the testimony of our conscience.*[56] One can read in the office of Saint Elizarius, no one saw him disturbed or agitated. No one ever saw him perturbed or annoyed by any of the many things that happened to him. Tell me, Christian, if there has ever been anyone in the midst of the affairs of the world, no matter how rich or exalted, who has never been observed to be perturbed or annoyed. Truly, it is a wonderful thing to live with a tranquil conscience. *Taste and see.*

Its Extrinsic Gentleness

Second, the yoke of the holy and divine law is sweet and gentle for a number of reasons that add new luster to the sweetness and intrinsic ease of the law, and which make it softer and softer. I think that the most outstanding of these reasons is realizing that God Himself ordained the law for us and orders us to fulfill it. Even if God's law contained nothing gentle in itself, merely thinking about that would always make it very gentle. Men often perform enthusiastically and easily tasks that are given them by a friend or by someone whose interests they wish to promote. And since our Lord is infinitely good, and since we owe Him so much and need Him so much, it follows that it ought to be easy for us to obey any command of His.

Let us recall, Christians, that when our Lord gave us the commands of love, He told us that love was the principal feature of the law, and he especially called our attention to this feature: *This is my commandment. I, however, say to you, love.*[57] And for the entire law as a whole He shows us the same thing, through

---

56. 2 Corinthians 1:12.
57. John 15:12; Matthew 5:44.

Isaiah: *Listen, my people and hear me, for the law will come forth from my lips.*[58] Let us listen again to the words of Jesus, *This is my commandment, that you love one another.* Realize that I am the one who is commanding you: *I, however, say to you.* Thus, considering that the Lord is giving us the law, will you not observe it with great gentleness?

What is harder and more grim than for a father to take the life of his own son? It is said that the Canaanites, Jebusites, Perizzites, and other peoples of the promised land took the lives of their own sons, with exception of the sons of the king, on many days each year. It is also said that in Carthage three hundred boys were sacrificed on one day. The Latins were said to kill and sacrifice one-tenth of the boys born during the year. In Mexico, it is said, every year twenty thousand hearts of boys who had been killed would be offered up. You will say, how could they have the heart to do such terrible things? The answer is simple. The idol whom each people had as their god ordered it. Well, then, if those barbarians were enraged enough to kill their own sons on the orders of some cruel gods, isn't it enough for you to observe the law of the Lord, knowing that the ordinances of the law are so good and its prescriptions so gentle?

Another circumstance which gives a new softness to the holy and divine law is the example of Christ. He Himself had no obligation to observe the law, yet He made Himself subject to it and observed it faithfully. *God sent His Son, born under the law. I did not come to abolish the law, but to fulfill it.*[59] Oh, what a circumstance this is! If we knew how to value this, how enthusiastically would we observe the law of God and live a holy life. Jesus Christ himself refers to this circumstance when He says, *Learn from me, and you will find rest for your souls.*[60] Learn from me, learn from my example, and you will find that you are refreshed when you walk. The spouse of the Song of Songs yearned for this example of her divine husband and promised to imitate it promptly: *Draw me after you. Let us make haste.*[61] The author of the Letter to the Hebrews encourages his readers with this example of Christ, as he says, *Let us lay aside every weight and the sin that clings so closely, and let us run with perseverance the race that is set before us, looking [to Jesus] the pioneer of our faith.*[62]

Another circumstance that makes the divine law and its observance easy and gentle is the presence of divine grace, with which our Lord nourishes and aids us. If we really knew the true value of this, what would it matter if the law of the Lord were hard in itself? Then, with the assistance of this divine grace, we

---

58. Isaiah 51:4.
59. Galatians 4:4.
60. Matthew 11:29.
61. Song of Songs 1:4.
62. Hebrews 12:1.

would accomplish everything quite easily. So says Saint Paul: with divine grace I dare all and I can do all. *I can do all things through Him who strengthens me.*[63] Whenever the yoke of the divine law might be heavy, the grace of God absorbs that burden and cancels it out. So Hugo interprets what the Holy Spirit says through Isaiah: *His burden will be removed from your shoulder, and His yoke will be destroyed from your neck.*[64]

Another aspect or circumstance that also makes the observance of the divine law more easy and gentle is the hope of heavenly glory. If we knew how to consider this aspect, that would enable us to suffer many sorrows and mortifications in this life. We would regard all of them together as sweeter than a honeycomb compared to the gentle and sweet gift of the glory which those who observe the law in this life finally reach. I do not want to trouble you by going on. So I will skip over many other paths through which the observance of the holy and divine law is made more gentle and easy through extrinsic ways. What I have already said is enough to demonstrate how gentle this law is both in itself and in various extrinsic circumstances and how gentle it is when the one who lays down the divine law is our God and Lord. *Gentle is the Lord. Gentle in the yoke He imposes.* So it is, Christians!

Third Sermon: Of the Gentleness of the Lord Even in the Sufferings He Sends Us: *Taste and See*, Psalm 33

A full and vibrant trumpet call ought to resound in this church today before I begin my sermon, for I am going to issue a public call and publish a royal decree. Congratulate yourselves a thousand times over, you happy vassals of that Monarch who continues, more and more, to demonstrate his great goodwill toward you and who loves you so tenderly. *That the Lord is good.*[65]

My public call is about the grand price of a coin with which on this very day you all ought to make yourselves rich. And what is this coin of such a high price? Christians, this coin is made up of the pains and labors which the Lord sends us in this life. Its worth is so grand that with it you can purchase heavenly glory. The Lord's infinite goodwill and love for you spurs Him to send us this coin. He does this to show us that He is above all sweet and gentle. *Taste and see. Gentle in the scourging of his sons.*

This is what the royal prophet is saying in Psalm 22: *Your rod and your staff comfort me.*[66] Lord, when I feel the rod of your tribulations ("Rod, that is, rod

---
63. Philippians 4:13.
64. Isaiah 10:27.
65. Psalm 34:9.
66. Psalm 23:4.

of tribulations," as Saint Bernard of Siena says in his commentary) I have experienced a great consolation within myself. The same saint adds this about these words: "True adversity has a sweet taste and bestows a prudent disposition on us." It is as if he said this: "The psalmist rightly declares that, in the rod and the staff with which the Lord afflicts us, I have found great consolation. For the trials and labors of this life have a very flavorful, sweet, and wonderful taste."

When the Lord punishes us, we are very correctly called sons: *In the scourging of His sons*. Indeed, the punishments of a father toward a son are not like the punishments of a tyrant, or even those of a king. Rather, they are punishments of pure love. When God punishes us, He shows us how much He loves us. And since a basic characteristic of love is generosity, the labors that He sends us are a pledge or a demonstration that He loves us as children.

Let us recall the eleventh chapter of the Gospel of Saint John. The sisters of Lazarus, Martha and Mary, sent a message to Jesus. *Lord, he whom you love is ill.*[67] Lord, look over here, the one you love so much is sick. It is important to note that Christ, who cured so many sick people, permitted his friend Lazarus to suffer that illness. But what happened afterward is even more significant. Jesus said, *This sickness is not unto death.*[68] This sickness is not fatal. However, Lazarus did die. And Jesus did not go to revive him until four days after his death. But if the Lord loved Lazarus, why did He not go sooner to cure him? He even postponed his departure, as one of the saints points out: "He delayed the healing."

Now let us reflect on all this. Christ truly loved Lazarus. But He also loved his sisters: *Jesus loved Martha and her sister and Lazarus.*[69] If Christ had cured Lazarus immediately or had revived him immediately after his death, Lazarus would have had a token of the love of Christ. But his sisters would not have suffered during those four days of mourning, and therefore they would not have had a demonstration of the love Christ had for them. So Aloysius wrote: "Tribulations in this life are a preeminent gift of God. There is no more certain sign of divine election and love."

But I see that we still have to answer the question, how can punishment and affliction be called "goodwill"? Look at it this way: our God is a doctor, and that is how He came into the world. On this earth our life is always prone to sickness because of the various evil humors of the sin of our first parents. So tell me, which doctor loves his patients—the one who treats them with bitter liquids and bleeding or the one who indulges his patient's whims and does not forbid anything that the patient's corrupted taste might long for? Certainly, you will answer, the

---

67. John 11:3.
68. John 11:4.
69. John 11:5.

first one. That is indeed true, and that is why God says to the troubled man, *I will be with him in trouble. I will rescue him and honor him.*[70]

Besides being a doctor, God is also a lathe operator, as can be deduced from one of the songs: *His hands are turned.*[71] What does the operator do? He places the wood which before was without form or beauty into the lathe. Or, he takes iron and removes the superfluous slag and gives it a form beautiful enough to be placed among the most beautiful gems of a palace. That is exactly what the Lord does to us, according to Saint Gregory of Nyssa: "God inserts the dregs of everything into his lathe and transforms what is superfluous matter into the Lord's portion."

The Lord has another profession as well—that of a glass worker or glassblower. As we read in Ezekiel, *I will leave you there and melt you.*[72] The glass worker takes a flint, places it in a fire, keeps it up in open air until it is melted and purified and becomes very fine glass. This is what the Lord does with you, because He loves you and desires your salvation.

Tribulations are the greatest riches, the highest gift from the Lord, the most gentle and desirable thing in this life. So our holy father Saint Francis said to his companion Fray Leon, that in this world nothing gives true happiness except trials borne for the love of God. He added, Fray Leon, even if a religious were a great philosopher, a great theologian and had mastered all the sciences of the world; even if he knew the qualities of all the herbs and trees of the world, the movement of the heavens, of the stars and the other heavenly bodies; even if he could work miracles like curing the sick or the deaf; even if he could raise someone from the dead; even if he were such a tremendous preacher that he could convert the whole world, and even if he were able to do a number of other things as well, still, in all of this, he would not have true joy in this world. For true joy consists in suffering patiently the travails of this life.

The learned Gerson[73] writes, "Although I might want to say everything I would think of in praise of tribulations, I would still not be able to expound its value completely. But I know that it certainly would not be necessary to read many books." And so, *Hail Mary.*

Taste and See

It is true that tribulations are not always paternal punishments from God. However, they generally stem from His goodwill and are aimed at the greater glory of the Lord or the greater spiritual benefit of the afflicted person. There is a large

---

70. Psalm 91:15.
71. Song of Songs 5:14.
72. Ezekiel 22:20.
73. Jean Charlier de Gerson (1363–1429) was a leading French theologian and academic.

difference between the tribulations that come from divine love and those that are sent by God as punishment. But at times the first type of tribulation can spark a most distressing set of ideas toward the person who is afflicted by them. So we see that after the apostle Paul had escaped the hardships of the sea, he was bitten by a very poisonous snake. His companions thought that this was divine vengeance and that he was a murderer: *This man must be a murderer. Though he escaped from the sea, justice has not allowed him to live.*[74] But shortly thereafter, when they saw that he did not die, they began to think of him almost as a God.

So, Christians, do not consider the trials and tribulations which you experience and you see others undergoing as punishment from God. Think of them instead as manifestations of the great compassion and gentle goodwill of the Lord. *Taste and see, etc. In the scourging of His sons.*

The trials of this world are widespread but gentle, for they flow from the Lord's impulse of love. Thus they have infinite worth. That is, they are gentle a priori and a posteriori. In both of these respects, I have to try, once again, to convince you of the gentleness of the Lord, of which the psalmist speaks: *Taste and see, etc. In the scourging of His sons.* This is the third rung of the ladder of glory.

In the first place, the gentleness of the tribulations of this life and the goodwill of the Lord in spreading them around are apparent to us a priori. For the word of God teaches us that sufferings come from the paternal and infinite love that the Lord has for us. So we encounter this passage in the letter to the Hebrews: *For the Lord disciplines those whom He loves, and scourges every child whom He accepts.*[75] The Lord afflicts those He loves, but He flogs the one He receives as a son. The Lord Himself says the same thing in the Apocalypse: *I reprove and discipline those whom I love.*[76]

Saint Gregory the Pope argues that there is a strong connection between the love of God for His chosen children and the mortification and difficulties He sends us. He says that those whom the Lord does not honor with such difficulties are carrying a large banner proclaiming that they are not among the number of the Lord's chosen children: "Those who are not numbered among the scourged are not numbered among the sons."

Therefore, that we are afflicted by the Lord with the travails of this life means that we are loved by Him as his own children. How could it not be a consolation to see ourselves with difficulties and travails! How could we not say with the Psalmist, *Your rod and your staff, etc.*, your rod and your staff console me.

But you will say, how can the tender love of a father for his child be reconciled with punishing and afflicting him? Actually, a harmony between love and

---

74. Acts 28:4.
75. Hebrews 12:6.
76. Revelation 3:19.

strictness is what characterizes a true father. It is precisely because the father loves him that he teaches him to obey. When he misbehaves, the father scolds and punishes him so that the son can correct his mistakes. Because he does not want his son to turn out wrong, he takes him out to the field to teach him to work. So that he might be able to defend himself, the father teaches him how to use weapons, and he takes great care that the son will not use them in any inappropriate way. The father continuously watches over his son's life and health. When he appears to be depressed, the father perks him up, counsels him, and helps him. Finally he makes him heir of all he possesses.

In this way, even though it might seem at first glance that the son is his father's slave, it becomes clear that he is his father's deeply beloved son. The divine father behaves in a similar way with men, who are his own sons. Perhaps in this vein Christ was able to address His own father in the words of David: *I am your servant, the son of your serving girl.*[77] I am your servant, the son of your servant, and also your son. First he presents himself as a servant, which was reflected in the way he worked and suffered. But then he gives himself the name of son, as if he were saying that the name "servant" springs from the glorious and loving title of "son." This is what the father Saint Anthony of Padua says in his commentary: "Because I am a servant of God, for that reason I am at the same time a son of God."

Oh Christians! What an honor the Lord bestows on us in this life. The tribulations He sends us are the clearest proof that He looks upon us as sons, that His love for us is boundless: *As a lily among thorns, so is my love.*[78] He loves us like a lily that struggles among thorns. Thus He shows us the endless abundance of his mercy.

The Holy Spirit affirms in Ecclesiastes 35:26 that God's mercy is the other side of the tribulations He sends us: *His mercy is welcome in times of tribulation.*[79] In a time of tribulation the mercy of the Lord is beautiful. And in the book of Tobit: *In the time of tribulation, you forgive sins.*[80] In the time of tribulation, you pardon our sins. The Prophet King said to the Lord, *In the day of tribulation, you will honor me.*[81] The apostle Paul wrote in the same vein to the Corinthians. *I am full of consolation, filled with joy in all of our tribulations.*[82]

Listen, then, faithful Christians! When you find yourselves hounded by the tribulations of this life, do not think that the Lord has forsaken you. Do not consider yourselves wretched. On the contrary, think of yourselves as most fortunate. For in this time you see, clearer than ever, how much the Lord loves you. If you only

---

77. Psalm 116:16.
78. Song of Songs 2:2.
79. Sirach 35:26.
80. Tobit 3:13.
81. Psalm 50:15.
82. 2 Corinthians 7:4.

knew how to appreciate that! Then you would be able to bear these tribulations with the greatest love and patience, and conform yourselves to the will of God.

This is how the apostles, instructed by the Majesty of Christ, looked at things. They bore tribulations very joyfully, and considered them as a great gift from the Lord: *As they left the council, they rejoiced.*[83] Other upright people looked at matters in the same way and gave repeated thanks to God for the tribulations they received. A notable case of this way of acting was a religious, a daughter of this monastery. One reads that she, seeing that the Lord was favoring her with trials and tribulations, used to pray in this manner: "Lord, how can you show so many favors to such an unworthy creature? Lord, I am only worthy of your sending me gifts and comforts. But I confess that my sins and ingratitude have rendered me completely unworthy of the tremendous favor you do for me, sending me trials and tribulations. May your infinite compassion and mercy be exalted forever." This is how the upright speak, and this corresponds to reality as it actually is.

David speaks of miserable and wretched sinners in Psalm 72: *For they have no pain; their bodies are sound and sleek. They are not in trouble as others are; they are not plagued like other people.*[84] There are no sufferings for them. They do not share the labors and the pains of the rest of mankind. And they will not be punished with them in this life. Saint Ambrose asks why God did not punish Cain for the death of his brother, why he did not extinguish his life or give him a more dreadful punishment. But then he answers: "He was judged unworthy of being punished." Since Cain was so evil, he was not worthy of God's punishment in this life.

But in regard to the just, it is completely appropriate and honorable that the Lord afflicts them, as San Juan Capistrano says. The apostle Paul was not so happy because he had been snatched up into the third heaven, that is, Paradise, as much as because he had suffered persecution and imprisonment for the love of God: *I do not say he was blessed because he had been caught up all the way into the third heaven and paradise, but because he had been cast into chains.* He adds that he was not so happy for having heard mysterious things which no man is able to explain in words, but for having been chained and jailed for the glory of the Lord: *I do not say he was blessed because he heard mysterious things, but because he bore chains.* Look at the apostle Saint Peter, wrapped in chains, surrounded by soldiers, bound for death. But look at how tranquil he was—he was sleeping! Oh apostle Peter! How were you able to sleep so calmly in the face of such tribulation? In this matter, the father Saint Hilary says: "The servants of God never rest more gently than when they are favored with trials and tribulations."

---

83. Acts 5:41. The rest of the verse is "that they were considered worthy to suffer reproach for the sake of the name [of Jesus]."
84. Psalms 73:4–5.

But it is even more important to note what Saint Chrysostom says about this place: "If anyone would ask me if I would prefer to be Peter bound to the angel who filled the jail with splendor and freed him from his chains, I would reply that I would much rather be Peter in chains rather than to be with that bright heavenly assembly." He continues, "For I understand that the gift of being bound in chains is greater than the ability to hold back the sun, shake the world, to subdue all of hell, and perform the other mighty tasks which the Angels were able to accomplish."

Well, then, Christians! Who is not going to have a tremendous love for the trials and tribulations with which the Lord, as a benign father, afflicts us in this life? Who is not going to embrace them with great zeal and to consider himself most fortunate to experience them? Who is not going to confess that God, in parceling them out to us, is sweet and gentle and that He is impelled to send them to us by his love?

When we have travails, we have God Himself at our side. *The Lord is near to the brokenhearted*.[85] If we are lukewarm and have difficulty bearing those travails, let us call upon the Lord. In His compassion, He will promptly listen. The royal prophet, based on his own experience, testifies to this: *In my distress I cried to the Lord and He answered me*.[86] The Lord sends us tribulations because he loves us. Because of that love, he makes our tribulations more gentle. *Taste and see*.

A Posteriori

In the second place, the tribulations are gentle because of the heavenly and eternal prize they allow us to reach. Let us begin by recalling what Mary Most Holy revealed to the Venerable Mother of Ágreda. The prize that comes from even the small travails we suffer patiently for the love of God, even though it might be nothing more than picking up a piece of straw from the floor, is beyond the capacity of the human tongue to describe or the human mind to comprehend.

Saint Paul addresses the Christians of Corinth in a similar way. See that even a very light travail lasting only a minute conducts us to an eternal height of glory: *For this slight momentary affliction is preparing us for an eternal weight of glory beyond all measure*.[87] Louis de Blois says, The slightest annoyance, tolerated for the love of God, is not only of tremendous value, but exceeds many other great instances of good works.[88] God knows the value of the trials and tribulations suffered in this life. If only we knew how to calculate their worth, how soft and wonderful we would find them to be!

---

85. Psalm 33:19.
86. Psalm 120:1.
87. 2 Corinthians 4:17.
88. Louis de Blois was a sixteenth-century Flemish monk and writer.

In the little book of my holy father Saint Francis, there is a passage in which they asked him how he could so joyfully tolerate the pain in his eyes and the other constant troubles and tribulations. The holy patriarch replied, "The reward of the glory I hope to enjoy through these trials is so great that whatever task, whatever illness, whatever humiliation, persecution, or mortification comes gives me the greatest delight and joy." The heavens let a hermit understand the prize which these travails would enable him to reach in this way. The hermit had to undertake a long walk to obtain water. So he thought that he would move his dwelling place closer to the fountain. But one day, while he was returning, carrying his pitcher, he heard a voice counting 1, 2, 3, 4. He stopped and looked around but he could not see anyone. So he resumed walking and the voice resumed counting, 5, 6, 7. He looked around again but still saw no one. But the voice spoke to him: I am an angel sent by God to count the steps you take, so that each step will be rewarded. So he moved his dwelling again, but this time he moved it farther away from the fountain, so that he would have to take more steps and thus increase his merits for heaven.

The father Saint Anthony of Padua meditates on these words of Deuteronomy: "They shall suck as milk the abundance of the sea."[89] He interprets them in this way. The righteous will enjoy the tribulations of the sea of this world as if they were the sweetest milk. Later he exclaims: "Oh, how sweet is the bitterness, how easy are the tribulations which the elect bear for the name of Christ!"

The most devout de Blois places these words in the mouth of Christ. "If all the hearts of all the people who ever lived, are living, or will live were joined together, they would not be able to support even the smallest part of the sweet prize which I am going to bestow on anyone who bears the slightest cross or tribulation patiently for the love of me."

Oh Christian! Who would not confess that the tribulations and pains of this life are also most soft because of the prize to which they lead and the effects they cause? *Taste and see. Gentle in the scourging of his children.* Well, then, Christians, let us listen to this and let us all say together. . . .[90]

Fourth Sermon: Of the Sweetness of the Lord in His Mercy

The lowly vassal of a prince will not be comforted by the prince's goodwill if it does not include forgiveness and pardon of the offenses which the vassal has committed against his lord. No matter how gentle his law, his words of admonishment, or his punishments might be, some sort of transgression of his law will usually occur. When this happens, the prince will be forced to adopt an exceedingly rigorous and strict reaction.

---

89. Deuteronomy 33:19.
90. The sermon ended with a common prayer, most likely the Hail Mary.

In this regard our Lord, *the God of all consolation,* whose goodwill we have already meditated upon, takes pride in being *a Father of mercy.*[91] This is the fourth rung on the mystical ladder to heaven. Today it falls to me to consider this step with you, so that we can all know more fully the gentleness of the Lord. *Taste and see the goodness of the Lord. Gentle in the forgiveness of sins.*

The Lord is benign and gentle when He generously pardons any offenses we have committed against Him. His infinite mercy consists in this above all else.

The Prophet King demonstrates this in Psalm 102:13 in these words: *As a father has compassion for his children, so the Lord has compassion for those who fear Him. For He knows how we were made.*[92] Just as a tender father is moved to pity because of the misfortunes of his children, so our God and Lord, in His infinite mercy, sympathizes with us because He realizes how fragile the clay is from which we have been formed. Oh, the name of father! How fitting for God, and how little deserved for men!

The compassion of the Lord also shines forth in the last words of our text: *For He knows how we were made.* The text does not mention the good deeds the Lord has done for us. It does not mention the free will He has given us. It does not mention the grace with which He helps us, and which would enable us never to offend Him. The text does not refer to the many gifts with which He has favored us and which ought to lead us to love Him always and serve Him promptly. All of these matters might induce the Lord to punish us for our ingratitude.

But what they evoke instead is the fragile nature of the clay from which we were formed. This leads the Lord to have compassion and mercy on us. Here indeed we see how much mercy is a part of the Lord.

The father Saint Anthony of Padua says, "Mercy is a wonderfully soft substance which the Lord sprinkles on the hearts of men." That is to say, the Lord, besides being sweet and gentle—*the Lord is gentle*—is also a father of compassion, a father of all mercy and consolation. Thus the church in its prayer says that the most characteristic attitudes of God are sympathy and forgiveness: *God, whose nature it is always to be merciful and to spare.*[93] And the man from Padua, whom I have just cited, says, "Although all the works of the world show forth and proclaim the divinity and boundless excellence of the Lord, none of them—indeed, not all of them together—do that so well as His infinite mercy." In other words, the Lord pours forth the abundance of his love with mercy. This is the point we shall treat today.

Ave María: Taste and See

There is nothing more unworthy or horrible than for someone to take the weapons which have been given to him for his own self-defense and use them to take

---
91. 2 Corinthians 1:3.
92. Psalm 103:13–14.
93. A prayer from the popular devotion the Litany of the Saints.

his own life. Well, then, the infinite mercy of God is the best weapon to defend the well-being of our own soul. This is all that we can desire in this mortal life. So what would it amount to if we used the mercy of God to remain in an evil life, in a life that barely conforms to the obligations each of us has?

Before I begin this point, I want to warn you that the Lord is greatly offended by those who do this. Everyone preaches that God is merciful and that we can therefore approach Him with confidence that He will pardon the sins we have committed. But the divine mercy should not be extolled to the extent that some do, who use it as an excuse to commit more sins. These people are completely unworthy of God's mercy and they ought to fear for their salvation.

This is what Saint John was speaking of in the Apocalypse, *Lord, who will not fear you?*[94] And listen to what he says: *For you alone are compassionate*. It would have been logical if he had said that the Lord should be feared because He is severe and strict. But Saint John is speaking of those who abuse the Lord's mercy and to use it as a pretext to commit more sins. These people should be afraid. Because this verse, *Who will not fear you?*, is directed at them.

I assume that no one here is using these excuses but instead that all of you want to hear of the greatness and gentleness of the Lord's infinite mercy to heighten your zeal to beg for forgiveness, to increase greatly your love for Him, and to bless and praise Him more.

Indeed, the Lord is gentle. *Taste and see*. He is gentle especially in the great mercy with which He pardons us whenever we approach Him. *Gentle in the forgiveness of sins*.

The gentle mercy of the Lord is as great as the grandeur of God himself. That is simply the way He is. This mercy is great and boundless both intensively and extensively, in terms of its intention and of its extension. In terms of intention, because of the intense and intrinsic affection with which He pardons us. In terms of extension, because of the great multitude of sins which God's mercy reaches. So I want to consider the gentleness of the Lord in terms of both of these aspects—intensive and extensive. Let us begin.

Intensive Mercy

First, the mercy of our God is grand and tremendously gentle in its intention. The delight and the love with which God pardons us is such that He seems a bit disturbed when He is not pardoning us. The father Saint Ambrose asked why, when He created the world, God did not rest until the seventh day. *He rested on the seventh day*.[95] Why did He not have to rest on the previous days? Why would

---

94. Revelation 15:4.
95. Genesis 2:1.

He need to rest at all, since it is certain that all the labors that He undertook on the previous days would not have been able to tire Him? Saint Ambrose responds in this way: *He rested on the seventh day because now He had someone whose sins He could forgive.* The Lord created man on the sixth day, and so on the seventh day He had someone He was able to pardon. He had someone for whom He was able to employ his attribute of mercy. This is why the Lord rested: He is infinitely pleased to exercise his mercy.

One has to notice that, as soon as the light was created, the Lord was so pleased that, differently from all his other works, He immediately certified it and it alone as good: *And God saw that the light was good.*[96] Since light illuminates everything else, it is really the creature in which the living reality of mercy can be best seen. As soon as it was created, it spread itself out to all other creatures without any exception. And this so delighted the benign and most merciful Lord that He immediately broke out in praise of light itself.

The Lord was in love with light because that creature so gently spread over everything. In doing so, it showed the flashes of divine mercy, as Psalm 144 says: *The Lord is gracious and merciful, slow to anger and abounding in steadfast love. The Lord is gentle to all, and His mercy is over all that He has made.*[97] The Lord's mercy is like light. As extensive as the darkness of sin might be in someone, as soon as a remorseful sinner approaches God, that light scatters the darkness "instantly," as the father Saint Bernard says, or *quickly*, as Jesus puts it in the parable of the prodigal son.[98] The Son of God Himself, when He became man, offered Himself to everyone as the light of the world: *I am the light of the world.*[99]

The father Saint Gregory says, "The mercy of the Lord is like a fountain that is always clear and polished, always flowing and delightful, always overflowing and purifying." The sacred text of Zacharias 13:1 points in the same direction: *On that day a fountain shall be opened for the house of David to cleanse them from sin.* This is how the Lord acts with us. He is solely spurred by the boundless love He has for us.

So the Lord says to us through the prophet Jeremiah: *I have loved you with an everlasting love; therefore I have drawn you, having mercy on you.*[100] I always love you and have loved you with an infinite love. In my infinite mercy I have taken care to draw you to me. Oh Christians! When we see the most intense pleasure with which the Lord grants us His mercy, who will refuse to give himself over completely to Him and draw near to Him? The Lord so enjoys pardoning us that it seems that giving Him an opportunity to do so is doing Him a favor, as if the mercy He has for us were actually for himself.

---

96. Genesis 1:4.
97. Psalm 145:8–9.
98. Luke 15:22.
99. John 8:12.
100. Jeremiah 31:3.

In this regard, let us listen to a story about a monk. He was a person who was never able to learn any prayer to commend himself to the Lord's mercy. He constantly heard the other monks in the choir chanting the words, "Have mercy on me, O God." He was only able to remember this one prayer, but he got it wrong: "Have mercy on your self, O God."[101] So he went around repeating this, "Have mercy on your self, O God. Have mercy on your self, O God." One time, the superior, passing by his dwelling, perceived a scent so sweet that it seemed the sweetness of the heavenly glory. So he called the monk and asked him what he was doing. He replied that he was such a wretch, that he only knew this one prayer, "Have mercy on your self, O God," and that he was praying it. The superior taught him to say, "Have mercy on me." The monk obeyed. But the superior stopped smelling that scent any more. So he ordered the monk to pray as he had before, and he was once again able to sense that heavenly scent. It seemed that the Lord wanted to make the monk understand how much it pleases Him to offer pardon, and how little effort is needed to approach His divine mercy.

The compassion with which the Lord pardons our many faults is extremely intense. The father Saint Anthony of Padua explains it with these sublime words: "Any virtue is most efficacious and delightful when it is experienced most perfectly. The divine mercy is greater than all other virtues since its perfection is infinite." But are not all virtues of God infinite? Faith tells us that they are. But then how can the saint say that infinity is a peculiar characteristic of mercy?

We have to make a distinction. The divine virtues can be considered in themselves. From this perspective, none is greater than any other, since infinite perfection is in all of them. But they can also be considered as they apply to creatures. From this perspective there can be a gradation of greater and less, because some can apply with greater intensity than others. So then, that wisest man from Padua says that the Lord applies his mercy with a greater intensity than any other virtue. Thus, the mercy of the Lord is the most efficacious and sweet of all the divine virtues.

Some words of David offer a fine confirmation of this: *For as high as the heavens are above the earth, so great is His mercy toward those who fear Him.*[102] The Lord's mercy toward those who fear Him corresponds to the height of the heavens above the earth. Two things cry out for comment here. First, it seems that those who fear God are upright, and thus do not offer an opportunity for the exercise of mercy. Second, once mercy is granted, it does not seem to need anything to support it, since it is not thin or brittle.

What this text means is that once mercy has been granted, the Lord keeps granting it with such generosity that it fills the small vessel of the soul with

---

101. In the well-known Latin phrases, which Serra probably used in the sermon, the difference between these two phrases is only one syllable: *Miserere mei* and *Miserere tui*.
102. Psalm 103:11.

the force of the inexhaustible ocean. Thus Saint John Chrysostom says, "The mercy of God, whenever it is encountered, is an immense sea, unfathomable and incomprehensible, and it exceeds all meaning and all created knowledge." The great Saint Anthony of Padua also considers this most intense sea of divine mercy and exclaims, "Oh, the height of divine clemency! How far are you from the depths of human intelligence?" Here perhaps everyone might better be able to say what Aristotle proclaimed on another occasion, "Oh infinite sea! Since we cannot embrace you, embrace us!"

Christians, the reluctance to punish, which the Lord demonstrated when He had to drown the world in the flood, comes from this divine goodwill: *The Lord was grieved to his heart as He said, "I will destroy man, whom I have created."*[103] Concerning this verse, the subtle master Saint Augustine comments that even though it is figuratively said that God created the world in six days, He actually created it in an instant. Despite this, for a hundred years before flooding the surface of the earth, He was issuing warnings about those forty days, hoping that people would repent and spare Him the necessity of punishing them. And after the flood, as if He regretted having employed such strong measures, He himself swore that He would never order another flood. As a witness to that oath, He placed the rainbow in place: *By my own self have I sworn. I will set my bow.*[104]

In a similar way, after He had destroyed the city of Tyre for its many faults, God ordered the prophet Ezekiel to show how the necessity of razing the city had pained Him: *Now, therefore, son of man, raise a lamentation over Tyre.*[105] And many other similar instances could be mentioned as well.

Pardoning even the greatest sinner with great gentleness greatly pleases the Lord. There is a story that one day such a great sinner went out into the field seething with rage and blaspheming against God. He issued this challenge. If God is strong enough to fight me, let Him try, and I will destroy Him! Do you think that the Lord came down to fight against that unhappy man? Instead, God arranged it that a document floated down with this message, "Say this, have mercy on me, Oh God." The man read it. He changed his mind and repented and the Lord granted him His infinite mercy. Saint Anthony of Padua rightly says, "Oh, the depth of the divine clemency!"

Extensive Mercy

The mercy of God is most gentle in its extension. It is the kind of divine mercy that extends itself to all men and women, no matter how many of them are sinners nor how many times they have sinned. God's mercy is not just for a certain

---

103. Genesis 6:6–7.
104. Genesis 22:16, 9:13.
105. Ezekiel 27:2.

time. No, it persists through all the centuries, as the psalmist says: *The mercy of the Lord is from everlasting to everlasting toward those who fear Him*.[106] The Lord's mercy extends from the beginning to the end of time. It is not restricted to a certain number of sins. Indeed, it hardly knows how to count: *His mercy is beyond measure*.[107] It is not limited to a certain type of person. It is open to everyone from the beginning, according to the Book of Wisdom: *You are merciful to all, for you can do all things*.[108] You have sympathy for everyone, because you can do everything. It does not just apply to a certain level of sinfulness. It is infinitely greater than the most enormous sin, as the prophet Joel says: *He is gracious and merciful, slow to anger, and abounding in mercy*.[109] The mercy of the Lord conquers every type of malice. In a word, it applies to everything, since it is boundless: *The mercy of the Lord is without end*.[110]

Christian, ponder and meditate upon the extent of the mercy of the Lord. In Sacred Scripture, the Holy Spirit talks much more of God's mercy than His justice. Thus, through the prophet Isaiah, the Spirit says: *The Spirit of the Lord has sent me to proclaim the year of the Lord's favor and the day of vengeance of our God*.[111] The Spirit of the Lord sent me to preach a year of mercy, and only one day of anger. And, as if even this might appear to be too strict, he adds, through the same prophet: *In the moment of indignation, hide your face from me and in my eternal mercy I will gather you*.[112] My people, in the moment of my anger, get away from me. In my constant times of mercy, I myself will seek you out. The divine anger lasts but an instant, but His mercy is eternal.

This exemplary extent of the divine mercy was what made the Doctor Saint Bonaventure exclaim, "Oh, the compassion of our God!" The soul sins, not simply one sin or a number of them, but countless times. Yet the Lord instantly returns and pardons each and every sin. Even more: if the sinner does not want to turn back to the Lord, God calls him so that he might return.

The civil laws say that if a crime is very bad and obvious, no lawyer ought to be given to the criminal. The law orders that if a criminal is arraigned but does not submit to the legal process, all of his property should be sequestered. And if a year goes by and he still does not submit, then his property is forfeit and no appeal is allowed. In book 4 of the Old Digest it is ordered that a person who has been summoned to court three times but still does not submit himself to the

---

106. Psalm 103:17.
107. Cf. Psalm 147:5.
108. Wisdom 11:23.
109. Joel 2:13.
110. Cf. Psalm 145:3.
111. Isaiah 61:2.
112. Cf. Isaiah 54:7–8.

legal process is declared in contempt and his property seized. If he is apprehended and the crime is serious enough, the penalty is death.[113]

These are the types of laws which earthly tribunals use. But the mercy of our God is based on a different system. The Lord is always our advocate: *We have an advocate with the Father, Jesus Christ the righteous.*[114] The Lord is lenient with us, not just for a year, but for many years. Whatever our faults might be, He pardons us: *I do not tell you to pardon seven times, but seventy times seven times.*[115]

Thus Saint Augustine says, "No one should distrust the compassion of God, for his mercy is greater than our distress." Saint Vincent Ferrer says that God would even pardon someone who killed one of the apostles. Remember Manassas, who turned to idolatry, persecuted those who remained faithful to God, and made the streets of Jerusalem run with innocent blood. He sawed in two the prophet Isaiah, whom God so loved, and committed many other atrocities. Yet at the end he repented and God granted him his mercy.

---

113. The reference is to the Code of Justinian. Trials and other legal proceedings are dealt with in books 5–11 of the Digest.
114. 1 John 2:1.
115. Matthew 18:22.

Glossary

Alabado — A Latin hymn the missionaries taught the Indians as part of morning prayer.

Alcalde (Indian) — The highest-ranking neophyte in the mission hierarchy. He was supposed to be elected by the neophytes, and he possessed a real, if limited, authority in supervising the mission Indians and in maintaining order.

Alférez — An ensign; the lowest-ranked military officer, approximately equal to the second lieutenant in a modern army.

Almud — Dry measure equal to 4.275 quarts. Also, a land measurement equivalent to about half an acre.

Arroba — A bulk measurement equal to approximately 25.36 pounds.

Arroyo — A creek or stream.

Asistencia — Mission outpost to which a priest would occasionally journey to say Mass or administer the sacraments. Sometimes called a *visita*.

Atole — A cooked mixture of water and ground, dried grains; a staple mission food.

Auto-da-fé — Literally, "act of faith." A public ceremony during which the sentences on those brought before the Spanish Inquisition were read and after which the sentences were executed by the secular authorities.

Caballero — A gentleman, horseman.

Cacique — An indigenous leader or chief.

Camino Real	A principal road or trail for mounted travelers or pack trains.
Cañada	A gully or ravine.
Cañón	A ravine, gorge, or canyon.
Capellán	A chaplain.
Carreta	An ox-drawn two-wheeled cart.
Casta	A system of racial classification prevalent in New Spain during the Colonial era.
Castillo	A fortress or coastal defense battery.
Catalán	A native of Catalonia, Spain. Also, the language spoken by these people.
Colegio apostólico	Apostolic college. Franciscan institution established in the New World for the training and sending of missionaries to unbaptized native peoples.
Comandante	A military commander.
Comisaría	Commissariat or branch of the army in charge of providing food and other supplies for the troops.
Comisario	The officer in charge of the warehouse. Also, an investigator of the Inquisition.
Congregación	A compact settlement of indigenous people administered by a missionary.
Convento	The mission building in which the priests' residence was located.
Converso	Baptized Catholics of Jewish or Muslim descent.
Corpus Christi	A Catholic feast day celebrated in honor of the Eucharist.
Corregidor	A member of an indigenous governing body charged with supervising the mission Indian population.
Cotón	Woolen shirt or blouse worn by neophytes.

Cuera	From the word *cuero*, which means "hide" or "leather." A heavy, knee-length, usually sleeveless jacket made up of a number of layers of buckskin or cowhide and bound at the edges with a strong seam. This distinctive armor garment gave the presidio soldier the name by which he was known for more than two centuries: *soldado de cuera*.
Curandera	A female practitioner of folk medicine.
Curato	A parish.
Discretorio	The council of advisers to the Guardián in a Franciscan religious house.
Don/Doña	A polite title of honor or respect.
Encomendero	The person to whom an encomienda was given.
Encomienda	Indians and lands granted to a conquistador or nobleman with the understanding that he would provide for the welfare and civilization of the Indians and their instruction in Christianity in return for their labor.
Escolta	The escort or squad of soldiers assigned to protect a missionary at a mission.
Excelentísimo	Literally, "Most Excellent." A term of respect.
Fanega	A dry measure of weight, the equivalent of about 1.6 bushels. Also a land measurement, equivalent to approximately 8.8 acres.
Fernandinos	Term used to refer to the Franciscans who were members of the Colegio Apostólico de San Fernando in Mexico City.
Fiscal	In the colonial government, the chief staff attorney in the viceroy's office. In the missions, a native officeholder whose duties involved seeing that Indians attended church services.
Fray: Friar	A member of the Franciscan Order.
Ganado	Livestock. *Ganado mayor* refers to cattle, and *ganado menor* refers to sheep, goats, or pigs.

Gente de razón	Literally, "people with the capacity to reason," meaning any non-Indian.
Gentile	A nonbaptized Indian.
Guardián	The head of a Franciscan religious community.
Habilitado	An officer in a Spanish regiment charged with its supplies or money; a quartermaster or paymaster.
Hacienda	A large estate.
Hechicera(o)	A witch or sorcerer; the pejorative name given to Native American shamans by missionaries.
Ilustrísimo(a)	Literally, "Most Illustrious." A term of respect.
Inquisidores	Inquisitors.
Judaizantes	Pejorative term to describe Jewish converts to Christianity who were suspected of not being true converts.
Junta	A congress, an assembly, a council; any meeting of persons to speak about business; a group used to administer or govern, usually ad interim.
Ladino(a)	Literally, "latinized." Referred to indigenous people who were in some fashion, most often linguistically and/or culturally, assimilated to Spanish ways.
League	A standard Spanish measure of distance, approximately 2.6 miles.
Lector	Literally, "reader." An academic title for someone who held a faculty position in a university.
Lobo(a)	A casta designation indicating ancestry that is both African and Indian.
Maestro de novicios	Novice master.
Mantillón	A rogue, rascal, trickster, etc.
Mayordomo	A foreman or supervisor of a mission under the priest, or of a ranch under the owner.
Mestizo	A person of mixed European and Indian heritage.

Metate	Slab of stone on which acorn seeds, corn, and other grains were ground.
Mulato(a)	A casta designation indicating ancestry that is both African and European. In colonial Latin America, mulato(a) could also mean an individual of mixed African and Indian ancestry.
Neófito	Neophyte, or recent convert; term used to describe the Christian mission Indians.
Patronato Real	The system through which the Spanish monarchy controlled ecclesiastical finances and personnel.
Pinole	Parched corn, ground and mixed with sugar and water for a drink. Also refers to the ground seeds of other plants.
Pozole	A thick soup of cornmeal, beans, common knee, marrow bones, and scrap of meat.
Propaganda Fide	Latin for Propagation of the Faith. The name of a Vatican congregation under whose auspices the Franciscan apostolic colleges were founded.
Predicador	Preacher.
Presidio	A frontier military garrison; the fortified location and community of such a garrison.
Pueblo	The populace; a village or town. The smallest municipal entity, often possessing a town council.
Pulque	A thick fermented alcoholic beverage made from various species of agave.
Quintal	A unit of measurement equal to 100 pounds.
Ramada	A simple structure made by setting fork posts in the ground as corners and laying other posts across them as a superstructure, roofed with thatch.
Ranchería	An Indian village or settlement, usually referring to the non-Christian Indians. It could also refer to an Indian village attached to a mission.
Real Hacienda	Royal treasury.

Rebozo	A shawl or wrap.
Reconquista	Reconquest.
Recopilación de Indias	Compilation of the laws of the kingdoms of the Indies.
Reducción	A mission or the process of missionization. The state of affairs resulting from the indigenous peoples' being grouped together closely at and around the missions.
Regidor	A member of the town council.
Repartimiento	A medieval system of dividing land and Indians, implemented by the Spanish in the colonization of the Indies, beginning in the early 1500s.
Representación	A report.
Salve Regina	A prayer to the Virgin Mary.
Síndico	A public attorney or advocate/representative of a mission. Among Franciscans, the síndico was the person, usually a non-Franciscan, who managed the order's funds, for the upkeep of its institutions, including its missions.
Sínodos	Annual stipends paid to the missionaries by the government of New Spain. In Alta California these stipends were financed from the Pious Fund, an endowment originally established by the Jesuits in the eighteenth century to support the Baja California missions.
Solar	House lot in a town.
Suerte	Track of town land on which to grow crops.
Su Ilustrísima	Literally, "Your [or His] Illustrious-ness." A term of respect.
Su Paternidad	Literally, "Your [or His] Paternity." A term of respect.
Su Señoría	Literally, "Your [or His] Lordship." A term of respect.
Te Deum Laudamus	A traditional Latin hymn of praise to God.
Teniente	A lieutenant, or the officer who was second in command of a military unit.

Tercio	A unit of measurement, equivalent to one-half a pack load.
Vale	"God be with you" or "Farewell" in Latin.
Vara	A measure of length, equivalent to 33.99 inches.
Villa	A royally chartered settlement with certain rights to self-government.
Visita	A station attached to a mission, which a priest would occasionally visit to administer the sacraments.
Visitador general	Visitor general. An inspector appointed to visit and report on a particular region, such as a viceroyalty.
Vuestra Merced	Literally, "Your Mercy" or "Your Grace." A term of respect.
Vuestra Reverencia	Literally, "Your Reverence." A term of respect.

Bibliography

Abbott, Don Paul, ed. *Rhetoric in the New World: Rhetorical Theory and Practice in Colonial Spanish America*. Columbia: University of South Carolina Press, 1996.
Ágreda, María de Jesús. *Mística ciudad de Dios: Vida de María*. Madrid: [s.n.], 1970.
Aguirre, Rodolfo. "La demanda de clérigos 'lenguas' del arzobispado de México, 1700–1749." *Estudios de Historia Novohispana* 35 (July 2006): 47–70.
Ahern, Maureen. "Martyrs and Idols: Performing Ritual Warfare on Early Missionary Frontiers in the Northwest." In *Religion in New Spain*, edited by Susan Schroeder and Stafford Poole, 279–97. Albuquerque: University of New Mexico Press, 2007.
Alegre, Francisco Javier. *Historia de la Compañía de Jesús en Nueva España*. 3 vols. Mexico City: Impr. de J. M. Lara, 1841.
Almada, Ignacio. *Breve historia de Sonora*. Mexico City: Colegio de México; Fideicomiso Historia de las Américas; Fondo de Cultura Económica, 2000.
Alomar Esteve, Gabriel. *Ensayos sobre historia de las Islas Baleares, hasta el año 1800*. Palma de Mallorca: Ediciones Cort, 1979.
Altamira, Juan Rodríguez de Albuerne. *Pacificación de los chichimecas de la Sierra Gorda y dictamen del auditor de guerra Marqués de Altamira*. Edited by Vargas Rea. Mexico City: Biblioteca Aportación Histórica, 1944.
Anderson, Kat. *Tending the Wild: Native American Knowledge and the Management of California's Natural Resources*. Berkeley: University of California Press, 2005.
Applegate, Richard. "Native California Concepts of the Afterlife." In *Flowers of the Wind: Papers on Ritual, Myth, and Symbolism in California and the Southwest*, edited by Thomas C. Blackburn, 105–19. Socorro, N.M.: Ballena Press, 1977.
Archer, Christon I. *The Army in Bourbon Mexico, 1760–1810*. Albuquerque: University of New Mexico Press, 1977.
Armas Briz, Luz Amelia, and Olivia Solís Hernández, eds. *Esclavos negros y mulatos en Querétaro, siglo 18: Antología documental*. Santiago de Querétaro: Gobierno del Estado de Querétaro; Oficialía Mayor; Archivo Histórico de Querétaro, 2001.
Armstrong, Regis J., OFM Cap., J. A. Wayne Hellmann, OFM Conv., and William J. Short, OFM, eds. *Francis of Assisi: Early Documents*. 4 vols. Hyde Park, N.Y.: New City Press, 1999.
Arricivita, Juan Domingo. *Apostolic Chronicle of Juan Domingo Arricivita: The Franciscan Mission Frontier in the Eighteenth Century in Arizona, Texas, and the Californias*. Translated by George P. Hammond and Agapito Rey. Revised and indexed by Vivian C. Fisher.

Introduction and notes by W. Michael Mathes. Berkeley: Academy of American Franciscan History, 1996.

Asencio, José. *Origen de los colegios apostólicos.* Guadalajara: Banco Industrial de Jalisco, 1947.

Bancroft, Hubert Howe. *California Pastoral, 1769–1848.* San Francisco: History Company, 1888.

———. *History of California.* 7 vols. San Francisco: History Company, 1884.

Barajas, Dení Trejo. "Declinación y crecimiento demográfico en Baja California, siglos 18 y 19: Una perspectiva desde los censos y padrones locales." *Historia Mexicana* 54, no. 3 (2005): 761–831.

Barr, Juliana. *Peace Came in the Form of a Woman: Indians and Spaniards in the Texas Borderlands.* Chapel Hill: University of North Carolina Press. Published in association with the William P. Clements Center for Southwest Studies, Southern Methodist University, 2007.

Bean, Lowell John, ed. *California Indian Shamanism.* Menlo Park, Calif.: Ballena Press, 1992.

———. *The Ohlone Past and Present: Native Americans of the San Francisco Bay Region.* Menlo Park, Calif.: Ballena Press, 1994.

Beebe, Rose Marie, and Robert M. Senkewicz. "Constructing California: Francisco Palóu's Life of Junípero Serra." In *They Came to El Llano Estacado: An Anthology of Essays Presented at the Franciscan Presence in the Borderlands of North America Conference,* edited by Félix D. Almaráz, 21–35. San Antonio: University of Texas at San Antonio, 2006.

———. *Guía de manuscritos concernientes a Baja California en las colecciones de la Biblioteca Bancroft.* Berkeley: University of California Library, 2002.

———. "Junípero Serra and the Santa Bárbara Channel." In *To Toil in That Vineyard of the Lord: Contemporary Scholarship on Junípero Serra,* edited by Rose Marie Beebe and Robert M. Senkewicz, 95–120. Berkeley: Academy of American Franciscan History, 2010.

———. *Lands of Promise and Despair: Chronicles of Early California, 1535–1846.* Berkeley and Santa Clara: Heyday Books and Santa Clara University, 2001.

———. "Revolt at Mission San Gabriel, October 25, 1785: Judicial Proceedings and Related Documents." *Boletín: Journal of the California Mission Studies Association* 24, no. 2 (2007): 15–29.

———, eds. *To Toil in That Vineyard of the Lord: Contemporary Scholarship on Junípero Serra.* Berkeley: Academy of American Franciscan History, 2010.

———. "Uncertainty on the Mission Frontier: Missionary Recruitment and Institutional Stability in Alta California in the 1790s." In *Francis in the Americas: Essays on the Franciscan Family in North and South America,* edited by John Frederick Schwaller, 301–28. Berkeley: Academy of American Franciscan History, 2005.

———. "What They Brought: The Alta California Franciscans before 1769." In *Alta California: Peoples in Motion, Identities in Formation, 1769–1850,* edited by Steven W. Hackel, 17–46. Berkeley: Published for Huntington-USC Institute on California and the West by University of California Press, Berkeley, California, and The Huntington Library, San Marino, California, 2010.

Beilharz, Edwin. *Felipe de Neve: First Governor of California.* San Francisco: California Historical Society, 1971.

Benavides, Alonso. *Benavides' Memorial of 1630.* Translated by Peter P. Forrestal. Washington, D.C.: Academy of American Franciscan History, 1954.

———. *Fray Alonso de Benavides' Revised Memorial of 1634.* Edited by Frederick Webb Hodge, George Peter Hammond, and Agapito Rey. Albuquerque: University of New Mexico Press, 1945.

———. *A Harvest of Reluctant Souls: The Memorial of Fray Alonso de Benavides, 1630.* Translated by Baker H. Morrow. Niwot: University Press of Colorado, 1996.

Bernabéu Albert, Salvador. "El diablo en California: Recepción y decadencia del maligno en el discuro misional jesuita." In *El septentrión novohispano: Ecohistoria, sociedades e imágenes de frontera,* edited by Salvador Bernabéu Albert, 139–76. Madrid: Consejo Superior de Investigaciones Científicas, 2000.

———. *Expulsados del infierno: El exilio de los misioneros jesuitas de la península Californiana, 1767–1768.* Madrid: Consejo Superior de Investigaciones Científicas, 2008.

Bernstein, Barton J. *Towards a New Past: Dissenting Essays in American History.* New York: Pantheon Books, 1968.

Blackburn, Thomas C. *Flowers of the Wind: Papers on Ritual, Myth, and Symbolism in California and the Southwest.* Socorro, N.M.: Ballena Press, 1977.

Blackburn, Thomas C., and Kat Anderson, eds. *Before the Wilderness: Environmental Management by Native Californians.* Menlo Park, Calif.: Ballena Press, 1993.

Bobb, Bernard E. *The Viceregency of Antonio María Bucareli in New Spain, 1771–1779.* Austin: University of Texas Press, 1962.

Bolton, Herbert Eugene, ed. *Anza's California Expeditions.* 5 vols. Berkeley: University of California Press, 1930.

———. *Spanish Exploration in the Southwest, 1542–1706.* New York: Charles Scribner's Sons, 1916.

Boneu Companys, Fernando. *Gaspar de Portolá: Explorer and Founder of California.* Translated by Alan K. Brown. Lérida: Instituto de Estudios Ilerdenses, 1983.

Bonner, Anthony, ed. *Doctor Illuminatus: A Ramón Llull Reader.* Princeton, N.J.: Princeton University Press, 1993.

Borges Morán, Pedro. *El envío de misioneros a América durante la época española.* Salamanca: Universidad Pontificia, 1977.

Braunstein, Baruch. *The Chuetas of Majorca: Conversos and the Inquisition of Majorca.* New York: Ktav, 1973.

Breschini, Gary S., and Trudy Haversat. *The Esselen Indians of the Big Sur Country: The Land and the People.* Salinas, Calif.: Coyote Press, 2004.

———. "Rumsen Seasonality and Population Dynamics." In *The Ohlone: Past and Present: Native Americans of the San Francisco Bay Region,* edited by Lowell John Bean, 183–201. Menlo Park, Calif.: Ballena Press, 1994.

Brockey, Liam Matthew. *Journey to the East: The Jesuit Mission to China, 1579–1724.* Cambridge, Mass.: Belknap Press of Harvard University Press, 2007.

Brown, Raphael, ed. *The Little Flowers of St. Francis.* Garden City, N.Y.: Image Books, 1958.

Brown, Tracy. "Conversion to Christianity in Colonial New Mexico: Pedagogy and Personhood in the Pueblo/Franciscan Encounter." *Catholic Southwest* 12 (June 2001): 29–50.

Campaner y Fuertes, Alvaro. *Cronicón Mayoricense: Noticias y relaciones históricas de Mallorca desde 1229 a 1800.* Juan Colamar y Salas, 1881.

Campbell, Leon G. *The Military and Society in Colonial Peru, 1750–1810.* Philadelphia: American Philosophical Society, 1978.

Cañizares, José de. "Putting a Lid on California: An Unpublished Diary of the Portolá Expedition." Edited by Virginia E. Thickens and Margaret Mollins. *California Historical Society Quarterly* 31, nos. 2, 3, 4 (1952): 109–24, 261–70, 343–54.

Cañizares-Esguerra, Jorge. *How to Write the History of the New World: Histories, Epistemologies, and Identities in the Eighteenth-Century Atlantic World*. Stanford: Stanford University Press, 2001.

Cantarellas Camps, Catalina. "La institucionalización de la enseñanza artística en Mallorca: La Academia de Nobles Artes (1778–1808)." *Mayurqa* 19, no. 1 (1979): 279–93.

Carr, Raymond, ed. *Spain: A History*. Oxford: Oxford University Press, 2000.

Carrasco Pizana, Pedro. *Los Otomíes: Cultura e historia prehispánica de los pueblos mesoamericanos de habla otomiana*. Toluca: Ediciones del Gobierno del Estado de México, 1986.

Carrico, Richard L. "Sociopolitical Aspects of the 1775 Revolt at Mission San Diego de Alcalá: An Ethnohistorical Approach." *Journal of San Diego History* 43, no. 3 (1997): 142–57.

———. *Strangers in a Stolen Land: Indians in San Diego County from Prehistory to the New Deal*. 2nd ed. San Diego: Sunbelt Publications, 2008.

Castillo, Edward D. "The Assassination of Padre Andrés Quintana by the Indians of Mission Santa Cruz in 1812: The Narrative of Lorenzo Asisara." *California History* 68, no. 3 (1989): 116–25.

———. "An Indian Account of the Decline and Collapse of Mexico's Hegemony over the Missionized Indians of California." *American Indian Quarterly* 13, no. 4 (October 1989): 391–408.

Castro, Manuel de. "Lenguas indígenas americanas transmitidas por los franciscanos del siglo 18." *Archivo Ibero-Americano* 52, nos. 205/208 (1992): 585–628.

Castro, Taurino Burón. "Texto autógrafo latino de fray Junípero Serra sobre Antonio Llinaz." *Archivo Ibero-Americano* 53, no. 209 (1993): 105–18.

Cather, Willa. *Death Comes for the Archbishop*. Lincoln: University of Nebraska Press, 1999.

Cavo, Andrés. *Historia de México, paleografiada del texto original y anotada*. Edited by Ernest J. Burrus. Mexico City: Editorial Patria, 1949.

Cervantes, Fernando. *The Devil in the New World: The Impact of Diabolism in New Spain*. New Haven, Conn.: Yale University Press, 1994.

Chauvet, Fidel de Jesús. *La iglesia de San Fernando de México y su extinto colegio apostólico*. Mexico City: Centro de Estudios Bernardino de Sahagún, 1980.

Chemín Bässler, Heidi. *Los pames septentrionales de San Luis Potosí*. Mexico City: Instituto Nacional Indigenista, 1984.

Cirino, André, and Josef Raischl, eds. *A Pilgrimage through the Franciscan Intellectual Tradition*. Canterbury: Franciscan International Study Centre, 2008.

Cisneros, Gerardo Lara. "Aculturación religiosa en Sierra Gorda: El Cristo viejo de Xichú." *Estudios de Historia Novohispana* 27 (June–December 2002): 59–89.

Clossey, Luke. *Salvation and Globalization in the Early Jesuit Missions*. New York: Cambridge University Press, 2008.

Cohn, Norman. *The Pursuit of the Millennium: Revolutionary Millenarians and Mystical Anarchists of the Middle Ages*. Oxford: Oxford University Press, 1970.

Colahan, Clark. "María de Jesús de Ágreda: The Sweetheart of the Holy Office." In *Women in the Inquisition: Spain and the New World*, edited by Mary E. Giles, 155–70. Baltimore: Johns Hopkins University Press, 1999.

———. *The Visions of Sor María de Ágreda: Writing Knowledge and Power*. Tucson: University of Arizona Press, 1994.

Colegio de San Fernando. *Representación al virrey para el reforme de las misiones de California*. Mexico City: Vargas Rea, 1946.

Connolly Miskwish, Michael. "The Changing Economy of the Kumeyaay." In *Memorias de balances y perspectivas de la antropología e historia de Baja California, 2002–2004*, 273–77. Mexicali: Instituto Nacional de Antropología e Historia, n.d.

Cook, Sherburne. *The Conflict between the California Indian and White Civilization*. Berkeley: University of California Press, 1976.

———. "The Conflict between the California Indian and White Civilization." *Ibero-Americana* 21–24 (1943).

———. "Population Trends among the California Mission Indians." *Ibero-Americana* 17 (1940).

Copleston, Frederick Charles. *Medieval Philosophy*. London: Methuen, 1980.

Córdoba y Salinas, Diego de. *Crónica franciscana de las provincias del Perú*. Edited by Lino Gómez Canedo. Washington, D.C.: Academy of American Franciscan History, 1957.

———. *Vida, virtudes, y milagros del apóstol del Perú el B.P. Fr. Francisco Solano*. Madrid: Imprenta Real, 1676.

Costo, Rupert, and Jeannette Henry Costo. *The Missions of California: A Legacy of Genocide*. San Francisco: Published by the Indian Historian Press for the American Indian Historical Society, 1987.

Covarrubias, José Enrique. *En busca del hombre útil: Un estudio comparativo del utilitarismo neomercantilista en México y Europa, 1748–1833*. Mexico City: Universidad Nacional Autónoma de México, 2005.

Crespí, Juan. *A Description of Distant Roads: Original Journals of the First Expedition into California, 1769–1770*. Edited by Alan K. Brown. San Diego: San Diego State University Press, 2001.

Crosby, Harry. *Antigua California: Mission and Colony on the Peninsular Frontier, 1697–1768*. Albuquerque: University of New Mexico Press, 1994.

———. "Defining and Manning the Portolá Expedition." *Boletín: Journal of the California Mission Studies Association* 22, no. 2 (Fall 2005): 4–21.

———. *Doomed to Fail: Gaspar de Portolá's First California Appointees*. San Diego: Institute for Regional Studies of the Californias, San Diego State University, 1989.

———. *Gateway to Alta California: The Expedition to San Diego, 1769*. San Diego: Sunbelt Publications, 2003.

Cruz, José Antonio. *Chichimecas, misioneros, soldados y terratenientes: Estrategias de colonización, control y poder en Querétaro y la Sierra Gorda, siglos 16–18*. Mexico City: Secretaría de Gobernación; Archivo General de la Nación, 2003.

Cruz González, Cristina. "Landscapes of Conversion: Franciscan Politics and Sacred Objects in Late Colonial Mexico." PhD diss., University of Chicago, 2009.

Culleton, James. *Indians and Pioneers of Old Monterey*. Fresno, Calif.: Academy of California Church History, 1950.

Cutter, Donald C. *California in 1792: A Spanish Naval Visit*. Norman: University of Oklahoma Press, 1990.

Daniel, Emmett Randolph. *The Franciscan Concept of Mission in the High Middle Ages*. Lexington: University Press of Kentucky, 1975.

Davin, Diego, ed. *Cartas edificantes, y curiosas, escritas de las misiones estranjeras, por algunos misioneros de la Compañía de Jesús: Traducidas del idioma francés por el padre Diego Davin*. Madrid: Imprenta en la oficina de la viuda de M. Fernández, 1753.

Delio, Ilia. *Crucified Love: Bonaventure's Mysticism of the Crucified Christ*. Quincy, Ill.: Franciscan Press, 1998.

Deverell, William, and David Igler, eds. *A Companion to California History*. Chichester, U.K.; Malden, Mass.: Wiley-Blackwell, 2008.

Donahue, William H. "Mary of Ágreda and the Southwest United States." *The Americas* 9, no. 3 (January 1, 1953): 291–314.

Driver, Harold E., and Wilhelmine Driver. "Ethnography and Acculturation of the Chichimeca-Jonaz of Northeast Mexico." *International Journal of American Linguistics* 29, no. 2, pt. 2 (April 1963). Publication of the Indiana University Research Center in Anthropology, Folklore, and Linguistics, 26. Bloomington: Indiana University, 1963.

DuBois, Constance Goddard. *The Religion of the Luiseño Indians of Southern California*. University of California Publications in American Archaeology and Ethnology, vol. 8. Berkeley: University Press, 1908.

Duggan, Marie Christine. "The Laws of the Market versus the Laws of God: Scholastic Doctrine and the Early California Economy." *History of Political Economy* 37, no. 2 (Summer 2005): 343–70.

———. "Market and Church on the Mexican Frontier: Alta California, 1769–1832." PhD diss., New School for Social Research, 2000.

Duhaut-Cilly, Auguste Bernard, and August Frugé. *A Voyage to California, the Sandwich Islands and around the World in the Years 1826–1829*. Edited by Neal Harlow. Berkeley: University of California Press, 1999.

Dunne, Peter Masten. *Black Robes in Lower California*. Berkeley: University of California Press, 1952.

Dwyer, Daniel Patrick. "Mystics in Mexico: A Study of Alumbrados in Colonial New Spain." PhD diss., Tulane University, 1995.

Ebright, Malcolm, and Rick Hendricks. *The Witches of Abiquiu: The Governor, the Priest, the Genízaro Indians, and the Devil*. Albuquerque: University of New Mexico Press, 2006.

Egido, Teófanes. "Religiosidad popular y taumaturgia del barroco (los milagros de la monja de Carrión)." In *Actas del II Congreso de Historia de Palencia: 27, 28 y 29 de abril de 1989*, edited by Congreso de Historia de Palencia, Tomo 3, volumen 1, Edad Moderna: 11–39. Palencia: Diputación Provincial de Palencia, Departamento de Cultura, 1990.

Eguilaz de Prado, Isabel. *Los indios del nordeste de Méjico en el siglo 18*. Seville: Facultad de Filosofía y Letras, Universidad de Sevilla, 1965.

Eire, Carlos M. N. "The Concept of Popular Religion." In *Local Religion in Colonial Mexico*, edited by Martin Austin Nesvig, 1–35. Albuquerque: University of New Mexico Press, 2006.

Elliott, J. H. *Spain, Europe and the Wider World, 1500–1800*. New Haven, Conn.: Yale University Press, 2009.

Encinas Moral, Angel, ed. *Diario de la expedición de Fray Junípero Serra: Desde la misión de Loreto a San Diego en 1769*. Epílogo y coedición de Teófilo Ruiz. Madrid: Miraguano Ediciones, 2011.

Engelhardt, Zephryn. *Mission San Carlos Borromeo (Carmelo: The Father of the Missions)*. Santa Barbara: Mission Santa Barbara, 1934.

———. *Mission San Luis Obispo in the Valley of the Bears*. Santa Barbara: Mission Santa Barbara, 1933.

———. *The Missions and Missionaries of California*. 4 vols. San Francisco: James H. Barry Company, 1908.

———. *San Antonio de Padua, the Mission in the Sierras*. Santa Barbara: Mission Santa Barbara, 1929.

———. *San Buenaventura, the Mission by the Sea*. Santa Barbara: Mission Santa Barbara, 1930.

———. *San Diego Mission*. San Francisco: James H. Barry Company, 1920.

———. *San Francisco or Mission Dolores*. Chicago: Franciscan Herald Press, 1924.

———. *San Gabriel Mission and the Beginnings of Los Angeles*. San Gabriel: Mission San Gabriel, 1927.

———. *San Juan Capistrano Mission*. Los Angeles: Standard Printing Company, 1922.

Engstrand, Iris Wilson, ed. "Pedro Fages and Miguel Costansó: Two Early Letters from San Diego in 1769." *Journal of San Diego History* 21, no. 2 (Spring 1975): 1–11.

Erickson, Bruce. "Violence and Manhood: Military Culture on the Northern Frontier of Colonial New Spain." PhD diss., University of New Mexico, 2001.

Escandell Bonet, Bartolomé. *Baleares y América*. Madrid: Editorial MAPFRE, 1992.

Espinosa, Isidro Félix de. *Crónica de los colegios de propaganda fide de la Nueva España*. Edited by Lino Gómez Canedo. Washington, D.C.: Academy of American Franciscan History, 1964.

Evans, William E. "The Confirmation Controversy of 1779, Serra vs. Neve: A Rationale." *Southern California Quarterly* 51, no. 2 (June 1969): 85–96.

Fages, Pedro. *A Historical, Political, and Natural Description of California*. Edited by Herbert Ingram Priestley. Berkeley: University of California Press, 1937.

Farriss, Nancy M. *Crown and Clergy in Colonial Mexico, 1759–1821: The Crisis of Ecclesiastical Privilege*. London: Athlone Press, 1968.

Fedewa, Marilyn. *María of Ágreda: Mystical Lady in Blue*. Albuquerque: University of New Mexico Press, 2009.

Fernández-Largo, Jacinto. "Junípero Serra, escotista inédito." In *Homo et mundus: Acta 5. Congressus Scotistici Internationalis, Salmanticae, 21–26 Septembris 1981*, edited by Camille Berube, 537–42. Studia Scholastico-Scotistica 8. Rome: Societas Internationalis Scotistica, 1984.

Fitch, A. H. *Junípero Serra: The Man and His Work*. Chicago: A. C. McClurg, 1914.

Fletcher, Richard. *The Barbarian Conversion: From Paganism to Christianity*. New York: H. Holt and Co., 1998.

Fogel, Daniel. *Junípero Serra, the Vatican and Enslavement Theology*. San Francisco: Ism Press, 1988.

Fogelquist, James. "The Discourse of Saints' Lives in Francisco Palóu's *Vida de Junípero Serra.*" *Americas Review* 24 (Spring–Summer 1997): 227–48.

Font, Pedro. *With Anza to California, 1775–1776: The Journal of Pedro Font, OFM*. Edited by Alan K. Brown. Norman: Arthur H. Clark Company / University of Oklahoma Press, 2011.

Font Obrador, Bartolomé. *El apóstol de California, sus albores*. Palma de Mallorca: Direcció General de Cultura, 1989.

———. *Fray Junípero Serra, doctor de gentiles*. Palma de Mallorca: Miquel Font, 1998.

———. *Joan Crespí: Explorador i cronista franciscà a l'Alta Califòrnia*. Palma de Mallorca: Ajuntament, 1994.

———. *Padre Viejo*. Mallorca: Edicions Miramar, 1991.

Font Obrador, Bartolomé, and Norman Neuerburg. *Fr. Junípero Serra: Mallorca, Mexico, Sierra Gorda, Californias*. Palma: Comissió de Cultura, Consell Insular de Mallorca, 1992.

Fontana, Bernard L., Edmond J. B. Faubert, and Barney T. Burns. *The Other Southwest: Indian Arts and Crafts of Northwestern Mexico*. Phoenix: Heard Museum, 1977.

Forbes, Mrs. A. S. C. *California Missions and Landmarks: El Camino Real*. The author, 1915.

Forbes, Alexander. *California: A History of Upper and Lower California from Their First Discovery to the Present Time*. London: Smith, Elder and Co., 1839.

Forbes, Jack D. "The Historian and the Indian: Racial Bias in American History." *The Americas* 19, no. 4 (April 1, 1963): 349–62.

———. "Historical Survey of the Indians of Sonora, 1821–1910." *Ethnohistory* 4, no. 4 (1957): 335–68.

———. "Unknown Athapaskans: The Identification of the Jano, Jocome, Jumano, Manso, Suma, and Other Indian Tribes of the Southwest." *Ethnohistory* 6, no. 2 (April 1, 1959): 97–159.

Forrestal, Peter P. "Venerable Antonio Margil de Jesús." *Mid-America* 14 (April 1932): 305–34.

Frost, Elsa Cecilia. "A New Millenarian, Georges Baudot: Review Article." *The Americas* 36, no. 4 (April 1980): 515–26.

Galaviz de Capdevielle, María Elena. "Descripción y pacificación de la Sierra Gorda." *Estudios de Historia Novohispana* 4 (1971): 113–49.

Gallardo Arias, Patricia. *Los pames coloniales: Un grupo de fronteras*. Mexico; San Luis Potosí: Centro de Investigaciones y Estudios Superiores en Antropología Social; Universidad Autónoma de San Luis Potosí: El Colegio de San Luis: Secretaría de Cultura del Estado de San Luis Potosí, 2011.

———. "La transgresión al ideal femenino cristiano y una acusación por brujería en Valle del Maíz." *Estudios de Historia Novohispana* 44 (June 2011): 77–111.

Galvin, John R., ed. *The First Spanish Entry into San Francisco Bay, 1775*. San Francisco: John Howell, 1971.

Gamble, Lynn H. *The Chumash World at European Contact: Power, Trade, and Feasting among Complex Hunter-Gatherers*. Berkeley: University of California Press, 2008.

Gamble, Lynn H., and Irma Carmen Zepeda. "Social Differentiation and Exchange among the Kumeyaay Indians during the Historic Period in California." *Historical Archaeology* 36, no. 2 (2002): 71–91.

García, Sebastián. "América en la legislación general de la orden franciscana. s. xviii." In *Los franciscanos en el nuevo mundo (siglo 18): Actas del IV congreso internacional sobre los franciscanos en el nuevo mundo, Cholula-Puebla del 22 al 27 de julio de 1991*, 629–89. Madrid: Deimos, 1993.

García Ugarte, Marta Eugenia. *Breve historia de Querétaro*. Mexico City: Colegio de México; Fideicomiso Historia de las Américas; Fondo de Cultura Económica, 1999.

Geiger, Maynard. "The Franciscan 'Mission' to San Fernando College, Mexico, 1749." *The Americas* 5, no. 1 (July 1948): 48–60.

———. *Franciscan Missionaries in Hispanic California, 1769–1848: A Biographical Dictionary*. San Marino: The Huntington Library, 1969.

———. "Fray Rafael Verger, OFM, and the California Mission Enterprise." *Southern California Quarterly* 49, no. 2 (1967): 205–31.

———. *The Indians of Mission Santa Barbara*. 2nd ed., revised by John R. Johnson. Santa Barbara: Santa Bárbara Mission Archive-Library, 2010.

———. "The Internal Organization and Activities of San Fernando College, Mexico (1734–1858)." *The Americas* 6, no. 1 (July 1949): 3–31.

———. "The Library of the Apostolic College of San Fernando, Mexico, in the Eighteenth and Nineteenth Centuries." *The Americas* 7, no. 4 (April 1, 1951): 425–34.

———. *The Life and Times of Fray Junípero Serra, OFM; or, The Man Who Never Turned Back, 1713–1784, a Biography*. 2 vols. Washington, D.C.: Academy of American Franciscan History, 1959.

———. "The Mallorcan Contribution to Franciscan California." *The Americas* 4, no. 2 (October 1947): 141–50.

———. "The Royal Presidio Chapel of San Carlos, Monterey, Capital of Colonial California." *The Americas* 9, no. 2 (October 1952): 207–11.

———. "The Scholastic Career and Preaching Apostolate of Fray Junípero Serra, OFM, S.T.D. (1730–1749)." *The Americas* 4, no. 1 (July 1947): 65–82.

———. *The Serra Trail in Picture and Story*. Santa Barbara: Franciscan Fathers of California, 1960.

———. "Spreading the News of the California Conquest." *Southern California Quarterly* 47, no. 4 (December 1965): 395–407.

Geiger, Maynard, and Clement W. Meighan. *As the Padres Saw Them: California Indian Life and Customs as Reported by the Franciscan Missionaries, 1813–1815*. Santa Barbara: Santa Bárbara Mission Archive Library.

Gerbi, Antonello. *The Dispute of the New World: The History of a Polemic, 1750–1900*. Translated by Jeremy Moyle. Pittsburgh: University of Pittsburgh Press, 2010.

Gerhard, Peter. *A Guide to the Historical Geography of New Spain*. Rev. ed. Norman: University of Oklahoma Press, 1993.

———. *The North Frontier of New Spain*. Rev. ed. Norman: University of Oklahoma Press, 1993.

Ginn, Sarah. "Creating Community in Spanish California: An Investigation of California Plainwares." PhD diss., University of California, Santa Cruz, 2009.

Golla, Victor. *California Indian Languages*. Berkeley: University of California Press, 2011.

Gómez Canedo, Lino. "Aspectos característicos de la acción franciscana en América." *Archivo Ibero-Americano* 48, no. 189 (1988): 441–72.

———. *De México a la Alta California, una gran epopeya misional.* Mexico City: Editorial Jus, 1969.

———. *Evangelización, cultura y promoción social: Ensayos y estudios críticos sobre la contribución franciscana a los orígenes cristianos de México: Siglos 16–18.* Mexico City: Editorial Porrúa, 1993.

———. *Evangelización y conquista: Experiencia franciscana en Hispanoamérica.* Mexico City: Editorial Porrúa, 1977.

———. "Franciscans in the Americas: A Comprehensive View." In *Franciscan Presence in the Americas: Essays on the Activities of the Franciscan Friars in the Americas, 1492–1900*, edited by Francisco Morales, 5–45. Potomac, Md.: Academy of American Franciscan History, 1983.

———. "Fray Junípero Serra y su noviciado misional en América (1750–1758)." In *Evangelización, cultura y promoción social: Ensayos y estudios críticos sobre la contribución franciscana a los orígenes cristianos de México: Siglos 16–18*, 570–99. Mexico City: Editorial Porrúa, 1993.

———. *Primeras exploraciones y poblamiento de Texas, 1686–1694.* Noticias Geográficas e Históricas del Noreste de México 3. Mexico City: Monterrey, 1968.

———. *Sierra Gorda, un típico enclave misional en el centro de México (siglos 17–18).* Querétaro: Ediciones del Gobierno del Estado de Querétaro, 1988.

Gonzalbo, Pilar. *Historia de la educación en la época colonial: El mundo indígena.* Mexico City: Colegio de México; Centro de Estudios Históricos, 1990.

González Marmolejo, Jorge René. *Misioneros del desierto: Estructura, organización y vida cotidiana de los colegios apostólicos de propaganda fide de la Nueva España, siglo 18.* Mexico City: Instituto Nacional de Antropología e Historia, 2009.

González Rodríguez, Jaime. "El sistema de reducciones." In *Historia de la Iglesia en Hispanoamérica y Filipinas (siglos 15–19)*, edited by Pedro Borges, 535–48. Madrid: Biblioteca de Autores Cristianos, 1992.

Gould, Lewis L. *The Spanish-American War and President McKinley.* Lawrence: University Press of Kansas, 1982.

Greenleaf, Richard E. *The Inquisition in Colonial Latin America: Selected Writings of Richard E. Greenleaf.* Edited by James Denson Riley. Berkeley: Academy of American Franciscan History, 2010.

Greer, Allan. "Conversion and Identity: Iroquois Christianity in Seventeenth-Century New France." In *Conversion: Old Worlds and New*, edited by Kenneth Mills and Anthony Grafton, 175–98. Rochester: University of Rochester Press, 2003.

Guerrero, Vladimir. *The Anza Trail and the Settling of California.* Santa Clara and Berkeley: Santa Clara University and Heyday Books, 2006.

Guest, Francis F. "The Cause of Junípero Serra." In "The Serra Report." BANC MSS 87/208c.

———. "An Examination of the Thesis of S. F. Cook on the Forced Conversion of Indians in the California Missions." *Southern California Quarterly* 61, no. 1 (1979): 1–77.

———. *Fermín Francisco de Lasuén (1736–1803): A Biography.* Washington, D.C.: Academy of American Franciscan History, 1973.

———. *Hispanic California Revisited: Essays by Francis F. Guest, OFM.* Edited by Doyce B. Nunis. Santa Barbara: Santa Bárbara Mission Archive-Library, 1996.

———. "Pedro Fages' Five Complaints against Junípero Serra." *The Californians* 8, no. 2 (August 1990): 39–48.

———. "Principles for an Interpretation of the History of the California Missions (1769–1893)." *Hispania Sacra* 40 (1988): 791–805.

Gunnarsdóttir, Ellen. *Mexican Karismata: The Baroque Vocation of Francisca de los Angeles, 1674–1744.* Lincoln: University of Nebraska Press, 2004.

———. "Una visionaria barroca de la provincia mexicana: Francisca de los Angeles (1674–1744)." In *Monjas y beatas: La escritura femenina en la espiritualidad barroca novohispana siglos 17 y 18,* edited by Asunción Lavrín and Rosalva Loreto López, 205–65. Mexico City: Universidad de las Américas-Puebla; Archivo General de la Nación, 2002.

H.H. [Helen Hunt Jackson]. "Father Junípero and His Work." *Century Magazine* 26, nos. 1 and 2 (1883): 3–19, 199–216.

Haas, Lisbeth. *Conquests and Historical Identities in California, 1769–1936.* Berkeley: University of California Press, 1995.

———. *Pablo Tac, Indigenous Scholar: Writing on Luiseño Language and Colonial History.* Berkeley: University of California Press, 2011.

Hackel, Steven W., ed. *Alta California: Peoples in Motion, Identities in Formation, 1769–1850.* Berkeley: Published for Huntington-USC Institute on California and the West by University of California Press, Berkeley, and The Huntington Library, San Marino, 2010.

———. *Children of Coyote Press, Missionaries of Saint Francis: Indian-Spanish Relations in Colonial California, 1769–1850.* Chapel Hill: Published for the Omohundro Institute of Early American History and Culture, Williamsburg, Va., by the University of North Carolina Press, 2005.

———. *Junípero Serra: California's Founding Father.* New York: Hill and Wang, 2013.

———. "Junípero Serra across the Generations." In *A Companion to California History,* edited by William Deverell and David Igler, 99–115. Malden, Mass.: Wiley-Blackwell, 2008.

———. "Junípero Serra's California Sacramental Community." In *To Toil in That Vineyard of the Lord: Contemporary Scholarship on Junípero Serra,* edited by Rose Marie Beebe and Robert Senkewicz, 75–93. Berkeley: Academy of American Franciscan History, 2010.

———. "Sources of Rebellion: Indian Testimony and the Mission San Gabriel Uprising of 1785." *Ethnohistory* 50, no. 4 (2003): 643–69.

———. "The Staff of Leadership: Indian Authority in the Missions of Alta California." *William and Mary Quarterly* 54, no. 2 (1997): 347–76.

Hackel, Steven W., and Hilary E. Wyss. "Print Culture and the Power of Native Literacy in California and New England Missions." In *Native Americans, Christianity, and the Reshaping of the American Religious Landscape,* edited by Joel W. Martin and Mark A. Nicholas, 201–21. Chapel Hill: University of North Carolina Press, 2010.

Hadley, Diana, Thomas H. Naylor, and Mardith Schuetz-Miller, eds. *The Presidio and Militia on the Northern Frontier of New Spain: A Documentary History. Volume Two, Part Two, the Central Corridor and the Texas Corridor, 1700–1765.* Tucson: University of Arizona Press, 1997.

Hämäläinen, Pekka. *The Comanche Empire*. New Haven, Conn.: Yale University Press, 2008.

Hanke, Lewis. *All Mankind Is One: A Study of the Disputation between Bartolomé de las Casas and Juan Ginés de Sepúlveda in 1550 on the Intellectual and Religious Capacity of the American Indians*. DeKalb: Northern Illinois University Press, 1974.

Harrison, Jay T. "Franciscan Concepts of the Congregated Mission and the Apostolic Ministry in Eighteenth-Century Texas." In *From La Florida to La California: Franciscan Evangelization in the Spanish Borderlands*, edited by Timothy J. Johnson and Gert Melville, 323–39. Berkeley: Academy of American Franciscan History, 2013.

Heizer, Robert F., ed. *California Indian Linguistic Records: The Mission Indian Vocabularies of H. W. Henshaw*. Berkeley: University of California Press, 1955.

Hernández Sánchez-Barba, Mario. *Monjas ilustres en la historia de España*. Madrid: Temas de Hoy, 1993.

Hickerson, Nancy P. *The Jumanos: Hunters and Traders of the South Plains*. Austin: University of Texas Press, 1994.

———. "The Visits of the 'Lady in Blue': An Episode in the History of the South Plains, 1629." *Journal of Anthropological Research* 46, no. 1 (1990): 67–90.

Hilton, Sylvia L. *Junípero Serra*. Madrid: Historia 16/Ediciones Quorum, 1987.

Hittell, John S. *A History of the City of San Francisco and Incidentally of the State of California*. San Francisco: Bancroft & Co., 1878.

Hyslop, Stephen G. *Contest for California: From Spanish Colonization to the American Conquest*. Norman: Arthur H. Clark Company / University of Oklahoma Press, 2012.

Ingham, Mary Beth. *The Harmony of Goodness: Mutuality and Moral Living according to John Duns Scotus*. Quincy, Ill.: Franciscan Press, 1996.

———. *The Philosophical Vision of John Duns Scotus: An Introduction*. Washington, D.C.: Catholic University of America Press, 2004.

———. *Scotus for Dunces: An Introduction to the Subtle Doctor*. St. Bonaventure, N.Y.: Franciscan Institute Publications, 2003.

Jackson, Helen Hunt. *Father Junípero and the Mission Indians of California*. Boston: Little, Brown & Co., 1902.

Jackson, Robert H. "The Chichimeca Frontier and the Evangelization of the Sierra Gorda, 1550–1770." *Estudios de Historia Novohispana* 47 (July–December 2012): 45–91.

———. "Demographic Patterns in the Missions of Northern Baja California." *Journal of California and Great Basin Anthropology* 5, nos. 1/2 (1983): 131–39.

———. "Epidemic Disease and Population Decline in the Baja California Missions, 1697–1834." *Southern California Quarterly* 63, no. 4 (1981): 308–46.

———. *Indian Population Decline: The Missions of Northwestern New Spain, 1687–1840*. Albuquerque: University of New Mexico Press, 1994.

———. "The Last Jesuit Censuses of the Pimería Alta Missions, 1761 and 1766." *Kiva* 46, no. 4 (1981): 243–72.

Jackson, Robert H., and Edward D. Castillo. *Indians, Franciscans, and Spanish Colonization: The Impact of the Mission System on California Indians*. Albuquerque: University of New Mexico Press, 1995.

Jayme, Luis. *Letter of Luis Jayme, OFM, San Diego, October 17, 1772.* Edited by Maynard Geiger. Los Angeles: Published for the San Diego Public Library by Dawson's Book Shop, 1970.

Jiménez, Alfredo. "El bárbaro en la mente y la voz del ilustrado: La frontera norte de Nueva España (s. xviii)." In *El gran norte mexicano: Indios, misioneros y pobladores entre el mito y la historia,* edited by Salvador Bernabéu Albert, 363–98. Seville: Consejo Superior de Investigaciones Científicas, 2009.

Jiménez de Wagenheim, Olga. *Puerto Rico: An Interpretive History from Pre-Columbian Times to 1900.* Princeton, N.J.: Markus Wiener Publishers, 1998.

Johnson, John R. "Chumash Social Organization: An Ethnohistoric Perspective." PhD diss. University of California, Santa Barbara, 1988.

Johnson, Norman S. "Franciscan Passions: Missions to the Muslims, Desire for Martyrdom and Institutional Identity in the Later Middle Ages." PhD diss., University of Chicago, 2010.

Johnson, Timothy J., and Gert Melville, eds. *From La Florida to La California: Franciscan Evangelization in the Spanish Borderlands.* Berkeley: Academy of American Franciscan History, 2013.

Johnston, Bernice Eastman. *California's Gabrielino Indians.* Los Angeles: Southwest Museum, 1962.

Jover Avellà, Gabriel, and Carles Manera Erbina. "Producción y productividad agrícolas en la Isla de Mallorca, 1590–1860." *Revista de Historia Económica / Journal of Iberian and Latin American Economic History* 27, no. 3 (December 2009): 463–98.

Kamen, Henry. *Inquisition and Society in Spain in the Sixteenth and Seventeenth Centuries.* Bloomington: Indiana University Press, 1985.

———. *The Spanish Inquisition: A Historical Revision.* New Haven, Conn.: Yale University Press, 1998.

———. "Vicissitudes of a World Power." In *Spain: A History,* edited by Raymond Carr. Oxford: Oxford University Press, 2000.

Katzew, Ilona. "'That This Should Be Published and Again in the Age of the Enlightenment?': Eighteenth-Century Debates about the Indian Body in Colonial Mexico." In *Race and Classification: The Case of Mexican America,* edited by Ilona Katzew, 73–118. Stanford: Stanford University Press, 2009.

Kaufman, David. "Rumsen Ohlone Folklore: Two Tales." *Journal of Folklore Research* 45, no. 3 (December 2008): 383–91.

Keen, Benjamin. *The Aztec Image in Western Thought.* New Brunswick, N.J.: Rutgers University Press, 1971.

Kendrick, Thomas Downing. *Mary of Ágreda: The Life and Legend of a Spanish Nun.* London: Routledge and Kegan Paul, 1967.

Kessell, John L. "Anza Damns the Missions: A Spanish Soldier's Criticism of Indian Policy, 1772." *Journal of Arizona History* 13, no. 1 (1972): 53–63.

———. "Friars versus Bureaucrats: The Mission as a Threatened Institution on the Arizona-Sonora Frontier, 1767–1842." *Western Historical Quarterly* 5, no. 2 (April 1974): 151–62.

———. "Miracles or Mystery: María de Ágreda's Ministry to the Jumano Indians of the Southwest in the 1620s." In *Great Mysteries of the American West,* edited by Ferenc Morton Szasz, 121–44. Golden, Colo.: Fulcrum, 1993.

Kovach, Francis J. *Scholastic Challenges to Some Mediaeval and Modern Ideas*. Stillwater, Okla.: Western Publications, 1987.

Kraft, Keith. "The Royal Eagle of the Pájaro River." *Branciforte* (January 1997): 77–78.

Kroeber, A. L. *The Chumash and Costanoan Languages*. University of California Publications in American Archaeology and Ethnology, vol. 9, no. 2. Berkeley: University Press, 1910.

Kropp, Phoebe S. *California Vieja: Culture and Memory in a Modern American Place*. Berkeley: University of California Press, 2006.

Kuethe, Allan J. *Military Reform and Society in New Granada, 1773–1808*. Gainesville: University Presses of Florida, 1978.

Kugel, Verónica. "¿Sincretismo o idolatría? Dos percepciones y una relación de fuerzas desigual en un documento del archivo parroquial de Cardonal (s. xviii)." *Estudios de Cultura Otopame* 3 (2002): 77–104.

Kurillo, Max, and Erline M. Tuttle. *California's El Camino Real and Its Historic Bells*. San Diego: Sunbelt Publications, 2000.

La Rose, Douglas J. "Political Geography and Colonialism in Mission Valley, San Diego: Spanish-Kumeyaay Interactions at Cosoy and the Presidio." *Society of California Archaeology Proceedings* 23 (2009), unpaginated volume.

Ladrón de Guevara, Antonio. *Noticias de los poblados de que se componen el Nuevo Reino de León*. Edited by Andrés Montemayor Hernández. Monterrey, 1969.

Lara, Jaime. *Christian Texts for Aztecs: Art and Liturgy in Colonial Mexico*. Notre Dame, Ind.: University of Notre Dame Press, 2008.

———. "The Sacramented Sun: Solar Eucharistic Worship in Colonial Latin America." In *El Cuerpo de Cristo: The Hispanic Presence in the U.S. Catholic Church*, edited by Peter J. Casarella and Raúl Gómez, SDS., 261–91. New York: Crossroad, 1998.

Lara Cisneros, Gerardo. *El cristianismo en el espejo indígena: Religiosidad en el occidente de la Sierra Gorda, siglo 18*. Mexico City: Archivo General de la Nación, 2002.

———. *El Cristo Viejo de Xichú: Resistencia y rebelión en la Sierra Gorda durante el siglo 18*. Mexico City: Conaculta; Dirección General de Cultural Populares, 2007.

———. "Xichu de Indios: Marginalidad y frontera cultural en Sierra Gorda, Mexico." *Locus: Revista de Historia* 7, no. 2 (2001): 29–51.

Larkin, Brian. "Liturgy, Devotion, and Religious Reform in Eighteenth-Century Mexico." *The Americas* 60, no. 4 (2004): 493–518.

Lasuén, Fermín. *Writings of Fermín Francisco de Lasuén*. Edited by Finbar Kenneally. 2 vols. Washington, D.C.: Academy of American Franciscan History, 1965.

Laverty, Philip. "The Ohlone/Costanoan-Esselen Nation of Monterey, California: Dispossession, Federal Neglect, and the Bitter Irony of the Federal Acknowledgment Process." *Wicazo Sa Review* 18, no. 2 (2003): 41–77.

———. "Recognizing Indians: Place, Identity, History, and the Federal Acknowledgment of the Ohlone/Costanoan-Esselen Nation." PhD diss., University of New Mexico, 2010.

Lazcano Sahagún, Carlos, ed. *Diario de fray Junípero Serra en su viaje de Loreto a San Diego*. Ensenada: Provincia Franciscana de San Pedro y San Pablo de Michoacán; Gobierno del Estado de Baja California; Fundación Barca; Museo de Historia de Ensenada, 2002.

———. *Pa-tai: La historia olvidada de Ensenada*. Ensenada: Museo de Historia de Ensenada; Seminario de Historia de Ensenada, 2000.

———. *La primera entrada: Descubrimiento del interior de la antigua California*. Ensenada: Fundación Barca; Museo de Historia de Ensenada; Seminario de Historia de Ensenada, 2000.

Lea, Henry Charles. *A History of the Inquisition of Spain*. 4 vols. New York: Macmillan, 1922.

León-Portilla, Miguel. *La California mexicana: Ensayos acerca de su historia*. Mexico; Mexicali: Universidad Nacional Autónoma de México; Instituto de Investigaciones Históricas; Universidad Autónoma de Baja California, 1995.

León Velazco, Lucila. "Conflictos de poder en la California misional (1768–1775)." In *Memoria 2001: Undécimo ciclo de conferencias, seminario de historia de Baja California*, 149–60. Mexicali: Instituto de Cultura de Baja California, n.d.

———. "Indígenas y misioneros en Baja California." In *Memorias de balances y perspectivas de la antropología e historia de Baja California 2002–2004*, 247–52. Mexicali: Instituto Nacional de Antropología e Historia, 2005.

———. "Los soldados de Baja California, 1697–1840: Procesos de interacción social en el noroeste novohispano." PhD diss., Universidad Autónoma de Baja California, 2013.

Linck, Wenceslaus. *Wenceslaus Linck's Diary of His 1766 Expedition to Northern Baja California*. Edited and translated by Ernest J. Burrus. Los Angeles: Dawson's Book Shop, 1966.

Lladó Ferragut, Jaime. "El siglo 17 en Mallorca." In *Historia de Mallorca*, edited by J. Mascaró Pasarius, 2:257A–288A. Palma de Mallorca: Mascaró Pasarius, 1975.

Loarca Castillo, Eduardo. *Fray Junípero Serra: Guía de las misiones barrocas del siglo 18 en la Sierra Gorda de Querétaro*. Querétaro: s.n., 1994.

———. *Fray Junípero Serra y sus misiones barrocas del siglo 18: Sierra Gorda de Querétaro*. Querétaro: s.n., 1984.

Lockhart, James, and Enrique Otte, eds. *Letters and People of the Spanish Indies, Sixteenth Century*. Cambridge: Cambridge University Press, 1976.

López Urrutia, Carlos. *El real ejército de California*. Madrid: Grupo Medusa Ediciones, 2000.

López-Velarde López, Benito. *Expansión geográfica franciscana en el hoy norte central y oriental de México*. Mexico City: Editorial Progreso, 1964.

Lummis, Charles. "Diary of Junípero Serra, Loreto to San Diego, March 28–June 30, 1769." *Out West* 16 (1902): 293–96, 399–406, 513–18, 635–42; 17 (1902): 69–76.

Lynch, John. *Bourbon Spain, 1700–1808*. Oxford: Basil Blackwell, 1989.

MacCawley, William. *The First Angelinos: The Gabrielino Indians of Los Angeles*. Banning and Novato: Malki Museum Press and Ballena Press, 1996.

Macías, John. "Of Spanish Myths and Mexican Realities: Racial and Social Development in San Gabriel, California, 1771–1971." PhD diss., Claremont Graduate University, 2012.

Maclean, Katie. "María de Ágreda, Spanish Mysticism and the Work of Spiritual Conquest." *Colonial Latin American Review* 17, no. 1 (June 2008): 29–48.

———. "The Mystic and the Moor-Slayer: Saint Teresa, Santiago and the Struggle for Spanish Identity." *Bulletin of Spanish Studies* 83, no. 7 (November 2006): 887–910.

———. "Transatlantic Mysticism: Women, Religion and Colonization." PhD diss., Duke University, 2002.

MacMullen, Ramsay. *Christianity and Paganism in the Fourth to Eighth Centuries*. New Haven, Conn.: Yale University Press, 1997.

Magnaghi, Russell M. *Indian Slavery, Labor, Evangelization, and Captivity in the Americas: An Annotated Bibliography*. Metuchen, N.J.: Scarecrow, 1998.

———. "San Blas: Spanish Gateway to the North Pacific." *Terrae Incognitae* 31 (1999): 42–48.
Manera, Carlos. "Manufactura téxtil y comercio en Mallorca, 1700–1830." *Revista de Historia Económica / Journal of Iberian and Latin American Economic History* 6, no. 3 (1988): 523–55.
———. "Mercado, producción agrícola y cambio económico en Mallorca durante el siglo 18." *Revista de Historia Económica / Journal of Iberian and Latin American Economic History* 9, no. 1 (January 1991): 69–101.
Mann, Kristin. *The Power of Song: Music and Dance in the Mission Communities of Northern New Spain, 1590–1810*. Stanford and Berkeley: Stanford University Press and Academy of American Franciscan History, 2010.
Manrique Castañeda, Leonardo. "Análisis preliminar del vocabulario pame de fray Juan Guadalupe Soriano." *Anales de Antropología* 12, no. 1 (1975).
Martínez, Iván. "The Banner of the Spanish Monarchy: The Political Use of the Immaculate Conception." In *Un privilegio sagrado: La concepción de María Inmaculada: celebración del dogma en México / A Sacred Privilege: The Conception of Mary Immaculate: The Celebration of Dogma in Mexico*, 123–54. Mexico City: Museo de la Basílica de Guadalupe, 2005.
Mascaró Pasarius, J., ed. *Historia de Mallorca*. 5 vols. Palma de Mallorca: Mascaró Pasarius, 1975.
Mason, William M. *The Census of 1790: A Demographic History of Colonial California*. Menlo Park, Calif.: Ballena Press, 1998.
———. "The Garrisons of San Diego Presidio: 1770–1794." *Journal of San Diego History* 24, no. 4 (1978): 399–424.
Mathes, W. Michael. "A Case of Idolatry among the Cochimí." *Masterkey* 48, no. 3 (1974): 98–107.
———. *Jesuítica Californiana 1681–1764: Impresos de los RR. PP. Eusebio Francisco Kino, Fernando Consag, Juan Antonio Balthasar, Juan Joseph de Villavicencio, y Francisco Zevallos de la Compañía de Jesús*. Madrid: Ediciones J. Porrúa Turanzas, 1998.
———. *The Land of Calafia: A Brief History of Peninsular California (1533–1848)*. Tecate: Corredor Histórico Carem, A.C., 2009.
———. *Las misiones de Baja California, 1683–1849 / The Missions of Baja California, 1683–1849*. La Paz: Editorial Aristos, 1977.
McAlister, Lyle N. *The "Fuero Militar" in New Spain, 1764–1800*. Gainesville: University of Florida Press, 1957.
McCarty, Kieran. "Apostolic Colleges of the Propagation of the Faith—Old and New World Background." *The Americas* 19, no. 1 (1962): 50–58.
———. "Before They Crossed the Great River: Cultural Backgrounds of the Spanish Franciscans of Texas." *Journal of Texas Catholic History and Culture* 3 (1992): 37–43.
McCloskey, Michael. *The Formative Years of the Missionary College of Santa Cruz of Querétaro, 1683–1733*. Washington, D.C.: Academy of American Franciscan History, 1955.
McCormack, Brian T. "Conjugal Violence, Sex, Sin, and Murder in the Mission Communities of Alta California." *Journal of the History of Sexuality* 16, no. 3 (2007): 391–415.
McEnroe, Sean F. "A Sleeping Army: The Military Origins of Interethnic Civic Structures on Mexico's Colonial Frontier." *Ethnohistory* 59, no. 1 (December 2012): 109–39.
McGroarty, John S. *California: Its History and Romance*. Los Angeles: Grafton Publishing, 1911.

McNeill, William H. *Transatlantic History*. Edited by Steven G. Reinhardt and Dennis Reinhartz. College Station: Published for the University of Texas at Arlington by Texas A&M University Press, 2006.

McRoskey, Racine. *The Missions of California, with Sketches of the Lives of St. Francis and Junípero Serra*. San Francisco: Philopolis, 1914.

Medina, José Toribio. *Historia del Tribunal del Santo Oficio de la Inquisición en México*. Santiago de Chile: Imprenta Elzevir, 1905.

Meigs, Peveril. *The Kiliwa Indians of Lower California*. Berkeley: University of California Press, 1939.

Mejía González, Alma Leticia. *Relación de la causa de Juana María, mulata: Esclava, mulata y hechicera: Historia inquisitorial de una mujer novohispana del siglo 18*. Mexico City: Colegio de México; Centro de Estudios Linguísticos y Literarios, 1996.

Melvin, Karen. *Building Colonial Cities of God: Mendicant Orders and Urban Culture in New Spain*. Stanford: Stanford University Press, 2012.

Mendoza Muñoz, Jesús. *El conde de Sierra Gorda don José de Escandón y la Helguera: Militar, noble y caballero*. Cadereyta de Montes, Querétaro: Fomento Histórico y Cultural de Cadereyta, 2005.

Miller, Benjamin Frank, and Claire Brackman Keane. *Miller-Keane Encyclopedia and Dictionary of Medicine, Nursing and Allied Health*. Philadelphia: Saunders, 1997.

Milliken, Randall. *Central Contra Costa Indians: An Ethnographic Study of the Clayton Area*. San Francisco: Holman & Associates, 1982.

———. *Ethnohistory of the Rumsen*. Papers in Northern California Anthropology 2. Berkeley: Northern California Anthropological Group, 1987.

———. "The Spatial Organization of Human Population on Central California's San Francisco Peninsula at the Spanish Arrival." MA thesis, Sonoma State University, 1983.

———. *A Time of Little Choice: The Disintegration of Tribal Culture in the San Francisco Bay Area, 1769–1810*. Menlo Park, Calif.: Ballena Press, 1995.

Moore, Kenneth. *Those of the Street: The Catholic-Jews of Mallorca*. Notre Dame, Ind.: University of Notre Dame Press, 1976.

Morales, Francisco. *Clero y política en México, 1767–1834: Algunas ideas sobre la autoridad, la independencia y la reforma eclesiástica*. Mexico City: Secretaría de Educación Pública, 1975.

———. "Franciscanos ante las religiones indígenas." In *Franciscanos en América: Quinientos años de presencia evangelizadora*, edited by Francisco Morales, 87–102. Mexico City: Conferencia Franciscana de Santa María de Guadalupe, 1993.

Morales Carrión, Arturo. *Puerto Rico, a Political and Cultural History*. New York and Nashville: W. W. Norton and American Association for State and Local History, 1983.

Morán, Pedro Borges. "Análisis sociológico de las expediciones de misioneros franciscanos a América." *Archivo Ibero-Americano* 46, no. 181 (1986): 443–72.

Morgado, Martin J. *Junípero Serra: A Pictorial Biography*. Monterey: Siempre Adelante Publishers, 1991.

———. *Junípero Serra's Legacy*. Pacific Grove, Calif.: Mount Carmel, 1987.

Mujal, Carlos León. "Out of the Apocalypse to Alta California: Franciscans in the New World (1524–1833)." PhD diss., University of California, Berkeley, 2002.

Müller, Anne. "Turning to the East: Medieval Franciscan Missions to Asia." In *From La Florida to La California: Franciscan Evangelization in the Spanish Borderlands*, edited by Timothy J. Johnson and Gert Melville, 35–45. Berkeley: Academy of American Franciscan History, 2013.

Museo de la Basílica de Guadalupe and Apostólico Colegio de Nuestra Señora de Guadalupe. *Un privilegio sagrado: La concepción de María Inmaculada: Celebración del dogma en México / A Sacred Privilege: The Conception of Mary Immaculate: The Celebration of Dogma in Mexico*. Mexico City: Museo de la Basílica de Guadalupe, 2005.

Nalle, Sara T. "Inquisitors, Priests, and the People during the Catholic Reformation in Spain." *Sixteenth Century Journal* 18, no. 4 (1987): 557–87.

Nava, L., and E. Fernando. *Otopames: Memoria del primer coloquio, Querétaro, 1995*. Mexico City: Universidad Nacional Autónoma de México; Instituto de Investigaciones Antropológicas, 2004.

Navajas Josa, Belén. "El Padre Kino y la Pimería. Aculturación y expansión en la frontera norte de Nueva España." PhD diss., Universidad Complutense de Madrid, 2009.

Navarro García, Luis. *Don José de Gálvez y la comandancia general de las Provincias Internas del norte de Nueva España*. Seville: Consejo Superior de Investigaciones Científicas, 1964.

Naylor, Thomas H., and Charles W. Polzer, eds. *Pedro de Rivera and the Military Regulations for Northern New Spain, 1724–1729: A Documentary History of His Frontier Inspection and the Reglamento de 1729*. Tucson: University of Arizona Press, 1988.

Neve, Felipe de. *Reglamento para el gobierno de la Provincia de Californias*. Edited by Salvador Bernabéu Albert. Madrid and La Paz: Doce Calles and Ayuntamiento de La Paz, 1994.

Newell, Quincy. *Constructing Lives at Mission San Francisco: Native Californians and Hispanic Colonists, 1776–1821*. Albuquerque: University of New Mexico Press, 2009.

Noel, Charles C. "Missionary Preachers in Spain: Teaching Social Virtue in the Eighteenth Century." *American Historical Review* 90, no. 4 (October 1985): 866–92.

Nunis, Doyce B., ed. *The Founding Documents of Los Angeles: A Bilingual Edition*. Los Angeles and Pasadena: Historical Society of Southern California and Zamorano Club of Los Angeles, 2004.

Nuttall, Donald A. "Light Cast upon Shadows: The Non-California Years of Don Pedro Fages." *California Historical Quarterly* 56, no. 3 (October 1977): 250–69.

———. "Pedro Fages and the Advance of the Northern Frontier of New Spain, 1767–1782." PhD diss., University of Southern California, 1964.

O'Brien, Eric, OFM, ed. "'Breve Método' of the College of San Fernando." *Provincial Annals* 7, no. 2 and 3 (April and July 1945): 3–12, 3–16.

Ocaranza, Fernando. *Capítulos de la historia franciscana, segunda serie*. Mexico City: (s.n.), 1934.

Omaechevarría, Ignacio. *Fr. Pablo José de Mugártegui en su marco social y misionero*. Bilbao: Desclée de Brouwer, 1959.

———. *Pedro Pérez de Mezquía, OFM: (1688–1764): Maestro y precursor de fray Junípero Serra en las misiones*. Vitoria: Imprenta del Montepío Diocesano, 1963.

O'Neil, Dennis H. "The Spanish Use of Glass Beads as Pacification Gifts among the Luiseño, Ipai, and Tipai of Southern California." *Pacific Coast Archaeological Society Quarterly* 28, no. 2 (March 1992): 1–17.

Oré, Luis Jerónimo de. *Relación de la vida y milagros de San Francisco Solano.* Edited by Noble David Cook. Lima: Pontificia Universidad Católica del Perú, Fondo Editorial, 1998.

Orellana, Antonio de, and N. de Diereville. *The Travels of Several Learned Missioners of the Society of Jesus, into Divers Parts of the Archipelago, India, China, and America.* London: R. Gosling, 1714.

Ortiz, Beverly O. "Chocheño and Rumsen Narratives: A Comparison." In *The Ohlone Past and Present: Native Americans of the San Francisco Bay Region*, edited by Lowell John Bean, 99–163. Menlo Park, Calif.: Ballena Press, 1994.

Osante, Patricia. "Del Cantábrico al Seno Mexicano: José de Escandón en Nueva España." In *El gran norte mexicano: Indios, misioneros y pobladores entre el mito y la historia*, edited by Salvador Bernabéu Albert, 331–61. Seville: Consejo Superior de Investigaciones Científicas, 2009.

———. *Orígenes del Nuevo Santander (1748–1772).* Mexico City; [Ciudad Victoria]: Universidad Nacional Autónoma de México, Instituto de Investigaciones Históricas ; Universidad Autónoma de Tamaulipas, 1997.

———. "Presencia misional en Nuevo Santander en la segunda mitad del siglo 18. Memoria de un infortunio." *Estudios de Historia Novohispana* 17 (1998): 107–35.

———. "Los problemas de la administración franciscana en las misiones sonorenses, 1768–1800." *Archivo Ibero-Americano* 52, no. 205 (1992): 277–92.

———. *Testimonio acerca de la causa formada en la colonia del Nuevo Santander al coronel Don José de Escandón.* Mexico City and Ciudad Victoria, Tamaulipas: Universidad Nacional Autónoma de México and Universidad Autónoma de Tamaulipas: Instituto Tamaulipeco para la Cultura y las Artes, 2000.

Osante, Patricia, and Rosalba Alcaraz Cienfuegos. *Nuevo Santander 1748–1766: Un acercamiento al origen de Tamaulipas.* Ciudad Victoria, Mexico: Gobierno del Estado de Tamaulipas, 1999.

Osio, Antonio María. *The History of Alta California: A Memoir of Mexican California.* Edited, translated, and annotated by Rose Marie Beebe and Robert M. Senkewicz. Madison: University of Wisconsin Press, 1996.

Owen, Roger C., Nancy E. Walstrom, and Ralph C. Michelsen. "Musical Culture and Ethnic Solidarity: A Baja California Case Study." *Journal of American Folklore* 82, no. 324 (1969): 99–111.

Owens, Sarah E. "Journeys to Dark Lands: Francisca de los Angeles' Bi-locations to the Remote Provinces of Eighteenth-Century New Spain." *Colonial Latin American Historical Review* 12, no. 2 (Spring 2003): 151–71.

Pagden, Anthony. *The Fall of Natural Man: The American Indian and the Origins of Comparative Ethnology.* Cambridge: Cambridge University Press, 1982.

Palóu, Francisco. *Cartas desde la península de California, 1768–1773.* Edited by José Luis Soto Pérez. Mexico City: Editorial Porrúa, 1994.

———. *Francisco Palóu's Life and Apostolic Labors of the Venerable Father Junípero Serra: Founder of the Franciscan Missions of California.* Edited by George Wharton James. Translated by C. Scott Williams. Pasadena: G. W. James, 1913.

———. *Historical Memoirs of New California.* Edited by Herbert Eugene Bolton. 4 vols. Berkeley: University of California Press, 1926.

———. *Palóu's Life of Fray Junípero Serra*. Edited and translated by Maynard J. Geiger. Washington, D.C.: Academy of American Franciscan History, 1955.

———. *Recopilación de noticias de la Antigua y de la Nueva California (1767–1783)*. Edited by José Luis Soto Pérez. 2 vols. Mexico City: Editorial Porrúa, 1998.

———. *Relación histórica de la vida y apostólicas tareas del venerable padre fray Junípero Serra, y de las misiones que fundó en la California Septentrional, y nuevos establecimientos de Monterey*. Mexico City: En la imprenta de don Felipe de Zúñiga y Ontiveros, 1787.

Parsons, Jeffrey R. "El norte-centro de México como zona de transición entre Mesoamérica y la gran chichimeca desde el formativo hasta el posclásico." *Estudios de Cultura Otopame* 1 (1998): 53–59.

Payeras, Mariano. *Writings of Mariano Payeras*. Edited by Donald C. Cutter. Santa Barbara: Bellerophon Books, 1995.

Peelo, Sarah Ginn. "Baptism among the Salinan Neophytes of Mission San Antonio de Padua: Investigating the Ecological Hypothesis." *Ethnohistory* 56, no. 4 (October 2009): 589–624.

Peers, E. Allison. *Ramón Lull: A Biography*. London: Society for Promoting Christian Knowledge, 1929.

Peña Montenegro, Alonso de la. *Itinerario para párrocos de indios*. Madrid: En la Oficina de Pedro Marín, 1771.

Pérez Villanueva, Joaquín. "Algo más sobre la Inquisición y sor María de Ágreda: La prodigiosa evangelización americana." *Hispania Sacra* 37, no. 76 (1985): 585–618.

Phillips, Carla Rahn. "Economy and Society in the Iberian Atlantic." In *Transatlantic History*, edited by Steven G. Reinhardt and Dennis Reinhartz, 19–39. College Station: Published for the University of Texas at Arlington by Texas A&M University Press, 2006.

———. *Six Galleons for the King of Spain: Imperial Defense in the Early Seventeenth Century*. Baltimore: Johns Hopkins University Press, 1986.

Phillips, George Harwood. *Vineyards and Vaqueros: Indian Labor and the Economic Expansion of Southern California, 1771–1877*. Norman: Arthur H. Clark Company / University of Oklahoma Press, 2010.

Pietschma, Horst. "Consideraciones en torno a protoliberalismo, reformas borbónicas y revolución: La Nueva España en el último tercio del siglo 18." In *Europa e Iberoamerica: Cinco siglos de intercambios: Actas 3*, edited by María J. Sarabia Viejo and Isabel Arenas-Frutos, 325–50. Seville: Asociación de Historiadores Latinoamericanistas Europeos: Consejería de Cultura y Medio Ambiente (Junta de Andalucía), 1992.

Pilarcik, Eric R. "Out of the Ruins: Rebuilding the Alta California Missions, 1880s to 1930s." MA thesis, Graduate Theological Union, 2010.

Pimentel, Francisco. *Lenguas indígenas de México*. Mexico City: Tipografía de Isidoro Epstein, 1875.

Piña Homs, Román. "Del decreto de Nueva Planta a las Cortes de Cádiz." In *Historia de Mallorca*, edited by J. Mascaró Pasarius, 2:289–384. Palma de Mallorca: Mascaró Pasarius, 1975.

Ponç i Fullana, Andreu. *Fr. Rafael Josep Verger i Suau*. Mallorca: Editorial Moll, 1990.

Ponce Aguilar, Antonio. *De cueva pintada a la modernidad: Historia de Baja California*. Tijuana: Imprecolor, 1999.

Priestley, Herbert Ingram. *José de Gálvez, Visitor-General of New Spain (1765–1771)*. Berkeley: University of California Press, 1916.

Quezada, Noemí. *Enfermedad y maleficio: El curandero en el México colonial*. Mexico City: Universidad Nacional Autónoma de México; Instituto de Investigaciones Antropológicas, 2000.

———. "The Inquisition's Repression of Curanderos." In *Cultural Encounters: The Impact of the Inquisition in Spain and the New World*, edited by Mary Elizabeth Perry and Anne J. Cruz. Berkeley: University of California Press, 1991.

Ramírez, David Piñera. *Visión histórica de la Frontera Norte de México*. Mexicali: Universidad Autónoma de Baja California; Centro de Investigaciones Históricas UNAM-UABC, 1994.

Rangel Silva, José Alfredo. *Capitanes a guerra, linajes de frontera: Ascenso y consolidación de las élites en el oriente de San Luis, 1617–1823*. Mexico City: El Colegio de México, 2008.

———. "El discurso de una frontera olvidada: El Valle del Maíz y las guerras contra los 'indios bárbaros,' 1735–1805." *Cultura y Representaciones Sociales* 2, no. 4 (April 2010).

———. "Herejías y disidencias en la frontera de Rioverde: Los Barragán en el siglo 18." *Revista de Indias* 70, no. 248 (May 2010): 155–84.

———. "Linaje y fortuna en una zona de frontera: Felipe Barragán y su familia." *Estudios de Historia Novohispana* 37 (July 2007): 123–66.

———. "Pames, franciscanos y estancieros en Rioverde, Valles y sur de Nuevo Santander, 1600–1800." *Relaciones: Estudios de Historia y Sociedad* 30, no. 120 (October 2009): 225–66.

Rea, Vargas. *Pacificación de los chichimecas de la Sierra Gorda y dictamen del auditor de guerra Marqués de Altamira*. Mexico City: Biblioteca Aportación Histórica, 1944.

Reff, Daniel T. "Contextualizing Missionary Discourse: The Benavides 'Memorials' of 1630 and 1634." *Journal of Anthropological Research* 50, no. 1 (1994): 51–67.

Rex Galindo, David. "Franciscanos e indios en la Alta California española: 1769–1822." *Espacio, Tiempo y Forma. Serie IV, Historia Moderna. Año 2007*, 20 (2007): 157–70.

———. "Propaganda Fide: Training Franciscan Missionaries in New Spain." PhD diss., Southern Methodist University, 2010.

Reyes, Bárbara. *Private Women, Public Lives: Gender and the Missions of the Californias*. Austin: University of Texas Press, 2009.

Río, Ignacio del. "La adjudicación de las misiones de la Antigua California a los padres dominicos." *Estudios de Historia Novohispana* 18 (January 1998): 69–82.

———. "Utopia in Baja California: The Dreams of José de Gálvez." Translated by Arturo Jiménez-Vera. *Journal of San Diego History* 18, no. 4 (Fall 1972): 1–13.

Ríos, Eduardo Enrique. *Life of Fray Antonio Margil, OFM*. Translated by Benedict Leutenegger. Washington, D.C.: Academy of American Franciscan History, 1959.

Rivera y Moncada, Fernando. *Diario del capitán comandante Fernando de Rivera y Moncada, con un apéndice documental*. 2 vols. Edited by Ernest J. Burrus. Madrid: Ediciones J. Porrúa Turanzas, 1967.

Robinson, Alfred. *Life in California: During a Residence of Several Years in That Territory*. New York: Wiley & Putnam, 1846.

Rodríguez Cruz, Águeda, OP, and Enrique Llamas, OCD. "La 'Mística ciudad de Dios' en el ambiente universitario y cultural de Salamanca en el siglo 17." *Estudios Marianos* 69, (2003): 272–301.

Rodríguez-Sala, María Luisa, ed. *De San Blas hasta la Alta California: Los viajes y diarios de Juan Joseph Pérez Hernández*. Mexico City: Universidad Autónoma de México; Centro de Investigaciones sobre América del Norte; Centro de Enseñanza para Extranjeros, 2006.

———. *Los gobernadores de las Californias, 1767–1804: Contribuciones a la expansión territorial y del conocimiento*. Mexico; Jalisco; Baja California: Instituto de Investigaciones Sociales, UNAM; Colegio de Jalisco; Estado de Baja California; Instituto de Cultura de Baja California; Universidad Autónoma de Baja California, 2003.

Rodríguez Tomp, Rosa. *Cautivos de Dios: Los cazadores-recolectores de Baja California durante el período colonial*. Mexico City: CIESAS; Instituto Nacional Indigenista, 2002.

Rowland, Donald W. "The Elizondo Expedition against the Indian Rebels of Sonora, 1765–1771." PhD diss., University of California, 1930.

Ruiz, Teófilo F. *A King Travels: Festive Traditions in Late Medieval and Early Modern Spain*. Princeton, N.J.: Princeton University Press, 2012.

Ruiz Zavala, Alipio. *Historia de la provincia agustiniana del Santísimo Nombre de Jesús de México*. 2 vols. Mexico City: Editorial Porrúa, 1984.

Russell, Craig. *From Serra to Sancho: Music and Pageantry in the California Missions*. New York: Oxford University Press, 2009.

Sáiz Díez, Félix. *Los colegios de Propaganda Fide en Hispanoamérica*. Lima: CETA, 1992.

Sales, Luis. *Observations on California, 1772–1790*. Translated and edited by Charles N. Rudkin. Los Angeles: Glen Dawson, 1956.

Salisbury, Neal. "Embracing Ambiguity: Native Peoples and Christianity in Seventeenth-Century North America." *Ethnohistory* 50, no. 2 (Spring 2003): 247–59.

Samaniego, José Ximénez. *Life of Venerable Sister Mary of Jesus—D. Ágreda, Poor Clare Nun*. Translated by Ubaldus de Pandolfi. Evansville, Ind.: Printed by the Keller-Crescent Printing and Engraving Co., 1910.

Samperio Gutiérrez, Hector. "Las misiones fernandinas de la Sierra Gorda." In *Sierra Gorda: Pasado y presente: Coloquio en homenaje a Lino Gómez Canedo, 1991*, edited by Lino Gómez Canedo. Querétaro: Fondo Editorial de Querétaro, 1994.

Sánchez, Joseph P. *Spanish Bluecoats: The Catalonian Volunteers in Northwestern New Spain, 1767–1810*. Albuquerque: University of New Mexico Press, 1990.

Sánchez Gil, Víctor. "Teología y teólogos franciscanos españoles en el siglo de la Ilustración." *Archivo Ibero-Americano* 42, no. 165 (1982): 703–50.

Sandos, James A. "Christianization among the Chumash: An Ethnohistoric Perspective." *American Indian Quarterly* 15, no. 1 (Winter 1991): 65–89.

———. "Converting California: Indians and Franciscans in the Missions." *Boletín: Journal of the California Mission Studies Association* 21, no. 2 (2004): 49–72.

———. *Converting California: Indians and Franciscans in the Missions*. New Haven, Conn.: Yale University Press, 2004.

———. "Junípero Serra, Canonization, and the California Indian Controversy." *Journal of Religious History* 15, no. 3 (February 1989): 311–29.

———. "Junípero Serra's Canonization and the Historical Record." *American Historical Review* 93, no. 5 (December 1988): 253–69.

Sandos, James A., and Patricia B. Sandos. "Chisli, Canuch, and Junípero Serra: Indian Responses to Missión San Diego, 1769–1788." In *To Toil in That Vineyard of the Lord:*

Contemporary Scholarship on Junípero Serra, edited by Rose Marie Beebe and Robert M. Senkewicz, 53–74. Berkeley: Academy of American Franciscan History, 2010.

Sanneh, Lamin O. *Translating the Message: The Missionary Impact on Culture*. Maryknoll, N.Y.: Orbis Books, 1989.

Santamaría Arández, Alvaro. "Mallorca en el siglo 14." In *Historia de Mallorca*, edited by J. Mascaró Pasarius, 2:225–80. Palma de Mallorca: Mascaró Pasarius, 1975.

Sauer, Carl, and Peveril Meigs. "Site and Culture at San Fernando de Velicatá." *University of California Publications in Geography* 2, no. 9 (1927): 271–302.

Saunt, Claudio. "'My Medicine Is Punishment': A Case of Torture in Early California, 1775–1776." *Ethnohistory* 57, no. 4 (Fall 2010): 679–708.

Scholes, France V. *Church and State in New Mexico, 1610–1650*. Albuquerque: University of New Mexico Press, 1937.

Schroeder, Susan, and Stafford Poole, eds. *Religion in New Spain*. Albuquerque: University of New Mexico Press, 2007.

Schwaller, John F., ed. *Francis in the Americas: Essays on the Franciscan Family in North and South America*. Berkeley: Academy of American Franciscan History, 2005.

Schwartz, Stuart B. *All Can Be Saved: Religious Tolerance and Salvation in the Iberian Atlantic World*. New Haven, Conn.: Yale University Press, 2008.

Seed, Patricia. *Ceremonies of Possession in Europe's Conquest of the New World, 1492–1640*. Cambridge: Cambridge University Press, 1995.

Selke, Angela. *The Conversos of Majorca: Life and Death in a Crypto-Jewish Community in Seventeenth-Century Spain*. Translated by Henry J. Maxwell. Jerusalem: Magnes Press, Hebrew University, 1986.

Semboloni, Lara. "Cacería de brujas en Coahuila, 1748–1751. 'De Villa en villa, sin Dios ni Santa María.'" *Historia Mexicana* 54, no. 2 (October 2004): 325–64.

Senkewicz, Robert M. "The Representation of Junípero Serra in California History." In *To Toil in That Vineyard of the Lord: Contemporary Scholarship on Junípero Serra*, edited by Rose Marie Beebe and Robert M. Senkewicz, 17–52. Berkeley: Academy of American Franciscan History, 2010.

Serra, Junípero. *A Letter of Junípero Serra to the Reverend Father Preacher Fray Fermín Francisco de Lasuén: A Bicentennial Discovery*. Edited by Francis Weber. Boston: D. R. Godine, 1970.

———. *Writings of Junípero Serra*. Edited by Antonine Tibesar. 4 vols. Washington, D.C.: Academy of American Franciscan History, 1955–66.

Shaul, David Leedom. "Two Mission Indian (Ohlone/Costanoan) Catechisms." September 5, 2012. http://www.wyominglinguistics.org/2012/09/05/chalon-and-rumsen-catechisms/.

Shipek, Florence C. "Kumeyaay Socio-political Structure." *Journal of California and Great Basin Anthropology* 4, no. 2 (1982): 296–303.

———. "A Native American Adaptation to Drought: The Kumeyaay as Seen in the San Diego Missions Records 1770–1798." *Ethnohistory* 28, no. 4 (1981): 295–312.

———. "A Strategy for Change: The Luiseño of Southern California." PhD diss., University of Hawaii, 1977.

Sierra Nava-Lasa, Luis. *El cardenal Lorenzana y la Ilustración*. Madrid: Fundación Universitaria Española, 1975.

Skowronek, Russell K. "Sifting the Evidence: Perceptions of Life at the Ohlone (Costanoan) Missions of Alta California." *Ethnohistory* 45, no. 4 (Fall 1998): 675–708.

Solís de la Torre, J. *Bárbaros y ermitaños: Chichimecas y agustinos en la Sierra Gorda, siglos 16–18*. Santiago de Querétaro: Gobierno del Estado de Querétaro, 2004.

Soustelle, Jacques. *La familia Otomí-Pame del centro de México*. Mexico City: UAEM; Ateneo del Estado de México; Instituto Mexiquense de Cultura, 1993.

Spier, Leslie. "Southern Diegueño Customs." *University of California Publications in American Archaeology and Ethnology* 20, no. 16 (1923): 297–358.

Stagg, Albert. *The First Bishop of Sonora: Antonio de los Reyes, OFM*. Tucson: University of Arizona Press, 1976.

Steckley, John, ed. *De Religione: Telling the Seventeenth-Century Jesuit Story in Huron to the Iroquois*. Norman: University of Oklahoma Press, 2004.

Stein, Stanley J., and Barbara H. Stein. *Apogee of Empire: Spain and New Spain in the Age of Charles III, 1759–1789*. Baltimore: Johns Hopkins University Press, 2003.

Stockel, H. Henrietta. *On the Bloody Road to Jesus: Christianity and the Chiricahua Apaches*. Albuquerque: University of New Mexico Press, 2004.

Super, John C. "Francisco Palóu: Historian and Biographer." *Inter-American Review of Bibliography* 40, no. 2 (1990): 194–206.

———. "Palóu: President of the Lower California Missions, 1769–1773." Ms., Santa Bárbara Mission Archive-Library.

———. "Querétaro Obrajes: Industry and Society in Provincial Mexico, 1600–1810." *Hispanic American Historical Review* 56, no. 2 (1976): 197–216.

Tapia Méndez, Aureliano. "Fray Rafael José Verger y Suau, Técnico de Misiones." *Humanitas* 16 (1975): 449–96.

Tar, Jane. "Flying through the Empire: The Visionary Journeys of Early Modern Nuns." In *Women's Voices and the Politics of the Spanish Empire: From Convent Cell to Imperial Court*, edited by Jennifer Lee Eich, Jeanne Gillespie, and Lucia G. Harrison, 263–302. New Orleans: University Press of the South, 2008.

Taylor, William. "'. . . de corazón pequeño y ánimo apocado' conceptos de los curas párrocos sobre los indios en la Nueva España del siglo 18." *Relaciones* 10, no. 39 (1989): 5–67.

———. Introduction to *Contested Visions in the Spanish Colonial World*, edited by Ilona Katzew, 15–27. Los Angeles: Los Angeles County Museum of Art; New Haven, Conn.: Yale University Press, 2011.

———. *Magistrates of the Sacred: Priests and Parishioners in Eighteenth-Century Mexico*. Stanford: Stanford University Press, 1996.

———. *Marvels and Miracles in Late Colonial Mexico: Three Texts in Context*. Albuquerque: University of New Mexico Press, 2011.

———. "Placing the Cross in Colonial Mexico." *The Americas* 69, no. 2 (October 2012): 145–78.

———. *Shrines and Miraculous Images: Religious Life in Mexico before the Reforma*. Albuquerque: University of New Mexico Press, 2010.

———. "Two Shrines of the Cristo Renovado: Religion and Peasant Politics in Late Colonial Mexico." *American Historical Review* 110, no. 4 (October 2005): 945–74.

Temple, Thomas Workman. "Two Letters from Sergeant José Francisco Ortega to Governor Felipe de Neve, September 4 and 5, 1781." *Historical Society of Southern California Quarterly* 22, no. 4 (December 1940): 121–30.

Thomas, Alfred Barnaby. *Teodoro de Croix and the Northern Frontier of New Spain, 1776–1783*. Norman: University of Oklahoma Press, 1941.

Thurman, Michael E. *The Naval Department of San Blas: New Spain's Bastion for Alta California and Nootka, 1767 to 1798*. Glendale, Calif.: Arthur H. Clark Company, 1967.

Tibesar, Antonine. "Editor's Note." *The Americas* 41.4 (1985): 426.

———, ed. *Junípero Serra and the Northwestern Mexican Frontier, 1750–1825*. Washington, D.C.: Academy of American Franciscan History, 1985.

Tinker, George E. *Missionary Conquest: The Gospel and Native American Cultural Genocide*. Minneapolis: Fortress Press, 1993.

Tormo Sanz, Leandro. "De Llull a Serra: Contribución de las Baleares al descubrimiento y cristianización de las Indias." *Missionalia Hispánica* 41, no. 120 (1984): 323–40.

Torre Curiel, José Refugio de la. *Twilight of the Mission Frontier: Shifting Interethnic Alliances and Social Organization in Sonora, 1768–1855*. Stanford: Stanford University Press; Berkeley: Academy of American Franciscan History, 2012.

Torrens y Nicolau, Francisco. *Bosquejo histórico del insigne franciscano, V.P.F. Junípero Serra, fundador y apóstol de la California septentrional*. Felanitx: Estab. tip. de B. Reus, 1913.

Torres Puga, Gabriel. *Los últimos años de la Inquisición en la Nueva España*. Mexico City: Miguel Angel Porrúa; CONACULTA-INAH, 2004.

Tous Meliá, Juan. *Palma a través de la cartografía (1596–1902)* Palma de Mallorca: Ajuntament de Palma, 2002.

Townsend, Camilla. *Pocahontas and the Powhatan Dilemma: An American Portrait*. New York: Hill and Wang, 2004.

Turner, Justin G. "Fray Crespí's Farewell to Old Spain." *Pacific Historian* 12, no. 3 (1968): 38–40.

Tutino, John. *Making a New World: Founding Capitalism in the Bajío and Spanish North America*. Durham, N.C.: Duke University Press, 2011.

Valle, Ivonne del. *Escribiendo desde los márgenes: Colonialismo y jesuitas en el siglo 18*. Mexico City: Siglo XXI Editores, 2009.

Vázquez Janeiro, Isaac. "Origen y significado de los colegios de misiones franciscanos." *Archivo Ibero-Americano* 50, no. 197 (1990): 725–71.

Velasco Mireles, Margarita, ed. *La Sierra Gorda: Documentos para su historia*. 2 vols. Mexico City: Instituto Nacional de Antropología e Historia, 1996–1997.

Velázquez, María del Carmen. *El marqués de Altamira y las provincias internas de Nueva España*. Mexico City: Colegio de México, Centro de Estudios Históricos, 1976.

Vernon, Edward W. *A Maritime History of Baja California*. Santa Barbara: Viejo Press, with the cooperation of the Maritime Museum of San Diego, 2009.

———. *Las Misiones Antiguas: The Spanish Missions of Baja California, 1683–1855*. Santa Barbara: Viejo Press, 2002.

Vetancurt, Agustín de. *Teatro mexicano: Descripción breve de los sucesos ejemplares de la Nueva-España en el Nuevo Mundo occidental de las Indias*. 4 vols. Madrid: Ediciones J. Porrúa Turanzas, 1960.

Vicedo, Salustiano. *La casa solariega de la familia Serra*. Petra, Mallorca: Apóstol y Civilizador, 1984.

———. *Convento de San Bernardino de Sena: La escuela del beato Junípero Serra*. Mallorca: Petra, 1991.

———. *Fray Francisco Palóu, OFM: Un mallorquín, fundador de San Francisco de California*. Valencia: Unión Misional Franciscana, 1992.

———. *El mallorquín Fray Juan Crespí, OFM: Misionero y explorador: Sus diarios*. Valencia: Unión Misional Franciscana, 1994.

Wade, Maria. *Missions, Missionaries, and Native Americans: Long-Term Processes and Daily Practices*. Gainesville: University Press of Florida, 2008.

Wagner, Henry Raup. *The Spanish Southwest, 1542–1794: An Annotated Bibliography*. Albuquerque: Quivira Society, 1937.

Waterman, T. T. "The Religious Practices of the Diegueño Indians." *University of California Publications in American Archaeology and Ethnology* 8, no. 6 (1910): 272–343.

Weber, David. *Bárbaros: Spaniards and Their Savages in the Age of Enlightenment*. New Haven, Conn.: Yale University Press, 2005.

———. *The Spanish Frontier in North America*. New Haven, Conn.: Yale University Press, 1992.

Weber, Francis J. *Blessed Fray Junípero Serra: An Outstanding California Hero*. Strasbourg, France: Éditions Du Signe, 2007.

———, ed. *A Marian Novena Attributed to Fray Junípero Serra*. Los Angeles: Archives of the Archdiocese of Los Angeles, 1988.

———, ed. *The Pride of the Missions: A Documentary History of San Gabriel Mission*. Hong Kong: Libra Press, 1979.

Weckmann, Luis. *The Medieval Heritage of Mexico*. Translated by Frances M. López-Morillas. New York: Fordham University Press, 1992.

Weddle, Robert S. *The San Sabá Mission: Spanish Pivot in Texas*. College Station: Texas A&M University Press, 1999.

Whitehead, Richard. *Citadel on the Channel: The Royal Presidio of Santa Barbara, Its Founding and Construction, 1782–1798*. Santa Barbara: Santa Barbara Trust for Historic Preservation; Spokane: Arthur H. Clark Company, 1996.

Xamena Fiol, Pedro. "El siglo 16." In *Historia de Mallorca*, edited by J. Mascaró Pasarius, 2:281–88. Palma de Mallorca: Mascaró Pasarius, 1975.

Zappia, Natale A. "Indigenous Borderlands: Livestock, Captivity, and Power in the Far West." *Pacific Historical Review* 81, no. 2 (2012): 193–220.

———. "The Interior World: Trading and Raiding in Native California, 1700–1863." PhD diss, University of California, Santa Cruz, 2008.

Zermeño P., Guillermo. *Cartas edificantes y curiosas de algunos misioneros jesuitas del siglo 17: Travesías, itinerarios, testimonios*. Mexico City: Universidad Iberoamericana, 2006.

Index

Page numbers in *italics* indicate illustrations.

Acayucán, 368
Achasta, 219, 220, 221, 225, 278–79, 296, 297n
Acosta, Juan de, 58
Ágreda, Sor María de Jesús, 77, 78; influence at Mission San Antonio, 225–26; Inquisition, 80–81; *La mística ciudad de Dios*, 81, 82, 83; Serra's view, 84, 105, 175, 176; woodcut, *177*
agriculture, 329; San Carlos, 401
alcaldes, 358, 359, 360, 362–63, 366–67, 368–71
Alcatraz occupation, 29
Alta California: debates over mission efforts, 354; later missionary-ranchers, 424; mission management criticized, 376; overview of missionary efforts, 242–43; rumors of Franciscan expulsion, 393; staffing of missions, 303–304; writings, 34–35. *See also* Missions (Alta California)
Anza, Juan Bautista de, 17; cattle for troops, 313; Cavaller selling corn to, 376; Colorado River battle, 328; delivers letter from Colegio to Serra, 343; Font with, 291n; guide, 209; Rivera y Moncada relationship, 331–32; at San Luis Obispo, 378, 378n

Apache peoples, 97–98, *99*
Areche, José de, 237
Aristotle, 58
Arriaga, Julián de, 385
Ascensión, Sor Luisa de la, 77, 80–81
Asunta pueblo, 355
atriums, 214
Augustinian missionaries, 85, 87
Automobile Club of Southern California, 319
Ayala, Juan Bautista de, 285

Baja California, *134*; Colegio renouncing missions, 374–75; Gálvez fiction about, 276–77; linguistic groups, *142*; significance of Serra's experience there, 133; Spanish presence, 141. *See also* Missions (Baja California)
Baltasar (Rumsen), 363–64, 366–67, 366n
Bancroft, Hubert Howe, 23–24, 27
baptisms: Baja California, 175, 176; by Dominicans, 78; first in Alta California, 223; of Indians en masse, 78, 84; instruction before, 376–77; Jesuits in Baja California, 141; Kumeyaay people, 329–30; María del Buen Año, 38, 40; Mission San Carlos de Monterey, 219; Rumsen people, 221–23;

493

baptisms *(continued)*
    San Carlos, 401, 402; San Diego, 210, 222; San Juan Capistrano, 338; Santa Clara, 410; Sierra Gorda, 94; Tongva people, 390; of young children, 219, 221, 223, 225
baptized Indians. *See* mission Indians
Barco, Miguel del, 276
Barragán, Rufino, 106–107, 108, 131–32
Barri, Felipe de (Phelipe Barry), 235, 282, 344, 385
Basterra, Dionisio, 162, 165–66
Bay of San Quintín, 183
Bay of Todos Santos, 208
beatification and canonization process, 30–32
Benavides, Alonso de, 77–78, 80–84, 177
Bernardino (Kumeyaay), 339, 340
Bernardino de Jesús (Rumsen), 223
bilocations, 77, 78, 80–81, 83, 84
biographies of Serra, 20–24
black saint, 66, 66n
Bolton, Herbert Eugene, 26
Botellas, Antonio, 71, 71n
Bourbon centralization, 46
Bourbon Reforms, 344–45; Gálvez appointed, 143; secularization, 96
Bravo, Marcelino, 292–93, 295–96
Brother Junípero, 42–45
Bucareli y Ursúa, Antonio María, 236–40, 239, 242, 304; Fages removal, 385; Neve appointment, 344; Provincias Internas, 354
bureaucracy, and Serra's workload, 371–72
Butrón, Manuel, 309–10

California: changes after Serra's death, 424; Serra as historical figure, 20
Cambón, Pedro, 232–34, 378n, 390
Campa, Miguel de la, 137, 152, 169, 172, 173
Canuch (Francisco), 328n, 329–32, 339–41
Cañizares, José, 187, 194, 411, 416
Cárcel de San Pedro (placename), 201
Carlos (Rumsen), 297

Carlos III, 141, 143
Carmel River, 215, 216, 217–18, 221
Carpio, Simón, 278, 279n
Carrillo, Mariano, 209, 229, 337
Castro, Francisco María de, 157, 157n
Catalán volunteers, 28, 143, 208, 209, 227, 229, 385
Cather, Willa, 27
cattle, 174, 277, 297; impact of, 225; inventory, 298; later importance, 424; Mission San Carlos, 404
Cavaller, José, 375–76, 378n
Chichimeca peoples, 213
Chisli (Carlos) 328n, 329–32, 339–41
Christianity, viewed by indigenous peoples, 324
chuetas, 48, 364
Chumash people: aid from, 18–19; artifacts, 382–83; assisting Serra's party, 18–19; Crespí reports, 379, 381; Engelhardt on, 27; as essential to Serra plan, 229; Fages on, 229; hostilities, 17–18; mission among, 379–90; Serra on, 383–85, 388; settlement map, *380*; soldiers inciting, 384; territory, 17
church buildings, 213, 214
Cipriano, 278–79, 296–97
city founding, 346
Cochimí people, 141, 172, 181; Jesuits and, 175
coercion and violence, sermons on, 57
Colegio Apostólico de Nuestra Señora de Guadalupe (Zacatecas), 75, 96
Colegio Apostólico de San Fernando: aims of, 88–89; Alta California missions, 302; complaints about Serra's leadership, 343; *custodia* arrangement, 392; experience with Sierra Gorda missions, 88; founding, 74, 75; later difficulties, 408–409; leadership, 61; management of California missions, 377; missions in Sierra Gorda and Baja California renounced, 374–75; Neve Reglamento,

358; orders for California missions, 133; protesting Neve Reglamento, 397; recruiting, 89, 408–409; reprimand instructions, 374–75; self-flagellation at, 105; Serra at, 21, 74, 75, 84–85, 85n, 101; Serra's offices at, 101; Texas missions, 97–98; trip from San Diego (1773), 236; view of secularization, 96–97
Colegio de Santa Cruz de Querétaro, 2, 75, 83, 84, 88; Sonoran missions, 135, 137; Texas missions, 97–98
colegios apostólicos, 73–77; Llinás's campaign, 83–84
colonialism, overview of impact, 19
Colorado River battle and missions, 341, 353
Columbus quincentenary controversy, 30–31
Comanche peoples, 98, 99, 102
Compostela, New Spain, 275–76
La Concepción, 140, 147
confirmations: authority to administer, 371–74, 373, 412; journey (1783), 399–400; Mission San Carlos, 402; Mission San Diego Indians, 339–40; Mission Santa Clara, 410; Neve on, 350–52; Ortega's children, 339; Vatican permission, 343, 371
congregation policy, 87, 213. See also Texas method
Consag, Fernando, 276
Convento de San Francisco (Palma, Mallorca), 49, 50
Convent of Santa Clara (Palma, Mallorca), 54, 319
conversion: Mallorcan experience, 48–49; Serra's hopes, 19
conversos in Mallorca, 47–49
Coronel, Juan Antonio, 229
Cortés, Hernán, 365, 368–69
Cosoy, 329
Crespí, Juan: Alta California, 206, 207, 242, 350; Baja California, 133, 152, 156–57; Carmel, 215, 216; on Chumash, 379; diary of Alta California expedition, 148, 194; former student, 51; Rivera y Moncada expedition, 147, 152, 155; Serra on, 399; death, 398–99
Cristóbal (Rumsen), 297
Cristo viejo cult, 85
Croix, Carlos Francisco de, 143, 236
Croix, Teodoro de, 353, 355, 391; Neve Reglamento, 357
custodia arrangement, 392–93, 399

demon worship charges, 91–92, 118–19
devil, pact with, 119, 124, 128, 130
Diego José (Rumsen), 221–23
Diego Rivera (Kumeyaay), 330–31, 339
Dimas Chiulchicup (Kumeyaay), 339
divine law, yoke of, 55
divine mercy, 59
doctrinas, 350–52, 354
Dominga de Jesús, 110, 112–17, 119, 123
Dominican Order, 393
Dumetz, Francisco, 232, 242, 258, 294–95, 303, 350, 397, 398

Echeveste, Juan José, 238–39, 239n, 278, 377
Echeveste Reglamento, 238–39, 239n, 296, 304, 308–309, 357
El Cajón (road), 168, 169
El Príncipe. See San Antonio (*El Príncipe*, packet boat)
encomienda, 212–13
Engelhardt, Zephyrin, 26
Enlightenment, 46–47, 214–15, 240
Ensenada de Todos Santos, 193
epidemic disease, 223–25, 292
Escandón, José de, 97; civil settlements near missions, 346; policy on missions, 212; pacification of Sierra Gorda, 86–88; rival of, 106; settlers, 345; treatment of Indians, 285
Esselen peoples, 279–81
evangelization, Chumash-Spanish bond, 19

Fages, Pedro, 231; background, 227; camp at San Diego, 205; cattle for Mission San Francisco, 298; cattle for troops, 313; on Chumash, 381; Chumash people, 17, 229; command style, 230–32; conflicts with Serra, 227, 229–30, 235; desertions, 232; as governor, 341, 391–92; on indigenous peoples, 229, 230; as military commander of Alta California, 227, 229; reappearance in California, 385; replaced as military commander, 41, 278, 391; report on California, 385; Rivera and, 277–78; Santa Bárbara mission approval, 410; Serra on removal of, 237, 238
Feijóo, Benito Jerónimo, 46–47
Fernando (Kumeyaay), 339
Fernando José (Rumsen), 221–23
Ferrer, Juan, 71, 72
Figuer, Juan, 393–96
Fitch, A. H., 26
flogging and whipping, 296, 297, 348, 363, 364–65, 368, 369
Fomear (Tongva), 233
Font, Pedro, on souls of unbaptized Indians, 291n
Forbes, Alexander, 22
Forbes, Jack D., 29
Franciscan Order: active in northern New Spain, 214; Baja California assignments, 135; Baja California mission affairs, 147; Huasteca, 106; Mallorca, 63, 63n, 64, 74; martyrdom, 61; missions in Sierra Gorda, 85; New Mexico, 77–78, 80–84; on Benavides, 81; Petra, 42; philosophical emphasis, 51–52; poverty vow, 301–302; Province of Jalisco, 135; recruiting in Spain, 60, 89; rumors of expulsion from Alta California, 393
Francisco (Rumsen), 222–23
Francis of Assisi, 19; Brother Junípero, 42, 44; feast day celebrated, 72, 72n; miracles, 84; signs of God's providence, 73–74

Fuente, Francisco de la, 80
Fuster, Vicente, 323–24, 330, 332, 397

Gálvez, José de, 145; Alta California plans, 141, 229, 276–77; on Baja California, 276–77; Fages's removal, 385; Guanajuato meeting, 138; moving Indians around, 162; Provincias Internas established, 343, 354; Serra meeting, 149–50; Serra relationship, 353, 354; *visitador general* post, 143
Gastón, Juan Ignacio, 160–61
Geiger, Maynard, 20, 28, 148
gentile, use of term, 170
Gerónimo (Rumsen), 297
Golden Gate Park statue, 25
Gómez, Francisco, 147, 150, 206, 211
González Vizcaíno, Juan, 109, 147, 150, 206, 209, 210
Guadalupe apparition, 107, 107n
Guadalupe shrine, 74
Guaycura people, 141, 144, 147, 276
Guest, Francis, 26

Hapsburg dynasty, 46, 52, 83
Hezeta, Bruno de, 301, 304, 312, 315
Historical Account of the Life and Apostolic Labors of the Venerable Father Fray Junípero Serra (1787), 21–22; translations into English, 25, 28
Hittell, John S., 23
Hittell, Theodore, 27
Huasteca region, 105–106, 111; witchcraft charges, 106, 112–28. *See also* Missions (Huasteca)

Ichxenta, 221, 352
Ignacio (Kumeyaay), 330
Ildefonso (Rumsen), 296–97
Immaculate Conception devotion, 52, 83, 94
Indian labor: agricultural, 285, 289; Escandón on, 87, 88; "legitimate," 285;

limits on, 285; Mission San Carlos, 402; work habits, 285, 286
indigenous peoples: alcalde election issue, 358–70; appropriating Spanish goods, 172, 197; captured individual, 179–81; child-rearing practices, 364–65; Christianity as verbal religion, 324; contrition and repentance as alien concepts, 59; earlier popular views, 27; fighting tactics, 331; historical perspective revised, 28; hostilities with settlers, 96; military control, 344–45; missionaries on role of, 346, 348; mission communities viewed by, 342; missions related, 29; negative views of, 58; philosophical discussions about, 58; population trends, 28–29; Portolá expedition, 172, 179–82; presidios and, 211–12; self-government plan, 358–70; Serra's observations, 33, 132, 133, 423; Spanish terms for, 170. *See also individual peoples by name*; punishment; flogging and whipping
indigenous peoples of Alta California, 190; appropriating Spanish goods, 197, 198; dancing at Mission San José, 292; encounters with, 181–89, 191–201; Engelhardt on, 27; hostility, 191–92, 193–94, 198, 199, 232, 233; indigenous officials, 358–70; on marriage among Christian Indians, 238; material culture, 192; Mission San Diego, 205, 208, 210; notions of baptism, 210; Santa Clara Valley, 149; Serra's zeal about, 230; "The Dancer," 187–89; traditional rituals, 290–91. *See also individual groups*
indigenous peoples of Baja California: as role models, 237–38; removal, 143–44; resistance to relocation, 162. *See also individual groups*
Inquisition: demon worship in Sierra Gorda, 91–92; duties in New Spain, 108–109; influence on Serra's thinking, 290,

291, 364; interrogating Spanish religious women, 80–81, 83; interrogation, 118; in Mallorca, 42, 47–49; Mexico City, 131; in New Mexico, 77–78; penitential garb, 66n; Pereli appointment, 130; Serra's report, 92–93; Serra's role, 48–49; traditional healers, 106, 107–108, 109–10; witchcraft in Huasteca, 106, 108–10, 112–28

Jackson, Helen Hunt, 24–25
James, George Wharton, 25
Jayme, Luis, 323, 324, 329, 330, 338–39, 356
Jesuits: Cochimí territory, 175; Compostela benefactor, 276; confirmations, 371; control over Baja California, 135, 138, 141; expulsion of, 133, 276, 344; Gálvez on, 143; northward expansion, 135, 214; Pious Fund, 141; travel accounts, 148
Jonace people, 85, 87, 88
José María Rivera (Kumeyaay), 330
Juan Evangelista (Rumsen), 221, 236, 246–48, 251, 264, 352
Juan Evangelista Benno (Cochimí), 160–61, 163, 209, 211, 221
Juncosa, Domingo, 375–76

Kiliwa people, 181, 186
Kumeyaay people, 141; appropriating Spanish goods, 172; baptisms, 329–30; hostilities, 210, 337, 340; killing a missionary, 323–24; language barrier, 210; lifeways, 329; Mission San Diego destroyed, 323–28; population trends, 29; Portolá expedition, 192–200; punishments after uprising, 332–33; San Diego encampment, 209–10; southern peoples, 342; views of missions, 342

La Asumpta (*ranchería*), 387
ladder (*escalera*) analogy, 319, 320–21, 323, 429–30

Ladrón de Guevara, Antonio de, 106, 108, 109, 125
language issues: Baja California linguistic groups, 142; baptizing indigenous children, 219, 221–23; communicating with Kumeyaay, 210; glossary of terms, 37, 459–65; importance of language, 34; languages taught at *colegios apostólicos*, 85, 93–94; living language approach, 36; official Spanish practice, 94; problem with evangelization, 230, 231; San Diego garrison, 210; Serra learning indigenous languages, 93
Las Casas, Bartolomé de, 78, 97, 213, 285
Lasuén, Fermín Francisco de: Alta California, 224; Baja California, 133, 162, 168, 171; Chumash people, 17–18; leniency for Carlos, 341; Mission San Juan Capistrano, 299; Monterey Presidio, 286
law of God, 56–57
Laws of Burgos, 212
leather-jacket soldiers (*soldados de cuera*): concubinage of, 261; under Fages, 227, 229; San Diego, 208, 209
Lenten sermons, 53–54
Linck, Wenceslaus, 171, 175, 181, 276
Llinás, Antonio, 74–75, 77, 83–84, 409
Llull, Ramón, 45–47
Luiseño people, 29
Lummis, Charles Fletcher, 25

Mallorca, 21, 39; cultural development, 46–47; economy 40–41; Llínas at, 74; Serra as Inquisitor in, 48–49; Serra's departure from, 59–66; Serra's early years in, 39–42; Serra's mathematician nephew in, 140–44; Serra's preaching in, 53–59; Serra's professorial career in, 45, 49–53; Serra's writings at, 34; student life in, 42–45; trade, 40
María Victoria (Rumsen), 278–79
Martínez, Antonio, 155, 156
martyrdom, 60–61, 98

McRoskey, Racine, 25
Media Villa y Ascona, Melchor de, 125, 126
Medinaveitia, Juan León de, 161–62
Mendieta, Gerónimo, 324
Mexico City: journey to, 236, 376; Serra's arrival, 19; Serra's first biography, 20; Serra's preaching, 102. *See also* Colegio Apostólico de San Fernando
Miguel (Kumeyaay), 330
military. *See names of individual commanders*; soldiers
military in Baja California, 135
military reforms, 344–45
Miller, Frank, 25
miracles: Inquisition, 80–81; San Sabá, 100. *See also* bilocations
Mishopshno, 381
missionaries: authority issue, 237; complaints about Serra's leadership, 343; control over baptized Indians, 359, 363; crises among, 393–96; criticisms of, 348; depression among, 162, 393–94; instructions on how to treat soldiers, 374; killed, 323–24, 333–34, 335, 338, 340; on role of native peoples, 346, 348; time-honored strategy for conversion, 383; travel, regulations on, 377
missionary career of Serra: appropriate role of military, 293–99; bureaucratic duties, 372; complaints about Serra's conduct, 375; final report, 400–406; management of missions, 376–77; mission president duties, 356; moving missionaries around, 374, 377, 378; non-Christian practices viewed, 364; as Padre Presidente, 377, 400–406; Palóu summary, 418; primary objective of missions, 319, 321; prohibition against communicating with colonial officials, 374, 377–78; recommendations to Viceroy Bucareli, 236–40; reprimand from *colegio*, 374–75; Rivera correspondence, 275, 278–96; Sierra Gorda, 85, 89, 91–98; significance

for Serra, 426; Spanish versus indigenous worldviews, 172; strict interpretations, 290, 291, 291n. *See also* Missions (Baja California); Missions (Huasteca); Missions (Sierra Gorda, New Spain); Sierra Gorda

mission Indians: food for, 314; livelihoods, 166; missionary control over, 359, 363; nudity, 402; recapture, 290–97, 330, 367–68; San Diego, 329; singing skills, 159; traditional rituals, 290–91; unable to feed selves, 157, 159. *See also* Indian labor

Missions (Alta California), 322; La Purísima Concepción de María Santísima, 321, 345, 362; San Antonio de Padua, 225, 242, 279, 301, 302–303, 307, 313, 370, 375, 400, 410, 412; San Buenaventura, 229, 233, 235, 321, 345, 355, 362, 379, 385, *386*, 388–90, 393, 397–400, 404, 409n; San Carlos Borromeo, 19, 21, 25, 26, 40, 215, 218, 221, 224, 242, 278, 280, 302–303, 305, 307, 323, 332, 341, 352, 364, 372, *373*, 379, 394–95, 399, 400–406, 411, 425; San Diego de Alcalá, 17, 165, 209, 222, 232, 235, 242, 302–303, 313, 323–28, 332–41, 356, 362, 364, 372, 393, 395, 397, 400; San Fernando Rey de España, 398; San Francisco de Asís (Dolores), 21, 291, 298, 299, 302–303, 372, 376, 394, 395, 398, *408*; San Gabriel Arcángel, 209, 230, 232–35, 242, 298, 302–303, 313, 326, 363–64, 369, 385, 390, 393, 398, 400, 405; San José, 291, 292; San Juan Capistrano, 196, 299, 302–303, 310, 321, 323, 325–26, 337, 338, 400; San Luis Obispo de Tolosa, 17, 234, 235, 242, 298, 302–303, 307, 313, 363, 369, 370, 375–76, 377, 378, 378n, 393, 400, 410, 412–13; San Luis Rey de Francia, 291, 293; Santa Bárbara, Virgen y Mártir, 26, 362, 387, 388, 389–90; Santa Clara de Asís, 345, 373, 394, 395, 406, *407*, 409–10; Santa Inés, Virgen y Mártir, 165. *See also* Alta California

Missions (Baja California), 136; Jesuit, 135, 138, 141; La Purísima Concepción de Cadegomó, 147, 152, 160, 162; Nuestra Señora de los Dolores Apaté, 144, 150; Nuestra Señora de Guadalupe de Huasinapí, 157, 159, 161, 163, 209, 211; Nuestra Señora de Loreto Conchó, 141, 144, 153, 155, 161, 206, 341; Nuestro Señor San Ignacio de Kadakaamán, 152, 161–62, *164*, 186; San Fernando Rey de España de Velicatá, 147, 152, 153, 169, 170, 171–72, 175, 176, 179, 181, 242, 277; San Francisco de Borja Adac, 162, 166, 168–69, 175, 176, 191, 278; San Francisco Javier de Viaggé-Biaundó, 144, 151, 153–55, 156; San José de Comondú, 155, 156, 156n, 157, *158*, 162; San José del Cabo Añuití, 141, 276; San Luis Gonzaga Chiriyaqui, 144, 152; Santa Gertrudis de Cadacamán, 162, *164*, 165–66, *167*, 169, 176, 209; Santa María de los Ángeles de Cabujakaamung, 141, 152, 161, 169–70, 176, 191, 211; Santa Rosalía de Mulegé, 159, 160, 161; Santiago de los Coras, 144; Todos Santos, 144, 147, 150

Missions (Huasteca), 105–106; Nuestra Señora de la Purísima Concepción, 106, 107; San José, 107, 132

Missions (Sierra Gorda, New Spain): Nuestra Señora de la Luz de Tancoyol, 129; San José de Vizarrón, 86, 87, 88; Santiago de Jalpan, 85, 87–88, 89, 91; Xilitla, 87

Missions (Texas), Santa Cruz de San Sabá, 21, 97–98, 99–100, 102, 137, 323, 327

missions: under Bourbon reforms, 344–45; buildings at San Carlos, 403–404; concept of, 211; *doctrinas* versus, 350–52, 354; Engelhardt on, 26–27; to facilitate travel, 319; failure of assimilation, 358; iconic portrayal, 24–25; indigenous death rate, 223–25; justifying to Croix, 356–57; later missionary-ranchers, 424;

missions *(continued)*
  long-term development, 353; Neve Reglamento on, 358; new or later, 310, 318–21, 334, 343, 345, 356–57, 387; official colonial views of, 21–22, 344–45, 358; origins of mission system, 212–13; physical aspects, 214; possible sites, 195–96, 202, 207; practical function, 346; rations for servants, 289–90, 301, 304–18; regional variations, 214; scholars on, 29; soldiers to new missions, 297; temporal needs, 237–38; as temporary, 214, 352. See also Texas method

La mística ciudad de Dios (María de Jesús de Ágreda), 81, 82, 83
Mixton Revolt, 213
Mojave peoples, 342
Monterey: harbor, 147; Indian man, *280*; indigenous population, 218–19; as new capital, 343; occupation of, 209; presidio and mission founded, 215; Serra's view of site, 215; taking possession of, 215, 217
Monterey expedition, 147, 148, 215–16, 227, 277
Montesino, Antonio de, 97
Montserrat, Joaquín de, 143
Morisca, Juana, 113–14
Mosqueda, José, 2
Mount Rubidoux cross, 25
mules, 299, 300, 313–14, 315, 316, 317; Alta California expedition, 160; Mission San Carlos, 404; Monterey, 281–84
Murguía, José Antonio de, 375, 395, 406–407, 408

Naguasajo, 332
National Statuary Collection, 20, 27
natural slavery argument, 58
Neve, Felipe de: air of confidence, 353; background, 344; criticisms of priests, 36–37, 352–53; Indian elections, 358–60, 363–64; inspector general appointment, 391; Jesuit expulsion, 34; meetings at Monterey Presidio, 349–52; Mission San Buenaventura, 388; as new governor, 344–45; new regime of, 343; Provincias Internas commandant, 391; punishing Carlos, 340–41; Quechán rebellion, 385–86; recommendations to Fages, 391; refusal with Santa Bárbara, 389; reimbursement for mules, 282–83, 284; Serra's authority for confirmations, 371; Serra's meeting with, 348, 349; Serra's relationship with, 21–22, 27, 348, 352–53, 358–60
Neve Reglamento, 357–58, 397
New Granada, 344, 345
New Laws, 212–13
New Mexico, 77–78, 80, 235
New Spain: city and town founding, 346; departure for, Mediterranean travels, 62; domestic missions, 102–105, 133; Huasteca region, 105–106; secularization of *doctrinas*, 352
Nicolás (Tongva), 363–64, 369
Nicolás Supelpex (Kumeyaay), 330
Nipaguay, 329
Noriega, Matías Antonio, 400, 417
North Africa, 40, 45, 48
Nuevo Santander, 96, 345

Oaxaca, 166
Ocio, Manuel de, 138, 147, 276, 277
Ohlone people, 278, 291, *331*
Olvera, Diego, 290
Olvera, Ignacio, 289, 290
Ortega, José Francisco de: allocation of mules, 281, 284; indigenous officials, 359, 361; Mission San Buenaventura founding, 386; offspring confirmed, 339; Portolá expedition, 174, 176, 200, 277; recapture of baptized Indians, 330; replacing Fages, 237; San Diego Indians, 338; Serra's request, 278; tent purchased from, 404; warnings about Indians, 198
Ortés de Velasco, José, 88, 89

Otopame cultural group, 85

Pach-hepas (Esselen), 280
Pai-Pai people/territory, 186–92, 376
Palóu, Francisco, 21–22; Baja California, 133, 153–55, 169; as biographer, 20, 21–22, 73, 93–95, 97, 108–109, 232, 234, 391; "Exemplary Death of Venerable Padre Junípero," 411–21; former student, 61; Guadalajara trip, 137; at Mission Santa Clara, 406, 409–10; on missions (Sierra Gorda, New Spain), 41–42; offices at Colegio de San Fernando, 102; Presidente of Baja California missions, 153, 242, 375; Rivera y Moncada expedition diary, 149; on Serra's zeal, 230
Pame people, 85–86, 87–88; devil seen as a Pame, 120, 121, 124, 132; *doctrina* serving, 352; Huasteca, 106, 107, 109; idol seized, 98; language, 93; Nuevo Santander, 96; population decline, 94–95
Pa'Mu, 337
Pangua, Francisco, 374, 376
Parrón, Fernando, 150, 206, 209, 211, 328
Pascuala de Nava, María, 109–10, 112–16, 117–28, 132; imprisonment and death, 130–31
Paterna, Antonio, 232
paternalism toward native peoples: alcaldes, 368; indigenous child-rearing practices versus, 364–65; neophytes as children, 356; parent-child analogy, 57–58; Serra's view of flogging, 348–49; theological basis for, 57–58
Patronato Real, 60, 86
Payeras, Mariano, 224
Peña, Tomás de la, 303, 395, 406
Perea, Estevan de, 77
Pereli, Miguel José, 130, 131
Pérez, Juan, 205, 206, 207
Pérez de Mezquía, Pedro, 61, 87, 89
Pericú people, 141, 144; revolt, 141
Peru, 391

Petaluma people, 291
Petra, 39–41, 42, 43, 61, 65–66; convent at, 101
Petra, Miguel de, 98, 240; letters to, 99–102, 240–44
Phelan, James, 25
Philippines, 25
Pieras, Miguel, 225–26
Pious Fund, 301
population decline, Pame people, 94–95
population studies, 28–29
Portolá expedition, 228; arrival at San Diego, 204–206; autographs of participants, 146; burricide, 192–93; command, 152; Fages, 227; gifts of tobacco, 173; Monterey, occupation of, 209; native versus Spanish foods, 172; route, 181; San Diego to Monterey, 211, 215–17; Serra's assessment, 207–208; Serra's diary account, 148–204; staging for, 169–70; warning shots, 181–82, 185
Portolá, Gaspar de, 139; Baja California role, 144, 147; changes to mission assignments, 137; on cowboy skills of soldiers, 165; Jesuits expelled, 276; Serra's remarks on Mission Santa Bárbara, 379; taking possession of Monterey, 215, 217
postal service, 318–21, 405
Powhatan Indians, 221
preaching: bureaucratic duties versus, 372; domestic missions, 102–105, 133; final Mass, 411–12; Llull feast day sermon, 47; Mallorca, 51, 53, 61; Mexico City, 102; Petra, Mallorca, 61; popular preaching exercises, 67–68; reputation, 104; San Juan, Puerto Rico, 67–68, 69–70, 70n; singing ability, 216n; theatrical pulpit persona, 68, 105
Presidios: capital moved, 343; Compostela origins, 275–76; corn rations, 212; defense of mission, 326–27; exile to, 341; Lasuén as chaplain, 286; layout, 350; Loreto Presidio, 147, 150, 151, 152;

Presidios (continued)
  mission surplus, 400–401; Monterey Presidio, 215, 227, 287; mules, 281–84; Neve-Serra meetings, 349–52; El Pitic Presidio, 385; plaza, 351; priest needed, 317; punishment of Indian deserters, 296–97; rations, 361; Rivera y Moncada at, 276, 278; San Diego Presidio, 277, 336; San Diego uprising, 333; San Francisco Presidio, 330; Santa Bárbara Presidio, 387, 388, 390, 404; uprising against mission, 333; use of flogging, 364

presidios: concept of, 211; Escandón policy, 212; physical structure, 212; Rivera report, 86, 212; Serra's relationship with, 22; soldiers' access to religious services, 305

Provincias Internas, 354–57; impact on Serra, 343

pueblos: Chumash, 381; congregation and reduction policies, 213, 214; historical roots, 345–46; Iberian view, 345–46, 381, 383; research on, 31; Serra on disadvantages, 356

punishment: for missionaries killed, 323–24, 333–34, 335, 338, 340; general pardon, 356; as gift from God, 57; indigenous officials, 368–70; need for missionary control over, 363, 364–65; recaptured baptized Indians, 296–97; Serra on flogging, 363, 364–65, 368–69

Quechán Indians, 341, 342; rebellion, 385
Querétaro, Provincial Regiment of, 344
Quinto Zúñiga, Josef Pío, 301

rancherías, 166; de San Juan, 194; use of term, 166n
reduction (*reducción*), policy of, 57, 213, 214; Neve on, 358; northern frontier, 214; Serra on, 357
regidores, 358, 360
religious orders, tensions among, 95, 213

Reyes, Antonio de los, 392
Rivera, Pedro de, 86, 212
Rivera y Moncada, Fernando de: Alta California expedition, 150–52, 157, 205, 277; Anza relationship, 331–32; appointment as military commander, 278; background, 275; career, 276; diary, 35, 275; excommunicated, 332; Indian labor issue, 285; killed in Colorado, 341, 354; Loreto leadership, 344; refusal to bring solders to Monterey, 229; replacing Fages, 278; San Diego uprising, 330–32
Robinson, Alfred, 22
Romeu, José Antonio, 385
Rosarito, 197–98
Rubí, Marqués de, 212
Rumsen people, 219; baptisms, 221–23; Carmel, 221; hostilities with Esselen, 280–81; village location, 220

San Antonio (*El Príncipe*, packet boat), 140, 150, 204, 211, 221; scurvy among crew, 205, 206; sent for supplies, 205
San Benvenuto, 199
San Blas: exile in, 333, 334, 335; port closure, 238
San Buenaventura (saint), 396
San Carlos (packet boat), 20, 147, 150, 151, 410, 412; Fages aboard, 227; reasons for delay, 206–207; San Diego, 204, 205, 209, 211; San Francisco Bay, 300; scurvy, 205, 206, 227; Serra friction with Rivera y Moncada, 284–89; ship chaplain, 397
Sancho, Juan, 157, 160
Sandham, Henry, 25
San Diego, 133; Baja California Indians, 209, 210, 211; early history, 328–30; encampment personnel, 209; expeditions, 148–204, 277; harbor, 147; indigenous settlements nearby, 205; region assessed, 207–208. *See also* Missions (Alta California)
San Fernando (saint), 185–86

San Francisco Bay exploration, 300
San Francisco Solano (placename), 197
San José (packet boat), 206
San José de Guadalupe pueblo, 330, 345, 347, 355
San Juan de Dios, 209
San Juan, Puerto Rico, 67, 69–70
Santa Bárbara Channel: Chumash confrontation, 17–18; establishment of mission and presidio, 379; importance, 379, 383; missions approved, 358, 362, 410; missions established, 385; presidio for, 345; projected mission, 232, 355; Spanish and indigenous communities (map), 389; third mission possible, 229. *See also* Missions (Alta California)
Santa Clara Valley, 149
Santa Cruz Presidio (Sonora), 385
Santa Margarita, 188
Santa María, Vicente de, 300, 397–98
Santiago, 300–301
Scholastic philosophy, 51–53, 285, 423
Scotus, John Duns, 49; Serra as follower, 49–50, 52, 285, 353, 372
secularization of the *doctrinas*, 352
secularization of the missions, 214–15; Engelhardt on, 26; Escandón on, 88, 95–96; religious view of, 96–97; Sierra Gorda, 88, 95
self-flagellation, 104–105, 365
self-identity, 33; as active missionary, 98; as Franciscan and Mallorcan, 45; Mallorcan identity, 47
Seri Indians, 227, 385
sermons: first sermon, 55–56; first sermon (text), 427–35; second sermon, 55–57; second sermon (text), 435–43; third sermon, 57–58; third sermon (text), 443–50; fourth sermon, 58–59; fourth sermon (text), 450–57; domestic missions, 104; funeral sermon (Mallorca), 51; Lenten, 53–55; sources for, 54
Serra Cause, 28, 29–30

Serra, Francesch, 63, 67, 100–101
settlers: Baja California, 135; as primary agents of Indian assimilation, 88; proposed sequence for, 357; Serra's view of, 131, 348; Sierra Gorda, 89, 95
sexual activity: Barragán and Inquisition, 107, 132; behavior of soldiers, 232, 329, 353, 363, 369, 394; mission Indians, 278–79; settlers and Indians, 132; traditional indigenous, 363, 367; witchcraft investigation, 120, 128
shamans, 187–88, *190*
ships, effect upon California, 424. *See also* San Antonio; San Carlos; San José; Santiago; Villasota
Shisholop, 381, 386
Sierra Gorda, 85–91, *90*; departure from, 97–98; economic activities, 41–42; Llinás initiative, 75; method of missionary practice, 236; missionaries to Baja California, 133; missions renounced, 375; Palóu at, 21; recapturing baptized Indians, 367; Serra as president of missions, 93; Serra on settlers, 89, 91; tensions among religious groups, 95; Villa de Herrera, 89, 91; writings during, 34. *See also* Missions (Sierra Gorda, New Spain)
sínodos, 302, 404, 405
Sitjar, Buenaventura, 225
Sociedad Económica de Amigos del País, 240
Solano, Francisco (saint), 59–60, 61, 68, 105, 368
soldiers: authority of missionaries, 237; conflicts with missionaries in Alta California, 282–84; conflicts with missionaries in New Spain, 47, 162, 235; desertions, 232, 238; inciting Chumash, 384; needed to staff missions, 348; relationships with missionaries, 162, 165; Serra's *mayordomo* plan, 238
Soler, Juan, 289, 290, 304, 307, 311–12, 315

Sonora: diocese created, 392; Fages at Santa Cruz Presidio, 385; former Jesuit missions, 135, 138; missions compared to Sierra Gorda, 135, 137, 138. *See also* Missions (Sonora)
Spain, map, 79
Spanish colonial empire, 19, 29
Spanish Revival, 24–25, 26, 28
Stanford, Jane, 25
Statuary Hall, 27
syncretism, 86

Taraval, Sebastián, 209
Tatlun, 271, 352
teaching, Mallorca, 45, 49–53
Texas: bilocations in, 84; Comanche attacks, 98, 99, 102; new missions in Apache territory, 97. *See also* Missions (Texas)
Texas method, 87; as tried-and-true, 353–54; Mission San Diego, 329; as "new method," 236–37; resistance to, 94–95
Toledo, Conrado, 290, 290n
Tongva people, 390
Toypurina, 364
traditional healers, 106, 107–108, 109–10, 119, 121, 123; Alta California, *190*
translation issues, 35–36, 37
Tucutnut, 221, 225, 296, 297n
Tuthill, Franklin, 27

Uchití people, 276
unbaptized native peoples: Alta California, 198, 218–19; Baja California, 135, 178–79; early contacts, 149; entering territory of, 170; first contact, 133, 152, 172; San Diego, 209–10; Spanish terms for, 170
urban planning, 346

Vatican, 80, 343, 371
Veracruz: landing at, 71–72; walk to Mexico City, 68, 73–74, 91
Verger, Rafael, 61, 230, 236, 241, 376
Vergerano, José María, 209, 210
Vila, Vicente, 205, 206
Villa de Valles, 85, 109
Villasota, 63, 67, 71–72
Virgil, 51
Vizcaíno expedition, 215
Vizcaíno, Father. *See* González Vizcaíno, Juan

Williams, C. Scott, 25
witchcraft charges, 91, 92–93; Huasteca, 106, 112–28
women: indigenous attracted by sacred painting, 232, 234; Kumeyaay women as spies, 198, 199; religious, 77, 78. *See also* witchcraft charges
writings considered, 34–37; diary of Portolá expedition, 148–204, *203*; Mallorca, 51; overview, 35; prayers to Mary, 103n. *See also* sermons

Xasauan, 280
Ximénez Santiago, José, 81, 83

Yuman-speaking people, 141

Zacatecas silver strikes, 211–12